ALSO BY AMERICA'S TEST KITCHEN

The Complete One Pot

Cooking for One

The Complete Summer Cookbook

Bowls

Vegetables Illustrated

The Side Dish Bible

Foolproof Fish

100 Techniques

Easy Everyday Keto

Everything Chocolate

The Perfect Pie

How to Cocktail

Spiced

The Ultimate Burger

The New Essentials Cookbook

Dinner Illustrated

Cook's Illustrated Revolutionary Recipes

Tasting Italy: A Culinary Journey

Cooking at Home with Bridget and Julia

The Complete Diabetes Cookbook

The Complete Slow Cooker

The Complete Make-Ahead Cookbook

The Complete Mediterranean Cookbook

The Complete Vegetarian Cookbook

The Complete Cooking for Two Cookbook

Just Add Sauce

How to Braise Everything

How to Roast Everything

Nutritious Delicious

What Good Cooks Know

Cook's Science

The Science of Good Cooking

The Perfect Cake

The Perfect Cookie

Bread Illustrated

Master of the Grill

Kitchen Smarts

Kitchen Hacks

100 Recipes: The Absolute Best Ways to Make the True Essentials

The New Family Cookbook

The America's Test Kitchen Cooking School Cookbook

The Cook's Illustrated Meat Book

The Cook's Illustrated Baking Book

The Cook's Illustrated Cookbook

The America's Test Kitchen Family Baking Book

America's Test Kitchen Twentieth Anniversary TV Show Cookbook

The Best of America's Test Kitchen (2007–2021 Editions)

The Complete America's Test Kitchen TV Show Cookbook 2001–2021

Mediterranean Instant Pot

Instant Pot Ace Blender Cookbook

Cook It in Your Dutch Oven

Sous Vide for Everybody

Air Fryer Perfection

Multicooker Perfection

Food Processor Perfection

Pressure Cooker Perfection

Vegan for Everybody

Naturally Sweet

Foolproof Preserving

Paleo Perfected

The How Can It Be Gluten-Free Cookbook: Volume 2

The How Can It Be Gluten-Free Cookbook

The Best Mexican Recipes

Slow Cooker Revolution Volume 2: The Easy-Prep Edition

Slow Cooker Revolution

The America's Test Kitchen D.I.Y. Cookbook

THE COOK'S ILLUSTRATED ALL-TIME BEST SERIES

All-Time Best Brunch

All-Time Best Dinners for Two

All-Time Best Sunday Suppers

All-Time Best Holiday Entertaining

All-Time Best Appetizers

All-Time Best Soups

COOK'S COUNTRY TITLES

Big Flavors from Italian America

One-Pan Wonders

Cook It in Cast Iron

Cook's Country Eats Local

The Complete Cook's Country TV Show Cookbook

FOR A FULL LISTING OF ALL OUR BOOKS

CooksIllustrated.com

AmericasTestKitchen.com

PRAISE FOR AMERICA'S TEST KITCHEN TITLES

"The book's depth, breadth, and practicality makes it a must-have for seafood lovers."

PUBLISHERS WEEKLY (STARRED REVIEW) ON FOOLPROOF FISH

"Another flawless entry in the America's Test Kitchen canon, Bowls guides readers of all culinary skill levels in composing one-bowl meals from a variety of cuisines."

BUZZFEED BOOKS ON BOWLS

Selected as the Cookbook Award Winner of 2019 in the Health and Special Diet Category

INTERNATIONAL ASSOCIATION OF CULINARY PROFESSIONALS (IACP) ON THE COMPLETE DIABETES COOKBOOK

"This book is a comprehensive, no-nonsense guide . . . a well-thought-out, clearly explained primer for every aspect of home baking."

THE WALL STREET JOURNAL ON THE COOK'S ILLUSTRATED BAKING BOOK

"The team at Cook's Illustrated magazine and America's Test Kitchen offers a real option for a cook who just wants to learn some new ways to encourage family and friends to explore today's sometimes-daunting vegetable universe. This is one of the most valuable vegetable cooking resources for the home chef since Marian Morash's beloved classic The Victory Garden Cookbook (1982)."

BOOKLIST (STARRED REVIEW) ON VEGETABLES ILLUSTRATED

"This is a wonderful, useful guide to healthy eating."

PUBLISHERS WEEKLY ON NUTRITIOUS DELICIOUS

"The Perfect Cookie. . . is, in a word, perfect. This is an important and substantial cookbook. . . . If you love cookies, but have been a tad shy to bake on your own, all your fears will be dissipated. This is one book you can use for years with magnificently happy results."

THE HUFFINGTON POST ON THE PERFECT COOKIE

Selected as one of the 10 Best New Cookbooks of 2017

THE LA TIMES ON THE PERFECT COOKIE

"The sum total of exhaustive experimentation . . . anyone interested in gluten-free cookery simply shouldn't be without it."

NIGELLA LAWSON ON THE HOW CAN IT BE GLUTEN-FREE COOKBOOK

"True to its name, this smart and endlessly enlightening cookbook is about as definitive as it's possible to get in the modern vegetarian realm."

MEN'S JOURNAL ON THE COMPLETE VEGETARIAN COOKBOOK

"A one-volume kitchen seminar, addressing in one smart chapter after another the sometimes surprising whys behind a cook's best practices. . . . You get the myth, the theory, the science, and the proof, all rigorously interrogated as only America's Test Kitchen can do."

NPR ON THE SCIENCE OF GOOD COOKING

"The 21st-century Fannie Farmer Cookbook or The Joy of Cooking. If you had to have one cookbook and that's all you could have, this one would do it."

CBS SAN FRANCISCO ON THE NEW FAMILY COOKBOOK

"Some 2,500 photos walk readers through 600 painstakingly tested recipes, leaving little room for error."

ASSOCIATED PRESS ON THE AMERICA'S TEST KITCHEN COOKING SCHOOL COOKBOOK

"It's all about technique and timing, and the ATK crew delivers their usual clear instructions to ensure success. . . . The thoughtful balance of practicality and imagination will inspire readers of all tastes and skill levels."

PUBLISHERS WEEKLY ON HOW TO ROAST EVERYTHING

"The go-to gift book for newlyweds, small families, or empty nesters."

ORLANDO SENTINEL ON THE COMPLETE COOKING FOR TWO COOKBOOK

"Some books impress by the sheer audacity of their ambition. Backed by the magazine's famed mission to test every recipe relentlessly until it is the best it can be, this nearly 900-page volume lands with an authoritative wallop."

CHICAGO TRIBUNE ON THE COOK'S ILLUSTRATED COOKBOOK

"This impressive installment from America's Test Kitchen equips readers with dozens of repertoire-worthy recipes. . . . This is a must-have for beginner cooks and more experienced ones who wish to sharpen their skills."

PUBLISHERS WEEKLY (STARRED REVIEW) ON THE NEW ESSENTIALS COOKBOOK

MEAT
illustrated

A FOOLPROOF GUIDE to Understanding
and Cooking with Cuts of All Kinds

Library of Congress Cataloging-in-Publication Data

Names: America's Test Kitchen (Firm), author.
Title: Meat illustrated : a foolproof guide to understanding and cooking
  with cuts of all kinds / America's Test Kitchen.
Other titles: Cook's illustrated.
Description: Boston, MA : America's Test Kitchen, [2020] | Includes index.
Identifiers: LCCN 2020030441 (print) | LCCN 2020030442 (ebook) | ISBN
  9781948703321 (hardcover) | ISBN 9781948703338 (epub)
Subjects: LCSH: Cooking (Meat) | LCGFT: Cookbooks.
Classification: LCC TX749 .M417 2020 (print) | LCC TX749 (ebook) | DDC
  641.6/6--dc23
LC record available at https://lccn.loc.gov/2020030441
LC ebook record available at https://lccn.loc.gov/2020030442

America's Test Kitchen
21 Drydock Avenue, Boston, MA 02210

Manufactured in the United States of America
10 9 8 7 6 5 4 3 2 1

Distributed by Penguin Random House Publisher Services
Tel: 800.733.3000

Pictured on front cover **Butter-Basted Rib Steak (page 69)**

Pictured on back cover **Sous Vide Pepper-Crusted Beef Roast (page 49), Crumb-Crusted Rack of Lamb (page 342), Grilled Lemongrass Pork Chops (page 227)**

Front and Back Cover Food Styling **Catrine Kelty**
Front and Back Cover Photography **Joseph Keller**

Editorial Director, Books **Adam Kowit**

Executive Food Editor **Dan Zuccarello**

Deputy Food Editor **Stephanie Pixley**

Executive Managing Editor **Debra Hudak**

Project Editor **Sacha Madadian**

Senior Editor **Joseph Gitter, Sara Mayer**

Assistant Editors **Tess Berger, Kelly Cormier, Brenna Donovan, and Sara Zatopek**

Editorial Assistant **Emily Rahravan**

Additional Editorial Support **Samantha Block, Christine Campbell, Sarah Ewald, April Poole**

Design Director **Lindsey Timko Chandler**

Deputy Art Director **Courtney Lentz**

Photography Director **Julie Bozzo Cote**

Photography Producer **Meredith Mulcahy**

Senior Staff Photographers **Steve Klise and Daniel J. van Ackere**

Staff Photographer **Kevin White**

Food Styling **Catrine Kelty, Chantal Lambeth, Kendra McNight, Ashley Moore, Marie Piraino, Elle Simone Scott**

Additional Photography Support **Melita Morales**

PHOTOSHOOT KITCHEN TEAM

Photo Team and Special Events Managers **Allison Berkey and Timothy McQuinn**

Lead Test Cook **Eric Haessler**

Assistant Test Cooks **Hannah Fenton, Jacqueline Gochenouer, Gina McCreadie, and Christa West**

Illustrations **John Burgoyne**

Senior Manager, Publishing Operations **Taylor Argenzio**

Imaging Manager **Lauren Robbins**

Production and Imaging Specialists **Tricia Neumyer, Dennis Noble, and Amanda Yong**

Copy Editor **Cheryl Redmond**

Proofreader **Ann-Marie Imbornoni**

Indexer **Elizabeth Parson**

Chief Creative Officer **Jack Bishop**

Executive Editorial Directors **Julia Collin Davison and Bridget Lancaster**

contents

welcome to
AMERICA'S TEST KITCHEN

This book has been tested, written, and edited by the folks at America's Test Kitchen, where curious cooks become confident cooks. Located in Boston's Seaport District in the historic Innovation and Design Building, it features 15,000 square feet of kitchen space including multiple photography and video studios. It is the home of *Cook's Illustrated* magazine and *Cook's Country* magazine and is the workday destination for more than 60 test cooks, editors, and cookware specialists. Our mission is to empower and inspire confidence, community, and creativity in the kitchen.

We start the process of testing a recipe with a complete lack of preconceptions, which means that we accept no claim, no technique, and no recipe at face value. We simply assemble as many variations as possible, test a half-dozen of the most promising, and taste the results blind. We then construct our own recipe and continue to test it, varying ingredients, techniques, and cooking times until we reach a consensus. As we like to say in the test kitchen, "We make the mistakes so you don't have to." The result, we hope, is the best version of a particular recipe, but we realize that only you can be the final judge of our success (or failure). We use the same rigorous approach when we test equipment and taste ingredients.

All of this would not be possible without a belief that good cooking, much like good music, is based on a foundation of objective technique. Some people like spicy foods and others don't, but there is a right way to sauté, there is a best way to cook a pot roast, and there are measurable scientific principles involved in producing perfectly beaten, stable egg whites. Our ultimate goal is to investigate the fundamental principles of cooking to give you the techniques, tools, and ingredients you need to become a better cook. It is as simple as that.

To see what goes on behind the scenes at *America's Test Kitchen,* check out our social media channels for kitchen snapshots, exclusive content, video tips, and much more. You can watch us work (in our actual test kitchen) by tuning in to America's Test Kitchen or *Cook's Country* on public television or on our websites. Download our award-winning podcast Proof, which goes beyond recipes to solve food mysteries (AmericasTestKitchen.com/proof), or listen to test kitchen experts on public radio (SplendidTable.org) to hear insights that illuminate the truth about real home cooking. Want to hone your cooking skills or finally learn how to bake—with an America's Test Kitchen test cook? Enroll in one of our online cooking classes. And you can engage the next generation of home cooks with kid-tested recipes from America's Test Kitchen Kids.

Our community of home recipe testers provides valuable feedback on recipes under development by ensuring that they are foolproof. You can help us investigate the how and why behind successful recipes from your home kitchen. (Sign up at AmericasTestKitchen. com/recipe_testing.)

However you choose to visit us, we welcome you into our kitchen, where you can stand by our side as we test our way to the best recipes in America.

facebook.com/AmericasTestKitchen
twitter.com/TestKitchen
youtube.com/AmericasTestKitchen
instagram.com/TestKitchen
pinterest.com/TestKitchen

AmericasTestKitchen.com
CooksIllustrated.com
CooksCountry.com
OnlineCookingSchool.com
AmericasTestKitchen.com/kids

introduction

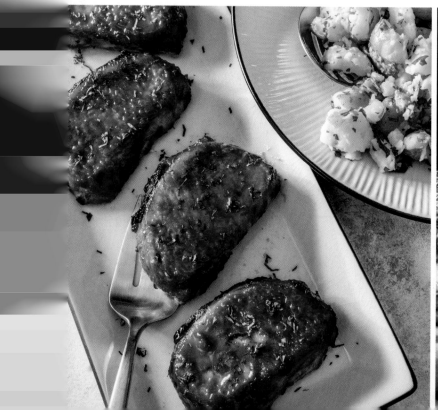

MEAT OF ANY KIND, whether a weeknight-friendly pork tenderloin roast or a prized special-occasion prime rib, a thick-cut veal chop or a hearty lamb burger, is a special kind of luxury, a privilege to eat, even if you eat it every day. It's also a nourishing gift, one that provides protein and essential nutrients. But because many of us eat meat routinely, this is easy to forget. There's a lot that goes into bringing meat from pasture (or elsewhere) to your plate. Breeds of animals are many, raising styles vary and affect the animal's taste and texture, wholesalers separate sides of meat into large primal cuts, butchers break large cuts down into smaller retail cuts, and, finally, you bring cuts home and cook them.

The very last step is where we come in: We develop foolproof recipes. You can be certain we'll reliably teach you the best way to cook meat—beef, veal, pork, lamb, and ground meat. But we want to shed light on the importance of the preceding steps. And so this isn't just a cookbook, it's also an invaluable handbook filled with detailed hand-drawn illustrations and organized by animal. For each animal, we present its primal cuts and hierarchy of retail cuts—roasts, steaks, and chops—along with the facts you need to make informed cooking decisions. Chuck roast, you'll find, is cut from the cow's shoulder and is tougher because the muscles are actively used for movement, so you'll want to cook it low and slow to tenderize. Lamb loin and rib chops can be used interchangeably (pan-sear or grill them) so you can improvise. Learn (and view) cut-specific techniques like trimming a rack of lamb to reduce its slightly gamy-tasting fat, or properly carving an unwieldy country ham.

Looking to branch out from the cuts you're used to? Have a new butcher shop in the neighborhood, or curious about a new cut in the case? This approach helps you grasp the must-know methods for your favorite cuts but also gives you the opportunity to read about new-to-you cuts so you're empowered to take advantage of the wide range of options that might look good wherever you're shopping. Cook what your eyes are drawn to—maybe the marbling on a big porterhouse looks particularly abundant one day, or your butcher just started displaying a blade-end pork loin roast next to the center-cut one—not just familiar standbys, like workaday steak tips and boneless pork chops. Become a confident carnivore, cooking up whatever appeals with ease.

If you are giving a cut a try for the first time, you'll be comforted to know it will come out perfectly, because each cut in this book is followed by recipes that cover every technique appropriate for it. The entry for flank steak, for example, will share that it takes well to pan searing, stir-frying, and grilling, and even braising. You'll find recipes for each cooking method, with Pan-Seared Flank Steak with Mustard-Chive Butter (page 166), Beef Stir-Fry with Bell Peppers and Black Pepper Sauce (page 169), Grilled Beef Satay (page 175), and Arrachera en Adobo (page 168), respectively.

A cut of meat is often a center-of-the-plate star, and we make it shine in satisfying recipes like Butter-Basted Rib Steak (page 69), where we spoon hot butter on the steaks from both sides so they come to temperature as they acquire a deep crust; meltingly tender Chinese Barbecue Roast Pork Shoulder (page 220), cooked for 6 hours so the collagen melts to lubricate the meat; and the quintessential Crumb-Crusted Rack of Lamb (page 342), spread with mustard so the crumbs adhere.

Meat can also have an impact when it doesn't sit in the middle of the plate and instead is an equal part of a whole meal. Vibrant dishes benefit from large and small additions of meat, sometimes for richness or savor rather than for bulk. We bring meat beyond centerpiece status with complete meals: Shake up surf and turf with Fried Brown Rice with Pork and Shrimp (page 258). Braise lamb shoulder chops in a Libyan-style chickpea and orzo soup called Sharba (page 337). Lemongrass Beef and Rice Noodles (page 154) is a fresh-tasting meal in a bowl, full of pleasing textures. An Italian pork, fennel, and lemon ragu (see page 228) coats ribbons of pappardelle surprisingly delicately. Egyptian Eggah with Ground Beef and Spinach (page 380) features bountiful spinach and leeks and spiced ground beef in a thick egg omelet.

Meat Illustrated has the answer to any kind of meat, manner of cooking, or style of recipe you prefer. Butchering is a craft; we hope this book does justice to the cuts that come from it, making cooking and eating meat more memorable, and more special.

Recipe List by Cut

Sometimes the purchase comes before the planning. Use this list to search for recipes you might like to make for the cut you have on hand.

Beef

▮ CHUCK
Chuck-Eye Roast
Barbecue Chuck Roast (51)
Best Beef Stew (45)
Bresato al Barolo (40)
Carne Guisada (47)
Chuck Roast in Foil (43)
Classic Pot Roast (40)
Boeuf Bourguignon (45)
Pot-au-Feu (42)
Pressure-Cooker Beef Stew with Tomatoes, Olives, and Orange Zest (48)
Rigatoni alla Genovese (46)
Roasted Beef Chuck with Horseradish-Parsley Sauce (44)
Shredded Barbecue Beef (51)
Slow-Cooker Pot Roast with Tomatoes and Red Wine (48)
Sous Vide Pepper-Crusted Beef Roast (49)

Chuck-Eye Steak
Grilled Chuck Steaks (52)

Top-Blade Roast
*good substitute for chuck-eye roast

Blade Steak
Braised Steaks with Root Vegetables (54)
Chipotle Beef Tamales (57)
Pressure-Cooker Beef and Barley Soup (54)
Thai Beef with Chiles and Shallots (56)
Ultimate Beef Chili (53)

Flat-Iron Steak
Smoked Herb-Rubbed Flat-Iron Steaks (59)

7-Bone Chuck Roast
*good substitute for chuck-eye roast

▮ RIB
First-Cut Standing Rib Roast
Best Roast Prime Rib (65)
Boneless Rib Roast with Yorkshire Pudding and Jus (65)
Grill-Smoked Prime Rib (67)
One-Pan Roasted Prime Rib and Vegetables (67)
Sous Vide Prime Rib (68)

Second-Cut Standing Rib Roast
*good substitute for first-cut standing rib roast

Rib Steak
Butter-Basted Rib Steak (69)

Double-Cut Bone-In Rib Steak
Grilled Cowboy-Cut Steaks (69)

Rib-Eye Steak
Bulgogi (71)
Grilled Bourbon Steaks (72)
Hibachi-Style Steaks and Vegetables (73)
Spice-Rubbed Rib Eyes (72)

▮ SHORT LOIN
Top Loin Roast
Holiday Strip Roast (80)

Boneless Strip Steak
Cast Iron Steaks with Herb Butter (83)
Garlic Steaks (85)
Grilled Argentine Steaks with Chimichurri Sauce (87)
Grilled Frozen Steaks with Arugula and Parmesan (86)
One-Pan Steak with Sweet Potatoes and Scallions (85)
Pressure-Cooker Beef Pho (90)
Quick Pan-Seared Strip Steaks (83)
Sous Vide Seared Steaks (89)
Steak Frites (86)

Thick-Cut Strip Steaks (80)
Ultimate Charcoal-Grilled Steaks (89)

Porterhouse Steak
Bistecca alla Fiorentina (93)
Grilled Steaks with Garlic Essence (93)
Grilled Thick-Cut Porterhouse Steaks (92)
Thick-Cut Porterhouse Steaks (92)

T-Bone Steak
*good substitute for porterhouse steak

▮ TENDERLOIN
Whole Beef Tenderloin
Green Peppercorn–Crusted Beef Tenderloin (98)
Peppercorn-Crusted Beef Tenderloin (98)
Pink Peppercorn–Crusted Beef Tenderloin (98)
White Peppercorn–Crusted Beef Tenderloin (98)

Center-Cut Beef Tenderloin Roast
Beef Wellington (102)
Grill-Roasted Beef Tenderloin (104)
Horseradish-Crusted Beef Tenderloin (100)
Roast Beef Tenderloin (98)
Roast Beef Tenderloin with Mushroom and Caramelized Onion Stuffing (101)

Filet Mignon
Bacon-Wrapped Filets Mignons (107)
Filets Mignons with Sage-Buttered Mushrooms and Black Pepper Polenta (105)
Grilled Filets Mignons (107)
Pepper-Crusted Filets Mignons (105)

▮ SIRLOIN
Top Sirloin Roast
Baltimore Pit Beef (114)
Beef en Cocotte with Caramelized Onions (112)

Veal Cutlets

Cotoletta alla Valdostana (204)
Veal Scaloppini with Lemon-Parsley
Sauce (203)
Veal Scaloppini with Porcini-Marsala
Sauce (203)

Veal Shanks

Osso Buco (204)
Pressure-Cooker Veal Shanks with
Sweet and Spicy Peperonata (206)
Sous Vide Osso Buco (205)

Pork

▮ BLADE SHOULDER
Bone-In Pork Butt Roast

Chinese Barbecue Roast Pork
Shoulder (220)
Cider-Braised Pork Roast (218)
Slow-Roasted Pork Shoulder with
Cherry Sauce (218)
Slow-Roasted Pork Shoulder with
Peach Sauce (218)

Boneless Pork Butt Roast

Carnitas (222)
Chile Verde con Cerdo (230)
Feijoada (230)
French Pork and White Bean
Casserole (229)
Homemade Sausages and Peppers (227)
Indoor Pulled Pork With Lexington
Vinegar Barbecue Sauce (227)
Indoor Pulled Pork with Sweet and
Tangy Barbecue Sauce (225)
Porchetta (222)
Ragù Bianco (228)
Pork Gyro (227)
Pressure-Cooker Shredded Pork
Tacos (232)
Slow-Cooker Southwestern Pork
Roast (221)
Sous Vide Char Siu (233)
South Carolina Pulled Pork (224)

Pork Butt Steaks

*we cut them from pork butt roast

Blade-Cut Pork Chops

Filipino Pork Adobo (235)
Grilled Lemongrass Pork Chops (237)
Red Wine–Braised Pork Chops (234)
Slow-Cooker Braised Pork Chops with
Campfire Beans (235)

▮ ARM SHOULDER
Picnic Shoulder Roast

Cuban-Style Grill-Roasted Pork (243)
Pork Pernil (240)

Smoked Picnic Ham

Glazed Picnic Ham (Smoked
Shoulder) (240)

▮ LOIN
Blade-End Pork Rib Roast

Barbecue Glazed Pork Roast (252)

Boneless Blade-End Pork Loin

Grill-Roasted Pork Loin (253)
Smoked Pork Loin with Dried-Fruit
Chutney (253)

Country-Style Ribs

Braised Ribs with Black-Eyed Peas and
Collard Greens (258)
Fried Brown Rice with Pork and
Shrimp (258)
Pork Lo Mein (263)
Posole (255)
Slow-Cooker Pork Pad Thai (264)
Slow-Cooker Spicy Pork Chili with
Black-Eyed Peas (257)
Slow-Cooker Sunday Gravy (256)
Pinchos Morunos (259)
Shu Mai (261)
Sweet and Tangy Grilled Country-Style
Pork Ribs (256)
Vietnamese Summer Rolls (260)

Center-Cut Pork Rib Roast

Grill-Roasted Bone-In Pork Rib Roast (266)
Slow-Roasted Bone-In Pork Rib Roast (264)

Pork Rib Chops

Caribbean Grilled Thin-Cut Pork
Chops (271)
Grilled Thin-Cut Pork Chops (271)
Indoor Barbecue Pork Chops (267)

Mediterranean Grilled Thin-Cut Pork
Chops (271)
Pan-Seared Thick-Cut Pork Chops (269)
Pan-Seared Thick-Cut Pork Chops with
Cilantro and Coconut Pan Sauce (269)
Pan-Seared Thick-Cut Pork Chops with
Garlic and Thyme Pan Sauce (269)
Sous Vide Thick-Cut Pork Chops (269)
Spicy Thai Grilled Thin-Cut Pork Chops (271)
Texas Thick-Cut Smoked Pork Chops (270)

Crown Roast

Crown Roast of Pork (266)

Center-Cut Pork Loin

Enchaud Perigordine (273)
Herb-Crusted Pork Loin (272)
Pressure-Cooker Pork Loin with Black
Mole Sauce (276)
Roast Pork Loin with Sweet Potatoes
and Cilantro Sauce (272)
Slow-Cooker Pork Loin With Warm Spiced
Chickpea Salad (275)

Boneless Pork Chops

Crispy Pan-Fried Pork Chops (277)
Crispy Pan-Fried Pork Chops with Spicy
Rub (277)
Crispy Pan-Fried Pork Chops with
Three-Pepper Rub (277)
Deviled Pork Chops (278)
Mustardy Apple Butter–Glazed Pork
Chops (277)
Pan-Seared Thick-Cut Boneless Pork Chops
with Peaches and Spinach (278)
Spicy Gochujang-Glazed Pork Chops (277)

Pork Tenderloin

Broiled Pork Tenderloin (280)
Grilled Pork Kebabs with Hoisin and
Five-Spice (285)
Grilled Pork Tenderloin with Grilled
Pineapple–Red Onion Salsa (284)
Mu Shu Pork (286)
Pepper-Crusted Pork Tenderloin
with Asparagus and Balsamic
Pan Sauce (279)
Perfect Pan-Seared Pork Tenderloin
Steaks (284)
Pork Medallions with Red Pepper
Sauce (283)

Meat Must-Knows

The four parts of this book break down the specifics for beef and veal, pork, and lamb cuts, and ground meat. But there are universal purchasing, prepping, and cooking steps. We cover those here.

BREAKING AN ANIMAL INTO CUTS

Animals are divided into large primal cuts (the shoulder of lamb or the rib of a cow, for example) at wholesale. These are the ones you see outlined in most animal drawings including our own, which are then cut into the smaller roasts (sometimes called sub-primals) and even smaller steaks and chops that we buy at retail. (For more information on butchery, see page 30.) This nomenclature is widely accepted but we use it more loosely in this book because it's less applicable in the home kitchen than it is at a slaughterhouse or butcher shop. Some cuts straddle two primals and don't fit neatly in a category (beef tenderloin, a favorite of many, for example, spans the short loin and the sirloin of the cow). Some don't make sense to discuss in culinary terms at the same time: A lamb shank cooks a lot differently than the leg to which it's attached. We're here to teach you about specific cuts you can commonly find and how best to cook them, so that's how we've organized the sections within chapters.

Each section opens with universal information about the larger wholesale cut and then follows with specifics about the roasts and steaks that come from there. Recipes that follow are tagged with the cut they call for. You can also refer to the chart beginning on page 2 to see recipes organized by cut so you know exactly where to go in the book once you come home with what looked good at the market.

PURCHASING AND STORING

The sections on beef, veal, pork, and lamb each tell you how to choose high-quality cuts, but there are also general shopping and storing tips to take to the market with you.

Pay Attention to Temperature
When you're picking meat from a case, you might have an eye on the cleanliness of the surroundings, but temperature is important, too. Is the packaging cool to the touch? Even at the farmers' market, meat should be stored under 40 degrees. On especially hot days, take advantage of your market's insulated shopping bags (or bring an insulated cooler bag—the type used to keep lunches cool). Of course, you can also keep a cooler in the trunk of your car. If you have a lot of items on your grocery list, make the meat counter one of your last stops, so the meat stays cooler until you can get it home.

Looks Matter
Meat should look moist but not sodden. For example, an excessive amount of juices inside a meat package, also called purge, can be an indication that the meat has been on the shelf for too long. As for color, red meat will appear mahogany or purplish when butchered but the flesh will turn bright red or pink once exposed to oxygen. Meat that has turned brown all the way through is on its way to spoiling. Avoid meat that has green spots—this is an indication of spoilage and bacteria. Note that shrink-wrapped cuts may be of varying sizes and thicknesses, which will have an adverse effect on cooking times. If possible, buy parts individually to make sure they're of similar size and thus cook through at the same rate.

Fat Is Flavor
Streaks of white throughout meat, especially beef, are an indication of marbling. The marbling is fat and adds flavor to meat. Don't confuse marbling with gristle. Gristle, which is often translucent rather than white, is connective tissue and does not break down upon cooking. Avoid cuts with visible gristle when possible. Note that some exterior fat is good, especially when selecting roasts. In the oven or on the grill, this fat will melt and flavor the meat. This is especially important when selecting relatively lean cuts like pork loin or beef brisket. However, excessive exterior fat will need to be trimmed, and since you're buying meat by the pound, more than ½ inch of exterior fat is generally too much.

Your Nose Knows
You know how fresh fish shouldn't smell overtly fishy? The same goes for meat. Truly fresh meat should have little aroma. Any strong off or sour odors indicate spoilage.

Meat Label Mastery
Does "pasture-raised" mean that the beef you're buying came from a cow that spent its days roaming a bucolic field? That may not be the case. Here are labeling terms that require explanation.

PASTURE-RAISED
The term "pasture-raised" is not regulated by the U.S. Department of Agriculture (USDA) and is not clearly defined in the industry. (The animals' access to a pasture may be very limited.) Geography may affect pasture raising; animals in colder climates might spend less time in the pasture than those in more temperate areas. A "pasture-raised" label can be an indication of quality, but to be sure, you should ask the producer how they define the term.

NO HORMONES AND NO ANTIBIOTICS

Beef may be labeled "no hormones administered" if the producer can provide documentation proving that the animal wasn't raised with hormones. The USDA prohibits all use of hormones (and steroids) with pork, so it technically doesn't require a label. The agency requires that if a "no hormones" label is used, it must be followed by the statement, "Federal regulations prohibit the use of hormones." In short, the label is an empty reassurance since the practice is prohibited for pork anyway. Similarly, it is not industry standard to use hormones on lamb. Like the "no hormones" label, the term "no antibiotics" can be applied if the producer provides documentation that the animal was not raised with antibiotics. This is useful for beef, pork, veal, and lamb (antibiotics can be administered to all four).

NATURAL

"Natural" simply means that the meat was minimally processed and contains no artificial ingredients. The USDA defines minimally processed meat as meat "processed in a manner that does not fundamentally alter the product." Our advice is to stick to buying your meat fresh if possible and skip the frozen food aisle; there's probably not much that's natural about frozen sliced sandwich "steak," burger patties, and bags of frozen meatballs.

ORGANIC

In contrast to "natural," the USDA's definition of "organic" is a bit more involved: Organic food is produced by farmers who emphasize the use of renewable resources and the conservation of soil and water to enhance environmental quality for future generations. Organic meat comes from animals that are given no antibiotics or growth hormones. Organic food is produced without using most conventional pesticides; fertilizers made with synthetic ingredients or sewage sludge; bioengineering; or ionizing radiation. Before a product can be labeled "organic," a government-approved certifier inspects the farm where the food is grown to make sure the farmer is following all the rules necessary to meet USDA organic standards. A farm must use organic processes for three years before it can become accredited.

Buy Bone-In or Boneless?

We see value in both bone-in and boneless cuts depending on how much effort you want to put into preparing, how long you're willing to wait for something to cook, and what you plan to do with the end result. We call for boneless meat often. However, it's true that bone-in meat tastes meatier. As bones are heated, they expel moisture, salt, amino acids, and nucleotides from the richly flavored marrow. Since those water-soluble flavor molecules must penetrate through a thick layer of bone to reach the meat, the diffusion process is slow and the amount of flavor contributed is not enormous—but it is detectable. When coupled with the considerable moisture- and flavor-enhancing benefits of the fat and connective tissue around the bones, the process certainly provides another good reason to opt for bone-in cuts of meat if you have the option in a recipe.

Keep It Cold

Meat should be refrigerated promptly after purchase and can remain refrigerated before cooking for up to three days. Smoked and cured products store for two weeks once opened, and ground meat, defrosted cuts, and cooked meat store for two days. A refrigerator thermometer will tell you if your fridge and freezer are working properly. Check the temperature of your refrigerator regularly to ensure that it is between 35 and 40 degrees; your freezer should be below zero degrees.

Keep in mind that the back of a refrigerator is the coldest, while the door is the least cold. Make sure that raw meat is stored well wrapped and never on shelves that are above other food, especially when thawing.

As for freezing meat, in general, meat tastes best if you've never frozen it. The slow process of freezing that occurs in a home freezer (as compared with a commercial freezer) causes large ice crystals to form. The crystals rupture the cell walls of the meat, permitting the release of juices during cooking. That said, if you're going to freeze meat, we've found that the best method is to remove it from its packaging, vacuum-seal it or wrap it well in plastic, and then place the meat in a zipper-lock bag and squeeze out excess air. If the cuts are small, like steaks or chops, we like to freeze them, uncovered, overnight on a baking sheet (this dries them out to prevent crystallization) before wrapping them tightly in plastic wrap and placing them in the zipper-lock bag. Meat can remain frozen for up to one month before cooking; however, if you own and use a vacuum sealer, you can store it for about three months.

A way to level-up freezing: Quick-chill the meat before placing it in the freezer. Why? The faster the meat freezes the smaller the ice crystals that form. We quick-chill items by using an ice bath with added salt. This works wonders for cuts like steaks, pork chops, or small roasts like tenderloins. Combine 1 cup of ice, 1 pound of salt, and ⅓ cup of water in a container. This is enough mixture to chill four steaks or chops. Wrap the meat in plastic wrap, place the pieces in a zipper-lock bag, and submerge the bag in the ice bath. Once the meat is frozen solid, remove the bag from the ice bath and transfer it to the freezer.

To prevent the growth of harmful bacteria when thawing frozen meat, we defrost thicker (1 inch or greater) cuts in the refrigerator and place thinner cuts on a heavy cast-iron or steel pan at room temperature; the metal's rapid heat transfer safely thaws the meat in about an hour. Have even less time? Soak cuts such as chops, steaks, and cutlets in hot water. Simply seal steaks or chops in zipper-lock bags and submerge the packages in very hot (140-degree) water. Cuts will take roughly 12 minutes to thaw, which is fast enough that the rate of bacterial growth falls into the "safe" category, and the meat doesn't start to cook. (Large roasts are not suitable for hot thawing.)

THE 1, 2, 3, 4s OF COOKING MEAT

Whether beef, veal, pork, or lamb is on the menu, there are universal prep steps that ensure the best—and safest—results. Follow one, two, three, and four for preparing anything from small steaks to weighty roasts.

1. PRACTICE SAFE PREPARATION

The safety considerations for preparing meat are different from those for preparing produce or pantry items. After all, meat has doneness temperatures (as opposed to that roasted carrot that you're not sticking a temperature probe in); even the very best, USDA-approved piece of meat naturally contains some bacteria that you can't see, taste, or smell. And you'll not only want to kill it through cooking (see page 11 for proper cooking temperatures), but also make sure it doesn't spread to other spots in your kitchen or other food items.

BUILDING BARRIERS

Try to keep things relatively contained when you're cooking with meat, choosing your space before you take the meat out of the package, reserving cutting boards just for meat prep, and covering items you'll place meat on, like a hard-to-clean kitchen scale, with plastic wrap.

WASH EVERYTHING—EXCEPT YOUR MEAT

Wash your hands, wash your sink regularly, wash your prep areas before and after cooking, wash your sponges to disinfect them. Do *not* wash your meat. This outdated practice of rinsing meat is more likely to spread contaminants around the sink (and perhaps onto nearby foods like lettuce sitting on the counter) than to send them down the drain. And our kitchen tests failed to demonstrate any flavor benefit to rinsing meat before cooking.

SEPARATE SALT AND PEPPER

Though bacteria can't live for more than a few minutes in direct contact with salt (which quickly dehydrates bacteria, leading to cell death), it can live on the edges of a box or shaker. To avoid contamination, grind pepper and place salt in small bowls. This way, you can reach into the bowl for seasoning without having to wash your hands every time you touch raw meat. Afterward, the bowls go right into the dishwasher.

2. SEASON WITH SENSE

You can cook a rib eye to a perfect medium-rare, and its browned exterior and beautiful rosy center are still nothing without seasoning. Salt has serious uses in meat cookery that you'll read about, but it also just makes food taste its best. And don't forget pepper, a perfect meat pairing.

FLAVOR FAT

Season fattier cuts of meat more generously than lean meat. Fat is flavorful—that's why we like it—but it can also dull the palate to other tastes. You need to use a heavier hand when seasoning fattier cuts "to taste."

SEASONING SHOWER

If you've seen chefs season meat, you know that they often sprinkle salt and pepper high above the food. This isn't just kitchen theatrics—this technique distributes the seasoning more evenly than if sprinkled close to the meat, where it will clump in spots.

START-TO-FINISH SEASONING

We season meat at different times during the cooking process so it blends in properly: Applying salt to meat before cooking improves flavor and, sometimes, texture. Salting a stew before braising ensures even, well-rounded seasoning, as salt's rate of diffusion increases with heat. Finally, it's crucial to taste a dish for seasoning before serving it. When adjusting seasonings after cooking, keep in mind that unlike salt, pepper has more punch when unheated; use it sparingly. Salt with some texture, like our go-to, Maldon sea salt, is a nice way to finish a slab of juicy prime rib or a lamb chop.

BRINING BASICS

Brining—soaking food in a solution of salt and water—is a pretreatment that can make lean meats juicy, tender, and flavorful throughout. During brining, salt moves from the area of greatest concentration (the surrounding liquid brine) to the area of lesser concentration (the interior of the food being brined), bringing the liquid with it in a process called osmosis. Meanwhile, the salt changes the structure of the proteins, so they're better able to hold on to the moisture received in osmosis, even after cooking. Through this process, the meat's structural integrity is compromised, which reduces toughness and results in a more tender product. And, of course, the method seasons meat to the very center.

We usually don't brine beef and lamb; brining can water down their robust taste. Many cuts of beef and lamb have enough fat to melt within the meat, making it juicy without help. Beef cuts that are leaner should ideally be cooked only to about 125 degrees (for medium-rare). In comparison, pork needs to be cooked to 145 degrees and is, therefore, in greater danger of drying out. So we often turn to brining for lean pork to keep it juicy.

You don't need much for brining; just your protein, table salt (the tiny grains dissolve more quickly in water than kosher salt), and a container. Brining formulas are provided in recipes, but if you're taking matters into your own hands, follow the general guidelines in the table on page 11 for salt-to-water rules for pork.

THE OTHER SALTING

Salting often simply means seasoning meat. But it has another meaning in the test kitchen, and that's the act of sprinkling meat with salt (we often use kosher for more even distribution of the larger grains) and then letting the meat rest and gain benefits much like those from brining. Why the need for this alternative pretreatment technique? The added moisture of a brine makes it tough to get browning and crisping on the surface of meat. And as stated, all that water can wash out the concentrated meaty flavor of beef and lamb.

When salt is applied to meat and left to sit for a spell, it first draws the moisture out to the surface through osmosis, where the liquid dissolves that applied salt. Drawing out moisture doesn't make the meat less moist, however. That's where time comes in. Once the salt dissolves in the surface moisture, it creates a superconcentrated brine, which moves into the meat. This migration causes muscle fibers to swell to make room for the liquid and dissolves other proteins, which then act like a sponge so that the meat soaks up and holds on to moisture during cooking. The meat tastes more like itself since it's reabsorbing its own juices, so the method is

Meat Prep Guide

Here are some guidelines to follow when pretreating meat in recipes that don't provide brining and salting instructions, as well as the proper temperatures for your desired meat doneness.

BRINING PORK CUTS

CUT	COLD WATER	TABLE SALT	TIME
Bone-In Pork Chops (up to 6)	1½ quarts	3 tablespoons	½ to 1 hour
Boneless Pork Chops (up to 6)	1½ quarts	3 tablespoons	½ to 1 hour
1 (2½- to 6-pound) Boneless Roast	2 quarts	¼ cup	1 to 1½ hours

SALTING MEAT CUTS

CUT	KOSHER SALT	TIME	METHOD
Steaks, Lamb Chops, Pork Chops	¾ teaspoons per 8-ounce steak or chop	1 hour	Apply salt evenly over surface and let rest at room temperature, uncovered, on a wire rack set in a rimmed baking sheet
Beef, Lamb, and Pork Roasts	1 teaspoon per pound	At least 4 hours or up to 24 hours (sometimes as long as 4 days!)	Apply salt evenly over surface, into crosshatches when applicable, wrap tightly with plastic wrap if recipe specifies so, and let rest in the refrigerator

MEAT DONENESS TEMPERATURES

CUT	DESIRED DONENESS	COOKING STOP TEMPERATURE	TEMPERATURE AFTER RESTING
Beef, Veal, and Lamb	Rare	115 to 120 degrees	120 to 125 degrees
	Medium-Rare	120 to 125 degrees	125 to 130 degrees
	Medium	130 to 135 degrees	135 to 140 degrees
	Medium-Well	140 to 145 degrees	145 to 150 degrees
	Well-Done	150 to 155 degrees	155 to 160 degrees
Pork	Medium	140 to 145 degrees	150 degrees
	Well-Done	150 to 155 degrees	160 degrees

Note: The doneness temperatures in this book represent the test kitchen's assessment of palatability weighed against safety. The basics from the USDA differ somewhat: Cook whole cuts of meat, including pork, to an internal temperature of at least 145 degrees and let rest for at least 3 minutes. Cook all ground meats to an internal temperature of at least 160 degrees. For more information on food safety from the USDA, visit www.fsis.usda.gov.

appropriate for beef and lamb, too. And because the cuts aren't overly moist, their surfaces can achieve good browning. Follow the general guidelines for salting in the table on page 11 when prepping beef, lamb, and pork.

THE MARINADE MYTH

Marinating is often regarded as a cure-all for bland, chewy meat. Years of testing have taught us that while it can bump up flavor, a marinade will never turn a tough cut tender. But with the right ingredients in the mix, marinating can enhance juiciness and add complexity. Successful marinating is all about getting as much of the soaking liquid flavors into (and on) the meat as possible. Brining in a saltwater solution is a way to create more juiciness. But to pump up flavor as well as juiciness, our marinades combine both approaches, with soaking liquids that not only contain lots of seasonings and flavorings but also enough salt—or a salt-containing ingredient like glutamate-rich, meaty-tasting soy sauce—that you might even call them "brinerades." This deepens their effectiveness. Marinating is most successful with thinner cuts of meat (since you'll never get a flavoring to penetrate far) and course-grained meats like flank steak which have channels for the flavor to physically enter.

Oil is another important marinade component. Most of the herbs and spices we add to marinades are oil-soluble, which means they only release their full flavor when mixed in oil. So, to get the most out of a marinade, include oil. Sugar or honey can boost complexity and make marinated foods brown better.

When we refrigerate marinated meat, we often do so in a zipper-lock bag so we can make sure the meat is fully surrounded by the salty elixir. We also flip the bag occasionally to evenly distribute the stuff. Sometimes we poke or score the meat first for more efficient penetration.

Many of the same rules apply for dry and wet rubs. You want to make sure your meat's surface can grab on to these seasoning agents: That could mean spraying leaner cuts with bonding oil (see page 118), or making crosshatches in the meat or a roast's fat cap and making sure seasonings enter the slits, which we do often.

3. COOK, ACCORDING TO THE RECIPE

Our recipes are formulated to marry a cut of meat with the best cooking technique (for more information on these techniques, see page 13), and each recipe explains why it turns out perfectly. Be sure to dry meats that will be seared, roasted, or grilled by patting with paper towels before cooking so that they'll brown properly. And cook to the "right" doneness temperature.

To some extent doneness temperatures are subjective—there's a reason you're asked your preference at a steakhouse. And to some extent they're not—if you want to be eating tasty meat. Pork, to be safe for consumption, must be cooked to 145 degrees, so there's not much wiggle room there—you can only go up. Veal is best at medium. For most of our beef and lamb recipes, we call for cooking meat to the degree we think is best for *most* cuts, which is medium-rare. We list the timing and temperature for this in our recipes. Some cuts taste better, however, at medium due to the composition of their muscle fibers. These include top sirloin steak, flap meat, and flank steak (for more information, see page 110).

That said, who are we to stop you from eating bloody-rare or brown-in-the-middle well-done meat? Follow the doneness table on page 11 for these temperatures and know that if a recipe calls for cooking to medium-rare, you'll need to keep the meat in the pan for less time for rare or more time for medium and beyond, to get your results.

Insert the probe of an instant-read thermometer deep into the meat, away from any bone, which throws off the reading. You can take two or three readings to make sure the entire piece of meat has reached the proper temperature. For smaller cuts, such as steaks and chops, take the temperature of the meat from the side, so you can easily reach the center. And check each piece.

Finally, don't forget about carryover cooking. Meat continues to rise in temperature as it rests, so we remove it from the oven below its desired serving temperature.

4. GIVE IT A REST

Much like a sweet-smelling tray of chocolate chip cookies, a hot juicy steak isn't something you want to wait to eat. But be patient. The purpose of resting meat is to allow the juices, which are driven to the center during cooking, to redistribute throughout the meat. As a result, meat that has rested will shed much less juice than meat sliced straight after cooking. To prove this, we grilled four steaks and let two rest while slicing into the other two immediately. The steaks that had rested for 10 minutes shed 40 percent less juice than the steaks sliced right after cooking. The meat on the unrested steaks also looked grayer and was not as tender. A thin steak or chop should rest for about 5 to 10 minutes, a thicker roast for about 15 to 20 minutes.

tenderize the meat. When the meat's temperature rises above 122 degrees, the action stops. So the longer the temperature is low, the more tenderizing can take place. Lower heat also reduces the temperature differential between the exterior and the interior of the meat, so you end up with meat that's more evenly cooked.

We tie many roasts with cooking twine before putting them in the oven. (Specific tying instructions are provided by cut throughout the book.) This can help uneven cuts roast more evenly. Some cuts are already even, like cylindrical beef tenderloin or bottom round roast; we use twine here to tie down the roast to even out the thickness.

Many times we give roasted meats a booster seat. Cooking on a roasting rack or on a wire rack set in a rimmed baking sheet means there isn't a side in contact with a pan that can overcook or overbrown, and instead the heat of the oven circulates around the roast, cooking it more evenly.

Sometimes quicker-cooking cuts won't brown enough from their shorter stint in the oven. In those cases (and since they're quicker-cooking, they're small enough to fit in a skillet), we'll sear them on the stovetop before or after cooking (depending on the recipe) to brown them to perfection.

Braising and Stewing

To braise means to cook the meat in a closed environment to break down its proteins and achieve ultratender results. While roasting uses dry heat to create flavor through changes to meat's proteins (in effect, it adds heat to food to make it taste good), braising unlocks the delicious flavor already inherent in the meat you're cooking: The tough collagen breaks down, tenderizing the meat, and making it taste distinctly of itself. Stewing is essentially the same thing, although we tend to use the term for braises of cubes of meat.

Steady cooking is braising's greatest benefit. Cooking in liquid maintains a temperature in the cooking vessel that can't possibly reach higher than 212 degrees, the boiling point of water. This allows and coaxes collagen—the main protein that makes up the chewy connective tissue that surrounds meat's muscle fibers—to melt into gelatin without the worry of one part of the meat cooking too slow or too fast on its path to tenderness. The gelatin lubricates the muscle fibers rather than holds them together (as collagen does), giving the protein a soft, tender texture. The gelatin also provides the braising liquid with the body to become a lustrous sauce for the amazing meat.

It's possible to braise in a covered pot on the stove, but we find that the direct heat of the burner is intense, specific, and often too efficient. The oven uses indirect and less efficient heat, which translates to gentle, even cooking. The cooking is low and slow, usually at an oven temperature of around 300 degrees depending on the recipe.

MANY WAYS TO MAKE MEAT

The techniques in meat cookery are numerous, some creative. We won't be cooking cuts solely with a professional blowtorch as is sometimes done in restaurants, for example, but we do grill steaks directly over the chimney starter of a charcoal grill for some of the best outdoor steaks (see page 89). We'll go to (reasonable) extremes for the best recipe, but below we list the techniques in meat cookery that we turn to again and again, and tell you why they're good for certain cuts. Throughout the book, we'll reference these techniques when we break down the cuts, listing what's best for what.

Roasting

Cooking meat in the oven lets the heat circulate around it while drying out the surface so that the Maillard reaction (see page 15) can occur and a roast can achieve the burnished browning we love to see at the center of the table. As far as active cooking methods go, it's one of the more hands-off, which is especially good for large, unwieldy roasts.

You'll notice we roast a lot of meats at a moderate temperature—nothing too scorching. In general, tender cuts, such as pork tenderloin, can be roasted in a moderately hot oven, say 300 to 375 degrees. Tougher cuts or those with lots of connective tissue benefit from oven temperatures of 300 degrees or lower. When the internal temperature of a piece of meat is kept below 122 degrees, enzymes in the meat effectively break down the muscle fibers to

A variation on braising in a pot is cooking en cocotte (French for covered cooking "in a casserole"). Here the liquid released from the meat itself creates a moist environment, in effect braising the item in its own juices. The muscle fibers break down and a shallow sauce forms, ultraconcentrated in flavor. Therefore you can serve a roast, a top sirloin roast (see page 109), or a leg of lamb (see page 348) with the fall-apart tenderness of a braise.

Broiling

The top-down cooking of broiling is good for recipes that cook quickly, where you want to get color or crust on the surface without drying out the meat out as might happen with the time required to sear it on all sides or roast it. This is a good method for pork tenderloin (see page 250), but it does require a watchful eye.

Pan Searing

We outline many creative ways to turn out the very best steaks and chops, but pan searing might be the first you think of for smaller cuts. Take to the stove with a pan and some oil and you're guaranteed a quick dinner. Not always so fast, though. Often for thick-cut steaks and chops (1½ to 1¾ inches thick), we've found it best to combine the stove with the oven, bringing the meat up to temperature in the oven and then quickly searing on the stove; this prevents a gray band of meat from occurring or, worse, a burned exterior and a raw interior if the exterior races ahead of the interior when it hits a scorching pan. There are a couple specialty methods that keep meat on the stove, however: Butter basting efficiently cooks meat from all sides when streams of superhot butter are spooned over the top in the pan (for more information, see page 69). Fast-flipping, where you flip a thick-cut steak or chop frequently, encourages heat to evenly access the meat from top to bottom and to carryover as the meat moves face-down to face-up. And of course, stir-frying is fast stovetop cooking that creates tender pieces of thinly sliced meat.

Once the meat is seared and resting and you're left with brown marks in the pan—fond—it can be nice to make a pan sauce to loosen them, as they're packed with meaty flavor. There are recipes for pan sauces accompanying meats throughout the book. Note that the idea that searing meat seals in juices is a fallacy. Searing does not lock in flavor; it only produces a great crust and flavorful fond.

Grilling

Every meat tastes good with char, and the technique can really concentrate the flavor of the meat's exterior. When we talk about grilling, we're mostly talking about cooking meats hot and fast. The temperature of the grill is somewhere between 400 and 500 degrees or higher and the meat cooks very quickly. By the time the exterior browns, the meat is cooked through. For thinner steaks and chops, you can grill over the coals of a hot fire. For thicker cuts, it can help to create a hot and a cool zone—the hot one for searing the meat and the cool one for cooking it through gently.

Grill Roasting

This is the grilling term we use for relatively large cuts of meat that are tender and require even enclosed cooking but nothing superprolonged, as they don't have a lot of collagen that needs breaking down. Grill-roasting temperatures typically range from 300 to 400 degrees, and cooking times are relatively short, usually less than 2 hours. The cooking is indirect: Food isn't placed over the coals or a lit burner, so the fire must be fashioned accordingly so that part of the grill has no fire at all. You can let the roasting meat pick up smoky flavor from the grill or charcoal alone, or you can add wood chips or chunks before cooking to amp up the woody smoke flavor.

Barbecuing

Barbecuing is the last outdoor grill technique. The goal is to impart a deep, intense smokiness while transforming chewy, tough, fatty cuts into tender, succulent meats. This means a long cooking time (usually several hours) over low heat—low and slow. This creates the ideal environment for collagen to break down and keeps the meat at a low temperature for as long as possible for optimal enzymatic activity. Although there is some debate among experts as to the proper heat level for barbecuing, we find a cooking temperature between 250 and 300 degrees to be optimal for most types of meats. Sometimes we place a small pan of water under the cooking grate to provide just a little moisture that prevents the surface of the meat from drying out. We also cover with the lid to prevent drying. Barbecue foods that cook for more than a couple of hours often require a fuel replenishment to keep the fire sufficiently hot. On a charcoal grill, this means adding fresh coals to the fire. Depending on the cut of meat, barbecuing can take the better part of a day on the grill and require monitoring and multiple fuel replenishments. For a simpler way that yields equally great results, we cook the food just long enough on the grill for it to pick up plenty of smoke; then, we move indoors and finish it in a low oven.

Slow Cooking

A slow-cooker pot does exactly that: cooks food slowly. And yet it saves the cook time by using more of it rather than less; with a relatively modest investment of up-front prep time, you can put the ingredients for dinner into the slow cooker, turn it on, and walk away for a few hours or a whole day. It's like braising to the extreme—the environment is ultramoist, ultralow in heat, and keeps the meat within a low temperature range for an ultralong time, for ultrasucculence. If you own a slow cooker, you'll find delicious slow-cooked recipes—from classic braises to "barbecue" meats—in this collection.

Electric Pressure Cooking

An electric pressure cooker (or a multicooker, which also slow-cooks) has intuitive controls for fast cooking yet with foolproof, hands-free results. There's no need to worry about your oven not being properly calibrated or your stovetop burner running too hot. Braises, stews, and numerous other traditionally long-cooked meat dishes become a weeknight option. How? When pressure cooking, you're cooking food with steam that's at a temperature up to 38 degrees higher than what's possible in a normal pot so collagen breaks down more efficiently. And dishes have maximum flavor; volatile flavor molecules can't escape the enclosed environment as they do from traditional stovetop cookware. Basically, the sealed pot means more flavor stays in the meat and jus or sauce.

Sous-Vide Cooking

A sous vide machine (also called an immersion circulator) is used to preheat a water bath to a precise temperature. Food is sealed in plastic bags and immersed in the bath. The food eventually reaches the same temperature as the water, which is often set to the ideal serving temperature of the final dish. For meat, there is usually a quick searing step before serving. This differs from conventional stovetop and oven methods, in which the heat used is much higher than the serving temperature of the food, making it imperative to remove the food at just the right moment, when it's done but not overcooked. But with sous vide there's usually no risk of overcooking, making it a game-changing technique for temperature-sensitive (and often expensive) meats like steak. The low cooking temperature ensures that the meat remains juicy; it's never dry. And dialing in the precise temperature creates exceptionally consistent results that can't be achieved with traditional methods. Long, slow cooking breaks down collagen to render even tough cuts such as chuck or pork shoulder extremely tender.

OVERCOOKING FOR A CAUSE

When you're low-and-slow roasting, braising, stewing, barbecuing, or slow cooking, you're essentially doing something you've been taught is bad: overcooking. In many cases, overcooking, however, is what makes collagen-rich, heavily marbled meats taste so good. Because when you're cooking, collagen doesn't even start to break down until the meat reaches 140 degrees—and it relaxes further once it reaches higher temperatures, preferably 160 to 190 degrees depending on the cut (see specific recipes). As meat heats, protein molecules bond together tighter, pushing out moisture; as the temperature creeps up, the meat is drier and seems tougher. But "overcook" a collagen-rich cut even more, past this point, and the collagen melts into gooey gelatin, which lubricates the muscle fibers, making the meat tender—even more tender than before the moisture was pushed out. Sure, large cuts cooked this way won't be rosy-pink inside, but they'll break to buttery, luscious pieces under your fork—a delight of its own.

WHY COOK HIGH AND HOT?

Based on the above, it sounds like cooking low and slow will give your meat first prize in succulence. But there's good reason to roast, sear, broil, and grill as well. First-prize flavor in meat often comes from browning. The process, specifically, is called the Maillard reaction, named after the French chemist who first described it in the early 1900s. The Maillard reaction occurs when the amino acids and sugars in the food, in this case meat, are subjected to heat, which causes them to combine. In turn, hundreds of different flavor compounds are created. These compounds break down to form yet more new flavor compounds, and so on, and so on.

When browning meat, you want a deep brown sear and a discernibly thick crust on all sides—best obtained by quick cooking over high heat. To ensure that meat browns properly, first make sure the meat is dry before it goes into the pan; pat it thoroughly with paper towels. Second, make sure the pan is hot by preheating it over high heat until the fat added to the pan is shimmering or almost smoking. Finally, make sure not to overcrowd the pan; there should be at least ¼ inch of space between the pieces of meat. If there isn't, the meat is likely to steam instead of brown. If need be, cook the meat in two or three batches.

There are some ways to achieve browning still if you are cooking low and slow, however. You can sear or sauté the meat before braising or stewing, or you can leave the lid off your Dutch oven for a spell when braising. The meat exposed at the top of the braise will dry and eventually brown from the oven's heat.

THE MEAT KITCHEN

Meat cookery requires the same arsenal of equipment and ingredients that you'd use for other savory cooking. We've outlined our picks for high-quality tools for butchering and preparing meat—tasks that can become difficult with inadequate equipment. As for the pantry, we recommend having a few basics on hand at all times (and you probably already do).

Oil

We recommend having vegetable oil and extra-virgin olive oil for cooking meat. The former is a cooking medium that works for every meat, the latter is a fine cooking medium as well, and a flavor finisher.

Butter

We usually sear meat in oil (butter's milk solids can burn), but butter is an excellent finisher as in Butter-Basted Rib Steak (page 69) where spooning hot melted butter over the meat promotes even cooking and enhances its richness. We also rub leaner cuts with butter before roasting, and we make flavorful compound butters (page 25) to finish meat dishes.

Salt

Keep at least table and kosher varieties for seasoning before cooking. In addition, consider buying flake sea salt to use as a final flourish and provide some nice crunch before serving.

Peppercorns

Buy whole black peppercorns to grind for seasoning meat with pepper. Always avoid dusty preground black pepper. For interest, pink, white, and green are nice to have on hand; we coat beef tenderloins with each variety (see page 98).

Spices and Rubs

You can rub meat with a single spice or a complex rub before cooking it for a flavorful crust. We have recipes for homemade spice rubs on page 20. You can make them and keep them at room temperature for a month.

Baking Soda

Does this ingredient sound unlike the others? Baking soda is actually helpful for recipes featuring small pieces of meat, like some stir-fries. Briefly soaking meat in a solution of baking soda and water raises the pH on the meat's surface, making it more difficult for the proteins to bond excessively, which keeps the meat tender and moist when it's cooked in high heat.

Equipment

BUTCHERY

CHEF'S KNIFE

A good chef's knife is an invaluable tool in the kitchen. We can't think of a meat recipe we don't use it for—this includes chopping vegetables and herbs, cutting tenderloins into medallions, butterflying a roast, and countless other tasks. In the test kitchen, we use our favorite, the **Victorinox Swiss Army Fibrox Pro 8" Chef's Knife** ($31), daily. Because a chef's knife is used so often, it is important to have one that fits comfortably in your hand, with a nonslip grip. It should be lightweight to allow for easy maneuvering. Thin, high-carbon stainless-steel blades are best for their long-lasting, super-sharp edges. And our highly recommended chef's knife is a downright bargain compared with others in the category.

PARING KNIFE

In the test kitchen, we use a paring knife for detailed work like trimming silverskin from meat. We like the balance of a lightweight handle with a comfortable grip. Blade sizes run the gamut from a stumpy 2¾ inches to as long as 5 inches. We prefer 3- to 3½-inch blades, like the one on our favorite paring knife, the **Victorinox Swiss Army Fibrox Pro 3¼" Spear Point Paring Knife** ($7), since longer blades compromise precision and agility. Slightly curved blades with sharply pointed tips are best for the widest number of tasks.

BONING KNIFE

Often, buying larger cuts of meat and butchering them yourself is more economical than buying precut meat; plus, you'll get more evenly sized pieces. If you choose to do this, a boning knife like the **Zwilling Pro 5.5" Flexible Boning Knife** ($110) can be a useful tool. A good boning knife should be at least 6 inches long, very sharp, and allow you to easily maneuver around joints and bones and trim fat and silverskin. Look for a narrow, straight blade.

MEAT CLEAVER

Meat cleavers can look intimidating, but we find that they are an important addition to the home kitchen, particularly when chopping meat and bones for stock. A good meat cleaver should do most of the chopping work for you, so look for one with a razor-sharp blade balanced by a comfortable handle. Our favorite is the **Shun Classic Meat Cleaver** ($160).

MEAT PREP

MEAT POUNDER

Since we often prefer to pound our own veal cutlets rather than buy uneven precut cutlets from the store, or to even out the butterflying on a leg of lamb, a meat pounder is an important piece of equipment. There are two styles of meat pounders: those with vertical handles and those with offset handles (i.e., horizontally oriented). We prefer vertical handles, which offer better leverage and control. In the test kitchen, we use the **Norpro GRIP-EZ Meat Pounder** ($19.99). Look for a meat pounder that weighs at least 1½ pounds.

KITCHEN TWINE

Good twine should stay tied without burning, fraying, or breaking. We prefer a center-fed cotton or linen twine, like **Librett Cotton Butcher's Twine** ($7), for its neat ties and ability to withstand all conditions without slipping. Make sure that your twine is labeled "food-safe" or "kitchen twine."

FAT SEPARATOR

A fat separator is an essential tool when performing tasks such as making gravy from the drippings of a roast or making a homemade stock into soup. We like the **Cuisipro Fat Separator** ($27) for its versatility and ease of use. It has a detachable canister that makes it the easiest separator to clean by hand. Since fat separators are often used with hot liquids, shock-resistant plastic is more suited to this task than glass.

INSTANT-READ THERMOMETER

Sight, touch, and experience are age-old ways to gauge when food is done, but for consistent results, nothing is as reliable as taking the food's internal temperature. We use our favorite **Thermoworks Thermapen Mk4** ($99) every day. An instant-read thermometer makes it easier to tell if your roast is fully cooked or still raw on the inside without having to cut into it, draining valuable juices. Instant-read thermometers register temperatures quickly and are easy to read. The size of the thermometer stem can make a big difference. A long stem (one that measures at least 4 inches) is necessary to reach the center of large roasts. Water-resistant thermometers are helpful as they're easier to clean and less likely to be damaged by spills.

REMOTE THERMOMETER

A remote thermometer allows you to monitor the temperature of your food from a distance. A temperature probe inserted into the meat connects to a base that rests outside the grill or oven, which communicates with a pager you carry with you. Almost all models will work from a distance of more than 100 feet, even behind walls. As with any thermometer, we value accuracy above all else, but we also prefer models that are intuitive and easy to use. We highly recommend the **ThermoWorks Smoke 2-Channel Alarm** ($99).

OVEN THERMOMETER

Unless you have your oven routinely calibrated, there is a good chance that its temperature readings may be off. Inaccurate temperatures will dramatically impact your food, leaving it underdone on the inside or overbrowned and tough. To avoid such problems, we recommend purchasing an inexpensive oven thermometer, like the **CDN Pro Accurate Oven Thermometer** ($9), and checking it once the oven is preheated. Look for a thermometer that mounts securely in the oven and has clearly marked numbers that make it easy to read quickly.

TONGS

We found that whether tong pincers are nonstick or not makes less difference than their shape. We prefer slightly concave pincers with wide, shallow scallops around the edges. Soft cushioning on the handles makes gripping easier and keeps them from overheating. We prefer a length of 12 inches, which keeps our hands far from the heat but is still easily maneuverable. Tongs should open and close easily and fit comfortably in your hand. In the test kitchen, we use **OXO Good Grips 12-Inch Tongs** ($13).

GRILL TONGS

When you're cooking over live fire, to keep you safe, you're going to want something longer than is practical for the kitchen. We like the longer version of our winning regular tongs, the **OXO Good Grips 16" Locking Tongs** ($15).

RIMMED BAKING SHEET

In the test kitchen, we use baking sheets for more than just baking. When buying baking sheets, look for ones that are light-colored and thick. A light-colored surface will heat and brown evenly. And a pan that isn't thick enough can buckle or transfer heat too intensely, burning the food. We prefer pans that are 18 by 13 inches with a 1-inch rim all around. And because they have so many different uses, we recommend having more than one. Our highly recommended rimmed baking sheet is the **Nordic Ware Baker's Half Sheet** ($20).

SKILLETS

Skillets are simply frying pans with low, flared sides. Their shape encourages evaporation, which is why skillets excel at searing, browning, and sauce reduction. We sear, sauté, shallow-fry, pan-roast, or even stir-fry in a skillet. In the test kitchen, we like to have three types of skillets on hand: traditional, cast-iron, and nonstick. Our favorite traditional skillet, the **All-Clad D3 Stainless 12" Fry Pan with Lid** ($130), is what we reach for when we want to create fond, the browned bits that are the foundation for great flavor in sautéed or pan-seared dishes. Cast-iron skillets are also useful for their excellent heat retention for high-heat cooking techniques such as frying and searing. And they actually improve with time and heavy use. Our favorite is the **Lodge Classic Cast Iron Skillet, 12"** ($41). For cooking delicate foods, like thin slices of meat in stir-fries, a nonstick skillet is ideal. Our favorite nonstick skillet is the **OXO Good Grips Non-Stick Pro 12" Open Frypan** ($60).

COOKING

DUTCH OVEN

A good Dutch oven is a kitchen essential. They're heavier and thicker than stockpots, allowing them to retain and conduct heat more effectively, and deeper than a skillet, so they can handle large cuts of meat and cooking liquid. These qualities make Dutch ovens the best choice for braises, pot roasts, and stews, especially as they can go on the stovetop to sear foods and then into the oven to finish cooking. Their tall sides make them useful for deep frying, and many cooks press Dutch ovens into service for jobs like boiling pasta. Our favorite pots are wide enough (at least 8 inches) to brown 3½ pounds of beef in three or four batches. We like **Le Creuset 7¼ Quart Round Dutch Oven** ($380). Our best buy is the **Cuisinart Chef's Classic Enameled Cast Iron Covered Casserole** ($72).

ROASTING PAN

A good roasting pan should be a sturdy, large workhorse, able to brown food evenly and withstand high-heat searing on the stovetop. We prefer durable tri-ply stainless-steel pans with a lighter finish, which allows monitoring of browning. Look for roomy, secure handles, which make maneuvering easier and safer. Most models come with a rack, which should fit snugly in the pan and not move or slide around. Our favorite roasting pan is the **Calphalon Contemporary Stainless Roasting Pan with Rack** ($140).

SERVING

CARVING FORK

Carving forks may seem like a basic tool, but differences between models can either help or hinder the meat-slicing process. Carving forks come in two styles: curved, with prongs that follow the shape of a roast, and bayonet style, with long, straight prongs. We prefer curved forks, like the **Mercer Cutlery Genesis 6-Inch High-Carbon Carving Fork** ($27), for their better sight lines and ability to hold roasts firmly while staying out of the knife's way. We also find that they can more easily transfer meat to a platter. Look for a carving fork that won't bend when lifting or turning heavy roasts, with a comfortable, nonslip handle.

SLICING KNIFE

The right knife can mean the difference between ragged, lopsided slices and professional, even ones. The heft, sharpness, length, and shape of a slicing knife all affect its cutting ability. We prefer an extra-long tapered blade that can cut through large roasts in one easy glide. It is also good to look for a rounded tip, which won't get caught on the way down. A Granton edge (which has small oval scallops carved out on both sides of the blade) makes for effortless slicing. In the test kitchen, we use the **Victorinox Swiss Army Fibrox Pro 12" Granton Slicing/Carving Knife** ($48).

CUTTING BOARD

Cutting boards are useful when dicing vegetables, performing other prep tasks, or slicing into smaller cuts of meat. The best ones have ample work space—at least 15 by 20 inches is best—and enough heft to keep them from slipping and sliding around. Our preferred cutting board is the **Teakhaus by Proteak Edge Grain Cutting Board** ($88).

CARVING BOARD

When it comes time to carve a finished roast, we reach for a spacious carving board. We value heavy, sturdy boards that won't move while we're carving. Look for a deep, wide trench to prevent juices from running over the sides. We prefer models with some kind of meat-anchoring mechanism—our favorite, the **J.K. Adams Maple Reversible Carving Board** ($85), has an oval-shaped central well where the meat can rest snugly.

STEAK KNIVES

The best steak knives have sturdy blades that won't wobble, even when cutting through thick pieces of meat. We find that serrated blades create jagged tears and don't make cutting any easier. We recommend buying steak knives with very sharp straight edges, like the **Victorinox Swiss Army 6-Piece Rosewood Steak Set, Spear Point, Straight Edge** ($130). Our best buy is the $28 **Chicago Cutlery Walnut Tradition 4-Piece Steak Knife Set.** Look for comfortable, smooth handles.

Eat with Meat

While there are many fully spiced, sauced, and seasoned dishes in this book, we provide flavor accompaniments for the centerpiece roasts and steaks you'll learn to perfect so you can dress up these cuts and taste them in new ways. You'll find spice rubs for treating meat before cooking and sauces to finish them with flair. For each we give suggestions on what kind of meat to serve them with, but feel free to experiment as you like.

Spice Rubs

Rubs, mixed together from pantry spices, are a simple path to complex flavor—just coat and cook, and the flavor blooms on the meat when exposed to the heat. We recommend using about 2 tablespoons of rub for steaks for four people, and ¼ cup for a roast for six. Rubs keep at room temperature for a month.

Barbecue Rub
Makes about ½ cup
Barbecue can mean a lot of things depending on the region of the country, and you see recipe-specific dry rubs in this book, but this spicy-sweet all-purpose rub is immediately recognizable as "barbecue" for beef and pork.

- 3 tablespoons chili powder
- 3 tablespoons packed brown sugar
- 2 teaspoons pepper
- ¾ teaspoon cayenne pepper

Combine all ingredients in bowl.

Classic Steak Rub
Makes about ½ cup
This popular steakhouse seasoning has an earthy, herbal bite.

- 2 tablespoons peppercorns
- 3 tablespoons coriander seeds
- 4 teaspoons dried dill
- 2 teaspoons red pepper flakes

Process peppercorns and coriander seeds in spice grinder until finely ground, about 30 seconds; transfer to small bowl. Stir in dill and pepper flakes.

Herbes de Provence
Makes about ½ cup
This delicate, aromatic blend of dried herbs from southern France is a good match for sweet, mild veal or pork.

- 2 tablespoons dried thyme
- 2 tablespoons dried marjoram
- 2 tablespoons dried rosemary
- 2 teaspoons fennel seeds

Combine all ingredients in bowl.

Five-Spice Powder
Makes about ½ cup
Chinese five-spice powder has a kick that offsets richness in recipes for beef, pork, and lamb.

- 5 teaspoons fennel seeds
- 4 teaspoons white peppercorns or 8 teaspoons Sichuan peppercorns
- 1 tablespoon whole cloves
- 8 star anise pods
- 1 (3-inch) cinnamon stick, broken into pieces

Process fennel seeds, peppercorns, and cloves in spice grinder until finely ground, about 30 seconds; transfer to small bowl. Process star anise and cinnamon in now-empty spice grinder until finely ground, about 30 seconds; transfer to bowl with other spices and stir to combine.

Jerk Rub
Makes about ½ cup
If you don't have time for a proper paste as in our Jerk Pork Ribs (page 296), stir up this flavorful rub to give anything fiery, fruity flavor.

- 5 teaspoons allspice berries
- 5 teaspoons black peppercorns
- 2 teaspoons dried thyme
- 3 tablespoons packed brown sugar
- 1 tablespoon garlic powder
- 2 teaspoons dry mustard
- 1 teaspoon cayenne pepper

Process allspice, peppercorns, and thyme in spice grinder until coarsely ground, about 30 seconds; transfer to small bowl. Stir in sugar, garlic powder, mustard, and cayenne.

Southwestern Rub
Makes about ½ cup
The flavors of the Southwest are classically bold and fiery but also warm and round, and this spice blend hits all the right notes for beef.

- 3 tablespoons cumin seeds
- 2 tablespoons coriander seeds
- ¾ teaspoon ground cinnamon
- 3 tablespoons chili powder
- ¾ teaspoon red pepper flakes

Process cumin seeds, coriander seeds, and cinnamon in spice grinder until finely ground, about 30 seconds; transfer to small bowl. Stir in chili powder and pepper flakes.

Herb Sauces

With their fresh flavors and vivid colors, herb sauces bring vibrancy and beauty to just about anything, often cutting through the richness of certain cuts of meat.

Salsa Verde
Makes about 1½ cups
Italian salsa verde is an all-purpose green sauce for just about any cut of meat, brightened with plenty of lemon juice.

- 4 cups fresh parsley leaves
- 2 slices hearty white sandwich bread, lightly toasted and cut into ½-inch pieces (1½ cups)
- ¼ cup capers, rinsed
- 4 anchovy fillets, rinsed
- 1 garlic clove, minced
- ¼ teaspoon table salt
- ¼ cup lemon juice (2 lemons)
- 1 cup extra-virgin olive oil

1. Pulse parsley, bread, capers, anchovies, garlic, and salt in food processor until finely chopped, about 5 pulses. Add lemon juice and pulse briefly to combine.

2. Transfer mixture to medium bowl and slowly whisk in oil until incorporated. Cover and let sit at room temperature for at least 1 hour to allow flavors to meld. Season with salt and pepper to taste. (Salsa verde can be refrigerated for up to 2 days. Bring to room temperature and whisk to recombine before serving.)

LEMON-BASIL SALSA VERDE
Substitute 2 cups fresh basil leaves for 2 cups of parsley. Add 1 teaspoon grated lemon zest to processor with parsley and increase garlic to 2 cloves.

SALSA VERDE WITH ARUGULA
Substitute 2 cups chopped arugula for 2 cups of parsley. Increase garlic to 2 cloves.

Chermoula
Makes about 1½ cups
This Moroccan cilantro and garlic dressing gets roundness from cumin and paprika.

- 2¼ cups fresh cilantro leaves
- 8 garlic cloves, minced
- 1½ teaspoons ground cumin
- 1½ teaspoons paprika
- ½ teaspoon cayenne pepper
- ½ teaspoon table salt
- 6 tablespoons lemon juice (2 lemons)
- ¾ cup extra-virgin olive oil

1. Pulse cilantro, garlic, cumin, paprika, cayenne, and salt in food processor until coarsely chopped, about 10 pulses. Add lemon juice and pulse briefly to combine.

2. Transfer mixture to medium bowl and slowly whisk in oil until incorporated. Cover and let sit at room temperature for at least 1 hour to allow flavors to meld. Season with salt and pepper to taste. (Sauce can be refrigerated for up to 2 days. Bring to room temperature and whisk to recombine before serving.)

Chimichurri
Makes about 1½ cups
This oil, vinegar, and herb sauce is a traditional Argentinian accompaniment to steak. Dried oregano adds depth to the freshness of parsley and cilantro, garlic gives the sauce bite, vinegar offers a clarifying vibrancy, and red pepper flakes pack a pleasing heat.

- ¼ cup hot tap water
- 2 teaspoons dried oregano
- 1 teaspoon table salt
- 1⅓ cups fresh parsley leaves
- ⅔ cup fresh cilantro leaves
- 6 garlic cloves, minced
- ½ teaspoon red pepper flakes
- ¼ cup red wine vinegar
- ½ cup extra-virgin olive oil

1. Combine hot water, oregano, and salt in small bowl; let sit for 5 minutes to soften oregano.

2. Pulse parsley, cilantro, garlic, and pepper flakes in food processor until coarsely chopped, about 10 pulses. Add water mixture and vinegar and pulse briefly to combine.

3. Transfer mixture to medium bowl and slowly whisk in oil until incorporated. Cover and let sit at room temperature for at least 1 hour to allow flavors to meld. Season with salt and pepper to taste. (Sauce can be refrigerated for up to 2 days. Bring to room temperature and whisk to recombine before serving.)

Mint Persillade
Makes about 1½ cups

This take on a French sauce makes a great accompaniment to lamb.

- 2½ cups fresh mint leaves
- 2½ cups fresh parsley leaves
- 6 garlic cloves, peeled
- 6 anchovy fillets, rinsed and patted dry
- 2 teaspoons grated lemon zest plus 2½ tablespoons juice
- ½ teaspoon table salt
- ⅛ teaspoon pepper
- ¾ cup extra-virgin olive oil

1. Pulse mint, parsley, garlic, anchovies, lemon zest, salt, and pepper in food processor until finely chopped, 15 to 20 pulses. Add lemon juice and pulse briefly to combine.

2. Transfer mixture to medium bowl and slowly whisk in oil until incorporated. Cover and let sit at room temperature for at least 1 hour to allow flavors to meld. Season with salt and pepper to taste. (Sauce can be refrigerated for up to 2 days. Bring to room temperature and whisk to recombine before serving.)

Gremolata
Makes about ⅓ cup

Used more as a finishing touch than a sauce, this mix of herbs and lemon zest is known for giving deeply savory Italian braises much-needed brightness with a stir, but you could find yourself sprinkling it on a number of beef, pork, lamb, or veal dishes for a pop of freshness in every bite.

- ¼ cup minced fresh parsley
- 3 garlic cloves, minced
- 2 teaspoons finely grated lemon zest

Combine all ingredients in small bowl.

Creamy Sauces

Eating meat is a treat, and sometimes an addition of a creamy sauce can gild the lily in the very best way. Other times, it can add richness and interest to leaner cuts. Creamy sauces can even be dairy-free; romesco is thickened with almonds and bread.

Hollandaise Sauce
Makes about 1¼ cups

Creamy, tangy hollandaise is an elegant classic accompaniment to luxurious beef steaks or slices of holiday-worthy roasts. It's important to make sure the butter is still hot (about 180 degrees) so that the egg yolks cook sufficiently. Serve this sauce immediately.

- 3 large egg yolks
- 2 tablespoons lemon juice
- ¼ teaspoon table salt
  Pinch cayenne pepper, plus extra for seasoning
- 16 tablespoons unsalted butter, melted and still hot (180 degrees)

Process egg yolks, lemon juice, salt, and cayenne in blender until frothy, about 10 seconds, scraping bottom and sides of blender jar as needed. With blender running, slowly add hot butter and process until hollandaise is emulsified, about 2 minutes. Adjust consistency with hot water as needed until sauce slowly drips from spoon. Season with salt and extra cayenne to taste.

Yogurt-Herb Sauce
Makes about 2 cups

This creamy yogurt sauce adds tang to beef and lamb dishes and can add cooling relief to heavily spiced dishes. Do not substitute low-fat or nonfat yogurt here.

- 2 cups plain whole-milk yogurt
- ¼ cup minced fresh parsley
- ¼ cup minced fresh chives
- 2 teaspoons grated lemon zest plus ¼ cup juice
- 2 garlic cloves, minced

Whisk all ingredients together in bowl and season with salt and pepper to taste. Cover and refrigerate for at least 30 minutes to allow flavors to meld. (Sauce can be refrigerated for up to 4 days.)

Za'atar Yogurt Sauce
Makes about 1 cup

The lemony herbal flavor of this yogurt sauce is great with gamy lamb but can also perk up rich beef dishes. It's a nice contrast to dishes with a lot of warm spices.

- 1 cup plain whole-milk yogurt
- 1 tablespoon za'atar
- 1 garlic clove, minced
- 1 teaspoon grated lemon zest plus 1 tablespoon juice

Whisk all ingredients together in bowl and season with salt and pepper to taste. Cover and refrigerate so flavors meld, about 30 minutes. (Sauce can be refrigerated for up to 4 days.)

Horseradish–Sour Cream Sauce
Makes about 1 cup

Horseradish adds heat and zip to a white sauce that's a classic with roast beef.

- ½ cup sour cream
- ½ cup prepared horseradish, drained
- ¾ teaspoon table salt
- ⅛ teaspoon pepper

Whisk sour cream, horseradish, salt, and pepper together in bowl. Cover and refrigerate for at least 30 minutes to allow flavors to meld. Season with salt and pepper to taste. (Sauce can be refrigerated for up to 2 days.)

Gorgonzola Vinaigrette
Makes about 1 cup

Blue cheese is a classic accompaniment to steak. This quick and easy no-cook steak sauce is disguised as a vinaigrette, the rich, creamy Gorgonzola balanced by white wine vinegar. For a creamier texture, buy a wedge of Gorgonzola cheese instead of a precrumbled product.

- 2 tablespoons white wine vinegar
- 2 teaspoons Dijon mustard
- ½ teaspoon kosher salt
- ⅛ teaspoon pepper
- ¼ cup extra-virgin olive oil

2 ounces Gorgonzola cheese, crumbled (½ cup)
1 small shallot, sliced thin
2 tablespoons chopped fresh parsley

Whisk vinegar, mustard, salt, and pepper together in bowl. Slowly whisk in oil until emulsified. Stir in Gorgonzola, shallot, and parsley.

Romesco
Makes about 2 cups
This bright but savory sauce is complexly flavored and best with beef and lamb.

1 slice hearty white sandwich bread, crusts removed, bread lightly toasted and cut into ½-inch pieces (½ cup)
3 tablespoons slivered almonds, toasted
1¾ cups jarred roasted red peppers, rinsed, patted dry, and chopped coarse
1 small tomato, cored, seeded, and chopped
2 tablespoons extra-virgin olive oil
1½ tablespoons sherry vinegar
1 large garlic clove, minced
½ teaspoon table salt
¼ teaspoon cayenne pepper

Process bread and almonds in food processor until finely ground, about 30 seconds. Add red peppers, tomato, oil, vinegar, garlic, salt, and cayenne. Process until smooth and mixture has texture similar to mayonnaise, 20 to 30 seconds, scraping down sides of bowl as needed. Season with salt and pepper to taste. (Sauce can be refrigerated for up to 2 days; bring to room temperature before serving.)

Spicy Avocado–Sour Cream
Makes about 1 cup
Level up beef and pork tacos with this rich sauce or serve with fajitas.

1 cup sour cream
½ avocado, cut into 1-inch pieces
1 jalapeño chile, stemmed, seeded, and chopped
1 teaspoon lime juice

Process all ingredients in food processor until smooth, scraping down sides of bowl as needed, and season with salt and pepper to taste. (Sauce can be refrigerated for up to 2 days.)

Classic Burger Sauce
Makes about 1 cup
This burger sauce has the sweetness, tang, and richness of the sauce served with your favorite fast-food burger—in a good way.

½ cup mayonnaise
¼ cup ketchup
2 teaspoons sweet pickle relish
2 teaspoons sugar
2 teaspoons distilled white vinegar
1 teaspoon pepper

Whisk all ingredients together in bowl. (Sauce can be refrigerated for up to 4 days; bring to room temperature before serving.)

Relishes

These (usually) chunky condiments make the perfect topping for burgers or filling for meat-based sandwiches.

Onion-Balsamic Relish
Makes about ⅔ cup
Make the ultimate steak or pork sandwich with this sweet-savory, jammy relish.

6 tablespoons extra-virgin olive oil
2 red onions, chopped fine
½ teaspoon table salt
4 garlic cloves, minced
¼ cup balsamic vinegar
¼ cup minced fresh mint
½ teaspoon pepper

1. Heat ¼ cup oil in medium saucepan over medium-low heat until shimmering. Add onions and salt and cook, stirring occasionally, until onions are very soft and lightly browned, about 20 minutes.

2. Stir in garlic and cook until fragrant, about 1 minute. Stir in vinegar and cook until syrupy, 30 to 60 seconds. Transfer onion mixture to bowl and let cool to room temperature, about 15 minutes. Stir in mint, pepper, and remaining 2 tablespoons oil. Season with salt and pepper to taste. (Relish can be refrigerated for up to 1 week; bring to room temperature before serving.)

Tangy Corn Relish
Makes about 2½ cups
This is great on steak sandwiches or in beef tacos but you can also top robust whole steaks with it.

¼ cup sugar
2 tablespoons all-purpose flour
1½ teaspoons table salt
1 teaspoon pepper
1 cup distilled white vinegar
2 tablespoons water
2 ears corn, kernels cut from cobs (1½ cups)
1 red bell pepper, stemmed, seeded, and chopped fine
½ onion, chopped fine
½ teaspoon yellow mustard seeds
¼ teaspoon celery seeds

Whisk sugar, flour, salt, and pepper together in large saucepan. Slowly whisk in vinegar and water until incorporated. Stir in corn, bell pepper, onion, mustard seeds, and celery seeds and bring to simmer. Cook, stirring occasionally, until vegetables are tender and mixture has thickened slightly and measures about 2½ cups, about 40 minutes. Transfer to bowl and let cool to room temperature, about 2 hours. (Relish can be refrigerated for up to 1 week; bring to room temperature before serving.)

Chutneys

These thick, tangy sauces, a staple of Indian cuisine, often contain fruit but they can vary widely and feature all kinds of ingredients. They range from chunky to smooth, and from mild to spicy.

Cilantro-Mint Chutney
Makes about 1 cup

This creamy chutney adds unique warmth and aroma to beef and lamb dishes. We prefer to use whole-milk yogurt here, but low-fat yogurt can be substituted; do not use nonfat yogurt.

2 cups fresh cilantro leaves
1 cup fresh mint leaves
⅓ cup plain whole-milk yogurt
¼ cup finely chopped onion
1 tablespoon lime juice
1½ teaspoons sugar
½ teaspoon ground cumin
¼ teaspoon table salt

Process all ingredients in food processor until smooth, about 20 seconds, scraping down sides of bowl as needed. (Chutney can be refrigerated for up to 2 days.)

Green Tomato Chutney
Makes about 2 cups

This sweet-tart chutney, given grassy warmth from coriander, is great with roasted beef or lamb.

2 pounds green tomatoes, cored and cut into 1-inch pieces
¾ cup sugar
¾ cup distilled white vinegar
1 teaspoon coriander seeds
1 teaspoon table salt
½ teaspoon red pepper flakes
¼ cup minced fresh chives
2 teaspoons lemon juice

Bring tomatoes, sugar, vinegar, coriander seeds, salt, and pepper flakes to simmer in medium saucepan. Cook until thickened and measures about 2 cups, about 40 minutes. Transfer to bowl and let cool to room temperature, about 2 hours. Stir in chives and lemon juice. (Chutney can be refrigerated for up to 1 week; bring to room temperature before serving.)

Red Bell Pepper Chutney
Makes about 2 cups

Lighten heavy dishes with this potent, bright, vegetal chutney.

1 tablespoon extra-virgin olive oil
1 red onion, chopped fine
4 red bell peppers, stemmed, seeded, and cut into ½-inch pieces
1 cup white wine vinegar
½ cup plus 2 tablespoons sugar
2 garlic cloves, peeled and smashed
1 (1-inch) piece ginger, peeled, sliced into thin coins, and smashed
1 teaspoon yellow mustard seeds
1 teaspoon table salt
½ teaspoon red pepper flakes
¼ cup minced fresh parsley

Heat oil in large saucepan over medium heat until shimmering. Add onion and cook until softened, about 5 minutes. Stir in bell peppers, vinegar, sugar, garlic, ginger, mustard seeds, salt, and pepper flakes. Bring to simmer and cook until thickened and measures about 2 cups, about 40 minutes. Transfer to bowl and let cool to room temperature, about 2 hours. Discard garlic and ginger, then stir in parsley. (Chutney can be refrigerated for up to 1 week; bring to room temperature before serving.)

Spiced Apple Chutney
Makes about 2 cups

Since apple and pork are perfect partners, we love this chutney with pork chops or roasts.

1 tablespoon vegetable oil
3 Granny Smith apples, peeled, cored, and chopped
1 shallot, minced
1 tablespoon grated fresh ginger
½ teaspoon cinnamon
¼ teaspoon nutmeg
⅓ cup white wine vinegar
½ cup apple jelly

Heat oil in 12-inch nonstick skillet over medium-high heat until shimmering. Cook apples until lightly browned, about 5 minutes. Stir in shallot, ginger, cinnamon, and nutmeg, and cook until fragrant, about 1 minute. Stir in vinegar and apple jelly, bring to simmer, and cook until thickened and measures about 2 cups, about 5 minutes. Transfer to bowl

and let cool completely, about 2 hours. (Chutney can be refrigerated for up to 1 week; bring to room temperature before serving.)

Pesto

Pesto doesn't have to be made just from basil and it isn't just for pasta; it can dress up just about everything. Stir into a meat-based soup or stew or dollop onto finished dishes. You could even spread some on a piece of meat before grilling. You can also thin pesto with lemon juice for a more dressing-like sauce.

Classic Basil Pesto
Makes about 1½ cups

This is the most traditional version and we love to have it on hand for several meat dishes; it can also fill roasts.

6 garlic cloves, unpeeled
½ cup pine nuts
4 cups fresh basil leaves
¼ cup fresh parsley leaves
1 cup extra-virgin olive oil
1 ounce Parmesan cheese, grated fine (½ cup)

1. Toast garlic in 8-inch skillet over medium heat, shaking skillet occasionally, until softened and spotty brown, about 8 minutes. When garlic is cool enough to handle, remove and discard skins and chop coarse. Meanwhile, toast pine nuts in now-empty skillet over medium heat, stirring often, until golden and fragrant, 4 to 5 minutes.

2. Place basil and parsley in 1-gallon zipper-lock bag. Pound bag with flat side of meat pounder or with rolling pin until all leaves are bruised.

3. Process garlic, pine nuts, and herbs in food processor until finely chopped, about 1 minute, scraping down sides of bowl as needed. With processor running, slowly add oil until incorporated. Transfer pesto to bowl, stir in Parmesan, and season with salt and pepper to taste. (Pesto can be

flavors blend, about 10 minutes, or roll into log and refrigerate. (Makes about ½ cup. Butter can be refrigerated in airtight container for up to 4 days or frozen, wrapped tightly in plastic wrap, for up to 2 months.)

Chipotle-Cilantro Compound Butter

- 2 teaspoons minced canned chipotle chile in adobo sauce, plus 2 teaspoons adobo sauce
- 4 teaspoons minced fresh cilantro
- 2 garlic cloves, minced
- 2 teaspoons honey
- 2 teaspoons grated lime zest

Chive-Lemon Miso Compound Butter

- ¼ cup white miso
- 2 teaspoons grated lemon zest plus 4 teaspoons juice
- ¼ teaspoon pepper
- ¼ cup minced fresh chives

Parsley-Caper Compound Butter

- ¼ cup minced fresh parsley
- 4 teaspoons capers, rinsed and minced

Parsley-Lemon Compound Butter

- ¼ cup minced fresh parsley
- 4 teaspoons grated lemon zest

Tarragon-Lime Compound Butter

- ¼ cup minced scallion
- 2 tablespoons minced fresh tarragon
- 4 teaspoons lime juice

Tapenade Compound Butter

- 10 pitted oil-cured black olives, chopped fine
- 1 anchovy fillet, rinsed and minced
- 1 tablespoon brandy
- 2 teaspoons minced fresh thyme
- 2 garlic cloves, minced
- ¼ teaspoon grated orange zest

refrigerated for up to 3 days or frozen for up to 3 months. To prevent browning, press plastic wrap flush to surface or top with thin layer of olive oil. Bring to room temperature before using.)

TOASTED WALNUT AND PARSLEY PESTO

Omit basil. Substitute 2 cups walnuts for pine nuts and increase parsley to ¾ cup.

Sun-Dried Tomato Pesto
Makes about 1½ cups
This pesto is great for filling rolled pork roasts. We prefer sun-dried tomatoes packed in oil over those that are packaged dried.

- 3 garlic cloves, unpeeled
- ¼ cup walnuts
- 1 cup oil-packed sun-dried tomatoes, patted dry and chopped
- ½ cup extra-virgin olive oil
- 1 ounce Parmesan cheese, grated fine (½ cup)

1. Toast garlic in 8-inch skillet over medium heat, shaking skillet occasionally, until softened and spotty brown, about 8 minutes. When garlic is cool enough to handle, remove and discard skins and chop coarsely. Meanwhile, toast walnuts in now-empty skillet over medium heat, stirring often, until golden and fragrant, 4 to 5 minutes.

2. Process garlic, walnuts, and tomatoes in food processor until finely chopped, about 1 minute, scraping down sides of bowl as needed. With processor running, slowly add oil until incorporated. Transfer pesto to bowl, stir in Parmesan, and season with salt and pepper to taste. (Pesto can be refrigerated for up to 3 days or frozen for up to 3 months. To prevent browning, press plastic wrap flush to surface or top with thin layer of olive oil. Bring to room temperature before using.)

Compound Butters

Compound butters—butter mixed with aromatic ingredients and spices—are a great accompaniment to simple seared steaks or oven roasts. As a dollop melts on the warm meat, it transforms into a sauce. We like to make a double or triple batch, roll it into a log, and store it in the freezer so that flavored butter is always just a slice away.

To make compound butter:
Whip 8 tablespoons softened unsalted butter in bowl with fork until light and fluffy. Mix in any of the following ingredient combinations and season with salt and pepper to taste. Cover in plastic wrap and let rest so

PART 1

beef
& veal

BEEF CUTS

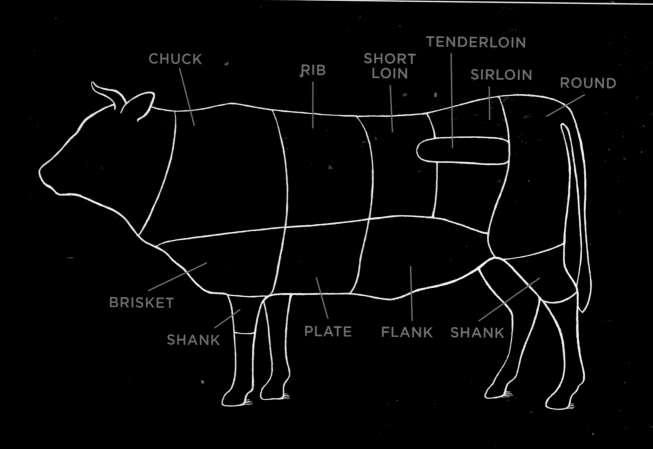

CHUCK

RIB

SHORT LOIN

TENDERLOIN

SIRLOIN

ROUND

BRISKET

SHANK

PLATE

FLANK

SHANK

WHILE MANY CLASSIC MEAT DISHES—centerpiece holiday roasts, perfectly seared, rosy steaks, juicy burgers, barbecuers' delights, many a meat-and-potatoes meal—can come in one form or another from any of the animals in this book, these must-have dishes are primarily associated with beef. You might coat a tenderloin in a horseradish crust for company during the holidays (see page 100), look forward to ordering a crusty rib eye (see page 69) when you go to a steakhouse, pile a beef burger (see page 127) high with your favorite toppings, seek out supreme brisket with an impressive smoke ring (see page 151), or cook a warming beef stew (see page 45) on a winter night. The meat for these timeless (and, we'd say, essential) recipes comes from the animal with the most primal cuts, each of which cooks a bit differently.

Beef is beloved for many reasons; in fact, our bodies just might be wired to crave it. It's long been part of our American eating history, especially since Spanish missionaries brought their cattle through the Southwest in the 18th century, which prompted the cattle drives that supported the nation's economy in the 19th century and further influenced the creation of the beef industry as we know it today. The success of that industry translated to ample amounts of beef on plates in restaurants and in home kitchens. Beef also offers some key nutrients: important B vitamins, including B6, B12, and niacin; abundant amino acids; zinc; and heme iron, the form of iron (unlike non-heme from plant-based sources) that our bodies most efficiently absorb. Also, depending on the area of the cow your cut comes from, beef can be rich in fat, intermuscular (fat running between muscles) and intramuscular (fat within the muscles), something we naturally crave—and, which, of course, is essential to life in reasonable amounts.

COUNT THE CATTLE

While our cow illustration on page 28 is fairly generic, there are different breeds of cattle that roam the world. (Note that a "cow," which we use casually as the singular for beef cattle, is technically a female, and a bull is a male.) Knowing what kind of cattle our meat comes from—and prizing it accordingly—isn't so much a part of our culture as it is in Europe (where you can find premium Piedmontese cattle, for example) or in Japan (home to fatty, marbled Kobe Waygu beef). But breed does matter even if it's not frequently publicized, or seen often on menus. The most important distinguishing factor among breeds is whether they are genetically better suited for milking or for beef production. Breed impacts what a cow looks like, how it grows and develops, its temperament, its resilience in various environmental conditions, and—of particular interest for a cookbook—the qualities of its meat, such as taste, marbling, and yield.

There are upwards of 100 breeds of beef cattle, but some are particularly noteworthy in the United States. The most popular breed is Angus, a source of high-quality beef. Dexter cattle are smaller than many other breeds, making them a more economical choice for breeders—they simply take up and need less space. They are a common choice for raising grass-fed beef because they do not need supplementary feeding. The all-purpose Randall Lineback cattle was bred in the United States more than 200 years ago for subsistence farming—but is now the rarest breed. Like snowflakes, Texas Longhorns, with their unmistakable long horns, rarely look alike, sporting different color combinations, and they're all-American cows descended from the first cattle brought to this country.

Butchery

Butchery has essentially existed for as long as animals have been killed for food. The term "butcher" traditionally refers to a person who kills and guts animals and then breaks the carcasses down into large sections, or primal cuts. Since the late 1800s, butchers have been mainly wholesalers who sell these primal cuts to retailers. It's not likely that the butchers at today's butcher shops kill, skin, or gut animals, although they are skilled in breaking them down (and telling you how to cook the cuts). Similarly, many grocery stores employ meat cutters who break down primal cuts into subprimals (large cuts such as bottom round) or smaller cuts (such as individual steaks) for cooking. For convenience, we refer to both of these groups of people as butchers.

Beef Grading

The U.S. Department of Agriculture (USDA) assigns different quality grades to beef, but most meat available to consumers is confined to three grades: prime, choice, and select. Grading is voluntary on the part of the meat-packer. If meat is graded, it should

Beef Grading

PRIME

Heavily marbled, tender, and flavorful.

bear a USDA stamp indicating the grade, though it may not be visible to the consumer. To grade meat, inspectors evaluate color, grain, surface texture, and fat content and distribution.

USDA prime beef is heavily marbled with intramuscular fat, which makes for a tender, flavorful steak. About 2 percent of graded beef is considered prime. Prime meats are most often served in restaurants or sold in high-end butcher shops or grocers. The majority of graded beef is choice. While the levels of marbling in choice beef can vary, it is generally moderately marbled with intramuscular fat. Select beef has little marbling.

Our blind tasting of all three grades of rib-eye steaks produced predictable results: Prime ranked first for its tender, buttery texture and rich flavor. Next came choice, with good meaty flavor and a chewier—but still quite good—texture. The tough and stringy select steak followed, with flavor that was barely acceptable. Our advice: When you're willing to splurge, go for prime steak, but a choice steak that exhibits a moderate amount of marbling is a fine, affordable option. Just steer clear of select-grade steak.

Beef Shopping

You've learned that very rich "prime" beef is the highest grade and that "select" isn't very good. But grade aside, what should you be looking for in beef? After all, beef grading is voluntary by the producer—a step taken if they'd like to pay to get the USDA's

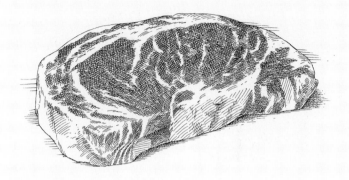

CHOICE

Moderately marbled, good flavor and value.

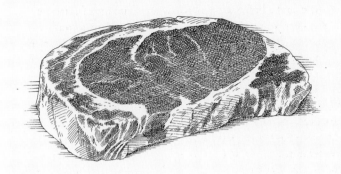

SELECT

Lightly marbled, tough, poor flavor.

grading stamp (and therefore perhaps enhance profitability). The USDA inspects all meat to make sure there isn't contamination or spoilage—so all beef at the store is good enough to eat.

Another way to distinguish beef is by branding. Branding can tell you the breed, if you happen to have an allegiance, or the beef producer. The meat may be labeled "Angus," for example, or with the name of a farm. You should also pay attention to color, grain, and, if possible, smell. The redder the beef, the shorter the time it's been on store shelves, as it darkens when exposed to oxygen. So bright red beef is a good sign, but beef that's slightly brownish is OK; it has probably been displayed for just a couple days more. Beef should look moist but not wet in the case, and packaged beef shouldn't contain a lot of liquid—this means it's been stored for too long or was previously frozen. The grain should be tight and even; broken grain could indicate poor handling. The beef should smell fresh and clean and not at all sour; any odor indicates spoilage. Especially avoid a green cast, which means bacteria has grown. (Note that blue dye on the surface of some cuts of beef is the ink used to stamp beef with its grade or breed and is made of edible food dye that is safe to eat.)

Organic Beef

The government regulates the use of the term "organic" on beef labels, but producers set their own guidelines when it comes to the term "natural." That means the labeling doesn't carry weight. If you want to ensure that you're buying meat raised without antibiotics or hormones and fed an organic diet (without meat or poultry by-products), then look for the USDA's organic seal.

FACTS ABOUT FEED

Most U.S. beef is raised on grain but grass-fed beef is becoming an increasingly popular option. Both types are good to eat. Here are the facts so you can make a choice that's right for you.

What's Grain-Fed Beef?

Cattle that are placed in feedlots for the last three to six months before slaughter and fattened on a diet of grains (usually soy- and corn-based) are considered "grain-fed." (Such animals may also be called "grain-finished," since prior to being sent to feedlots, the cows existed on a grass or pasture diet.) Since the 1950s, the vast majority of cattle raised for beef in the United States have been fattened this way. Grains are higher in protein and starch, which not only help the cow fatten faster, but also make the beef richer and fattier.

What's Grass-Fed Beef?

Beef labeled "grass-fed" comes from cows that have eaten a grass or pasture diet for some of their lives. In order to use the label, producers must provide documentation to the Food Safety Inspection Service (FSIS) of the USDA, detailing the accuracy of their claims. Note: A grass-fed label does not necessarily mean the animals foraged outdoors for most of their lives; grazed on organic grass; or that antibiotics or hormones were omitted from the feed. It doesn't assume organic beef and therefore isn't automatically appropriate if you choose to adhere to an organic diet. And all cattle consume grass for some time in their lives so only beef labeled "100 percent grass-fed" has eaten only grass for its entire life. You likely won't taste a difference between beef in the two different grass-fed categories (some grass versus only grass), but the latter label is a clearer indicator of what you're getting.

Is Grass-Fed Beef More Healthful Than Grain-Fed Beef?

Because of the difference in the cattle's diet, grass-fed beef is leaner than grain-fed beef. Grass-fed beef is also higher in certain vitamins, minerals, antioxidants, and omega-3 fatty acids. Furthermore, grass-fed beef also contains twice the amount of conjugated linoleic acid (CLA) isomers, a small family of fatty acids that purportedly fight cancer and lower the risk of diabetes.

Which Tastes Better—Grass-Fed or Grain-Fed Beef?

Grain-fed beef has long been promoted as a richer and fattier option, while grass-fed beef has been criticized for its leanness,

for being chewy, and for having a gamey taste. To judge for ourselves, we compared grass- and grain-fed strip steaks and rib-eye steaks. Tasters could not detect differences in the leaner strip steaks, but they did notice differences in the fattier rib eyes: The grain-fed beef had a "mild" flavor, while the grass-fed steaks had more complex, "nutty" undertones. Interestingly, preferences were evenly split as to which option is better. What accounts for the apparent turnaround in beef that used to be maligned? The answer may lie in new measures introduced in recent years that have made grass-fed beef taste more appealing, including "finishing" the beef on forage like clover that imparts a sweeter profile. Perhaps even more significant is that an increasing number of grass-fed beef producers have decided to dry-age (all of the steaks we tasted were dry-aged for 21 days). This process concentrates beefy flavor and dramatically increases tenderness in both grass-fed as well as grain-fed beef. (Read on for more information on dry-aging.)

Cooking Grass-Fed Beef

Because it's leaner, grass-fed beef cooks faster than grain-fed beef, according to many sources. To put this claim to the test, we cooked seven grain-fed prime strip steaks alongside seven grass-fed strip steaks (grass-fed beef is not graded). Though the grass-fed steaks rose in temperature a bit more quickly than the grain-fed in all but one of the tests, the difference between the quickest and the slowest steak was 4 minutes or less, and all of the samples cooked within our given time range.

DRY-AGED BEEF

Dry-aged steak is touted as having a far more tender texture and richer, beefier flavors than unaged beef. Its price—40 to 100 percent more than unaged meat—would certainly suggest a superior product. Here's a breakdown of what's really going on.

How Dry Aging Works

Dry aging is basically controlled decomposition. It typically starts with large cuts with bones and fat caps left fully intact. These are held in humidity-controlled refrigerated rooms where air can circulate around the beef, pulling moisture from its exposed surfaces. As the beef ages, water evaporates out of it, which concentrates its flavor. Meanwhile, enzymes slowly break down collagen and muscle protein, enhancing tenderness, and desirable molds grow on the meat's surface, creating additional protein-snipping enzymes. The breakdown of protein and fat also generates a slew of new nutty, savory, and even desirably cheesy flavors and aromas that deepen and transform the beef's taste. At the end of aging, a thin pellicle of dried, hardened flesh will have formed on the meat's exterior; this, along with the molds and oxidized fat, are trimmed away, and the beef is then cut into individual steaks.

How to Shop for Dry-Aged Beef

Dry-aged beef is expensive; between moisture evaporation and the trimming away of dried moldy parts, a dry-aged cut can lose more than 30 percent of its original weight. This, along with the time spent in dedicated refrigerators, contribute to this beef's premium price.

Unsurprisingly, the more aged it is, the more expensive it will be and beef can be aged for as long as 120 days. We think the sweet spot (and economical choice) for dry aging is four to six weeks. That's when the meat will have become significantly more tender, with richer, beefier flavors. More advanced dry aging produces steak with a heightened gamy, cheesy flavor. If you're up for that,

look for meat that's been aged for more than six weeks. As for steak dry-aged for just two weeks—why bother? You'll be paying a lot more for a product that's barely different from steak that hasn't been dry-aged.

ANIMAL AGE

Dry aging occurs once an animal is processed, but the age of the cattle the meat came from also matters for flavor. A younger steer (that is, a less mature or physiologically strained one) generally tastes better than a mature one. Maturity can be determined most easily by the condition of the bones, particularly by the chine bone. Animals with more flexible cartilage than rigid bone are younger and generally more palatable. Hypermasculine mature bulls are low in beefiness.

VEAL

Veal can be controversial: It's the meat from young calves and therefore ultratender. Many people are opposed to milk-fed veal because the calves are confined to small stalls before being butchered. In veal, "natural" means something different and more specific than it does in beef. "Natural" is the official term used to inform the consumer that the calves are allowed to move freely, without the confines of the stalls. Natural veal is also generally raised on grass (the calves can forage) and without hormones or antibiotics.

Moral issues aside, the differences in how the calves are raised create differences in the texture and flavor of the veal. Natural veal is darker, meatier, and more like beef. Milk-fed veal is paler in color, more tender, and milder in flavor. When we grilled both types of veal chops in the test kitchen, each had its supporters. Several tasters preferred the meatier, more intense flavor of the natural veal. They thought the milk-fed veal seemed bland in comparison. Other tasters preferred the softer texture and milder flavor of the milk-fed veal. They felt that the natural veal tasted like "wimpy" beef and that the milk-fed chops had the mild, sweet flavor they expected from veal.

The grading you see in beef doesn't exist for veal. Most-always-tender veal lacks the attributes (deep color, marbling) that are used to grade beef. Ever delicate, veal should be stored for only a day or two before using it to ensure freshness.

CHUCK

HARD-WORKING AND HARDY, the chuck comprises the cow's lower neck, shoulder (this is the main chuck section that we work with), and upper arm. That's a lot of meat. The nomenclature is indeed a bit confusing since much of "the chuck" is called, well, chuck.

Used by the cow for movement and weight support, the chuck consists of complex (they run across the square chuck at various angles), hard-acting muscles that, in addition to being flavorful, can be tough, with the much-exercised shoulder muscles being the toughest. Tough doesn't have to be a meat pejorative, however; you can cook most any piece of meat to a desirable texture if you choose the right technique. The chuck is strewn with a balanced amount of flavorful fat, and chewy connective tissue that holds the muscles together. Does fat and chewy tissue sound unpleasant? While an overabundance might be, they're not unpleasant when cuts from the chuck enter a pot, braise or stew so that fat slowly enriches and flavors the meat, and that connective tissue degenerates into gelatin that lubricates the meat. These processes turn a cut of meat that was once tight and tough into something luscious, sometimes even, when this outcome is desirable, fall-apart tender. (To boot, in a traditional braise, gelatin adds glossy body to the braising liquid to become a luxurious sauce.) Finally, the chuck creates great ground beef because of its mix of flavor and fat. (For more information on ground meat, see pages 364–368.)

Chuck-Eye Roast

Cost: ■■▢▢ Flavor: ■■■▢

Best cooking methods: braise, stew, slow cook, sous vide
Texture: very tender if cooked low and slow
Alternative names: chuck center roast, chuck-eye roll, inside chuck roll, boneless chuck fillet, America's beef roast

There's a large, boneless section of chuck that lies between the shoulder blade of the cow and the ribs and backbone known as the chuck roll. Weighing in at around 20 pounds, this portion contains some of the more tender muscles of the chuck and so it's frequently fabricated into a top section that we discuss here, the chuck-eye roast, and a bottom section, the chuck under blade (which is also cut into coarse-grained steaks) that we don't use in the test kitchen.

We prize the chuck-eye roast, and it's our most commonly used cut from the chuck for its supremely tender texture. The boneless chuck-eye roast is cut from the center of the first five ribs (the term "eye" refers to any center-cut piece of meat). Unlike other roasts from the chuck, which may feature multiple small muscle groups separated by lots of hard fat and connective tissue, the chuck eye has a more limited number of large muscle groups that run along the center of the shoulder. It is a continuation of the same muscles that make up the rib eye (see page 62), one of the most flavorful and tender cuts of beef. With fewer muscle groups, this roast has less intramuscular fat and connective tissue to trim away than other parts of the chuck, so it's easier to prep (a compact, uniform shape helps here, too); it also has a higher yield of meat for the money.

Since this deep-flavored cut is our very top choice from the cow for stewing and braising, it's also great in the slow cooker—in fact, its range is remarkably impressive. It creates the quintessential Classic Pot Roast (page 40); breaks into tender pieces to create a saucy Genovese beef and onion ragu for rigatoni (see page 46); can be barbecued, with proper technique (for more information see page 51); and, if a very low temperature is used, can even be roasted for a flavorful, affordable Roasted Beef Chuck with Horseradish-Parsley Sauce (page 44), an exception to our moist cooking rule. Look for a well-marbled cut for maximum flavor.

MEAT PREP *Trimming and Tying Chuck-Eye Roast*

1. Pull roast apart at major seam (delineated by line of fat) into 2 halves. Use knife as necessary.

2. Using knife, remove large knobs of fat from each piece, leaving thin layer of fat on meat.

3a. To create 1 evenly shaped roast, place pieces back together along major seam. Tie back together with kitchen twine at 1-inch intervals.

3b. For 2 smaller roasts, tie 3 pieces of kitchen twine around each piece to keep meat from falling apart.

SHOULDER SECOND-BESTS

Sometimes, despite one of its alternative names being "America's beef roast," hinting at its status as a stew star, chuck-eye roast is hard to find: Its proximity to the rib eye allows butchers to portion and sell chuck-eye steaks (see page 36) as a less expensive alternative to boneless rib-eye steaks, whittling away at the available chuck-eye roast. If your butcher can't fashion you a 3- to 4-pound chuck-eye roast, you can try cuts with similar flavor and texture. We like the top-blade roast (see page 37), which is closer to the shoulder blade so it takes slightly longer to cook, or the 7-bone chuck roast (see page 38). Finally, while their size prevents them from being a whole-roast alternative, boneless short ribs (see page 177) are an excellent (albeit more expensive) choice for cutting into cubes for stews.

A TALE OF (ONE OR) TWO ROASTS

Chuck-eye roast has a natural seam running down it. As this interior area is known for some sinewy fat that can take away from the elegance of a final dish, the seam makes it convenient to separate the two lobes of meat and trim away any undesirables before cooking. Take some twine and tie it back together for one cleaned-up roast. Or, for faster cooking or more surface area exposure, cook as two roasts, as called for in some recipes.

"STEW MEAT"

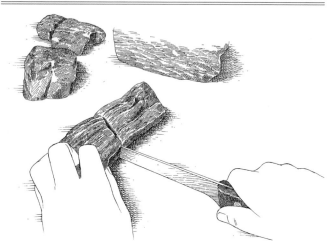

Prepackaged beef stew meat is convenient—but not very good. In most markets, the pieces are much too small and they're unevenly butchered, so smaller pieces overcook by the time larger ones are done. Even more problematic is the meat itself. Sometimes it comes from the most-desired chuck eye, sometimes from tougher areas of the chuck like the under blade, but often packages contain scraps from the clod or all over the animal, many of which are not very flavorful. Instead, we cut a chuck-eye roast into stew meat ourselves in large chunks, usually 1½ to 2 inches; we think bigger chunks make a better stew because they're satisfying and less likely to overcook. Trim any hard knobs of white fat as you work. Don't bother trimming soft, thin lines of fat—they will melt during the stewing process and lubricate the meat; you can always skim the final stew. (That said, don't be surprised if you have a good number of trimmings—count on roughly ½ pound of trimmings for every 4 pounds of meat.)

Chuck-Eye Steak

Cost: ■■□□ **Flavor:** ■■■□
Best cooking methods: grill
Texture: lean, some chew
Alternative names: shoulder steaks, London broil

We like chuck-eye steaks as they're cut from the portion of the chuck-eye roast that's a continuation of the muscle from which luxe rib-eye steaks are cut. They've risen in popularity as a still-tender but much less expensive alternative. We've found that chuck-eye steaks bought in the store can be inconsistent in size and shape, so they cook at different rates. We prefer to purchase a boneless chuck-eye roast and cut it into steaks ourselves. We like to grill our chuck-eye steaks (see page 52)—this allows us to char them hot and fast on both sides and then move them to a cooler area of the grill to cook through to medium-rare. Slicing the meat against the grain reduces chewiness.

MEAT PREP *Butchering Chuck-Eye Steak*

1. Separate chuck-eye roast into 2 pieces along natural seam. Turn each piece on its side and cut in half lengthwise against grain.

2. Remove silverskin and trim fat to ¼-inch thickness.

Top-Blade Roast

Cost: ▪▪◻◻ Flavor: ▪▪▪◻
Best cooking methods: braise, stew, slow cook, sous vide
Texture: tender if cooked low and slow
Alternative names: chuck roast first cut, blade roast, top chuck roast

Recall that we said the beef chuck includes a large portion called the chuck roll from which the chuck eye and the chuck under blade are cut (see page 35). The remainder, the other large subprimal is called the chuck clod. "Clod" might imply that this portion isn't exactly desirable. But one of its five distinct muscles, the top blade, is quite tender. The top-blade roast is a broad, flat cut well marbled with fat and connective tissue, which makes it very juicy and flavorful. Even after thorough braising, this roast retains a distinctive strip of connective tissue, but it's not unpleasant to eat. It's not our go-to, but it's our favorite substitute for the chuck-eye roast. It needs to be tied to even out its shape.

Blade Steak

Cost: ▪▪◻◻ Flavor: ▪▪▪◻
Best cooking methods: braise, stew, stir-fry, slow cook
Texture: tender once braised
Alternative names: Top-blade steak

Cut across the top blade and you get blade steaks. They have a big, beefy flavor and, unlike some fattier cuts that require several hours of cooking, they get nice and tender with just about an hour of simmering. The underrated cut is incredibly affordable because of the top blade's line of gristle that runs down the middle, but when slowly cooked these steaks turn fall-apart tender, and you can easily remove the gristle, yielding a richly flavored, beefy steak. Alternatively, depending on the preparation, you may choose to remove the gristle before cooking. You can slice blade steaks thin to become tender in a meaty stir-fry like Stir-Fried Thai Beef with Chiles and Shallots (page 56) or cut them into pieces to be braised for recipes like chili (see page 53), and they're great when you want to braise whole steaks rather than sear them, as in Braised Steaks with Root Vegetables (page 54). You can substitute flat-iron steaks in most applications and flank steak if you're slicing the steaks for stir-fries.

MEAT PREP *Trimming Blade Steak*

1. Halve each steak lengthwise, leaving gristle on 1 half. **2.** Cut gristle away.

MEAT PREP *Preparing Blade Steak for Stir-Fries*

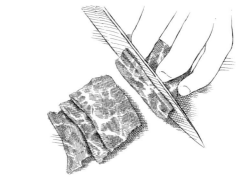

Slice meat on bias into ¼-inch-thick strips.

Flat-Iron Steak

Cost: ▪▪◻◻ Flavor: ▪▪▪◻
Best Cooking Methods: seared or grilled
Texture: tender
Alternative names: Top-blade steak

Flat-iron steak is cut from the top blade, lengthwise atop the line of gristle, so there's none in the steak. In addition to the lack of gristle, this steak is protected from the cow's shoulder movements so it's surprisingly, and profoundly, tender—it can be grilled (see page 59) or seared, unlike blade steak, which should most often be braised. Just make sure to cook it until medium to break down enough connective tissue for tenderness.

7-Bone Chuck Roast

Cost: ■■▢▢ Flavor: ■■■▢

Best cooking methods: braise, stew, slow cook, sous vide
Texture: rich, very beefy, a bit less tender than chuck-eye roast
Alternative names: 7-bone steak

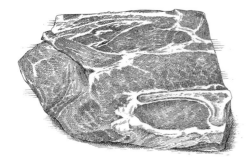

We love the chuck-eye roast but we mention the 7-bone chuck roast because it's a classic—a well-marbled cut with an incredibly beefy flavor. Unlike the squarer chuck-eye roast, it's not cut horizontally but is cut vertically through the chuck into 2-inch-wide pieces. (Thus, it doesn't contain seven bones but rather its bone structure can look like the number 7.) This means it can contain any number of muscles and portions of the chuck so some are more tender than others. Because it's only 2 inches thick, it requires less liquid and less time to braise. If you want a bone-in chuck roast, this is what you should buy. Do not buy a 7-bone roast that weighs more than 3½ pounds, as it will not fit in a Dutch oven; make sure to adjust the liquid in your recipe as necessary.

OTHER CUTS FROM THE CHUCK

We've expanded on cuts we use in our recipes (or ones that are good substitutes), but the large, complex chuck contains other cuts. These include the ultrachewy, bouncy chuck shoulder roast and the full-of-fat under-blade roast.

NOT FOR THE BACKYARD BARBECUER

Beyond in the context of the top-blade roast, we haven't discussed the chuck clod, but it's so expansive we want to mention it again. The large boneless cut from the shoulder naturally requires the lowest and slowest of cooking so it's the dream cut for some in the barbecue circuit; it delivers supremely beefy flavor when coated with spicy black pepper and cayenne, well seasoned with salt, and tossed on the grill. Long overshadowed in the world of Texas barbecue by fattier but less intensely meaty brisket, it's also one of the most economical cuts of meat around. But that doesn't mean *we're* going to cook it. Why not? Well, it weighs a hulking 13 to 21 pounds. We successfully barbecued a boneless chuck-eye roast instead to mimic the flavor of a clod achieved by the pros. See how on page 51.

Bresato al Barolo

CLASSIC POT ROAST

Serves 6 to 8 | chuck-eye roast

WHY THIS RECIPE WORKS Pot roast is the quintessential chuck-eye roast recipe and the most fundamental example of a hearty, comforting braise. Slow-cooking an economical roast in liquid with vegetables and aromatics until it's succulent is an accessible technique. We wanted to achieve a supremely tender roast along with a deliciously savory sauce to spoon over the top. For the braising liquid, equal amounts of beef and chicken broth tasted best, and we added just enough water for the liquid to come about halfway up the sides of the roast and prevent it from drying out. When it comes to cooking pot roast, there are two typical approaches: Cook it on the stove or in the oven. It was too difficult to maintain a steady, low temperature on the stove with the flame from below, so we transferred the Dutch oven, covered with foil under the lid for a tight seal, to a 300-degree oven where the roast could cook more evenly for moist, flavorful meat. Use a good-quality, medium-bodied wine, such as a Côtes du Rhône or a Pinot Noir, for this dish.

- 1 (3½- to 4-pound) boneless beef chuck-eye roast, trimmed and tied at 1-inch intervals
- 2 tablespoons vegetable oil
- 1 onion, chopped fine
- 1 small carrot, peeled and chopped
- 1 small celery rib, chopped
- 2 garlic cloves, minced
- 2 teaspoons sugar
- 1 cup chicken broth
- 1 cup beef broth
- 1 sprig fresh thyme
- ¼ cup dry red wine

1. Adjust oven rack to middle position and heat oven to 300 degrees. Pat roast dry with paper towels and season with salt and pepper.

2. Heat oil in Dutch oven over medium-high heat until shimmering. Brown roast on all sides, 8 to 10 minutes, reducing heat if fat begins to smoke; transfer roast to large plate.

3. Reduce heat to medium; add onion, carrot, and celery to pot and cook, stirring occasionally, until beginning to brown, 6 to 8 minutes. Add garlic and sugar; cook until fragrant, about 30 seconds. Add chicken broth, beef broth, and thyme sprig, scraping up any browned bits.

4. Return roast and any accumulated juices to pot; add enough water to come halfway up sides of roast. Bring liquid to simmer over medium heat. Place large piece of aluminum foil over pot and cover tightly with lid; transfer pot to oven. Cook, turning roast every 30 minutes, until fully tender and fork slips easily in and out of meat, 3½ to 4 hours.

5. Transfer roast to carving board and tent with foil. Let liquid in pot settle for about 5 minutes, then use wide spoon to skim fat from surface; discard thyme sprig. Bring liquid to boil over high heat and cook until reduced to about 1½ cups, about 8 minutes. Add wine to pot and cook until reduced to 1½ cups, about 2 minutes. Season with salt and pepper to taste.

6. Remove twine from roast. Slice meat against grain into ½-inch-thick slices or pull apart into large pieces. Transfer meat to platter and pour about ½ cup sauce over meat. Serve, passing remaining sauce separately.

VARIATION

Pot Roast with Root Vegetables

Add 1½ pounds carrots, sliced ½ inch thick; 1½ pounds small red potatoes, halved if larger than 1½ inches in diameter; and 1 pound parsnips, sliced ½ inch thick, to Dutch oven after cooking beef for about 3 hours, submerging them in liquid. Continue to cook until vegetables are almost tender, 30 minutes to 1 hour longer. Transfer roast to carving board and tent with aluminum foil. Let liquid in pot settle for about 5 minutes, then use wide spoon to skim fat from surface; remove thyme sprig. Add wine and salt and pepper to taste; boil over high heat until vegetables are tender, 5 to 10 minutes. Using slotted spoon, transfer vegetables to warmed serving platter. Slice meat against grain into ½-inch-thick slices or pull apart into large pieces; transfer meat to bowl or platter with vegetables and pour about ½ cup sauce over meat and vegetables. Serve, passing remaining sauce separately.

BRESATO AL BAROLO

Serves 6 | chuck-eye roast

WHY THIS RECIPE WORKS Bresato al Barolo is a hearty yet elegant braise enjoyed in households across the Piedmont region of Italy for special occasions. This pot roast is supreme because it's cooked in a full bottle of Barolo, often called the king of wines. Rich, full-bodied, and velvety, the wine reduces to an ultraluxurious and complex-tasting sauce that can't be achieved with a lighter-bodied wine. This dish's purpose is to highlight this ingredient, so we sought to do justice to this regal wine. We separated the meat at the seam to create two roasts, which cooked quicker than one large roast, and bathed them in the luxe wine sauce. We kept the aromatics simple, and to temper the Barolo's bold flavor, we also added a can of diced tomatoes, plus just ½ teaspoon of sugar to balance the wine's acidity. After 3 hours of braising in a low oven, a dark, full-flavored, and lustrous sauce bestowed nobility on our humble chuck-eye roast.

TUTORIAL
Bresato al Barolo

A braised roast is a distinct comfort. Most share similar steps: preparing the meat, browning the meat, cooking the aromatics, combining with liquid, and braising.

1. Pull apart chuck-eye roast at its major seam. Trim away excess fat and gristle.

2. Pat beef dry with paper towels and season with pepper. Using 3 pieces of kitchen twine for each piece of beef, tie crosswise to form even roasts.

3. Brown roasts on all sides in cooked pancetta fat, 8 to 10 minutes. Transfer roasts to large plate.

4. Add onions, carrots, and celery to fat left in pot and cook over medium heat until softened and lightly browned, 6 to 8 minutes. Stir in garlic, tomato paste, flour, sugar, and pancetta and cook for 1 minute. Slowly whisk in wine.

5. Stir in tomatoes and herbs. Nestle roasts into pot along with any accumulated juices and bring to boil. Place aluminum foil over pot and cover with lid; transfer to oven. Cook, turning roasts every 45 minutes, until beef is tender and fork slips easily in and out of meat, about 3 hours.

6. Bring liquid in pot to boil and cook, whisking vigorously to help vegetables break down, until reduced to about 3½ cups, about 18 minutes. Remove twine from roasts. Slice meat against grain into ½-inch-thick slices. Serve with sauce.

1 (3½- to 4-pound) boneless beef chuck-eye roast,
   pulled apart at seams and trimmed
2 (¼-inch-thick) slices pancetta (4 ounces), cut into
   ¼-inch pieces
2 onions, chopped
2 carrots, peeled and chopped
2 celery ribs, chopped
3 garlic cloves, minced
1 tablespoon tomato paste
1 tablespoon all-purpose flour
½ teaspoon sugar
1 (750-ml) bottle Barolo wine
1 (14.5-ounce) can diced tomatoes, drained
10 sprigs fresh parsley
1 sprig fresh rosemary
1 sprig fresh thyme, plus 1 teaspoon minced

1. Adjust oven rack to middle position and heat oven to 300 degrees. Pat beef dry with paper towels and season generously with pepper. Using 3 pieces of kitchen twine for each piece of beef, tie cross-wise to form even roasts.

2. Cook pancetta in Dutch oven over medium-low heat until browned and fat is rendered, about 8 minutes. Using slotted spoon, transfer pancetta to bowl. Pour off all but 2 tablespoons fat from pot. Heat fat left in pot over medium-high heat until just smoking. Brown roasts on all sides, 8 to 10 minutes; transfer roasts to large plate.

3. Add onions, carrots, and celery to fat left in pot and cook over medium heat until softened and lightly browned, 6 to 8 minutes. Stir in garlic, tomato paste, flour, sugar, and pancetta and cook until fragrant, about 1 minute. Slowly whisk in wine, scraping up any browned bits and smoothing out any lumps. Stir in tomatoes, parsley sprigs, rosemary sprig, and thyme sprig. Nestle roasts into pot along with any accumulated juices and bring to boil. Place large sheet of aluminum foil over pot and cover tightly with lid; transfer pot to oven. Cook, turning roasts every 45 minutes, until beef is tender and fork slips easily in and out of meat, about 3 hours.

4. Transfer roasts to carving board and tent with foil. Let liquid in pot settle for 5 minutes, then use wide spoon to skim fat from surface. Stir in minced thyme. Bring liquid to boil and cook, whisking vigorously to help vegetables break down, until thickened and reduced to about 3½ cups, about 18 minutes. Strain sauce through fine-mesh strainer into bowl, pressing on solids to extract as much liquid as possible; you should have about 1½ cups strained sauce (if necessary, return strained sauce to pot and continue to boil until sauce reduces to 1½ cups). Discard solids. Season sauce with salt and pepper to taste. Remove twine from roasts. Slice meat against grain ½ inch thick. Transfer meat to platter. Spoon half of sauce over meat and serve, passing remaining sauce separately.

POT-AU-FEU

Serves 6 to 8 | chuck-eye roast

WHY THIS RECIPE WORKS Though a bit vintage, pot-au-feu (which translates literally as "pot on the fire"), a dish of tender meat and vegetables, a rich broth, and a robust sauce, has been celebrated in France since its Revolution. It's typically made with many meats, but we had the temperament for just one. While we love chuck, the broth, was coming up short. Adding marrow bones with the boneless roast gave our broth a beguiling mix of butteriness and body. Marrow bones (also called soup bones) can be found in the freezer section or the meat counter at most supermarkets. Use small red potatoes measuring 1 to 2 inches in diameter.

MEAT
1 (3½- to 4-pound) boneless beef chuck-eye roast,
   pulled apart at seams and trimmed
1 tablespoon kosher salt
1½ pounds marrow bones
1 onion, quartered
1 celery rib, sliced thin
3 bay leaves
1 teaspoon black peppercorns
4 cups water

PARSLEY SAUCE
⅔ cup minced fresh parsley
¼ cup Dijon mustard
¼ cup minced fresh chives
3 tablespoons white wine vinegar
10 cornichons, minced
1½ teaspoons pepper

VEGETABLES
1 pound small red potatoes, halved
1 pound carrots, halved crosswise, thick halves quartered
   lengthwise, thin halves halved lengthwise
1 pound asparagus, trimmed

   Flake sea salt

1. **For the meat:** Adjust oven rack to lower-middle position and heat oven to 300 degrees. Sprinkle beef with kosher salt. Using 3 pieces of kitchen twine per piece, tie each into loaf shape. Place roasts, bones, onion, celery, bay leaves, and peppercorns in Dutch oven. Add enough water to come halfway up roasts. Bring to simmer over high heat. Partially cover pot and transfer to oven. Cook until beef is tender and fork slips easily in and out of meat (beef should not be shreddable), 3¼ to 3¾ hours, flipping roasts halfway through cooking.

2. **For the parsley sauce:** While roasts cook, combine all ingredients in bowl. Cover and set aside.

Chuck Roast in Foil

CHUCK ROAST IN FOIL

Serves 4 to 6 | chuck-eye roast

WHY THIS RECIPE WORKS Remember your elders' pot roast, the old family recipe? Many times this is a relatively lazy roast that involves rubbing a chuck roast with onion soup mix, wrapping it in foil, and cooking it in the oven until tender. While we like the ease of this dish, we aren't fans of its artificial, salty taste. To develop really oniony flavor with ease, we started with onion powder and salt, but ditched the monosodium glutamate in favor of soy sauce, which enhanced the roast's beefy flavor. Brown sugar added sweetness and depth, while a surprise ingredient, a little espresso powder, provided toasty complexity. Dividing the roast into two halves allowed us to apply more of the flavorful spice rub. You will need an 18-inch-wide roll of heavy-duty aluminum foil for wrapping the roast. Use small red potatoes measuring 1 to 2 inches in diameter.

RUB

- 3 tablespoons cornstarch
- 4 teaspoons onion powder
- 2 teaspoons packed light brown sugar
- 2 teaspoons table salt
- 1 teaspoon pepper
- 1 teaspoon garlic powder
- 1 teaspoon instant espresso powder
- 1 teaspoon dried thyme
- ½ teaspoon celery seeds

CHUCK ROAST

- 1 (4-pound) boneless beef chuck-eye roast, pulled apart at seams, fat trimmed to ¼ inch, and tied at 1-inch intervals
- 2 onions, peeled and quartered
- 1 pound small red potatoes, quartered
- 4 carrots, peeled and cut into 1½-inch pieces
- 2 bay leaves
- 2 tablespoons soy sauce

1. For the rub: Adjust oven rack to lower-middle position and heat oven to 300 degrees. Combine all ingredients in small bowl.

2. For the chuck roast: Pat roast dry with paper towels. Place two 30 by 18-inch sheets of heavy-duty aluminum foil perpendicular to each other inside large roasting pan. Place onions, potatoes, carrots, and bay leaves in center of foil and drizzle with soy sauce. Set roasts on top of vegetables. Rub roasts all over with rub. Fold opposite corners of foil toward each other and crimp edges tightly to seal. Transfer pan to oven and cook until meat is completely tender, about 4½ hours.

3. Remove pot from oven and turn off oven. Transfer roasts to large platter, cover tightly with aluminum foil, and return to oven to keep warm. Transfer bones to cutting board; use handle of spoon to extract marrow. Mince marrow to paste and add 2 tablespoons marrow to parsley sauce (reserve any remaining marrow for other applications). Using ladle or large spoon, skim fat from surface of broth and discard fat. Strain broth through fine-mesh strainer into large liquid measuring cup; add water to equal 6 cups. Return broth to pot. (Meat can be returned to broth, cooled, and refrigerated for up to 2 days. Skim fat from cold broth, then gently reheat and proceed with recipe.)

4. For the vegetables: Add potatoes to broth and bring to simmer over high heat. Reduce heat to medium and simmer for 6 minutes. Add carrots and cook 10 minutes longer. Add asparagus and continue to cook until all vegetables are tender, 3 to 5 minutes longer.

5. Using slotted spoon, transfer vegetables to large bowl. Toss with 3 tablespoons parsley sauce and season with salt and pepper to taste. Season broth with salt to taste.

6. Transfer roasts to carving board. Remove twine. Slice meat against grain ½ inch thick. Divide beef and vegetables among shallow bowls. Dollop beef with parsley sauce, drizzle with ⅓ cup broth, and sprinkle with sea salt. Serve, passing remaining parsley sauce and extra sea salt separately.

3. Remove roasts from foil pouch and place on carving board. Tent beef with foil and let rest for 20 minutes. Remove onions and bay leaves. Using slotted spoon, place carrots and potatoes on serving platter. Strain contents of roasting pan through fine-mesh strainer into fat separator. Let liquid settle, then pour defatted pan juices into serving bowl.

4. Remove twine from roasts. Slice roasts thin against grain and transfer to platter with vegetables. Pour ½ cup pan juices over meat. Serve with remaining pan juices.

ROASTED BEEF CHUCK WITH HORSERADISH-PARSLEY SAUCE

Serves 8 to 10 | chuck-eye roast

WHY THIS RECIPE WORKS We cover grand, holiday-worthy roasts aplenty in this collection, but a centerpiece beef roast doesn't need to break the bank. Chuck-eye roast boasts big, beefy flavor that can stand up to a deliciously assertive sauce—and it rings in at about a third of the price of your typical tenderloin. Since chuck-eye roast is our choice for braising, we made sure to take the low-and-slow concept to the dry heat of the oven—and we needed to cook the roast beyond medium-rare, to 145 degrees so the connective tissue could begin to break down enough. We pulled the roast apart at the seam, trimmed it, and tied it back together to make one evenly shaped, impressive-looking main course. Salting the roast and refrigerating it for up to a day further improved flavor and texture. To drizzle over the top, we made a spicy, herby sauce that was a cross between a traditional creamy horseradish sauce and a more vibrant, fresh parsley sauce. Buy refrigerated prepared horseradish, not the self-stable kind, which contains preservatives and additives.

BEEF

- 1 (5-pound) boneless beef chuck-eye roast, trimmed
- 2 tablespoons kosher salt
- 2 teaspoons pepper
- 2 tablespoons extra-virgin olive oil

SAUCE

- 1 cup fresh parsley leaves
- ¼ cup prepared horseradish
- 1 shallot, chopped
- 2 tablespoons capers, rinsed
- 1 tablespoon lemon juice
- 1 garlic clove, minced
- ½ teaspoon kosher salt
- ¾ cup extra-virgin olive oil

Best Beef Stew

1. For the beef: Pull roast into 2 pieces at major seam delineated by line of white fat, cutting with boning knife as needed. Using knife, remove large knobs of fat from each piece.

2. Sprinkle beef all over with salt and pepper. Place pieces back together along major seam. Tie together with kitchen twine at 1-inch intervals to create 1 evenly shaped roast. Wrap tightly in plastic wrap and refrigerate for 18 to 24 hours.

3. Adjust oven rack to lower-middle position and heat oven to 275 degrees. Set wire rack in rimmed baking sheet. Unwrap roast and rub all over with oil. Place roast on prepared wire rack. Transfer sheet to oven and roast until meat registers 145 to 150 degrees, 3¼ to 3¾ hours. Transfer roast to carving board, tent with aluminum foil, and let rest for 45 minutes.

4. For the sauce: Meanwhile, pulse parsley, horseradish, shallot, capers, lemon juice, garlic, and salt in food processor until parsley is finely chopped, 6 to 8 pulses, scraping down sides of bowl as needed. Transfer to bowl and stir in oil until combined. Season with salt to taste; set aside. (Sauce can be refrigerated for up to 2 days. Bring to room temperature before serving.)

5. Slice roast thin against grain, removing twine as you go so roast stays intact. Serve, passing sauce separately.

BEST BEEF STEW

Serves 6 to 8 | chuck-eye roast

WHY THIS RECIPE WORKS Every culture has its unique version of beef stew, but for this all-American version, we didn't want to settle for the commonplace. We sought a superlatively rich-tasting but approachable stew with tender meat, flavorful vegetables, and a rich brown gravy. We planned to take a no-holds-barred attitude toward the ingredient list. We browned chuck-eye roast that we cut into cubes, taking care not to crowd the meat in the pan. Along with traditional stew components like onion, carrots, garlic, red wine, and chicken broth, we added glutamate-rich tomato paste, anchovies, and salt pork. Glutamates are compounds that give meat its savory taste, and they contribute considerable flavor to the dish. To mimic the luxurious, mouth-coating texture of beef stews made with homemade stock, we included powdered gelatin and flour. Use a good-quality, medium-bodied red wine, such as a Côtes du Rhône or Pinot Noir, for this stew. Look for salt pork that is roughly 75 percent lean.

- 2 garlic cloves, minced
- 4 anchovy fillets, rinsed and minced
- 1 tablespoon tomato paste
- 1 (4-pound) boneless beef chuck-eye roast, pulled apart at seams, trimmed, and cut into 1½-inch pieces
- 2 tablespoons vegetable oil, divided
- 1 large onion, halved and sliced ⅛ inch thick
- 4 carrots, peeled and cut into 1-inch pieces
- ¼ cup all-purpose flour
- 2 cups red wine
- 2 cups chicken broth
- 4 ounces salt pork, rinsed
- 2 bay leaves
- 4 sprigs fresh thyme
- 1 pound Yukon Gold potatoes, cut into 1-inch pieces
- 1½ cups frozen pearl onions, thawed
- 2 teaspoons unflavored gelatin
- ½ cup water
- 1 cup frozen peas, thawed

1. Adjust oven rack to lower-middle position and heat oven to 300 degrees. Combine garlic and anchovies in small bowl; press with back of fork to form paste. Stir in tomato paste and set aside.

2. Pat beef dry with paper towels (do not season). Heat 1 tablespoon oil in Dutch oven over high heat until just smoking. Add half of beef and cook until well browned on all sides, about 8 minutes; transfer to large plate. Repeat with remaining 1 tablespoon oil and remaining beef, leaving second batch of beef in pot after browning.

3. Reduce heat to medium and return first batch of beef to pot. Stir in onion and carrots and cook, scraping up any browned bits, until onion is softened, 1 to 2 minutes. Add garlic mixture and cook, stirring constantly, until fragrant, about 30 seconds. Add flour and cook, stirring constantly, until no dry flour remains, about 30 seconds.

4. Slowly add wine, scraping up any browned bits. Increase heat to high and simmer until wine is thickened and slightly reduced, about 2 minutes. Stir in broth, salt pork, bay leaves, and thyme sprigs. Bring to simmer and cover; transfer pot to oven. Cook for 1½ hours.

5. Remove pot from oven; discard salt pork, bay leaves, and thyme sprigs. Stir in potatoes, cover, return pot to oven, and continue to cook until potatoes are almost tender, about 45 minutes.

6. Using wide spoon, skim fat from surface of stew. Stir in pearl onions; cook over medium heat until potatoes and pearl onions are cooked through and fork slips easily in and out of beef (meat should not be falling apart), about 15 minutes. Meanwhile, sprinkle gelatin over water in bowl and let sit until gelatin softens, about 5 minutes.

7. Increase heat to high, stir in gelatin mixture and peas, and simmer until gelatin is fully dissolved and stew is thickened, about 3 minutes. Season with salt and pepper to taste, and serve.

BOEUF BOURGUIGNON

Serves 6 to 8 | chuck-eye roast

WHY THIS RECIPE WORKS A defining dish of French cuisine, boeuf Bourguignon, or beef Burgundy, is the ultimate rich and satisfying beef stew. By gently simmering chunks of meat in broth and a good amount of red wine, you end up with fork-tender beef and a braising liquid that becomes a silky, full-bodied sauce. We wanted that without the work that traditional recipes require: browning beef, cooking garnishes, braising, combining, cooking further. To eliminate the time-consuming step of searing the beef, we cooked the stew uncovered in a roasting pan in the oven so the exposed meat browned as it braised. We also used the oven to render the salt pork and caramelize the traditional mushroom and onion garnish. Adding anchovy paste and dried porcini mushrooms enhanced the meaty savoriness of the dish. If the pearl onions have a papery outer coating, remove it by rinsing them in warm water and gently squeezing individual onions between your fingertips. Two minced anchovy fillets can be used in place of the anchovy paste.

1 (4-pound) boneless beef chuck-eye roast, pulled apart at seams, trimmed, and cut into 1½-inch pieces, scraps reserved
1½ teaspoons table salt
6 ounces salt pork, cut into ¼-inch pieces
3 tablespoons unsalted butter, divided
1 pound cremini mushrooms, trimmed and halved if medium or quartered if large
1½ cups frozen pearl onions, thawed
1 tablespoon sugar
⅓ cup all-purpose flour
4 cups beef broth
1 (750-ml) bottle red Burgundy or Pinot Noir, divided
5 teaspoons unflavored gelatin
1 tablespoon tomato paste
1 teaspoon anchovy paste
2 onions, chopped coarse
2 carrots, peeled and cut into 2-inch lengths
1 garlic head, cloves separated, unpeeled, and smashed
½ ounce dried porcini mushrooms, rinsed
10 sprigs fresh parsley, plus 3 tablespoons minced
6 sprigs fresh thyme
2 bay leaves
½ teaspoon black peppercorns

1. Toss beef and salt together in bowl; let sit at room temperature for 30 minutes.

2. Adjust oven racks to lower-middle and lowest positions and heat oven to 500 degrees. Place beef scraps, salt pork, and 2 tablespoons butter in large roasting pan. Roast on upper rack until well browned and fat is rendered, 15 to 20 minutes.

3. While beef scraps and salt pork roast, toss cremini mushrooms, pearl onions, sugar, and remaining 1 tablespoon butter on rimmed baking sheet. Roast on lower rack, stirring occasionally, until moisture released by mushrooms evaporates and vegetables are lightly glazed, 15 to 20 minutes. Transfer vegetables to large bowl, cover, and refrigerate.

4. Remove roasting pan from oven and reduce temperature to 325 degrees. Sprinkle flour over rendered fat and whisk until no dry flour remains. Whisk in broth, 2 cups wine, gelatin, tomato paste, and anchovy paste until combined. Add onions, carrots, garlic, porcini mushrooms, parsley sprigs, thyme sprigs, bay leaves, and peppercorns to pan. Arrange beef in single layer on top of vegetables. Add water as needed to come three-quarters up sides of beef pieces (beef should not be submerged). Return roasting pan to oven and cook until meat is tender, 3 to 3½ hours, stirring after 1½ hours and adding water to keep meat at least half-submerged.

5. Using slotted spoon, transfer beef to bowl with cremini mushrooms and pearl onions; cover and set aside. Strain braising liquid through fine-mesh strainer set over large bowl, pressing on solids to extract as much liquid as possible; discard solids. Stir in remaining wine. Let liquid settle for 10 minutes, then use wide spoon to skim fat from surface.

6. Transfer liquid to Dutch oven and bring mixture to boil over medium-high heat. Simmer briskly, stirring occasionally, until sauce has thickened to consistency of heavy cream, 15 to 20 minutes. Reduce heat to medium-low, stir in beef and mushroom-onion mixture, cover, and cook until just heated through, 5 to 8 minutes. Season with salt and pepper to taste. Stir in minced parsley and serve.

RIGATONI ALLA GENOVESE

Serves 6 to 8 | chuck-eye roast

WHY THIS RECIPE WORKS This rich, supple beef and onion ragu was born out of thrift in 16th-century Naples. La Genovese began as a combination of beef and aromatic vegetables that was cooked to make two meals: a meal of cooked beef and a savory sauce for pasta. Onions are the foundation of this deeply flavorful sauce. To eliminate the need for stirring and monitoring during cooking, we moved the process from the stovetop to the oven. A surprising ingredient—water—extracted maximum flavor from the onions, turning them to a sweet, delicious, pleasantly pulpy sauce. We also added tomato paste for a boost of flavor and color. To encourage the sauce to cling to the pasta, we vigorously stirred the two together so that the starch from the pasta added body to the sauce.

1 (1- to 1¼-pound) boneless beef chuck-eye roast, cut into 4 pieces and trimmed of large pieces of fat
1 teaspoon kosher salt, plus salt for cooking pasta
½ teaspoon pepper
2 ounces pancetta, cut into ½-inch pieces
2 ounces salami, cut into ½-inch pieces
1 small carrot, peeled and cut into ½-inch pieces
1 small celery rib, cut into ½-inch pieces
2½ pounds onions, halved and cut into 1-inch pieces
2 tablespoons tomato paste
1 cup dry white wine, divided
2 tablespoons minced fresh marjoram, divided
1 pound rigatoni
1 ounce Pecorino Romano cheese, grated (½ cup), plus extra for serving

1. Sprinkle beef with salt and pepper and set aside. Adjust oven rack to lower-middle position and heat oven to 300 degrees.

Carne Guisada

CARNE GUISADA

Serves 8 to 10 | chuck-eye roast

WHY THIS RECIPE WORKS Braised beef and potatoes is as classic as, well, meat and potatoes. The Texas version, carne guisada, is a bold, satisfying stew flavored with tomato, chiles, and warm spices. It's commonly served as tacos or as a stew with beans, rice, or tortillas on the side. Multiple varieties of chiles can be easier to find in Texas than in other areas of the U.S., so we seasoned the stew with a simple but delicious mix of chili powder, oregano, cumin, and coriander—no fresh chiles necessary. Choosing chicken broth for our braising liquid let the flavor of what would become meltingly tender beef shine—there were already strong flavors in this stew. We added the potatoes and bell peppers partway through cooking to guarantee the vegetables were tender but that they didn't disintegrate. Finally, cutting back on the amount of liquid and adding a tablespoon of flour gave our stew the perfect texture.

3 pounds boneless beef chuck-eye roast, trimmed and cut into 1-inch pieces
2 tablespoons vegetable oil
2 onions, chopped
1 teaspoon table salt
2 tablespoons tomato paste
4 garlic cloves, minced
1 tablespoon chili powder
1 tablespoon dried oregano
2 teaspoons ground coriander
1½ teaspoons ground cumin
1 tablespoon all-purpose flour
1 (14.5-ounce) can diced tomatoes, drained
1 cup chicken broth
1 pound Yukon Gold potatoes, peeled and cut into ½-inch pieces
2 green bell peppers, stemmed, seeded, and cut into ¼-inch strips
24 flour tortillas, warmed
Fresh cilantro leaves
Lime wedges

2. Process pancetta and salami in food processor until ground to paste, about 30 seconds, scraping down sides of bowl as needed. Add carrot and celery and process 30 seconds longer, scraping down sides of bowl as needed. Transfer paste to Dutch oven and set aside. Pulse onions in now-empty processor in 2 batches, until ⅛- to ¼-inch pieces form, 8 to 10 pulses per batch. Cook pancetta mixture over medium heat, stirring frequently, until fat is rendered and fond begins to form on bottom of pot, about 5 minutes. Add tomato paste and cook, stirring constantly, until browned, about 90 seconds. Stir in 2 cups water, scraping up any browned bits. Stir in onions and bring to boil. Stir in ½ cup wine and 1 tablespoon marjoram. Add beef and push into onions to ensure that it is submerged. Transfer to oven and cook, uncovered, until beef is fully tender, 2 to 2½ hours.

3. Transfer beef to carving board. Place pot over medium heat and cook, stirring frequently, until mixture is almost completely dry. Stir in remaining ½ cup wine and cook for 2 minutes, stirring occasionally. Using 2 forks, shred beef into bite-size pieces. Stir beef and remaining 1 tablespoon marjoram into sauce and season with salt and pepper to taste. Remove from heat, cover, and keep warm.

4. Bring 4 quarts water to boil in large pot. Add pasta and 2 tablespoons salt and cook, stirring often, until just al dente. Drain pasta and add to sauce. Add Pecorino and stir vigorously over low heat until sauce is slightly thickened and pasta is fully tender, 1 to 2 minutes. Serve, passing extra Pecorino separately.

1. Adjust oven rack to lower-middle position and heat oven to 325 degrees. Pat beef dry with paper towels and season with salt and pepper. Heat oil in Dutch oven over medium-high heat until just smoking. Add half of beef and cook until browned on all sides, 7 to 10 minutes; transfer to plate.

2. Reduce heat to medium-low, add onions and salt to pot, and cook until softened, about 5 minutes. Stir in tomato paste, garlic, chili powder, oregano, coriander, and cumin and cook until fragrant, about 30 seconds. Stir in flour and cook for 1 minute. Stir in tomatoes and broth and bring to simmer, scraping up any browned bits. Stir in all of beef and any accumulated juices and cover; transfer pot to oven. Cook for 1½ hours.

3. Remove pot from oven and stir in potatoes and bell peppers. Cover, return pot to oven, and continue to cook until beef and potatoes are tender, about 45 minutes longer.

4. Season with salt and pepper to taste. Spoon small amount of stew into center of each tortilla, top with cilantro, and serve with lime wedges.

SLOW-COOKER POT ROAST WITH TOMATOES AND RED WINE

Serves 8 to 10 | chuck-eye roast
Cooking time: 9 to 10 hours on low or 6 to 7 hours on high

WHY THIS RECIPE WORKS A slow cooker, with its even and moist heat, is the perfect environment for braising a pot roast until fork-tender. As we already have a recipe for a classic pot roast (see page 40), we thought we'd put a deeply flavored spin on this roast with the addition of red wine, oregano, tomatoes, red pepper flakes, and dried porcini mushrooms. To get loads of flavor into our roast we first browned the meat in a skillet and then sautéed some bacon and aromatics. Deglazing the skillet with wine helped capture all the flavorful browned bits. We often divide a chuck roast into two smaller ones and that was ideal for the slow cooker; they fit perfectly and cooked evenly, yielding fork-tender meat more consistently than if cooked as one whole roast.

1 (4- to 5-pound) boneless beef chuck-eye roast, pulled apart at seams and trimmed
2 tablespoons extra-virgin olive oil
8 slices bacon, chopped
2 onions, chopped
4 carrots, peeled and cut into 1-inch pieces
6 garlic cloves, minced
½ ounce dried porcini mushrooms, rinsed and minced
2 tablespoons minced fresh oregano or 2 teaspoons dried
2 tablespoons tomato paste
½ teaspoon red pepper flakes
½ cup dry red wine
1 (28-ounce) can crushed tomatoes
1 cup chicken broth
2 bay leaves
¼ cup minced fresh parsley

1. Pat beef dry with paper towels and season with salt and pepper. Tie 3 pieces of kitchen twine around each piece of beef to create 2 evenly shaped roasts. Heat oil in 12-inch skillet over medium-high heat until just smoking. Brown roasts on all sides, 7 to 10 minutes; transfer to plate.

2. Add bacon to now-empty skillet and cook over medium heat until crisp, 5 to 7 minutes. Using slotted spoon, transfer bacon to slow cooker. Pour off all but 2 tablespoons fat from skillet.

3. Add onions and carrots to fat left in skillet and cook over medium heat until softened and lightly browned, 8 to 10 minutes. Stir in garlic, mushrooms, oregano, tomato paste, and pepper flakes and cook until fragrant, about 30 seconds. Stir in wine, scraping up any browned bits; transfer to slow cooker.

4. Stir tomatoes, broth, and bay leaves into slow cooker. Nestle roasts into slow cooker, adding any accumulated juices. Cover and cook until beef is tender and fork slips easily in and out of meat, 9 to 10 hours on low or 6 to 7 hours on high.

5. Transfer roasts to carving board, tent with aluminum foil, and let rest for 20 minutes.

6. Discard bay leaves. Using large spoon, skim fat from surface of sauce. Stir in parsley and season with salt and pepper to taste.

7. Remove twine from roasts. Slice meat against grain ½ inch thick and arrange on platter. Spoon 1 cup sauce over meat and serve, passing remaining sauce separately.

PRESSURE-COOKER BEEF STEW WITH TOMATOES, OLIVES, AND ORANGE ZEST

Serves 4 to 6 | chuck-eye roast

WHY THIS RECIPE WORKS We wanted a beef stew that we could make on a weeknight—one that would be mostly hands-off but would still produce tender meat and a thick, luxurious gravy. That's where the electric pressure cooker came in. We could start stewing as soon as we got home and be eating a normally long-cooked dinner in short order. The moist heat effortlessly tenderized chuck-eye roast, and we found we could skip the time-consuming browning of the beef by sautéing our aromatics to create plenty of fond and adding a hefty amount of savory soy sauce and tomato paste. Flour helped thicken the stew to give it good body. For an alternative to the traditional beef stew profile (see page 45), we turned to the flavors of Provence; tomatoes added interest to the braising liquid and olives provided briny bites throughout. A subtle aroma of orange perfumed the whole comforting dish.

1 tablespoon vegetable oil
1 onion, chopped fine
½ teaspoon table salt
¼ cup all-purpose flour
¼ cup tomato paste

Sous Vide Pepper-Crusted Beef Roast

SOUS VIDE PEPPER-CRUSTED BEEF ROAST

Serves 10 to 12 | chuck-eye roast
Sous vide time: 18 to 24 hours

WHY THIS RECIPE WORKS When it comes to holiday beef roasts, chuck isn't really known for being the go-to for medium-rare resplendence (we're looking at you, prime rib). With most traditional methods of cooking, you have two options: low and slow until it's tender or braised and broken down. Both methods turn out a great dish; neither gives you medium-rare. But with sous vide we can have it all: a fork-tender, juicy, medium-rare chuck roast. Circulating the roast at a low temperature for 24 hours allows enough time to break down intramuscular collagen, tenderizing the meat while preserving a rosy, medium-rare interior from edge to edge. We paired this roast with a generous herb crust, which goes well with our Yogurt-Herb Sauce (page 22). We prefer a combination of all three different peppercorns here, but you can use a single type.

1 (5-pound) boneless beef chuck-eye roast, trimmed
4 teaspoons kosher salt
2 tablespoons vegetable oil
1 egg white
¼ cup coarsely ground black, green, and pink peppercorns
2 tablespoons flake sea salt

1. Pull roast into 2 pieces at major seam delineated by line of white fat, cutting with boning knife as needed. Using knife, remove large knobs of fat from each piece. Sprinkle beef all over with salt. Place pieces back together along major seam. Tie together with kitchen twine at 1-inch intervals to create 1 evenly shaped roast. Transfer roast to large plate and refrigerate, uncovered, at least 24 hours or up to 96 hours.

2. Using sous vide circulator, heat water to 133°F in 12-quart container. Heat oil in 12-inch skillet over medium-high heat until just smoking. Brown roast on all sides, 6 to 8 minutes. Season roast with pepper and place in 2-gallon zipper-lock freezer bag. Seal bag, pressing out as much air as possible. Gently lower bag into prepared water bath until roast is fully submerged, and then clip top corner of bag to side of water bath container, allowing remaining air bubbles to rise to top of bag. Reopen 1 corner of zipper, release remaining air bubbles, and reseal bag. Cover and cook for at least 18 hours or up to 24 hours.

3. Adjust oven rack to middle position and heat oven to 475°F. Set wire rack in aluminum foil–lined rimmed baking sheet and spray with vegetable spray. Transfer roast to prepared rack and let rest for 10 to 15 minutes. Pat roast dry with paper towels.

1 (2-inch) strip orange zest
2 teaspoons herbes de Provence
2 cups beef broth, plus extra as needed
2 tablespoons soy sauce
2 pounds boneless beef chuck-eye roast, pulled apart at seams, trimmed, and cut into 1-inch pieces
2 (15-ounce) cans chopped tomatoes, drained
1 pound red potatoes, unpeeled, cut into 1-inch pieces
1 cup kalamata olives, pitted and halved
2 tablespoons minced fresh parsley

1. Using highest sauté or browning function, heat oil in electric pressure cooker until shimmering. Add onion and salt and cook until onion is softened, 3 to 5 minutes. Stir in flour, tomato paste, orange zest, and herbes de Provence and cook until fragrant, about 1 minute. Slowly whisk in broth and soy sauce, scraping up any browned bits and smoothing out any lumps. Season beef with salt and pepper and stir into electric pressure cooker along with tomatoes and potatoes.

2. Lock lid in place and close pressure release valve. Select high pressure cook function and cook for 25 minutes. Turn off pressure cooker and quick-release pressure. Carefully remove lid, allowing steam to escape away from you.

3. Stir in olives and let sit until heated through, about 2 minutes. Adjust consistency with extra hot broth as needed. Stir in parsley and season with salt and pepper to taste. Discard orange zest and serve.

TUTORIAL
Sous Vide Pepper-Crusted Beef Roast

Sous-viding your classic holiday roast may not have been your go-to in the past, but if you follow our steps, it's the most foolproof way to turn out a perfect roast, even with chuck-eye roast.

1. Sprinkle beef with salt. Tie pieces together with kitchen twine at 1-inch intervals to create 1 evenly shaped roast.

2. Using sous vide circulator, heat water to 133°F in 12-quart container. Heat oil in 12-inch skillet over medium-high heat until just smoking. Brown roast on all sides, 6 to 8 minutes.

3. Season roast with pepper and place in 2-gallon zipper-lock freezer bag. Seal bag, pressing out as much air as possible.

4. Gently lower bag into prepared water bath until roast is fully submerged, and then clip top corner of bag to side of water bath container, allowing remaining air bubbles to rise to top of bag.

5. Reopen 1 corner of zipper, release remaining air bubbles, and reseal bag. Cover and cook for at least 18 hours or up to 24 hours.

6. Brush cooked roast on all sides with egg white mixture, then coat with peppercorn mixture, pressing to adhere. Roast until surface is evenly browned and fragrant, 15 to 20 minutes, rotating sheet halfway through roasting.

4. Whisk egg white in bowl until frothy, about 30 seconds. Combine peppercorns and flake sea salt in shallow dish. Brush roast on all sides with egg white, then coat with peppercorn mixture, pressing to adhere. Return roast to prepared rack and roast until surface is evenly browned and fragrant, 15 to 20 minutes, rotating sheet halfway through roasting.

5. Transfer roast to carving board. Remove twine from roast. Slice meat against grain ½ inch thick; serve.

VARIATIONS

Rosemary–Mustard Seed Crusted Roast Beef
Process ¼ cup mustard seeds and 3 tablespoons peppercorns in spice grinder until coarsely ground. Transfer to shallow dish and stir in ⅓ cup chopped rosemary. Substitute rosemary mixture for peppercorns.

Za'atar-Crusted Roast Beef
Substitute ½ cup za'atar for peppercorns.

BARBECUE CHUCK ROAST

Serves 8 to 10 | chuck-eye roast

WHY THIS RECIPE WORKS Beef shoulder clod (see page 38), a sacred cut in some corners of Texas, delivers supremely beefy flavor underneath a coal-colored crust spiced with black pepper, cayenne, and salt. However, it often tips the scales at somewhere between 13 and 21 pounds. To make a more manageable version, we used chuck-eye roast. Salting the roast overnight seasoned it throughout. Cooking the roast over indirect heat on a hot grill outfitted with a packet of soaked wood chips infused the beef with smoky flavor. Cooked to 140 degrees, when a deep brown crust encased just a touch of pink in the center, the meat was chewy. We pushed it farther and pulled the roast off the grill when it registered 155 degrees, at which point the chewiness gave way to buttery tenderness. Slicing it paper-thin also ensured tenderness. If you'd like to use wood chunks instead of wood chips when using a charcoal grill, substitute two medium wood chunks, soaked in water for 1 hour, for the wood chip packet. Leftovers go well on slices of hearty white bread.

1½ tablespoons kosher salt
1½ teaspoons pepper
¼ teaspoon cayenne pepper
1 (5-pound) boneless beef chuck-eye roast, trimmed
2 cups wood chips

1. Combine salt, pepper, and cayenne in bowl. Pat roast dry with paper towels. Place roast on large sheet of plastic wrap and rub all over with spice mixture. Wrap tightly in plastic and refrigerate for 18 to 24 hours.

2. Just before grilling, soak wood chips in water for 15 minutes, then drain. Using large piece of heavy-duty aluminum foil, wrap soaked chips in 8 by 4½-inch foil packet. (Make sure chips do not poke holes in sides or bottom of packet.) Cut 2 evenly spaced 2-inch slits in top of packet.

3a. For a charcoal grill: Open bottom vent completely. Light large chimney starter filled with charcoal briquettes (6 quarts). When top coals are partially covered with ash, pour evenly over half of grill. Place wood chip packet on coals. Set cooking grate in place, cover, and open lid vent completely. Heat grill until hot and wood chips are smoking, about 5 minutes.

3b. For a gas grill: Remove cooking grate and place wood chip packet directly on primary burner. Set grate in place, turn all burners to high, cover, and heat grill until hot and wood chips are smoking, about 15 minutes. Leave primary burner on high and turn off other burner(s). (Adjust primary burner [or, if using 3-burner grill, primary burner and second burner] as needed to maintain grill temperature of 350 degrees.)

4. Clean and oil cooking grate. Unwrap roast and place on cooler side of grill; cover (position lid vent directly over roast if using charcoal) and cook until meat registers 155 to 160 degrees, 2 to 2½ hours. Transfer roast to carving board, tent with foil, and let rest for 20 minutes. Slice meat thin against grain and serve.

SHREDDED BARBECUE BEEF

Serves 8 to 10 | chuck-eye roast

WHY THIS RECIPE WORKS For big grill flavor for our backyard beef without a big time commitment, we cut a chuck-eye roast into quarters. The smaller pieces of beef absorbed more smoke flavor and cooked much faster. After cooking the meat in a disposable roasting pan on the cooler side of the grill for a few hours, we flipped all four pieces, wrapped the pan in foil, and placed the roast in the oven to finish cooking. For a barbecue sauce with richer flavor, we sautéed the onions in beef fat from the pan. Chili powder and pepper added bite, while ketchup, vinegar, coffee, Worcestershire sauce, brown sugar, and the beef juices rounded out the flavors.

BEEF
1 tablespoon table salt
1 tablespoon pepper
1 teaspoon cayenne pepper
1 (5- to 6-pound) boneless beef chuck-eye roast, trimmed
1 (13 by 9-inch) disposable aluminum roasting pan
3 cups wood chips, soaked in water for 15 minutes and drained

BARBECUE SAUCE

    1 onion, chopped fine
    4 garlic cloves, minced
  ½ teaspoon chili powder
1¼ cups ketchup
  ¾ cup brewed coffee
  ½ cup cider vinegar
  ½ cup packed brown sugar
    3 tablespoons Worcestershire sauce
  ½ teaspoon pepper

1. For the beef: Combine salt, pepper, and cayenne in small bowl. Cut roast into quarters and remove any excess fat and gristle. Rub beef all over with salt mixture and transfer to disposable pan. (Rubbed beef can be covered tightly with plastic wrap and refrigerated for up to 24 hours.) Using 2 large pieces of heavy-duty aluminum foil, wrap soaked chips in two 8 by 4½-inch foil packets. (Make sure chips do not poke holes in sides or bottoms of packets.) Cut 2 evenly spaced 2-inch slits in top of each packet.

2a. For a charcoal grill: Open bottom vent halfway. Light large chimney starter half filled with charcoal briquettes (3 quarts). When top coals are partially covered with ash, pour into steeply banked pile against side of grill. Place wood chip packets on coals. Set cooking grate in place, cover, and open lid vent halfway. Heat grill until hot and wood chips are smoking, about 5 minutes.

2b. For a gas grill: Remove cooking grate and place wood chip packets directly on primary burner. Set grate in place, turn all burners to high, cover, and heat grill until hot and wood chips are smoking, about 15 minutes. Turn primary burner to medium and turn off other burner(s). (Adjust primary burner as needed to maintain grill temperature of 275 degrees.)

3. Place disposable pan with beef on cooler side of grill and cook, covered, until meat is deep red and smoky, about 2 hours. During final 20 minutes of cooking, adjust oven rack to lower-middle position and heat oven to 300 degrees. Flip beef in disposable pan, cover pan tightly with foil, and roast in oven until fork slips easily in and out of beef, 2 to 3 hours. Transfer beef to large bowl, tent with foil, and let rest for 30 minutes. While beef rests, skim fat from beef juices in disposable pan using wide spoon; reserve 2 tablespoons fat. Strain defatted beef juices; reserve ½ cup juices.

4. For the barbecue sauce: Combine reserved fat and onion in saucepan and cook over medium heat until onion has softened, about 10 minutes. Add garlic and chili powder and cook until fragrant, about 30 seconds. Stir in ketchup, coffee, vinegar, sugar, Worcestershire, pepper, and reserved beef juices and simmer until thickened, about 15 minutes. Using 2 forks, pull beef into bite-size pieces, discarding any excess fat or gristle. Toss meat with ½ cup barbecue sauce. Serve, passing remaining sauce separately.

Shredded Barbecue Beef

GRILLED CHUCK STEAKS

Serves 4 | chuck-eye steak

WHY THIS RECIPE WORKS We thought it was time to give affordable, flavorful chuck a chance for our next steak dinner. We had the best luck when we created hotter and cooler cooking areas: We could sear the steaks over the hotter side of the grill and then move them to the cooler area to cook through without burning the exteriors. Brushing the steaks with oil right before cooking created even better char. Slicing the cooked meat thin against the grain minimized the chewiness. For a satisfying spice rub, chipotle chile powder provided a suitably assertive, complex base. Granulated garlic and coriander added complementary flavors, and cocoa powder lent great depth, with brown sugar helping to smooth out the bitter edges. When we rubbed the steaks and refrigerated them for at least 6 (or up to 24) hours, the salt and spice flavor was much more pervasive. Choose a roast without too much fat at the seam.

    1 tablespoon kosher salt
    1 tablespoon chipotle chile powder
    1 teaspoon unsweetened cocoa powder
    1 teaspoon packed brown sugar
  ½ teaspoon ground coriander
  ½ teaspoon granulated garlic
    1 (2½- to 3-pound) boneless beef chuck-eye roast
    2 tablespoons vegetable oil

1. Combine salt, chile powder, cocoa, sugar, coriander, and granulated garlic in bowl. Separate roast into 2 pieces along natural seam. Turn each piece on its side and cut in half lengthwise against grain. Remove silverskin and trim fat to ¼-inch thickness. Pat steaks dry with paper towels and rub with spice mixture. Transfer steaks to zipper-lock bag and refrigerate for at least 6 hours or up to 24 hours.

2a. For a charcoal grill: Open bottom vent halfway. Light large chimney starter filled with charcoal briquettes (6 quarts). When top coals are partially covered with ash, pour evenly over half of grill. Set cooking grate in place, cover, and open lid vent halfway. Heat grill until hot, about 5 minutes.

2b. For a gas grill: Turn all burners to high, cover, and heat grill until hot, about 15 minutes. Turn primary burner to medium-high and other burner(s) to medium-low.

3. Clean and oil cooking grate. Brush steaks all over with oil. Place steaks on hotter side of grill and cook (covered if using gas) until well charred, about 5 minutes per side. Move steaks to cooler side of grill and continue to cook (covered if using gas) until steaks register 120 to 125 degrees (for medium-rare), 5 to 8 minutes longer.

4. Transfer steaks to carving board, tent with aluminum foil, and let rest for 10 minutes. Slice steaks thin against the grain. Serve.

ULTIMATE BEEF CHILI

Serves 6 to 8 | blade steak

WHY THIS RECIPE WORKS Our goal in creating an ultimate chili was to determine which of chili experts' "secret ingredients" were spot-on—and which were expendable. Meaty blade steaks stayed in big chunks in our finished chili. For complex chile flavor, we traded commercial chili powder for ground dried ancho and arbol chiles; for grassy heat, we added fresh jalapeños. Beer and chicken broth outperformed red wine and coffee as the liquid components. For balancing sweetness, light molasses was better than offbeat ingredients like prunes and Coca-Cola. Finally, a small amount of cornmeal thickened better than pasty flour or gloppy peanut butter. Because much of the chili flavor is held in the fat of this dish, we stirred in the fat that rose to the top rather than discard it. You can substitute dried New Mexican or guajillo chiles for the anchos; each dried arbol may be replaced with ⅛ teaspoon cayenne pepper. If you prefer not to work with any whole dried chiles, the anchos and arbols can be replaced with ½ cup commercial chili powder and ¼ to ½ teaspoon cayenne pepper, though the texture of the chili will be slightly compromised.

8 ounces (1¼ cups) dried pinto beans, picked over and rinsed
1½ teaspoons table salt, divided, plus salt for soaking beans
6 dried ancho chiles, stemmed, seeded, and torn into 1-inch pieces
2–4 dried arbol chiles, stemmed, seeded, and halved
3 tablespoons cornmeal
2 teaspoons dried oregano
2 teaspoons ground cumin
2 teaspoons unsweetened cocoa powder
2½ cups chicken broth, divided
2 onions, cut into ¾-inch pieces
3 small jalapeño chiles, stemmed, seeded, and cut into ½-inch pieces
3 tablespoons vegetable oil, divided
4 garlic cloves, minced
1 (14.5-ounce) can diced tomatoes
2 teaspoons molasses
3½ pounds blade steak, ¾ inch thick, trimmed and cut into ¾-inch pieces
1½ cups mild lager, such as Budweiser, divided

1. Combine 4 quarts water, beans, and 3 tablespoons salt in Dutch oven and bring to boil over high heat. Remove pot from heat, cover, and let stand for 1 hour. Drain and rinse well.

2. Adjust oven rack to lower-middle position and heat oven to 300 degrees. Place anchos in 12-inch skillet over medium-high heat; toast, stirring frequently, until flesh is fragrant, 4 to 6 minutes, reducing heat if chiles begin to smoke. Transfer to food processor and let cool (do not clean skillet).

3. Add arbols, cornmeal, oregano, cumin, cocoa, and ½ teaspoon salt to processor with toasted anchos; process until finely ground, about 2 minutes. With processor running, slowly add ½ cup broth until smooth paste forms, about 45 seconds, scraping down sides of bowl as needed. Transfer paste to small bowl. Pulse onions in now-empty processor until coarsely chopped, about 4 pulses. Add jalapeños and pulse until consistency of chunky salsa, about 4 pulses, scraping down sides of bowl as needed.

4. Heat 1 tablespoon oil in Dutch oven over medium-high heat. Add onion mixture and cook, stirring occasionally, until moisture has evaporated and vegetables are softened, 7 to 9 minutes. Add garlic and cook until fragrant, about 1 minute. Add tomatoes and their juice, molasses, and chile paste; stir until thoroughly combined. Add beans and remaining 2 cups broth; bring to boil, then reduce heat to low and simmer.

5. Meanwhile, heat 1 tablespoon oil in now-empty skillet over medium-high heat until shimmering. Pat beef dry with paper towels and sprinkle with remaining 1 teaspoon salt. Brown half of beef on all sides, about 10 minutes; transfer to pot. Add ¾ cup beer to skillet, scraping up any browned bits, and bring to simmer. Transfer beer to pot. Repeat with remaining 1 tablespoon oil, remaining beef, and remaining ¾ cup beer; transfer to pot. Stir to combine and return mixture to simmer.

6. Cover pot; transfer to oven. Cook until meat and beans are fully tender, 1½ to 2 hours. Let chili stand, uncovered, for 10 minutes. Stir well, season with salt to taste, and serve.

BRAISED STEAKS WITH ROOT VEGETABLES

Serves 6 | blade steak

WHY THIS RECIPE WORKS Steak isn't always about the thick crust from a hard, fast sear. Tough blade steaks turn meltingly tender when simmered in liquid, which produces an accompanying sauce full of beefy flavor. To achieve this effect, we purposely "overcooked" the meat—a 2-hour braise allowed nearly all of the fat and connective tissue to dissolve, giving each bite a soft, silky texture. We seared the meat to get the browning we'd expect on steaks and set it aside while we built a balanced braising liquid. Then we returned the steaks to the pot and let them simmer in the oven undisturbed until the final 30 minutes of cooking when we added potatoes, carrots, and parsnips to make this an easy one-pot meal. At the very end we reduced the braising liquid to spoon over both the steaks and vegetables before serving. Make sure to buy steaks that are about the same size to ensure even cooking.

- 6 (6-ounce) blade steaks, ¾ to 1 inch thick, trimmed
- 4 teaspoons vegetable oil, divided
- 2 onions, halved and sliced thin
- 3 garlic cloves, minced
- 1 tablespoon minced fresh thyme or 1 teaspoon dried
- 1½ cups beef broth
- 1 cup water
- ½ cup dry white wine
- 12 ounces red potatoes, cut into ¾-inch pieces
- 4 carrots, peeled and sliced ½ inch thick
- 4 parsnips, peeled and sliced ½ inch thick
- 2 tablespoons minced fresh parsley
- 1 tablespoon fresh lemon juice

1. Adjust oven rack to lower-middle position and heat oven to 325 degrees. Pat steaks dry with paper towels and season with salt and pepper.

2. Heat 2 teaspoons oil in Dutch oven over medium-high heat until smoking. Brown steaks well on all sides, 7 to 10 minutes; transfer steaks to large plate.

3. Add remaining 2 teaspoons oil to pot and heat over medium heat until shimmering. Add onions and cook until softened, 8 to 10 minutes. Stir in garlic and thyme and cook until fragrant, about 30 seconds. Stir in broth, water, and wine, scraping up any browned bits, and bring to simmer.

4. Nestle steaks, along with any accumulated juices, into pot. Spoon sauce over steak. Return to simmer and cover; transfer pot to oven. Cook for 1½ hours.

5. Add potatoes, carrots, and parsnips to pot and continue to cook until steak and vegetables are tender, about 30 minutes. Transfer steaks and vegetables to large platter, tent with aluminum foil, and let rest while finishing sauce.

6. Simmer sauce over medium-high heat until slightly thickened, 2 to 4 minutes. Off heat, stir in parsley and lemon juice and season with salt and pepper to taste. Spoon sauce over steaks and vegetables and serve.

VARIATION

Braised Steaks with Mushrooms and Tomatoes
Omit carrots and parsnips. Before cooking onions in step 3, add 4 chopped portobello mushroom caps and cook, covered, until they begin to soften and release their liquid, about 5 minutes. Remove lid, add onions, and cook until onions and mushrooms are softened and browned, 10 to 12 minutes. Reduce water to ½ cup, substitute 2 teaspoons minced fresh rosemary for thyme, and add 1 (14.5-ounce) can diced tomatoes with their juice with broth.

PRESSURE-COOKER BEEF AND BARLEY SOUP

Serves 6 to 8 | blade steak

WHY THIS RECIPE WORKS Beef and barley soup should be packed with tender beef and have nicely al dente grains. We have the ultimate version on page 193, but this comfort food should be often-accessible. Since blade steaks are smaller and thinner than a roast, they cooked to perfect tenderness at the same rate as the barley in an electric pressure cooker. Even better, we didn't need to spend time browning the steaks; we could simply brown the mushrooms and aromatics for a deeply flavored base. A generous amount of soy sauce helped to boost the brew's savory flavor. Since pearl barley can absorb a lot of liquid, we were judicious in the amount we added to the soup. A modest ½ cup lent the soup a velvety texture without turning it into a thick stew. Do

Braised Steaks with Root Vegetables

not substitute hulled, hull-less, quick-cooking, or presteamed barley (read the ingredient list on the package to determine this) in this recipe.

1 tablespoon vegetable oil
8 ounces cremini mushrooms, trimmed and sliced ½ inch thick
1 onion, chopped fine
2 celery ribs, cut into ½-inch pieces
½ teaspoon table salt
2 tablespoons all-purpose flour
2 tablespoons tomato paste
2 teaspoons minced fresh thyme or ½ teaspoon dried
6 cups beef broth
2 tablespoons soy sauce
3 carrots, peeled and cut into ½-inch pieces
½ cup pearl barley
1 pound boneless beef blade steaks, trimmed and cut into ½-inch pieces
2 tablespoons minced fresh parsley

1. Using highest sauté or browning function, heat oil in electric pressure cooker until shimmering. Add mushrooms, onion, celery, and salt and cook until vegetables are softened, 6 to 8 minutes. Stir in flour, tomato paste, and thyme and cook until fragrant, about 1 minute. Slowly whisk in broth, soy sauce, carrots, and barley, scraping up any browned bits and smoothing out any lumps. Season beef with salt and pepper and stir into pressure cooker.

2. Lock lid in place and close pressure release valve. Select high pressure cook function and cook for 20 minutes. Turn off multicooker and quick-release pressure. Carefully remove lid, allowing steam to escape away from you. Stir in parsley and season with salt and pepper to taste. Serve.

THAI BEEF WITH CHILES AND SHALLOTS

Serves 4 | blade steak

WHY THIS RECIPE WORKS Two types of chiles bring the heat to this complexly flavored Thai stir-fry: a generous amount of sliced serrano chiles, plus Asian chili-garlic sauce, an easily controllable heat source. Ultrabeefy blade steaks needed only 15 minutes in a fish sauce marinade to develop flavor. We browned the steaks, stir-fried the serranos and shallots, and combined everything with a sauce. Fresh herbs stirred in at the end added brightness, and peanuts made for a crunchy garnish. White pepper lends this stir-fry a unique flavor; do not substitute black pepper. Serve with steamed jasmine rice.

Thai Beef with Chiles and Shallots

BEEF
1 tablespoon fish sauce
1 teaspoon packed light brown sugar
¾ teaspoon ground coriander
⅛ teaspoon ground white pepper
2 pounds beef blade steaks, trimmed and sliced crosswise ¼ inch thick

SAUCE AND GARNISH
2 tablespoons fish sauce
2 tablespoons rice vinegar
2 tablespoons water
1 tablespoon packed light brown sugar
1 tablespoon Asian chili-garlic sauce
3 tablespoons vegetable oil, divided
3 garlic cloves, minced
3 serrano chiles, stemmed, seeded, and sliced thin
3 shallots, peeled, quartered, and layers separated
½ cup fresh mint leaves, torn
½ cup fresh cilantro leaves
⅓ cup dry-roasted peanuts, chopped
Lime wedges

1. **For the beef:** Combine fish sauce, sugar, coriander, and white pepper in large bowl. Add beef, toss well to coat, and let sit for 15 minutes.

2. For the sauce and garnish: Whisk fish sauce, vinegar, water, sugar, and chili-garlic sauce in small bowl until sugar dissolves; set aside. In second small bowl, combine 1 teaspoon oil and garlic; set aside.

3. Heat 2 teaspoons oil in 12-inch nonstick skillet over high heat until just smoking. Add one-third of beef in single layer and cook, without stirring, for 2 minutes. Stir beef and continue to cook until browned, about 30 seconds; transfer to bowl. Repeat with 4 teaspoons oil and remaining beef in 2 batches; transfer to bowl.

4. Heat remaining 2 teaspoons oil in now-empty skillet over medium heat until shimmering. Add serranos and shallots and cook, stirring frequently, until beginning to soften, 3 to 4 minutes. Push chile mixture to sides of skillet. Add garlic mixture to center and cook, mashing mixture into pan, until fragrant, about 30 seconds. Stir mixture into chile mixture.

5. Return beef and any accumulated juices to skillet; toss to combine. Add fish sauce mixture, increase heat to high, and cook, stirring constantly, until thickened and slightly reduced, about 30 seconds. Off heat, stir in half of mint and cilantro. Sprinkle with peanuts and remaining herbs. Serve with lime wedges.

CHIPOTLE BEEF TAMALES

Makes 18 tamales; serves 6 to 8 | blade steak

WHY THIS RECIPE WORKS For a punchy filling for our steamed corn cakes, we turned to blade steaks, which turned meltingly tender with the extended cooking, and we liked them with the smoky, spicy flavor of chipotle chiles. Tamale dough can be hard to source. Easy-to-find grits and masa harina, brought together with water and lard plus butter for flavor, were a good texture match; corn kernels added pops of sweet freshness. We steamed the corn husk-wrapped parcels in a steamer basket to create warm, moist meat-filled cakes. For an accurate measurement of boiling water, bring a full kettle of water to a boil and then measure out the desired amount.

FILLING

- 4 dried ancho chiles, stemmed, seeded, and torn into ½-inch pieces (1 cup)
- 3 tablespoons vegetable oil
- 1 large onion, chopped
- 6 garlic cloves, minced
- 1½ tablespoons minced canned chipotle chile in adobo sauce
- 1 teaspoon dried oregano
- 1 teaspoon sugar, plus extra as needed
- 1 teaspoon table salt

- ¾ teaspoon ground cumin
- ½ teaspoon ground cinnamon
- ⅛ teaspoon ground cloves
- 3 cups beef broth
- 1¾ pounds blade steak, trimmed
- 1½ tablespoons red wine vinegar

TAMALES

- 1 cup plus 2 tablespoons quick grits
- 1½ cups boiling water
- 1 cup (4 ounces) plus 2 tablespoons masa harina
- 20 large dried corn husks
- 1½ cups frozen corn, thawed
- 6 tablespoons unsalted butter, cut into ½-inch cubes and softened
- 6 tablespoons lard, softened
- 1 tablespoon sugar
- 2¼ teaspoons baking powder
- ¾ teaspoon table salt

1. For the filling: Toast anchos in 12-inch skillet over medium heat, stirring frequently, until fragrant, 2 to 6 minutes; transfer to bowl.

2. Heat oil in now-empty skillet over medium heat until shimmering. Add onion and cook until softened, 5 to 7 minutes. Stir in garlic, chipotle, oregano, sugar, salt, cumin, cinnamon, cloves, and toasted chiles and cook for 30 seconds. Stir in broth and simmer until slightly reduced, about 10 minutes. Transfer mixture to blender and process until smooth, about 20 seconds; return to skillet.

3. Season beef with salt and pepper, nestle into skillet, and bring to simmer over medium heat. Cover, reduce heat to low, and cook until beef is very tender, about 1½ hours. Transfer beef to carving board and let cool slightly. Using 2 forks, shred beef into small pieces. Stir vinegar into sauce and season with salt, pepper, and sugar to taste. Toss shredded beef with 1 cup sauce.

4. For the tamales: Meanwhile, place grits in medium bowl, whisk in boiling water, and let stand until water is mostly absorbed, about 10 minutes. Stir in masa harina, cover, and let cool to room temperature, about 20 minutes. Meanwhile, place husks in large bowl, cover with hot water, and let soak until pliable, about 30 minutes.

5. Process masa dough, corn, butter, lard, sugar, baking powder, and salt together in food processor until mixture is light, sticky, and very smooth, about 1 minute, scraping down sides as necessary. Remove husks from water and pat dry with dish towel. Working with 1 husk at a time, lay on counter, cupped side up,

Smoked Herb-Rubbed Flat-Iron Steaks

with long side facing you and wide end on right side. Spread ¼ cup tamale dough into 4-inch square over bottom right-hand corner, pushing it flush to bottom edge but leaving ¼-inch border at wide edge. Mound 2 scant tablespoons filling in line across center of dough, parallel to bottom edge. Roll husk away from you and over filling, so that dough surrounds filling and forms cylinder. Fold up tapered end, leaving top open, and transfer seam side down to platter.

6. Fit large pot or Dutch oven with steamer basket, removing feet from steamer basket if pot is short. Fill pot with water until it just touches bottom of basket and bring to boil. Gently lay tamales in basket with open ends facing up and seam sides facing out. Cover and steam, checking water level often and adding additional water as needed, until tamales easily come free from husks, about 1 hour. Transfer tamales to large platter. Reheat remaining sauce from filling in covered bowl in microwave, about 30 seconds, and serve with tamales.

SMOKED HERB-RUBBED FLAT-IRON STEAKS

Serves 4 to 6 | flat-iron steak

WHY THIS RECIPE WORKS In the world of smoking meat, you don't often see small cuts of beef, but smoking steaks can lend them complexity. Too much smoke can overwhelm the quick-cooking meat's delicate flavor but marbled, beefy-tasting flat-iron steaks can stand up. We found that the key was using a small amount of wood chips and cooking the steaks quickly over direct heat so that they were just kissed with smoke. Coating the steaks with an herb-spice rub lent an extra layer of flavor that complemented the smoke. We also grilled lemons to serve with the steaks for a hit of brightness. We like hickory chips in this recipe, but other kinds of wood chips will work. Use 1½ cups of wood chips if using a gas grill.

- 2 teaspoons dried thyme
- 1 teaspoon dried rosemary
- ¾ teaspoon fennel seeds
- ½ teaspoon black peppercorns
- ¼ teaspoon red pepper flakes
- 4 (6- to 8-ounce) flat-iron steaks, ¾ to 1 inch thick, trimmed
- 1 tablespoon kosher salt
- 1–1½ cups wood chips
    Vegetable oil spray
- 2 lemons, quartered lengthwise

1. Grind thyme, rosemary, fennel seeds, peppercorns, and pepper flakes in spice grinder or with mortar and pestle until coarsely ground. Transfer to small bowl. Pat steaks dry with paper towels. Rub steaks evenly on both sides with salt and place on wire rack set in rimmed baking sheet. Let stand at room temperature for 1 hour.

2. Using large piece of heavy-duty aluminum foil, wrap wood chips (1 cup if using charcoal; 1½ cups if using gas) in 8 by 4½-inch foil packet. (Make sure chips do not poke holes in sides or bottom of packet.) Cut 2 evenly spaced 2-inch slits in top of packet.

3a. For a charcoal grill: Open bottom vent completely. Light large chimney starter filled with charcoal briquettes (6 quarts). When top coals are partially covered with ash, pour evenly over half of grill. Place wood chip packet on coals. Set cooking grate in place, cover, and open lid vent completely. Heat grill until hot and wood chips are smoking, about 5 minutes.

3b. For a gas grill: Remove cooking grate and place wood chip packet directly on primary burner. Set grate in place, turn all burners to high, cover, and heat grill until hot and wood chips are smoking, about 15 minutes. Leave primary burner on high and turn other burner(s) to medium.

4. Clean and oil cooking grate. Sprinkle half of herb rub evenly over 1 side of steaks; press to adhere. Lightly spray herb-rubbed side of steaks with oil spray, about 3 seconds. Flip steaks and repeat with remaining herb rub and oil spray. Place lemons and steaks on hotter side of grill, cover (position lid vent over steaks if using charcoal), and cook both until well browned on both sides and meat registers 130 to 135 degrees (for medium), 4 to 6 minutes per side. (If steaks are fully charred before reaching desired temperature, move to cooler side of grill, cover, and continue to cook.) Transfer lemons and steaks to clean wire rack set in rimmed baking sheet, tent with foil, and let rest for 10 minutes. Transfer steaks to cutting board. Slice steaks thin against grain and serve with lemons.

RIB

THE COW HAS 26 RIBS, 13 on each side, but the rib primal of the cow holds only seven of them, back ribs 6 through 12. If you're looking for that prized balance of cuts that are exquisitely beefy yet still tender, these are the ribs that matter to you. Located behind the chuck (home to ribs 1 through 5), the rib primal gifts us some of the money cuts, like standing rib roast (it's called *prime* rib for a reason) and the luxurious rib-eye steaks. The major muscle that runs along the rib (the longissimus dorsi or rib eye) supports the cow's backbone; to compare the rib to its shoulder neighbor, it's much more tender for two reasons, lack of exercise and lack of complex cross-cutting muscles. Combine that with rich marbling and you get some very delicious beef.

MAGIC MARBLING

You know that swirls of creamy fat coursing through bright red meat is a sign of greatness, and because rib cuts are most famous for it, we wanted to break down why it's so great. Marbling is a more delicious word for intramuscular fat, and it gives meat lubricating moisture and flavor. (That's why the tenderloin, though supremely tender, lacks the depth of the rib primal—it's super-lean and absent of marbling.) It's because of this network of fat that the rib reigns supreme for many beef-eaters. Prime rib is, after all, the unmatched beef roast and rib steaks are a favorite of many. (For more information on marbling, see pages 7 and 30.)

First-Cut Standing Rib Roast

Cost: ▪▫▫▫ **Flavor:** ▪▫▫▫

Best cooking methods: roast, grill roast, sous vide
Texture: very tender, fine-textured
Alternative names: large end rib roast

For a table-appropriate roast, butchers cut a rib roast into two distinct cuts, first and second cut. They're both *prime* rib, but the more desirable of the two cuts consists of ribs 10 through 12, the portion closer to the loin primal. It's considered more desirable because it contains the large, single rib-eye muscle and is less fatty than the second cut.

There aren't many recipes that mess with this good thing. Standing rib roast is typically served roasted and cut into slabs, ideally still rosy and hit with generous salt. There's no need to treat this luxurious cut with moist cooking techniques like braising or gussy it up with too many competing flavors. Rib roasts are also available boneless.

PRIME PRIME RIB

As you learned on page 30, the USDA grades beef as prime, choice, or select. "Prime" rib doesn't mean a roast with a USDA prime designation, however, and is something of a misnomer. (That's why we prefer to call for "standing rib roast.") Prime rib was originally used to refer to the most desirable portions of the rib section. That means that prime-grade prime rib is the best of the best, costing more per pound, naturally, than choice prime rib. Additionally, some butchers offer dry-aged prime rib. (For more on dry aging, see page 33.) Dry aging adds even more cost per pound. To find out if prime-grade prime rib is worth the premium, we cooked several prime-grade, choice-grade, and dry-aged rib roasts. In the entire lot, there were no outright losers, but the experiment was telling. First, we don't recommend spending the extra cash on dry aging here; we found that its nuances were lost on this already great roast. On the other hand, in most cases the prime cuts beat out the choice cuts in terms of superior marbling and, thus, superior flavor and texture. Given that this meal will be a splurge no matter how you slice it, springing for prime beef makes sense, although a choice roast will be almost as good.

MEAT PREP *Carving Standing Rib Roast*

Slice meat ¾ inch thick. Sprinkle slices with flake sea salt if desired.

Second-Cut Standing Rib Roast

Cost: ▪▪▫▫   **Flavor:** ▪▪▫▫
Best cooking methods: roast, grill roast, sous vide
Texture: slightly less tender than first-cut
Alternative names: prime rib, beef rib roast, loin end, small end, rib-eye roast, Newport roast

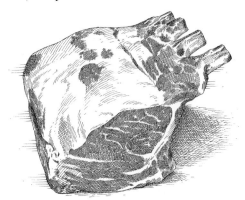

In the case of prime rib, second-cut might be second best, but it's still pretty darn good. It consists of ribs 6 through 8 or 9; closer to the chuck end of the cow, this cut becomes more multimuscled, and since muscles are surrounded by fat, this means a fattier roast. While the more regularly formed loin end is usually favored for its superior tenderness, we know that some fat, of course, is good and this cut is tremendously flavorful because of its more plentiful soft pockets of fat, as well as a more generous fat cap that bastes it as it cooks. Maybe you'll prefer the second best.

Rib Steak

Cost: ▪▪▫▫   **Flavor:** ▪▪▫▫
Best cooking methods: roast, pan sear, grill
Texture: tender
Alternative names: bone-in rib steak

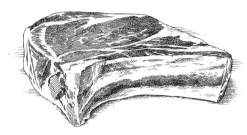

Less common than the boneless rib-eye steak, a rib steak is a steak cut from the aforementioned standing rib roasts, with the curved rib bone attached. Think a big slab of prime rib. This big steak requires ultraefficient ways to cook it so its best qualities shine—most notably, the interior needs to cook evenly as quickly as the exterior takes to become beautifully browned. (Thinner steaks often have the opposite problem.) We butter-baste them on page 69 to transfer heat through the medium of fat to ensure even cooking: nice browning and perfect interior doneness.

SHOULD YOU LET STEAKS COME TO ROOM TEMPERATURE BEFORE COOKING?

Some cooks rest a refrigerated steak on the counter to start raising its internal temperature from around 40 degrees toward its target cooked temperature (125 degrees for medium-rare, for example) before they introduce the steak to a hot pan. The theory is that with "warmer" meat, the middle can come up to temperature before a dry gray band of overcooked meat can develop under the crust during cooking, a particular problem with thick-cut steaks. But does a 1- or 2-hour rest at room temperature actually increase the internal temperature of a steak enough to make a difference? (Resting the meat longer is not advisable, since it puts it in the food safety "danger zone" as defined by the U.S. Department of Agriculture.) The short answer: No. For 1-inch-thick rib-eye steaks, the temperature increased from 41 degrees to only 52 degrees after an hour and rose to 62 degrees after 2 hours. When we pan-seared these samples and compared them with steaks cooked directly from the refrigerator, the gray banding was identical and there was no noticeable difference in their taste or texture. To avoid a gray band for thick-cut steaks, we sometimes warm the steaks to around 95 degrees in a low oven before searing them. The process takes anywhere from 30 to 50 minutes depending on the steak, but it's worth it, warming the steak sufficiently so that the searing time is very quick, producing steaks with little to no gray banding.

Double-Cut Bone-In Rib Steak

Cost: ▪▪■■ Flavor: ▪■■■
Best cooking methods: grill
Texture: appealing chew
Alternative names: cowboy steak

Great for the grill, these steaks—individually expensive 1½-pound or greater, bone-in behemoths—can be up to double the thickness of conventional rib-eye steaks and their longer cooking time means they soak up lots of smoky grill flavor. The larger and thicker a steak is, the more difficult it is to get a nice brown sear and a perfectly cooked interior to happen at the same time (learn how on page 77), which is why we turn to a grill where we can create multiple heating zones.

THE MOST FLAVORFUL PART OF THE COW?

The exterior band of fat and meat on a bone-in rib steak is called the deckle; connoisseurs say it's the most flavorful part of the cow and you get double the delicious in a double-cut rib steak. This flavor transfers to the meat but you can also gnaw on the bone; we won't tell. And while this yields some tasty bites, you can also find this delicious part of the cow, also known as the rib-eye cap, spinalis dorsi, or "butcher's butter," for purchase at a good butcher shop, trimmed from the entire rib-portion of the cow's ribs. Just don't expect this prized piece to be inexpensive.

Rib-Eye Steak

Cost: ▪■■■ Flavor: ▪■■■
Best cooking methods: pan sear, grill, sous vide
Texture: smooth, fine texture, appealing chew
Alternative names: beauty steak, Delmonico steak, Spencer steak, Scotch filet, entrecôte

A rib-eye steak is a rib steak with the bone removed—essentially a boneless piece of prime rib. The steak has an oval shape with a narrow strip of meat that curves around one end. Rib-eye steaks, like other steaks from the rib section, contain large pockets of fat and have a rich, smooth texture. This pricey steak is tender and juicy, with a pronounced beefiness. Weighing in at around a pound, one steak typically serves two.

DRY-AGING STEAK AT HOME

Sometimes an option at a high-end meat market, sometimes a way of leveling up at the steakhouse, "dry aging" is supposed to mean more valuable meat (for more information, see page 33). In commercial dry-aging, butchers hold large primal cuts of beef (typically the rib or short loin sections) for as long as 120 days in humid refrigerators ranging between 32 and 40 degrees. (The humidity is necessary to prevent the meat's exterior from drying out too much.)

Does dry-aged beef need to be confined to special occasions? We tried replicating these results at home on a smaller scale. We bought rib-eye and strip steaks and stored them in the back of the refrigerator, where the temperature is coldest. Since home refrigerators are less humid, we wrapped the steaks in cheesecloth and put them on a wire rack to allow air to pass through while also preventing excessive dehydration and checked them after four days (the longest length of time we felt comfortable storing raw beef in a home fridge). Their edges looked appropriately dried out, so we pan-seared the home-aged steaks and tasted them alongside a batch of the same commercially dry-aged cuts. Our findings? Sure enough, four days of dry-aging in a home fridge gave the steaks a comparably smoky flavor and dense, tender texture—and at a much lower price tag.

Best Roast Prime Rib

BEST ROAST PRIME RIB

Serves 8 to 10 | first-cut standing rib roast

WHY THIS RECIPE WORKS Keep it simple: Roasting lets a prime rib's extraordinary flavor shine. With prime rib, salt is even more essential than it typically is. We salted our roast way in advance (as long as four days!); this seasoned the thick roast to the core and dried out the exterior so that it developed a prized deeply browned crust when we seared it. We first removed the meat from the bones to make searing easier. Then we tied the roast back to the bones to ensure more even cooking. A very low oven temperature allowed the meat's enzymes to act as natural tenderizers, and a quick trip under the broiler right before serving restored the glorious crispness the crust lost while the meat was resting. A longer salting time is preferable. If the roast has not reached the correct temperature in the time range specified in step 4, reheat the oven to 200 degrees for 5 minutes, shut it off, and continue to cook the roast until it reaches the desired temperature.

- 1 (7-pound) first-cut beef standing rib roast (3 bones), with ½-inch fat cap
- 2 tablespoons kosher salt
- 2 teaspoons vegetable oil

1. Using sharp knife, cut beef from bones. Cut slits 1 inch apart in crosshatch pattern in fat cap of roast, being careful not to cut into beef. Rub 2 tablespoons salt thoroughly over roast and into slits. Place beef back on bones (to save space in refrigerator) and refrigerate, uncovered, for at least 24 hours or up to 4 days.

2. Adjust oven rack to middle position and heat oven to 200 degrees. Heat oil in 12-inch skillet over high heat until just smoking. Remove beef from bones. Sear top and sides of roast until browned, 6 to 8 minutes; do not sear side of roast that was cut from bones.

3. Fit roast back onto bones, let cool for 10 minutes, then tie together with kitchen twine between bones. Transfer roast, fat side up, to wire rack set in rimmed baking sheet and season with pepper. Roast until beef registers 110 degrees, 3 to 4 hours.

4. Turn oven off and leave roast in oven, without opening door, until beef registers 120 to 125 degrees (for medium-rare), 30 minutes to 1¼ hours. Remove roast from oven (leave roast on sheet) and let rest for at least 30 minutes or up to 1¼ hours.

5. Adjust oven rack 8 inches from broiler element and heat broiler. Place 3-inch aluminum foil ball under ribs to elevate fat cap. Broil until top of roast is well browned and crisp, 2 to 8 minutes. Transfer roast to carving board. Remove twine and remove meat from ribs. Slice roast ¾ inch thick. Serve.

BONELESS RIB ROAST WITH YORKSHIRE PUDDING AND JUS

Serves 10 to 12 | boneless rib roast

WHY THIS RECIPE WORKS A traditional British Sunday dinner can consist of a beef roast and Yorkshire pudding. Neither component is particularly fuss-free, but we made them so. We started with a richly marbled, easy-to-carve boneless rib roast and used rendered fat from the roast and trimmings for an ultrasavory Yorkshire pudding. For juicy, well-seasoned meat, we salted the roast a day in advance and cooked it in a low 250-degree oven. Letting the Yorkshire pudding batter sit while the roast cooked allowed the gluten in the batter to relax, so the pudding could rise more quickly in the oven when we poured it into the searing-hot roasting pan. A quick, savory jus completed the meal. If you're using a dark roasting pan, reduce the pudding's cooking time by 5 minutes. A longer salting time is preferable.

ROAST AND PUDDING
- 1 (5- to 5½-pound) first-cut boneless beef rib roast, with ½-inch fat cap
- 3 tablespoons kosher salt, divided
- 2½ cups all-purpose flour
- 4 cups milk
- 4 large eggs
- 1 tablespoon vegetable oil, plus extra as needed

JUS
- 1 onion, chopped fine
- 1 teaspoon cornstarch
- 2½ cups beef broth
- 1 sprig fresh thyme

1. **For the roast and pudding:** Using sharp knife, trim roast's fat cap to ¼-inch thickness; refrigerate trimmings. Cut slits 1 inch apart in crosshatch pattern in fat cap of roast, being careful not to cut into beef. Rub 2 tablespoons salt thoroughly over roast and into slits. Refrigerate, uncovered, for at least 24 hours or up to 4 days.

2. Adjust oven rack to lower-middle position and heat oven to 250 degrees. Spray large roasting pan with vegetable oil spray. Cut reserved trimmings into ½-inch pieces. Place 3 ounces (about ¾ cup) trimmings in bottom of pan. Set V-rack over trimmings in pan and spray with oil spray. Season roast with pepper and place fat side up on V-rack. Roast until beef registers 120 to 125 degrees (for medium-rare), 2½ to 3 hours.

3. Meanwhile, combine flour and remaining 1 tablespoon salt in large bowl. Whisk milk and eggs in second bowl until fully combined. Slowly whisk milk mixture into flour mixture until smooth. Cover with plastic wrap and let rest for 1 hour.

Best Roast Prime Rib

Prime rib is the ultimate splurge dish. Since this treat is often reserved for a celebration, we show the steps to making it come out absolutely perfect.

1. Using sharp knife, cut beef from bones.

2. Cut slits 1 inch apart in crosshatch pattern in fat cap of roast, being careful not to cut into beef. Rub 2 tablespoons salt thoroughly over roast and into slits. Refrigerate for at least 24 hours or up to 4 days.

3. Heat oil in 12-inch skillet over high heat until just smoking. Remove beef from bones. Sear top and sides of roast until browned, 6 to 8 minutes; do not sear side of roast that was cut from bones.

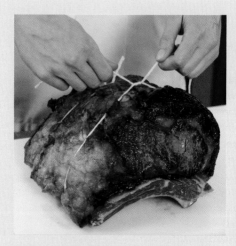

4. Fit roast back onto bones, let cool for 10 minutes, then tie together with kitchen twine between bones. Roast at 200 degrees until beef registers 110 degrees, 3 to 4 hours. Let rest for at least 30 minutes or up to 1¼ hours.

5. Place 3-inch aluminum foil ball under ribs to elevate fat cap. Broil until top of roast is well browned and crisp, 2 to 8 minutes.

6. Transfer roast to carving board, remove twine, and remove beef from ribs. Slice meat ¾ inch thick.

4. Transfer V-rack with roast to carving board and let rest for 1 hour. Remove solids in pan, leaving liquid fat behind (there should be about 6 tablespoons; if not, supplement with vegetable oil). Increase oven temperature to 425 degrees.

5. When oven reaches 425 degrees, return pan to oven and heat until fat is just smoking, 3 to 5 minutes. Rewhisk batter and pour into center of pan. Bake until pudding is dark golden brown and edges are crisp, 40 to 45 minutes.

6. While pudding bakes, pat roast dry with paper towels. Heat oil in 12-inch skillet over medium-high heat until just smoking. Brown roast well on all sides, 8 to 12 minutes. Transfer roast to carving board.

7. **For the jus:** Return now-empty skillet to medium-high heat, add onion, and cook until softened, about 5 minutes, scraping up any browned bits. Whisk cornstarch into broth. Add broth mixture and thyme sprig to skillet and bring to boil. Reduce heat to medium-low and simmer until reduced by half, about 7 minutes. Strain jus through fine-mesh strainer set over small saucepan; discard solids. Cover and keep warm.

8. Slice roast into ¾-inch-thick slices. Cut pudding into squares in pan. Serve roast with pudding and jus.

ONE-PAN ROASTED PRIME RIB AND VEGETABLES

Serves 8 to 10 | first-cut standing rib roast

WHY THIS RECIPE WORKS A big prime rib roast might not sound like the ingredient to star in a one-pan meal, but we made an impressive dish with perfectly cooked prime rib and hearty vegetables, yes, in one pan. After cooking the prime rib through slowly, we simply roasted a mix of root vegetables and brussels sprouts in the flavorful beef drippings as the meat rested. Adding the meat back to the pan with the browned, tender vegetables for a final stint under the broiler turned the outside of the roast crispy and golden and brought the whole dish together. We ended up with a feast fit for a holiday—with only one pan to wash. A longer salting time is preferable.

- 1 (7-pound) first-cut beef standing rib roast (3 bones), with ½-inch fat cap
- 2 tablespoons plus 1 teaspoon kosher salt, divided Vegetable oil
- 2 pounds carrots, peeled, cut into 2-inch lengths, halved or quartered lengthwise to create ½-inch-diameter pieces
- 1 pound parsnips, peeled and sliced ½ inch thick on bias
- 1 pound brussels sprouts, trimmed and halved
- 1 red onion, halved and sliced through root end into ½-inch wedges
- 2 teaspoons minced fresh thyme
- ½ teaspoon pepper

1. Using sharp knife, cut 1-inch crosshatch pattern in roast's fat cap, being careful not to cut into beef. Rub 2 tablespoons salt over entire roast and into slits. Refrigerate, uncovered, for at least 24 hours or up to 4 days.

2. Adjust oven rack to lower-middle position and heat oven to 250 degrees. Set V-rack in large roasting pan and spray with vegetable oil spray. Season roast with pepper and arrange, fat side up, on prepared V-rack. Roast until beef registers 120 to 125 degrees (for medium-rare), 3 to 3½ hours. Transfer V-rack with roast to carving board and let rest for 1 hour.

3. Meanwhile, increase oven temperature to 425 degrees. Using fork, remove solids in pan, leaving liquid fat behind (there should be about 2 tablespoons; if not, supplement with vegetable oil). Toss carrots, parsnips, brussels sprouts, onion, thyme, pepper, and remaining 1 teaspoon salt with fat in pan. Roast vegetables until tender and browned, 45 to 50 minutes, redistributing halfway through cooking.

4. Remove pan from oven and heat broiler. Carefully nestle V-rack with roast among vegetables in pan. Broil roast until fat cap is evenly browned, rotating pan as necessary, about 5 minutes. Transfer roast to carving board, carve meat from bones, and slice ¾ inch thick. Season vegetables with salt and pepper to taste. Serve beef with vegetables.

GRILL-SMOKED PRIME RIB

Serves 8 to 10 | first-cut standing rib roast

WHY THIS RECIPE WORKS If you think roasted prime rib is as good as it gets, you have to try grill smoking. This method offers prime treatment for prime rib, giving it a well-charred salty crust and ultratender meat—along with lovely smoky flavor that doesn't outshine the delicious meat. Since bones protect the meat from overbrowning, we removed the bones for carving convenience and then tied them back onto the meat for grilling. To get the color and flavor we wanted, we quickly seared the fat-covered sides on the hotter side of a half-grill fire before slow-roasting the meat bone side down on the cooler side.

- 1 (7-pound) first-cut beef standing rib roast (3 or 4 bones), with ⅛-inch fat cap
- 1 tablespoon vegetable oil
- ¼ cup kosher salt, for salting beef
- 2 cups wood chips
- 1 (16 by 12-inch) disposable aluminum roasting pan (if using charcoal)

1. Using sharp knife, cut beef from bones. Pat roast dry with paper towels, rub with oil, and season with pepper. Spread ¼ cup salt on rimmed baking sheet and press roast into salt to coat evenly on all sides. Place meat back on ribs so bones fit exactly where they were cut; tie meat to bones with 2 lengths of kitchen twine. Refrigerate roast, uncovered, for 1 hour, then let sit at room temperature for 2 hours.

2. Just before grilling, soak wood chips in water for 15 minutes, then drain. Using large piece of heavy-duty aluminum foil, wrap soaked chips in 8 by 4½-inch foil packet. (Make sure chips do not poke holes in sides or bottom of packet.) Cut 2 evenly spaced 2-inch slits in top of packet.

3a. For a charcoal grill: Open bottom vent halfway and place disposable pan on 1 side of grill. Light large chimney starter two-thirds filled with charcoal briquettes (4 quarts). When top coals are partially covered with ash, pour evenly over other side of grill. Set cooking grate in place, cover, and open lid vent halfway. Heat grill until hot, about 5 minutes.

3b. For a gas grill: Turn all burners to high, cover, and heat grill until hot, about 15 minutes. Turn primary burner to medium and turn off other burner(s). (Adjust primary burner [or, if using 3-burner grill, primary burner and second burner] as needed to maintain grill temperature of 325 degrees.)

4. Clean and oil cooking grate. Place roast on hotter side of grill and cook (covered if using gas) until well browned on all sides, 10 to 15 minutes, turning as needed. (If flare-ups occur, move roast to cooler side of grill until flames die down.)

5. Transfer roast to second rimmed baking sheet. If using charcoal, remove cooking grate and place wood chip packet on pile of coals; set cooking grate in place. If using gas, remove cooking grate and place wood chip packet directly on primary burner; set cooking grate in place. Place roast on cooler side of grill, bone side down, with tips of bones pointed away from fire. Cover (position lid vent over meat if using charcoal) and cook until meat registers 120 to 125 degrees (for medium-rare), 2 to 2½ hours.

6. Transfer roast to carving board and let rest for 30 minutes. Remove twine and remove beef from ribs. Slice roast into ½-inch-thick slices. Serve.

SOUS VIDE PRIME RIB

Serves 6 to 8 | first-cut standing rib roast
Sous vide time: 16 to 24 hours

WHY THIS RECIPE WORKS Given prime rib's celebratory status and high price tag, you're going to want to cook it well. Sous vide allows you to do that every time. We started by salting the roast and letting it sit overnight. Presearing the roast built flavor before it went into its low-temperature bath. After 16 to 24 hours at 133°F, the roast's connective tissue had broken down, producing its trademark buttery texture—but extra buttery. A flash under the broiler crisped up the fat cap to create a nice crust.

1 (7-pound) first-cut beef standing rib roast (3 bones)
2 tablespoons kosher salt
1 tablespoon vegetable oil

1. Using sharp knife, cut beef from bones. Cut slits 1 inch apart in crosshatch pattern in fat cap of roast, being careful not to cut into beef. Rub salt over entire roast and into slits. Place beef back on bones (to save space in refrigerator) and refrigerate, uncovered, for at least 24 hours or up to 4 days.

2. Using sous vide circulator, bring water to 133°F in 12-quart container.

3. Remove beef from bones; set aside bones. Heat oil in 12-inch skillet over medium-high heat until just smoking. Sear sides and top of roast until browned, 6 to 8 minutes; do not sear side where roast was cut from bone. Fit roast back onto bones, let cool for 10 minutes, then tie together with kitchen twine between bones.

4. Season roast with pepper and place in 2-gallon zipper-lock freezer bag. Seal bag, pressing out as much air as possible. Gently lower bag into prepared water bath until roast is fully submerged, and then clip top corner of bag to side of water bath container, allowing remaining air bubbles to rise to top of bag. Reopen 1 corner of zipper, release remaining air bubbles, and reseal bag. Cover and cook for at least 16 hours or up to 24 hours.

5. Adjust oven rack to middle position and heat broiler. Set wire rack in aluminum foil–lined rimmed baking sheet and spray with vegetable spray. Transfer roast, fat side up, to prepared rack and let rest for 10 to 15 minutes. Pat roast dry with paper towels. Broil until surface of roast is browned and crisp, 4 to 8 minutes. Transfer roast to carving board and discard ribs. Slice meat into ¾-inch-thick slices. Serve.

Butter-Basted Rib Steak

1 shallot, peeled and quartered through root end
2 garlic cloves, lightly crushed and peeled
5 sprigs fresh thyme

1. Pat steak dry with paper towels and sprinkle with pepper and salt. Heat oil in 12-inch skillet over medium-high heat until just smoking. Place steak in skillet and cook for 30 seconds. Flip steak and continue to cook for 30 seconds. Continue flipping steak every 30 seconds for 3 more minutes.

2. Slide steak to back of skillet, opposite handle, and add butter to front of skillet. Once butter has melted and begun to foam, add shallot, garlic, and thyme sprigs. Holding skillet handle, tilt skillet so butter pools near base of handle. Use metal spoon to continuously spoon butter and aromatics over steak, concentrating on areas where crust is less browned. Baste steak, flipping it every 30 seconds, until steak registers 120 to 125 degrees (for medium-rare), 1 to 2 minutes.

3. Remove skillet from heat and transfer steak to cutting board; tent with aluminum foil and let rest for 10 minutes. Discard aromatics from pan and transfer butter mixture to small bowl. Cut meat from bone (if bone-in), slice steak thin against grain, and serve with butter mixture.

VARIATIONS

Butter-Basted Rib Steak with Coffee-Chile Butter
Substitute 2 tablespoons whole coffee beans, cracked, for garlic and ½ teaspoon red pepper flakes for thyme.

Butter-Basted Rib Steak with Rosemary-Orange Butter
Substitute 8 (2-inch) strips orange zest for garlic and 1 sprig fresh rosemary for thyme.

BUTTER-BASTED RIB STEAK

Serves 2 | rib or rib-eye steak

WHY THIS RECIPE WORKS There's steak, and then there's pan-seared, butter-basted rib steak. These processes serve different purposes and the second isn't just for flavor. Searing involves cooking the surface of meat at a high temperature to create a browned crust. Basting requires continuously spooning hot fat over the steak to continue cooking it evenly. To prevent a gray band from forming under the crust (an indicator of overcooked, dried-out meat), we also repeatedly flipped the steak as it seared. Why? A hot skillet cooks food from the bottom up. When a protein is flipped, some heat from the seared side dissipates into the air, but lingering residual heat continues to cook the protein from the top down. The more a protein is flipped, the more it cooks from both sides. Our hot basting liquid—butter infused with shallot, garlic, and thyme—also helped the steak to cook from the top down and boosted its rich flavor.

1 (1¼-pound) bone-in rib steak or (1-pound) boneless rib-eye steak, 1½ inches thick, trimmed
1 teaspoon pepper
½ teaspoon table salt
1 tablespoon extra-virgin olive oil
3 tablespoons unsalted butter

GRILLED COWBOY-CUT STEAKS

Serves 4 to 6 | double-cut bone-in rib steak

WHY THIS RECIPE WORKS Oversized, cowboy-cut rib eyes offer big, beefy flavor, but cooking the huge steaks all the way through while achieving a flavorful seared crust is challenging. We used a bare minimum of seasonings—salt, pepper, and oil—to highlight the flavor of the steaks. To cook them, we opted for a low-and-slow approach to start. To keep the fire burning long enough, we layered unlit coals under lit ones. We let the steaks come to room temperature before grilling them to cut down on cooking time and then slow-roasted the steaks on the cooler side of the grill until they were almost done. A quick sear over hot coals gave them a flavorful dark crust. Don't start grilling until the steaks' internal temperatures have reached 55 degrees. Otherwise, the times and temperatures in this recipe will be inaccurate.

TUTORIAL
Butter-Basted Rib Steak

Butter-basting a rib steak is an exercise in luxury—and just a great way to cook
a thick steak. Learn how to make this luxe steak.

1. Pat steak dry with paper towels and sprinkle with pepper and salt. Heat oil in 12-inch skillet over medium-high heat until just smoking. Place steak in skillet and cook for 30 seconds.

2. Flip steak and continue to cook for 30 seconds. Continue flipping steak every 30 seconds for 3 more minutes.

3. Slide steak to back of skillet, opposite handle, and add butter to front of skillet. Once butter has melted and begun to foam, add shallot, garlic, and thyme sprigs.

4. Holding skillet handle, tilt skillet so butter pools near base of handle.

5. Baste steak, flipping it every 30 seconds, until steak registers 120 to 125 degrees (for medium-rare), 1 to 2 minutes.

6. Remove skillet from heat and transfer steak to cutting board; tent with aluminum foil and let rest for 10 minutes. Discard aromatics from pan and transfer butter mixture to small bowl. Slice steak thin and serve with butter mixture.

2 (1¼- to 1½-pound) double-cut bone-in rib steaks,
  1¾ to 2 inches thick, trimmed
4 teaspoons kosher salt
2 teaspoons vegetable oil
2 teaspoons pepper

1. Set wire rack in rimmed baking sheet. Pat steaks dry with paper towels and sprinkle all over with salt. Place steaks on prepared rack and let stand at room temperature until meat registers 55 degrees, about 1 hour. Rub steaks with oil and sprinkle with pepper.

2a. For a charcoal grill: Open bottom vent halfway. Arrange 4 quarts unlit charcoal briquettes in even layer over half of grill. Light large chimney starter one-third filled with charcoal briquettes (2 quarts). When top coals are partially covered with ash, pour evenly over unlit coals. Set cooking grate in place, cover, and open lid vent halfway. Heat grill until hot, about 5 minutes.

2b. For a gas grill: Turn all burners to high, cover, and heat grill until hot, about 15 minutes. Turn primary burner to medium-low and turn off other burner(s). Adjust primary burner as needed to maintain grill temperature of 300 degrees.

3. Clean and oil cooking grate. Place steaks on cooler side of grill with bones facing fire. Cover and cook until steaks register 75 degrees, 10 to 20 minutes. Flip steaks, keeping bones facing fire. Cover and continue to cook until steaks register 95 degrees, 10 to 20 minutes.

4. If using charcoal, slide steaks to hotter part of grill. If using gas, remove steaks from grill, turn primary burner to high, and heat until hot, about 5 minutes; place steaks over primary burner. Cover and cook until well browned and steaks register 120 to 125 degrees (for medium-rare), about 4 minutes per side. Transfer steaks to clean wire rack set in rimmed baking sheet, tent with foil, and let rest for 15 minutes. Transfer steaks to cutting board and cut meat from bone. Slice steaks against grain into ½-inch-thick slices. Serve.

BULGOGI

Serves 4 | rib-eye steak

WHY THIS RECIPE WORKS Served with rice, spicy sauce, and pickles, this Korean staple of thinly sliced marinated beef comes together to make a complete meal—and cooks up in less than 5 minutes. Rib-eye steak offered the right combination of a marbled interior and rich beef flavor. As the meat is supposed to be superthin, we froze it in pieces to make it easier to shave. A test kitchen step, soaking the meat in a baking soda solution

for just 5 minutes, tenderized it. Soy sauce, garlic, sesame oil, pepper, and chopped onion brought savory undertones to the typically sweet marinade, tempering its intense flavor. A quick savory-spicy sauce, ssamjang, and daikon pickles offered flavor and textural contrast. To save time, prepare the pickles and chile sauce while the steak freezes. You can substitute 2 cups of bean sprouts and one cucumber, peeled, quartered lengthwise, seeded, and sliced thin on the bias, for the daikon, if desired. It's worth seeking out the Korean fermented bean pastes doenjang and gochujang, which are sold in Asian markets and online. If you can't find them, you can substitute red or white miso for the doenjang and sriracha for the gochujang. You can eat bulgogi with rice and kimchi or wrap small portions of beef in lettuce leaves with sauce.

PICKLES
1 cup rice vinegar
2 tablespoons sugar
1½ teaspoons table salt
1 pound daikon radish, peeled and cut into 1½-inch-long matchsticks

SSAMJANG
4 scallions, white and light green parts only, minced
¼ cup doenjang
1 tablespoon gochujang
1 tablespoon water
2 teaspoons sugar
2 teaspoons toasted sesame oil
1 garlic clove, minced

BEEF
1 (1¼-pound) boneless rib-eye steak, cut crosswise into 1½-inch-wide pieces and trimmed
1 tablespoon water
¼ teaspoon baking soda
¼ cup chopped onion
¼ cup sugar
3 tablespoons soy sauce
4 garlic cloves, peeled
1 tablespoon toasted sesame oil
¼ teaspoon pepper
2 teaspoons vegetable oil
4 scallions, dark green parts only, cut into 1½-inch pieces

1. For the pickles: Whisk vinegar, sugar, and salt together in medium bowl. Add daikon and toss to combine. Gently press on daikon to submerge. Cover and refrigerate for at least 30 minutes or up to 24 hours.

2. For the ssamjang: Combine all ingredients in small bowl. Cover and set aside. (Sauce can be refrigerated for up to 3 days.)

3. **For the beef:** Place beef on large plate and freeze until very firm, 35 to 40 minutes. Once firm, stand each piece on 1 cut side on cutting board and, using sharp knife, shave beef against grain as thin as possible. (Slices needn't be perfectly intact.) Combine water and baking soda in medium bowl. Add beef and toss to coat. Let sit at room temperature for 5 minutes.

4. Meanwhile, process onion, sugar, soy sauce, garlic, sesame oil, and pepper in food processor until smooth, about 30 seconds, scraping down sides of bowl as needed. Add onion mixture to beef and toss to evenly coat.

5. Heat vegetable oil in 12-inch nonstick skillet over medium-high heat until shimmering. Add beef mixture in even layer and cook, without stirring, until browned on 1 side, about 1 minute. Stir and continue to cook until beef is no longer pink, 3 to 4 minutes longer. Add scallion greens and cook, stirring constantly, until fragrant, about 30 seconds. Transfer to platter. Serve with pickles and ssamjang.

Bulgogi

SPICE-RUBBED RIB EYES

Serves 4 to 6 | rib-eye steak

WHY THIS RECIPE WORKS We like spice on rib-eye steaks; the steaks are rich and beefy enough to stand up to the bold (but not overly aggressive) spice crust and thick enough to provide the perfect ratio of interior meat to exterior spice, ensuring the right mix of flavors and textures in every bite. Spice blends have a tendency to burn and can fall off during cooking—but we wanted a crust that was superflavorful, not superburnt. To get one, we continually flipped the steaks, thus ensuring that each side of the steaks was exposed to the heat in short intervals. And by not patting the steaks dry before applying the spice blend (as most recipes call for), we let the moisture from the meat act as a glue to help the spices stick. For even more insurance, we used a fork to flip the steaks, rather than tongs or a spatula, to keep the spice crust in place.

  1 tablespoon black peppercorns
  2 tablespoons chopped fresh rosemary
  1 tablespoon kosher salt
  2 teaspoons ground coriander
  2 teaspoons grated lemon zest
1½ teaspoons dry mustard
  1 teaspoon red pepper flakes
  2 (1-pound) boneless rib-eye steaks, 1½ inches thick, trimmed
  1 tablespoon vegetable oil

1. Place peppercorns in zipper-lock bag and seal bag. Using rolling pin, crush peppercorns coarse. Combine peppercorns, rosemary, salt, coriander, lemon zest, mustard, and pepper flakes in bowl. Season steaks all over, including sides, with spice mixture, pressing to adhere. (Use all of spice mixture.)

2. Set wire rack in rimmed baking sheet. Heat oil in 12-inch nonstick skillet over medium heat until just smoking. Add steaks and cook, flipping steaks with fork every 2 minutes, until well browned and meat registers 120 to 125 degrees (for medium-rare), 10 to 13 minutes. Transfer steaks to prepared rack, tent with aluminum foil, and let rest for 5 minutes. Transfer steaks to cutting board. Slice against grain and serve.

GRILLED BOURBON STEAKS

Serves 6 to 8 | rib-eye steak

WHY THIS RECIPE WORKS Why marinate rib eyes in bourbon? Why not? The bourbon not only enhances the beef's meatiness but its sugars also increase flavorful charring. To maximize the steaks' flavor, we soaked four hefty rib eyes in a mixture of bourbon, Worcestershire sauce, shallot, and garlic; a 1:1 ratio of Worcestershire to bourbon delivered meat that was seasoned throughout with complex flavor and a balanced amount of salinity. After marinating the meat for 4 hours, we fired up the grill, brushed the steaks with oil and a liberal dose of salt and pepper, and cooked them to a juicy medium-rare. The boozy marinade really delivered, giving us sweet-savory flavors and perfect char. Use a bourbon you'd be happy drinking.

1 cup bourbon
1 cup Worcestershire sauce
1 shallot, minced
2 garlic cloves, minced
2 teaspoons kosher salt
2 teaspoons pepper
4 (1-pound) boneless rib-eye steaks, 1 to 1½ inches thick, trimmed
2 tablespoons vegetable oil

1. Whisk bourbon, Worcestershire, shallot, garlic, salt, and pepper together in bowl. Place 2 steaks in each of two 1-gallon zipper-lock bags and divide bourbon mixture between bags, about 1 cup each. Seal bags, turn to distribute marinade, and refrigerate for at least 4 hours or up to 24 hours, flipping occasionally.

2. Remove steaks from marinade and pat dry with paper towels; discard marinade. Brush steaks all over with oil and season liberally with salt and pepper.

3a. For a charcoal grill: Open bottom vent completely. Light large chimney starter filled with charcoal briquettes (6 quarts). When top coals are partially covered with ash, pour evenly over grill. Set cooking grate in place, cover, and open lid vent completely. Heat grill until hot, about 5 minutes.

3b. For a gas grill: Turn all burners to high, cover, and heat grill until hot, about 15 minutes. Turn all burners to medium-high.

4. Clean and oil cooking grate. Place steaks on grill and cook (covered if using gas) until well charred and meat registers 120 to 125 degrees (for medium-rare), 6 to 8 minutes per side.

5. Transfer steaks to wire rack set in rimmed baking sheet, tent with aluminum foil, and let rest for 10 minutes. Serve.

HIBACHI-STYLE STEAKS AND VEGETABLES

Serves 4 | rib-eye steak

WHY THIS RECIPE WORKS We wanted to deliver all the savory-sweet appeal of a hibachi steakhouse dinner at home. To mimic the powerful heat of the flattop, we chose to cook in a large cast-iron skillet; we avoided overcrowding by cooking

the steak and vegetables separately. After cooking the steaks, to give the vegetables a superflavorful start, we added them in the steak drippings in the still-hot skillet. We finished the sliced steaks and perfectly browned shiitakes, onion, and zucchini with a rich, savory soy-garlic butter. We like to serve the steak and vegetables with Simple Hibachi-Style Fried Rice and Yum-Yum Sauce, White Mustard Sauce, and/or Sweet Ginger Sauce (recipes follow). If using a nonstick skillet, heat the oil in the skillet over medium-high heat until just smoking before adding the steaks in step 2.

3 tablespoons unsalted butter, melted
2 tablespoons soy sauce
2 garlic cloves, minced
2 (1-pound) boneless rib-eye steaks, 1½ to 1¾ inches thick, trimmed
1¼ teaspoons white pepper, divided
1 teaspoon table salt, divided
1 tablespoon vegetable oil
2 zucchini (8 ounces each), halved lengthwise and sliced ¾ inch thick
2 onions, cut into ¾-inch pieces
6 ounces shiitake mushrooms, stemmed and halved if small or quartered if large
2 tablespoons mirin

1. Combine melted butter, soy sauce, and garlic in bowl; set aside. Pat steaks dry with paper towels and sprinkle with 1 teaspoon white pepper and ¾ teaspoon salt.

2. Heat 12-inch cast-iron skillet over medium-high heat for 5 minutes. Add oil to skillet and swirl to coat. Add steaks and cook, flipping steaks every 2 minutes, until well browned and meat registers 120 to 125 degrees (for medium-rare), 10 to 13 minutes. Transfer steaks to carving board, tent with aluminum foil, and let rest.

3. While steaks rest, add zucchini, onions, mushrooms, remaining ¼ teaspoon white pepper, and remaining ¼ teaspoon salt to fat left in skillet and stir to combine. Pat vegetables into even layer and cook over medium-high heat, without stirring, until beginning to brown, about 3 minutes. Stir and continue to cook 2 minutes longer. Add mirin and 2 tablespoons soy-garlic butter to skillet and continue to cook until liquid has evaporated and vegetables are well browned, about 2 minutes longer.

4. Transfer vegetables to serving platter. Slice steaks against grain ¼ inch thick and transfer to platter with vegetables. Drizzle steaks with remaining soy-garlic butter. Serve.

Hibachi-Style Steaks and Vegetables

Simple Hibachi-Style Fried Rice

Mirin can be found in your supermarket's Asian foods section. Black pepper can be substituted for the white pepper, if desired.

1½ cups long-grain white rice
3 large eggs
1 teaspoon toasted sesame oil
¼ teaspoon table salt
¼ teaspoon white pepper
1 tablespoon unsalted butter, softened
1 garlic clove, minced
1 tablespoon vegetable oil
4 scallions, sliced ¼ inch thick
1½ tablespoons soy sauce
1½ tablespoons mirin

1. Bring 3 quarts water to boil in large saucepan over high heat. Add rice and cook, stirring occasionally, until just cooked through, about 12 minutes. Drain rice in fine-mesh strainer or colander. Whisk eggs, sesame oil, salt, and white pepper together in bowl; set aside. Combine butter and garlic in second bowl; set aside.

2. Heat vegetable oil in 12-inch nonstick skillet over medium-high heat until shimmering. Add egg mixture and stir with rubber spatula until set but still wet, about 15 seconds.

3. Add scallions and rice and cook until sizzling and popping loudly, about 3 minutes. Add soy sauce and mirin and cook, stirring constantly, until thoroughly combined, about 2 minutes. Stir in garlic butter until incorporated. Serve.

Yum-Yum Sauce

Makes about ¾ cup; serves 4
White miso can be substituted for the red miso, if desired.

½ cup mayonnaise
2 tablespoons water
1 tablespoon unsalted butter, melted
1 tablespoon red miso
1 teaspoon tomato paste
¼ teaspoon cayenne pepper
¼ teaspoon paprika
¼ teaspoon table salt

Whisk all ingredients together in bowl.

White Mustard Sauce

Makes about ⅔ cup; serves 4
Be sure to use toasted sesame oil here. If you prefer a spicier sauce, add more dry mustard.

½ cup heavy cream
2 tablespoons soy sauce
1½ teaspoons dry mustard
1½ teaspoons toasted sesame oil
1 teaspoon sugar

Vigorously whisk all ingredients in bowl until combined and slightly thickened.

Sweet Ginger Sauce

Makes about ¾ cup; serves 4
Be sure to use unseasoned rice vinegar here.

½ cup chopped onion
3 tablespoons sugar
3 tablespoons rice vinegar
3 tablespoons soy sauce
1 (¾-inch) piece ginger, peeled and chopped

Process all ingredients in blender until smooth, about 15 seconds, scraping down sides of blender jar as needed.

SHORT LOIN

THE LOIN IS A WONDERFULLY complex primal of the cow (there's a lot of good stuff here), so we break it down a bit, starting here with the front part, the part closest to the rib (see page 61), the short loin. (You'll learn about the end part of the loin, the sirloin, on pages 108–127.) The short loin extends from the last rib through the midsection of the animal to the hip area. Beef lovers often praise steaks from this region for being tender and juicy since the muscles get little exercise; they can be cooked hot and fast. Short loin cuts are just a bit more mild in beefy flavor and a bit more tender than rib cuts.

The short loin contains parts of two major muscles, the tenderloin (see pages 94–107 where we give this cut special attention) and the larger shell muscle, which has more robust flavor and more fat. The T-bone and porterhouse steaks (see page 78) contain portions of both the tenderloin and shell muscles, separated by a piece of lumbar vertebra; these steaks are cut (if the tenderloin hasn't been removed) from the short loin. Young cattle are generally more desirable for their tenderness; due to the presence of this spinal section, these steaks by law in the United States can come only from cows that are younger than 30 months old, so they have those flavor and texture advantages.

Top Loin Roast

Cost: ◼◼▮▮ Flavor: ◼◼▮▮
Best cooking methods: roast
Texture: tender and juicy
Alternative names: strip roast

You're probably familiar with a strip steak—this tastes like that delicious steak in roast form. The well-marbled, tender meat and ample fat cap make it a great, less expensive alternative to other premium roasts, such as prime rib. Another advantage? It's boneless and uniform, which makes it easy to cook and slice. The rib end, the part of the top loin that lies closer to the rib, is slightly more tender. You'll want to trim the roast's fat cap only to ¼ inch so that it flavors the meat and forms an appealing crisp exterior.

MEAT PREP *Making a Uniform Top Loin Roast*

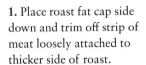

1. Place roast fat cap side down and trim off strip of meat loosely attached to thicker side of roast.

2. Rotate roast 180 degrees and trim off strip of meat and fat from narrow side of roast. (Save trimmings if called for in recipe.)

Boneless Strip Steak

Cost: ◼◼▮▮ Flavor: ◼◼▮▮
Best cooking methods: pan sear, grill, sous vide
Texture: well-marbled, firm textured, and pleasantly chewy-tender
Alternative names: ambassador steak, top loin steak, shell steak, sirloin strip steak, Kansas City strip steak, New York strip steak, Texas strip steak, boneless club steak

A steakhouse standard and a steak-eater favorite, with its balanced fat content (it's rich but not overwhelming) and manageable size, this moderately expensive cut is available both boneless and bone-in although it's much more commonly found boneless. Cut from the top loin roast, these steaks are well-marbled, but more lean than rib-eye steaks, with a tight grain and a pleasantly chewy texture. This cut is so popular all over the country that it has a host of alternative names. Whatever you call it, it has big beefy flavor and is one of the most satisfying steaks.

CONSIDERATIONS FOR COOKING THICK STEAKS

We consider a strip steak a thick-cut steak, one almost as thick as it is wide. This can make it difficult to keep the perimeter from overcooking (and a gray band from forming) while the very center of the steak comes up to the desired temperature. How do we achieve a good crust and a medium-rare center for these steaks?

Method #1: Reverse Searing

Searing thick-cut steaks quickly keeps the meat directly under the crust from turning gray. But although a quick, hot sear might get the outer rim in shape, it doesn't give the steak enough time in the pan to come to temperature at the center. So we start the steak in the oven to warm it up slowly to a temperature just shy of our desired temperature; this also dries the outside of the steaks thoroughly—more thoroughly than patting them dry with paper towels—so they are perfectly cooked in the flash it takes to then brown them in the skillet on the stovetop. See Thick-Cut Strip Steaks (page 80).

Method #2: Shortcut Searing

This fast-flipping method also allows a crust to form without the steak sitting for too long in the same place—but all in one skillet. It requires a more watchful eye than reverse searing but takes less time—it's the method to choose for a busy weeknight.

Here we use a nonstick or carbon steel skillet so the savory brown crust sticks to the steak and not to the pan—and so we don't need oil, additional fat that can smoke or splatter. We start the steak in the opposite of what's expected—a cold skillet. Skipping preheating the pan allows the interiors to heat up gradually. Flipping often—every 2 minutes—rather than patiently leaving the steak alone, as old-school wisdom may suggest, cooks the steaks from the bottom up and the top down so their interiors warm evenly and their crust builds gradually for edge-to-edge rosiness. See Quick Pan-Seared Strip Steaks (page 83).

Method #3: Cooking in Cast Iron

Your grandparents' favorite pan might be the very best for cooking a thick-cut steak. Taking longer to reach the proper temperature than a traditional skillet (its thermal conductivity—the ability to transfer heat from one part of the metal to another—is lower), but holding heat much more effectively, its temperature drop is minimal, even when a relatively cold steak is added to the pan, and the steak browns better. Retaining heat extremely well, cast iron produces the ultimate brown sear in rapid time—the goal. The trick is to make sure that the pan preheats thoroughly and evenly, which we do in a very hot oven (not on the stovetop) so the heat reaches the pan from all directions and there are no hot spots. Once the pan is hot, we set it over a moderate flame to maintain the heat and to avoid creating an overly thick crust on the steak. Combining this with the faster flipping of method two creates a gorgeous steak that's evenly cooked. See Cast Iron Steaks with Herb Butter (page 83).

Method #4: From Frozen

Come home from work, take a rock-hard steak from the freezer, and clunk it in a hot pan. What sounds like a recipe for disaster is in fact a final road to thick-cut steak success, if frozen is what you have. When we seared frozen (no sitting on the counter) strip steaks as well as frozen-then-thawed steaks on both sides and then transferred them to a low oven to finish, the frozen steaks browned just as well, had thinner bands of gray, overcooked meat under the crust, and tasted juicier than the thawed steaks.

How did this happen? A fully frozen steak is extremely cold, which prevents overcooking in the time the surface reaches the very high temperatures necessary for browning reactions. And since meat muscle fibers begin to squeeze out a significant amount of moisture when cooked to temperatures higher than 140 degrees, the steaks with more gray banding (and therefore more overcooking) were drier.

A fresh steak will always give you the best texture, but if you have frozen steaks, this is a smooth road to well-cooked thick-cut steaks. There are a couple ways to ensure success with this technique. First, freeze your steaks properly (see page 8) to prevent a layer of ice from forming and causing dangerous flare-ups in a hot oiled pan (or on the grill; see page 86). Second, use more oil, to a depth of about ⅛ inch, than you would for conventional searing. This will allow the oil to reach and transfer heat to the more abundant crevices of a frozen steak as well as provide a larger heat reserve and therefore better recovery when the frozen steak is added to the pan so its temperature doesn't drop too much, inhibiting browning.

T-Bone Steak

Cost: ▪▪▫▫ **Flavor:** ▪▪▫▫
Best cooking methods: pan sear, grill
Texture: tender-chewy on the larger strip side with a noticeable grain
Alternative names: none

A classic grilling steak, this cut is named for the T-shaped bone that runs through the meat. This bone separates two muscles, the flavorful strip (or shell) on the left of the illustration above and the buttery tenderloin on the right. Some see this form as creating a best-of-both-worlds steak in terms of flavor and texture.

Porterhouse Steak

Cost: ■■▮▮ Flavor: ■■▮▮

Best cooking methods: pan sear, grill
Texture: great balance of pleasant chew and buttery fine-grained tenderloin
Alternative names: king steak

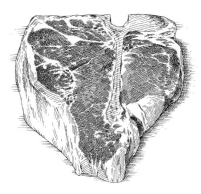

A porterhouse steak is really just a huge T-bone steak—usually large enough to serve two people. Because of its size (it's normally cut thicker than the T-bone), you'll often see it served sliced up for portioning purposes. The T-bone is cut from the front of the short loin, which captures the tapered part of the tenderloin; the tenderloin portion of the porterhouse is larger than it is on the T-bone, because the porterhouse is cut farther back. This larger tenderloin portion gives the porterhouse a higher price tag. In fact, there are rules to this prized cut: The USDA requires a steak's tenderloin portion to measure 1¼ inches or greater from bone to edge for it to be classified "porterhouse."

MEAT PREP *Slicing T-Bone and Porterhouse Steaks*

1. Cut along bone to remove strip section.

2. Turn steak around and cut tenderloin section off bone.

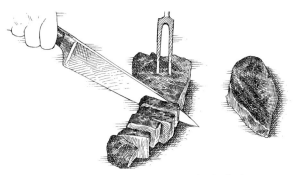

3. Cut each piece crosswise into ¼-inch-thick slices.

TENDER AND SENSITIVE

The beauty of a two-part steak: the best of all worlds for taste and texture. The difficulty: cooking the hearty cut evenly. The lean tenderloin portion can dry out in the time it takes to cook the more-marbled strip section, and the high heat needed to brown the exterior of a steak widens this disparity. On the grill, we can protect our more-sensitive tenderloin portion of a T-bone or porterhouse steak by giving it a little extra love. We position the meat so that the tenderloin faces the cooler side of the grill, with the bone between the tenderloin and the fire. This allows the delicate tenderloin to cook at a slightly slower rate and stay tender and juicy.

HOLIDAY STRIP ROAST

Serves 8 to 10 | top loin roast

WHY THIS RECIPE WORKS For an occasion-worthy, beefy top-loin roast, we wanted a seared crust and an interior that was cooked to a perfect medium-rare throughout, but most recipes we found could only give us one or the other. Gently roasting the beef in a low oven until it was almost done and then setting it under the broiler for a few minutes achieved both results beautifully without the hassle of pan searing. Scoring the fat cap before cooking helped the fat to render and created a crisp, craggy surface that looked as good as it tasted. We maximized flavor by combining the spice rubs and herb rubs we saw called for in other recipes, opting for a single spice-herb rub that we let sit on the meat overnight (along with plenty of salt). We like to serve this perfectly seasoned, flavorful roast with a bright, fresh Salsa Verde (page 21) to complement the rich meat.

- 1 (5- to 6-pound) boneless top loin roast, fat trimmed to ¼ inch
- 2 tablespoons peppercorns
- 1 tablespoon coriander seeds
- 1 tablespoon yellow mustard seeds
- 3 tablespoons extra-virgin olive oil
- 2 tablespoons kosher salt
- 2 tablespoons chopped fresh rosemary
- 1 teaspoon red pepper flakes

1. Pat roast dry with paper towels. Using sharp knife, cut ½-inch crosshatch pattern in fat cap, being careful not to cut into meat. Tie kitchen twine around roast at 2-inch intervals. Grind peppercorns, coriander seeds, and mustard seeds to texture of coarse sand in spice grinder. Combine spice mixture, oil, salt, rosemary, and pepper flakes in bowl and stir until thick paste forms. Rub paste all over roast and into crosshatch. Wrap roast with plastic wrap and refrigerate for 6 to 24 hours.

2. Set wire rack in rimmed baking sheet. One hour before cooking, unwrap meat and place on prepared rack, fat side up. Adjust oven rack to middle position and heat oven to 275 degrees. Transfer roast to oven and cook until meat registers 115 degrees, about 1½ hours, rotating sheet halfway through cooking. Remove roast from oven and heat broiler.

3. Return roast to oven and broil on middle oven rack until fat cap is deep brown and interior of roast registers 120 to 125 degrees (for medium-rare), 3 to 5 minutes. Transfer to carving board, tent with aluminum foil, and let rest for 20 minutes. Remove twine from roast. Slice meat thin against grain. Serve.

THICK-CUT STRIP STEAKS

Serves 4 | boneless strip steak

WHY THIS RECIPE WORKS One of the best ways to cook a thick steak—without it forming a gray band beneath the browned crust before the center cooks through—is to sear it at the end of cooking, rather than at the beginning. We began by cooking the steaks in a 275-degree oven, which allowed them to warm through gently and also dried the surface of the meat thoroughly—essential for a well-browned crust. When the steaks met the hot skillet, they developed a beautiful browned crust in minutes while the interiors stayed pink, juicy, and tender. To complete these steakhouse-favorite steaks, we like to serve them in steakhouse preparations, with Red Wine–Mushroom Pan Sauce, Sun-Dried Tomato Relish, or Tequila-Poblano Pan Sauce (recipes follow). Make the sauce while the steak rests and spoon over steak.

- 2 (1-pound) boneless strip steaks, 1½ to 1¾ inches thick, trimmed
- 1 tablespoon vegetable oil

1. Adjust oven rack to middle position and heat oven to 275 degrees. Pat steaks dry with paper towels. Cut each steak in half crosswise to create four 8-ounce steaks. Season steaks with salt and pepper; gently press sides of steaks until uniform 1½ inches thick.

2. Place steaks on wire rack set in rimmed baking sheet. Cook until meat registers 90 to 95 degrees (for rare to medium-rare), 20 to 25 minutes, 25 to 30 minutes.

3. Heat oil in 12-inch skillet over high heat until just smoking. Place steaks in skillet and cook until well browned and crusty, 1½ to 2 minutes, lifting once halfway through cooking to redistribute fat underneath each steak. (Reduce heat if fond begins to burn.) Using tongs, flip steaks and cook until well browned on second side, 2 to 2½ minutes. Transfer all steaks to clean wire rack set in rimmed baking sheet and reduce heat to medium. Using tongs, stand 2 steaks on their sides. Holding steaks together, return to skillet and sear on all sides until browned, about 1½ minutes. Return steaks to wire rack and tent with aluminum foil. Repeat with remaining 2 steaks. Let steaks rest for 10 minutes, then serve.

Thick-Cut Strip Steaks

Red Wine–Mushroom Pan Sauce

Makes about 1 cup; serves 4

Prepare all the ingredients for the pan sauce while the steaks are in the oven.

- 1 tablespoon vegetable oil
- 8 ounces white mushrooms, trimmed and sliced thin
- 1 small shallot, minced
- 1 cup dry red wine
- ½ cup chicken broth
- 1 tablespoon balsamic vinegar
- 1 teaspoon Dijon mustard
- 2 tablespoons unsalted butter, cut into 4 pieces and chilled
- 1 teaspoon minced fresh thyme

While steaks rest, pour off fat from skillet. Heat oil over medium-high heat until just smoking. Add mushrooms and cook, stirring occasionally, until beginning to brown and liquid has evaporated, about 5 minutes. Add shallot and cook, stirring frequently, until beginning to soften, about 1 minute. Increase heat to high; add red wine and broth, scraping bottom of skillet with wooden spoon to loosen any browned bits. Simmer rapidly until liquid and mushrooms are reduced to 1 cup, about 6 minutes. Add vinegar, mustard, and any steak juices; cook until thickened, about 1 minute. Off heat, whisk in butter and thyme; season with salt and pepper to taste.

Sun-Dried Tomato Relish

Makes ½ cup; serves 4

Prepare all the ingredients for the relish while the steaks are in the oven.

- ½ cup chicken broth
  Pinch red pepper flakes
- 2 tablespoons oil-packed sun-dried tomatoes, rinsed and chopped
- 1 tablespoon capers, rinsed and chopped
- 1 tablespoon extra-virgin olive oil
- 2 teaspoons lemon juice
- 1 teaspoon honey
- 2 tablespoons chopped fresh parsley
- 1 tablespoon minced fresh mint

While steaks rest, pour off fat from skillet and return to high heat. Add broth, scraping up any browned bits. Add pepper flakes and boil until liquid is reduced to 2 tablespoons, about 5 minutes. Add any steak juices to skillet. Add tomatoes, capers, oil, lemon juice, and honey to skillet and swirl vigorously to emulsify. Off heat, stir in parsley and mint. Season with salt and pepper to taste.

Quick Pan-Seared Strip Steaks

Tequila-Poblano Pan Sauce

Makes ⅔ cup; serves 4

Prepare all the ingredients for the pan sauce while the steaks are in the oven. Before flambéing, be sure to roll up long shirtsleeves, tie back long hair, and turn off the exhaust fan and any lit burners.

- 1 small shallot, minced
- 1 poblano chile, stemmed, seeded, and chopped fine
- ½ teaspoon ground cumin
- ½ cup white tequila, divided
- ½ cup chicken broth
- 1 tablespoon lime juice, divided
- 3 tablespoons unsalted butter, cut into 3 pieces and chilled
- 1 tablespoon chopped fresh cilantro

While steaks rest, pour off all but 1 tablespoon fat from skillet. Return pan to high heat and add shallot and poblano; cook, stirring frequently, until lightly browned and fragrant, 1 to 2 minutes. Add cumin and continue to cook for 30 seconds. Transfer pan contents to bowl. Off heat, add all but 2 teaspoons tequila to now-empty skillet, and let warm through, about 5 seconds. Wave lit match over pan until tequila ignites, then shake pan to distribute flames. When flames subside, add broth and 2 teaspoons lime juice. Reduce to ⅓ cup, about 6 minutes. Add remaining 2 teaspoons tequila, remaining 1 teaspoon lime juice, and any steak juices to pan. Remove from heat and whisk in butter, cilantro, and poblano and shallot; season with salt and pepper to taste.

QUICK PAN-SEARED STRIP STEAKS

Serves 4 | boneless strip steak

WHY THIS RECIPE WORKS We love our recipe for Thick-Cut Strip Steaks (page 80), but sometimes sticking to just using a skillet is most convenient—if the method doesn't spray the kitchen with oil. To devise a fast, mess-free way of achieving deeply seared, rosy meat, we started the steaks in a "cold" (not preheated) nonstick skillet, turning the heat first to high and then lowering it to medium, and flipping the steaks every 2 minutes. The meat's temperature increased gradually, allowing a crust to build up on the outside without overcooking the interior. And the dual temperatures produced sizzle without smoke. Because we were cooking in a nonstick skillet, it wasn't necessary to lubricate the skillet with oil, and the well-marbled meat exuded enough fat to achieve a good sear. Before serving, we sliced the steaks and sprinkled them with flake sea salt so that every bite was well seasoned. If you have time, salt the steaks for 45 minutes or up to 24 hours before cooking: Sprinkle each of the steaks with 1 teaspoon of kosher salt, refrigerate them, and pat them dry with paper towels before cooking.

> 2   (12- to 16-ounce) boneless strip steaks, 1½ inches thick, trimmed
> 1   teaspoon pepper

1. Pat steaks dry with paper towels and sprinkle both sides with pepper. Place steaks 1 inch apart in cold 12-inch nonstick skillet. Place skillet over high heat and cook steaks for 2 minutes. Flip steaks and cook on second side for 2 minutes. (Neither side of steaks will be browned at this point.)

2. Flip steaks, reduce heat to medium, and continue to cook, flipping steaks every 2 minutes, until browned and meat registers 120 to 125 degrees (for medium-rare), 4 to 10 minutes longer. (Steaks should be sizzling gently; if not, increase heat slightly. Reduce heat if skillet starts to smoke.)

3. Transfer steaks to cutting board and let rest for 5 minutes. Slice steaks against grain, season with flake sea salt to taste, and serve.

CAST IRON STEAKS WITH HERB BUTTER

Serves 4 | boneless strip steak

WHY THIS RECIPE WORKS A cast-iron skillet, with its evenly heated cooking surface can give a steak a great sear. To get the heat-retaining pan hot, we preheated it in the oven. This gave us time to prepare a zesty compound butter and let the steaks (we chose boneless strip steak for its big, beefy flavor) come to room temperature, which helped them cook more quickly and evenly. Flipping the steaks frequently led to a shorter cooking time and a smaller gray band of dry, overcooked meat just under the surface. A favorite pan did it again, producing perfectly browned, crisp crust and a juicy, evenly cooked interior.

> 2   (1-pound) boneless strip steaks, 1½ inches thick, trimmed
> 4   tablespoons unsalted butter, softened
> 2   tablespoons minced shallot
> 1   tablespoon minced fresh parsley
> 1   tablespoon minced fresh chives
> 1   garlic clove, minced
> ¼   teaspoon pepper
> 2   tablespoons vegetable oil

1. Adjust oven rack to middle position, place 12-inch cast-iron skillet on rack, and heat oven to 500 degrees. Meanwhile, season steaks with salt and let sit at room temperature. Mix butter, shallot, parsley, chives, garlic, and pepper together in bowl; set aside.

2. When oven reaches 500 degrees, pat steaks dry with paper towels and season with pepper. Using pot holders, remove skillet from oven and place over medium-high heat; turn off oven. Being careful of hot skillet handle, add oil and heat until just smoking. Cook steaks, without moving, until lightly browned on first side, about 2 minutes. Flip steaks and continue to cook until lightly browned on second side, about 2 minutes.

3. Flip steaks, reduce heat to medium-low, and cook, flipping every 2 minutes, until steaks are well browned and meat registers 120 to 125 degrees (for medium-rare), 7 to 9 minutes. Transfer steaks to cutting board, dollop 2 tablespoons herb butter on each steak, tent with aluminum foil, and let rest for 5 to 10 minutes. Slice steaks against grain ½ inch thick and serve.

VARIATION

Cast Iron Steaks with Blue Cheese–Chive Butter
Omit herb butter and serve steaks with Blue Cheese–Chive Butter (page 106).

Garlic Steaks

GARLIC STEAKS

Serves 4 | boneless strip steak

WHY THIS RECIPE WORKS For perfectly cooked steaks with over-the-top garlic flavor, we began by coating boneless strip steaks in a pungent mix of minced garlic, salt, and olive oil and letting them rest in the mixture in the refrigerator. By briefly cooking smashed garlic cloves in extra-virgin olive oil on the stovetop, we created a garlic oil for both searing the steaks and whipping up an emulsified garlic-butter sauce. Adding a bit of raw garlic to the sauce contributed freshness and bite to the mellowed toasted garlic. Finally, we garnished the steaks with the toasted garlic cloves for textural contrast and yet another layer of garlic flavor—there's no such thing as too much.

STEAKS

¼ cup extra-virgin olive oil
6 garlic cloves, minced
1 tablespoon kosher salt, divided
1½ teaspoons pepper, divided
2 (1-pound) boneless strip steaks, 1½ inches thick, trimmed

GARLIC SAUCE AND TOASTED GARLIC

4 tablespoons unsalted butter, softened
7 garlic cloves (1 minced, 6 smashed and peeled)
½ teaspoon kosher salt
¼ teaspoon pepper
¼ cup extra-virgin olive oil
2 sprigs fresh thyme

1. For the steaks: Combine oil, garlic, 2 teaspoons salt, and 1 teaspoon pepper in 1-gallon zipper-lock bag. Place steaks in bag and seal. Turn bag to evenly coat steaks. Refrigerate for at least 4 hours or up to 24 hours. Rinse steaks under cold water to remove any pieces of garlic; discard oil mixture. Pat steaks dry with paper towels. Sprinkle steaks with remaining 1 teaspoon salt and remaining ½ teaspoon pepper; set aside.

2. For the garlic sauce and toasted garlic: Combine butter, minced garlic, salt, and pepper in bowl. Heat oil, thyme sprigs, and smashed garlic in 12-inch nonstick skillet over medium heat until garlic has softened and turned light brown, about 5 minutes, flipping garlic as needed to ensure even browning. Remove garlic from skillet with slotted spoon and set aside; discard thyme sprigs. Add 2 tablespoons garlic oil to butter mixture and whisk until emulsified and creamy. Set aside.

3. Heat remaining 2 tablespoons garlic oil in skillet over medium heat until just smoking. Add steaks and cook, flipping every 2 minutes, until well browned and meat registers 120 to 125 degrees (for medium-rare), 12 to 16 minutes. Transfer steaks to cutting board, tent with aluminum foil, and let rest for 10 minutes. Rewhisk sauce to make fluid again. Slice steaks thin against grain and serve with sauce and reserved garlic cloves.

ONE-PAN STEAK WITH SWEET POTATOES AND SCALLIONS

Serves 4 | boneless strip steak

WHY THIS RECIPE WORKS Cooking strip steaks in a blazing-hot skillet will get you a great steak. But we wanted to make a complete dinner for four and dirty only one pan. We simulated pan-searing the steaks by preheating a rimmed baking sheet before placing the steaks onto it to cook quickly. This produced a satisfying sizzle and, with an extra boost from a spice rub, a flavorful crust on one side of the steaks. Jump-starting the sweet potatoes while heating the sheet for the steaks allowed everything to come out of the oven at the same time. Use all the coffee rub on the steak. It aids in browning as well as adding flavor. Remove only the root hairs from the scallions.

1½ pounds sweet potatoes, unpeeled, cut lengthwise into 1-inch wedges
2 tablespoons extra-virgin olive oil, divided
1 tablespoon table salt, divided
2¼ teaspoons pepper, divided
16 scallions, trimmed
2 tablespoons packed dark brown sugar
1 tablespoon finely ground coffee
1 tablespoon chili powder
2 (1-pound) boneless strip steaks, 1½ to 1¾ inches thick
10 radishes, trimmed and sliced thin
1 tablespoon lime juice, plus lime wedges for serving

1. Adjust oven rack to lower-middle position and heat oven to 450 degrees. Toss potatoes, 1½ tablespoons oil, 1 teaspoon salt, and 1 teaspoon pepper together in large bowl. Arrange potatoes skin side down in single layer on half of rimmed baking sheet. Roast until potatoes begin to soften, about 25 minutes.

2. Meanwhile, toss scallions with remaining 1½ teaspoons oil, ¼ teaspoon salt, and ¼ teaspoon pepper in now-empty bowl. Mix sugar, coffee, chili powder, 1½ teaspoons salt, and remaining 1 teaspoon pepper together in small bowl. Pat steaks dry with paper towels, then sprinkle all over with coffee mixture.

3. Arrange scallions on top of potatoes. Place steaks on empty side of sheet. Roast until potatoes are fully tender and meat registers 120 to 125 degrees (for medium-rare), 12 to 15 minutes. Transfer steaks bottom side up to cutting board, tent with aluminum foil, and let rest for 5 minutes. Toss radishes, lime juice, and remaining ¼ teaspoon salt together in bowl. Slice steaks thin against grain and serve with potatoes, scallions, radishes, and lime wedges.

STEAK FRITES

Serves 4 | boneless strip steak

WHY THIS RECIPE WORKS Restaurants employ people at different stations to make this bistro classic: One person cooks the steak, another person cooks the fries. But at home, where often there isn't a sous chef, we needed a way to make both components simultaneously. We wanted a french fry recipe that used half the oil and required no double frying, so we tried submerging the potatoes in cold oil before frying them over high heat until browned. With lower-starch potatoes such as Yukon Golds, the results were crispy exteriors and creamy interiors. How to time things so we could eat everything hot? First, we started the fries on the stove. Shortly after the oil began to bubble, we placed a skillet with a tablespoon of oil over medium-high heat. Once the oil started to smoke, we added the steaks. After 4 to 7 minutes per side, the steaks were ready to move to the cutting board to rest—just in time to return to the pot of oil and give the fries a stir. Once the steaks rested (about 10 minutes), the fries were done.

Steak Frites

4 tablespoons unsalted butter, softened
1 shallot, minced
1 tablespoon minced fresh parsley
1 garlic clove, minced
½ teaspoon kosher salt
¼ teaspoon pepper
2½ pounds large Yukon Gold potatoes, unpeeled
1½ quarts plus 1 tablespoon peanut or vegetable oil, divided
2 (1-pound) boneless strip steaks, 1¼ to 1½ inches thick, trimmed and halved crosswise

1. Mash butter, shallot, parsley, garlic, salt, and pepper together in bowl; set aside compound butter.

2. Square off potatoes by cutting ¼-inch-thick slice from each of their 4 long sides; discard slices. Cut potatoes lengthwise into ¼-inch-thick planks. Stack 3 or 4 planks and cut into ¼-inch-thick fries. Repeat with remaining planks. (Do not place fries in water.)

3. Line rimmed baking sheet with triple layer of paper towels. Combine potatoes and 1½ quarts oil in large Dutch oven. Cook over high heat until oil is vigorously bubbling, about 5 minutes. Continue to cook, without stirring potatoes, until potatoes are limp but exteriors are beginning to firm up, about 15 minutes. Using tongs, stir potatoes, gently scraping up any that stick, and continue to cook, stirring occasionally, until golden and crispy, 7 to 10 minutes longer.

4. Meanwhile, pat steaks dry with paper towels and season with salt and pepper. Heat remaining 1 tablespoon oil in 12-inch skillet over medium-high heat until just smoking. Add steaks and cook until well browned and meat registers 120 to 125

degrees (for medium-rare), 4 to 7 minutes per side. Transfer steaks to platter, top each with compound butter, tent with aluminum foil, and let rest for 10 minutes.

5. Using spider skimmer or slotted spoon, transfer fries to prepared sheet and season with salt. Serve fries with steaks.

GRILLED FROZEN STEAKS WITH ARUGULA AND PARMESAN

Serves 4 | boneless strip steak

WHY THIS RECIPE WORKS Rather than follow the convention of thawing frozen steaks before grilling them, we discovered that we could cook steaks straight from the freezer for ease—and with extraordinary results. Strip steaks were perfect because they were flavorful (important since a marinade or spice rub wasn't an option) and thick. We took advantage of the steaks' ultrachilled state and started them over a hot fire to develop a well-browned crust on both sides without interior overcooking; we then slid them to the cooler side of the grill to cook until they reached the desired internal temperature. (For more information on freezing steaks, see page 8.) To make a meal we sliced the rich steaks and served them with lemony dressed peppery arugula and shredded Parmesan.

2 **(1-pound) frozen boneless strip steaks, 1½ inches thick, trimmed**
6 **tablespoons extra-virgin olive oil**
2 **tablespoons lemon juice, plus lemon wedges for serving**
¾ **teaspoon table salt**
¼ **teaspoon pepper**
8 **ounces (8 cups) baby arugula**
2 **ounces Parmesan cheese, shredded (⅔ cup)**

1a. For a charcoal grill: Open bottom vent completely. Light large chimney starter mounded with charcoal briquettes (7 quarts). When top coals are partially covered with ash, pour evenly over half of grill. Set cooking grate in place, cover, and open lid vent completely. Heat grill until hot, about 5 minutes.

1b. For a gas grill: Turn all burners to high, cover, and heat grill until hot, about 15 minutes. Leave primary burner on high and turn off other burner(s).

2. Clean and oil cooking grate. Place steaks on hotter side of grill and cook (covered if using gas) until browned and charred on first side, 5 to 7 minutes. Flip steaks, season with salt and pepper, and cook until browned and charred on second side, 5 to 7 minutes. Flip steaks again, season with salt and pepper, and move to cooler side of grill, arranging so steaks are about 6 inches from heat source. Continue to cook until meat registers 120 to 125 degrees (for medium-rare), 10 to 15 minutes longer. Transfer steaks to wire rack set in rimmed baking sheet and let rest for 5 minutes.

3. Transfer steaks to cutting board. Slice steaks thin against grain. Fan slices on either side of platter. Whisk oil, lemon juice, salt, and pepper together in large bowl. Add arugula and three-quarters of Parmesan and toss to combine. Arrange arugula down center of platter, allowing it to overlap steak. Sprinkle remaining Parmesan over steak and arugula. Serve with lemon wedges.

GRILLED ARGENTINE STEAKS WITH CHIMICHURRI SAUCE

Serves 6 to 8 | boneless strip steak

WHY THIS RECIPE WORKS A fresh, herb-packed chimichurri sauce complementing rich, smoky, ultracharred grilled caveman-size steaks is an Argentine favorite: Oregano, parsley, cilantro, garlic, red pepper flakes, and red wine vinegar add up to a vibrant, bold sauce that cuts through the richness of the steaks. Boneless strip steaks are generally smaller than Argentine cuts, so we formulated the recipe accordingly. We rubbed

the steaks with salt and used the freezer as a dehydrator to evaporate the surface moisture; this, along with rubbing the steaks with cornstarch, helped them develop the trademark substantial browned exterior of this grilled dish. If you'd like to use wood chunks instead of wood chips when using a charcoal grill, substitute four medium wood chunks, soaked in water for 1 hour, for the wood chip packets.

CHIMICHURRI SAUCE
¼ **cup hot water**
2 **teaspoons dried oregano**
1 **teaspoon table salt**
1⅓ **cups fresh parsley leaves**
⅔ **cup fresh cilantro leaves**
6 **garlic cloves, minced**
½ **teaspoon red pepper flakes**
¼ **cup red wine vinegar**
½ **cup extra-virgin olive oil**

STEAKS
1 **tablespoon cornstarch**
1½ **teaspoons table salt**
4 **(1-pound) boneless strip steaks, 1½ inches thick, trimmed**
4 **cups wood chips**
1 **(9-inch) disposable aluminum pie plate (if using gas)**

1. For the chimichurri sauce: Combine water, oregano, and salt in small bowl and let sit until oregano is softened, about 15 minutes. Pulse parsley, cilantro, garlic, and pepper flakes in food processor until coarsely chopped, about 10 pulses. Add water mixture and vinegar and pulse to combine. Transfer mixture to bowl and slowly whisk in oil until combined. Cover and let sit at room temperature for 1 hour. (Chimichurri sauce can be refrigerated for up to 3 days.)

2. For the steaks: Meanwhile, combine cornstarch and 1½ teaspoons salt in bowl. Pat steaks dry with paper towels and place on wire rack set in rimmed baking sheet. Rub entire surface of steaks with cornstarch mixture and place steaks in freezer, uncovered, until very firm, about 30 minutes. Just before grilling, soak wood chips in water for 15 minutes, then drain. Using 2 large pieces of heavy-duty aluminum foil, wrap soaked chips in two 8 by 4½-inch foil packets. (Make sure chips do not poke holes in sides or bottom of packets.) Cut 2 evenly spaced 2-inch slits in top of each packet.

3a. For a charcoal grill: Open bottom vent halfway. Light large chimney starter filled with charcoal briquettes (6 quarts). When top coals are partially covered with ash, pour evenly over grill. Place wood chip packets on coals. Set cooking grate in place, cover, and open lid vent halfway. Heat grill until hot and wood chips are smoking, about 5 minutes.

TUTORIAL
Ultimate Charcoal-Grilled Steaks

This grill setup isn't the norm—cooking with the charcoal chimney instead of using it only to heat coals—but normal isn't necessary for the best charcoal-grilled steaks.

1. Place steak halves with tapered ends flat on counter and pass two 12-inch metal skewers, spaced 1½ inches apart, horizontally through steaks, making sure to keep ¼-inch space between steak halves.

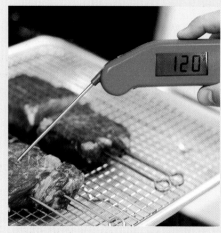

2. Cook skewered steaks in 200-degree oven until centers of steaks register 120 degrees, flipping steaks halfway through cooking and removing them as they come to temperature, 1½ hours to 1 hour 50 minutes.

3. Light large chimney starter half filled with charcoal briquettes (3 quarts). Place lit chimney on grill grate or on top of bricks. When top coals are completely covered with ash, uncover steaks and pat dry with paper towels.

4. Using tongs, place 1 set of steaks directly over chimney so skewers rest on rim of chimney (steaks will be suspended over coals).

5. Cook until both sides are well browned and charred, about 1 minute per side. Using tongs, return first set of steaks to wire rack in sheet, season with pepper, and tent with foil.

6. Repeat with second set of skewered steaks. Remove skewers from steaks and serve.

3b. For a gas grill: Turn all burners to high, cover, and heat grill until hot, about 15 minutes. Leave all burners on high. Place wood chunks in disposable aluminum pie plate and set on cooking grate. Close lid and heat until wood chunks begin to smoke, about 5 minutes.

4. Clean and oil cooking grate. Season steaks with pepper. Place steaks on grill, cover, and cook until beginning to brown, 2 to 3 minutes per side.

5. Flip steaks and cook, uncovered, until well browned on first side, 2 to 4 minutes. Flip steaks and continue to cook until meat registers 120 to 125 degrees (for medium-rare), 2 to 6 minutes longer.

6. Transfer steaks to cutting board, tent with foil, and let rest for 5 to 10 minutes. Slice steaks against grain ¼ inch thick. Serve, passing chimichurri sauce separately.

ULTIMATE CHARCOAL-GRILLED STEAKS

Serves 4 | boneless strip steaks

WHY THIS RECIPE WORKS For this recipe, we came across a novel technique for cooking over a live fire that relied on a charcoal chimney starter not just to light the coals but to actually do the cooking. Turns out, this method creates a grilled steak with a killer crust and perfectly cooked meat from edge to edge. We started the steaks with a slow cook in the oven to give them a head start and allow the salt to deeply season them, and then we finished them right over the chimney, stabilized with metal skewers. It felt like camping— with much better food. You will need a charcoal chimney starter with a 7½-inch diameter and four 12-inch metal skewers for this recipe. If your chimney starter has a smaller diameter, skewer each steak individually and cook in four batches. During cooking, the lit chimney can be placed on the grill grate or set on top of bricks.

- 2 **(1-pound) boneless strip steaks, 1¾ inches thick, fat caps removed**
- 2 **teaspoons kosher salt**

1. Adjust oven rack to middle position and heat oven to 200 degrees. Cut each steak in half crosswise to create four 8-ounce steaks. Cut ¹⁄₁₆-inch-deep slits, spaced ¼ inch apart, in crosshatch pattern on both sides of each steak. Sprinkle both sides of each steak with ½ teaspoon salt. Place steak halves with tapered ends flat on counter and pass two 12-inch metal skewers, spaced 1½ inches apart, horizontally through steaks, making sure to keep ¼-inch space between steak halves. Repeat skewering with remaining steak halves.

2. Place skewered steaks on wire rack set in rimmed baking sheet, transfer to oven, and cook until centers of steaks register 120 degrees (for medium-rare), flipping steaks halfway through cooking and removing them as they come to temperature, 1½ hours to 1 hour 50 minutes. Tent skewered steaks (still on rack) with aluminum foil.

3. Light large chimney starter half filled with charcoal briquettes (3 quarts). Place lit chimney on grill grate or on top of bricks. When top coals are completely covered with ash, uncover steaks (reserving foil) and pat dry with paper towels. Using tongs, place 1 set of steaks directly over chimney so skewers rest on rim of chimney (steaks will be suspended over coals). Cook until both sides are well browned and charred, about 1 minute per side. Using tongs, return first set of steaks to wire rack in sheet, season with pepper, and tent with reserved foil. Repeat with second set of skewered steaks. Remove skewers from steaks and serve.

SOUS VIDE SEARED STEAKS

Serves 4 | boneless strip steaks
Sous vide time: 1½ to 3 hours

WHY THIS RECIPE WORKS Cooking steaks sous vide is a game changer. The water bath technique takes all the guesswork and stress out of the dinner-preparation equation. Steaks are cooked to the same temperature, and thus the same doneness all the way through. This eliminates the gray band of overcooked meat around the exterior of steaks, which can occur with searing methods. Once your steaks are taken out of the water bath, all that's left to do is to give them a quick sear in a screaming-hot pan to trigger Maillard browning (see page 15). You can use other tender steaks (rib eye, shell sirloin, top sirloin, and tenderloin) in this recipe; avoid tougher cuts such as top round, bottom round, blade, and flank, as they would require a longer cook time. Serve with Red Wine–Peppercorn Pan Sauce (recipe follows), if desired; make the sauce while the steak rests and spoon over steak immediately after making.

- 2 **(1-pound) boneless strip steaks, 1 to 1½ inches thick, trimmed**
- 7 **tablespoons vegetable oil, divided**

1. Using sous vide circulator, bring water to 130°F in 7-quart container. Season steaks with salt and pepper. Place steaks and ¼ cup oil in 1-gallon zipper-lock freezer bag and toss to coat. Arrange steaks in single layer and seal bag, pressing out as much air as possible. Gently lower bag into prepared water bath until steaks are fully submerged, and then clip top corner of bag to side of water bath container, allowing remaining air bubbles to rise to top of bag. Reopen 1 corner of zipper, release remaining air bubbles, and reseal bag. Cover and cook for at least 1½ hours or up to 3 hours.

3. Transfer steaks to paper towel–lined plate and let rest for 5 to 10 minutes. Pat steaks dry with paper towels. Heat remaining 3 tablespoons oil in 12-inch skillet over medium-high heat until just smoking. Sear steaks until well browned, about 1 minute per side. Transfer to cutting board and slice ½ inch thick. Serve.

Red Wine–Peppercorn Pan Sauce

Makes about ½ cup; serves 4
Note that this recipe is meant to be started after you have seared the steaks. Use a good quality medium-bodied wine, such as a Côtes du Rhône or Pinot Noir, for this sauce.

       Vegetable oil, if needed
    1 large shallot, minced
    ½ cup dry red wine
    ¾ cup chicken broth
    2 teaspoons packed brown sugar
    3 tablespoons unsalted butter, cut into 3 pieces and chilled
    1 teaspoon coarsely ground pepper
    ¼ teaspoon balsamic vinegar

1. Pour off all but 1 tablespoon fat from skillet used to sear steak. (If necessary, add oil to equal 1 tablespoon.) Add shallot and cook over medium heat until softened, 1 to 2 minutes. Stir in wine, scraping up any browned bits. Bring to simmer and cook until wine is reduced to glaze, about 3 minutes.

2. Stir in broth and sugar and simmer until reduced to ⅓ cup, 4 to 6 minutes. Off heat, whisk in butter, 1 piece at a time, until melted and sauce is thickened and glossy. Whisk in pepper, vinegar, and any accumulated meat juices. Season with salt to taste.

PRESSURE-COOKER BEEF PHO

Serves 4 to 6 | boneless strip steak

WHY THIS RECIPE WORKS The most important element of this Vietnamese soup is its fragrant, beefy broth. The electric pressure cooker is a perfect vessel for extracting flavor from beef bones to make one. For a savory boost, we browned the bones in the microwave before cooking them and added flavorful trimmings from our steak to the cooker. To give the broth its signature clear appearance, we strained and defatted it after cooking. The rest of the soup components were simple. We soaked rice noodles and then finished cooking them right in the broth. And we thinly sliced tender strip steak and ladled the hot broth over the slices, which cooked them just enough. Look for noodles that are about ⅛ inch wide; these are often labeled "small." Don't use Thai Kitchen Stir-Fry Rice Noodles; they are too thick and don't adequately soak up the broth.

    3 pounds beef bones
    2 onions, quartered through root end
    ¼ cup fish sauce, plus extra for serving
    1 (4-inch) piece ginger, peeled and sliced into ⅛-inch-thick rounds
    1 cinnamon stick
    6 star anise pods
    6 whole cloves
    1 tablespoon table salt
    1 teaspoon black peppercorns
    1 (1-pound) boneless strip steak, 1½ to 1¾ inches thick, trimmed and halved crosswise, trimmings reserved
 14–16 ounces (⅛-inch-wide) rice noodles
    ⅓ cup chopped fresh cilantro
    3 scallions, sliced thin (optional)
       Bean sprouts
       Fresh Thai or Italian basil sprigs
       Lime wedges
       Hoisin sauce
       Sriracha sauce

1. Arrange beef bones on paper towel–lined plate and microwave (in batches, if microwave is small) until well browned, 8 to 10 minutes. Add bones and 6 onion quarters to electric pressure cooker. Slice remaining 2 onion quarters as thin as possible and set aside for serving. Add 2 quarts water, fish sauce, ginger, cinnamon stick, star anise, cloves, salt, peppercorns, and reserved steak trimmings to pressure cooker.

2. Lock lid in place and close pressure release valve. Select high pressure cook function and cook for 1½ hours. Turn off pressure cooker and let pressure release naturally for 15 minutes. Quick-release any remaining pressure, then carefully remove lid, allowing steam to escape away from you.

3. Meanwhile, place steak on large plate and freeze until very firm, 35 to 45 minutes. Once firm, cut against grain into ⅛-inch-thick slices. Return steak to plate and refrigerate until needed.

4. Place noodles in large container and cover with hot tap water. Soak until noodles are pliable, 10 to 15 minutes; drain noodles.

5. Bring broth to boil using highest sauté or browning function. Add noodles and cook until softened, about 90 seconds. Turn off pressure cooker. Using tongs, divide noodles between individual serving bowls. Divide steak among bowls, shingling slices on top of noodles. Pile reserved onion slices on top of steak slices and sprinkle with cilantro and scallions, if using. Ladle hot broth into each bowl. Serve immediately, passing bean sprouts, basil sprigs, lime wedges, hoisin, sriracha, and extra fish sauce separately.

Pressure-Cooker Beef Pho

THICK-CUT PORTERHOUSE STEAKS

Serves 6 to 8 | porterhouse steak

WHY THIS RECIPE WORKS Mammoth porterhouse steaks make a spectacular centerpiece. But mammoth isn't easy to cook and unevenly cooked steaks aren't all that spectacular. To help our porterhouse steaks stay pink, juicy, and tender throughout, we arranged the steaks on a wire rack set in a rimmed baking sheet and then roasted them in a low, 275-degree oven before searing them to gradually bring them up to temperature. Because the steaks were elevated on the rack, hot air circulated all around them and the steaks cooked more evenly from all sides. This method also dried the steaks' exterior so that the final sear in a ripping-hot pan happened fast and furiously, further reducing the chance of overcooking. You can substitute a T-bone steak.

- 2 (2½- to 3-pound) porterhouse steaks, 2 inches thick, trimmed
- 3 tablespoons vegetable oil

1. Adjust oven rack to middle position and heat oven to 275 degrees. Set wire rack in aluminum foil–lined rimmed baking sheet. Pat steaks dry with paper towels and season liberally with kosher salt and pepper. Place steaks side by side on prepared rack with tenderloins facing center, about 1 inch apart. Transfer steaks to oven. Cook until thermometer inserted sideways 3 inches from tip of strip side of steak registers 115 to 120 degrees (for medium-rare), 1 hour 10 minutes to 1½ hours, rotating sheet halfway through cooking.

2. Pat steaks dry with paper towels. Heat oil in 12-inch skillet over high heat until just smoking. Place 1 steak in skillet and sear until well browned, about 2 minutes per side, lifting occasionally to redistribute oil. Using tongs, stand steak upright to sear edges, 1 to 2 minutes. Return steak to wire rack, tent with foil, and repeat with remaining steak. Let steaks rest for 10 minutes.

3. Transfer steaks to carving board. Carve strip steaks and tenderloins from bones. Place T-bone on platter. Slice steaks thin against grain, then reassemble sliced steaks on both sides of bones. Season with salt and pepper to taste. Serve.

GRILLED THICK-CUT PORTERHOUSE STEAKS

Serves 6 to 8 | porterhouse steak

WHY THIS RECIPE WORKS Grilling thick-cut porterhouse steaks doesn't have to be intimidating. Setting up a half-grill fire with a cooler side and a hotter side allowed us to control the amount of crusty exterior and achieve a rosy interior for

Grilled Thick-Cut Porterhouse Steaks

these steaks. We grilled the steaks directly over the coals to char them before moving them to the cooler side of the grill to finish. To protect the lean tenderloin portion, we positioned the steaks with the tenderloins facing the cooler side of the grill. The T-shaped bone in the middle acted as a heat shield, further protecting the tenderloins. Finally, we got the most accurate temperature reading near the tapered tip of the strip portion. A drizzle of melted butter added restrained elegance. Flare-ups may occur when grilling over charcoal. If the flames become constant, slide the steaks to the cooler side of the grill until the flames die down. You can substitute a T-bone steak.

- 2 (2½- to 3-pound) porterhouse steaks, 2 inches thick, fat trimmed to ¼ inch
- 4¼ teaspoons kosher salt, divided
- 4 teaspoons extra-virgin olive oil (if using gas)
- 2 teaspoons pepper
- 3 tablespoons unsalted butter, melted

1. Pat steaks dry with paper towels and sprinkle each side of each steak with 1 teaspoon salt. Transfer steaks to large plate and refrigerate, uncovered, for at least 1 hour or up to 24 hours.

2a. For a charcoal grill: Open bottom vent completely. Light large chimney starter filled with charcoal briquettes (6 quarts). When top coals are partially covered with ash, pour evenly over half of grill. Set cooking grate in place, cover, and open lid vent completely. Heat grill until hot, about 5 minutes.

2b. For a gas grill: Turn all burners to high, cover, and heat grill until hot, about 15 minutes. Leave primary burner on high and turn off other burner(s). (Adjust primary burner [or, if using 3-burner grill, primary burner and second burner] as needed to maintain grill temperature of 450 degrees.)

3. Pat steaks dry with paper towels. If using gas, brush each side of each steak with 1 teaspoon oil. Sprinkle each side of each steak with ½ teaspoon pepper.

4. Clean and oil cooking grate. Place steaks on hotter side of grill, with tenderloins facing cooler side. Cook (covered if using gas) until evenly charred on first side, 6 to 8 minutes. Flip steaks and position so tenderloins are still facing cooler side of grill. Continue to cook (covered if using gas) until evenly charred on second side, 6 to 8 minutes longer.

5. Flip steaks and transfer to cooler side of grill, with bone side facing fire. Cover and cook until thermometer inserted 3 inches from tip of strip side of steak registers 115 to 120 degrees (for medium-rare), 8 to 12 minutes, flipping halfway through cooking. Transfer steaks to wire rack set in rimmed baking sheet, tent with aluminum foil, and let rest for 10 minutes.

6. Stir remaining ¼ teaspoon salt into melted butter. Transfer steaks to carving board. Carve strips and tenderloins from bones. Place T-bone on platter. Slice steaks thin against grain, then reassemble sliced steaks around bones. Drizzle with melted butter and season with salt and pepper to taste. Serve.

BISTECCA ALLA FIORENTINA

Serves 6 to 8 | porterhouse steak

WHY THIS RECIPE WORKS Simple preparation is a hallmark of Tuscan cooking. Take, for example, Tuscany's famous bistecca alla Fiorentina, a thick-cut porterhouse steak usually sourced from the Chianina cows of Valdichiana, grilled to perfection, and drizzled with olive oil and served with lemon. Our established method for grilling porterhouses (see Grilled Thick-Cut Porterhouse Steaks) makes domestic steaks taste just as good. The oil is almost as important as the steak here; we drizzled on the oil after slicing—just before serving—to preserve its delicate flavors. A squeeze of lemon juice at the table cut through the richness. Flare-ups may occur when grilling over charcoal. If the flames become constant, slide the steaks to the cooler side of the grill until the flames die down. You can substitute a T-bone steak.

2 (2½- to 3-pound) porterhouse steaks, 2 inches thick, fat trimmed to ¼ inch
4 teaspoons kosher salt
4 teaspoons extra-virgin olive oil (if using gas), plus extra for drizzling
2 teaspoons pepper
Lemon wedges

1. Pat steaks dry with paper towels and sprinkle each side of each steak with 1 teaspoon salt. Transfer steaks to large plate and refrigerate, uncovered, for at least 1 hour or up to 24 hours.

2a. For a charcoal grill: Open bottom vent completely. Light large chimney starter filled with charcoal briquettes (6 quarts). When top coals are partially covered with ash, pour evenly over half of grill. Set cooking grate in place, cover, and open lid vent completely. Heat grill until hot, about 5 minutes.

2b. For a gas grill: Turn all burners to high, cover, and heat grill until hot, about 15 minutes. Leave primary burner on high and turn off other burner(s). (Adjust primary burner [or, if using 3-burner grill, primary burner and second burner] as needed to maintain grill temperature of 450 degrees.)

3. Pat steaks dry with paper towels. If using gas, brush each side of each steak with 1 teaspoon oil. Sprinkle each side of each steak with ½ teaspoon pepper.

4. Clean and oil cooking grate. Place steaks on hotter side of grill, with tenderloins facing cooler side. Cook (covered if using gas) until evenly charred on first side, 6 to 8 minutes. Flip steaks and position so tenderloins are still facing cooler side of grill. Continue to cook (covered if using gas) until evenly charred on second side, 6 to 8 minutes.

5. Flip steaks and transfer to cooler side of grill, with bone side facing hotter side. Cover and cook until thermometer inserted 3 inches from tip of strip side of steak registers 115 to 120 degrees (for medium-rare), 8 to 12 minutes, flipping steaks halfway through cooking. Transfer steaks to wire rack set in rimmed baking sheet, tent with aluminum foil, and let rest for 10 to 15 minutes.

6. Transfer steaks to carving board. Carve strips and tenderloins from bones. Place T-bone on platter. Slice steaks thin against grain, then reassemble sliced steaks around bones. Drizzle with extra olive oil and season with salt and pepper to taste. Serve with lemon wedges.

VARIATION

Grilled Steaks with Garlic Essence
Rub 1 halved garlic clove over bone and meat on each side of steaks before seasoning with salt and pepper in step 1.

TENDERLOIN

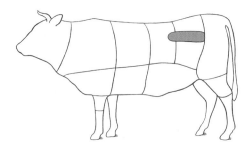

BEEF TENDERLOIN, WITH ITS SUPERLATIVELY tender texture, comes with a host of luxe associations: higher price tags, holiday traditions, fancy preparations (think Beef Wellington [see page 102]). We're still in loin territory here: Running through the short loin and the sirloin, located just under the cow's spine, the tenderloin comes by its namesake texture because the muscle is essentially immobile. Its prized status in the world of beef cuts is a bit curious: Prime rib (see page 61), after all, is often served in juicy, bone-in slabs that are tender but also decadently beefy. A short loin roast (see page 77) is like a strip steak in roast form. But though tenderloin's texture, barely requiring a knife to cut through, is truly unrivaled by any other part of the cow, this cut is decidedly low on flavor. Chalk up its appeal to the high value Americans place on tenderness. It also makes the perfect canvas for a number of flavors. And we can up its richness with butters, sauces, and other goodies. Another reason for tenderloin attraction: its even cylindrical shape, more even and cylindrical if you choose the center cut (see page 96). The tenderloin can be cut into smaller roasts and steaks.

Whole Beef Tenderloin

Cost: ■■□□ Flavor: ■■□□

Best cooking methods: roast, grill roast, sous vide
Texture: very tender and fine
Alternative names: whole filet, full tenderloin roast, filet mignon roast

You can buy the whole tenderloin muscle, a piece of beef that should weigh around 5 pounds and serve 12 to 16 people. Unpeeled tenderloins come with a thick layer of exterior fat still attached, which should be removed. Peeled roasts have scattered patches of fat that need not be removed (in the case of lean tenderloin, that fat can help the cause). All whole tenderloin roasts sport silverskin, a shiny strip of connective tissue that doesn't break down during cooking and that needs to be removed, ideally with a flexible boning knife (see page 17). (You'll see this again in pork tenderloin on page 250.) Tenderloin is incredibly lean with little intramuscular fat, so it dries out easily if overcooked. The supremely fine texture—its most majestic quality—makes a tenderloin very easy to carve. A whole tenderloin isn't completely even: The portion at the front of the short loin is tapered, thin, and pointy; the portion at the rear, nearest the sirloin, is fatter. We typically tuck the thin tail under the roast to even out the shape and prevent overcooking of that small portion.

Trimming the Tenderloin

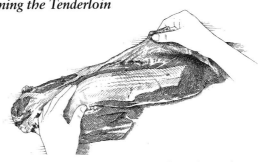

1. Pull away outer layer of fat to expose fatty chain of meat.

2. Pull chain of fat away from roast, cut it off, and discard chain.

3. Scrape silverskin at creases in thick end to expose lobes.

4. Trim silverskin by slicing under it and cutting upward. Remove remaining silverskin in creases at thick end.

5. Turn tenderloin over and remove fat from underside.

Tying the Tenderloin

1. Tuck tail end of tenderloin 2 to 4 inches under roast to create more even shape.

2. Tie with kitchen twine to secure tail end. Tie remainder of tenderloin at 1-inch intervals.

PUNCHING UP TENDERLOIN

Beef tenderloin is so desirable because of its texture but if you're into big, beefy flavor, it might not do it for you. That's why you'll see tenderloin used in rich applications—topped with mushrooms and wrapped in pastry or served with compound butter, for example. Here are some ways we boost our beef's flavor.

Sauce It Up: Herb sauces brighten all kinds of beef but tenderloin is particularly nice with something richer. Eggy, almost-custardy, and punchy hollandaise adds richness by the spoonful to recipes like Peppercorn-Crusted Beef Tenderloin (page 98). A creamy (and traditional) horseradish sauce gives spice along with richness (see page 22).

Give It a Crust: Coating tenderloin with peppercorns (in any color of the rainbow; see page 98) or encapsulating it in a crumb crust (see page 100) provides bonus flavor—plus appealing contrasting texture.

Wrap It Up: Pastry-covered Beef Wellington (page 102) is a holiday classic, or you can wrap filets mignons in bacon for smoky flavor and extra fat (see page 107).

Stuff It: If you butterfly a tenderloin you can stuff it with a flavorful filling like caramelized onions (see page 101) and roll it up for extra flavor throughout the roast.

Grill It: This one's a no-brainer: A kiss of grill fire will make anything taste more robust.

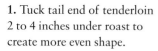

Center-Cut Beef Tenderloin Roast

Cost: ◾◾◻◻ **Flavor:** ◾◻◻◻
Best cooking methods: roast, grill roast, sous vide
Texture: ultrabuttery and the most tender roast
Alternative names: Châteaubriand

Beef tenderloin is an agreeable cylindrical cut, but if working with it is like driving a Mercedes, working with a center cut, often called the Châteaubriand, is like having a personal driver. This is the most tender part of the most tender cut and it's completely even in shape and thickness from end to end (and therefore even in cooking) and trimmed clean. If we don't need to feed a crowd (a center cut weighs anywhere from 2 to 4 pounds, as opposed to 6 pounds for the whole tenderloin), it's our top tenderloin.

Filet Mignon

Cost: ◾◾◾◻ **Flavor:** ◾◻◻◻
Best cooking methods: pan sear, grill, sous vide
Texture: ultrabuttery and the most tender steak
Alternative names: Tenderloin steak, filet de boeuf

When the tenderloin is cut into steaks, it's very expensive, as Americans prize tenderness in their steaks above all else. Filets are cut from the narrow end of the tenderloin (below the head) and are 1 to 2 inches thick. They're buttery-smooth and very tender, and lean, with very mild beef flavor. Filets mignons are very low in marbling, so when shopping, if you notice filets with more marbling remember that's a desirable feature and purchase accordingly.

HIGH-TICKET TIPS

Sirloin steak tips (cut from flap meat; see page 110) are a relatively affordable cut, but tenderloin tips—called tournedos, or sometimes tenderloin tails—are "steak tips" for when money isn't an object. Think of them as little filets mignons, but they're cut from the most narrow part of the tapered end. At about 1 inch across and very nicely trimmed, they can be used for the most tender steak tips, kebabs, or stir-fry you've ever had.

Roast Beef Tenderloin

PEPPERCORN-CRUSTED BEEF TENDERLOIN

Serves 4 to 6 | whole beef tenderloin

WHY THIS RECIPE WORKS This most tender centerpiece roast is luxurious to eat but benefits from something special to bolster its meek flavor. A peppercorn crust is impressive and does just the trick. And we offer variations with more than just the standard black peppercorns (pungent white; floral, fruity pink; briny green). For a tender, rosy roast with a spicy, yet not harsh-tasting, crust that didn't fall off, we relied on a few tricks. Rubbing the raw tenderloin with an abrasive mixture of kosher salt, sugar, and baking soda transformed its surface into a magnet for the pepper crust. To tame the heat of the pepper crust, we simmered cracked peppercorns in oil and then strained them from the oil. To replace some of the subtler flavor notes we had simmered away, we added some orange zest and nutmeg to the mix. With the crust in place, we gently roasted the tenderloin at 300 degrees until it was perfectly rosy on the interior. Sift the cracked peppercorns through a fine-mesh strainer. We like to serve the roast with Hollandaise Sauce (page 22).

1½ tablespoons kosher salt
1½ teaspoons sugar
¼ teaspoon baking soda
½ cup plus 1 tablespoon extra-virgin olive oil
½ cup coarsely cracked black peppercorns
1 tablespoon grated orange zest
½ teaspoon ground nutmeg
1 (6-pound) whole beef tenderloin, trimmed

1. Adjust oven rack to middle position and heat oven to 300 degrees. Set wire rack in rimmed baking sheet. Combine salt, sugar, and baking soda in bowl; set aside. Heat 6 table-spoons oil and peppercorns in small saucepan over low heat until faint bubbles appear. Cook at bare simmer, swirling sauce-pan occasionally, until pepper is fragrant, 7 to 10 minutes. Strain peppercorn mixture through fine-mesh strainer and discard oil. Mix peppercorns with orange zest, nutmeg, and remaining 3 tablespoons oil.

2. Set tenderloin on sheet of plastic wrap. Sprinkle salt mixture evenly over surface of tenderloin and rub into tenderloin until surface is tacky. Tuck tail end of tenderloin under about 6 inches to create more even shape. Rub top and sides of tenderloin with peppercorn mixture, pressing to make sure peppercorns adhere. Spray three 12-inch lengths of kitchen twine with vegetable oil spray; tie head of tenderloin crosswise at 2-inch intervals to maintain even shape.

3. Transfer tenderloin to prepared wire rack, keeping tail end tucked under. Roast until thickest part of meat registers about 120 to 125 degrees (for medium-rare) (thinner parts will be

slightly more done), 1 hour to 1 hour 10 minutes. Transfer to carving board and let rest for 30 minutes. Remove twine from roast. Slice meat ½ inch thick. Serve.

VARIATIONS

Green Peppercorn–Crusted Beef Tenderloin
Substitute dried green peppercorns for black peppercorns.

Pink Peppercorn–Crusted Beef Tenderloin
Substitute pink peppercorns for black peppercorns; reduce cook-ing time to 3 to 5 minutes in step 1.

White Peppercorn–Crusted Beef Tenderloin
Substitute white peppercorns for black peppercorns.

ROAST BEEF TENDERLOIN

Serves 4 | center-cut beef tenderloin roast

WHY THIS RECIPE WORKS A simple preparation lets center-cut beef tenderloin's supreme tenderness shine. We tied the roast at even intervals to ensure even cooking and then we lavished it with softened butter to boost its mild flavor. To cook the neat piece of meat, we used a reverse-sear method, first roasting the meat and then finishing it on the stovetop. A fairly low 300-degree oven minimized the temperature differential between the exterior and interior, allowing for gentle, even cooking. This approach also dried out the meat's surface, so it seared very quickly in the skillet—and had no chance to overcook. We slathered the cooked roast with a compound butter (yes, more butter) with the classic flavors of shallots and herbs as it rested, which instantly created a rich sauce.

BEEF
1 (2-pound) center-cut beef tenderloin roast, trimmed and tied at 1½-inch intervals
2 teaspoons kosher salt
1 teaspoon pepper
2 tablespoons unsalted butter, softened
1 tablespoon vegetable oil

SHALLOT AND PARSLEY BUTTER
4 tablespoons unsalted butter, softened
½ shallot, minced
1 tablespoon minced fresh parsley
1 garlic clove, minced
¼ teaspoon table salt
¼ teaspoon pepper

1. **For the beef:** Sprinkle roast evenly with salt, cover loosely with plastic wrap, and let stand at room temperature for 1 hour. Adjust oven rack to middle position and heat oven to 300 degrees.

TUTORIAL
Peppercorn-Crusted Beef Tenderloin

Pick your peppercorn variety, tame its bite, and then make it stick to your tenderloin roast by following our steps.

1. Heat oil and peppercorns in small saucepan over low heat until faint bubbles appear. Cook at bare simmer until pepper is fragrant, 7 to 10 minutes. Strain peppercorns and mix with orange zest, nutmeg, and remaining 3 tablespoons oil.

2. Set tenderloin on sheet of plastic wrap. Sprinkle salt mixture evenly over surface of tenderloin and rub into tenderloin until surface is tacky.

3. Tuck tail end of tenderloin under about 6 inches to create more even shape.

4. Rub top and sides of tenderloin with peppercorn mixture, pressing to make sure peppercorns adhere.

5. Spray three 12-inch lengths of kitchen twine with vegetable oil spray; tie head of tenderloin crosswise at 2-inch intervals to maintain even shape.

6. Roast until thickest part of meat registers about 120 degrees (for rare) or about 125 degrees (for medium-rare), 1 hour to 1 hour 10 minutes.

2. For the shallot and parsley butter: Meanwhile, combine all ingredients in bowl and let rest to blend flavors, about 10 minutes. Wrap in plastic wrap, roll into log, and refrigerate until serving.

3. Pat roast dry with paper towels. Sprinkle roast evenly with pepper and spread softened butter evenly over surface. Transfer roast to wire rack set in rimmed baking sheet. Roast until beef registers 120 to 125 degrees (for medium-rare), 40 to 55 minutes, flipping roast halfway through roasting.

4. Heat oil in 12-inch skillet over medium-high heat until just smoking. Brown roast well on all sides, about 8 minutes. Transfer roast to carving board and spread 2 tablespoons flavored butter evenly over top of roast; let rest for 30 minutes. Remove twine from roast. Slice meat ½ inch thick. Serve, passing remaining flavored butter separately.

HORSERADISH-CRUSTED BEEF TENDERLOIN

Serves 6 | center-cut beef tenderloin roast

WHY THIS RECIPE WORKS Spicy, pungent horseradish is a classic pairing for mild beef tenderloin, often introduced to the roast in the form of a crust. To give our crust crunch in addition to flavor, we bound prepared horseradish with bread crumbs as well as potato sticks, which we quickly cooked to a crisp ourselves. So that such a hefty crust would stay put, we added gelatin. This was the best adhesive, as meat and gelatin are made of linear proteins that form tight bonds with each other so the coating stayed firmly on the meat. To prevent the crisp crust from turning soggy, we let the meat rest after searing it so that its juices could drain off before we coated the roast. We then coated only the top and sides of the tenderloin with the bread-crumb coating, leaving an "opening" on the bottom for any additional juices to escape. Add the gelatin to the horseradish paste at the last moment or the mixture will become unspreadable.

ROAST
- 1 (2-pound) center-cut beef tenderloin roast, trimmed
- 1 tablespoon plus ¼ teaspoon kosher salt, divided
- 3 tablespoons panko bread crumbs
- 1 cup plus 2 teaspoons vegetable oil, divided
- 1¼ teaspoons pepper
- 1 small russet potato (about 6 ounces), peeled and grated
- ¼ cup prepared horseradish, drained, divided
- 1½ teaspoons mayonnaise
- 1½ teaspoons Dijon mustard
- ½ teaspoon unflavored gelatin
- 1 small shallot, minced

- 2 garlic cloves, minced
- 2 tablespoons minced fresh parsley
- ½ teaspoon minced fresh thyme

HORSERADISH CREAM SAUCE
- ½ cup heavy cream
- ½ cup prepared horseradish
- 1 teaspoon table salt
- ⅛ teaspoon pepper

1. For the roast: Sprinkle roast with 1 tablespoon salt, cover with plastic wrap, and let sit at room temperature for 1 hour or refrigerate for up to 24 hours. (If refrigerating, let roast sit at room temperature for 1 hour before cooking.)

2. Adjust oven rack to middle position and heat oven to 400 degrees. Combine panko, 2 teaspoons oil, ¼ teaspoon pepper, and remaining ¼ teaspoon salt in 12-inch nonstick skillet. Cook over medium heat, stirring frequently, until deep golden brown, 3 to 5 minutes. Transfer to rimmed baking sheet and let cool to room temperature, about 15 minutes.

3. Wipe skillet clean with paper towels. Rinse grated potato in colander under cold water, then squeeze dry in kitchen towel. Transfer potato and remaining 1 cup oil to now-empty skillet. Cook over high heat, stirring frequently, until potato is golden brown and crisp, 6 to 8 minutes.

4. Using slotted spoon, transfer potato to paper towel–lined plate and season lightly with salt. Reserve 1 tablespoon oil from skillet and discard remainder. Let potato cool for 5 minutes, then crush until coarsely ground. Transfer ground potato to sheet with panko mixture and toss to combine. (Panko-potato mixture can be stored at room temperature for up to 1 day.)

5. Pat roast dry with paper towels and sprinkle with remaining 1 teaspoon pepper. Heat reserved 1 tablespoon oil in again-empty skillet over medium-high heat until just smoking. Brown roast on all sides, 8 to 10 minutes. Transfer to wire rack set in second rimmed baking sheet and let rest for 10 minutes.

6. Just before coating tenderloin, combine 2 tablespoons horseradish, mayonnaise, mustard, and gelatin in small bowl. Toss bread crumb–potato mixture with shallot, garlic, parsley, thyme, and remaining 2 tablespoons horseradish. Spread horseradish-mayonnaise paste on top and sides of roast, leaving bottom and ends bare. Roll coated sides of roast in bread-crumb mixture, pressing gently so crumbs adhere in even layer that just covers horseradish paste; pat off any excess.

7. Return tenderloin to rack and roast until it registers 120 to 125 degrees (for medium-rare), 25 to 30 minutes.

Roast Beef Tenderloin with Mushroom and Caramelized Onion Stuffing

with some Madeira. The roast can be stuffed, rolled, tied, and refrigerated up to 24 hours in advance; make sure to let it come to room temperature before putting it into the oven. This recipe can be doubled to make two roasts. Sear the roasts one after the other, cleaning the pan and adding new oil after searing the first roast. Both pieces of meat can be roasted on the same rack.

STUFFING

- 8 ounces cremini mushrooms, trimmed and broken into rough pieces
- 1 tablespoon unsalted butter
- 2 teaspoons extra-virgin olive oil
- 1 onion, halved and sliced ¼ inch thick
- ½ teaspoon kosher salt
- ⅛ teaspoon pepper
- 1 garlic clove, minced
- ½ cup Madeira or sweet Marsala wine

ROAST

- 1 (2- to 3-pound) center-cut beef tenderloin roast, trimmed
- ½ cup baby spinach
- 3 tablespoons extra-virgin olive oil, divided
- 1½ teaspoons kosher salt
- 1½ teaspoons pepper

HERB BUTTER

- 4 tablespoons unsalted butter, softened
- 1 tablespoon whole-grain mustard
- 1 tablespoon chopped fresh parsley
- 1 garlic clove, minced
- ¾ teaspoon chopped fresh thyme
- ¼ teaspoon kosher salt
- ⅛ teaspoon pepper

8. **For the horseradish cream sauce:** Meanwhile, whisk cream in medium bowl until thickened but not yet holding soft peaks, 1 to 2 minutes. Gently fold in horseradish, salt, and pepper. Cover and refrigerate for at least 30 minutes or up to 1 hour.

9. Transfer roast to carving board and let rest for 20 minutes. Slice meat ½ inch thick and serve with sauce.

ROAST BEEF TENDERLOIN WITH MUSHROOM AND CARAMELIZED ONION STUFFING

Serves 4 to 6 | center-cut beef tenderloin roast

WHY THIS RECIPE WORKS While a center-cut beef tenderloin is special on its own, a rich stuffing is an ultraluxe way to add flavor on special occasions. We wanted something savory to amp up the meatiness and a little sweetness to offset the savor. We started by butterflying a center-cut tenderloin. This cut's cylindrical shape made it easy to stuff and encouraged even cooking. To achieve an intensely flavored filling without having to pack in a lot of stuffing, we turned to woodsy cremini mushrooms and caramelized onions, which we cooked down

1. **For the stuffing:** Pulse mushrooms in food processor until coarsely chopped, about 6 pulses. Heat butter and oil in 12-inch nonstick skillet over medium-high heat until butter is melted. Add onion, salt, and pepper; cook, stirring occasionally, until onion is softened, about 5 minutes. Add mushrooms and cook, stirring occasionally, until all moisture has evaporated, 5 to 7 minutes. Reduce heat to medium and continue to cook, stirring frequently, until vegetables are deeply browned and sticky, about 10 minutes. Stir in garlic and cook until fragrant, 30 seconds. Stir in Madeira, scraping bottom of skillet to loosen any browned bits, and cook until liquid has evaporated, 2 to 3 minutes. Transfer mushroom mixture to plate and let cool completely.

2. **For the roast:** Position roast fat side up. Insert knife one-third of way up from bottom of roast along 1 long side and cut horizontally, stopping ½ inch before edge. Open up flap. Keeping

knife parallel to cutting board, cut through thicker portion of roast about ½ inch from bottom of roast, keeping knife level with first cut and stopping about ½ inch before edge. Open up this flap. If uneven, cover with plastic wrap and use meat pounder to even out. Season cut side of roast with salt and pepper. Spread cooled mushroom mixture over interior of roast, leaving ½-inch border on all sides; lay spinach on top of stuffing. Roll roast lengthwise and tie at 1½-inch intervals with kitchen twine.

3. Stir 1 tablespoon oil, salt, and pepper together in small bowl. Rub roast with oil mixture and let stand at room temperature for at least 1 hour or up to 2 hours.

4. Adjust oven rack to middle position and heat oven to 450 degrees. Heat remaining 2 tablespoons oil in 12-inch skillet over medium-high heat until just smoking. Brown roast well on all sides, 8 to 10 minutes. Transfer to wire rack set in rimmed baking sheet and place in oven. Roast until beef registers 120 to 125 degrees (for medium-rare), 20 to 22 minutes.

5. For the herb butter: Meanwhile, combine all ingredients in bowl. Transfer roast to carving board; spread half of butter evenly over top of roast and let rest for 20 minutes. Remove twine from roast. Slice meat ½ inch thick. Serve with remaining butter.

BEEF WELLINGTON

Serves 8 to 10 | center-cut beef tenderloin roast

WHY THIS RECIPE WORKS It's no secret: When it comes to meat dishes, beef Wellington, a substantial piece of tenderloin swathed in fine pâté and mushroom duxelles and bundled in a cloak of flaky, golden puff pastry is a definite project. Just reading the description should tell you that it's worth it, but we wanted to cut the fuss as much as possible. First task to eliminate: making the pâté. Homemade versions can be grainy, while store-bought pâté was smooth and luxurious. Making a rich, moist duxelles—chopped mushrooms sautéed with butter and shallots and cooked down into an intense, nubby hash—took less than 15 minutes with the help of the food processor. Moisture is the enemy of soggy pastry so we took serious (but easy) measures to mitigate it. First, we dry-aged the tenderloin in the refrigerator for two days (for more information on dry aging, see page 33)—hands-off work. Then we seared the tenderloin before wrapping it in store-bought puff pastry. Searing also ensured that the tenderloin cooked properly in the time the pastry became beautifully golden. Be sure to use a smooth-textured pâté, not a coarse country pâté.

DRY-AGED TENDERLOIN
1 (3- to 4-pound) center-cut beef tenderloin roast, about 12 inches long and 4 inches in diameter, trimmed

WELLINGTON
3 tablespoons extra-virgin olive oil
2 teaspoons table salt
2 teaspoons pepper
5 ounces fine pâté, mashed until smooth
1 pound puff pastry
1 large egg
1 recipe Duxelles (recipe follows)

1. **For the dry-aged tenderloin:** Place roast on wire rack set in rimmed baking sheet and refrigerate, uncovered, for 48 hours.

2. **For the Wellington:** Rub tenderloin with 2 tablespoons oil, then sprinkle with salt and pepper and lightly rub into meat. Heat remaining 1 tablespoon oil in 12-inch heavy-bottomed skillet over high heat until smoking.

3. Set tenderloin in skillet, curving it to fit if necessary, and sear on first side, without moving it, until well browned, about 1 minute, pressing down on meat so that bottom of roast makes full contact with pan. Using tongs, rotate tenderloin and brown on all sides, about 1 minute per side. Remove hot tenderloin from skillet, wrap tightly in plastic wrap, and refrigerate for at least 4 hours or up to 24 hours.

4. Unwrap tenderloin. Using small spatula, spread pâté over top and sides of tenderloin; set aside.

5. Dust large sheet of parchment paper with flour. Unwrap puff pastry and place on parchment; dust puff pastry lightly with flour and cover with second large sheet of parchment. Roll into 15 by 12-inch rectangle, mending cracks as you roll. Remove top sheet of parchment and, using sharp knife, trim two 1-inch bands off long side to form 15 by 10-inch rectangle; refrigerate bands on parchment-lined plate. (If dough is soft and sticky or tears easily, slide parchment with pastry onto baking sheet and freeze until firm, about 10 minutes.)

6. Line rimmed baking sheet with parchment paper and spray lightly with vegetable oil spray; set aside. Beat egg with 1 tablespoon water; set aside.

7. Remove plastic from duxelles. Invert duxelles onto puff pastry; peel off parchment. Place tenderloin, pâté side down, on duxelles-covered dough. Brush edges of dough lightly with egg wash. Encase tenderloin in dough, wrapping tightly. (There should be about 1-inch overlap forming seam; if overlap is excessive, trim

Beef Wellington

with scissors.) Carefully invert dough-wrapped tenderloin onto prepared sheet and brush dough lightly with egg wash; refrigerate, uncovered, for 30 minutes.

8. Adjust oven rack to lowest position and heat oven to 450 degrees. Bake Wellington until light golden brown, about 15 minutes, then arrange dough bands into ribbons or leaves on top. Continue to bake until Wellington is deep golden brown and thermometer inserted in center registers 120 degrees (for medium-rare), 15 to 20 minutes. Let stand for 10 minutes, transfer to carving board, and slice ½ inch thick. Serve.

Duxelles
Makes about 1 cup
The mushrooms should not be ground so fine as to release moisture. Madeira is a fortified wine made from both red and white grapes and additional alcohol that enhances the mushrooms' natural umami flavor.

- 1 pound white mushrooms, trimmed and quartered
- 3 tablespoons unsalted butter
- 2 large shallots, minced
- 2 tablespoons heavy cream
- 1 teaspoon Madeira (optional)
- 1 teaspoon table salt
- ½ teaspoon pepper
- 1 tablespoon minced fresh thyme

1. Process half of mushrooms in food processor until chopped uniformly fine, about 10 pulses, scraping down sides of bowl after 5 pulses. Transfer chopped mushrooms to medium bowl and repeat with remaining mushrooms.

2. Melt butter in 12-inch skillet over medium-low heat. Add shallots and cook, stirring frequently, until softened, 3 to 5 minutes.

3. Stir in mushrooms, increase heat to medium-high, and cook, stirring frequently, until most of liquid has evaporated, 7 to 10 minutes. Add cream; Madeira, if using; salt; and pepper and cook until mixture is dry, about 3 minutes. Off heat, stir in thyme.

4. Line rimmed baking sheet with parchment paper; turn out duxelles onto sheet and, using rubber spatula, spread into 10 by 8-inch rectangle of even thickness. Cover duxelles with plastic wrap and refrigerate until completely cold, at least 2 hours or up to 24 hours.

GRILL-ROASTED BEEF TENDERLOIN

Serves 6 | center-cut beef tenderloin roast
WHY THIS RECIPE WORKS Beef tenderloin isn't just for winter holidays and gatherings; it can make fancy summer fare, too. But it doesn't taste as smoky as other beef cuts on the grill. That's because much of the signature grilled flavor in fattier cuts is created as fat drippings break down into flavorful compounds that condense on the food above, and lean tenderloin doesn't generate those drippings. Our solution brought in the bacon. But we didn't wrap the roast in it as you might guess—that was too distractingly porky. Instead, we laced strips onto a skewer and allowed their fat to render slowly near the beef while it roasted to create those drippings and thus a steady stream of smoke to flavor the beef. We like to serve the tenderloin with Chermoula (page 21).

- 2¼ teaspoons kosher salt
- 2 teaspoons vegetable oil
- 1 teaspoon pepper
- 1 teaspoon baking soda
- 1 (3-pound) center-cut beef tenderloin roast, trimmed and tied at 1½-inch intervals
- 3 slices bacon

1. Combine salt, oil, pepper, and baking soda in small bowl. Rub mixture evenly over roast and let sit while preparing grill.

2. Stack bacon slices. Keeping slices stacked, thread 12-inch metal skewer through bacon 6 or 7 times to create accordion shape. Push stack together to compact into about 2-inch length.

3a. **For a charcoal grill:** Open bottom vent halfway. Light large chimney starter two-thirds filled with charcoal briquettes (4 quarts). When top coals are partially covered with ash, pour evenly over half of grill. Set cooking grate in place, cover, and open lid vent halfway. Heat grill until hot, about 5 minutes.

3b. **For a gas grill:** Turn all burners to high, cover, and heat grill until hot, about 15 minutes. Turn primary burner to medium and turn off other burner(s). (Adjust primary burner as needed to maintain grill temperature of 300 degrees.)

4. Clean and oil cooking grate. Place roast on hotter side of grill and cook until lightly browned on all sides, about 12 minutes. Slide roast to cooler side of grill, arranging so roast is about 7 inches from heat source. Place skewered bacon on hotter side of grill. (For charcoal, place near center of grill, above edge of coals. For gas, place above heat diffuser of primary burner.

Filets Mignons with Sage-Buttered Mushrooms and Black Pepper Polenta

2 minutes ensured even cooking—since filet is so lean, it's especially important not to overcook it. To limit the number of dishes, we cooked the mushrooms in the same pan that we used for the steak; as a bonus, the mushrooms picked up meaty steak flavor. You can substitute white mushrooms for the cremini.

> 3 cups water
> 2 teaspoons pepper, divided
> ¾ cup instant polenta
> 2 ounces Parmesan cheese, grated (1 cup)
> 6 tablespoons unsalted butter, divided
> 1¼ teaspoons table salt, divided
> 4 (6- to 8-ounce) center-cut filets mignons, trimmed
> 1 pound cremini mushrooms, trimmed and sliced thin
> 1 tablespoon minced fresh sage
> 2 garlic cloves, minced

1. Bring water and 1½ teaspoons pepper to boil in large saucepan over high heat. Whisk in polenta, reduce heat to medium-low, and cook until thickened, about 3 minutes. Off heat, stir in Parmesan, 2 tablespoons butter, and ½ teaspoon salt. Cover to keep warm.

2. Meanwhile, pat steaks dry with paper towels and sprinkle with ½ teaspoon salt and remaining ½ teaspoon pepper. Melt 1 tablespoon butter in 12-inch nonstick skillet over medium-high heat. Add steaks and cook, flipping every 2 minutes, until meat registers 120 to 125 degrees (for medium-rare), 10 to 12 minutes. Transfer to plate and tent with aluminum foil.

3. Melt 2 tablespoons butter in now-empty skillet. Add mushrooms and remaining ¼ teaspoon salt and cook until mushrooms are well browned, about 6 minutes. Off heat, stir in sage, garlic, and remaining 1 tablespoon butter until mushrooms are well coated. Serve steaks with polenta and mushrooms.

Bacon should be 4 to 6 inches from roast and drippings should fall on coals or heat diffuser and produce steady stream of smoke and minimal flare-ups. If flare-ups are large or frequent, slide bacon skewer 1 inch toward roast.)

5. Cover and cook until beef registers 120 to 125 degrees (for medium-rare), 50 minutes to 1¼ hours. Transfer roast to carving board and let rest for 30 minutes. Remove twine from roast. Slice meat into ½-inch-thick slices and serve.

FILETS MIGNONS WITH SAGE-BUTTERED MUSHROOMS AND BLACK PEPPER POLENTA

Serves 4 | filet mignon

WHY THIS RECIPE WORKS Filet mignon might seem like a steak you'd likely order at a steakhouse, but it doesn't have to sit at the center of an empty white plate. Its mild, crowd-pleasing flavor and unfailing tenderness make it a good choice for a complete weeknight dinner that feels satisfying and luxurious. We paired filets with earthy sage-buttered mushrooms and a comforting black pepper polenta that carried a complementary bite. Flipping the filets every

PEPPER-CRUSTED FILETS MIGNONS

Serves 4 | filet mignon

WHY THIS RECIPE WORKS As with our Peppercorn-Crusted Beef Tenderloin (page 98), pepper punches up the flavor of filets mignons here. The peppercorns adhere much easier to the smaller, uniform steaks so there's less preparation, meaning we could have this bistro-style dinner on the table quickly. We merely needed to crush the peppercorns so they distributed evenly, briefly mellow their flavor with a simmer in oil, and then rub the steaks with the resulting pepper paste. We started the steaks in a skillet to achieve a pepper crust that nicely contrasted with the soft beef, and then we finished the steaks in the oven until they reached temperature. For a milder pepper flavor, drain the cooled peppercorns in a fine-mesh strainer in step 1, toss them with 5 tablespoons of fresh oil, add the salt, and proceed. Serve the steaks with our Blue Cheese–Chive Butter or Port-Cherry Reduction (recipes follow).

5 tablespoons black peppercorns, crushed
5 tablespoons plus 2 teaspoons extra-virgin olive oil, divided
1 tablespoon kosher salt
4 (7- to 8-ounce) center-cut filets mignons, 1½ to 2 inches thick, trimmed

1. Heat peppercorns and 5 tablespoons oil in small saucepan over low heat until faint bubbles appear. Continue to cook at bare simmer, swirling pan occasionally, until pepper is fragrant, 7 to 10 minutes. Remove from heat and set aside to cool. When mixture has cooled completely, add salt and stir to combine. Rub steaks with peppercorn mixture, thoroughly coating top and bottom of each steak. Cover steaks with plastic wrap and press gently to make sure peppercorns adhere; let stand at room temperature for 1 hour.

2. Meanwhile, adjust oven rack to middle position, place baking sheet on rack, and heat oven to 450 degrees. When oven reaches 450 degrees, heat remaining 2 teaspoons oil in 12-inch skillet over medium-high heat until just smoking. Place steaks in skillet and cook, without moving them, until dark brown crust has formed, 3 to 4 minutes. Using tongs, turn steaks and cook until well browned on second side, about 3 minutes.

3. Off heat, transfer steaks to hot sheet in oven. Roast until meat registers 120 to 125 degrees (for medium-rare), 4 to 6 minutes. Transfer steaks to wire rack, tent with aluminum foil, and let rest for 5 minutes before serving.

SERVE WITH
Blue Cheese–Chive Butter
Makes about ½ cup; serves 4
Our favorite supermarket blue cheese is Stella Blue. Spoon 1 to 2 tablespoons of the butter over the steaks while they're resting.

1½ ounces mild blue cheese, crumbled (⅓ cup), room temperature
3 tablespoons unsalted butter, softened
⅛ teaspoon table salt
2 tablespoons minced fresh chives

Combine blue cheese, butter, and salt in medium bowl and mix with stiff rubber spatula until smooth. Fold in chives.

Pepper-Crusted Filets Mignons

Port-Cherry Reduction
Makes about 1 cup; serves 4
Pass this sauce at the table.

1½ cups port
½ cup balsamic vinegar
½ cup dried tart cherries
1 large shallot, minced
2 sprigs fresh thyme
1 tablespoon unsalted butter

1. Combine port, balsamic vinegar, cherries, shallot, and thyme in medium saucepan; simmer over medium-low heat until liquid is reduced to ⅓ cup, about 30 minutes. Cover and set aside.

2. While steaks are resting, reheat sauce. Off heat, remove thyme, then whisk in butter until melted. Season with salt to taste.

BACON-WRAPPED FILETS MIGNONS

Serves 4 | filet mignon

WHY THIS RECIPE WORKS Wrapping filets mignons in bacon is a surefire way to add flavor (and fat). The trick would be getting perfectly cooked steaks and crispy slices of bacon at the same time, as flabby bacon wouldn't do. But bacon fat takes time to render. By slowly cooking the wrapped filets in a low oven until they were just shy of medium-rare, we ensured that they were perfectly cooked before giving the bacon the attention it needed. After being rendered slightly in the oven, the bacon was ready for a quick trip to the skillet to finish crisping; using the edges of the skillet to stand the steaks on their sides, we were able to get fully seared steaks with crisp, smoky wrappers. We like to serve the steaks with bright, pungent Gorgonzola Vinaigrette (page 22).

- 2 teaspoons kosher salt
- 1 teaspoon pepper
- 1 (2-pound) center-cut beef tenderloin roast, trimmed
- 4 slices bacon
- 1 tablespoon vegetable oil

1. Adjust oven rack to middle position and heat oven to 275 degrees. Set wire rack in rimmed baking sheet. Combine salt and pepper in bowl. Cut tenderloin crosswise into 4 equal steaks. Pat steaks dry with paper towels and sprinkle evenly with salt mixture.

2. Working with 1 steak at a time, wrap 1 slice bacon around circumference of steak, stretching as needed, and secure overlapping ends with toothpick inserted horizontally. Place steaks on prepared wire rack. Roast until steaks register 115 degrees (for medium-rare), 40 to 50 minutes.

3. Heat oil in 12-inch nonstick skillet over medium-high heat until just smoking. Position steaks on sides in skillet with bacon seam side down and nestled into rounded corners of skillet. Cook until bacon is evenly browned, rotating steaks as needed, about 5 minutes. Position steaks flat side down in center of skillet and cook until steaks are well browned on tops and bottoms, 1 to 2 minutes per side.

4. Transfer steaks to platter, tent with aluminum foil, and let rest for 10 minutes. Gently remove toothpicks, leaving bacon intact. Serve.

GRILLED FILETS MIGNONS

Serves 4 | filet mignon

WHY THIS RECIPE WORKS Filet mignon is the Superman of tenderness, yet its flavor is as mild as Clark Kent, so it's great when grilled. The fire sears the exterior of the steaks, concentrating the flavor by forming a deep brown, crisp, aromatic crust. A very hot fire was essential, but the thick steaks cooked over consistently high heat burned. Instead, we turned to a two-level fire. We seared the steaks first over high heat and then finished cooking them through on the cooler side. Rubbing the steaks with olive oil before grilling improved browning and added flavor. For an accurate temperature reading of the steaks, insert the probe from the side and make sure that the tip of the probe doesn't go past the center of the steak. To add a little richness to the steaks, we like to apply a compound butter (see page 25) while they're still warm, so the melted butter drips down the sides of the steaks.

- 4 (7- to 8-ounce) center-cut filets mignons, 1½ to 2 inches thick, trimmed
- 4 teaspoons extra-virgin olive oil

1a. For a charcoal grill: Open bottom vent completely. Light large chimney starter filled with charcoal briquettes (6 quarts). When top coals are partially covered with ash, pour two-thirds evenly over half of grill, then pour remaining coals over other half of grill. Set cooking grate in place, cover, and open lid vent completely. Heat grill until hot, about 5 minutes.

1b. For a gas grill: Turn all burners to high, cover, and heat grill until hot, about 15 minutes. Leave all burners on high.

2. Meanwhile, pat steaks dry with paper towels and lightly rub with oil. Season steaks with salt and pepper.

3. Clean and oil cooking grate. Place steaks on grill (on hotter side if using charcoal) and cook (covered if using gas) until well browned on both sides, 4 to 6 minutes, flipping halfway through cooking. Move steaks to cooler side of grill (if using charcoal) or turn all burners to medium (if using gas) and continue to cook (covered if using gas), until meat registers 115 to 120 degrees (for rare) or 120 to 125 degrees (for medium-rare), 5 to 9 minutes longer.

4. Transfer steaks to serving platter, tent with aluminum foil, and let rest for 10 minutes before serving.

SIRLOIN

THE FINAL BIG LOIN SECTION, the end part, at the cow's hip, is the sirloin. It's tougher than the short loin because the muscles get more exercise. The sirloin is a lot about straddling lines: It lives sandwiched between the luxurious short loin and the tough and less-desirable rump. And to further complicate things, it's typically demarcated by yet another line, a natural seam separating it into a top sirloin (the top sirloin butt) and a bottom sirloin (the bottom sirloin butt) and made up of a bunch of different muscles. We prefer the top; it's lean but it's closer in taste and texture to the short loin and can make a really nice roast. The bottom gets tougher still as it's closer to the rear legs. Both portions are relatively inexpensive. Just watch out: Sometimes there's no differentiation in labeling and everything from here is called "sirloin." Ask questions when labeling is unclear. If you're buying steaks they're much more likely to be cut with the grain into boneless steaks, though the sirloin can be cut against the grain into bone-in steaks.

Top Sirloin Roast

Cost: ■■▯▯   Flavor: ■■▯▯
Best cooking methods: roast, braise, grill roast
Texture: succulent and tender beyond the line of gristle
Alternative names: Top butt, center-cut roast

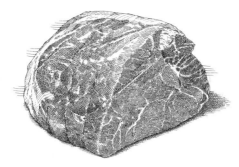

This top cut from the hip area tastes incredibly meaty and has plenty of marbling, which makes for a succulent roast. Aside from the vein of gristle that runs through it, which is slightly unpleasant to eat, the roast is tender and juicy, with big, beefy flavor. Other parts of the sirloin are lean and tough, but with its balance of beefy flavor and affordable pricing, the top sirloin roast is one of our favorite inexpensive roasts. It should come in at about 8 inches square and 4 inches tall at the center, with one side that tapers into a narrower end and two sides that slope, with no fat cap and a reasonable amount of marbling. We cook it gently to ensure even cooking with no gray band on the roast. Another trick for even cooking? Cutting it into two roasts along the line of gristle. This is our holiday centerpiece supersaver (see page 112).

MEAT PREP *Preparing a Top Sirloin Roast*

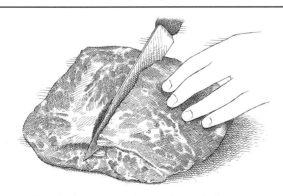

Cut roast lengthwise along grain into 2 equal pieces.

Top Sirloin Steak

Cost: ■■▯▯   Flavor: ■■▯▯
Best cooking methods: pan sear, grill
Texture: tender, juicy
Alternative names: New York sirloin steak, shell sirloin steak, sirloin butt steak

Like the top sirloin roast, which we like very much, top sirloin steak boasts a unique combination of tenderness with pleasant chew, affordability, and meatiness. That makes it an economical cut to cube for kebabs but also perfectly good for a weekday steak as in Steak and Potato Salad (page 117). Preparations like Steak Marsala (page 117) are particularly helpful because the glutamate content of the mushrooms intensifies the flavor of the meat. We also mastered grilling techniques for this cut, making it stand up to more expensive steaks (see page 118).

This steak can come in a range of sizes and can often be quite large, so be sure to purchase according to the recipe specs. Avoid cuts that taper drastically on one end. It's very commonly called a shell sirloin steak in the Northeast, so you may know this bargain cut by that name if you're from that area. When this steak has a bone in it, it's called a round-bone steak. We do not cook with round-bone steaks. Bear in mind that even those tasters who usually prefer rare beef preferred these steaks cooked medium-rare or, better yet, medium because the texture is firmer and not quite so chewy.

Tri-Tip Roast

Cost: ■■▯▯▯ Flavor: ■■▯▯▯
Best cooking methods: pan sear, grill roast
Texture: moist, a bit spongy
Alternative names: bottom sirloin steak, California cut, triangle roast

If you're not from California you may not have heard of the triangular (go figure) tri-tip roast—cooking it is a West Coast tradition. (Butchers on the East Coast sometimes cut it up into sirloin tips or faux steak tips.) But we think it deserves wider attention as it has nice marbling. This small, boomerang-shaped cut of beef from the bottom sirloin is tender and moist if not overcooked but can have a spongy texture.

Flap Meat

Cost: ■■▯▯▯ Flavor: ■■▯▯▯
Best cooking methods: pan sear, grill
Texture: loose grain, can be chewy
Alternative names: sirloin steak tip, faux hanger, bavette

Most cuts of meat go by more than one name, but flap meat (found next to the tri-tip) is particularly confusing. It's often called steak tips (especially in New England), but it can be purchased whole and cooked as a sirloin steak, cut into strips, or cooked in cubes as steak tips would imply. However, steak tips (the cube kind) can also, misleadingly, be cut from random parts of the cow. To ensure authenticity (and sirloin flavor), we like to buy larger pieces of flap meat (a whole piece of flap meat weighs about 2½ pounds, from ½ inch to 1½ inches thick) and cut it ourselves. Though not particularly tender, this steak has a distinct grain and a robust beefiness. Slice it thin against the grain after cooking. When cooked as tips, it's particularly appealing because of the higher ratio of crust to interior—if you're into steak with good sear. We also like grinding meat for burgers from flap meat for the right fat content and texture. (For more information on grinding your own meat, see page 367.)

MEAT PREP *Cutting Flap Meat into Steak Tips*

1. Trim meat.

2. Cut meat into 2-inch pieces.

OVERCOOKED STEAKS?

Our apologies if you fall into this category, but it's no secret that big beef eaters don't have a high opinion of people who order their steaks at a doneness higher than medium-rare. We tend to agree—but flap meat, like top sirloin steak (see page 109), is an exception and we think you should cook it to at least medium-rare if not medium.

Several factors contribute to the toughness or tenderness of meat, but primary among them is the size of the meat fibers (the thicker and longer they are the harder they are to bite through). Flap meat looks striated because the fibers are very thick and packed very tightly in bundles. This makes them tough when cooked to rare. Cooking past medium-rare tenderizes thick-fibered meat because the muscle fibers shrink in diameter by about 25 percent at 130 degrees, which makes them easier to chew through. However, there's a stopping point: If you cook thick-fibered meat (like steak tips) beyond medium to 140 degrees, the shrinking muscle fibers will squeeze out moisture, making the meat dry and tough. Thus, we prefer to aim for the sweet spot, between 130 and 135 degrees, with long-fibered meats like flap meat.

GRAIN GAINS

Steak tips, with their distinctive longitudinal grain, can have more chew than other steaks, but are also better at soaking up flavor. Marinades don't do much for tenderizing meat, but they can flavor it—if they can penetrate (see page 12). With all those empty spaces between meat fibers, steak tips effectively absorb a flavorful bath. Likewise, skirt steak (see page153) and flank steak (see page 165) are great candidates for marinating.

Coffee-Chipotle Top Sirloin Roast

COFFEE-CHIPOTLE TOP SIRLOIN ROAST

Serves 8 to 10 | top sirloin roast

WHY THIS RECIPE WORKS A robust spice rub can transform an already-extraordinary top sirloin roast into an even more impressive centerpiece. Cutting the roast in half and then tying each half along its length reduced the cooking time and created more surface area for our tangy, subtly spicy rub made from garlic, anchovy, coffee, chipotle, and spices—a bold complement to the beefy cut. For a flavorful, attractive exterior, we seared the roasts, rubbed them (so that the paste wouldn't burn on the stovetop), and increased the oven temperature at the end of cooking to deepen the paste's color and flavor and crisp up the crust. A finishing sprinkle of salt after slicing brought the flavors to life. A longer salting time is preferable. Do not omit the anchovies; they provide depth of flavor.

- 1 (5- to 6-pound) center-cut top sirloin roast, trimmed
- 2 tablespoons kosher salt
- 4 teaspoons plus ¼ cup extra-virgin olive oil, divided
- 4 garlic cloves, minced
- 6 anchovy fillets, rinsed and patted dry
- 1 tablespoon ground coffee
- 1 tablespoon minced canned chipotle chile in adobo sauce
- 2 teaspoons ground coriander
- 2 teaspoons paprika
- 1 teaspoon unsweetened cocoa powder
- 1 teaspoon dry mustard
- 1 teaspoon pepper

1. Cut roast lengthwise along grain into 2 equal pieces. Rub 1 tablespoon salt over each piece and tie securely with kitchen twine at 1½-inch intervals. Transfer roasts to plate and refrigerate, uncovered, for at least 24 hours or up to 3 days.

2. Adjust oven rack to middle position and heat oven to 225 degrees. Pat roasts dry with paper towels. Heat 2 teaspoons oil in 12-inch skillet over high heat until just smoking. Brown 1 roast on all sides, 6 to 8 minutes; transfer to clean plate. Repeat with 2 teaspoons oil and remaining roast; transfer to plate. Let cool for 10 minutes.

3. Meanwhile, process garlic, anchovies, coffee, chipotle, coriander, paprika, cocoa, mustard, pepper, and remaining ¼ cup oil in food processor until smooth paste forms, about 30 seconds, scraping down sides of bowl as needed. Transfer roasts, fat side up, to wire rack set in rimmed baking sheet and rub evenly with paste. Roast until beef registers 120 to 125 degrees (for medium-rare), 2 to 2¼ hours. Remove roasts from oven, tent with aluminum foil, and let rest on rack for 30 minutes.

4. Heat oven to 500 degrees. Discard foil and remove twine from roasts. Return roasts to oven and cook until exteriors are well browned, 6 to 8 minutes. Transfer roasts to carving board. Slice meat against grain ¼ inch thick. Sprinkle with flake sea salt to taste. Serve.

VARIATION

Rosemary-Garlic Top Sirloin Roast

Omit coffee, chipotle, coriander, paprika, cocoa, and mustard. In step 3, process 3 tablespoons chopped fresh rosemary with garlic, anchovies, and remaining ¼ cup oil in food processor until smooth paste forms, about 30 seconds, scraping down sides of bowl as needed. Add pepper and ¼ teaspoon red pepper flakes and pulse to combine, 2 to 3 pulses. Proceed with recipe as directed.

BEEF EN COCOTTE WITH CARAMELIZED ONIONS

Serves 6 to 8 | top sirloin roast

WHY THIS RECIPE WORKS Cooking en cocotte (cooking in a casserole) is a French technique similar to braising. It uses a covered pot, a low oven temperature, and an extended cooking time to yield tender, flavorful meat or poultry, but no liquid is added to the pot. Instead, the meat cooks in its own juices. Without added liquid, cooking en cocotte does the job quicker than traditional braising—so quickly that more marbled chuck roast doesn't have a chance to break down enough in this method. Beefy top sirloin, however, works great. We balanced the beefy flavors with the sweetness of caramelized onions, cooking the onions after we seared the beef. To boost their flavor, we added some garlic and then deglazed the pot with sherry, scraping up the fond as the liquid reduced. We cooked the roast on top of the onions; when they were done we added chicken broth to the onions and reduced the mixture to a flavorful sauce. Trim the beef well so that the sauce isn't greasy.

- 1 (3- to 4-pound) center-cut top sirloin roast, trimmed and tied once around middle
- 3 tablespoons vegetable oil, divided
- 3 onions, halved, and sliced thin
- 3 garlic cloves, peeled and crushed
- ¼ cup dry sherry
- 2 cups chicken broth
- 1 tablespoon unsalted butter

1. Adjust oven rack to lowest position and heat oven to 250 degrees. Pat roast dry with paper towels and season with salt and pepper.

**Beef en Cocotte with Creamy
Mushroom Barley**

BEEF EN COCOTTE WITH CREAMY MUSHROOM BARLEY

Serves 6 | top sirloin roast

WHY THIS RECIPE WORKS We push the limits of what you might think can come out of one Dutch oven with this ultraimpressive beef roast that cooks along with a risotto-like savory mushroom barley side—it comes together like magic. We browned the roast in the Dutch oven, removed it, and then started the mushroom-barley mixture in the drippings. Once all the ingredients were incorporated, we returned the roast to the pot, sealed it, covered it, and let both components cook in the oven. To make the barley even more creamy we finished it with Parmesan. And Salsa Verde (page 21) was a bright, surprising finishing component to offset the savor that we don't think is optional. Trim the beef well to keep the barley from turning greasy.

1 (3- to 4-pound) center-cut top sirloin roast, trimmed and tied around middle
3 tablespoons vegetable oil, divided
8 ounces white mushrooms, trimmed and sliced thin
1¼ cups pearl barley, rinsed
1 onion, chopped
½ ounce dried porcini mushrooms, rinsed and minced
3 garlic cloves, minced
1 tablespoon tomato paste
1 teaspoon minced fresh thyme or ¼ teaspoon dried
3 tablespoons cognac
2 cups beef broth
1 cup chicken broth
1 cup water
1 ounce Parmesan cheese, grated (½ cup)

1. Adjust oven rack to lowest position and heat oven to 250 degrees. Pat roast dry with paper towels and season with salt and pepper. Heat 2 tablespoons oil in Dutch oven over medium-high heat until just smoking. Add roast and brown on all sides, 7 to 10 minutes; transfer to plate.

2. Add white mushrooms, barley, onion, porcini mushrooms, and remaining 1 tablespoon oil to now-empty pot and cook over medium heat until onion is softened, 5 to 7 minutes. Stir in garlic, tomato paste, and thyme and cook until fragrant, about 30 seconds. Stir in cognac, scraping up any browned bits, and cook until almost completely evaporated, about 30 seconds. Stir in beef broth, chicken broth, and water and bring to simmer.

3. Off heat, return roast and any accumulated juices to pot. Place large sheet of aluminum foil over pot and press to seal, then cover tightly with lid. Transfer pot to oven and cook until beef registers 120 to 125 degrees (for medium-rare), 1 hour to 1 hour 20 minutes. Remove pot from oven. Transfer roast to carving board, tent with foil, and let rest for 20 minutes.

2. Heat 2 tablespoons oil in Dutch oven over medium-high heat until just smoking. Brown roast on all sides, 7 to 10 minutes, reducing heat if pot begins to scorch. Transfer beef to large plate.

3. Add remaining 1 tablespoon oil to pot and heat over medium heat until shimmering. Add onions and garlic, cover, and cook until softened and wet, about 5 minutes. Remove lid and continue to cook onions, stirring often, until dry and well browned, 10 to 12 minutes. Stir in sherry, scraping up any browned bits, and cook until almost all of liquid has evaporated, about 1 minute.

4. Off heat, nestle beef into pot and add any accumulated juices. Place large sheet of aluminum foil over pot and cover tightly with lid; transfer pot to oven. Cook until very center of the roast registers 120 to 125 degrees (for medium-rare), 20 to 30 minutes.

5. Transfer roast to carving board, tent with foil, and let rest for 20 minutes. Stir broth into onions and simmer over medium-high heat until slightly thickened, about 2 minutes. Off heat, whisk in butter, season with salt and pepper to taste, and cover to keep warm.

6. Remove twine from roast. Slice meat against grain ¼ inch thick and transfer to serving platter. Spoon sauce over meat and serve.

(If barley is underdone, continue to cook over medium heat, adding water as needed, until tender.) Stir Parmesan into barley mixture and cook over medium heat until creamy, 1 to 2 minutes. Season with salt and pepper to taste, and cover to keep warm. Remove twine from roast. Slice meat against grain ¼ inch thick. Serve.

BALTIMORE PIT BEEF

Serves 10 | top sirloin roast

WHY THIS RECIPE WORKS Pit beef is Baltimore's high-heat, fast-paced answer to the slow smoking of barbecue farther south. A massive spice-rubbed roast is grilled over a hot fire until it's charred and a rosy medium-rare on the inside. The meat is shaved paper thin, piled onto a kaiser roll, and topped with tiger sauce, a local horseradish-spiked mayonnaise. We cut a top sirloin roast in half and slow-cooked the meat on the cooler side of a half-grill fire; an aluminum foil shield provided protection so it didn't dry out. Then, for the most char, we generously seared the roasts on all sides over the hotter side.

TIGER SAUCE
- ½ cup mayonnaise
- ½ cup hot prepared horseradish, drained
- 1 teaspoon lemon juice
- 1 garlic clove, minced

PIT BEEF
- 4 teaspoons kosher salt
- 1 tablespoon paprika
- 1 tablespoon pepper
- 1 teaspoon garlic powder
- 1 teaspoon dried oregano
- ¼ teaspoon cayenne pepper
- 1 (4- to 5-pound) center-cut top sirloin roast, trimmed and halved crosswise
- 10 kaiser rolls
- 1 onion, sliced thin

1. For the tiger sauce: Whisk all ingredients together in bowl. Season with salt and pepper to taste. (Sauce can be refrigerated for up to 2 days.)

2. For the pit beef: Combine salt, paprika, pepper, garlic powder, oregano, and cayenne in bowl. Pat roasts dry with paper towels and rub with 2 tablespoons seasoning mixture. Wrap meat tightly with plastic wrap and refrigerate for 6 to 24 hours.

3a. For a charcoal grill: Open bottom vent halfway. Light large chimney starter filled with charcoal briquettes (6 quarts). When top coals are partially covered with ash, pour evenly over half of grill. Set cooking grate in place, cover, and open lid vent halfway. Heat grill until hot, about 5 minutes.

3b. For a gas grill: Turn all burners to high, cover, and heat grill until hot, about 15 minutes. Leave primary burner on high and turn other burner(s) off.

4. Clean and oil cooking grate. Unwrap roasts and place end to end on long side of 18 by 12-inch sheet of aluminum foil. Loosely fold opposite long side of foil around top of roasts. Place meat on cool part of grill with foil-covered side closest to heat source. Cover (positioning lid vent over meat if using charcoal) and cook until meat registers 100 degrees, 45 minutes to 1 hour.

5. Transfer roasts to plate and discard foil. Turn all burners to high if using gas. If using charcoal, carefully remove cooking grate and light large chimney starter three-quarters filled with charcoal briquettes (4½ quarts). When top coals are partially covered with ash, pour evenly over spent coals. Set cooking grate in place and cover. Heat grill until hot, about 5 minutes.

6. Pat roasts dry with paper towels and rub with remaining spice mixture. Place meat on hot part of grill. Cook (covered if using gas), turning occasionally, until charred on all sides and meat registers 120 to 125 degrees (for medium-rare), 10 to 20 minutes. Transfer roasts to carving board, tent with foil, and let rest for 15 minutes. Slice roasts thin against grain. Transfer sliced beef to rolls, top with onion slices, and drizzle with sauce. Serve.

PAN-SEARED INEXPENSIVE STEAKS

Serves 4 | top sirloin steak

WHY THIS RECIPE WORKS Steaks for searing don't need to be the pricey picks at the market. Top sirloin steak may not get four stars for flavor from us, but it does sear up superbly. We used a pan-searing technique of heating oil in a skillet until it began smoking, cooking the steaks over medium-high heat on one side, and then reducing the heat to medium when we flipped the steaks. This approach ensured a nice sear on both sides without overcooking or allowing the fond on the bottom of the pan to burn; once deglazed, the fond added great flavor to a pan sauce in one of our two variations that keep this accessible steak dinner interesting—affordability with flair.

- 2 tablespoons vegetable oil
- 2 (1-pound) boneless top sirloin steaks, 1¼ inches thick, trimmed

1. Pat steaks dry with paper towels and season with salt and pepper. Heat oil in 12-inch skillet over medium-high heat until just smoking. Place steaks in skillet; cook, without moving steaks, until well browned, about 2 minutes. Using tongs, flip

Pan-Seared Inexpensive Steaks

and meat registers 120 to 125 degrees (for medium-rare) or 130 to 135 degrees (for medium), 5 to 6 minutes. Transfer steaks to cutting board, tent with aluminum foil, and let rest for 12 minutes.

2. Pour off all but 1 tablespoon fat from skillet. Add shallot and cook, stirring frequently, over low heat until beginning to brown, 2 to 3 minutes. Add wine and increase heat to medium-high; simmer rapidly, scraping up any browned bits, until liquid is reduced to glaze, about 30 seconds. Add broth and simmer until reduced to ¼ cup, about 3 minutes. Add cream and any accumulated steak juices; cook until heated through, about 1 minute. Stir in mustard and season with salt and pepper to taste. Slice steak against grain on bias ¼ inch thick. Spoon sauce over steaks and serve.

Pan-Seared Inexpensive Steaks with Tomato-Caper Pan Sauce

- 2 (1-pound) boneless top sirloin steaks, 1¼ inches thick, trimmed
- 2 tablespoons vegetable oil
- 1 shallot, minced
- 1 teaspoon all-purpose flour
- 2 tablespoons dry white wine
- 1 cup chicken broth
- 1 ripe tomato, cored, seeded, and cut into ¼-inch pieces
- 2 tablespoons capers, rinsed
- ¼ cup minced fresh parsley

1. Pat steaks dry with paper towels and season with salt and pepper. Heat oil in 12-inch skillet over medium-high heat until just smoking. Place steaks in skillet and cook, without moving them, until well browned, about 2 minutes. Using tongs, flip steaks; reduce heat to medium. Cook until well browned on second side and meat registers 120 to 125 degrees (for medium-rare) or 130 to 135 degrees (for medium), 5 to 6 minutes. Transfer steaks to cutting board, tent with aluminum foil, and let rest for 12 to 15 minutes.

2. Pour off all but 1 tablespoon fat from skillet. Add shallot and cook, stirring frequently, over low heat until beginning to brown, 2 to 3 minutes. Sprinkle flour over shallot and cook, stirring constantly, until combined, about 1 minute. Add wine and increase heat to medium-high; simmer rapidly, scraping up any browned bits, until liquid is reduced to glaze, about 30 seconds. Add broth and simmer until reduced to ⅔ cup, about 4 minutes. Reduce heat to medium; add tomato, capers, and any accumulated steak juices and cook until flavors are blended, about 1 minute. Stir in parsley and season with salt and pepper to taste. Slice steak against grain on bias ¼ inch thick. Spoon sauce over steaks and serve.

steaks; reduce heat to medium. Cook until well browned on second side and meat registers 120 to 125 degrees (for medium-rare) or 130 to 135 degrees (for medium), 5 to 6 minutes.

2. Transfer steaks to cutting board and tent with foil; let rest for 12 minutes. Slice steak against grain on bias ¼ inch thick and serve immediately.

VARIATIONS
Pan-Seared Inexpensive Steaks with Mustard-Cream Pan Sauce

- 2 (1-pound) boneless top sirloin steaks, 1¼ inches thick, trimmed
- 2 tablespoons vegetable oil
- 1 shallot, minced
- 2 tablespoons dry white wine
- ½ cup chicken broth
- 6 tablespoons heavy cream
- 3 tablespoons whole-grain Dijon mustard

1. Pat steaks dry with paper towels and season with salt and pepper. Heat oil in 12-inch skillet over medium-high heat until just smoking. Place steaks in skillet and cook, without moving them, until well browned, about 2 minutes. Using tongs, flip steaks; reduce heat to medium. Cook until well browned on second side

Steak Marsala

STEAK MARSALA

Serves 4 to 6 | top sirloin steak

WHY THIS RECIPE WORKS You may be used to buttery, sweet, and savory Marsala sauce partnered with chicken cutlets. What about with steak? Steak Marsala, we found, was doubly grand, pairing full-flavored beef and mushrooms with a perfectly complementary rich wine sauce. To amplify the savoriness of the cremini mushrooms, we added rehydrated dried porcini mushrooms, which contributed a deep complexity. A healthy dose of sweet Marsala provided the perfect amount of deep smokiness to the sauce, and butter, lemon, and parsley rounded out the flavors.

  1 cup chicken broth, divided
  ½ ounce dried porcini mushrooms, rinsed
  3 tablespoons extra-virgin olive oil, divided
 12 ounces cremini mushrooms, trimmed and sliced thin
  ½ teaspoon table salt, divided
  ½ teaspoon pepper, divided
  4 (6-ounce) boneless top sirloin steaks, trimmed
  1 shallot, minced
  1 tablespoon all-purpose flour
  3 garlic cloves, minced
  1 teaspoon minced fresh rosemary
  ¾ cup plus 1 tablespoon sweet Marsala, divided
  4 tablespoons unsalted butter, cut into 4 pieces and chilled
  1 tablespoon minced fresh parsley
  2 teaspoons lemon juice

1. Microwave ½ cup broth and porcini mushrooms in covered bowl until steaming, about 1 minute. Let sit until softened, about 5 minutes. Drain porcini mushrooms in fine-mesh strainer lined with coffee filter, reserve liquid, and chop porcini mushrooms fine.

2. Heat 1 tablespoon oil in 12-inch nonstick skillet over medium-high heat until shimmering. Add cremini mushrooms, ¼ teaspoon salt, and ¼ teaspoon pepper and cook, covered, until mushrooms release their liquid, about 3 minutes. Uncover and continue to cook, stirring occasionally, until liquid has evaporated and mushrooms are well browned, about 8 minutes longer. Transfer to bowl; cover to keep warm.

3. Pat steaks dry with paper towels and season with salt and pepper. Add 1 tablespoon oil to now-empty skillet and heat over medium heat until just smoking. Add steaks and cook until well browned on first side, about 4 minutes. Flip steaks and cook until well browned on second side and meat registers 120 to 125 degrees (for medium-rare) or 130 to 135 (for medium), 4 to 6 minutes. Transfer steaks to carving board and tent with aluminum foil.

4. Heat remaining 1 tablespoon oil in now-empty skillet over medium-high heat until shimmering. Add shallot, flour, garlic, rosemary, porcini mushrooms, remaining ¼ teaspoon salt, and remaining ¼ teaspoon pepper and cook until shallot is beginning to soften, about 1 minute. Stir in ¾ cup Marsala, reserved porcini mushroom soaking liquid, and remaining ½ cup broth. Cook until reduced to 1 cup, 5 to 7 minutes.

5. Reduce heat to low and whisk in butter, 1 piece at a time, until emulsified. Stir in parsley, lemon juice, cremini mushrooms, and remaining 1 tablespoon Marsala. Season with salt and pepper to taste. Slice steaks thin against grain and transfer to warm platter. Spoon sauce over steaks and serve.

STEAK AND POTATO SALAD

Serves 4 | top sirloin steak

WHY THIS RECIPE WORKS Meat and potatoes are a common hearty-dinner craving, but this classic combination doesn't need to be a heavy affair. Instead of steak and fries or a roast and mashed potatoes, we combined the two in a salad with crisp, refreshing romaine and a zingy red wine vinaigrette. The dish came together quickly: We seared a beefy top sirloin steak in a skillet and, at the same time, jump-started the potatoes in the microwave so they cooked through. When the steak was done we moved the potatoes into the empty skillet and then quickly browned them. We served the sliced steak with the potatoes atop the lettuce. This salad is as satisfying as your classic meat and potatoes, with some extra freshness.

DRESSING
  3 tablespoons red wine vinegar
  3 tablespoons water
  1 shallot, minced
  2 tablespoons extra-virgin olive oil
  1 tablespoon honey
  1 tablespoon whole-grain mustard
  1 garlic clove, minced
  ½ teaspoon minced fresh thyme
  ¼ teaspoon salt
  ⅛ teaspoon pepper

SALAD
  1 (1-pound) boneless top sirloin steak, 1¼ inches thick, trimmed of all visible fat
  ⅛ teaspoon table salt
  ⅛ teaspoon pepper
  1 tablespoon canola oil, divided
  1 pound red potatoes, unpeeled, cut into ¾-inch-thick wedges
  3 romaine lettuce hearts (18 ounces), torn into bite-size pieces
  ⅓ cup thinly sliced red onion

1. **For the dressing:** Whisk all ingredients together in small bowl and set aside.

2. **For the salad:** Pat steak dry with paper towels and sprinkle with salt and pepper. Heat 2 teaspoons oil in 12-inch nonstick skillet over medium-high heat until just smoking. Add steak and cook until well browned on first side, about 3 minutes. Flip steak, reduce heat to medium, and continue to cook until meat registers 120 to 125 degrees (for medium-rare), 5 to 7 minutes longer.

3. Transfer steak to cutting board, tent with aluminum foil, and let rest for 10 minutes.

4. While steak is cooking, combine potatoes and remaining 1 teaspoon oil in large bowl and toss to coat. Cover and microwave until potatoes are tender, 5 to 10 minutes, shaking bowl halfway through microwaving.

5. Heat oil left in skillet over medium-high heat until just smoking. Add potatoes in single layer and cook until well browned on both sides, about 5 minutes. Season with salt and pepper to taste.

6. Slice steak against grain ¼ inch thick. Whisk dressing to recombine. Combine lettuce, onion, and ½ cup dressing in large bowl and toss to coat. Divide lettuce mixture evenly among 4 plates, top with steak and potatoes, and drizzle with remaining dressing. Serve.

GRILLED STEAK WITH NEW MEXICAN CHILE RUB

Serves 6 to 8 | top sirloin steak

WHY THIS RECIPE WORKS Cuts from the middle of the steer (such as rib eyes and porterhouses), with their tender texture and big beef flavor, need little more than salt, pepper, and a few minutes over a hot fire to render them impressive. Other cuts don't have the benefit of as much fat to give them flavor. Sirloin steaks' chewier texture and almost gamy flavor are inspiration for applying a spice rub, but the steaks exude little fat to bond with the spices, and the rub can fall off in chunks. We found clever solutions: First we made crosshatch slits in the steaks to help the spices grab on. Then we made a pungent wet rub with tomato paste and fish sauce, spread it over the steaks, and let them sit so their surface became tacky (and so the glutamate-rich rub delivered deep flavor). We sprayed the steaks with vegetable oil before cooking to serve as a glue for the dry spice rub whose flavor bloomed during cooking in the oil.

STEAK
- 2 teaspoons tomato paste
- 2 teaspoons fish sauce
- 1½ teaspoons kosher salt
- ½ teaspoon onion powder
- ½ teaspoon garlic powder
- 2 (1½- to 1¾-pound) top sirloin steaks, 1 to 1¼ inches thick, trimmed

SPICE RUB
- 2 dried New Mexican chiles, stemmed, seeded, and torn into ½-inch pieces (½ cup)
- 4 teaspoons cumin seeds
- 4 teaspoons coriander seeds
- ½ teaspoon red pepper flakes
- ½ teaspoon black peppercorns
- 1 tablespoon sugar
- 1 tablespoon paprika
- ¼ teaspoon ground cloves
  Vegetable oil spray

1. **For the steak:** Combine tomato paste, fish sauce, salt, onion powder, and garlic powder in bowl. Pat steaks dry with paper towels. Using sharp knife cut ½-inch crosshatch pattern, ¹⁄₁₆ inch deep, on both sides of steaks. Rub tomato paste mixture evenly on both sides of steaks. Place steaks on wire rack set in rimmed baking sheet; let stand at room temperature for at least 1 hour. After 30 minutes, prepare grill.

2. **For the spice rub:** Toast chiles, cumin, coriander, pepper flakes, and peppercorns in 10-inch skillet over medium-low heat, stirring frequently, until just beginning to smoke, 3 to 4 minutes. Transfer to plate to cool, about 5 minutes. Grind spices in spice grinder or in mortar with pestle until coarsely ground. Transfer spices to bowl and stir in sugar, paprika, and cloves.

3a. **For a charcoal grill:** Open bottom vent completely. Light large chimney starter mounded with charcoal briquettes (7 quarts). When top coals are partially covered with ash, pour two-thirds evenly over grill, then pour remaining coals over half of grill. Set cooking grate in place, cover, and open lid vent completely. Heat grill until hot, about 5 minutes.

3b. **For a gas grill:** Turn all burners to high, cover, and heat grill until hot, about 15 minutes. Leave primary burner on high and turn other burner(s) to medium.

4. Clean and oil cooking grate. Sprinkle half of spice rub evenly over 1 side of steaks and press to adhere until spice rub is fully moistened. Lightly spray rubbed side of steak with oil spray, about 3 seconds. Flip steaks and repeat process of sprinkling with spice rub and coating with vegetable oil spray on second side.

TUTORIAL
Grilled Steak with New Mexican Chile Rub

We came up with some clever techniques for a lean steak with a spice crust that sticks and stays put during grilling.

1. Cut ½-inch crosshatch pattern, ⅟₁₆ inch deep, on both sides of steaks.

2. Rub tomato paste mixture evenly on both sides of steaks. Place steaks on wire rack set in rimmed baking sheet; let stand at room temperature for at least 1 hour.

3. Toast chiles, cumin, coriander, pepper flakes, and peppercorns in 10-inch skillet over medium-low heat, stirring frequently, until just beginning to smoke, 3 to 4 minutes. Let cool and grind until coarsely ground. Stir in sugar, paprika, and cloves.

4. Sprinkle half of spice rub evenly over 1 side of steaks and press to adhere until spice rub is fully moistened.

5. Lightly spray rubbed side of steak with oil spray, about 3 seconds. Flip steaks and repeat process of sprinkling with spice rub and coating with vegetable oil spray on second side.

6. Place steaks over hotter side of grill and cook until browned and charred on both sides and center registers 120 to 125 degrees (for medium-rare) or 130 to 135 degrees (for medium), 3 to 4 minutes per side.

5. Place steaks over hotter side of grill and cook until browned and charred on both sides and center registers 120 to 125 degrees (for medium-rare) or 130 to 135 degrees (for medium), 3 to 4 minutes per side. If steaks have not reached desired temperature, move to cooler side of grill and continue to cook. Transfer steaks to clean wire rack set in rimmed baking sheet, tent with aluminum foil, and let rest for 10 minutes. Slice steaks thin against grain and serve.

BARBECUE TRI-TIP

Serves 4 to 6 | tri-tip roast

WHY THIS RECIPE WORKS In California, tri-tips are typically cooked over high heat and seasoned simply. This produces a charred exterior and very rare center, but we wanted the outside cooked less and the inside cooked more for a more evenly cooked product. To achieve this we pushed all the coals in our grill to one side. The meat developed a flavorful crust over the hotter side before we roasted it gently on the cooler side. For nuanced smokiness, we added a wood chip packet to the fire before moving the meat to the cooler side. Poking holes in the meat's surface and spreading on a simple garlicky marinade infused the beef with deep flavor. A longer marinating time is preferable. This garlicky, smoky beef needs no adornment but is traditionally accompanied by fresh tomato salsa; we like to serve it with Santa Maria Salsa (recipe follows).

2 tablespoons vegetable oil
6 garlic cloves, minced
1½ teaspoons kosher salt
1 (2-pound) beef tri-tip roast, trimmed
1 teaspoon pepper
¾ teaspoon garlic salt
2 cups wood chips

1. Combine oil, garlic, and salt in bowl. Pat beef dry with paper towels, poke each side about 20 times with fork, then rub evenly with oil-garlic mixture. Wrap beef in plastic wrap and let sit at room temperature for 1 hour or refrigerate for up to 24 hours.

2. Unwrap beef, wipe off garlic paste using paper towels, and season with pepper and garlic salt. Just before grilling, soak wood chips in water for 15 minutes, then drain. Using large piece of heavy-duty aluminum foil, wrap soaked chips in 8 by 4½-inch foil packet. (Make sure chips do not poke holes in sides or bottom of packet.) Cut 2 evenly spaced 2-inch slits in top of packet.

3a. For a charcoal grill: Open bottom vent halfway. Light large chimney starter filled with charcoal briquettes (6 quarts). When top coals are partially covered with ash, pour evenly over half of grill. Set cooking grate in place, cover, and open lid vent halfway. Heat grill until hot, about 5 minutes.

3b. For a gas grill: Turn all burners to high, cover, and heat grill until hot, about 15 minutes. Leave all burners on high.

4. Clean and oil cooking grate. Place roast on hotter side of grill. Cook (covered if using gas), turning as needed, until well browned on all sides, 8 to 10 minutes. Transfer roast to plate.

5. Remove cooking grate and place wood chip packet directly on coals or primary burner. Set cooking grate in place, cover, and let chips begin to smoke, about 5 minutes. If using gas, leave primary burner on high and turn off other burner(s).

6. Place roast on cooler side of grill. Cover (position lid vent over meat if using charcoal) and cook until beef registers 120 to 125 degrees (for medium-rare), about 20 minutes. Transfer roast to carving board and let rest for 20 minutes. Slice meat thin against grain and serve.

SERVE WITH
Santa Maria Salsa

Makes about 4 cups; serves 4 to 6
The distinct texture of each ingredient is part of this salsa's appeal, so we don't recommend using a food processor.

2 pounds tomatoes, cored and chopped
2 teaspoons table salt, for salting tomatoes
2 jalapeño chiles, stemmed, seeded, and chopped fine
1 small red onion, chopped fine
1 celery rib, chopped fine
¼ cup lime juice (2 limes)
¼ cup chopped fresh cilantro
1 garlic clove, minced
⅛ teaspoon dried oregano
⅛ teaspoon Worcestershire sauce

1. Place tomatoes in strainer set over bowl and sprinkle with salt; let drain for 30 minutes. Discard liquid. Meanwhile, combine jalapeños, onion, celery, lime juice, cilantro, garlic, oregano, and Worcestershire in large bowl.

2. Add drained tomatoes to jalapeño mixture and toss to combine. Cover with plastic wrap and let stand at room temperature for 1 hour. (Salsa can be refrigerated for up to 2 days.)

1. Bring water, 1 tablespoon oil, and ½ teaspoon salt to boil in small saucepan over high heat. Remove from heat, stir in couscous, cover, and let sit for 5 minutes. Add 1 teaspoon orange zest and fluff with fork. Set aside and let cool uncovered. Cut away peel and pith from orange. Quarter orange, then slice crosswise; set aside.

2. Sprinkle beef with ½ teaspoon salt and ½ teaspoon pepper. Heat 1 tablespoon oil in 12-inch nonstick skillet over medium-high heat until just smoking. Add beef and cook until browned on all sides and meat registers 120 to 125 degrees (for medium-rare) or 130 to 135 degrees (for medium), 8 to 12 minutes. Transfer beef to cutting board and tent with aluminum foil.

3. Whisk lemon juice, remaining 3 tablespoons oil, remaining ½ teaspoon orange zest, remaining ½ teaspoon salt, and remaining ¼ teaspoon pepper together in large bowl. Add arugula, Parmesan, pine nuts, couscous, and orange slices and toss to combine. Slice steak thin against grain. Serve steak with salad.

SIRLOIN STEAK WITH COUSCOUS SALAD

Serves 4 | flap meat

WHY THIS RECIPE WORKS There's a reason arugula goes nicely with steak; the peppery arugula cuts through the richness of the beef. In this quick, hearty, dinner-worthy salad, we combine seared larger pieces of flap meat, arugula, and couscous (for satisfying heft). Sweet-tart orange slices counterbalanced the seared steak further; shaved Parmesan contributed salty bite; and pine nuts added mellow richness and textural contrast. Adding orange zest to the warm couscous bloomed its oils so its flavor infused the couscous.

- ½ cup water
- 5 tablespoons extra-virgin olive oil, divided
- 1½ teaspoons table salt, divided
- ½ cup couscous
- 1½ teaspoons orange zest, divided, plus 1 large orange
- 1½ pounds flap meat, cut with grain into 3 equal pieces, trimmed
- ¾ teaspoon pepper, divided
- 2 tablespoons lemon juice
- 5 ounces (5 cups) baby arugula
- 2 ounces Parmesan cheese, shaved with vegetable peeler
- ¼ cup pine nuts, toasted

MONGOLIAN BEEF

Serves 4 to 6 | flap meat

WHY THIS RECIPE WORKS We brought this Chinese American restaurant dish with roots in Taiwan into our kitchen so we could often enjoy the crispy fried beef tossed with chiles in a salty-sweet sauce. We began by freezing the beef—flap meat worked best—to make for easier slicing. We then sliced the beef ⅛ inch thick and quickly fried it in peanut (or vegetable) oil. We let the sauce—made up of water, brown sugar, and soy sauce—cook down for a few minutes, resulting in a balanced sweet and salty glaze that perfectly coated each piece of meat. Freezing the strips of beef makes them firm and allows you to slice them thin. Ask your butcher for a 1½-pound piece of flap meat instead of already-cut steak tips, which are more difficult to slice thin. If you can't find dried arbol chiles, you can substitute small dried Asian chiles or ¾ teaspoon of red pepper flakes. Serve with white rice.

- 1½ pounds beef flap meat, trimmed
- ½ cup cornstarch
- 3 cups peanut or vegetable oil
- 4 scallions, white parts minced, green parts cut into 1-inch pieces
- 2–4 dried arbol chiles (each about 2 inches long), stemmed and halved crosswise
- 4 garlic cloves, minced
- 1 tablespoon grated fresh ginger
- ¾ cup water
- ⅔ cup packed brown sugar
- 6 tablespoons soy sauce

Mongolian Beef

1. Cut beef with grain into 2½- to 3-inch-wide strips and place strips on large plate; freeze until firm, about 15 minutes. Cut strips crosswise against grain ⅛ inch thick. Toss beef with cornstarch in bowl; set aside.

2. Set wire rack in rimmed baking sheet. Heat oil in large Dutch oven over medium-high heat to 375 degrees. Add one-third of beef and fry until browned and crispy, about 4 minutes, stirring occasionally to keep pieces from sticking together. Adjust burner, if necessary, to maintain oil temperature between 350 and 375 degrees. Using spider skimmer or slotted spoon, transfer beef to prepared rack. Return oil to 375 degrees and repeat with remaining beef in 2 batches.

3. Transfer 1 tablespoon frying oil to 12-inch nonstick skillet and heat over medium-high heat until shimmering. Add scallion whites, arbols, garlic, and ginger and cook until fragrant, about 30 seconds. Stir in water, sugar, and soy sauce and bring to vigorous simmer. Cook until sauce is thickened and reduced to 1¼ cups, 6 to 8 minutes. Add beef and scallion greens to sauce and cook, tossing constantly, until sauce coats beef, about 1 minute. Transfer to platter and serve.

STEAK TIPS WITH MUSHROOM-ONION GRAVY

Serves 4 to 6 | flap meat

This classic supper promises juicy beef and hearty flavors but often delivers overcooked meat in a generic brown sauce or a greasy, gloppy gravy. To rescue the dish, we started with tender sirloin steak tips. To build flavor without adding any fat, we marinated the tips in a mixture of sugar for sweetness and soy sauce for saltiness. Browning the beef in a skillet left behind plenty of flavorful browned bits with which we could build a rich gravy. Cremini mushrooms can be used in place of the white mushrooms. This dish can be served over rice or mashed potatoes, or with egg noodles.

- 1 tablespoon soy sauce
- 1 teaspoon sugar
- 1½ pounds flap meat, trimmed and cut into 1½-inch chunks
- 1¾ cups beef broth, divided
- ¼ ounce dried porcini mushrooms, rinsed
- ½ teaspoon pepper
- 2 tablespoons vegetable oil, divided
- 1 pound white mushrooms, trimmed and sliced ¼ inch thick
- ½ teaspoon table salt, divided
- 1 large onion, halved and sliced thin
- 4 teaspoons all-purpose flour
- 1 garlic clove, minced
- ½ teaspoon minced fresh thyme
- 1 tablespoon chopped fresh parsley

1. Combine soy sauce and sugar in medium bowl. Add beef, toss well, and marinate for at least 30 minutes or up to 1 hour, tossing once more.

2. Meanwhile, microwave ¼ cup broth and porcini mushrooms in covered bowl until steaming, about 1 minute. Let sit until softened, about 5 minutes. Drain porcini mushrooms in fine-mesh strainer lined with coffee filter, reserve liquid, and mince porcini mushrooms. Set aside porcini mushrooms and liquid.

3. Pat beef dry with paper towels and sprinkle with pepper. Heat 1 tablespoon oil in 12-inch skillet over medium-high heat until just smoking. Add beef and cook until well browned on all sides, 6 to 8 minutes. Transfer to large plate and set aside.

4. Add remaining 1 tablespoon oil to now-empty skillet and heat over medium-high heat. Add white mushrooms, minced porcini mushrooms, and ¼ teaspoon salt; cook, stirring frequently, until all liquid has evaporated and mushrooms start to brown, 7 to 9 minutes, scraping up any browned bits. Add onion and remaining ¼ teaspoon salt; cook, stirring frequently, until onion begins to brown and dark bits form on pan bottom, 6 to 8 minutes longer. Add flour, garlic, and thyme; cook, stirring constantly, until vegetables are coated with flour mixture, about 1 minute. Stir in porcini soaking liquid and remaining 1½ cups broth, scraping up any browned bits, and bring to boil.

5. Nestle beef into mushroom-onion mixture and add any accumulated juices to skillet. Reduce heat to medium-low and simmer until beef registers 130 to 135 degrees (for medium), 3 to 5 minutes, turning beef several times. Season with salt and pepper to taste, sprinkle with parsley, and serve.

STEAK TIPS WITH CHARRO BEANS

Serves 4 | flap meat

WHY THIS RECIPE WORKS Charro beans are a traditional Mexican recipe commonly served alongside carne asada. Though skirt steak is our preferred choice for carne asada on the grill, the steaks can measure up to a foot long, and we wanted a weeknight dinner that could be made on the stovetop. Steak tips were a more manageable option that still delivered the meatiness we wanted. Quick-pickled red onion and jalapeño added brightness and spice to the mild beans and rich, savory steak, and an array of Mexican-inspired spices delivered big flavor. Cooking the beans in the skillet used for the steak infused them with even more flavor for a unified dish. We like to garnish this dish with fresh cilantro leaves.

½ small red onion, sliced thin
¼ cup distilled white vinegar
1 small jalapeño chile, stemmed, seeded, and sliced thin
2 pounds flap meat, trimmed and cut into 2-inch chunks
3½ teaspoons kosher salt, divided
2½ teaspoons ground cumin, divided
1½ teaspoons pepper, divided
2 tablespoons vegetable oil
3 garlic cloves, minced
3 (15-ounce) cans pinto beans, rinsed
1½ cups chicken broth

1. Combine onion, vinegar, and jalapeño in small bowl. Cover and microwave until hot, about 2 minutes; set aside.

2. Sprinkle beef with 2 teaspoons salt, ½ teaspoon cumin, and 1 teaspoon pepper. Heat oil in 12-inch nonstick skillet over medium-high heat until just smoking. Add beef and cook until browned on all sides and meat registers 130 to 135 degrees (for medium), 7 to 10 minutes. Transfer beef to large plate and tent with foil.

3. Reduce heat to medium, add garlic and remaining 2 teaspoons cumin to now-empty skillet, and cook until fragrant, about 30 seconds. Stir in beans, broth, remaining 1½ teaspoons salt, and remaining ½ teaspoon pepper. Using potato masher, lightly mash beans until about one-quarter of beans are broken down. Bring to simmer and cook until thickened and liquid is fully incorporated into bean mixture, about 4 minutes. Serve steak with beans and pickled onion mixture.

BEEF SHASHLIK

Serves 4 to 6 | flap meat

WHY THIS RECIPE WORKS Shashlik—a favorite in the Brighton Beach neighborhood of Brooklyn, New York, and a popular street food in Russia, Kazakhstan, and the Caucasus—is a flame-grilled kebab with juicy, well-charred meat that's been flavored with a potent marinade. For our version, we opted for sirloin steak tips, which have big, beefy flavor. Their loose grain also enabled them to soak up more of the marinade; our version blended tangy red wine vinegar, neutral vegetable oil, and chopped onion and garlic with a harmonious array of warm spices. Adding a little sugar and grilling the steak tips over a hot fire ensured delicious charring despite the relatively wet marinade. A sweet, tangy sauce of caramelized onion and tart yogurt provided the perfect complement to the flame-kissed beef.

MARINADE
½ cup coarsely chopped onion
¼ cup vegetable oil
2 tablespoons red wine vinegar
4 garlic cloves
1 tablespoon soy sauce
1 tablespoon kosher salt
1 tablespoon sugar
1 teaspoon ground cumin
½ teaspoon pepper
½ teaspoon ground coriander
¼ teaspoon ground cinnamon
¼ teaspoon cayenne pepper
1 bay leaf, crumbled

BEEF AND SAUCE
2 pounds flap meat, trimmed and cut into 1-inch pieces
1 onion, chopped fine
⅓ cup water
1 tablespoon vegetable oil
½ cup plain whole-milk yogurt
⅓ cup chopped fresh cilantro
2 teaspoons lemon juice
6 (10-inch) wooden skewers, soaked in water for at least 30 minutes

1. **For the marinade:** Process all ingredients in blender until smooth, about 30 seconds. Measure out 2 tablespoons marinade and set aside.

2. **For the beef and sauce:** Combine beef and remaining marinade in 1-gallon zipper-lock bag. Press out air, seal bag, and turn to coat beef in marinade. Refrigerate for 1 to 2 hours.

3. While beef marinates, combine onion, water, oil, and reserved marinade in 10-inch skillet. Cover and cook over medium-high heat until liquid has evaporated and onion is beginning to brown, 5 to 7 minutes, stirring occasionally. Uncover, reduce heat to medium, and continue to cook until onion is well browned, 8 to 10 minutes longer. Transfer onion to bowl and stir in yogurt, cilantro, and lemon juice. Season with salt and pepper to taste.

4. Thread beef tightly onto skewers, leaving ends of skewers slightly exposed.

5a. **For a charcoal grill:** Open bottom vent completely. Light large chimney starter mounded with charcoal briquettes (7 quarts). When top coals are partially covered with ash, pour evenly over half of grill. Set cooking grate in place, cover, and open lid vent completely. Heat grill until hot, about 5 minutes.

5b. **For a gas grill:** Turn all burners to high, cover, and heat grill until hot, about 15 minutes. Leave all burners on high.

Beef Shashlik

6. Clean and oil cooking grate. Arrange kebabs on grill (over hotter side if using charcoal) and cook (covered if using gas), turning every 2 to 3 minutes, until beef is well browned, charred around edges, and registers between 135 and 145 degrees, 8 to 12 minutes. Transfer kebabs to platter, tent with aluminum foil, and let rest for 5 minutes. Serve with sauce.

GRILLED BEEF TERIYAKI

Serves 4 | flap meat

WHY THIS RECIPE WORKS The meaty, caramelized flavor of teriyaki is a treasure of this Japanese American dish. But if care isn't taken, attempts to make this restaurant dish at home can result in chewy, flavorless meat shellacked with a saccharine-sweet sauce. To beef things up, we turned to a marinade that would help the beef stay juicy on the grill and promote browning. Soy sauce contributed saltiness and savoriness, sugar and mirin added balanced sweetness, and scallions and ginger gave it an aromatic boost. Grilling sirloin steak tips over high heat produced well-charred, slightly smoky meat, and slicing the meat against the grain before grilling it gave us better texture and helped the glaze adhere firmly to each piece. Serve this dish with white rice.

STEAK
- 2 pounds flap meat, trimmed
- ⅓ cup soy sauce
- ¼ cup mirin
- 2 scallions, white parts minced, green parts sliced thin on bias
- 2 tablespoons vegetable oil
- 3 garlic cloves, minced
- 1 tablespoon grated fresh ginger
- 1 tablespoon sugar
- 1 teaspoon grated orange zest

SAUCE
- ½ cup sugar
- ½ cup sake or vermouth
- ½ cup mirin
- ⅓ cup soy sauce
- 1 teaspoon grated fresh ginger
- 1 teaspoon cornstarch

1. **For the steak:** Cut meat with grain into 2 or 3 even pieces. (If total length of meat is 12 inches or less, cut into 2 pieces. If more than 12 inches, cut into 3 pieces.) Holding knife at 45-degree angle to meat, cut each piece against grain into four or five ½-inch-thick slices. Combine soy sauce, mirin, scallion whites, oil, garlic, ginger, sugar, and orange zest in bowl. Place beef in 1-gallon zipper-lock bag and pour marinade into bag; toss beef to coat. Seal bag, pressing out as much air as possible, and refrigerate for 30 minutes to 1 hour, flipping bag every 15 minutes.

2a. **For a charcoal grill:** Open bottom vent completely. Light large chimney starter filled with charcoal briquettes (6 quarts). When top coals are partially covered with ash, pour evenly over half of grill. Set cooking grate in place, cover, and open lid vent completely. Heat grill until hot, about 5 minutes.

2b. **For a gas grill:** Turn all burners to high, cover, and heat grill until hot, about 15 minutes. Leave all burners on high.

3. **For the sauce:** Meanwhile, whisk all ingredients together in small saucepan and bring to simmer over medium heat. Cook until syrupy and reduced to 1 cup, 12 to 15 minutes. Set aside ¾ cup sauce.

4. Clean and oil cooking grate. Remove beef from marinade and pat dry with paper towels. Place beef on grill (on hotter side if using charcoal) and cook (covered if using gas) until dark brown, 6 to 8 minutes, flipping halfway through cooking. Brush beef with 2 tablespoons sauce, flip, and cook for 30 seconds. Brush beef with remaining 2 tablespoons sauce, flip, and continue to cook 30 seconds longer. Transfer beef to platter, tent with aluminum foil, and let rest for 5 to 10 minutes. Sprinkle with scallion greens and serve, passing reserved sauce separately.

Juicy Pub-Style Burgers

JUICY PUB-STYLE BURGERS

Serves 4 | flap meat

WHY THIS RECIPE WORKS In our quest for the ideal hearty pub-style burger, we found that grinding our own beef (for more on ground meat, see pages 364–368) was the best way to get big, beefy flavor and rich texture. For a taste of the pub, we started by freezing meaty sirloin steak tips, which made them easier to grind in a food processor to just the right coarse texture. To up the fat content on this leaner-than-chuck cut, we mixed in a little melted butter, which improved richness and juiciness. Lightly packing the patties gave the burgers enough structure without overworking the meat and making the burgers bouncy. We used a two-step cooking process to do the beef justice: The stovetop provided intense heat for searing, and the oven's ambient heat allowed a gentle, even finish for the perfect juicy center. A quick "special sauce" jazzed up the basic burger, and premium (but simple) additions made appealing variations. For the best flavor, season the burgers aggressively just before cooking. Use a food processor with a capacity of 7 to 14 cups.

SAUCE

- ¾ cup mayonnaise
- 2 tablespoons soy sauce
- 1 tablespoon packed dark brown sugar
- 1 tablespoon Worcestershire sauce
- 1 tablespoon minced fresh chives
- 1 garlic clove, minced
- ¾ teaspoon pepper

BURGERS

- 2 pounds flap meat, trimmed and cut into ½-inch pieces
- 4 tablespoons unsalted butter, melted and cooled
- 1 teaspoon pepper
- 1 teaspoon vegetable oil
- 4 large hamburger buns, toasted and buttered

1. For the sauce: Whisk all ingredients together in bowl; refrigerate until ready to serve.

2. For the burgers: Arrange beef in single layer in rimmed baking sheet and freeze until very firm and starting to harden around edges but still pliable, about 35 minutes.

3. Working in 4 batches, pulse beef in food processor until finely ground into ¹⁄₁₆-inch pieces, about 20 pulses, stopping to redistribute meat as needed; return to sheet. Spread beef over sheet, discarding long strands of gristle and large chunks of fat.

4. Adjust oven rack to middle position and heat oven to 300 degrees. Drizzle beef with melted butter, sprinkle with pepper, and gently toss with fork to combine. Divide beef into 4 lightly packed balls, then gently flatten into ¾-inch-thick burgers. Refrigerate until ready to cook. (Burgers can be covered and refrigerated for up to 1 day.)

5. Season 1 side of burgers with salt and pepper. Using spatula, gently flip patties and season other side. Heat oil in 12-inch skillet over high heat until just smoking. Using spatula, transfer burgers to skillet and cook, without moving, for 2 minutes. Flip burgers and continue to cook for 2 minutes. Transfer to rimmed baking sheet and bake until burgers register 120 to 125 degrees (for medium-rare), 3 to 5 minutes. Transfer burgers to platter and let rest for 5 minutes before serving on buns with sauce.

VARIATIONS

Juicy Pub-Style Burgers with Crispy Shallots and Blue Cheese

Heat ½ cup vegetable oil and 3 thinly sliced shallots in medium saucepan over high heat; cook, stirring frequently, until shallots are golden, about 8 minutes. Using slotted spoon, transfer shallots to paper towel–lined plate, season with salt, and let drain until crispy, about 5 minutes. (Shallots can be stored at room temperature for up to 3 days.) Top each burger with ¼ cup crumbled blue cheese before transferring to oven. Top with shallots before serving.

Juicy Pub-Style Burgers with Peppered Bacon and Aged Cheddar

Before cooking burgers, lay 6 slices of bacon in rimmed baking sheet. Sprinkle with 2 teaspoons coarsely ground pepper. Place second rimmed baking sheet on top of bacon. Bake in 375-degree oven until bacon is crisp, 15 to 20 minutes; transfer to paper towel–lined plate and let cool. Cut bacon in half crosswise. Before finishing burgers in oven, top with ¼ cup shredded aged cheddar cheese. Top with bacon before serving.

Juicy Pub-Style Burgers with Pan-Roasted Mushrooms and Gruyère

Heat 2 tablespoons vegetable oil in a 12-inch skillet over medium-high heat until just smoking. Add 10 ounces thinly sliced cremini mushrooms, ¼ teaspoon table salt, and ¼ teaspoon pepper; cook, stirring frequently, until browned, 5 to 7 minutes. Add 1 minced shallot and 2 teaspoons minced thyme and cook until fragrant. Remove the skillet from the heat and stir in 2 tablespoons dry sherry. Top each burger with 1 ounce grated Gruyère cheese before transferring to the oven. Top with mushrooms before serving.

ROUND

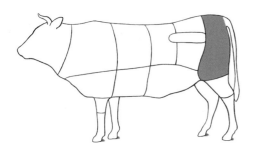

WE DON'T JUMP FOR THE round to round out a meal. This area of the cow—the rump and hind legs (the very back of the cow, as round designates in any animal)—is quite lean, incredibly light in flavor, and not too tender, as the muscles here get so much exercise in movement. But while we generally prefer cuts from other parts of the cow, top round makes a classic roast beef with success—if you slice it very thin. The bottom is better left for stewing. They're worth considering for their superlow cost for roast beef and, in one case, incredibly even shape that translates to incredibly even cooking, a distinct benefit when making roast beef. Let's get around to breaking down the round.

Top Round Roast

Cost: ◼◻◻◻ **Flavor:** ◼◼◻◻
Best cooking methods: roast
Texture: on the tough side
Alternative names: top round first cut, top round steak roast

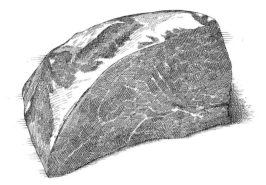

This affordable roast is a common choice in supermarkets. It's very similar to the top sirloin roast, with good flavor, texture, and juiciness. It can be overly chewy if sliced thick. Top round can be cut into steaks, though they're not a cut we love. In steak preparations, top round borders on tough and livery-tasting—except for in our Grilled London Broil (page 131), where the grill works wonders for an affordable meal.

Bottom Round Roast

Cost: ◼◻◻◻ **Flavor:** ◼◻◻◻
Best cooking methods: stew, roast
Texture: chewy
Alternative names: round roast, bottom round pot roast, bottom round oven roast, outside round.

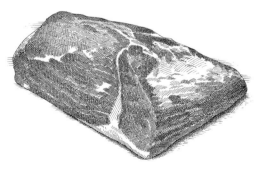

While relatively beefy, this cut can be rubbery and chewy and needs to be given tender loving care. But it's a very economical, common cut so we teach you how to break down its connective tissue in our recipe on page 131. This cut is least chewy when cooked to medium.

Boneless Eye-Round Roast

Cost: ◼◻◻◻ **Flavor:** ◼◻◻◻
Best cooking methods: roast
Texture: on the tough side
Alternative names: round eye pot roast

This boneless roast is quite inexpensive but not as flavorful as the top cuts. Why it's a common go-to: It has a nice even shape that slices easily—the quintessential-looking roast beef. In order to make this lean cut as tender as possible, roast it in a very low oven. When we're using it in an application where we need to slice it thin, we cook it to medium; this makes the meat firmer and easy to cut into clean, very thin tender slices to pile on a sandwich.

WHAT'S LONDON BROIL?

Coined in the early 1930s at Keen's Chophouse in New York City, the term "London broil" doesn't refer to a particular cut of meat at all, even though one might be labeled as such. Rather, it's a generic label bandied about by butchers to sell large, cheap, unfamiliar steaks that might otherwise be ignored by customers. Over the years, a number of different steaks have been called London broil. For a while, flank steak was the most common, but flank's popularity bumped its price out of the London broil range. Now, you'll mostly see top round steak, bottom round steak, and chuck steak labeled as London broil.

Grilled London Broil

GRILLED LONDON BROIL

Serves 4 | top round steak

WHY THIS RECIPE WORKS We were determined to tackle London broil (see page 129), another name for inexpensive but robustly flavored steak—and to like it. How did we do it? We grilled marinated steak over the hotter side of a half-grill fire and flipped it every minute to prevent a gray band of overcooked meat from forming, but flipping the steak so often inhibited charring. To remedy this without sacrificing a rosy interior, we crosshatched both sides of the steak to create thin ridges that would crisp up quickly. We also added a simple spice rub that crusted nicely on the grill. This lean steak will be very dry if overcooked.

1. (1½- to 2-pound) top round steak, 1½ inches thick, trimmed
½ cup soy sauce
2 tablespoons balsamic vinegar
2 tablespoons ketchup
2 tablespoons chopped fresh sage
5 garlic cloves, minced
1½ tablespoons vegetable oil
1 teaspoon chopped fresh rosemary
1½ teaspoons coarsely ground pepper
1 teaspoon paprika

1. Using sharp knife, cut ½-inch crosshatch pattern, ¼ inch deep, on both sides of steak. Place steak in 1-gallon zipper-lock bag. Combine soy sauce, vinegar, ketchup, sage, garlic, oil, and rosemary in blender and process until garlic and herbs are finely chopped, about 30 seconds. Add marinade to bag with steak, seal, and turn to coat. Let sit at room temperature for 2 hours or refrigerate for up to 8 hours. (If refrigerated, bring steak to room temperature before grilling.)

2a. For a charcoal grill: Open bottom vent completely. Light large chimney starter filled with charcoal briquettes (6 quarts). When top coals are partially covered with ash, pour evenly over half of grill. Set cooking grate in place, cover, and open lid vent completely. Heat grill until hot, about 5 minutes.

2b. For a gas grill: Turn all burners to high, cover, and heat grill until hot, about 15 minutes. Leave all burners on high.

3. Combine pepper and paprika in bowl. Remove steak from marinade, pat dry with paper towels, and season with pepper mixture.

4. Clean and oil cooking grate. Place steak on grill (on hotter side if using charcoal) and cook for 1 minute. Flip and grill on second side for 1 minute. Repeat, flipping every minute, until steak registers 120 to 125 degrees (for medium-rare), 5 to 8 minutes. Transfer to carving board, tent with aluminum foil, and let rest for 10 minutes. Slice steak thin against grain and serve.

BOTTOM ROUND ROAST BEEF WITH ZIP-STYLE SAUCE

Serves 8 | bottom round roast

WHY THIS RECIPE WORKS Bottom round roast is typically a fairly bland, chewy cut—as we've said, not our favorite. But if you treat it correctly, it has a chance at being tender and juicy. Salting the meat in advance helped make it more juicy and flavorful throughout, and a woodsy herbed crust of thyme, rosemary, salt, and pepper contributed enough flavor to make browning unnecessary. We roasted the beef in a 250-degree oven, tenderizing the meat by slowly breaking down its tough connective tissue. After about 2 hours, we turned off the oven and let the roast gradually finish cooking. We served the roast with our take on Detroit zip sauce, a combination of butter, Worcestershire sauce, garlic, rosemary, and thyme. This was the last step in zipping up bottom round roast. Because the sauce contains butter, it will solidify as it cools, so it's best kept warm for serving.

BEEF
1 (4-pound) boneless beef bottom round roast, trimmed and tied at 1½-inch intervals
1 tablespoon kosher salt, divided
1 tablespoon minced fresh rosemary
1 tablespoon minced fresh thyme
2 teaspoons pepper
2 tablespoons vegetable oil

ZIP-STYLE SAUCE
8 tablespoons unsalted butter
½ cup Worcestershire sauce
2 garlic cloves, minced
2 teaspoons minced fresh rosemary
1 teaspoon minced fresh thyme
½ teaspoon kosher salt
½ teaspoon pepper

1. **For the beef:** Pat roast dry with paper towels and rub with 2 teaspoons salt. Refrigerate, uncovered, for at least 1 hour or up to 24 hours.

2. Adjust oven rack to middle position and heat oven to 250 degrees. Set wire rack in rimmed baking sheet. Combine rosemary, thyme, pepper, and remaining 1 teaspoon salt in bowl.

3. Pat roast dry with paper towels. Rub roast all over with oil and sprinkle with herb mixture; place fat side up on prepared rack. Transfer to oven and cook until beef registers 120 degrees, 1¾ hours to 2¼ hours. Turn off oven and leave roast in oven, without opening door, until beef registers 130 to 135 degrees (for medium), 20 to 30 minutes. Transfer roast to carving board and let rest for 30 minutes.

4. For the zip-style sauce: Meanwhile, bring all sauce ingredients to bare simmer in small saucepan over medium heat, whisking constantly. Remove from heat, cover, and keep warm. Slice roast thin against grain. Serve with sauce.

SLOW-ROAST BEEF

Serves 6 to 8 | boneless eye-round roast

WHY THIS RECIPE WORKS For many, the modest roast beef go-to is an eye-round roast. Despite its low price, it has a uniform shape that guarantees even cooking so we wanted to make it work. Searing the meat before roasting, as well as salting it as much as 24 hours before cooking, vastly improved its flavor. Similar to the method for our bottom round roast (see page 131), we roasted the meat at a very low 225 degrees and then turned off the oven toward the end of cooking. This approach allowed the meat's enzymes to act as natural tenderizers, breaking down the tough connective tissue. If the roast has not reached the desired temperature in the time specified in step 4, reheat the oven to 225 degrees for 5 minutes, then shut it off and continue to cook the roast to the desired temperature. We like to serve this roast with Horseradish–Sour Cream Sauce (page 22).

  1 (3½- to 4½-pound) boneless eye-round roast, trimmed
  4 teaspoons kosher salt
  2 teaspoons plus 1 tablespoon vegetable oil, divided
  2 teaspoons pepper

1. Rub roast thoroughly with salt, wrap in plastic wrap, and refrigerate for at least 18 or up to 24 hours.

2. Adjust oven rack to middle position and heat oven to 225 degrees. Pat roast dry with paper towels, rub with 2 teaspoons oil, and sprinkle with pepper.

3. Heat remaining 1 tablespoon oil in 12-inch skillet over medium-high heat until just smoking. Brown roast well on all sides, 12 to 16 minutes; reduce heat if pan begins to scorch. Transfer roast to wire rack set in rimmed baking sheet and roast until meat registers 115 degrees (for medium-rare), 1¼ to 1¾ hours.

4. Turn off oven and leave roast in oven, without opening door, until meat registers 120 to 125 degrees (for medium-rare), 30 to 40 minutes.

5. Transfer roast to carving board and let rest for 15 to 20 minutes. Slice meat as thin as possible against the grain and serve.

SMOKED ROAST BEEF

Serves 6 to 8 | boneless eye-round roast

WHY THIS RECIPE WORKS Deep, rich, and flavorful, this beef has evenly cooked meat that is pink throughout, along with smoky grill flavor—that's a lot to like. A paste made of herbs, salt, and ketchup tenderized the meat and amplified its beefiness. We first slow-cooked the roast over indirect heat using a foil shield to moderate the temperature. Then we reloaded the grill with fresh coals while the roast rested so we could create a nicely charred crust over a fresh, hot fire. If using charcoal, you will need to light two fires, the first to smoke the meat, and the second to sear it after a rest. If using a gas grill, simply turn it off between uses. If you'd like to use wood chunks instead of wood chips when using a charcoal grill, substitute one medium wood chunk, soaked in water for 1 hour, for the wood chip packet. You don't need to rest the meat again after step 5; it can be served immediately.

  2 tablespoons ketchup
  4 teaspoons table salt
  2 teaspoons pepper
  ½ teaspoon dried thyme
  ½ teaspoon dried oregano
  ½ teaspoon dried rosemary
  1 (4-pound) boneless eye-round roast, trimmed
  1 cup wood chips
  2 teaspoons vegetable oil

1. Combine ketchup, salt, pepper, thyme, oregano, and rosemary in bowl. Rub ketchup mixture all over roast, then wrap roast in plastic wrap and refrigerate for at least 6 hours or up to 24 hours. Just before grilling, soak wood chips in water for 15 minutes, then drain. Using large piece of heavy-duty aluminum foil, wrap chips in 8 by 4½-inch foil packet. (Make sure chips do not poke holes in sides or bottom of packet.) Cut 2 evenly spaced 2-inch slits in top of packet.

2a. For a charcoal grill: Open bottom vent halfway. Light large chimney starter half filled with charcoal briquettes (3 quarts). When top coals are partially covered with ash, pour into steeply banked pile against side of grill. Place wood chip packet on coals. Set cooking grate in place, cover, and open lid vent halfway. Heat grill until hot and wood chips are smoking, about 5 minutes.

2b. For a gas grill: Remove cooking grate and place wood chip packet directly on primary burner. Set cooking grate in place, turn all burners to high, cover, and heat grill until hot and wood chips are smoking, about 15 minutes. Turn primary burner to medium-high and turn off other burner(s). (Adjust primary burner [or, if using 3-burner grill, primary burner and second burner] as needed to maintain grill temperature of 325 degrees.)

TUTORIAL
Smoked Roast Beef

Taking roast beef outside and adding a layer of smoke makes the classic into something completely new and improved when you follow these steps.

1. Rub ketchup mixture all over roast, then wrap roast in plastic wrap and refrigerate for at least 6 hours or up to 24 hours.

2. Make two ½-inch folds on long side of 18-inch length of foil to form reinforced edge. Place foil in center of cooking grate, with reinforced edge over hotter side. Place roast on cooler side of grill so that it covers one-third of foil. Lift, bend, and tuck edges of foil to shield roast.

3. Cook, covered, until meat registers 120 to 125 degrees (for medium-rare), 1½ to 1¾ hours. Remove roast from grill, transfer to wire rack, and tent with foil. Let roast rest for 30 minutes to 1 hour.

4. Brush roast all over with oil.

5. Grill directly over coals, turning frequently, until charred on all sides, 8 to 12 minutes.

6. Transfer meat to carving board, slice thin, and serve.

3. Set wire rack in rimmed baking sheet. Unwrap roast. Make two ½-inch folds on long side of 18-inch length of foil to form reinforced edge. Place foil in center of cooking grate, with reinforced edge over hotter side of grill. Place roast on cooler side of grill so that it covers one-third of foil. Lift and bend edges of foil to shield roast, tucking in edges. Cook, covered, until meat registers 120 to 125 degrees (for medium-rare), 1 ½ to 1 ¾ hours. Remove roast from grill, transfer to prepared wire rack, and tent with foil. Let roast rest for 30 minutes or up to 1 hour.

4a. For a charcoal grill: Open bottom vent completely. Light large chimney starter filled with charcoal briquettes (6 quarts). When top coals are partially covered with ash, pour into pile over spent coals. Set cooking grate in place, cover, and open lid vent completely. Heat grill until hot, about 5 minutes.

4b. For a gas grill: Turn all burners to high, cover, and heat grill until hot, about 5 minutes. Leave all burners on high.

5. Clean and oil cooking grate. Brush roast all over with oil. Grill (directly over coals if using charcoal; covered if using gas), turning frequently, until charred on all sides, 8 to 12 minutes. Transfer meat to carving board, slice thin, and serve.

BEEF ON WECK SANDWICHES

Makes 8 sandwiches | boneless eye-round roast

WHY THIS RECIPE WORKS To make Buffalo's signature sandwich, beef on weck, a salty roll called a kummelweck (we approximate one here) is piled high with thinly sliced roast beef, jus, and horseradish sauce. We wanted to make enough sandwiches to feed a crowd, so we'd need a sizable cut. Lean, inexpensive eye round proved to be just right. We usually cook eye round at a low temperature to gently break down its connective tissue but we didn't want an hour-plus cooking time for a humble sandwich; dividing the roast into two long strips cut the cooking time in half. Cooking the roast to medium made it easier to slice thin, and it was still tender and flavorful. A savory jus—tossed with the meat to prevent the bun from getting too soggy—and a quick horseradish sauce brought everything together.

HORSERADISH SAUCE
½ cup prepared horseradish, drained
1 tablespoon sour cream
1 tablespoon mayonnaise

BEEF
1 (2- to 2½-pound) boneless eye-round roast, trimmed
5 teaspoons vegetable oil, divided
2 teaspoons kosher salt
2 teaspoons pepper
2 teaspoons minced fresh thyme
¼ cup prepared horseradish, drained

JUS
1 onion, chopped fine
1 teaspoon vegetable oil
1 teaspoon cornstarch
2½ cups beef broth
1 sprig fresh thyme

WECK
8 kaiser rolls, split
2 teaspoons caraway seeds
1½ teaspoons kosher salt
2 tablespoons water
½ teaspoon cornstarch

1. For the horseradish sauce: Combine horseradish, sour cream, and mayonnaise in bowl; set aside.

2. For the beef: Adjust oven rack to middle position and heat oven to 275 degrees. Cut roast in half lengthwise to make 2 even-size roasts. Rub each roast with 1 teaspoon oil and season each with 1 teaspoon salt, 1 teaspoon pepper, and 1 teaspoon thyme. Tie roasts with kitchen twine at 1-inch intervals.

3. Heat remaining 1 tablespoon oil in 12-inch ovensafe skillet over medium-high heat until just smoking. Add both roasts and cook until browned on all sides, 6 to 8 minutes. Transfer skillet to oven and cook until roasts register 130 degrees, 28 to 32 minutes. Transfer roasts to carving board, tent with aluminum foil, and let rest for at least 30 minutes or up to 1 hour. Reserve skillet and any meat drippings. Increase oven temperature to 400 degrees.

4. For the jus: Return skillet with meat drippings to medium-high heat (skillet handle will be hot) and add onion and oil. Cook until onion is just softened, about 3 minutes, scraping up any browned bits. Whisk cornstarch into broth. Add broth mixture and thyme sprig to skillet and bring to boil. Reduce heat to medium-low and simmer until reduced by half and slightly thickened, about 7 minutes. Strain jus through fine-mesh strainer set over small saucepan; discard solids. Cover and keep warm.

Beef on Weck Sandwiches

Slow-Cooker Roast Beef with
Warm Garden Potato Salad

5. **For the weck:** Place rolls on rimmed baking sheet. Combine caraway seeds and salt in bowl. Whisk water and cornstarch together in separate bowl. Microwave cornstarch mixture until consistency of glue, about 30 seconds. Brush cornstarch mixture on roll tops, then sprinkle with caraway mixture. Bake until caraway mixture is set and rolls are crusty, about 7 minutes.

6. Slice roasts as thin as possible against grain. Toss sliced meat, ⅓ cup jus, and horseradish together in bowl and season with salt and pepper to taste. Sandwich meat mixture in rolls (about ½ cup per roll). Serve with horseradish sauce and individual portions of jus for dipping.

SLOW-COOKER ROAST BEEF WITH WARM GARDEN POTATO SALAD

Serves 8 to 10 | boneless eye-round roast
Cooking time: 1 to 2 hours on low

WHY THIS RECIPE WORKS A roast beef and vegetable dinner is surprisingly well suited for the slow cooker. As with many slow-cooker recipes, prep steps made it perfect: A quick sear in a skillet gave the roast a flavorful dark crust before we cooked it all the way through in the slow cooker at a low temperature to ensure an even doneness and a rosy color throughout. Microwaving the potatoes first allowed them to finish cooking in the slow cooker at the same time as the roast. However, we wanted a green element, too. To keep a side of green beans crisp-tender, we left them out of the slow cooker and simply steamed them in the microwave. Then we combined them with the potatoes in a flavorful salad. You will need an oval slow cooker for this recipe. Check the roast's temperature after 1 hour of cooking and continue to monitor until it registers 120 to 125 degrees (for medium-rare).

1 (4-pound) boneless eye-round roast, trimmed
4¾ teaspoons kosher salt, divided
2 pounds Yukon Gold potatoes, unpeeled, cut into 1-inch pieces
7 tablespoons extra-virgin olive oil, divided
1½ teaspoons garlic powder
2 pounds green beans, trimmed and cut on bias into 1-inch lengths
¼ cup chopped fresh parsley
1 shallot, minced
2 tablespoons white wine vinegar
2 tablespoons Dijon mustard
2 tablespoons minced fresh chives
⅛ teaspoon pepper

1. Sprinkle roast with 4 teaspoons salt. Wrap tightly in plastic wrap and refrigerate for at least 18 hours or up to 24 hours.

2. Microwave potatoes, 1 tablespoon oil, and ½ teaspoon salt in covered bowl, stirring occasionally, until almost tender, 8 to 10 minutes; transfer to slow cooker.

3. Pat roast dry with paper towels. Rub with 1 tablespoon oil, sprinkle with garlic powder, and season with pepper. Heat 1 tablespoon oil in 12-inch skillet over medium-high heat until just smoking. Brown roast on all sides, 7 to 10 minutes. Place roast on top of potatoes, cover, and cook until beef registers 120 to 125 degrees (for medium-rare), 1 to 2 hours on low.

4. Transfer roast to carving board, tent with aluminum foil, and let rest for 20 minutes.

5. While roast rests, microwave green beans and ¼ cup water in large covered bowl, stirring occasionally, until crisp-tender, 8 to 10 minutes. Drain green beans and return to now-empty bowl. Drain potatoes and transfer to bowl with green beans.

6. Whisk parsley, shallot, vinegar, mustard, chives, pepper, remaining ¼ cup oil, and remaining ¼ teaspoon salt together in small bowl. Pour dressing over vegetables and gently toss to combine. Season with salt and pepper to taste. Slice roast thin against grain. Serve with potato salad.

BRISKET

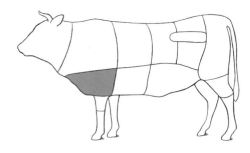

RUNNING ALONG THE UNDERSIDE OF the cow is the breast, home to the tough but terrific brisket. Coarse-grained and tough on the counter, it can be turned tender by the sorcery of slow braising or grill-roasting. Brisket is known primarily as a centerpiece winter dish, sauced with a savory gravy, or as one of the cornerstone cuts for barbecue. It is also brined (see pages 147 and 148 for corned or barbecue beef). This large, rectangular cut weighs about 13 pounds, so it's often divided into two subcuts: the flat cut (on the left side in this brisket) and the point cut (on the right side). We most often cook with one of these subcuts (specifically the flat cut), but our recipe for Texas Barbecue Brisket (page 181) uses the whole cut, for when you have a crowd you can feed.

THE TOUGHEST OF THE TOUGH

Braising gives tough cuts—think chuck cuts or top sirloin roast—the beat-down. And yet, brisket still often takes twice as long as most boneless roasts of the same weight to reach tenderness (when it does, it's well worth it). Why is brisket so darn stubborn? We've always thought that's because brisket has more chewy collagen (the main component in meat's connective tissue) than other cuts; the collagen needs more time to convert to soft gelatin for the meat to fully tenderize. But when we braise brisket, the braising liquid is actually quite thin rather than silky and unctuous, the way you'd expect liquid full of gelatin to be. Is there something else at work? Collagen is most abundant in muscles that get the most exercise. For this reason, brisket (from the breast, which supports 60 percent of the cow's weight) is naturally higher in collagen than chuck. But over time, exercise creates cross-links in collagen that transform it from a soluble form to a stronger and more insoluble form. Insoluble collagen can only weaken and soften with prolonged exposure to heat; it won't break down into gelatin and thus won't create full-bodied juices (sometimes we'll bolster them with gelatin; see page 142). So the brisket breakdown is indeed long because of collagen—you just don't see that in the liquid in the pan.

REFRIGERATOR REST

Serving company? Braised brisket can actually benefit from being cooled down and stored in the refrigerator overnight before reheating and serving for a convenience boost. The coarse-grained meat continues to soak up sauce as it sits for a juicier, more tender brisket. But the refrigerator rest also allows you to slice the meat without it falling apart or shredding. This is perfect if you're cooking brisket for a crowd: Making this dish a day ahead reduces the stress of timing in the kitchen, and the neatly sliced brisket creates a much more elegant spread on the serving platter.

Flat-Cut Brisket

Cost: ◼◼◻◻   **Flavor:** ◼◼◻◻
Best cooking methods: braise, barbecue
Texture: tough, then tender once slow cooked
Alternative names: middle cut, center cut, front cut, nose cut, first cut.

The flat-cut side of the brisket is leaner, thinner, more uniform in shape, and more widely available. When shopping for one, because it is leaner, make sure you see a decent fat cap on top. Because it is what you'll most likely find, we call for it in our recipes.

TRIM BRISKET—BARELY

The cap on a brisket contains all that fat and connective tissue that bastes the brisket and breaks down to keep it moist. Make sure you purchase a brisket with a fat cap and don't trim it more than is called for in the recipe, usually ¼ inch at the thinnest, often between ⅓ and ½ inch, depending on the application. (Too thick and it could create an overly greasy sauce during braising.)

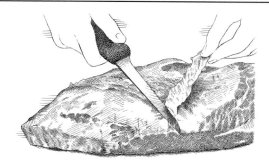

Using sharp knife, trim brisket's fat cap to thickness called for in recipe.

Point-Cut Brisket

Cost: ■■ □ □   **Flavor:** ■■ □ □
Best cooking methods: braise, barbecue
Texture: tough, then tender once slow-cooked, juicy
Alternative names: second cut, deckle cut

The fattier, thicker, nobby well-marbled pointed end of the brisket will take longer to cook but will be more succulent. It's hard to find so we don't call for it in our recipes, but you can purchase it and use it in our recipes if you can find it. It is a bit less attractive and uniform than the flat-cut brisket when sliced.

WHOLE BRISKET: BARBECUE BEHEMOTH

You can buy a whole 13-pound brisket, and it's a staple of the barbecue circuit. While it's often not practical for the home cook, it's delicious if you do it right, cooking it low and slow and letting it soak up smoke. See our recipe for Texas Barbecue Brisket on page 151.

WHY IS BRISKET PINK?

Championship barbecue brisket always contains a thick smoke ring—the pink layer just beneath the meat's surface. Smoke doesn't play much of a role—it's actually caused by reactions that occur when meat is cooked for a long time at a low temperature in a closed chamber. The fire emits gases that dissolve in the moisture on the surface of the meat to create new compounds similar to the nitrates that keep deli meats pink. We found that placing a pan of water in the grill added enough moisture for a proper smoke ring. That's also why long brining for corned beef (and the pink salt cure) turns it uniformly pretty in pink from edge of a slice to edge (see page 147).

Braised Brisket with Pomegranate, Cumin, and Cilantro

BRISKET CARBONNADE

Serves 6 | flat-cut brisket

WHY THIS RECIPE WORKS To combine two favorite dishes—braised brisket and onions and carbonnade à la flamande, the famous Belgian beef stew made with beer—we started by browning a flat-cut beef brisket. Weighing the meat down with a Dutch oven ensured an evenly browned crust and created plenty of flavorful fond in the skillet. Slicing the onions thick prevented them from turning to mush during the 3 hours that the meat needed to tenderize in the oven, and adding a raw pureed onion to the mix thickened and flavored the sauce. Along with the beer, cider vinegar, mustard, and a little brown sugar rounded out the flavors of the sauce. Letting the brisket rest in the juices for an hour ensured that it was moist and tender. We like wheat beers, lagers, and pilsners in this recipe.

- 4 large onions
- 1 (3½-pound) beef brisket, flat cut, fat trimmed to ¼ inch
- 2 tablespoons vegetable oil, divided
- ½ teaspoon table salt
- 1 tablespoon tomato paste
- 2 garlic cloves, minced
- 1 tablespoon all-purpose flour
- 1½ cups beer
- 4 sprigs fresh thyme
- 2 bay leaves
- 1 tablespoon packed brown sugar
- 1 tablespoon cider vinegar
- 1 teaspoon Dijon mustard

1. Adjust oven rack to lower-middle position and heat oven to 325 degrees. Halve and slice 3 onions ½ inch thick. Puree remaining onion in food processor, about 10 seconds. Pat brisket dry with paper towels and season liberally with salt and pepper. Heat 1 tablespoon oil in 12-inch skillet over medium-high heat until just smoking. Place brisket in skillet, weigh down with Dutch oven or cast-iron skillet, and cook until well browned, about 4 minutes per side. Transfer brisket to 13 by 9-inch baking dish.

2. Heat remaining 1 tablespoon oil in now-empty skillet over medium heat until shimmering. Add sliced onions and salt and cook, stirring occasionally, until soft and golden brown, about 15 minutes. Stir in tomato paste and garlic and cook until fragrant, about 30 seconds. Stir in flour until onions are evenly coated and flour is lightly browned, about 2 minutes. Stir in pureed onion and cook until mixture has thickened, about 2 minutes. Stir in beer, thyme sprigs, bay leaves, sugar, and vinegar, scraping up any browned bits. Increase heat to medium-high and bring to boil.

3. Pour onion mixture over brisket and cover dish tightly with aluminum foil. Bake until brisket is tender and fork easily slips in and out of meat, about 3 hours. Let brisket rest in liquid, uncovered, for 1 hour.

4. Transfer brisket to carving board. Skim fat from top of sauce with large spoon and discard thyme sprigs and bay leaves. Whisk mustard into sauce and season with salt and pepper to taste. Slice meat against grain into ¼-inch-thick slices and return to dish with sauce. Serve.

BRAISED BRISKET WITH POMEGRANATE, CUMIN, AND CILANTRO

Serves 6 to 8 | flat-cut brisket

WHY THIS RECIPE WORKS For a modern take on a timeless cooking method, braising brisket, we wanted to spare no detail and create the ultimate brisket dish—one that stood apart from the rest for a special occasion. We started by salting the meat (halved lengthwise for quicker cooking and easier slicing and poked all over to allow the salt to penetrate) and letting it sit for at least 16 hours, which helped it retain moisture as it cooked; the salt also seasoned it. From there, we brought the meat to 180 degrees—in the sweet range for the collagen breakdown that is necessary for the meat to turn tender—relatively quickly in a 325-degree oven and then lowered the oven temperature to 250 degrees so that the brisket finished cooking gently. We reduced the braising liquid (chicken broth, pomegranate juice, lots of onions and garlic, anchovies, tomato paste, herbs, and spices) to achieve rich flavor and build body. If you have a probe thermometer, we recommend using it to monitor the temperature of the brisket as it cooks.

- 1 (4- to 5-pound) beef brisket, flat cut, fat trimmed to ¼ inch
- 5 teaspoons kosher salt
- 2 tablespoons vegetable oil
- 2 large onions, chopped
- ¼ teaspoon baking soda
- 6 garlic cloves, minced
- 4 anchovy fillets, rinsed, patted dry, and minced to paste
- 1 tablespoon tomato paste
- 1 tablespoon ground cumin
- 1½ teaspoons ground cardamom
- ½ teaspoon pepper
- ⅛ teaspoon cayenne pepper
- ¼ cup all-purpose flour
- 2 cups pomegranate juice
- 1½ cups chicken broth
- 3 bay leaves
- 2 tablespoons unflavored gelatin
- 1 cup pomegranate seeds
- 3 tablespoons chopped fresh cilantro

TUTORIAL

Braised Brisket with Pomegranate, Cumin, and Cilantro

We braise brisket a couple different ways—this is the least traditional but it makes the ultimate brisket to serve for a special occasion.

1. Cut brisket in half lengthwise with grain. Poke each roast 20 times, pushing all the way through roast. Flip roasts and repeat on second side. Sprinkle roasts with salt, wrap in plastic, and refrigerate for 16 to 48 hours.

2. Place roasts in pan with sauce mixture. Cover pan tightly with aluminum foil, transfer to oven, and cook until meat registers 180 to 185 degrees at center, about 1½ hours.

3. Reduce oven temperature to 250 degrees and continue to cook until fork slips easily in and out of meat, 2 to 2½ hours longer. Transfer roasts to baking sheet and wrap sheet tightly in foil.

4. Strain braising liquid through fine-mesh strainer, pressing on solids to extract as much liquid as possible; discard solids. Let settle and skim fat from surface. Return defatted liquid to pan.

5. Increase oven temperature to 400 degrees. Return pan to oven and cook, stirring occasionally, until liquid is reduced by about one-third, 30 to 40 minutes. Draw liquid up sides of pan and scrape browned bits around edges of pan into liquid.

6. Pour sauce over sliced brisket, tent platter with foil and let stand for 5 to 10 minutes to warm brisket through. Sprinkle with pomegranate seeds and cilantro and serve.

1. Place brisket, fat side down, on cutting board and cut in half lengthwise with grain. Using paring knife or metal skewer, poke each roast 20 times, pushing all the way through roast. Flip roasts and repeat on second side.

2. Sprinkle each roast evenly on all sides with 2½ teaspoons salt. Wrap each roast in plastic wrap and refrigerate for at least 16 hours or up to 48 hours.

3. Adjust oven rack to middle position and heat oven to 325 degrees. Heat oil in large roasting pan over medium heat until shimmering. Add onions and baking soda and cook, stirring frequently, until onions have started to soften and break down, 4 to 5 minutes. Add garlic and cook until fragrant, about 30 seconds. Stir in anchovies, tomato paste, cumin, cardamom, pepper, and cayenne. Add flour and cook, stirring constantly, until onions are evenly coated and flour begins to stick to pan, about 2 minutes. Stir in pomegranate juice, broth, and bay leaves, scraping up any browned bits. Stir in gelatin. Increase heat to medium-high and bring to boil.

4. Unwrap roasts and place in pan. Cover pan tightly with aluminum foil, transfer to oven, and cook until meat registers 180 to 185 degrees at center, about 1½ hours. Reduce oven temperature to 250 degrees and continue to cook until fork slips easily in and out of meat, 2 to 2½ hours longer. Transfer roasts to baking sheet and wrap sheet tightly in foil.

5. Strain braising liquid through fine-mesh strainer set over large bowl, pressing on solids to extract as much liquid as possible; discard solids. Let liquid settle for 10 minutes. Using wide, shallow spoon, skim fat from surface and discard. Wipe roasting pan clean with paper towels and return defatted liquid to pan.

6. Increase oven temperature to 400 degrees. Return pan to oven and cook, stirring occasionally, until liquid is reduced by about one-third, 30 to 40 minutes. Remove pan from oven and use wooden spoon to draw liquid up sides of pan and scrape browned bits around edges of pan into liquid.

7. Transfer roasts to carving board and slice against grain into ¼-inch-thick slices; transfer to wide platter. Season sauce with salt and pepper to taste and pour over brisket. Tent platter with foil and let stand for 5 to 10 minutes to warm brisket through. Sprinkle with pomegranate seeds and cilantro and serve.

To make ahead: Follow recipe through step 6 and let sauce and brisket cool completely. Cover and refrigerate sauce and roasts separately for up to 2 days. To serve, slice each roast against grain ¼ inch thick and transfer to 13 by 9-inch baking dish. Heat sauce in small saucepan over medium heat until just simmering. Pour sauce over brisket, cover dish with aluminum foil, and cook in 325-degree oven until meat is heated through, about 20 minutes.

BRISKET WITH PASILLA CHILE SAUCE

Serves 6 | flat-cut brisket

WHY THIS RECIPE WORKS Looking for a brisket repertoire with some complex heat, we decided to make a tender, juicy beef brisket with the complex flavors of Mexico's southern region of Oaxaca. To ensure that our brisket turned out tender, we cooked it fat side up so it would self-baste as it cooked, and we covered it with foil to hold in moisture. We infused our aromatic cooking liquid with toasted mild but deep-flavored and multidimensional pasilla chiles—the prime chile of Oaxaca—and lots of herbs and spices typically used in Mexico, dried oregano, ground cumin, dried thyme, ground coriander, and ground cloves. Blending the cooking liquid to a smooth consistency made an ample quantity of rich sauce to spoon over the meat. You will need 18-inch-wide heavy-duty aluminum foil for this recipe.

1 (3½-pound) beef brisket, flat cut, fat trimmed to ¼ inch
1 tablespoon table salt
4 pasilla chiles, stemmed, seeded, and torn into ½-inch pieces (1 cup)
1 tablespoon vegetable oil
2 onions, chopped
8 garlic cloves, peeled and smashed
1 tablespoon dried oregano
2 teaspoons ground cumin
2 teaspoons dried thyme
1 teaspoon ground coriander
1 teaspoon pepper
¼ teaspoon ground cloves
1 cup chicken broth
1 (28-ounce) can diced tomatoes

1. Poke holes all over brisket with fork and rub with salt. Wrap brisket in plastic wrap and refrigerate for at least 6 or up to 24 hours.

2. Adjust oven rack to lower-middle position and heat oven to 325 degrees. Pat brisket dry with paper towels and season with pepper. Toast pasillas in 12-inch skillet over medium heat, stirring frequently, until fragrant, 2 to 6 minutes; transfer to bowl.

3. Heat oil in now-empty skillet over medium-high heat until just smoking. Lay brisket in skillet, place heavy Dutch oven on top, and cook until well browned on both sides, about 4 minutes per side; transfer to platter.

Brisket with Pasilla Chile Sauce

4. Pour off all but 1 tablespoon fat from skillet. Add onions and cook over medium heat until softened, 8 to 10 minutes. Stir in garlic, oregano, cumin, thyme, coriander, pepper, and cloves and cook until fragrant, about 1 minute. Stir in broth, tomatoes and their juice, and toasted chiles, scraping up any browned bits, and bring to simmer. Transfer to 13 by 9-inch baking dish.

5. Nestle browned brisket, fat side up, into dish and spoon some sauce over top. Cover dish tightly with aluminum foil and bake until tender and fork easily slips in and out of meat, 3½ to 4 hours. Remove dish from oven and let brisket rest, covered, for 1 hour.

6. Transfer brisket to carving board and tent with foil. Strain cooking liquid through fine-mesh strainer into bowl; transfer solids to blender. Let liquid settle for 5 minutes, then skim fat from surface. Add defatted liquid to blender and puree until smooth, about 2 minutes. Season sauce with salt and pepper to taste.

7. Slice brisket against grain ¼ inch thick and return to baking dish. Pour sauce over top and serve. (Brisket can be refrigerated for up to 2 days; reheat, covered, in 350-degree oven for 45 minutes before serving.)

SLOW-COOKER BARBECUE BRISKET

Serves 10 to 12 | flat-cut brisket
Cooking time: 9 to 10 hours on low or 6 to 7 hours on high

WHY THIS RECIPE WORKS To make a tender and moist barbecue brisket with robust smoke flavor, not outside, but in the slow cooker, we started out with a simple spice rub, often the hallmark of great barbecue. Salt, pepper, brown sugar, cumin, and paprika built the backbone of flavor while chipotle chiles provided smokiness. To allow the rub to penetrate the meat we pierced the brisket all over with a fork and then refrigerated it overnight. We microwaved onions, more chipotles, tomato paste, garlic, and chili powder and added them to the slow cooker, along with a little water to bump up the flavor even more. The resulting braising liquid was sweet, smoky, and spicy; all we needed to do to finish the sauce was stir in ketchup, vinegar, and liquid smoke for a barbecue sauce. Do not use point-cut brisket in this recipe. You will need an oval slow cooker for this recipe.

½ cup packed dark brown sugar
3 tablespoons minced canned chipotle chile in adobo sauce, divided
1 tablespoon ground cumin
1 tablespoon paprika
2 teaspoons pepper
1 teaspoon table salt
1 (5-pound) beef brisket, flat cut, fat trimmed to ¼ inch
2 onions, chopped fine
2 tablespoons tomato paste
4 garlic cloves, minced
1 tablespoon vegetable oil
1 tablespoon chili powder
½ cup water
¼ cup ketchup
1 tablespoon cider vinegar
¼ teaspoon liquid smoke

1. Combine sugar, 2 tablespoons chipotle, cumin, paprika, pepper, and salt in bowl. Using fork, prick brisket all over. Rub sugar mixture over brisket, wrap tightly in plastic wrap, and refrigerate for at least 8 or up to 24 hours.

2. Microwave onions, tomato paste, garlic, oil, chili powder, and remaining 1 tablespoon chipotle in bowl, stirring occasionally, until onions are softened, about 5 minutes; transfer to slow cooker. Stir in water. Unwrap brisket and nestle fat side up into slow cooker. Spoon portion of onion mixture over brisket. Cover and cook until beef is tender, 9 to 10 hours on low or 6 to 7 hours on high.

3. Transfer brisket to carving board, tent with aluminum foil, and let rest for 20 minutes.

4. Using large spoon, skim fat from surface of sauce. Whisk in ketchup, vinegar, and liquid smoke. Season with salt and pepper to taste. Slice brisket against grain ½ inch thick and arrange on serving dish. Spoon 1 cup sauce over brisket and serve, passing remaining sauce separately.

ROPA VIEJA

Serves 6 to 8 | flat-cut brisket

WHY THIS RECIPE WORKS Comforting Cuban ropa vieja, with its luscious shredded beef, traditionally involves making a beef stock and then using the meat and some of the liquid to make a separate sauté with onion, pepper, and spices. To do without making stock, we combined the two steps, opting for a Dutch oven braise, which ensured that all the beef's flavorful juices ended up in the final dish. Though untraditional, brisket has the right mix of beefy flavor and collagen to guarantee tender, flavorful, juicy shreds. We cut the brisket ahead of time into 2-inch-wide strips, which sped up cooking and made shredding a breeze. To mimic the meatiness that commonly comes from an MSG-spiked seasoning blend, we seared the meat before braising and added glutamate-rich anchovies to the mix. We found that slowly caramelizing the onion and pepper strips mimicked the deep flavor of a traditional sofrito without requiring an extra step. Briny chopped green olives and a splash of white vinegar brought all the flavors into sharp focus.

1 (2-pound) beef brisket, flat cut, fat trimmed to ¼ inch
5 tablespoons vegetable oil, divided
2 onions, halved and sliced thin
2 red bell peppers, stemmed, seeded, and sliced into ¼-inch-wide strips
2 anchovy fillets, rinsed, patted dry, and minced
4 garlic cloves, minced
2 teaspoons ground cumin
1½ teaspoons dried oregano
½ cup dry white wine
2 cups chicken broth
1 (8-ounce) can tomato sauce
2 bay leaves
¾ cup pitted green olives, chopped coarse
¾ teaspoon white wine vinegar, plus extra for seasoning

Ropa Vieja

1. Adjust oven rack to middle position and heat oven to 300 degrees. Cut brisket against grain into 2-inch-wide strips. Cut any strips longer than 5 inches in half crosswise. Season beef on all sides with salt and pepper.

2. Heat ¼ cup oil in Dutch oven over medium-high heat until just smoking. Brown beef on all sides, 7 to 10 minutes; transfer to large plate and set aside. Add onions and bell peppers and cook until softened and pan bottom develops fond, 10 to 15 minutes. Transfer vegetables to bowl and set aside.

3. Add remaining 1 tablespoon oil to now-empty pot, then add anchovies, garlic, cumin, and oregano and cook until fragrant, about 30 seconds. Stir in wine, scraping up any browned bits, and cook until mostly evaporated, about 1 minute. Stir in broth, tomato sauce, and bay leaves. Return beef and any accumulated juices to pot and bring to simmer over high heat. Transfer to oven and cook, covered, until beef is just tender, 2 to 2¼ hours, flipping meat halfway through cooking.

4. Transfer beef to cutting board; when cool enough to handle, shred into ¼-inch-thick pieces. Meanwhile, add olives and reserved vegetables to pot and bring to boil over medium-high heat; simmer until thickened and measures 4 cups, 5 to 7 minutes. Stir in beef. Add vinegar. Season with salt, pepper, and extra vinegar to taste. Serve.

RUSSIAN BEEF AND CABBAGE SOUP

Serves 4 to 6 | flat-cut brisket

WHY THIS RECIPE WORKS This stick-to-your-ribs winter soup can take all day to prepare; we wanted a version that maximized flavor and minimized time. Traditional recipes call for simmering a single hunk of brisket in water, but this method yielded bland meat and broth. A mixture of store-bought beef and chicken broths yielded a balanced stock that was meaty but mild enough to let the soup's other components shine. Chopping the brisket into cubes saved even more time. If you can't find savoy cabbage at your supermarket, you can substitute regular green cabbage; however, it has a less delicate texture. We prefer the flavor of sauerkraut that is packaged in plastic bags and refrigerated to the stuff stocked on supermarket shelves in cans and jars; resealed in its plastic bag, leftover sauerkraut will keep in the refrigerator for weeks.

1 pound beef brisket, flat cut, trimmed and cut into ½-inch pieces
2 tablespoons vegetable oil, divided
1 onion, chopped
3 garlic cloves, minced
4 cups beef broth
4 cups chicken broth
2 bay leaves
2 carrots, peeled and cut into ½-inch pieces
½ small head savoy cabbage, quartered, cored, and shredded into ¼-inch-thick pieces
½ cup sauerkraut, rinsed
2 tablespoons minced fresh dill
Sour cream

1. Pat beef dry with paper towels and season with salt and pepper. Heat 2 teaspoons oil in Dutch oven over medium-high heat until just smoking. Brown half of beef on all sides, 5 to 7 minutes. (Reduce heat if fond begins to burn.) Transfer browned beef to medium bowl. Repeat with 2 teaspoons oil and remaining beef; transfer to bowl.

2. Heat remaining 2 teaspoons oil in pot over medium heat until shimmering. Add onion and cook until softened, 5 to 7 minutes. Stir in garlic and cook until fragrant, about 30 seconds. Stir in beef broth and chicken broth, scraping up any browned bits. Stir in bay leaves and browned meat with any accumulated juices. Bring to boil, then cover, reduce to gentle simmer, and cook for 30 minutes.

3. Stir in carrots, cabbage, and sauerkraut. Cover partially (leaving pot open about 1 inch) and simmer gently until beef and vegetables are tender, 30 to 40 minutes longer. Off heat, discard bay leaves. Stir in dill, season with salt and pepper to taste, and serve, passing sour cream separately.

HOME-CORNED BEEF AND VEGETABLES

Serves 8 to 10 | flat-cut brisket

WHY THIS RECIPE WORKS Making corned beef—a New England and a St. Patrick's Day favorite—at home is actually quite simple. We soaked a flat-cut brisket for six days in a brine made with both table and pink curing salt; after the soak, the seasoning had penetrated to the core of the meat. To break down the brisket's abundant collagen, we gently simmered the meat in a low oven, adding classic corned beef accompaniments to the pot while the meat rested. Pink curing salt #1, which can be purchased online or in stores specializing in meat curing, is a mixture of table salt and nitrites; it is also called Prague Powder #1, Insta Cure #1, or DQ Curing Salt #1. In addition to the pink salt, we use table salt here. Purchase a uniformly thick brisket. The brisket will look gray after curing but will turn pink once cooked.

CORNED BEEF
1 (4½- to 5-pound) beef brisket, flat cut
¾ cup table salt for brining
½ cup packed brown sugar for brining
2 teaspoons pink curing kosher salt #1 for brining
6 garlic cloves, peeled, divided
2 tablespoons black peppercorns, divided
1 tablespoon coriander seeds
6 bay leaves, divided
5 allspice berries

VEGETABLES
6 carrots, peeled, halved crosswise, thick ends halved lengthwise
1½ pounds small red potatoes, unpeeled
1 head green cabbage (2 pounds), uncored, cut into 8 wedges

1. For the corned beef: Trim fat on surface of brisket to ⅛ inch. Dissolve salt, sugar, and curing salt in 4 quarts water in large container. Add brisket, 3 garlic cloves, 1 tablespoon peppercorns, coriander seeds, 4 bay leaves, and allspice berries to brine. Weigh brisket down with plate, cover, and refrigerate for 6 days.

2. Adjust oven rack to middle position and heat oven to 275 degrees. Remove brisket from brine, rinse, and pat dry with paper towels. Cut 8-inch square triple thickness of cheesecloth. Place remaining 3 garlic cloves, remaining 1 tablespoon peppercorns, and remaining 2 bay leaves in center of cheesecloth and tie into bundle with kitchen twine. Place brisket, spice bundle, and 2 quarts water in Dutch oven. (Brisket may not lie flat but will shrink slightly as it cooks.) Bring to simmer over high heat, cover, and transfer to oven. Cook until fork inserted into thickest part of brisket slides in and out with ease, 2½ to 3 hours. Remove pot from oven and turn off oven. Transfer brisket to large ovensafe platter, ladle 1 cup of cooking liquid over meat, cover, and return to oven to keep warm.

3. **For the vegetables:** Add carrots and potatoes to pot and bring to simmer over high heat. Reduce heat to medium-low, cover, and simmer until vegetables begin to soften, 7 to 10 minutes. Add cabbage to pot, increase heat to high, and return to simmer. Reduce heat to low, cover, and simmer until all vegetables are tender, 12 to 15 minutes.

4. While vegetables cook, transfer beef to carving board. Slice against grain ¼ inch thick. Return beef to platter. Using slotted spoon, transfer vegetables to platter with beef. Moisten with additional broth and serve.

BARBECUE BURNT ENDS

Serves 8 to 10 | flat-cut brisket

WHY THIS RECIPE WORKS Real burnt ends are all about moist meat and charred bark, but most pit masters use point-cut brisket. To make the leaner, more widely available flat-cut brisket work, we cut it into strips and brined it for maximum moisture and flavor. Three hours of smoke on the grill—with a water pan for more moisture—followed by a few more hours in a low oven ensured a fully tender brisket with plenty of char. We cut the meat into cubes before tossing it with homemade sauce. Look for a brisket with a significant fat cap. The meat can be brined ahead of time, transferred to a zipper-lock bag, and refrigerated for up to a day. If you don't have ½ cup of juices from the rested brisket, supplement with beef broth.

BRISKET AND RUB

  2 cups kosher salt for brining
 ½ cup granulated sugar for brining
  1 (5- to 6-pound) beef brisket, flat cut, untrimmed
 ¼ cup packed brown sugar
  2 tablespoons pepper
  1 tablespoon kosher salt
  4 cups wood chips

  1 (13 by 9-inch) disposable aluminum roasting pan (if using charcoal) or 2 (8½ by 6-inch) disposable aluminum pans (if using gas)

BARBECUE SAUCE

 ¾ cup ketchup
 ¼ cup packed brown sugar
  2 tablespoons cider vinegar
  2 tablespoons Worcestershire sauce
  2 teaspoons granulated garlic
 ¼ teaspoon cayenne pepper

1. **For the brisket and rub:** Dissolve 2 cups salt and granulated sugar in 4 quarts cold water in large container. Slice brisket with grain into 1½-inch-thick strips. Add brisket strips to brine, cover, and refrigerate for 2 hours. Remove brisket from brine and pat dry with paper towels.

2. Combine brown sugar, pepper, and salt in bowl. Season brisket all over with rub. Just before grilling, soak wood chips in water for 15 minutes, then drain. Using 2 large pieces of heavy-duty aluminum foil, wrap chips in two 8 by 4½-inch foil packets. (Make sure chips do not poke holes in sides or bottoms of packets.) Cut 2 evenly spaced 2-inch slits in top of each packet.

3a. **For a charcoal grill:** Open bottom vent halfway and place disposable pan filled with 2 quarts water on 1 side of grill, with long side of pan facing center of grill. Arrange 3 quarts unlit charcoal briquettes on opposite side of grill and place 1 wood chip packet on coals. Light large chimney starter filled halfway with charcoal briquettes (3 quarts). When top coals are partially covered with ash, pour evenly over unlit coals and wood chip packet. Place remaining wood chip packet on lit coals. Set cooking grate in place, cover, and open lid vent halfway. Heat grill until hot and wood chips are smoking, about 5 minutes.

3b. **For a gas grill:** Add ½ cup ice cubes to 1 wood chip packet. Remove cooking grate and place both wood chip packets directly on primary burner; place disposable pans each filled with 2 cups water directly on secondary burner(s). Set grate in place, turn all burners to high, cover, and heat grill until hot and wood chips are smoking, about 15 minutes. Leave primary burner on high and turn off other burner(s). (Adjust primary burner as needed to maintain grill temperature of 275 to 300 degrees.)

4. Clean and oil cooking grate. Arrange brisket on cooler side of grill as far from heat source as possible. Cover (positioning lid vent over brisket for charcoal) and cook without opening for 3 hours.

5. Adjust oven rack to middle position and heat oven to 275 degrees. Remove brisket from grill and transfer to rimmed baking sheet. Cover sheet tightly with foil. Roast until fork slips easily in and out of meat and meat registers 210 degrees, about 2 hours. Remove from oven, leave covered, and let rest for 1 hour. Remove foil, transfer brisket to carving board, and pour accumulated juices into fat separator.

6. **For the barbecue sauce:** Combine ketchup, sugar, vinegar, Worcestershire, granulated garlic, cayenne, and ½ cup defatted brisket juices in medium saucepan. Bring to simmer over medium heat and cook until slightly thickened, about 5 minutes.

7. Cut brisket strips crosswise into 1- to 2-inch chunks. Combine brisket chunks and barbecue sauce in large bowl and toss to combine. Serve.

Barbecue Burnt Ends

TUTORIAL
Texas Barbecue Brisket

Braising may be our most used technique for cooking brisket, but you'd never be able to do that with a whole brisket. This is for the barbecue—invite a crowd.

1. Set up charcoal snake with 2 sets of 58 briquettes, 2 briquettes wide by 2 briquettes high. Starting 4 inches from 1 end of snake, evenly space wood chunks on top of snake.

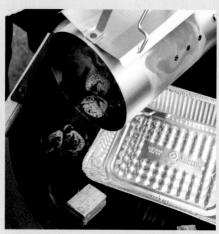

2. Place disposable pan in center of grill; fill with 6 cups water. Pour hot coals over only 1 end of snake.

3. Place brisket, fat side down, directly over water pan, with point end facing gap in snake. Insert temperature probe into side of upper third of point. Cook to 170 degrees.

4. Wrap brisket tightly with layer of foil, minimizing air pockets between foil and brisket. Rotate brisket 90 degrees and wrap with second layer of foil so it is airtight. Make mark on foil to keep track of fat/point side.

5. Pour unlit briquettes halfway around perimeter of grill over gap and spent coals. Return brisket to grill over water pan, with point facing where gap in snake used to be. Reinsert probe. Cook to 205 degrees.

6. Transfer brisket to cooler. Close cooler and let rest for 2 to 3 hours. Slice against grain and serve.

TEXAS BARBECUE BRISKET

Serves 12 to 15 | whole brisket

WHY THIS RECIPE WORKS We wanted to re-create a Texas-style smoked whole brisket on a charcoal grill with a tender, juicy interior encased in a dark, peppery bark. Yes, a whole brisket at home. The key to our success? A grill setup called a charcoal snake. This C-shaped array of smoldering briquettes provided low, slow, indirect heat to the center of the grill for upwards of 6 hours, so we needed to refuel only once during the exceptionally long cooking time. Cooking the brisket fat side down gave it a protective barrier against the direct heat of the fire. And wrapping the brisket in foil toward the end of its cooking time and letting it rest in a cooler for 2 hours before serving helped keep it ultramoist and juicy. We developed this recipe using a 22-inch Weber Kettle charcoal grill.

1 (10- to 12-pound) whole beef brisket, untrimmed
¼ cup kosher salt
¼ cup pepper
5 (3-inch) wood chunks
1 (13 by 9-inch) disposable aluminum pan

1. With brisket positioned point side up, use sharp knife to trim fat cap to ½- to ¼-inch thickness. Remove excess fat from deep pocket where flat and point are attached. Trim and discard short edge of flat if less than 1 inch thick. Flip brisket and remove any large deposits of fat from underside.

2. Combine salt and pepper in bowl. Place brisket on rimmed baking sheet and sprinkle all over with salt mixture. Cover loosely with plastic wrap and refrigerate for at least 12 or up to 24 hours.

3. Open bottom vent completely. Set up charcoal snake: Arrange 58 briquettes, 2 briquettes wide, around perimeter of grill, over-lapping slightly so briquettes are touching, leaving 8-inch gap between ends of snake. Place second layer of 58 briquettes, also 2 briquettes wide, on top of first. (Completed snake should be 2 briquettes wide by 2 briquettes high.)

4. Starting 4 inches from 1 end of snake, evenly space wood chunks on top of snake. Place disposable pan in center of grill. Fill disposable pan with 6 cups water. Light chimney starter filled with 10 briquettes (pile briquettes on 1 side of chimney). When coals are partially covered with ash, pour over 1 end of snake. (Make sure lit coals touch only 1 end of snake.)

5. Set cooking grate in place. Clean and oil cooking grate. Place brisket, fat side down, directly over water pan, with point end facing gap in snake. Insert temperature probe into side of upper third of point. Cover grill, open lid vent completely, and position lid vent over gap in snake. Cook, undisturbed and without lifting lid, until meat registers 170 degrees, 4 to 5 hours.

6. Place 2 large sheets of aluminum foil on rimmed baking sheet. Remove temperature probe from brisket. Using oven mitts, lift brisket and transfer to center of foil, fat side down. Wrap brisket tightly with first layer of foil, minimizing air pockets between foil and brisket. Rotate brisket 90 degrees and wrap with second layer of foil. (Use additional foil, if necessary, to completely wrap brisket.) Make small mark on foil with marker to keep track of fat/point side. Foil wrap should be airtight.

7. Remove cooking grate. Starting at still-unlit end of snake, pour 3 quarts unlit briquettes about halfway around perimeter of grill over gap and spent coals. Replace cooking grate. Return foil-wrapped brisket to grill over water pan, fat side down, with point end facing where gap in snake used to be. Reinsert temperature probe into point. Cover grill and continue to cook until meat registers 205 degrees, 1 to 2 hours longer.

8. Remove temperature probe. Transfer foil-wrapped brisket to cooler, point side up. Close cooler and let rest for at least 2 hours or up to 3 hours. Transfer brisket to carving board, unwrap, and position fat side up. Slice flat against grain ¼ inch thick, stopping once you reach base of point. Rotate point 90 degrees and slice point against grain (perpendicular to first cut) ⅜ inch thick. Serve.

PLATE

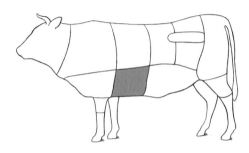

SITUATED UNDER THE RIB, the plate has an attractive fat content, which translates to juicy steak, giant beef plate ribs, and the most succulent short ribs. (Short ribs can come from other parts of the cow as well; for more information on short ribs see page 176.) Sometimes this area of the cow is called the short plate because it doesn't contain the brisket and is therefore not the whole underbelly of the cow. We use two very different cuts from this primal: thin, flavorful skirt steak, a favorite, and bigger-than-big beef ribs.

Skirt Steak

Cost: ▪▪▫▫▫   Flavor: ▪▪▪▫▫
Best cooking methods: braise, sear, grill
Texture: tender with decent chew
Alternative names: fajita steak, Philadelphia steak

Long, thin, ribbon-like skirt steak might be a bit unassuming but it's a surprising star—juicy and full of beefy flavor. And when we say long we mean it: Skirt steaks are often rolled up for packaging because when they are unrolled, the steaks can be nearly 2 feet long. This cut is the original choice for fajitas, although most cooks now use easier-to-find flank steak (see page 165). And it deserves great and varied treatments; although it can be cooked like flank steak, skirt steak has more connective tissue and is fattier and juicier. Look for it at better markets and butcher shops. If you can find skirt steak, it comes from two different muscles and some butchers might sell an inside cut and an outside cut. The more desirable outside skirt steak measures 3 to 4 inches wide and ½ to 1 inch thick. Avoid the inside skirt steak, which typically measures 5 to 7 inches wide and ¼ to ½ inch thick, as it is very chewy. Skirt steaks are most tender cooked to medium; because they have large muscle fibers, they take more force to bite through and therefore benefit from longer cooking so the muscle fibers can shrink in diameter.

GREAT GRAINS

The grain is really the best way to tell the difference between skirt steak and nearby flank steak (also long and thin; see page 165). Although we prefer the beefier flavor of skirt steak, it's not as widely available as flank steak. How do you tell the steaks apart? Skirt steak is narrower, and the grain runs crosswise. Flank steak is wider, and the grain runs lengthwise.

Skirt Steak

Flank Steak

Beef Plate Ribs

Cost: ▪▪▪▫▫   Flavor: ▪▪▪▫▫
Best cooking methods: barbecue
Texture: succulent, juicy
Alternative names: none

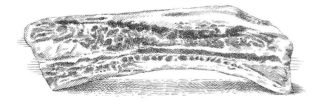

If you've ever gone to a Texas barbecue joint and seen long ribs almost hanging off metal serving trays, you're likely looking at beef plate ribs. These big ribs rate as "going all out" for barbecue—they're the meatiest ribs on the cow. They are marbled with fat and collagen; over low, slow heat, they achieve a tender, juicy texture. They are rarely available prepackaged, so these ribs are a special-order supper from your butcher.

PAN-SEARED SKIRT STEAK WITH ZUCCHINI AND SCALLION SAUCE

Serves 4 | skirt steak

WHY THIS RECIPE WORKS You might think of the grill for skirt steak, but pan searing can yield rosy steaks with deeply browned, flavorful crusts—no grill required. We wanted a quick and convenient weeknight dinner that would deliver big flavor, so we decided to serve our steaks with a vibrant, no-cook sauce. We started with fresh parsley leaves and then added scallions for a unique allium bite. Tangy Dijon mustard and red wine vinegar packed a punch that cut through the richness of the steak, and olive oil and a bit of water provided enough liquid for the sauce to blend up easily to a smooth consistency. While the steaks rested (to ensure that they would retain their juiciness), we cooked up a quick side of zucchini using the sauce.

- 1 cup fresh parsley leaves
- 8 scallions, white parts minced, green parts cut into 1-inch pieces
- ½ cup plus 3 tablespoons extra-virgin olive oil, divided
- ¼ cup water
- 4 teaspoons red wine vinegar
- 1 tablespoon Dijon mustard
- ½ teaspoon table salt
- ½ teaspoon pepper
- 1 (1½-pound) skirt steak, trimmed and cut into 4 equal pieces
- 2 medium zucchini, cut into ½-inch chunks

1. Process parsley, scallion greens, ½ cup oil, water, vinegar, mustard, salt, and pepper in blender until smooth, about 1 minute. Set aside.

2. Pat steak dry with paper towels and season with salt and pepper. Heat 2 tablespoons oil in 12-inch nonstick skillet over medium-high heat until just smoking. Cook steak until well browned and meat registers 120 to 125 degrees (for medium-rare), about 2 minutes per side. Transfer steak to cutting board and tent with foil.

3. While steak is resting, add remaining 1 tablespoon oil and zucchini to now-empty skillet and cook over medium-high heat, without stirring, until zucchini is well browned, about 2 minutes. Stir and continue to cook until softened, about 3 minutes. Off heat, add scallion whites and 2 tablespoons scallion sauce and stir to coat zucchini. Season with salt and pepper to taste. Slice steak thin against grain. Serve with zucchini and remaining scallion sauce.

BUN BO XAO

Serves 4 | skirt steak

WHY THIS RECIPE WORKS This Vietnamese dish is a savory, aromatic salad composed of rice noodles topped with pickled and fresh vegetables, herbs, lemongrass beef, and peanuts. It's all about the contrasting hues and textures of the ingredients when they're layered in the bowl. Raw vegetables add color and crunch, peanuts add even more textural contrast, and the Thai basil and mint leaves both add freshness and brightness. The dish is served at room temperature, which makes it forgiving for weeknight cooks. We prefer the unique flavor of Thai basil, but Italian basil can be used in its place. Be sure to drain the noodles thoroughly in step 2 to avoid diluting the flavors of the sauce.

- ¼ cup fish sauce, divided
- 1 lemongrass stalk, trimmed to bottom 6 inches and minced(5 teaspoons), divided
- 4 teaspoons vegetable oil, divided
- 1 tablespoon sugar, divided
- 1½ teaspoons Asian chili-garlic sauce, divided
- 1 pound skirt steak, trimmed and cut with grain into 3equalpieces
- 8 ounces rice vermicelli
- 1 carrot, peeled and shredded
- 1 cucumber, peeled, seeded, and cut into 2-inch-long matchsticks
- 2 ounces (1 cup) bean sprouts
- ¼ cup lime juice (2 limes), plus lime wedges for serving
- ¼ cup fresh Thai basil leaves
- ¼ cup fresh mint leaves
- 2 tablespoons chopped dry-roasted peanuts

1. Whisk 1½ teaspoons fish sauce, 1 tablespoon lemongrass, 1 tablespoon oil, 1 teaspoon sugar, and ½ teaspoon chili-garlic sauce together in medium bowl. Add steak to bowl with lemongrass mixture and toss to coat. Transfer steak to cutting board, cover with plastic wrap, and pound ¼ inch thick; return to bowl.

2. Bring 2 quarts water to boil in large saucepan. Off heat, add noodles to hot water and let stand until tender, about 5 minutes. Drain noodles in colander and rinse under cold running water until water runs clear. Drain well and divide among 4 individual serving bowls. Divide carrot, cucumber, and bean sprouts evenly over noodles in serving bowls.

3. Heat remaining 1 teaspoon oil in 12-inch skillet over medium-high heat until just smoking. Cook steak until well browned and meat registers 130 degrees, 2 to 3 minutes per side. Transfer steak to cutting board and tent with aluminum foil.

Bun Bo Xao

4. While steak is resting, whisk lime juice, remaining 3½ tablespoons fish sauce, remaining 2 teaspoons lemongrass, remaining 2 teaspoons sugar, and remaining 1 teaspoon chili-garlic in bowl until sugar is dissolved; set aside.

5. Slice steak thin against grain and divide evenly over noodles and vegetables in bowls. Whisk any accumulated juices from steak into sauce and drizzle 2 tablespoons sauce evenly over each bowl. Sprinkle with basil, mint, and peanuts. Serve with lime wedges.

STEAK TACO SALAD

Serves 4 | skirt steak

WHY THIS RECIPE WORKS We were after a fresher take on a taco salad, one featuring sliced steak, beans, and avocado heaped over shredded lettuce. We liked skirt here because its meaty flavor and textured exterior stood up to seasonings. For the greens, chopped romaine had the best crunch. An avocado did double duty as a salad topping and as the base of an ultracreamy, vibrantly fresh dressing. To make it a taco salad, we needed chips, but cutting fresh corn tortillas into strips and frying them was a little too much work for a simple salad. Store-bought tortilla chips added a salty crunch but lacked richness. Even better was another chip-aisle staple, Fritos, which brought a huge crunch and loads of corn flavor.

PICO DE GALLO

  1 tomato, cored and chopped
  2 tablespoons finely chopped red onion
  2 tablespoons chopped fresh cilantro
  2 teaspoons minced jalapeño chile
1½ teaspoons lime juice
  ¼ teaspoon table salt

DRESSING

  ½ ripe avocado
  ½ cup buttermilk
  2 tablespoons chopped fresh cilantro
1½ tablespoons lime juice
  1 garlic clove, minced
  1 teaspoon table salt
  ¼ teaspoon pepper

STEAK

  ¾ teaspoon chili powder
  ½ teaspoon ground cumin
  ½ teaspoon table salt
  ½ teaspoon pepper
  1 (1-pound) skirt steak, trimmed and cut crosswise into 4 equal pieces
  1 tablespoon vegetable oil

Steak Taco Salad

SALAD

  1 (15-ounce) can pinto beans, rinsed
  2 romaine lettuce hearts (12 ounces), cut into 1-inch pieces
  4 ounces Monterey Jack cheese, shredded (1 cup), divided
  ½ ripe avocado, cut into ½-inch pieces
  1 cup Fritos corn chips

1. For the pico de gallo: Combine all ingredients in bowl and set aside.

2. For the dressing: Process all ingredients in blender until smooth, about 60 seconds.

3. For the steak: Combine chili powder, cumin, salt, and pepper in bowl. Sprinkle steaks with spice mixture. Heat oil in 12-inch nonstick skillet over medium-high heat until just smoking. Cook steaks until well browned and meat registers 135 degrees (for medium), 2 to 4 minutes per side. Transfer steaks to carving board, tent with aluminum foil, and let rest for 5 minutes.

4. For the salad: Toss beans, lettuce, and ½ cup Monterey Jack with dressing in large bowl. Season with salt and pepper to taste. Transfer to large serving platter. Slice steaks thin against grain. Layer avocado, pico de gallo, steak, and remaining ½ cup Monterey Jack on top of lettuce mixture. Scatter chips around salad. Serve.

PHILLY CHEESESTEAKS

Serves 4 | skirt steak

WHY THIS RECIPE WORKS To get a real Philly cheesesteak, you have to go to Philadelphia. Or do you? In restaurants, these sandwiches are made using a meat slicer, a flat-top griddle, and pricey rib eye—all three of which were out of the question for a sandwich made at home. The task required coming up with a simple and economical way to mimic the superthinly shaved slivers of rib eye. We found that when partially frozen, skirt steak's thin profile and open-grained texture made for easy slicing, and its flavor was nearest to rib eye but without the sandwich sticker shock. Melty, gooey American cheese was essential, but we took the nontraditional route of adding Parmesan for sharpness to balance out the mild American. Top these sandwiches with chopped pickled hot peppers, sautéed onions or bell peppers, sweet relish, or hot sauce.

2 pounds skirt steak, trimmed and cut with grain into 3-inch-wide strips
4 (8-inch) Italian sub rolls, split lengthwise
2 tablespoons vegetable oil, divided
½ teaspoon table salt
⅛ teaspoon pepper
¼ cup grated Parmesan cheese
8 slices white American cheese (8 ounces)

1. Place steak pieces on large plate or baking sheet and freeze until very firm, about 1 hour.

2. Meanwhile, adjust oven rack to middle position and heat oven to 400 degrees. Spread split rolls on baking sheet and toast until lightly browned, 5 to 10 minutes.

3. Using sharp knife, shave steak pieces as thin as possible against grain. Mound meat on cutting board and chop coarse with knife 10 to 20 times.

4. Heat 1 tablespoon oil in 12-inch nonstick skillet over high heat until just smoking. Add half of meat in even layer and cook without stirring until well browned on 1 side, 4 to 5 minutes. Stir and continue to cook until meat is no longer pink, 1 to 2 minutes. Transfer meat to colander set in large bowl. Wipe out skillet with paper towel. Repeat with remaining 1 tablespoon oil and remaining sliced meat.

5. Return now-empty skillet to medium heat. Drain excess moisture from meat. Return meat to skillet (discard any liquid in bowl) and add salt and pepper. Heat, stirring constantly, until meat is warmed through, 1 to 2 minutes. Reduce heat to low, sprinkle with Parmesan, and shingle slices of American cheese over meat. Allow cheeses to melt, about 2 minutes. Using heatproof spatula or wooden spoon, fold melted cheese into meat thoroughly. Divide mixture evenly among toasted rolls. Serve immediately.

CORNISH PASTIES

Serves 6 | skirt steak

WHY THIS RECIPE WORKS Upper Midwesterners have divided opinions about this coal miner's classic, but we think everyone would agree these handheld turnovers should be rich and flaky, not tough and dry. For the best version, we tossed the uncooked meat and vegetables (onion, potato, and rutabaga) with a little flour before wrapping the filling tightly in our dough rounds. The flour combined with the filling's exuded juices as the pasties baked to create the gravy right inside the crust. Garlic and fresh thyme punched up the flavor of the filling. To ensure easy dough assembly, we used sour cream to make it both pliable and rip-resistant. You can substitute turnips for rutabagas. The pasties fit best on the baking sheet when placed crosswise in two rows of three. Serve the pasties with ketchup, if desired.

CRUST
⅔ cup sour cream, chilled
1 large egg, lightly beaten
3 cups (15 ounces) all-purpose flour
1¾ teaspoons table salt
16 tablespoons unsalted butter, cut into ½-inch pieces and chilled

FILLING
1 tablespoon unsalted butter
1 onion, chopped fine
2¼ teaspoons table salt, divided
1 tablespoon minced fresh thyme
2 garlic cloves, minced
1¼ pounds skirt steak, trimmed and cut into ½-inch pieces
10 ounces russet potatoes, peeled and cut into ½-inch pieces
10 ounces rutabaga, peeled and cut into ½-inch pieces
¾ teaspoon pepper
¼ cup all-purpose flour

1 large egg

1. **For the crust:** Whisk sour cream and egg together in small bowl. Process flour and salt in food processor until combined, about 3 seconds. Add butter and pulse until only pea-size pieces remain, about 10 pulses. Add half of sour cream mixture and pulse until combined, about 5 pulses. Add remaining sour cream mixture and pulse until dough begins to form, about 15 pulses.

2. Transfer mixture to lightly floured counter and knead briefly until dough comes together. Form dough into 6-inch disk, wrap tightly in plastic wrap, and refrigerate for 30 minutes. (Dough can be refrigerated for up to 24 hours; let chilled dough sit on counter for 15 minutes to soften before rolling.)

TUTORIAL
Cornish Pasties

Why have a fruit turnover when you can have a supersavory steak-and-potato-filled one.
That's essentially what a Cornish pasty is. Follow these steps for forming them.

1. Combine onion mixture, steak, potatoes, rutabaga, pepper, and salt in bowl. Add flour and toss to coat.

2. Remove dough from refrigerator and cut into 6 equal pieces (about 5 ounces each); cover with plastic wrap.

3. Working with 1 piece of dough at a time, roll into 10 by 8-inch oval (about ⅛ inch thick) on lightly floured counter.

4. Place 1 portion filling in center of dough. Moisten edges of dough with water, then fold narrow end of oval over filling to form half-moon shape. Press dough around filling to adhere.

5. Trim any ragged edges, then crimp edges with fork to seal; transfer to prepared sheet.

6. Cut 1-inch vent hole on top of each pasty. Brush pasties with egg wash. Bake until crust is golden brown and filling is bubbling up through vent hole, about 45 minutes, rotating sheet halfway through baking.

3. For the filling: Melt butter in 10-inch skillet over medium heat. Add onion and ¼ teaspoon salt and cook until softened, about 5 minutes. Add thyme and garlic and cook until fragrant, about 30 seconds. Let cool slightly, about 5 minutes. Combine cooled onion mixture, steak, potatoes, rutabaga, pepper, and remaining 2 teaspoons salt in bowl. Add flour and toss to coat.

4. Adjust oven rack to upper-middle position and heat oven to 375 degrees. Line rimmed baking sheet with parchment paper. Remove dough from refrigerator and cut into 6 equal pieces (about 5 ounces each); cover with plastic wrap. Divide filling into 6 equal portions, about 1 heaping cup each.

5. Working with 1 piece of dough at a time, roll into 10 by 8-inch oval (about ⅛ inch thick) on lightly floured counter. Place 1 portion filling in center of dough. Moisten edges of dough with water, then fold narrow end of oval over filling to form half-moon shape. Press dough around filling to adhere.

6. Trim any ragged edges, then crimp edges with fork to seal; transfer to prepared sheet. (For more decorative edge, trim any ragged edges and, starting at 1 end, pinch and slightly twist dough diagonally across seam between your thumb and index finger. Continue pinching and twisting dough around seam.) Repeat with remaining dough and filling.

7. Using paring knife, cut 1-inch vent hole on top of each pasty. Whisk egg and 2 teaspoons water in bowl. Brush pasties with egg wash. Bake until crust is golden brown and filling is bubbling up through vent hole, about 45 minutes, rotating sheet halfway through baking. Transfer pasties to wire rack and let cool for 10 minutes before serving.

GRILLED MOJO-MARINATED SKIRT STEAK

Serves 4 to 6 | skirt steak

WHY THIS RECIPE WORKS Skirt steak has ample surface area so we decided to make the most of it by submerging it in a citrusy, garlicky Latin American mojo marinade and grilling it for tons of char. Soy sauce in the marinade seasoned the meat, and its glutamates enhanced the meat's beefiness. We rubbed a thin coating of baking soda over the steaks to guarantee great browning. To emphasize the mojo flavor, we boiled the leftover marinade to make it food-safe and turned it into a sauce that we drizzled over the steaks.

6 garlic cloves, minced
2 tablespoons soy sauce
1 teaspoon grated lime zest plus ¼ cup juice (2 limes), divided
1 teaspoon ground cumin
1 teaspoon dried oregano
¾ teaspoon table salt
½ teaspoon grated orange zest plus ½ cup juice
¼ teaspoon red pepper flakes
2 pounds skirt steak, trimmed and cut with grain into 6- to 8-inch-long steaks
2 tablespoons extra-virgin olive oil, divided
1 teaspoon baking soda

1. Combine garlic, soy sauce, 2 tablespoons lime juice, cumin, oregano, salt, orange juice, and pepper flakes in 13 by 9-inch baking dish. Place steaks in dish. Flip steaks to coat both sides with marinade. Cover and refrigerate for 1 hour, flipping steaks halfway through refrigerating.

2. Remove steaks from marinade and transfer marinade to small saucepan. Pat steaks dry with paper towels. Combine 1 tablespoon oil and baking soda in small bowl. Rub oil mixture evenly onto both sides of each steak.

3. Bring marinade to boil over high heat and boil for 30 seconds. Transfer to bowl and stir in lime zest, remaining 2 tablespoons lime juice, orange zest, and remaining 1 tablespoon oil. Set aside sauce.

4a. For a charcoal grill: Open bottom vent completely. Light large chimney starter filled with charcoal briquettes (6 quarts). When top coals are partially covered with ash, pour evenly over half of grill. Set cooking grate in place, cover, and open lid vent completely. Heat grill until hot, about 5 minutes.

4b. For a gas grill: Turn all burners to high, cover, and heat grill until hot, about 15 minutes. Turn off 1 burner (if using grill with more than 2 burners, turn off burner farthest from primary burner) and leave other burner(s) on high.

5. Clean and oil cooking grate. Cook steaks on hotter side of grill until well browned and meat registers 130 to 135 degrees (for medium), 2 to 4 minutes per side. (Move steaks to cooler side of grill before taking temperature to prevent them from overcooking.) Transfer steaks to cutting board, tent with aluminum foil, and let rest for 10 minutes. Cut steaks against grain on bias ½ inch thick. Arrange slices on platter, drizzle with 2 tablespoons sauce, and serve, passing extra sauce separately.

GRILLED STEAK FAJITAS

Serves 6 | skirt steak

WHY THIS RECIPE WORKS For such a popular dish, fajitas have been treated terribly in Tex-Mex restaurants. We set out to bring them back to glory. The ideal fajitas should be a simple affair featuring tender strips of beef nestled into soft flour tortillas along with some onions and bell peppers. To ensure that the bell peppers and onion were perfectly softened but not mushy, we seared them over a hot fire and then moved them to a disposable aluminum pan on the cooler side of the grill to gently steam. We opted to use skirt steak, the classic (and some say only) choice for fajitas. For the best flavor, we whipped up a marinade of salty soy sauce, vegetable oil, garlic, and sweet-tangy pineapple juice. The soy sauce amped meatiness and the pineapple juice added fruitiness. We reserved some of this marinade to toss with the grilled bell peppers and onion. Serve the fajitas with pico de gallo, avocado pieces or guacamole, sour cream, and lime wedges. One (6-ounce) can of pineapple juice will yield ¾ cup. We cook the skirt steak to between medium and medium-well so that it's firmer and easier to eat among the vegetables in tortillas.

- ¾ cup pineapple juice
- ½ cup plus 1 tablespoon vegetable oil, divided
- ¼ cup soy sauce
- 3 garlic cloves, minced
- 2 pounds skirt steak, trimmed and cut crosswise into 6 equal pieces
- 3 yellow, red, orange, or green bell peppers
- 1 large red onion, sliced into ½-inch-thick rounds
- ¾ teaspoon table salt
- ½ teaspoon pepper
- 12 (6-inch) flour tortillas
- 1 (13 by 9-inch) disposable aluminum pan
- 1 tablespoon chopped fresh cilantro

1. Whisk pineapple juice, ½ cup oil, soy sauce, and garlic together in bowl. Reserve ¼ cup marinade. Transfer remaining 1¼ cups marinade to 1-gallon zipper-lock bag. Add steak, press out air, seal bag, and turn to distribute marinade. Refrigerate for at least 2 hours or up to 24 hours.

2. Using paring knife, cut around stems of bell peppers and remove cores and seeds. Push toothpick horizontally through each onion round to keep rings intact while grilling. Brush bell peppers and onion evenly with remaining 1 tablespoon oil and season with salt and pepper. Remove steak from marinade and pat dry with paper towels; discard marinade. Sprinkle steak with salt and pepper. Wrap tortillas in aluminum foil; set aside.

3a. For a charcoal grill: Open bottom vent completely. Light large chimney starter filled with charcoal briquettes (6 quarts). When top coals are partially covered with ash, pour evenly over half of grill. Set cooking grate in place, cover, and open lid vent completely. Heat grill until hot, about 5 minutes.

3b. For a gas grill: Turn all burners to high, cover, and heat grill until hot, about 15 minutes. Leave primary burner on high and turn other burner(s) to low.

4. Clean and oil cooking grate. Place bell peppers and onion on hotter side of grill and place tortilla packet on cooler side of grill. Cook (covered if using gas) until vegetables are char-streaked and tender, 8 to 13 minutes, flipping and moving as needed for even cooking, and until tortillas are warmed through, about 10 minutes, flipping halfway through cooking.

5. Remove tortillas from grill; keep wrapped and set aside. Transfer vegetables to disposable pan, cover pan tightly with foil, and place on cooler side of grill. (If using gas, cover grill and allow hotter side to reheat for 5 minutes.) Place steak on hotter side of grill and cook (covered if using gas) until charred and meat registers 135 to 140 degrees, 2 to 4 minutes per side. Transfer steak to cutting board and tent with foil. Remove disposable pan from grill.

6. Carefully remove foil from disposable pan (steam may escape). Slice bell peppers into thin strips. Remove toothpicks from onion rounds and separate rings. Return vegetables to disposable pan and toss with cilantro and reserved marinade. Season with salt and pepper to taste. Slice steak thin against grain. Transfer steak and vegetables to serving platter. Serve with tortillas.

GRILLED STEAK SANDWICHES

Serves 4 | skirt steak

WHY THIS RECIPE WORKS Packing tons of beefy flavor and taking only about 5 minutes to grill to doneness over a hot fire, skirt steak is the perfect choice for this classic, most satisfying lunch. We wanted to make sure assembling the sandwiches would be a breeze, so we whipped up a quick, bold, complementary blue cheese sauce before heading out to the grill. Along with crumbled blue cheese—the sauce's star ingredient—we added creamy mayonnaise, tangy balsamic vinegar, Dijon mustard, and a bit of black pepper to a food processor and blitzed the mixture so that it was smooth and spreadable. When the steak finished cooking, we let it rest briefly as we toasted sturdy ciabatta rolls right on the grill. All that was left to do was assemble. We prefer these sandwiches on ciabatta, but any sub rolls can be substituted.

Grilled Steak Sandwiches

TUTORIAL
Texas Smoked Beef Ribs

Become a barbecue pit master and man a grill of these mammoth ribs with confidence, with these steps.

1. Trim ribs of excess exterior fat. Set up grill with charcoal snake (see page 150).

2. Starting 4 inches from 1 end of snake, evenly space wood chunks on top. Place disposable pan in center of grill so short end of pan faces gap. Fill with 4 cups water.

3. Light chimney starter filled with 15 briquettes (pile on 1 side of chimney to make them easier to ignite). When coals are partially covered with ash, pour over 1 end of snake.

4. Position ribs next to each other, bone side down, crosswise over disposable pan and gap in snake.

5. Cover grill, position lid vent over gap in snake, and open lid vent completely. Cook undisturbed until rack of ribs overhanging gap in snake registers 210 degrees in meatiest portion, 5½ to 6¼ hours.

6. Transfer ribs to carving board, tent with aluminum foil, and let rest for 30 minutes. Cut ribs between bones and serve.

¾ cup mayonnaise
3 ounces blue cheese, crumbled (¾ cup)
1 tablespoon balsamic vinegar
1 tablespoon Dijon mustard
¼ teaspoon pepper
1 (1-pound) skirt steak, cut crosswise into 4 equal pieces and trimmed
4 ciabatta sandwich rolls, halved lengthwise
¼ cup extra-virgin olive oil
2 ounces (2 cups) baby arugula
1 small red onion, halved and sliced thin

1. Process mayonnaise, blue cheese, vinegar, mustard, and pepper in food processor until smooth, about 30 seconds. Set aside blue cheese sauce.

2. Pat steak dry with paper towels and season with salt and pepper. Brush cut sides of rolls with oil.

3a. **For a charcoal grill:** Open bottom vent halfway. Light large chimney starter filled with charcoal briquettes (6 quarts). When top coals are partially covered with ash, pour evenly over half of grill. Set cooking grate in place, cover, and open lid vent halfway. Heat grill until hot, about 5 minutes.

3b. **For a gas grill:** Turn all burners to high, cover, and heat grill until hot, about 15 minutes. Leave all burners on high.

4. Clean and oil cooking grate. Grill steak until meat registers 125 degrees (for medium-rare), 2 to 3 minutes per side. Transfer steak to cutting board and tent with foil. Grill rolls, cut side down, until lightly toasted, 1 to 2 minutes.

5. Slice steak thin against grain. Spread blue cheese sauce on rolls. Divide steak, arugula, and onion evenly among rolls. Serve.

TEXAS SMOKED BEEF RIBS

Serves 4 | beef plate ribs

WHY THIS RECIPE WORKS Mammoth Texas-style beef ribs are intimidating—so big they look like they came off a T. rex. But beneath the dark, peppery crust and pink smoke ring is succulent, tender beef so flavorful that barbecue sauce is unnecessary. To smoke these ribs on a humble charcoal grill rather than a huge smoker with temperature controls, we brought back the charcoal snake from our Texas Barbecue Brisket (page 151). This allowed us to surround the thick ribs

with indirect heat for upwards of 6 hours, and the wood chips on top provided steady smoke to infuse the meat with flavor. Cooking the ribs all the way to 210 degrees, so that the meat hung out above 180 degrees for a long time, ensured that the collagen melted properly. Our wait was rewarded with ultratender, juicy, and, yes, mammoth ribs. We developed this recipe using a 22-inch Weber Kettle charcoal grill.

3 tablespoons kosher salt
3 tablespoons pepper
2 (4- to 5-pound) racks beef plate ribs, 1 to 1½ inches of meat on top of bone, trimmed
5 (3-inch) wood chunks
1 (13 by 9-inch) disposable aluminum pan

1. Combine salt and pepper in bowl, then sprinkle ribs all over with salt-pepper mixture.

2. Open bottom vent completely. Set up charcoal snake: Arrange 60 briquettes, 2 briquettes wide, around perimeter of grill, overlapping slightly so briquettes are touching, leaving 8-inch gap between ends of snake. Place second layer of 60 briquettes, also 2 briquettes wide, on top of first. (Completed snake should be 2 briquettes wide by 2 briquettes high.)

3. Starting 4 inches from 1 end of snake, evenly space wood chunks on top of snake. Place disposable pan in center of grill so short end of pan faces gap in snake. Fill disposable pan with 4 cups water. Light chimney starter filled with 15 briquettes (pile briquettes on 1 side of chimney to make them easier to ignite). When coals are partially covered with ash, pour over 1 end of snake. (Make sure lit coals touch only 1 end of snake.)

4. Set cooking grate in place. Clean and oil cooking grate. Position ribs next to each other on cooking grate, bone side down, crosswise over disposable pan and gap in snake (they will be off-center; this is OK). Cover grill, position lid vent over gap in snake, and open lid vent completely. Cook undisturbed until rack of ribs overhanging gap in snake registers 210 degrees in meatiest portion, 5½ to 6¼ hours. Transfer ribs to carving board, tent with aluminum foil, and let rest for 30 minutes. Cut ribs between bones and serve.

FLANK

WHEN YOU TAKE A LOOK at the flank's placement on the cow, you'll understand why flank steak is less fatty and juicy than the cut it's often compared with, skirt steak. The plate, where skirt steak comes from (see page 152), is located under the prized, marbled rib, whereas the flank is located under the leaner loin. But flank steak has plenty of beefy flavor and is a great multipurpose choice when you want to be economical—or anytime. It is a perfect slicing steak; that is, it's great in a tortilla (see page 166), on a salad (see page 172), or in a noodle dish (see page 170). You can even braise it (see page 168)—yes, it's fairly lean, but it has enough collagen to break down to turn it from tough to tender, and it doesn't add any flavor-muting greasiness to sauces.

Flank Steak

Cost: ▪▪▫▫ **Flavor:** ▪▪▪▫
Best cooking methods: pan sear, grill, stir fry
Texture: slightly chewy
Alternative names: jiffy steak

Flank steak is a large, flat cut from the underside of the cow, with a distinct longitudinal grain—the muscle fibers are quite thick, as with skirt steak, and quite long, spanning the length of the long steak. Flank steak is thin and cooks quickly, making it ideal for the grill. Although very flavorful, flank steak is slightly chewy. Like some other thick-grained steaks, it's best cooked not a smidge less than medium-rare or a smidge past medium—or it will be tough or dry, respectively. And it should always be sliced thin against the grain. Flank steak's distinct grain makes it an excellent candidate for marinating.

SLICING STEAK

We've identified, especially for particular cuts, that slicing steak against the grain—that is, perpendicular to the orientation of the muscle fibers—makes relatively tough steaks more tender. How much more tender? We conducted an exacting experiment to find out. We cooked a whole flank steak sous vide to 130 degrees, cut equally thick slices both with and against the grain, and used an ultrasensitive piece of equipment called a CT3 Texture Analyzer from Brookfield Engineering to test how much force was required to "bite" into the slices. We repeated the experiment three times and averaged the results. We also duplicated the tests with a more tender piece of strip loin.

The results: Flank steak slices carved against the grain required 383 grams of force to "bite" 5 millimeters into the meat, while slices carved with the grain required a whopping 1,729 grams of force—more than four times as much—to travel the same distance. The reason comes down to grain. Flank steak contains wide muscle fibers and a relatively high proportion of connective tissue that make it chewy. Slicing it against the grain shortened those muscle fibers, making it easier to chew. Slicing against the grain also dramatically narrowed the gap in tenderness between the strip and flank steaks: Flank steak sliced with the grain was 193 percent tougher than strip steak sliced with the grain, but that difference dropped to just 16 percent when both types of steak were sliced against the grain. So while all cuts benefit from slicing against the grain, it's especially important when slicing flank steak. In fact, slicing a flank steak properly can make it tender enough to rival premium steaks.

Note that there are slicing considerations when working with raw flank steak as well. We really only cook the long steak whole when we're at the grill, where it fits without us having to cram it in a pan. Inside, a steak that long, with such a distinct long grain, can shrink and buckle when it hits a hot pan, so we slice it before cooking. Sometimes that means into individual steaks, as in Pan-Seared Flank Steak with Mustard-Chive Butter (page 166). In this case we cut *with* the grain to slice the steak in half and then against the grain to cut each half into a mini tender flank steak. For stir-fries like Yakisoba with Beef, Shiitakes, and Cabbage (page 170), we first slice the steak into long strips lengthwise and then into thin slices crosswise (against the grain) to ensure they'll be tender before they even hit the pan.

MEAT PREP *Slicing Flank Steak*

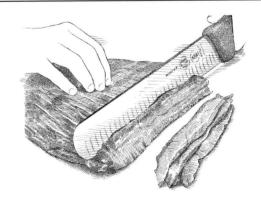

Slice flank steak thin against grain.

PAN-SEARED FLANK STEAK WITH MUSTARD-CHIVE BUTTER

Serves 4 to 6 | flank steak

WHY THIS RECIPE WORKS Thin flank steak is easy to overcook. What's more, the long muscle fibers tend to contract when seared, causing the steak to buckle and resist browning. We wanted an indoor cooking method that produced a juicy, well-browned flank steak cooked to an even rosy interior color. We cut the steak into portions that would fit neatly in a 12-inch skillet and sprinkled them with sugar to boost browning. Then we baked the steaks in a very low oven until they reached 120 degrees and seared them in a skillet for a flavorful crust. While they were in the skillet, we flipped the steaks several times to even out the contraction of the muscle fibers that makes them buckle. A compound butter topping enriched the lean steaks before serving. Open the oven as infrequently as possible in step 1. If the meat is not yet up to temperature, wait at least 5 minutes before taking its temperature again.

1 (1½- to 1¾-pound) flank steak, trimmed
2 teaspoons kosher salt
1 teaspoon sugar
½ teaspoon pepper
3 tablespoons unsalted butter, softened
3 tablespoons chopped fresh chives, divided
2 teaspoons Dijon mustard
½ teaspoon grated lemon zest plus 1 teaspoon juice
2 tablespoons vegetable oil

1. Adjust oven rack to middle position and heat oven to 225 degrees. Pat steak dry with paper towels. Cut steak in half lengthwise. Cut each piece in half crosswise to create 4 steaks. Combine salt, sugar, and pepper in small bowl. Sprinkle half of salt mixture on 1 side of steaks and press gently to adhere. Flip steaks and repeat with remaining salt mixture. Place steaks on wire rack set in rimmed baking sheet; transfer sheet to oven. Cook until thermometer inserted through side into center of thickest steak registers 120 degrees, 30 to 40 minutes.

2. Meanwhile, combine butter, 1 tablespoon chives, mustard, and lemon zest and juice in small bowl.

3. Heat oil in 12-inch skillet over medium-high heat until just smoking. Sear steaks, flipping every 1 minute, until brown crust forms on both sides, 4 minutes total. (Do not move steaks between flips.) Return steaks to wire rack and let rest for 10 minutes.

4. Transfer steaks to cutting board with grain running from left to right. Spread 1½ teaspoons butter mixture on top of each steak. Slice steaks as thin as possible against grain. Transfer sliced steaks to warm platter, dot with remaining butter mixture, sprinkle with remaining 2 tablespoons chives, and serve.

VARIATIONS

Pan-Seared Flank Steak with Garlic-Anchovy Butter

Substitute 3 tablespoons chopped fresh parsley and 1 anchovy fillet, rinsed and minced to paste, for chives, Dijon mustard, and lemon zest and juice in step 2.

Pan-Seared Flank Steak with Sriracha-Lime Butter

Substitute 3 tablespoons chopped fresh cilantro, 1 tablespoon sriracha, and ½ teaspoon grated lime zest plus 1 teaspoon juice for chives, Dijon mustard, and lemon zest and juice in step 2.

STEAK TACOS

Serves 4 | flank steak

WHY THIS RECIPE WORKS Grilled steak tacos are great, but we wanted an indoor recipe to make taco Tuesday a year-round possibility. As it did for our pan-seared flank steak recipe, a sprinkling of sugar gave the beefy flank steak the browned exterior and crisp edges characteristic of grilled meat. A deeply flavorful oil-based herb paste of cilantro, scallions, garlic, jalapeño, and cumin provided its own bright flavor boost. Piercing the steak and rubbing it with the herb paste before cooking allowed the flavors to fully penetrate the meat, and mixing the cooked steak with the remaining herb paste let bright flavor soak in. Serve with chopped tomatoes, chopped onion, and diced avocado, if desired.

½ cup fresh cilantro leaves, plus extra for serving
3 scallions, chopped coarse
3 garlic cloves, chopped coarse
1 jalapeño chile, stemmed and chopped coarse
½ teaspoon ground cumin
6 tablespoons vegetable oil, divided
1 tablespoon lime juice
1 (1½- to 1¾-pound) flank steak, trimmed
1½ teaspoons table salt
½ teaspoon sugar
½ teaspoon pepper
12 (6-inch) corn tortillas, warmed
Lime wedges

1. Pulse cilantro, scallions, garlic, jalapeño, and cumin in food processor until finely chopped, 10 to 12 pulses. Add ¼ cup oil and process until mixture is smooth, about 15 seconds, scraping down bowl as needed. Transfer 2 tablespoons herb paste to medium bowl and stir in lime juice; set aside for serving.

2. Cut steak with grain into 4 pieces. Using dinner fork, poke each piece of steak 10 to 12 times on each side. Place steaks in large baking dish, rub thoroughly with salt, then coat with remaining herb paste. Cover and refrigerate for 30 minutes to 1 hour.

TUTORIAL
Pan-Seared Flank Steak with Mustard-Chive Butter

One steak becomes four to fit in the skillet and prevent buckling. Here's how to divide and cook the steaks.

1. Cut steak in half lengthwise.

2. Cut each piece in half crosswise to create 4 steaks.

3. Sprinkle half of salt mixture on 1 side of steaks and press gently to adhere. Flip steaks and repeat. Transfer steaks to oven and cook until thermometer inserted into center of thickest steak registers 120 degrees, 30 to 40 minutes.

4. Heat oil in 12-inch skillet over medium-high heat until just smoking. Sear steaks, flipping every 1 minute, until brown crust forms on both sides. Return steaks to wire rack and let rest for 10 minutes.

5. Transfer steaks to cutting board with grain running from left to right. Spread 1½ teaspoons butter mixture on top of each steak.

6. Slice steaks as thin as possible against grain. Transfer sliced steaks to warm platter, dot with remaining butter mixture and sprinkle with remaining 2 tablespoons chives, and serve.

3. Scrape herb paste off steaks and sprinkle with sugar and pepper. Heat remaining 2 tablespoons oil in 12-inch nonstick skillet over medium-high heat until just smoking. Cook steaks, turning as needed, until well browned on all sides and meat registers 120 to 125 degrees (for medium-rare), 4 to 6 minutes. Transfer steaks to cutting board and let rest for 5 minutes.

4. Slice steaks thin against grain, add to bowl with reserved herb paste, and toss to coat. Season with salt and pepper to taste. Serve with warm tortillas, extra cilantro, and lime wedges.

BRACIOLE

Serves 4 to 6 | flank steak

WHY THIS RECIPE WORKS Braciole—thin beef rolled around a savory, slightly sweet filling and then browned and simmered in tomato sauce—is a staple for many Italian Americans. For our take, we pounded flank steak to an even ½-inch thickness. Many recipes call for a bread-based filling, but these were stodgy. A simple mixture of sweet raisins, fresh parsley and basil, and savory Parmesan cheese held together well, and brushing the meat with oil before applying the filling helped it stay put while we rolled the steak. A quick sear gave the meat bundle nice browning, and a long braise in a quick homemade tomato sauce infused it with more flavor and kept it tender. Some supermarkets sell meat labeled specifically for braciole, but we recommend buying flank steak and trimming it yourself. Look for flank steak of even thickness, without tapered ends. Braciole is usually served with pasta; our recipe makes enough sauce for at least 1 pound of pasta.

- 1 (2-pound) flank steak, trimmed
- ¼ cup extra-virgin olive oil
- 10 garlic cloves, sliced thin
- ½ cup golden raisins, chopped coarse
- 1 ounce Parmesan cheese, grated (½ cup), plus extra for serving
- ½ cup chopped fresh basil, divided
- ¼ cup chopped fresh parsley
- 1 teaspoon dried oregano, divided
- ½ teaspoon red pepper flakes, divided
- ¾ teaspoon pepper
- ½ teaspoon table salt
- 1 onion, chopped
- 3 tablespoons tomato paste
- 2 (28-ounce) cans crushed tomatoes

1. Adjust oven rack to middle position and heat oven to 325 degrees. Position steak on cutting board so long edge is parallel to counter edge. Cover with plastic wrap and pound to even ½-inch thickness. Trim any ragged edges to create rough rectangle about 11 by 9 inches. Pat steak dry with paper towels.

2. Combine oil and garlic in bowl and microwave until fragrant, about 1 minute. Let cool slightly, then remove garlic from oil with fork. Separately reserve garlic and garlic oil. Combine raisins, Parmesan, ¼ cup basil, parsley, ½ teaspoon oregano, ¼ teaspoon pepper flakes, and half of garlic in bowl.

3. Brush exposed side of steak with 1 tablespoon garlic oil and sprinkle with pepper and salt. Spread raisin mixture evenly over steak, pressing to adhere, leaving 1-inch border along top edge. Starting from bottom edge and rolling away from you, roll steak into tight log, finally resting it seam side down. Tie braciole crosswise with kitchen twine at 1-inch intervals.

4. Heat 1 tablespoon garlic oil in 12-inch nonstick skillet over medium-high heat until just smoking. Add braciole, seam side down, and cook until lightly browned all over, about 5 minutes. Transfer to 13 by 9-inch baking dish.

5. Reduce heat to medium and add onion, remaining garlic oil, remaining ½ teaspoon oregano, and remaining ¼ teaspoon pepper flakes to now-empty skillet. Cook until onion just begins to soften, about 3 minutes. Stir in tomato paste and remaining garlic and cook until fragrant and tomato paste is lightly browned, about 1 minute. Stir in tomatoes, bring to simmer, and pour sauce over braciole. Cover dish tightly with aluminum foil and bake until fork slips easily in and out of braciole, 1½ to 1¾ hours. Transfer dish to wire rack, spoon sauce over braciole, re-cover, and let rest in sauce for 30 minutes.

6. Transfer braciole to carving board, seam side down. Discard twine and slice braciole ¾ inch thick. Stir remaining ¼ cup basil into sauce and season with salt and pepper to taste. Ladle 2 cups sauce onto platter. Transfer braciole slices to platter. Serve, passing remaining sauce and extra Parmesan separately.

ARRACHERA EN ADOBO

Serves 4 to 6 | flank steak

WHY THIS RECIPE WORKS Arrachera en adobo, a chili-like dish of steak stewed in a pungent adobo sauce and eaten up with flour tortillas, is a gem of Mexican American cuisine that's virtually unknown outside Texas. Spicy, garlicky, sweet, sour, meaty, fruity, and rich, this complex dish is at once comforting and invigorating. For a simple adobo sauce that still had that characteristic complexity, we used two kinds of dried chiles—fruity anchos (dried poblanos) and bitter, earthy pasillas. Seeding the chiles tamed their heat, while toasting them enhanced their flavor. Blending the rehydrated chiles with lime juice, chicken broth, oregano, and salsa verde—a green salsa made from tomatillos—created a rich yet tangy sauce. Flank steak is leaner than a typical stewing cut and thus won't make the sauce too greasy—it's perfect here. We used jarred

Braciole

1. **For the adobo:** Adjust oven rack to lower-middle position and heat oven to 350 degrees. Arrange anchos and pasillas on rimmed baking sheet and bake until fragrant, about 5 minutes. Immediately transfer chiles to bowl and cover with hot tap water. Let stand until chiles are softened and pliable, about 5 minutes; drain.

2. Process salsa verde, broth, orange juice, sugar, lime juice, oregano, salt, pepper, and drained chiles in blender until smooth, 1 to 2 minutes; set aside.

3. **For the flank steak:** Reduce oven temperature to 300 degrees. Pat beef dry with paper towels and sprinkle with ½ teaspoon salt and pepper. Heat 1 tablespoon oil in Dutch oven over medium-high heat until just smoking. Add half of beef and cook, stirring occasionally, until well browned on all sides, 6 to 9 minutes. (Adjust heat, if necessary, to keep bottom of pot from scorching.) Using slotted spoon, transfer beef to large bowl. Repeat with remaining 1 tablespoon oil and remaining beef.

4. Add onion and remaining ½ teaspoon salt to now-empty pot. Reduce heat to medium and cook, stirring occasionally, until golden brown, 3 to 5 minutes, scraping up any browned bits. Add garlic and cumin and cook until fragrant, about 30 seconds. Stir in adobo, beef, and any accumulated juices until well incorporated and bring mixture to simmer.

5. Cover pot; transfer to oven. Cook until beef is tender and sauce has thickened, about 1½ hours. Season with salt and pepper to taste. Sprinkle with queso fresco and cilantro and serve with tortillas.

salsa verde for ease; our favorite is from Frontera. If queso fresco is unavailable, you can substitute farmer's cheese or a mild feta. This dish is also great served over rice.

ADOBO

1½ ounces dried ancho chiles, stemmed and seeded
1 ounce dried pasilla chiles, stemmed and seeded
¾ cup salsa verde
¾ cup chicken broth
½ cup orange juice
⅓ cup packed brown sugar
¼ cup lime juice (2 limes)
1½ teaspoons dried oregano
1 teaspoon table salt
½ teaspoon pepper

FLANK STEAK

2½–3 pounds flank steak, trimmed and cut into 1½-inch cubes
1 teaspoon table salt, divided
½ teaspoon pepper
2 tablespoons vegetable oil, divided
1 onion, chopped fine
8 garlic cloves, minced
1 tablespoon ground cumin
4 ounces queso fresco, crumbled (1 cup)
½ cup coarsely chopped fresh cilantro
12 (8-inch) flour tortillas, warmed

BEEF STIR-FRY WITH BELL PEPPERS AND BLACK PEPPER SAUCE

Serves 4 | flank steak

WHY THIS RECIPE WORKS Flank steak is often used for stir-fries but in order for it to have the velvety, meltingly tender texture of beef found in restaurants, we had to treat it properly. The first step was cutting it against the grain into bite-size pieces, so it had a pleasant chew—without being chewy. Adding some cornstarch to the marinade before flash-searing the beef gave it a plush coating that comes from the Chinese technique called "velveting." In traditional velveting, the meat gets marinated in an egg white–and–cornstarch mixture and then is blanched. But adding in a baking soda soak, which we use to tenderize meat (see page 16), allowed us to forgo the messy egg and extra step, respectively. We tied the stir-fry together with a spicy-sweet-salty sauce made from soy and oyster sauces, brown sugar, and black pepper. Serve with steamed white rice.

1 pound flank steak, trimmed
5 tablespoons water, divided
¼ teaspoon baking soda
3 tablespoons soy sauce, divided
3 tablespoons Shaoxing wine or dry sherry, divided
1 tablespoon cornstarch, divided
2½ teaspoons packed light brown sugar, divided
1 tablespoon oyster sauce
2 teaspoons rice vinegar
2 teaspoons coarsely ground pepper
1½ teaspoons toasted sesame oil
3 tablespoons plus 1 teaspoon vegetable oil, divided
1 red bell pepper, stemmed, seeded, and cut into
   ¼-inch-wide strips
1 green bell pepper, stemmed, seeded, and cut into
   ¼-inch-wide strips
6 scallions, white parts sliced thin on bias, green parts
   cut into 2-inch pieces
3 garlic cloves, minced
1 tablespoon grated fresh ginger

1. Cut steak lengthwise with grain into 2- to 2½-inch strips. Cut each strip crosswise against grain into ¼-inch-thick slices. Combine 1 tablespoon water and baking soda in medium bowl. Add beef and toss to coat. Let stand at room temperature for 5 minutes.

2. Whisk 1 tablespoon soy sauce, 1 tablespoon sherry, 1½ teaspoons cornstarch, and ½ teaspoon sugar together in small bowl. Add soy sauce mixture to beef, stir to coat, and let sit at room temperature for 15 to 30 minutes.

3. Whisk oyster sauce, vinegar, pepper, sesame oil, remaining ¼ cup water, remaining 2 tablespoons soy sauce, remaining 2 tablespoons sherry, remaining 1½ teaspoons cornstarch, and remaining 2 teaspoons sugar together in second bowl.

4. Heat 2 teaspoons vegetable oil in 12-inch nonstick skillet over high heat until just smoking. Add half of beef in single layer. Cook, without stirring, for 1 minute. Continue to cook, stirring occasionally, until spotty brown on both sides, about 1 minute longer. Transfer to bowl. Repeat with 2 teaspoons vegetable oil and remaining beef.

5. Return skillet to high heat, add 2 teaspoons vegetable oil, and heat until just smoking. Add bell peppers and scallion greens and cook, stirring occasionally, until vegetables are spotty brown and crisp-tender, about 4 minutes. Transfer vegetables to bowl with beef.

Yakisoba with Beef, Shiitakes, and Cabbage

6. Return now-empty skillet to medium-high heat and add remaining 4 teaspoons vegetable oil, garlic, ginger, and scallion whites. Cook, stirring frequently, until lightly browned, about 2 minutes. Return beef and vegetables to skillet and stir to combine.

7. Whisk sauce to recombine. Add to skillet and cook, stirring constantly, until sauce is thickened, about 30 seconds. Serve immediately.

YAKISOBA WITH BEEF, SHIITAKES, AND CABBAGE

Serves 4 to 6 | flank steak

WHY THIS RECIPE WORKS Springy noodles in a bold, complex sauce make yakisoba a standout among noodle stir-fries. For our version, we needed a readily available substitute for hard-to-find chewy yakisoba noodles. Lo mein noodles, which also contain an alkaline ingredient that gives them some elasticity, fit the bill perfectly. We undercooked them to enhance their chew and rinsed them with cold water to remove surface starches and make them appropriately slick. As in our Beef Stir-Fry with Bell Peppers and Black Pepper Sauce, baking soda raised the meat's pH, preventing its proteins from binding excessively and ensuring that each piece was tender and juicy. This recipe calls for lo mein noodles, but use yakisoba noodles if you can find them and follow the same cooking directions. Garnish the noodles with pickled ginger (often found in the refrigerated section of the grocery store near the tofu) and our Sesame-Orange Spice Blend (recipe follows) or, if you can find it, commercial shichimi togarashi.

12 ounces flank steak, trimmed
⅛ teaspoon baking soda
¼ cup ketchup
¼ cup soy sauce
2 tablespoons Worcestershire sauce
1½ tablespoons packed brown sugar
3 garlic cloves, minced
3 anchovy fillets, rinsed, patted dry, and minced
1 teaspoon rice vinegar
1 pound fresh or 8 ounces dried lo mein noodles
1 tablespoon vegetable oil, divided
6 ounces shiitake mushrooms, stemmed and sliced ¼ inch thick
1 carrot, peeled and sliced on bias ⅛ inch thick
¾ cup chicken broth, divided
6 cups napa cabbage, sliced crosswise into ½-inch strips
7 scallions, cut on bias into 1-inch pieces

1. Cut steak lengthwise with grain into 2- to 2½-inch strips. Cut each strip crosswise against grain into ¼-inch-thick slices. Combine 1 tablespoon water and baking soda in medium bowl. Add beef and toss to coat. Let stand at room temperature for 5 minutes.

2. Whisk ketchup, soy sauce, Worcestershire, sugar, garlic, anchovies, and vinegar together in second bowl. Stir 2 tablespoons sauce into beef mixture and set aside remaining sauce.

3. Bring 4 quarts water to boil in large pot. Add noodles and cook, stirring often, until almost tender (centers should still be firm with slightly opaque dot), 3 to 10 minutes (cooking time will vary depending on whether you are using fresh or dried noodles). Drain noodles and rinse under cold running water until water runs clear. Drain well and set aside.

4. Heat ½ teaspoon oil in 12-inch nonstick skillet over high heat until just smoking. Add mushrooms and carrot and cook, stirring occasionally, until vegetables are spotty brown, 2 to 3 minutes. Add ¼ cup broth to skillet and cook until all liquid has evaporated and vegetables are tender, about 30 seconds. Transfer vegetables to third bowl.

5. Return skillet to high heat, add ½ teaspoon oil, and heat until beginning to smoke. Add cabbage and scallions and cook, without stirring, for 30 seconds. Cook, stirring occasionally, until cabbage and scallions are spotty brown and crisp-tender, 2 to 3 minutes. Transfer to bowl with mushrooms and carrot.

6. Return skillet to high heat, add 1 teaspoon oil, and heat until beginning to smoke. Add half of beef mixture in single layer. Cook, without stirring, for 30 seconds. Cook, stirring occasionally, until beef is spotty brown, 1 to 2 minutes. Transfer to bowl with vegetables. Repeat with remaining beef mixture and remaining 1 teaspoon oil.

7. Return skillet to high heat; add reserved sauce, noodles, and remaining ½ cup broth. Cook, scraping up any browned bits, until noodles are warmed through, about 1 minute. Transfer noodles to bowl with vegetables and beef and toss to combine. Season with salt to taste, and serve immediately.

SERVE WITH
Sesame-Orange Spice Blend
Makes ¼ cup; serves 4 to 6
In addition to garnishing our stir-fry, this blend makes a great seasoning for eggs, rice, and fish.

¾ teaspoon grated orange zest
2 teaspoons sesame seeds
1½ teaspoons paprika
1 teaspoon pepper
¼ teaspoon garlic powder
¼ teaspoon ground ginger
⅛ teaspoon cayenne pepper

Place orange zest in small bowl and microwave, stirring every 20 seconds, until zest is dry and no longer clumping together, 1½ minutes to 2½ minutes. Stir in sesame seeds, paprika, pepper, garlic powder, ginger, and cayenne. (Spice blend can be stored in refrigerator for up to 1 week.)

FLANK STEAK WITH RED CURRY POTATOES

Serves 4 | flank steak
WHY THIS RECIPE WORKS Curry pastes are powerhouse ingredients that can add aromatic complexity and interest to an otherwise straightforward dish—they don't have to be relegated to stew-like curries. We wanted to use red curry paste (store-bought to avoid a laundry list of ingredients) to add interest to mild potatoes and serve them alongside a pan-seared skirt steak for a classic meat-and-potatoes dinner with a twist. The store-bought paste carried the flavors of lemongrass, galangal, and makrut lime leaves, and we augmented it with fresh ginger, garlic, fish sauce, and coconut milk for potatoes with creaminess and complexity that were ready to star alongside perfectly cooked flank steak.

1½ pounds small Yukon Gold potatoes, unpeeled, quartered
3 tablespoons vegetable oil, divided
1 (1½-pound) flank steak, trimmed and halved lengthwise
¼ cup red curry paste
1 tablespoon grated fresh ginger
2 garlic cloves, minced
1 cup canned coconut milk
2 teaspoons fish sauce
2 tablespoons fresh cilantro leaves

1. Combine potatoes and 2 tablespoons oil in large bowl. Cover and microwave until potatoes are nearly tender, about 7 minutes; set aside.

2. Pat steak dry with paper towels and season with salt and pepper. Heat remaining 1 tablespoon oil in 12-inch nonstick skillet over medium-high heat until just smoking. Cook steak until well browned and meat registers 120 to 125 degrees (for medium-rare), 5 to 7 minutes per side. Transfer steak to cutting board, tent with foil, and let rest for 5 minutes. Wipe out skillet with paper towels.

3. Add curry paste, ginger, and garlic to now-empty skillet and cook over medium-high heat until fragrant, about 30 seconds. Stir in coconut milk, fish sauce, and parcooked potatoes and bring to simmer. Cook until potatoes are tender, about 3 minutes. Slice steak thin against grain on bias. Serve with curried potatoes and sprinkle with cilantro.

NAM TOK

Serves 4 to 6 | flank steak

WHY THIS RECIPE WORKS In the best versions of this Thai grilled beef salad, the cuisine's five signature flavor elements—hot, sour, salty, sweet, and bitter—come into balance, making for a light but satisfying dish that's traditionally served with steamed jasmine rice. We captured those flavors in the dressing for our grilled flank steak and sliced cucumber: To a base of fish sauce, lime juice, sugar, and water, we added a Thai chile and a mix of toasted cayenne and paprika, which added earthy, fruity red pepper flavor. If fresh Thai chiles are unavailable, substitute ½ serrano chile. Don't skip the toasted rice; it's integral to the texture and flavor of the dish. Any variety of white rice can be used. Toasted rice powder (kao kua) can also be found in many Asian markets; substitute 1 tablespoon rice powder for the white rice.

1 teaspoon paprika
1 teaspoon cayenne pepper
1 tablespoon white rice
3 tablespoons lime juice (2 limes)

Nam Tok

2 tablespoons fish sauce
2 tablespoons water
½ teaspoon sugar
1 (1½-pound) flank steak, trimmed
1 seedless English cucumber, sliced ¼-inch-thick on bias
4 shallots, sliced thin
1½ cups fresh mint leaves, torn
1½ cups fresh cilantro leaves
1 Thai chile, stemmed, seeded, and sliced thin into rounds

1. Heat paprika and cayenne in 8-inch skillet over medium heat; cook, shaking pan, until fragrant, about 1 minute. Transfer to small bowl. Return skillet to medium-high heat, add rice and toast, stirring constantly, until deep golden brown, about 5 minutes. Transfer to small bowl and let cool for 5 minutes. Grind rice with spice grinder, mini food processor, or mortar and pestle until it resembles fine meal, 10 to 30 seconds (you should have about 1 tablespoon rice powder).

2. Whisk lime juice, fish sauce, water, sugar, and ¼ teaspoon toasted paprika mixture in large bowl and set aside.

3a. For a charcoal grill: Open bottom vent completely. Light large chimney starter filled with charcoal briquettes (6 quarts). When top coals are partially covered with ash, pour in even layer over half of grill. Set cooking grate in place, cover, and open lid vent completely. Heat grill until hot, about 5 minutes.

3b. For a gas grill: Turn all burners to high, cover, and heat grill until hot, about 15 minutes. Leave primary burner on high and turn off other burner(s).

4. Clean and oil cooking grate. Season steak with salt and coarsely ground white pepper. Place steak on hotter side of grill and cook until beginning to char and beads of moisture appear on outer edges of meat, 5 to 6 minutes. Flip steak and continue to cook until meat registers 120 to 125 degrees (for medium-rare), about 5 minutes longer. Transfer to cutting board, tent with aluminum foil, and let rest for 10 minutes (or allow to cool to room temperature, about 1 hour).

5. Line large platter with cucumber slices. Slice steak against grain on bias ¼ inch thick. Transfer sliced steak to bowl with fish sauce mixture. Add shallots, mint, cilantro, chile, and half of rice powder and toss to combine. Arrange steak over cucumber-lined platter. Serve, passing remaining rice powder and remaining toasted paprika mixture separately.

NEGIMAKI

Serves 8 to 10 as an appetizer or 4 to 6 as a main dish | flank steak

WHY THIS RECIPE WORKS Negimaki pairs grilled beef flavor with the elegant presentation of sushi—grilled steak surrounds pieces of scallions. For our version, we sliced flank steak (frozen briefly for easier slicing) on the bias, pounded the pieces thin, and formed meat "wrappers" that we topped with halved scallions. After forming and securing the rolls, we grilled them over a hot fire, turning for even browning and brushing them with a salty-sweet teriyaki-like glaze. The meat slices were too thin to probe for doneness, so instead we took the temperature of the scallion core; when it registered from 150 to 155 degrees, the meat was properly cooked. Finally, we sliced the rolls into bite-size pieces, drizzled them with extra glaze, and sprinkled them with toasted sesame seeds. Look for a flank steak that is as rectangular as possible, as this will yield the most uniform slices. You may end up with extra slices of steak; you can grill these alongside the rolls or make several smaller rolls. Serve either as an appetizer or as a main dish with steamed rice and a vegetable.

  1 (2-pound) flank steak, trimmed
  ½ cup soy sauce
  ¼ cup sugar
  3 tablespoons mirin
  3 tablespoons sake
 16 scallions, trimmed and halved crosswise
  1 tablespoon sesame seeds, toasted

1. Place steak on large plate and freeze until firm, about 30 minutes.

2. Bring soy sauce, sugar, mirin, and sake to simmer in small saucepan over high heat, stirring to dissolve sugar. Reduce heat to medium and cook until slightly syrupy and reduced to ½ cup, 3 to 5 minutes. Divide evenly between 2 bowls and let cool. Cover 1 bowl with plastic wrap and set aside for serving.

3. Place steak on cutting board. Starting at narrow, tapered end, slice steak against grain on bias ⅜ inch thick until width of steak is 7 inches (depending on size of steak, you will need to remove 2 to 3 slices until steak measures 7 inches across). Cut steak in half lengthwise. Continue to slice each half against grain on bias. You should have at least 24 slices. Pound each slice to ³⁄₁₆-inch thickness between 2 sheets of plastic.

4. Arrange 3 slices on cutting board with short side of slices facing you, overlapping slices by ¼ inch and alternating tapered ends as needed, to form rough rectangle that measures 4 to 6 inches wide and at least 4 inches long. Place 4 scallion halves along edge of rectangle nearest to edge of counter, with white tips slightly hanging over edges of steak on either side. Starting from bottom edge and rolling away from you, roll into tight cylinder. Insert 3 equally spaced toothpicks into end flaps and through center of roll. Transfer roll to platter and repeat with remaining steak and scallions. (Assembled rolls can be refrigerated for up to 24 hours.)

5a. For a charcoal grill: Open bottom vent completely. Light large chimney starter three-quarters filled with charcoal briquettes (4½ quarts). When top coals are partially covered with ash, pour evenly over half of grill. Set cooking grate in place, cover, and open lid vent completely. Heat grill until hot, about 5 minutes.

5b. For a gas grill: Turn all burners to high, cover, and heat grill until hot, about 15 minutes. Leave all burners on high.

6. Clean and oil cooking grate. Place rolls on grill (over coals if using charcoal) and cook until first side is beginning to char, 4 to 6 minutes. Flip rolls, brush cooked side with glaze, and cook until second side is beginning to char, 4 to 6 minutes. Cook remaining 2 sides, glazing after each turn, until all 4 sides of rolls are evenly charred and thermometer inserted from end of roll into scallions at core registers 150 to 155 degrees, 16 to 24 minutes total. Transfer rolls to cutting board, tent with aluminum foil, and let rest for 5 minutes. Discard remaining glaze.

7. Remove toothpicks from rolls and cut rolls crosswise into ¾-inch-long pieces. Arrange rolls cut side down on clean platter, drizzle with 2 tablespoons reserved glaze, sprinkle with sesame seeds, and serve, passing remaining reserved glaze separately.

TUTORIAL
Negimaki

Fashion a piece of flank steak into a completely different form with these flavorful Japanese steak-and-scallion rolls.

1. Place steak on cutting board. Starting at narrow, tapered end, slice steak against grain on bias ⅜ inch thick until width of steak is 7 inches.

2. Cut steak in half lengthwise. Continue to slice each half against grain on bias. You should have at least 24 slices.

3. Pound each slice to 3/16-inch thickness between 2 sheets of plastic.

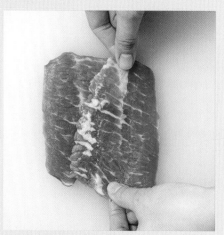

4. Arrange 3 slices with short side of slices facing you, overlapping slices by ¼ inch to form rectangle that measures 4 to 6 inches wide and at least 4 inches long.

5. Place 4 scallion halves along edge of rectangle nearest to edge of counter, with white tips slightly hanging over edges of steak. Roll into tight cylinder.

6. Insert 3 equally spaced toothpicks into end flaps and through center of roll. Repeat with remaining steak.

GRILLED BEEF SATAY

Serves 6 | flank steak

WHY THIS RECIPE WORKS This Southeast Asian street food is made by grilling kebabs of assertively flavored meat over a hot fire. Flank steak is perfect for an at-home version because its fat is evenly distributed and it has a symmetrical shape. We cut the steak against the grain and then threaded the strips onto skewers. A simple marinade of vegetable oil, sugar, and fish sauce seasoned the meat without turning its exterior mealy (a problem we had when incorporating ginger into the marinade, thanks to an enzyme in ginger that breaks down protein). Incorporating the ginger into a basting sauce and brushing it over the kebabs while they cooked infused the meat with the bold, aromatic flavors characteristic of great satay. You will need ten to twelve 12-inch metal skewers for this recipe, or you can substitute bamboo skewers that have been soaked in water for 30 minutes. The disposable aluminum roasting pan used for charcoal grilling should be at least 2¾ inches deep. Serve with Peanut Sauce (recipe follows).

BASTING SAUCE

- ¾ cup canned coconut milk
- 3 tablespoons packed dark brown sugar
- 3 tablespoons fish sauce
- 2 tablespoons vegetable oil
- 3 shallots, minced
- 2 lemongrass stalks, trimmed to bottom 6 inches and minced
- 2 tablespoons grated fresh ginger
- 1½ teaspoons ground coriander
- ¾ teaspoon red pepper flakes
- ½ teaspoon ground cumin
- ½ teaspoon table salt

BEEF

- 2 tablespoons vegetable oil
- 2 tablespoons packed dark brown sugar
- 1 tablespoon fish sauce
- 1 (1½- to 1¾-pound) flank steak, trimmed, halved lengthwise, and cut against grain on slight bias ¼ inch thick
- 1 (13 by 9-inch) disposable aluminum roasting pan (if using charcoal)

1. For the basting sauce: Whisk all ingredients together in medium bowl. Transfer one-third of sauce to small bowl (to brush on raw meat) and set both bowls aside.

2. For the beef: Whisk oil, sugar, and fish sauce together in medium bowl. Toss beef with marinade and let stand at room temperature for 30 minutes. Weave beef onto 12-inch metal skewers, 2 to 4 pieces per skewer, leaving 1½ inches at top and bottom of skewer exposed. You should have 10 to 12 skewers.

3a. For a charcoal grill: Poke twelve ½-inch holes in bottom of disposable pan. Open bottom vent completely and place disposable pan in center of grill. Light large chimney starter mounded with charcoal briquettes (7 quarts). When top coals are partially covered with ash, pour into disposable pan. Set cooking grate over coals with bars parallel to long side of disposable pan, cover, and open lid vent completely. Heat grill until hot, about 5 minutes.

3b. For a gas grill: Turn all burners to high, cover, and heat grill until hot, about 15 minutes. Leave all burners on high.

4. Clean and oil cooking grate. Place beef skewers on grill (directly over coals if using charcoal) perpendicular to grate bars. Brush meat with all of basting sauce in small bowl (reserved for raw meat) and cook (covered if using gas) until browned, about 3 minutes. Flip skewers, brush with half of remaining basting sauce in medium bowl, and cook until browned on second side, about 3 minutes. Brush meat with remaining basting sauce and cook 1 minute longer. Transfer to large platter and serve.

SERVE WITH
Peanut Sauce
Makes about 1½ cups; serves 6

- 1 tablespoon vegetable oil
- 1 tablespoon Thai red curry paste
- 1 tablespoon packed dark brown sugar
- 2 garlic cloves, minced
- 1 cup canned regular or light coconut milk
- ⅓ cup chunky peanut butter
- ¼ cup dry-roasted peanuts, chopped
- 1 tablespoon lime juice
- 1 tablespoon fish sauce
- 1 teaspoon soy sauce

Heat oil in small saucepan over medium heat until shimmering. Add curry paste, sugar, and garlic; cook, stirring constantly, until fragrant, about 1 minute. Add coconut milk and bring to simmer. Whisk in peanut butter until smooth. Off heat, stir in peanuts, lime juice, fish sauce, and soy sauce. Let cool completely.

SHORT RIBS

WHILE MOST SHORT RIBS THAT you purchase at the store come from the plate or chuck, these meaty short ends of ribs can technically be cut from anywhere along the rib section of the cow. That includes higher up toward the back, from the chuck area, or from the forward midsection. (That's why you see the chuck, rib, brisket, and plate primals highlighted.) The fat content will be different depending on the corresponding primal cut, but in no case is this ever a lean cut. All short ribs have incredibly beefy flavor. With the multiple ways you can cut and use them, we think they deserve their own spotlight as a category of beef in this book. There are two classifications of short ribs, English-style and flanken-style. Both types are full of collagen and connective tissue, which require slow cooking to break down—once that happens, the ribs are equally good and tender, meltingly so. But flanken-style ribs tend to be more expensive and harder to find, so you'll see we call for English-style in our recipes. We also have recipes that call for boneless short ribs in cases where the flavorful bone would get in the way (see "The Bold and the Boneless" for more information).

English-Style Short Ribs

Cost: ■■▢▢   **Flavor:** ■■■▢
Best cooking methods: braise, stew, grill, grill roast
Texture: succulent
Alternative names: short ribs

Cut parallel to the bone, English-style short ribs feature a rectangular slab of meat attached to one side of the bone. They can be purchased boneless, or you can remove the meat from the bone yourself.

THE BOLD AND THE BONELESS

Sure, we love the flavor a bone provides meat. And if you make a braise (see page 178) with bone-in short ribs, you're bound to end up with a luscious, glossy sauce full of body. But there are lots of benefits to boneless when it comes to short ribs—much of this because the meat itself is plenty fatty and so very deep in flavor.

Slice the meat for a luxe curry (see page 181) above and beyond those made with thin steaks.

Braise and then shred for a saucy ragu (see page 182) or a taco (see page 185) filling with a high meat yield.

Cut into chunks for a meat pie filling (see page 184) or a stew with sophistication.

Serve individual pot roasts by cooking boneless ribs and plating one per person (see page 182).

Cut them and pound them into even pieces for the grill for our easy-to-eat-version of Kalbi (page 186) with the very best texture.

MEAT PREP *Removing Short Ribs from the Bone*

1. Remove meat from bone, positioning chef's knife as close as possible to bone.

2. Trim excess hard fat and silverskin from both sides of meat.

Flanken-Style Short Ribs

Cost: ■■▢▢   **Flavor:** ■■■▢
Best cooking methods: braise, barbecue
Texture: succulent
Alternative names: Korean-style short ribs

Cut thin across the rib bones and found mainly in butcher shops, flanken-style ribs are a bit more complex in construction than English-style ones; they look like ladders with shorter pieces of meat attached at intervals to the bone. It is harder to get the meat off the bone. While we lean towards English-style, as they are easier to eat (and find), flanken-style ribs can often be substituted with some alterations to cook time.

RED WINE–BRAISED SHORT RIBS WITH BACON, PARSNIPS, AND PEARL ONIONS

Serves 6 | English-style short ribs

WHY THIS RECIPE WORKS Traditional bone-in braised short ribs are a luxurious and elegant treat. They're a terrific option for entertaining because you can make them ahead—in fact, it's actually best to rest them overnight before serving. Most recipes call for cumbersome stovetop browning, but we wanted a simpler option. We opted to brown the short ribs all at once in the oven, which allowed the ribs to spend more time in the heat, maximizing the amount of fat rendered (and minimizing the greasiness of our final sauce). To supplement the flavor, we made sure to add a lot of savory ingredients to the mix—garlic, red wine, rosemary, thyme, and tomato paste made the cut. We let the ribs rest to allow any additional fat to separate out and solidify. Once solidified, the fat was easy to scoop off the top; we then re-employed the braising liquid to finish cooking the vegetables and rewarm the ribs. Crisped bacon and sautéed pearl onions and parsnips added crunch and sweetness to our tender, succulent short ribs.

SHORT RIBS

- 6 pounds bone-in English-style short ribs, trimmed
- 3 cups dry red wine
- 3 large onions, chopped
- 2 carrots, peeled and chopped
- 1 large celery rib, chopped
- 9 garlic cloves, chopped
- ¼ cup all-purpose flour
- 4 cups chicken broth
- 1 (14.5-ounce) can diced tomatoes, drained
- 1½ tablespoons minced fresh rosemary
- 1 tablespoon minced fresh thyme
- 3 bay leaves
- 1 teaspoon tomato paste

BACON, PARSNIPS, AND PEARL ONIONS

- 6 slices bacon, cut into ¼-inch pieces
- 10 ounces parsnips, peeled and cut on bias into ¾-inch pieces
- 8 ounces frozen pearl onions
- ¼ teaspoon sugar
- ¼ teaspoon table salt
- 6 tablespoons chopped fresh parsley

1. For the short ribs: Adjust oven rack to lower-middle position and heat oven to 450 degrees. Arrange short ribs bone side down in single layer in large roasting pan; season with salt and pepper. Roast until meat begins to brown, about 45 minutes; drain off all liquid and fat. Return short ribs to oven and continue to roast until meat is well browned, 15 to 20 minutes longer. Transfer short ribs to large plate. Pour rendered fat into small bowl.

2. Reduce oven temperature to 300 degrees. Place now-empty pan over 2 burners set at medium heat; add wine and bring to simmer, scraping up any browned bits. Set aside.

3. Heat 2 tablespoons reserved fat in Dutch oven over medium-high heat; add onions, carrots, and celery and cook, stirring occasionally, until vegetables soften, about 12 minutes. Add garlic and cook until fragrant, about 30 seconds. Stir in flour until combined, about 45 seconds. Stir in broth, tomatoes, rosemary, thyme, bay leaves, tomato paste, and reserved wine. Season with salt and pepper to taste. Bring to boil and add short ribs, completely submerging meat in liquid. Return to boil and cover; transfer pot to oven. Cook until short ribs are tender, 2 to 2½ hours. Transfer pot to wire rack and let cool, partially covered, until warm, about 2 hours.

4. Transfer short ribs to serving platter, removing any vegetables that cling to meat; discard loose bones that have fallen away from meat. Strain braising liquid through fine-mesh strainer set over bowl, pressing on solids to extract all liquid; discard solids. Refrigerate short ribs and liquid separately, covered with plastic wrap, for at least 8 hours or up to 3 days.

5. For the bacon, parsnips, and pearl onions: Cook bacon over medium heat in Dutch oven until just crispy, 8 to 10 minutes; using slotted spoon, transfer bacon to paper towel–lined plate. Add parsnips, onions, sugar, and salt to pot; increase heat to high and cook, stirring occasionally, until browned, about 5 minutes.

6. Spoon off and discard solidified fat from reserved braising liquid. Add defatted liquid to pot and bring to simmer, stirring occasionally; season with salt and pepper to taste. Submerge short ribs in liquid and return to simmer. Reduce heat to medium and cook, partially covered, until short ribs are heated through and vegetables are tender, about 5 minutes; gently stir in bacon. Divide short ribs and sauce among serving bowls, sprinkle each bowl with 1 tablespoon parsley, and serve.

POMEGRANATE-BRAISED BEEF SHORT RIBS WITH PRUNES AND SESAME

Serves 6 | English-style short ribs

WHY THIS RECIPE WORKS Meltingly tender classic braised short ribs take a trip to the Mediterranean with this spin that features a warm-spiced sweet-but-tart sauce made with pomegranate juice and prunes. A good dose—2 tablespoons—of the warm spice blend ras el hanout added a pleasing, piquant aroma; we bloomed it by sautéing it with our onions and carrots to bring out its warmth from the start. Rather than

Red Wine-Braised Short Ribs with Bacon, Parsnips, and Pearl Onions

simply brown the ribs, we started by roasting them in the oven; this rendered a significant amount of fat that we could discard. After braising, we defatted the cooking liquid and then blended it with the vegetables and some of the prunes to create a velvety sauce. We added the remaining prunes to the sauce and garnished the dish with toasted sesame seeds and cilantro.

4 pounds bone-in English-style short ribs, trimmed
4 cups unsweetened pomegranate juice
1 cup water
2 tablespoons extra-virgin olive oil
1 onion, chopped fine
1 carrot, peeled and chopped fine
¼ teaspoon table salt
2 tablespoons ras el hanout
4 garlic cloves, minced
¾ cup prunes, halved
1 tablespoon red wine vinegar
2 tablespoons toasted sesame seeds
2 tablespoons chopped fresh cilantro

1. Adjust oven rack to lower-middle position and heat oven to 450 degrees. Pat ribs dry with paper towels and season with salt and pepper. Arrange ribs, bone side down, in single layer in large roasting pan and roast until meat begins to brown, about 45 minutes.

2. Discard any accumulated fat and juices in pan and continue to roast until meat is well browned, 15 to 20 minutes. Transfer ribs to bowl and tent with aluminum foil; set aside. Stir pomegranate juice and water into now-empty pan, scraping up any browned bits; set aside.

3. Reduce oven temperature to 300 degrees. Heat oil in Dutch oven over medium heat until shimmering. Add onion, carrot, and salt and cook until softened, about 5 minutes. Stir in ras el hanout and garlic and cook until fragrant, about 30 seconds.

4. Stir in pomegranate mixture from roasting pan and half of prunes and bring to simmer. Nestle ribs, bone side up, into pot and return to simmer. Cover, transfer pot to oven, and cook until ribs are tender, about 2½ hours.

5. Using pot holders, remove pot from oven. Being careful of hot pot handles, transfer ribs to bowl; discard any loose bones and tent with aluminum foil. Strain braising liquid through fine-mesh strainer into fat separator; transfer solids to blender. Let braising liquid settle for 5 minutes, then pour defatted liquid into blender with solids and process until smooth, about 1 minute.

Panang Beef Curry

6. Transfer sauce to now-empty pot and stir in vinegar and remaining prunes. Return ribs and any accumulated juices to pot, bring to gentle simmer over medium heat, and cook, spooning sauce over ribs occasionally, until heated through, about 5 minutes. Season with salt and pepper to taste. Transfer ribs to serving platter, spoon 1 cup sauce over top, and sprinkle with sesame seeds and cilantro. Serve, passing remaining sauce separately.

BRAISED BONELESS BEEF SHORT RIBS

Serves 6 | boneless beef short ribs

WHY THIS RECIPE WORKS Braised short ribs are a warm, hearty dinner on a cold day—but they often take a fair amount of that day to execute. We wanted to cut the usual long cooking time so that short ribs, with a silky, grease-free sauce, could make more frequent appearances at our dinner table. The first, easiest step to eliminating hours of cooking was starting with boneless short ribs. The only problem with omitting bones is that our braising liquid lacked the viscosity usually provided by them, so we added powdered gelatin to get a silky sauce that nicely napped the ribs. Wine, once reduced, added depth and intensity to the braise, and to supplement it, we chose beef broth to balance the wine. Make sure that the ribs are at least 4 inches long and 1 inch thick. We recommend a bold red wine such as a Cabernet Sauvignon.

3½ pounds boneless beef short ribs, trimmed
2 teaspoons kosher salt
1 teaspoon pepper
2 tablespoons vegetable oil, divided
2 large onions, sliced thin
1 tablespoon tomato paste
6 garlic cloves, peeled
2 cups red wine
1 cup beef broth
4 large carrots, peeled and cut into 2-inch pieces
4 sprigs fresh thyme
1 bay leaf
½ teaspoon unflavored gelatin

1. Adjust oven rack to lower-middle position and heat oven to 300 degrees. Pat short ribs dry with paper towels and sprinkle with salt and pepper. Heat 1 tablespoon oil in Dutch oven over medium-high heat until smoking. Add half of short ribs and cook, without moving them, until well browned, 4 to 6 minutes. Turn short ribs and continue to cook on second side until well browned, 4 to 6 minutes longer, reducing heat if fat begins to smoke. Transfer short ribs to bowl. Repeat with remaining 1 tablespoon oil and remaining short ribs.

2. Reduce heat to medium, add onions, and cook, stirring occasionally, until softened and beginning to brown, 12 to 15 minutes. (If onions begin to darken too quickly, add 1 to 2 tablespoons water to pot.) Add tomato paste and cook, stirring constantly, until it browns on sides and bottom of pot, about 2 minutes. Add garlic and cook until fragrant, about 30 seconds. Increase heat to medium-high, add wine, and simmer, scraping up any browned bits, until reduced by half, 8 to 10 minutes. Add broth, carrots, thyme sprigs, and bay leaf. Add short ribs and any accumulated juices to pot, cover, and bring to simmer; transfer pot to oven. Cook, turning short ribs twice during cooking, until fork slips easily in and out of meat, 2 to 2½ hours.

3. Sprinkle gelatin over ¼ cup water in bowl and let sit until gelatin softens, about 5 minutes. Using tongs, transfer short ribs and carrots to serving platter and tent with aluminum foil. Strain cooking liquid through fine-mesh strainer into fat separator or bowl, pressing on solids to extract as much liquid as possible; discard solids. Let liquid settle for 5 minutes, then skim fat from surface. Return cooking liquid to pot and cook over medium heat until reduced to 1 cup, 5 to 10 minutes. Remove from heat and stir in gelatin mixture; season with salt and pepper to taste. Pour sauce over short ribs and serve.

VARIATION
Braised Boneless Beef Short Ribs with Guinness and Prunes
Substitute 1 cup full-flavored porter or stout for wine and omit wine reduction time in step 2. Add ⅓ cup pitted prunes to pot along with broth.

PANANG BEEF CURRY

Serves 6 | boneless beef short ribs
WHY THIS RECIPE WORKS Savory-sweet, deeply rich and fragrant, panang curry is a velvety, coconut milk–spiked curry often made beef. To flavor ours, we used jarred red curry paste and doctored it up with the distinct flavors of this dish: makrut lime leaves, fish sauce, sugar, fresh chile, and peanuts. Thinly slicing boneless beef short ribs before cooking delivered a luscious fall-apart texture in just over an hour of hands-off cooking time. Cooking the beef separately until it was tender and only then adding it to the sauce ensured that its flavor didn't overpower the dish. Red curry pastes from different brands vary in spiciness, so start by adding 2 tablespoons and then taste the sauce and add up to 2 tablespoons more. Makrut lime leaves are sometimes sold as kaffir lime leaves. If you can't find them, substitute three 3-inch strips each of lemon zest and lime zest, adding them to the sauce with the beef in step 2 (remove the zest strips before serving). Do not substitute light coconut milk here. Serve this rich dish with rice and vegetables.

2 pounds boneless beef short ribs, trimmed
2 tablespoons vegetable oil
2–4 tablespoons Thai red curry paste
1 (14-ounce) can unsweetened coconut milk
4 teaspoons fish sauce
2 teaspoons sugar
1 Thai red chile, halved lengthwise (optional)
6 makrut lime leaves, middle vein removed, sliced thin
⅓ cup unsalted dry-roasted peanuts, chopped fine

1. Cut each rib crosswise with grain into 3 equal pieces. Slice each piece ¼ inch thick against grain. Place beef in large saucepan and add water to cover. Bring to boil over high heat. Cover, reduce heat to low, and cook until beef is fork-tender, 1 to 1¼ hours. Using slotted spoon, transfer beef to bowl; discard water. (Beef can refrigerated for up to 24 hours; when ready to use, add it to curry as directed in step 2.)

2. Heat oil in 12-inch nonstick skillet over medium heat until shimmering. Add 2 tablespoons curry paste and cook, stirring frequently, until paste is fragrant and darkens in color to brick red, 5 to 8 minutes. Add coconut milk, fish sauce, sugar, and chile, if using; stir to combine and to dissolve sugar. Taste sauce and add up to 2 tablespoons more curry paste to achieve desired spiciness. Add beef, stir to coat with sauce, and bring to simmer.

3. Rapidly simmer, stirring occasionally, until sauce is thickened and reduced by half and coats beef, 12 to 15 minutes. (Sauce should be quite thick, and streaks of oil will appear. Sauce will continue to thicken as it cools.) Add makrut lime leaves and simmer until fragrant, 1 to 2 minutes. Transfer to serving platter, sprinkle with peanuts, and serve.

BEEF SHORT RIB RAGU

Serves 4 to 6 | boneless beef short ribs

WHY THIS RECIPE WORKS Preparing a typical Sunday gravy is an all-day affair that can involve multiple meats. For the same flavor in much less time, we chose to use a single cut, intensely beefy boneless short ribs, which gave the ragu a velvety texture. For deep savor, we paired the ribs with porcini mushrooms, tomato paste, and anchovies—all umami powerhouses. Removing the lid partway through cooking facilitated browning, enhancing the meat's flavor. Finally, many Italian beef ragus call for a touch of warm spices, a nod to the spice route that passed through Italy from the 15th to the 17th century. Just ½ teaspoon of five-spice powder (a mix of cinnamon, cloves, fennel, white pepper, and star anise) contributed sweet and warm flavors. This recipe yields enough to sauce 1 pound of pasta or a batch of polenta (our favorite way to serve it). This recipe can be doubled.

1½ cups beef broth, divided
 ½ ounce dried porcini mushrooms, rinsed
 1 tablespoon extra-virgin olive oil
 1 onion, chopped fine
 2 garlic cloves, minced
 1 tablespoon tomato paste
 3 anchovy fillets, rinsed, patted dry, and minced
 ½ teaspoon five-spice powder
 ½ cup dry red wine
 1 (14.5-ounce) can whole peeled tomatoes, drained with juice reserved, chopped fine
 2 pounds boneless beef short ribs, trimmed
 ¾ teaspoon table salt

1. Adjust oven rack to middle position and heat oven to 350 degrees. Microwave ½ cup broth and mushrooms in covered bowl until steaming, about 1 minute. Let sit until softened, about 5 minutes. Drain mushrooms in fine-mesh strainer lined with coffee filter, pressing to extract all liquid; reserve liquid and chop mushrooms fine.

2. Heat oil in Dutch oven over medium heat until shimmering. Add onion and cook, stirring occasionally, until softened, about 5 minutes. Add garlic and cook until fragrant, about 1 minute. Add tomato paste, anchovies, and five-spice powder and cook, stirring frequently, until mixture has darkened and fond forms on pot bottom, 3 to 4 minutes. Add wine, increase heat to medium-high, and bring to simmer, scraping up any browned bits. Continue to cook, stirring frequently, until wine is reduced and pot is almost dry, 2 to 4 minutes. Add tomatoes and reserved juice, remaining 1 cup broth, reserved mushroom soaking liquid, and mushrooms and bring to simmer.

3. Toss beef with salt and season with pepper. Add beef to pot and cover; transfer pot to oven. Cook for 1 hour.

4. Uncover and continue to cook until beef is tender, 1 to 1¼ hours longer.

5. Remove pot from oven; using slotted spoon, transfer beef to cutting board and let cool for 5 minutes. Using 2 forks, shred beef into bite-size pieces, discarding any large pieces of fat or connective tissue. Using large spoon, skim off any excess fat that has risen to surface of sauce. Return beef to sauce and season with salt and pepper to taste. Serve.

SOUS VIDE SHORT RIB "POT ROAST"

Serves 4 | boneless beef short ribs
Sous vide time: 20 to 24 hours

WHY THIS RECIPE WORKS As you've seen, short ribs are most often braised since they're full of tough collagen and intramuscular fat. To achieve this texture while cooking sous vide, we opted for a higher-temperature water bath (160°F). This broke down collagen, tenderizing the meat while keeping it moist and preserving a medium-rosy interior from edge to edge. To make things even easier, we front-loaded the work. We quickly seared the short ribs and then built a sauce with traditional pot roast ingredients, mirepoix, tomato paste, red wine, beef broth, and herbs. We then bagged up the beef and sauce together for their sous vide bath. Afterward, we strained the sauce and briefly reduced it on the stovetop, poured it over the tender short ribs, and finished the dish with a sprinkling of fresh parsley. Easy pot roast—no pot or roasting required. Make sure that the ribs are at least 4 inches long and 1 inch thick. Be sure to double-bag the ribs to protect against seam failure.

3½ pounds boneless beef short ribs, trimmed
 2 tablespoons vegetable oil, divided
 1 large onion, chopped
 2 celery ribs, chopped
 1 carrot, peeled and chopped
 ¼ teaspoon table salt
 ¼ teaspoon pepper
 1 tablespoon tomato paste
 1 garlic clove, minced
 1 cup dry red wine
 1 cup beef broth
 8 sprigs fresh thyme
 2 bay leaves
 2 tablespoons minced fresh parsley

Beef Short Rib Ragu

1. Using sous vide circulator, bring water to 160°F in 7-quart container.

2. Pat ribs dry with paper towels and season with salt and pepper. Heat 1 tablespoon oil in Dutch oven over medium-high heat until just smoking. Brown half of ribs on all sides, 8 to 12 minutes; transfer to plate. Repeat with remaining 1 tablespoon oil and ribs.

3. Add onion, celery, carrot, salt, and pepper to fat left in pot and cook over medium heat until softened and lightly browned, 8 to 10 minutes. Stir in tomato paste and garlic and cook until fragrant, about 1 minute. Stir in wine, scraping up any browned bits, and cook until reduced by half, 2 to 4 minutes. Stir in broth and simmer for 2 minutes. Transfer mixture to blender and process until smooth, about 1 minute.

4. Divide ribs, sauce, thyme sprigs, and bay leaves between two 1-gallon zipper-lock freezer bags and toss to coat. Arrange ribs in single layer and seal bags, pressing out as much air as possible. Place each bag in second 1-gallon zipper-lock freezer bag and seal bags. Gently lower bags into prepared water bath until ribs are fully submerged, and then clip top corner of each bag to side of water bath container, allowing remaining air bubbles to rise to top of bag. Reopen 1 corner of each zipper, release remaining air bubbles, and reseal bags. Cover and cook for at least 20 hours or up to 24 hours.

5. Using tongs, transfer ribs to serving dish. Tent with aluminum foil and let rest while finishing sauce. Strain cooking liquid through fine-mesh strainer into medium saucepan, pressing on solids to extract as much liquid as possible; discard solids. Bring to simmer over medium heat and cook until reduced to 2 cups, 4 to 6 minutes. Season with salt and pepper to taste. Spoon sauce over ribs, sprinkle with parsley, and serve.

To make ahead: Short ribs can be rapidly chilled in ice bath (see page 13) and then refrigerated in zipper-lock bags after step 4 for up to 3 days. To reheat, return sealed bags to water bath set to 160°F, and let sit for 30 minutes. Proceed with step 5.

PRESSURE-COOKER TAMARIND BRAISED BEEF SHORT RIBS

Serves 4 | boneless short ribs

WHY THIS RECIPE WORKS Beefy short ribs pair perfectly with intensely flavored sauces, so for this recipe we opted for sweet-tart tamarind as a foil to the ultrarich meat. Boneless ribs were well suited to serving whole with a drizzle-able sauce, so we started there. To make our sauce, we browned some onion and garlic and then added easy-to-find tamarind juice concentrate along with white wine for acidity, soy sauce for depth, and brown sugar and warm spices for a rounded flavor. Without the extra gelatin from the bones, our flavorful sauce needed some additional body after pressure cooking, so we finished it with a cornstarch slurry for a supple texture. Serve with rice.

1 tablespoon vegetable oil
1 onion, chopped
2 garlic cloves, minced
1 teaspoon pepper
½ cup dry white wine
⅓ cup tamarind juice concentrate
2 tablespoons soy sauce
2 tablespoons packed dark brown sugar
2 cinnamon sticks
1 teaspoon allspice berries
2½ pounds boneless short ribs, 1½ to 2 inches thick, 1 to 1½ inches wide, and 4 to 5 inches long, trimmed
¼ cup water
1 tablespoon cornstarch
1 tablespoon balsamic vinegar
1 tablespoon shredded fresh basil

1. Using highest sauté or browning function, heat oil in electric pressure cooker until shimmering. Add onion and cook until softened and lightly browned, 5 to 7 minutes. Stir in garlic and pepper and cook until fragrant, about 30 seconds. Stir in wine,

tamarind juice concentrate, soy sauce, sugar, cinnamon sticks, and allspice berries, scraping up any browned bits. Season short ribs with pepper and nestle into pressure cooker.

2. Lock lid in place and close pressure release valve. Select high pressure cook function and cook for 1 hour 35 minutes. Turn off pressure cooker and let pressure release naturally for 15 minutes. Quick-release any remaining pressure, then carefully remove lid, allowing steam to escape away from you.

3. Transfer short ribs to platter, tent with aluminum foil, and let rest while finishing sauce.

4. Strain braising liquid through fine-mesh strainer into fat separator and let settle for 5 minutes. Return defatted liquid to now-empty pressure cooker and cook using highest sauté or browning function until reduced to about 1 cup, 10 to 15 minutes. Whisk water and cornstarch together in bowl, then whisk mixture into sauce and continue to cook until thickened, about 1 minute. Turn off pressure cooker. Stir in vinegar and season with salt and pepper to taste. Spoon sauce over short ribs, sprinkle with basil, and serve.

PUB-STYLE STEAK AND ALE PIE

Serves 6 | boneless beef short ribs

WHY THIS RECIPE WORKS Intensely savory steak pie is a British comfort food. Pie takes time for a manageable version, we skipped browning the meat and browned the mushrooms and onion instead, building a flavorful fond from the vegetables. Adding flour early in the process and limiting the amount of stock we added to the pot meant that the gravy formed as the meat cooked and we could bypass a sauce-building step. An egg added structure to our pastry dough, making it sturdy enough to go over the filling while it was hot. The dough baked up flaky and substantial. Don't substitute bone-in short ribs; their yield is too variable. Instead, use a 4-pound chuck-eye roast, well trimmed of fat. If you don't have a deep-dish pie plate, use an 8 by 8-inch baking dish and roll the pie dough into a 10-inch square. We prefer pale and brown ales for this recipe.

FILLING
- 3 tablespoons water
- ½ teaspoon baking soda
- 3 pounds boneless beef short ribs, trimmed and cut into ¾-inch chunks
- ½ teaspoon table salt
- ½ teaspoon pepper
- 2 slices bacon, chopped

- 1 pound cremini mushrooms, trimmed and halved if medium or quartered if large
- 1½ cups beef broth, divided
- 1 large onion, chopped
- 1 garlic clove, minced
- ½ teaspoon dried thyme
- ¼ cup all-purpose flour
- ¾ cup beer

CRUST
- 1 large egg, lightly beaten
- ¼ cup sour cream, chilled
- 1¼ cups (6¼ ounces) all-purpose flour
- ½ teaspoon table salt
- 6 tablespoons unsalted butter, cut into ½-inch pieces and chilled

1. **For the filling:** Combine water and baking soda in large bowl. Add beef, salt, and pepper and toss to combine. Adjust oven rack to lower-middle position and heat oven to 350 degrees.

2. Cook bacon in large Dutch oven over high heat, stirring occasionally, until partially rendered but not browned, about 3 minutes. Add mushrooms and ¼ cup broth and stir to coat. Cover and cook, stirring occasionally, until mushrooms are reduced to about half their original volume, about 5 minutes. Add onion, garlic, and thyme and cook, uncovered, stirring occasionally, until onion is softened and fond begins to form on bottom of pot, 3 to 5 minutes. Sprinkle flour over mushroom mixture and stir until all flour is moistened. Cook, stirring occasionally, until fond is deep brown, 2 to 4 minutes. Stir in beer and remaining 1¼ cups broth, scraping up any browned bits. Stir in beef and bring to simmer, pressing as much beef as possible below surface of liquid. Cover pot tightly with aluminum foil, then lid; transfer to oven. Cook for 1 hour.

3. Remove lid and discard foil. Stir filling, cover, return to oven, and continue to cook until beef is tender and liquid is thick enough to coat beef, 15 to 30 minutes longer. Transfer filling to deep-dish pie plate. (Once cool, filling can be covered with plastic wrap and refrigerated for up to 2 days.) Increase oven temperature to 400 degrees.

4. **For the crust:** While filling is cooking, measure out 2 tablespoons beaten egg and set aside. Whisk remaining egg and sour cream together in bowl. Process flour and salt in food processor until combined, about 3 seconds. Add butter and pulse until only pea-size pieces remain, about 10 pulses. Add half of sour cream mixture and pulse until combined, about 5 pulses. Add remaining sour cream mixture and pulse until dough begins to form, about 10 pulses. Transfer mixture to lightly floured counter and knead briefly until dough comes together. Form into 4-inch disk, wrap in plastic, and refrigerate for at least 1 hour or up to 2 days.

Carne Deshebrada

5. Roll dough into 11-inch round on lightly floured counter. Using knife or 1-inch round biscuit cutter, cut round from center of dough. Drape dough over filling (it's OK if filling is hot). Trim overhang to ½ inch beyond lip of plate. Tuck overhang under itself; folded edge should be flush with edge of plate. Crimp dough evenly around edge of plate using your fingers or press with tines of fork to seal. Brush crust with reserved egg. Place pie on rimmed baking sheet. Bake until filling is bubbling and crust is deep golden brown and crisp, 25 to 30 minutes. (If filling has been refrigerated, increase baking time by 15 minutes and cover with foil for last 15 minutes to prevent overbrowning.) Let cool for 10 minutes before serving.

CARNE DESHEBRADA

Serves 6 to 8 | boneless beef short ribs

WHY THIS RECIPE WORKS Carne deshebrada, or "shredded beef," is a common offering at Mexican taco stands. It's made by braising a large cut of beef until ultratender, shredding it, and then tossing it with a flavorful rojo sauce made with tomatoes and/or dried chiles. Although short ribs are a bit nontraditional, their beefy flavor made them an excellent choice. To achieve flavorful browning, we raised the beef up out of the braising liquid by resting it on onion rounds. Next, we created a braising liquid that would infuse the beef with flavor and later act as a base for our rojo sauce. Beer and cider

vinegar provided depth and brightness, and tomato paste boosted savory flavor. Smoky-sweet ancho chiles gave the sauce a gentle kick. Cumin, cinnamon, cloves, oregano, and bay leaves added warmth and complexity. Once the beef had finished cooking, we pureed the braising liquid into a smooth, luxurious sauce. A bright, tangy slaw complemented the rich meat. Use a full-bodied lager or ale such as Dos Equis or Sierra Nevada.

1½ cups beer
  4 dried ancho chiles, stemmed, seeded, and torn into ½-inch pieces (1 cup)
½ cup cider vinegar
  2 tablespoons tomato paste
  6 garlic cloves, lightly crushed and peeled
  3 bay leaves
  2 teaspoons ground cumin
  2 teaspoons dried oregano
  2 teaspoons table salt
½ teaspoon pepper
½ teaspoon ground cloves
½ teaspoon ground cinnamon
  1 large onion, sliced into ½-inch-thick rounds
  3 pounds boneless beef short ribs, trimmed and cut into 2-inch cubes
 18 (6-inch) corn tortillas, warmed
  1 recipe Cabbage-Carrot Slaw (recipe follows)
  4 ounces queso fresco, crumbled (1 cup)
    Lime wedges

1. Adjust oven rack to lower-middle position and heat oven to 325 degrees. Combine beer, anchos, vinegar, tomato paste, garlic, bay leaves, cumin, oregano, salt, pepper, cloves, and cinnamon in Dutch oven. Arrange onion rounds in single layer on bottom of pot. Place beef on top of onion rounds in single layer. Cover and cook until meat is well browned and tender, 2½ to 3 hours.

2. Using slotted spoon, transfer beef to large bowl, tent with aluminum foil, and set aside. Strain liquid through fine-mesh strainer into 2-cup liquid measuring cup (do not wash pot). Discard onion rounds and bay leaves. Transfer remaining solids to blender. Let strained liquid settle for 5 minutes, then skim any fat from surface. Add water as needed to equal 1 cup. Pour liquid into blender with reserved solids and blend until smooth, about 2 minutes. Transfer sauce to now-empty pot.

3. Using 2 forks, shred beef into bite-size pieces. Bring sauce to simmer over medium heat. Add beef and stir to coat. Season with salt to taste. (Beef can be refrigerated for up to 2 days; gently reheat before serving.)

4. Spoon small amount of beef into each warm tortilla and serve, passing slaw, queso fresco, and lime wedges separately.

SERVE WITH
Cabbage-Carrot Slaw
Makes about 8 cups; serves 6 to 8
- 1 cup cider vinegar
- ½ cup water
- 1 tablespoon sugar
- 1½ teaspoons table salt
- ½ head green cabbage, cored and sliced thin (6 cups)
- 1 onion, sliced thin
- 1 large carrot, peeled and shredded
- 1 jalapeño chile, stemmed, seeded, and minced
- 1 teaspoon dried oregano
- 1 cup chopped fresh cilantro

Whisk vinegar, water, sugar, and salt in large bowl until sugar is dissolved. Add cabbage, onion, carrot, jalapeño, and oregano and toss to combine. Cover and refrigerate for at least 1 hour or up to 24 hours. Drain slaw and stir in cilantro right before serving.

KALBI

Serves 4 to 6 | English-style short ribs
WHY THIS RECIPE WORKS Korean cooks can transform short ribs, which take time to break down, into tender barbecue beef, known as kalbi, in just minutes. Most Korean recipes use hard-to-find flanken-style short ribs; we opted for English-style short ribs and butchered them for quick cooking. We made four slices from each rib, evening them out with a quick pounding. Pureed pear, a common ingredient in kalbi recipes, served as a tenderizing agent in our marinade. We cooked the short ribs over high heat, moving them to the cooler side of our two-level grill fire when flare-ups occurred, to achieve a quick char without making the meat tough. Make sure to buy English-style ribs that have at least 1 inch of meat on top of the bone, avoiding ones that have little meat and large bones. Alternatively, 2½ pounds of thinly sliced Korean-style ribs can be used (no butchering is required), but if using charcoal, reduce to 3 quarts. Serve with rice, kimchi, and, gochujang. Traditionally, all these ingredients are wrapped in a lettuce leaf with the meat and eaten like a taco.

- 5 pounds bone-in English-style beef short ribs
- 1 ripe pear, peeled, halved, cored, and chopped coarse
- ½ cup soy sauce
- 6 tablespoons sugar
- 2 tablespoons toasted sesame oil
- 6 garlic cloves, peeled
- 4 teaspoons grated fresh ginger
- 1 tablespoon rice vinegar
- 3 scallions, sliced thin
- ½ teaspoon red pepper flakes (optional)

1. Remove meat from bones of ribs, trim, and slice widthwise at angle into ½- to ¾-inch-thick pieces. Pound pieces between plastic wrap to ¼-inch thickness.

2. Process pear, soy sauce, sugar, oil, garlic, ginger, and vinegar in food processor until smooth, 20 to 30 seconds. Transfer to medium bowl and stir in scallions and pepper flakes, if using.

3. Spread one-third of marinade in 13 by 9-inch baking dish. Place half of meat in single layer over marinade. Pour half of remaining marinade over meat, followed by remaining meat and remaining marinade. Cover tightly with plastic wrap and refrigerate for at least 4 hours or up to 12 hours, turning meat once or twice.

4a. For a charcoal grill: Open bottom vent completely. Light large chimney starter two-thirds filled with charcoal briquettes (4 quarts). When top coals are partially covered with ash, pour into even layer over half of grill. Set cooking grate in place, cover, and open lid vent completely. Heat grill until hot, about 5 minutes.

4b. For a gas grill: Turn all burners to high, cover, and heat grill until hot, about 15 minutes. Leave primary burner on high and turn off other burner(s).

5. Clean and oil cooking grate. Place half of meat on hotter side of grill and cook (covered if using gas), turning every 2 to 3 minutes, until well browned on both sides, 8 to 13 minutes. Move first batch of meat to cooler side of grill and repeat browning with second batch.

6. Transfer second batch of meat to serving platter. Return first batch of meat to hotter side of grill and warm for 30 seconds; transfer to serving platter and serve.

GRILL-ROASTED BEEF SHORT RIBS

Serves 4 to 6 | English-style short ribs
WHY THIS RECIPE WORKS Beef short ribs lend themselves naturally to the moist heat and long, slow cooking of a braise, which breaks down their abundant collagen, but we wondered if we could adapt this flavorful cut, whole, to the grill. To cut down on the time and tending they'd require on the grill, we jump-started the cooking in the oven, where the fat rendered from the ribs and their tough, chewy collagen began to transform into moisture-retaining gelatin. A bold spice rub balanced the richness of the ribs. We then headed out to the grill to complete the cooking and develop a nicely browned crust. Slowly cooking the ribs over a low fire and brushing them with one of our tangy glazes gave them a burnished exterior

Kalbi

evenly over ribs. Cover baking dish tightly with aluminum foil. Cook until thickest ribs register 165 to 170 degrees, 1½ to 2 hours.

3a. For a charcoal grill: Open bottom vent halfway. Arrange 2 quarts unlit charcoal briquettes into steeply banked pile against side of grill. Light large chimney starter half filled with charcoal briquettes (3 quarts). When top coals are partially covered with ash, pour on top of unlit charcoal to cover one-third of grill with coals steeply banked against side of grill. Set cooking grate in place, cover, and open lid vent halfway. Heat grill until hot, about 5 minutes.

3b. For a gas grill: Turn all burners to high, cover, and heat grill until hot, about 15 minutes. Turn primary burner to medium and turn off other burner(s). (Adjust primary burner as needed to maintain grill temperature of 275 to 300 degrees.)

4. Clean and oil cooking grate. Place short ribs, bone side down, on cooler side of grill about 2 inches from flames. Brush with ¼ cup glaze. Cover and cook until ribs register 195 degrees, 1¾ to 2¼ hours, rotating and brushing ribs with ¼ cup glaze every 30 minutes. Transfer ribs to large platter, tent with foil, and let rest for 5 to 10 minutes before serving.

GLAZES
Mustard Glaze
Makes 1 cup; serves 4 to 6
- ½ cup Dijon mustard
- ½ cup red wine vinegar
- ¼ cup packed brown sugar
- 1 teaspoon reserved spice rub
- ⅛ teaspoon cayenne pepper

Whisk all ingredients together in bowl.

Blackberry Glaze
Makes 1 cup; serves 4 to 6
- 10 ounces (2 cups) fresh or frozen blackberries
- ½ cup ketchup
- ¼ cup bourbon
- 2 tablespoons packed brown sugar
- 1½ tablespoons soy sauce
- 1 teaspoon reserved spice rub
- ⅛ teaspoon cayenne pepper

Bring all ingredients to simmer in small saucepan over medium-high heat. Simmer, stirring frequently to break up blackberries, until reduced to 1¼ cups, about 10 minutes. Strain through fine-mesh strainer, pressing on solids to extract as much liquid as possible. Discard solids.

and a tender but still substantial texture. Make sure to choose ribs that are 4 to 6 inches in length and have at least 1 inch of meat on top of the bone.

SPICE RUB
- 2 tablespoons kosher salt
- 1 tablespoon packed brown sugar
- 2 teaspoons pepper
- 2 teaspoons ground cumin
- 2 teaspoons garlic powder
- 1¼ teaspoons paprika
- ¾ teaspoon ground fennel
- ⅛ teaspoon cayenne pepper

SHORT RIBS
- 5 pounds bone-in English-style beef short ribs, trimmed
- 2 tablespoons red wine vinegar
- 1 recipe glaze (recipes follow)

1. For the spice rub: Combine all ingredients in bowl. Measure out 1 teaspoon rub and set aside for glaze.

2. For the short ribs: Adjust oven rack to middle position and heat oven to 300 degrees. Pat ribs dry. Sprinkle ribs with spice rub, pressing into all sides of ribs. Arrange ribs bone side down in 13 by 9-inch baking dish, placing thicker ribs around perimeter of baking dish and thinner ribs in center. Sprinkle vinegar

Grilled Boneless Short Ribs
with Argentine Pepper Sauce

Hoisin-Tamarind Glaze

Makes 1 cup; serves 4 to 6
Tamarind paste can be found in well-stocked supermarkets or
in Asian markets.

1 cup water
⅓ cup hoisin sauce
¼ cup tamarind paste
1 (2-inch) piece ginger, peeled and sliced into ½-inch-thick
    rounds
1 teaspoon reserved spice rub
⅛ teaspoon cayenne pepper

Bring all ingredients to simmer in small saucepan over medium-
high heat. Simmer, stirring frequently, until reduced to 1¼ cups,
about 10 minutes. Strain through fine-mesh strainer, pressing on
solids to extract as much liquid as possible. Discard solids.

GRILLED BONELESS SHORT RIBS WITH ARGENTINE PEPPER SAUCE

Serves 4 to 6 | boneless beef short ribs

WHY THIS RECIPE WORKS For a change from cooked-all-the-
way-through tear-apart short ribs, we took them to the grill
for meat that was tender, smoky, and medium-rare, like steaks.
To do so, we set up the grill with two heat zones. To render as
much fat as possible, we grilled the ribs covered on the cooler
side of the grill, positioned over a smoking wood chip packet,
before moving them to the hotter side to develop a nice sear.
To cut the ribs' richness, we served them with a sauce based on
Argentinian criolla. We cooked sweet red bell pepper with red
onion, olive oil, garlic, paprika, cumin, and cayenne and then
added fresh cilantro and lemon juice for an acidic kick.

2½–3 pounds boneless beef short ribs, 1½ to 2 inches thick,
    2 inches wide, and 4 to 5 inches long, trimmed
3½ teaspoons kosher salt, divided
1½ cups wood chips
½ cup finely chopped red bell pepper
⅓ cup finely chopped red onion
¼ cup extra-virgin olive oil
3 garlic cloves, minced
1 teaspoon paprika
½ teaspoon ground cumin
¼ teaspoon cayenne pepper

⅓ cup minced fresh cilantro
2 tablespoons lemon juice
1 (13 by 9-inch) disposable aluminum roasting pan (if using
    charcoal)

1. Pat beef dry with paper towels and sprinkle all over with
1 tablespoon salt. Let sit at room temperature for at least 1 hour.
Just before grilling, soak wood chips in water for 15 minutes,
then drain.

2. Meanwhile, combine bell pepper, onion, oil, garlic, paprika,
cumin, cayenne, and remaining ½ teaspoon salt in small saucepan. Cook over medium-high heat until vegetables are softened,
about 5 minutes. Remove from heat and stir in cilantro and
lemon juice. Transfer to bowl and set aside.

3a. For a charcoal grill: Using large piece of heavy-duty aluminum foil, wrap soaked chips in 12 by 10-inch foil packet. (Make
sure chips do not poke holes in sides or bottom of packet.) Cut
3 evenly spaced 2-inch slits in top of packet. Open bottom vent
completely. Light large chimney starter mounded with charcoal
briquettes (7 quarts). When top coals are partially covered with
ash, pour two-thirds evenly over half of grill, then pour remaining coals over other half of grill. Place wood chip packet on
smaller pile of coals, set cooking grate in place, cover, and open
lid vent completely. Heat grill until hot and wood chips are
smoking, about 5 minutes.

3b. For a gas grill: Using large piece of heavy-duty aluminum
foil, wrap soaked chips in 8 by 4½-inch foil packet. (Make sure
chips do not poke holes in sides or bottom of packet.) Cut
2 evenly spaced 2-inch slits in top of packet. Remove cooking
grate and place wood chip packet directly on primary burner.
Set grate in place, turn all burners to high, cover, and heat
grill until hot and wood chips are smoking, about 15 minutes.
Turn primary burner to medium and secondary burner(s) to
medium-high.

4. Clean and oil cooking grate. Season beef with pepper. Place beef
on grill directly over foil packet. Cover beef with disposable pan if
using charcoal (if using gas, close lid) and cook for 5 minutes. Flip
beef and cook 5 minutes longer, covering in same manner.

5. Slide beef to hotter side of grill and cook, covered if using
gas, until well browned on all sides and beef registers 125 degrees,
4 to 8 minutes, turning often. Transfer beef to carving board,
tent with foil, and let rest for 10 minutes. Slice beef as thin as
possible against grain. Serve with pepper sauce.

SHANKS AND OXTAILS

DON'T FORGET THE LIMBS. Beyond the main body of the cow are cuts that make some of the richest, silkiest stews you can make—and they're incredibly economical. These often-forgotten parts are worth cooking with. Beef shanks and oxtails are particularly practical not only because they make rich broths and sauces full of body, but also because after slow cooking, their meat tastes luxurious (belying its low price). Once these cuts have been used for the base of a dish, you can shred the meat to serve as part of the meal or simply eat the meat off the bone. As a bonus, the bones on both shanks and oxtails are packed with rich, flavorful marrow that's easy to access so it really supplements braises with savor and body.

Beef Shanks

Cost: ■■□□ Flavor: ■■■□
Best cooking methods: braise
Texture: succulent
Alternative names: center beef shanks

This upper part of the cow's legs puts in a lot of work to make the cow move. Tough work means tough, sinewy meat—unless the cut is slowly braised. Then it breaks down into something incredibly tender and luscious, thanks to connective tissue that liquefies, lubricating the meat and imparting silky richness to the cooking liquid. While many cuts rich in connective tissue are also quite fatty, meaning that their liquid requires careful defatting, beef shanks are actually quite lean so their sauce forms clean and clear. All this connective tissue means beef shanks don't cook quickly but the wait is worth it. And for homemade beef stock (see page 193), it's your best bet, combining the affordability you want in a cut used to make this ingredient with the plentiful collagen that produces a broth with great body (and nourishment). Beef shanks are sold as both long cut (more connective tissue) and cross cut (less connective tissue), as well as with or without the bone. We prefer long cut because it contains more collagen, but cross cut can be used; remove the bones before cooking and reduce the cooking time by about half an hour.

Oxtails

Cost: ■■□□ Flavor: ■■■□
Best cooking methods: braise
Texture: rich and ultratender
Alternative names: none

You might not think of an animal's tail as edible but when you cut it crosswise, you get oxtails—and we think they're highly underrated in the U.S. They're incredibly rich, full of marrow that's easily accessible to be coaxed out, and they cook to a tender softness—even more tender than a short rib. There was a time when humans were lest wasteful, when we ate every portion of beef we could—eating oxtails is a holdover from that time. As they are called oxtails, they can be the tails of oxen—castrated mature bulls that are mainly used for hard labor. What you're buying in the store, however, will generally be those from regular beef cattle. You can find them in a good supermarket and surely at a butcher but since they're mainly used for braising, you can substitute the other beefy, tissue-abundant cut, beef shanks, in most recipes, and vice versa.

BUYING OXTAILS

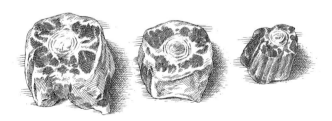

Depending on which part of the tail they come from, oxtail pieces can vary in diameter from ¾ inch to 4 inches. (Thicker pieces are cut close to the body; thinner pieces come from the end of the tail.) Try to buy oxtail packages with pieces approximately 2 inches thick and between 2 and 4 inches in diameter; they will yield more meat for your dish. Thicker pieces also lend more flavor to the broth with more marrow that can be extracted. It's fine to use a few small pieces; just don't rely on them exclusively.

ETLI KURU FASULYE

Serves 6 to 8 | oxtails

WHY THIS RECIPE WORKS Oxtails get star status in our spin on a Turkish dish, etli kuru fasulye, or "white beans with meat," and the white beans are a creamy, nutty counterpoint to hearty oxtails. To be sure our braise didn't turn out greasy, we started by roasting the oxtails in the oven for an hour, rather than browning them in a Dutch oven; this way, we rendered and discarded a significant amount of fat (about a half-cup!). The braising liquid got its character from a simple yet flavorful trio: sweet whole tomatoes, warm and earthy Aleppo pepper, and pungent oregano. Try to buy oxtails that are approximately 2 inches thick and 2 to 4 inches in diameter. Oxtails can often be found in the freezer section of the grocery store; if using frozen oxtails, thaw them completely before using.

4 pounds oxtails, trimmed
4 cups chicken broth
2 tablespoons extra-virgin olive oil
1 onion, chopped fine
1 carrot, peeled and chopped fine
6 garlic cloves, minced
2 tablespoons tomato paste
2 tablespoons ground dried Aleppo pepper
1 tablespoon minced fresh oregano, divided
1 (28-ounce) can whole peeled tomatoes
1 (15-ounce) can navy beans, rinsed
1 tablespoon sherry vinegar

1. Adjust oven rack to lower-middle position and heat oven to 450 degrees. Pat oxtails dry with paper towels and season with salt and pepper. Arrange oxtails cut side down in single layer in large roasting pan and roast until meat begins to brown, about 45 minutes.

2. Discard any accumulated fat and juices in pan and continue to roast until meat is well browned, 15 to 20 minutes. Transfer oxtails to bowl and tent with aluminum foil; set aside. Stir chicken broth into pan, scraping up any browned bits; set aside.

3. Reduce oven temperature to 300 degrees. Heat oil in Dutch oven over medium heat until shimmering. Add onion and carrot and cook until softened, about 5 minutes. Stir in garlic, tomato paste, Aleppo pepper, and 1 teaspoon oregano and cook until fragrant, about 30 seconds.

4. Stir in broth mixture from roasting pan and tomatoes and their juice and bring to simmer. Nestle oxtails into pot, bring to simmer, and cover; transfer pot to oven. Cook until oxtails are tender and fork slips easily in and out of meat, about 3 hours.

Alcatra

5. Transfer oxtails to bowl and tent with foil. Strain braising liquid through fine-mesh strainer into fat separator; return solids to now-empty pot. Let braising liquid settle for 5 minutes, then pour defatted liquid into pot with solids.

6. Stir in beans, vinegar, and remaining 2 teaspoons oregano. Return oxtails and any accumulated juices to pot, bring to gentle simmer over medium heat, and cook until oxtails and beans are heated through, about 5 minutes. Season with salt and pepper to taste. Transfer oxtails to serving platter and spoon 1 cup sauce over top. Serve, passing remaining sauce separately.

ALCATRA

Serves 8 | long-cut beef shanks

WHY THIS RECIPE WORKS Alcatra, a simple and meaty Portuguese beef stew, features tender chunks of beef braised with onions, garlic, spices, and wine. Beef shanks were a great option for our version because it's lean (which meant the cooking liquid didn't need to be skimmed) and full of collagen, which broke down into gelatin and gave the sauce full body. Submerging the sliced onions completely in the liquid under the meat caused them to form a meaty-tasting compound that amped up the savory flavor of the broth, and smoky-sweet Spanish chorizo sausage matched up perfectly with the other flavors in the stew. You can substitute 4 pounds of bone-in cross-cut shanks if that's all you can find. Remove the bones before cooking and save them for another use. Cross-cut shanks cook more quickly, so check the stew for doneness in step 2 after 3 hours.

   3 pounds boneless long-cut beef shanks
   1 teaspoon table salt
   5 garlic cloves, peeled and smashed
   5 allspice berries
   4 bay leaves
1½ teaspoons peppercorns
   2 large onions, halved and sliced thin
2¼ cups dry white wine
   ¼ teaspoon ground cinnamon
   8 ounces Spanish-style chorizo sausage, cut into
       ¼-inch-thick rounds

1. Adjust oven rack to middle position and heat oven to 325 degrees. Trim away any fat or large pieces of connective tissue from exterior of shanks (silverskin can be left on meat). Cut each shank crosswise into 2½-inch pieces. Sprinkle meat with salt.

2. Cut 8-inch square triple thickness of cheesecloth. Place garlic, allspice berries, bay leaves, and peppercorns in center of cheesecloth and tie into bundle with kitchen twine. Arrange onions and spice bundle in Dutch oven in even layer. Add wine and cinnamon. Arrange shank pieces in single layer on top of onions. Cover and cook until beef is tender, about 3½ hours.

3. Remove pot from oven and add chorizo. Using tongs, flip each piece of beef over, making sure that chorizo is submerged. Cover and let stand until chorizo is warmed through, about 20 minutes. Discard spice bundle. Season with salt and pepper to taste, and serve.

RICH BEEF STOCK

Makes about 8 cups | cross-cut beef shanks
WHY THIS RECIPE WORKS Restaurant cooks often adhere to time-consuming routines for making beef stock that aren't practical for home chefs. Our method simplifies the process. Of all the beef cuts we've covered, we think beef shanks are the very best for making stock; their abundant connective tissue breaks down as the broth simmers and contributes a velvety richness. Simmering the bones along with the meat (we call for a generous 6 pounds of shanks for 2 quarts of stock) ensured that the stock was ultrabeefy. If the broth is refrigerated, the fat hardens on the surface and is very easy to remove. To defat hot broth, we recommend using a ladle or fat separator.

   1 tablespoon vegetable oil, plus extra as needed
   1 large onion, chopped
   6 pounds cross-cut beef shanks, meat cut from bone
       in large chunks
   ½ cup dry red wine
   2 quarts boiling water
   2 bay leaves
   ½ teaspoon table salt

1. Heat oil in large stockpot or Dutch oven over medium-high heat until shimmering. Add onion and cook, stirring occasionally, until slightly softened, 2 to 3 minutes. Transfer to large bowl.

2. Brown beef and bones on all sides in 3 or 4 batches, about 5 minutes per batch, adding extra oil as necessary, up to 1 tablespoon. Transfer to bowl with onions.

3. Add wine to now-empty pot and cook, scraping up browned bits with wooden spoon, until reduced to about 3 tablespoons, about 2 minutes. Return browned beef, bones, and onion to pot; reduce heat to low; and cook, covered, until beef releases juices, about 20 minutes. Meanwhile, bring 2 quarts water to boil in medium saucepan.

4. Increase heat to high. Add boiling water, bay leaves, and salt to pot; return mixture to boil, then reduce heat to low and simmer, covered, until meat is tender and stock is flavorful, 1½ to 2 hours, occasionally skimming foam off surface. Strain, discarding bones and onion and reserving beef for another use. Skim fat from surface of stock before using. (Stock can be refrigerated for up to 4 days or frozen for up to 6 months.)

BEEF BARLEY SOUP WITH MUSHROOMS AND THYME

Makes about 8 cups | cross-cut beef shanks
WHY THIS RECIPE WORKS A big bonus of making your own beef stock from beef shanks (besides avoiding tinny-tasting supermarket stock) is the soft, tender meat that results—perfect for shredding and adding to a classic soup with your stock more deeply flavored than the norm. There's no need to discard that meat. Mushrooms complement and boost beefy flavor, so we used them for an even meatier-tasting soup. The sweetness of requisite onion and carrot counterbalanced all the savor nicely. Mulling over barley choices, we settled on pearl barley because it's quick-cooking; it was done in the 45 minutes we needed to simmer all the ingredients together to a cohesive soup. Adding fresh thyme early on in the process allowed its robust flavor to infuse the broth evenly while diced tomatoes added complexity and some acidity and helped balance the heartiness of the barley. You will need the stock and 2 cups of cooked beef from Rich Beef Stock for this recipe.

Hearty Beef Shank and Vegetable Soup

2 tablespoons vegetable oil
1 onion, chopped
2 carrots, peeled and chopped
12 ounces white mushrooms, trimmed and sliced thin
1 recipe Rich Beef Stock (page 193), plus 2 cups meat, shredded into bite-size pieces
½ cup canned diced tomatoes, drained
½ cup pearl barley
1½ teaspoons minced fresh thyme or ½ teaspoon dried
¼ cup minced fresh parsley

1. Heat 1 tablespoon oil in stockpot or Dutch oven over medium heat until shimmering. Add onion and carrots and cook until vegetables are almost soft, 3 to 4 minutes. Add remaining 1 tablespoon oil and mushrooms and cook until mushrooms soften and liquid evaporates, 4 to 5 minutes longer.

2. Add beef stock and meat, tomatoes, barley, and thyme. Bring to boil, then reduce heat to low; simmer until barley is just tender, 45 to 50 minutes. Stir in parsley, season with salt and pepper to taste, and serve.

HEARTY BEEF SHANK AND VEGETABLE SOUP

Serves 6 to 8 | cross-cut beef shanks

WHY THIS RECIPE WORKS Bulalo, a Filipino soup of beef shanks and vegetables, is traditionally cooked in a cauldron until the beef's collagen and marrow melt to create luscious flavor. For a streamlined version with the same impact, we started by frying sliced garlic in a Dutch oven and then browned the shanks in the flavorful leftover oil. Next we built a rich broth using onion, ginger, garlic, black peppercorns, fish sauce, and water. Letting everything simmer for about 2 hours helped break down the collagen and fats, producing ultratender meat. Corn and cabbage are traditional additions, but some recipes also add green beans, potatoes, and sweet onions. We tested various vegetable combinations and ultimately landed on corn, napa cabbage, and potatoes. Adding the potatoes to the Dutch oven with the napa cabbage kept them from becoming too mushy. We like serving bulalo with scallions, fish sauce, vinegar, and chili oil. Look for beef shanks that are 2 inches thick and 2 to 4 inches in diameter. Use a Dutch oven that holds 6 quarts or more for this recipe.

¼ cup vegetable oil
12 garlic cloves, peeled (6 sliced thin, 6 crushed)
4 pounds cross-cut beef shanks, trimmed
1 tablespoon table salt, divided
1 onion, quartered
1 (4-inch) piece ginger, sliced into thin rounds
1 tablespoon black peppercorns

3½ quarts water
2 tablespoons fish sauce, plus extra for seasoning
2 ears corn, husks and silk removed, cut into 1-inch lengths
1 pound Yukon Gold potatoes, unpeeled, cut into 1-inch pieces
½ head napa cabbage, cored and sliced thin (8 cups)
2 scallions, sliced thin on bias
White cane vinegar or distilled white vinegar
Chili oil

1. Cook vegetable oil and sliced garlic in Dutch oven over medium heat, stirring frequently, until garlic is crisp and light golden brown, about 3 minutes. Using slotted spoon, transfer garlic to paper towel–lined plate and season with salt to taste; set aside for serving. Pour off and reserve oil left in pot.

2. Pat beef shanks dry with paper towels and sprinkle with 1 teaspoon salt. Heat 1 tablespoon reserved oil in now-empty pot over medium-high heat until just smoking. Brown half of shanks on all sides, about 8 minutes; transfer to bowl. Repeat with 1 tablespoon reserved oil and remaining shanks; transfer to bowl. Discard any remaining reserved oil.

3. Add onion, ginger, peppercorns, and crushed garlic to fat left in pot and cook until fragrant, about 1 minute. Return shanks and any accumulated juices to pot. Cover, reduce heat to low, and cook until beef releases additional juices, about 15 minutes, scraping bottom of pot occasionally to release fond.

4. Add water, fish sauce, and remaining 2 teaspoons salt and bring to boil. Reduce heat to low, partially cover, and simmer, skimming away foam as needed, until meat is tender and broth is flavorful, 1½ to 2 hours.

5. Transfer shanks to cutting board and let cool slightly. Using 2 forks, shred beef into bite-size pieces. Reserve shank bones and discard excess fat and connective tissue.

6. Set fine-mesh strainer over large bowl or container and line with triple layer of cheesecloth. Strain broth through prepared strainer and let settle for 5 minutes. Using wide, shallow spoon, skim excess fat from surface of broth. (You should have 12 cups broth; add extra water as needed to equal 12 cups. Broth, shredded beef, and reserved bones can be refrigerated separately for up to 4 days.)

7. Return broth to now-empty pot and bring to simmer over medium-high heat. Add corn and cook until tender, about 15 minutes. Stir in potatoes and cabbage and cook until tender, about 8 minutes. Off heat, stir in beef and reserved bones and let sit until heated through, about 5 minutes. Season with extra fish sauce to taste. Sprinkle individual portions with scallions and reserved garlic chips and serve, passing vinegar and chili oil separately.

VEAL

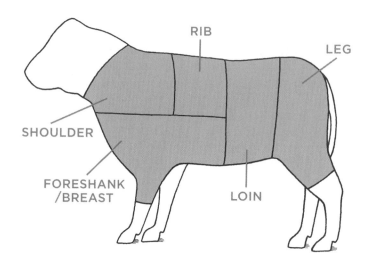

RIB

LEG

SHOULDER

FORESHANK
/BREAST

LOIN

VEAL HAS LONG BEEN REVERED in Europe for its supreme tenderness and delicate flavor; here in the United States, it's not as popular and is seen in restaurants more often than home kitchens. But veal doesn't have to be fancy (or pricey); you can make veal dishes easily at home. The delicate meat takes well to delicate flavors—often those from France—and more collagen-rich veal cuts, like those from the shoulder and shank, are nice when stewed. Since veal are immature beef cattle, their anatomy, while broken down more simply, is very similar to that of more mature cattle: The primal cuts are the same, with the exception that the underside of the animal is grouped into one primal cut rather than three, and the back half of the animal (the sirloin and leg) is combined into one primal cut. And there are fewer cuts created from the primals. Some are iconic, the shanks used for osso buco (page 204) or the cutlets breaded for tender scaloppini (see page 203), for instance. A rib chop makes an impressive grilled dish. Read more on how we cook with veal cuts.

Shoulder Roast

Cost: ■■▪▪ **Flavor:** ■■▪▪
Best cooking methods: braise, stew
Texture: tender after cooking
Alternative names: rolled shoulder roast

The veal shoulder area includes the front of the animal and runs from the neck through the fifth rib. Cuts from the shoulder are moderately tough and better suited to stewing than grilling. Many markets sell cutlets cut from the shoulder but they will buckle in the pan; we avoid them and prefer cutlets from the leg. Tougher chops also come from this area but they're too tough and gristle-y to be worth cooking. We cook with the shoulder roast frequently. It's our favorite choice for stews since the roast is meaty and does not contain too much gristle or fat. This boneless roast is usually sold in netting at the market.

Veal Rib Chops

Cost: ■■■▪ **Flavor:** ■■■▪
Best cooking methods: pan sear, grill
Texture: tender, fine-grained, and juicy
Alternative names: none

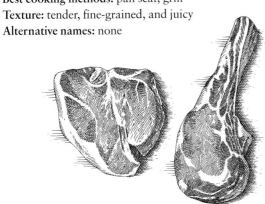

As with beef rib, veal rib (we cook rib chops) is prized—its flavor is meatier than other areas of the mild animal, and it's incredibly juicy, with meat that's almost creamy when done right. Rib chops are quite the treat. They're cooked like steak, not braised, so they aren't cooked through fully. We prefer them cooked to medium—with a trace of pink just at the center. Rib chops can be cut very thick or very thin. We like them somewhere in the middle—a hulking chop might seem appealing but it's hard to cook evenly. (There are T-bone-shaped veal chops as well, cut from the loin, but they're leaner and less flavorful at the same price tag, so we do not cook them.)

Veal Cutlets

Cost: ■■■▪ **Flavor:** ■■▪▪
Best cooking methods: pan-fry
Texture: tender if cut properly from the leg
Alternative names: birdies, scaloppine, scallops, escalopes, schnitzel

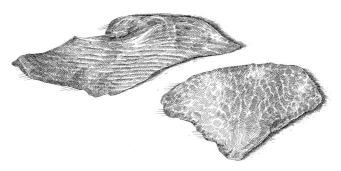

Quick to cook, low on prep, cutlets are busy-weeknight-friendly. A basic cooking procedure usually goes something like this: Gently pound the cutlets, quickly sauté them, and serve them with a basic pan sauce. Likely one of the most well-known and easily accessible cuts to veal novices, cutlets usually (but not always; see "Buying Veal Cutlets") come from the veal's leg, the largest primal of the animal, comprising almost 50 percent of its body (it's the name for the whole hind portion of the veal). This is the most common use of veal leg although you can find recipes for leg roasts.

BUYING VEAL CUTLETS

Veal cutlets for multipurpose cooking should ideally be cut from the upper top round portion of the leg, which is lean and has no muscle separation. Many supermarkets do not butcher the meat properly, cutting it with the grain, not across the grain, as is best. When shopping, look for cutlets in which no linear striation is evident. These lines are an indication that the veal has been cut with the grain and will be tough. Instead, the cutlet should have a smooth surface. If your market doesn't offer cutlets that look this, consider cutting your own cutlets (see "Cutting Veal Cutlets").

In addition to cutlets from the leg, markets also sell cutlets cut from the shoulder. If you're lucky enough to find the origin of your cutlets labeled and they're from the shoulder, avoid them; they'll buckle in the pan and we don't recommend them.

SCALOPPINI SPECIAL

This dish, featuring buttery-tender veal cutlets, was traditionally made with cutlets butchered carefully and specifically for it: yes, scaloppini (or scallops, escalopes, or even schnitzel) often fashioned from the prized veal loin rather than leg cuts. A good butcher will slice scaloppini by hand, most often now from the top round as with other cutlets, though you can sometimes find loin cuts, especially in restaurants—and pay top dollar for them. The butcher will carefully remove any fibers and connective tissue that would be chewy when cooked. A supermarket will not do this. You can use leg cutlets you find at the supermarket but if you're feeling crafty, we recommend fashioning ultratender cutlets yourself from a boneless round roast. That said, our recipe solution (see "Meat Tenderizer in the 2020s?") allows you to make this prized recipe successfully with the cutlets you have.

MEAT PREP *Cutting Veal Cutlets*

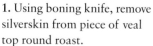

1. Using boning knife, remove silverskin from piece of veal top round roast.

2. Using long slicing knife, cut slices on the bias and against the grain that are between ¼ and ½ inch thick.

MEAT TENDERIZER IN THE 2020s?

The whole animal is generally fairly tender thanks to its young age, but the veal leg, naturally, does a lot of work and the shoulder (a source of inferior cutlets) does even more. So unlike other commonly cooked cutlets (say, from chicken breasts), veal cutlets don't always come to you supremely tender. For other meats, we salt, brine, soak in baking soda, or cut in a specific fashion to upgrade a cut's texture ourselves. To tenderize veal cutlets, we tried a common veal trick, soaking in milk, to no avail. Breaking out an old-fashioned Jaccard (a hand meat-tenderizing tool with many thin blades that puncture the meat) made the cutlets look like raggedy Salisbury steak. In the end, we found that an inexpensive supermarket product, powdered meat tenderizer (which contains bromelain as an active ingredient, along with salt and sugar), worked wonders on veal cutlets. A pinch of powder (Adolph's brand is common) turned reasonably priced supermarket cutlets

into cutlets every bit as tender as those found in restaurants, where cutlets are often crafted from the loin (see "Scaloppini Special") or even carefully from meltingly tender rib chops. So the shaker meant no home butchering and no high price tag—not bad for a tenderizer that costs pennies per use.

Veal Shanks

Cost: ▪▪▫▫   **Flavor:** ▪▪▪▫
Best cooking methods: braise
Texture: tender and rich after braising
Alternative names: osso buco

Cut crosswise from the front legs, the shanks contain both meat and bone. Depending on the butcher, shanks can vary in thickness and diameter, so shop carefully. Although they're sometimes sold boneless, you want shanks with the marrow-packed bone, which adds flavor to the braising medium. The most famous veal shank dish puts shanks on full display, Milanese-style: rich, hearty Osso Buco (page 204). We provide standard, sous vide, and electric pressure-cooker versions. Shanks become fall-off-the-bone tender, so we like to tie each one; this special dish deserves a special presentation, with meat served on the bone.

MEAT PREP *Tying Veal Shanks*

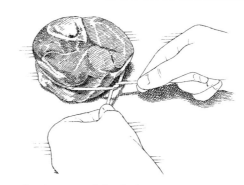

Tie piece of twine around the thickest portion of each shank.

Pan-Seared Veal Chops with Spinach and Gremolata

ITALIAN VEAL STEW

Serves 6 | boneless shoulder roast

WHY THIS RECIPE WORKS Osso Buco (page 204) is a favorite of ours but Italian flavors can serve deliciously with veal in a simpler stew, with meaty cubes of veal—a veal version of Italian beef stews. We started by cutting the roast into bite-size pieces and browning it on the stove in a Dutch oven. We knew our cubed meat would cook faster than veal shanks, and after experimenting with varying times and temperatures, we determined that 1½ to 1¾ hours in a 300-degree oven rendered ideal results, fork-tender, flavorful meat. To compensate for the lack of gelatin from the shanks, we thickened the stew with a bit of flour. Serve this stew over polenta, risotto, mashed potatoes, or buttered noodles.

- 2 pounds boneless veal shoulder roast, trimmed and cut into 1-inch pieces
- 3 tablespoons extra-virgin olive oil
- 2 onions, cut into ½-inch pieces
- 2 carrots, peeled and cut into ½-inch pieces
- 2 celery ribs, cut into ½-inch dice
- 6 garlic cloves, minced
- 2 tablespoons all-purpose flour
- ¾ cup dry white wine
- 1½ cups chicken broth
- 1 (14.5-ounce) can diced tomatoes, drained
- 2 bay leaves
- 1 recipe Gremolata (page 22)

1. Adjust oven rack to middle position and heat oven to 300 degrees.

2. Season veal with salt and pepper. Heat 1 tablespoon oil in Dutch oven over medium-high heat until just smoking. Add half of veal and cook, stirring frequently, until it has released juices and is lightly browned, 4 to 6 minutes. Transfer veal to plate and set aside. Repeat with 1 tablespoon oil and remaining veal.

3. Add remaining 1 tablespoon oil to pot and heat over medium heat until shimmering. Add onions, carrots, and celery and cook, scraping bottom of pot occasionally with wooden spoon, until onions are soft and lightly browned, 6 to 10 minutes. Add garlic and cook until fragrant, 10 to 30 seconds. Add flour and cook for 20 seconds. Add wine, scraping up any bits on bottom of pot, and simmer until thickened. Increase heat to high and add broth, stirring constantly and scraping pan edges. Add tomatoes, bay leaves, and veal along with any accumulated juices and bring to simmer. Cover and place pot in oven. Cook until veal is tender and easily pierced with paring knife, 1½ to 1¾ hours. (Stew can be covered and refrigerated for up to 3 days; reheat over medium-low heat.)

4. Remove pot from oven and stir in gremolata. Let stand, covered, for 5 minutes. Season with salt and pepper to taste, and serve.

BLANQUETTE DE VEAU

Serves 6 | boneless shoulder roast

WHY THIS RECIPE WORKS Veal's subtle, delicate nature is a welcome change of pace from other meats, but this quality also makes it tricky to cook, as it's easily overwhelmed. The French have solved this problem with a family of lightly flavored—and lightly colored—cream-enriched stews called blanquettes de veau. They are unusual in that browning isn't a goal; in fact, coloring is considered a defect. Sound bland? Far from it. The flavors are refreshingly clear. To start we blanched the veal, as is traditional. This removes any gray "scum"—proteins released by the meat when it's heated. To streamline the rest of the recipe, we simply stirred the blanched veal into a sauce of chicken broth, shallots, and white wine, and then cooked it in a moderate oven until the meat was tender. We added the vegetables to the pot about halfway through cooking and finished with tarragon, parsley, and cream.

- 2 pounds boneless veal shoulder roast, trimmed and cut into 1-inch pieces
- 3 tablespoons unsalted butter
- 4 large shallots, minced
- ¼ teaspoon table salt
- 2 garlic cloves, minced
- 2 tablespoons all-purpose flour
- ¾ cup dry white wine or dry vermouth
- 1½ cups chicken broth
- 2 bay leaves
- 1 large fennel bulb, stalks discarded, bulb halved, cored, and cut into ¼-inch-thick strips
- 3 carrots, peeled and sliced ¼ inch thick
- 1 cup frozen peas
- ½ cup heavy cream
- 1 tablespoon minced fresh parsley
- 2 teaspoons minced fresh tarragon
- 2 teaspoons lemon juice

1. Adjust oven rack to middle position and heat oven to 300 degrees.

2. Bring veal and 8 cups water to simmer in Dutch oven over high heat. Reduce heat to medium-low and simmer for 5 minutes. Skim foam from surface, then drain veal in colander, discarding cooking liquid. Rinse veal briefly, then set aside to drain.

3. Rinse and dry pot and return to stove. Melt butter in pot over medium heat. Add shallots and salt and cook until shallots have softened, 3 to 5 minutes. Stir in garlic and cook until fragrant, 30 seconds. Stir in flour and cook for 30 seconds. Add wine, scraping up any browned bits; simmer until thickened. Increase heat to high and add broth, stirring constantly and scraping pan edges. Add bay leaves and veal, bring to simmer, and cover; transfer pot to oven. Cook for 1 hour.

4. Remove pot from oven and stir in fennel and carrots. Continue to cook until meat and vegetables are just tender, 30 to 45 minutes longer.

5. Remove pot from oven. Stir in peas, cream, parsley, and tarragon. Cover and let stand for 5 minutes. Discard bay leaves and stir in lemon juice. Season with salt and pepper to taste, and serve immediately.

PAN-SEARED VEAL CHOPS

Serves 4 | rib chops

WHY THIS RECIPE WORKS Tossing pricey veal chops into a smoking-hot pan takes a bit of courage on the part of the cook. Without precise timing and a properly heated pan, a lot can go wrong in a hurry. But a perfectly pan-seared veal chop, with a thick, brown crust yielding to a juicy, tender interior, is well worth the careful stoveside attention it requires. It was important we get our specs right: We opted for 8- to 12-ounce cuts that were 1 to 1½ inches thick. Thinner than that and the meat was overcooked before it had formed a good crust. Any thicker and the chops were well-done and dry with a clear line of undercooked meat in the center. We found that once our chops did hit the pan, it was critical not to move them for several minutes; otherwise, the veal tended to stick. Make sure to let the cooked chops rest, tented with aluminum foil, for 5 minutes before serving.

    4 (8- to 12-ounce) bone-in veal rib chops, 1 to 1½ inches thick, trimmed
    2 teaspoons vegetable oil
       Lemon wedges

1. Pat chops dry with paper towels and season with salt and pepper. Heat oil in 12-inch skillet over medium-high heat until just smoking. Lay chops in skillet and cook, without moving them, until well browned, 4 to 5 minutes. Using tongs, flip chops. Reduce heat to medium and continue to cook until chops register 130 to 135 degrees, 8 to 12 minutes longer.

2. Transfer chops to large plate, tent with aluminum foil, and let rest for 5 minutes. Serve immediately with lemon wedges.

VARIATION
Pan-Seared Veal Chops with Spinach and Gremolata

Make the Gremolata (page 22) before searing the chops. Then, while the chops rest, you can wilt the spinach in the skillet used for the chops. You will need three bunches of flat-leaf spinach, each weighing about 10 ounces.

While chops rest, heat 1 tablespoon extra-virgin olive oil in now-empty skillet over medium-high heat. Add 4 quarts washed, dried, and torn flat-leaf spinach leaves, a handful at a time. Use tongs to stir and coat spinach with oil. Continue to stir with tongs until spinach is uniformly wilted, about 2 minutes longer. Sprinkle spinach with 2 teaspoons lemon juice and season with salt and pepper to taste. Divide spinach among 4 plates, top each with 1 chop, and top each chop with spoonful of gremolata. Serve immediately.

GRILLED VEAL RIB CHOPS

Serves 6 | rib chops

WHY THIS RECIPE WORKS A grilled veal chop, when done right, is impressive to serve: Deeply browned, rich, and juicy, the chops require little adornment. But simple presentation doesn't always mean simple preparation, and charred, dried-out veal chops are an expensive disappointment. We wanted to guarantee perfect results every time, so we looked for chops of medium thickness—this helped ensure moist chops with a nice golden crust. A two-level fire allowed us to sear the chops on the hotter side to develop a crust before finishing them on the cooler side. Although these chops were great seasoned with just salt and pepper, we also loved coating them in flavorful pastes before grilling—an herby Mediterranean paste and an umami-packed dried porcini paste were equally delicious variations. Be sure to trim the veal chops of excess fat to prevent flare-ups. Keep a squirt bottle filled with water on hand to spray flare-ups that may still occur. We like to serve these chops over a bed of arugula.

    6 bone-in veal rib chops, about 1¼ inches thick, trimmed

1a. For a charcoal grill: Open bottom vent completely. Light large chimney starter filled with charcoal briquettes (6 quarts). When top coals are partially covered with ash, pour two-thirds evenly over half of grill, then pour remaining coals over other half of grill. Set cooking grate in place, cover, and open lid vent completely. Heat grill until hot, about 5 minutes.

1b. For a gas grill: Turn all burners to high, cover, and heat grill until hot, about 15 minutes. Leave primary burner on high and turn other burner(s) to medium.

Veal Scaloppini with Lemon-Parsley Sauce

2. Clean and oil cooking grate. Season chops evenly with salt and pepper.

3. Grill chops (covered if using gas) over hotter side of grill until browned, about 2 minutes on each side. (If flare-ups occur, slide chops briefly to cooler side of grill and, if necessary, extinguish flames with squirt bottle.) Move chops to cooler side of grill. Continue grilling, turning once, until meat is still rosy pink at center and registers 130 to 135 degrees (for medium), 10 to 11 minutes.

4. Remove chops from grill and let rest for 5 minutes before serving.

VARIATIONS

Grilled Veal Chops with Herb Paste

If you don't have all the herbs in the recipe, feel free to use additional amounts of what you do have to make up the difference.

Mix 6 tablespoons extra-virgin olive oil, 5 minced garlic cloves, 2 tablespoons minced fresh parsley, 1 tablespoon minced fresh sage, 1 tablespoon minced fresh thyme, 1 tablespoon minced fresh rosemary, and 1 tablespoon minced fresh oregano together in small bowl. Season with salt and pepper to taste. Rub chops with herb paste. Grill as directed and serve with lemon wedges.

Porcini-Rubbed Grilled Veal Rib Chops

Grind ¾ ounce dried porcini mushrooms to powder in spice grinder. Mix ground mushrooms with 9 tablespoons extra-virgin olive oil, 3 minced garlic cloves, 1½ teaspoons table salt, and ½ teaspoon ground black pepper in small bowl. Rub chops with mushroom paste. Do not season chops with salt and pepper before grilling. Grill as directed.

VEAL SCALOPPINI WITH LEMON-PARSLEY SAUCE

Serves 4 | veal cutlets

WHY THIS RECIPE WORKS Veal scaloppini is a classic restaurant dish that's remarkably simple to prepare. Gently pound the cutlets, quickly sauté them, and serve them with a basic pan sauce. While this should be a great candidate for the home kitchen, supermarket cutlets can be tough. We tried every tenderizing trick in the book and landed on a decidedly unglamourous product, powdered meat tenderizer (for more information, see page 198). The meat was tender but cooking the cutlets was still a challenge—we wanted nicely browned cutlets but flouring and browning both sides overcooked the

quick-cooking meat. The answer? We floured and browned just one side of the cutlet and cooked the second, unfloured side only briefly. If the cutlets are thinner than ¼ inch, pound them to an even ⅛-inch thickness and then fold them in half. The meat tenderizer turns tough supermarket cutlets into cutlets every bit as tender as those found in restaurants; do not omit it. Because the meat tenderizer contains sodium, salting the cutlets is unnecessary. For superior cutlets, slice the cutlets yourself (see page 198).

LEMON-PARSLEY SAUCE

- 2 teaspoons vegetable oil
- 2 shallots, minced
- 1½ cups chicken broth
- 2 tablespoons minced fresh parsley
- 2 tablespoons unsalted butter, cut into 4 pieces
- 1–2 tablespoons lemon juice

VEAL CUTLETS

- 1½ pounds veal cutlets, ¼ inch thick
- ¾ teaspoon unseasoned meat tenderizer
- ⅛ teaspoon pepper
- ½ cup all-purpose flour
- 3 tablespoons vegetable oil, divided

1. For the lemon-parsley sauce: Heat oil in medium saucepan over medium-high heat until shimmering. Add shallots and cook until beginning to soften, about 1 minute. Add broth and increase heat to high; simmer until liquid is reduced to ¾ cup, about 8 minutes. Set aside.

2. For the veal cutlets: Pat cutlets dry with paper towels. Sprinkle tenderizer and pepper evenly on both sides of cutlets.

3. Spread flour in rimmed baking sheet in thin, even layer. Heat 1 tablespoon oil in 12-inch nonstick skillet over high heat until just smoking. Dredge first batch of cutlets in flour on 1 side only, shake off excess, and place in skillet, floured side down, making sure cutlets do not overlap. Cook, without moving cutlets, until well browned, 1 to 1½ minutes. Using tongs, flip cutlets and cook until second sides are no longer pink, about 30 seconds. Transfer cutlets to platter and tent with aluminum foil. Repeat with remaining cutlets in 2 batches, using 1 tablespoon oil for each batch. (If skillet becomes too dark after cooking second batch, rinse before continuing.)

4. Pour sauce into now-empty skillet and bring to simmer, scraping up any browned bits. Off heat, whisk in parsley, butter, and 1 tablespoon lemon juice and season with salt, pepper, and up to 1 tablespoon additional lemon juice to taste. Serve with cutlets.

VARIATION
Veal Scaloppini with Porcini-Marsala Sauce

Omit Lemon-Parsley Sauce. Microwave ½ cup water and ⅓ ounce rinsed dried porcini mushrooms in covered bowl until steaming, about 1 minute. Let sit until softened, about 5 minutes. Drain mushrooms in fine-mesh strainer lined with coffee filter, reserve liquid, and cut mushrooms into ¼-inch pieces. Set aside mushrooms and liquid. Heat 2 teaspoons vegetable oil in medium saucepan over medium-high heat until shimmering. Add 2 minced shallots and cook until beginning to soften, about 1 minute. Off heat, add 1 cup dry Marsala. Return saucepan to high heat; simmer rapidly until liquid is reduced to ½ cup, about 4 minutes. Add mushrooms and reserved soaking liquid and simmer until liquid is again reduced to ½ cup, about 4 minutes. Add 1½ cups chicken broth and simmer until liquid is reduced to 1 cup, about 8 minutes. Set aside. After cooking cutlets, pour sauce into empty skillet and bring to simmer, scraping up any browned bits. Off heat, whisk in 2 tablespoons butter, cut into 4 pieces, and 1 tablespoon minced chives and season with salt and pepper to taste. Serve with cutlets.

COTOLETTA ALLA VALDOSTANA

Serves 4 | veal cutlets

WHY THIS RECIPE WORKS In the Alpine region of Valle d'Aosta, food is rich and hearty for mountain living. There butter is preferred to olive oil, and creamy cheeses—a product of the region's vast milk supply—are cherished. Cotoletta alla Valdostana is a prime example of the hearty fare. A small amount of veal becomes a filling meal when stuffed with decadent prosciutto and fontina cheese. While traditional recipes vary in preparation, we followed a simple, neat approach. We pounded a veal cutlet until thin and tender, topped it with cheese and prosciutto, and then placed another piece of veal on top. We breaded this veal "sandwich" and cooked it until crispy. Lemon wedges are the only addition this dish needs, but you can serve it over arugula.

- 4 (3-ounce) veal cutlets, about ¼ inch thick, halved crosswise
- 2 ounces fontina cheese, shredded (½ cup)
- 4 thin slices Prosciutto di Parma (2 ounces)
- 2 large eggs
- 2 tablespoons all-purpose flour
- 1½ cups panko bread crumbs
- 8 tablespoons unsalted butter
  Lemon wedges

1. Pat 2 cutlet halves dry with paper towels and place between 2 layers of plastic wrap. Pound cutlets into rough 5 by 4-inch rectangles, about ⅛ inch thick, using meat pounder. Place 2 tablespoons fontina in center of 1 cutlet half, leaving ¼-inch border around edge. Lay 1 slice prosciutto on top of fontina, folding it as needed to prevent any overhang. Place second cutlet half over prosciutto. Gently press down on cutlets to compress layers, then press along edges to seal. Repeat with remaining cutlet halves, fontina, and prosciutto.

2. Whisk eggs and flour in shallow dish until smooth. Spread panko in second shallow dish. Working with 1 stuffed cutlet at a time, carefully dip in egg mixture, allowing excess to drip off. Dredge in panko to coat both sides, pressing gently so crumbs adhere. Place breaded cutlets in single layer on wire rack set in rimmed baking sheet and let sit for 5 minutes.

3. Melt butter in 12-inch nonstick skillet over medium heat (do not let butter brown). Place cutlets in skillet; cook until deep golden brown and crisp on first side, 3 to 6 minutes. Gently flip cutlets using 2 spatulas and continue to cook until deep golden brown and crisp on second side, about 4 minutes, adjusting burner as needed to prevent scorching. Transfer cutlets to paper towel–lined plate; blot dry. Season with salt and pepper to taste. Serve immediately with lemon wedges.

OSSO BUCO

Serves 6 | veal shanks

WHY THIS RECIPE WORKS In osso buco, slow, steady cooking renders veal shanks remarkably tender and turns a simple broth of carrots, onion, celery, wine, and stock into a velvety sauce. Each diner gets an individual shank; for some, the best part is the luscious bone marrow, which diners use a small spoon to extract. We sought to create a flavorful braising liquid and cooking technique that produced a rich sauce true to this venerable recipe; aromatics deepened the flavor of store-bought stock. We oven-braised the shanks, which was the easiest cooking method, and the natural reduction that took place left just the right amount of liquid in the pot. Tying the shanks around the equator kept the meat attached to the bone for an attractive presentation. Many recipes suggest flouring the veal before browning it, but we got better flavor when we simply seared the meat, liberally seasoned with salt and pepper. We stirred a traditional accompaniment, gremolata, a mixture of minced garlic, parsley, and lemon zest, into the sauce to brighten the hearty dish.

6 (14- to 16-ounce) veal shanks, 1½ inches thick
6 tablespoons extra-virgin olive oil, divided
2½ cups dry white wine, divided
2 onions, chopped
2 carrots, peeled and chopped
2 celery ribs, chopped
6 garlic cloves, minced
2 cups chicken broth
1 (14.5-ounce) can diced tomatoes, drained
2 bay leaves
1 recipe Gremolata (page 22)

1. Adjust oven rack to lower-middle position and heat oven to 325 degrees. Pat shanks dry with paper towels and season with salt and pepper. Tie piece of twine around thickest portion of each shank to keep meat attached to bone while cooking. Heat 2 tablespoons oil in Dutch oven over medium-high heat until just smoking. Brown half of shanks on all sides, 8 to 10 minutes; transfer to large bowl. Repeat with 2 tablespoons oil and remaining shanks; transfer to bowl. Off heat, add 1½ cups wine to now-empty pot and scrape up any browned bits. Pour liquid into bowl with shanks.

2. Heat remaining 2 tablespoons oil in again-empty pot until shimmering. Add onions, carrots, and celery and cook until vegetables are softened and lightly browned, 8 to 10 minutes. Stir in garlic and cook until lightly browned, about 1 minute. Stir in broth, tomatoes, bay leaves, and remaining 1 cup wine and bring to simmer. Nestle shanks into pot along with deglazing liquid. Cover pot, leaving lid slightly ajar, and transfer pot to oven. Cook until veal is tender and fork slips easily in and out of meat, but meat is not falling off bone, about 2 hours.

3. Remove pot from oven and discard bay leaves. Stir half of gremolata into braising liquid and season with salt and pepper to taste. Let sit for 5 minutes.

4. Transfer shanks to individual bowls and discard twine. Ladle braising liquid over shanks and sprinkle with remaining gremolata. Serve.

SOUS VIDE OSSO BUCO

Serves 4 | veal shanks
Sous vide time: 24 to 26 hours

WHY THIS RECIPE WORKS The traditional osso buco preparation is a long-simmering braise. By cooking our osso buco sous vide, we made a version that's relatively hands-off. First, we seared the shanks in a bit of vegetable oil to develop some good browning in our pan and on our meat. We reduced a sauce of onion, carrot, celery, garlic, dry white wine, and tomato to create a paste, which we threw right into the bag

with our shanks. As the shanks cooked, juices accumulated and rehydrated the paste, resulting in a velvety sauce with tons of meaty flavor. After 24 hours, nearly all the fat and collagen had rendered, and we were left with fork-tender, fall-apart meat. Be sure to double-bag the shanks to protect against seam failure.

1 large onion, chopped
2 carrots, peeled and chopped
2 celery ribs, chopped
8 garlic cloves, minced
1 (14.5-ounce) can diced tomatoes, drained
4 (12-ounce) veal shanks, 2 inches thick, trimmed and tied around equator
¼ cup vegetable oil, divided
¾ teaspoon table salt
¾ teaspoon pepper
2 tablespoons tomato paste
1¼ cups dry white wine
4 bay leaves
¼ cup chopped fresh parsley

1. Using sous vide circulator, bring water to 176°F in 7-quart container.

2. Pulse onion, carrots, celery, and garlic in food processor until finely chopped, 12 to 14 pulses; transfer to bowl. Pulse tomatoes in now-empty processor until finely chopped, 8 to 10 pulses.

3. Pat shanks dry with paper towels and season with salt and pepper. Heat 2 tablespoons oil in 12-inch skillet over medium-high heat until just smoking. Brown shanks, 3 to 4 minutes per side; transfer to plate.

4. Heat remaining 2 tablespoons oil in now-empty skillet over medium heat until shimmering. Add vegetable mixture, salt, and pepper and cook until softened and lightly browned, 16 to 20 minutes.

5. Stir in tomato paste and cook until fragrant, about 1 minute. Stir in wine, scraping up any browned bits, and cook until almost completely evaporated, 4 to 6 minutes. Stir in tomatoes and cook until mixture is thick and lightly browned, 16 to 20 minutes.

6. Transfer mixture to 2-gallon zipper-lock freezer bag. Add shanks and bay leaves and toss to coat. Arrange shanks in single layer and seal bag, pressing out as much air as possible. Place bag in second 2-gallon zipper-lock freezer bag and seal bag. Gently lower bag into prepared water bath until shanks are fully submerged, and then clip top corner of bag to side of water bath container, allowing remaining air bubbles to rise to top of bag. Reopen 1 corner of zipper, release remaining air bubbles, and reseal bag. Cover and cook for at least 24 hours or up to 26 hours.

7. Transfer shanks to serving dish, leaving sauce in bag. Discard bay leaves. Stir parsley into sauce and season with salt and pepper to taste. Pour sauce over shanks and serve.

To make ahead: Shanks can be rapidly chilled in ice bath and then refrigerated in zipper-lock bag after step 6 for up to 3 days. To reheat, return sealed bag to water bath set to 176°F for 1 hour and then proceed with step 7.

PRESSURE-COOKER VEAL SHANKS WITH SWEET AND SPICY PEPERONATA

Serves 6 | veal shanks

WHY THIS RECIPE WORKS We set out to create a modern spin on osso buco using a pressure cooker and some different additions. To serve six people, we used good-size shanks and tied them around the equator to keep the meat attached to the bones. Browning the shanks in two batches built savory fond and prevented overcrowding in the cooker, while deglazing the pan with wine enhanced the flavor of the meat. While the finishing dollop of gremolata usually does the work of offsetting some of the veal's richness, we decided on a different Italian specialty, a sweet and spicy peperonata, a classic condiment of stewed bell peppers, onions, and tomatoes, which we brightened up with capers and caper brine. We tried cooking our peperonata with the veal shanks, but the peppers became too soft and lost their brightness with the extended cooking time. Instead, we cooked our peperonata at the end, while the veal shanks rested. Just 15 minutes using the sauté function were enough to meld the peperonata's flavors while keeping everything fresh-tasting. Serve with risotto, polenta, or mashed potatoes.

6 (14- to 16-ounce) veal shanks, 1½ inches thick, trimmed and tied around equator
¼ cup extra-virgin olive oil, divided
3 sprigs fresh thyme
8 garlic cloves, minced, divided
¾ cup dry white wine
1 bay leaf
4 red or yellow bell peppers, stemmed, seeded, and cut into ¼-inch-wide strips
1 onion, halved and sliced thin
1 (14.5-ounce) can diced tomatoes, drained
¼ cup raisins
2 tablespoons tomato paste
¼ teaspoon red pepper flakes
¼ teaspoon table salt
2 tablespoons capers plus 4 teaspoons caper brine
½ cup chopped fresh basil

1. Pat shanks dry with paper towels and season with salt and pepper. Using highest sauté or browning function, heat 2 tablespoons oil in electric pressure cooker for 5 minutes (or until just smoking). Brown half of shanks on 1 side, 4 to 6 minutes; transfer to plate. Repeat with remaining shanks; transfer to plate.

2. Add thyme sprigs and half of garlic to fat left in pressure cooker and cook until fragrant, about 30 seconds. Stir in wine and bay leaf, scraping up any browned bits. Nestle shanks into pressure cooker (shanks will overlap slightly), adding any accumulated juices.

3. Lock lid in place and close pressure release valve. Select high pressure cook function and cook for 1 hour. Turn off pressure cooker and let pressure release naturally for 15 minutes. Quick-release any remaining pressure, then carefully remove lid, allowing steam to escape away from you.

4. Transfer shanks to serving dish and discard twine. Tent with aluminum foil and let rest while cooking peperonata. Discard cooking liquid and wipe pressure cooker clean with paper towels.

5. Using highest sauté or browning function, heat remaining 2 tablespoons oil in pressure cooker until shimmering. Add bell peppers, onion, tomatoes, raisins, tomato paste, pepper flakes, salt, and remaining garlic. Cover and cook, stirring occasionally, until vegetables are softened, 10 to 15 minutes. Turn off pressure cooker. Stir in capers and brine and season with salt and pepper to taste. Spoon peperonata over shanks and sprinkle with basil. Serve.

Sous Vide Osso Buco

PART 2

pork

PORK CUTS

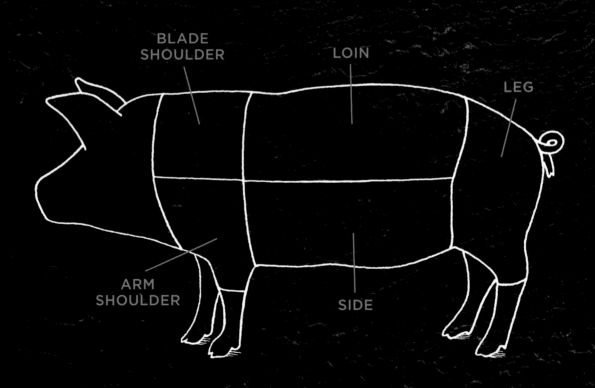

BLADE SHOULDER

LOIN

LEG

ARM SHOULDER

SIDE

PORK IS THE MOST BELOVED meat internationally, though it's the runner-up to beef in popularity in the United States. While beef's flavor lives on a simple spectrum from milder with little fat to beefier with more fat, pork possesses a range of flavors, depending on where the cut is from: Pork can be mild and almost poultry-like if from the loin, fatty and unctuous around the belly, sweet and robust from the shoulder, meaty and rich from the back end. Because it has these exciting and varied flavors, you can season and serve pork with a lot of interesting ingredients. Pork's nutritional selling points: It's rich in vitamin B6, niacin, phosphorous, selenium, thiamine, and zinc. And like most meat, it will efficiently help you reach your iron needs. While some parts of the pig are fatty, many cuts are quite lean and suitable for a healthful diet. As for the fat itself, you might be glad to know it's higher in unsaturated fatty acids than the fat from other meats. It *is* higher in cholesterol, however.

No matter where on the pig they're from, the noteworthy cuts are large roasts: pork chops for braising, searing, or grilling; pork ribs for barbecuing or indoor slow cooking in the oven; and holiday hams and bacon. Pork sold raw is a blank canvas, like most meat, but it's also often sold wet- or dry-cured or smoked.

Pork is popular around the world not only for its flavor but also for practicality. Historically, pigs were a good choice for sustenance, as their low-moisture meat took extremely well to curing; pork products could be preserved to be eaten during hard times and times of migration. Originally foreign to American land, pigs are thought to have first arrived with Spanish conquistador Hernando de Soto, and when English settlers brought them again later, they thrived. The settlers fed the pigs their abundant corn, which fattened them to something much meatier than scrawnier European pigs, and their high amount of fat grew to be a most favored trait in the marketplace.

(continued)

Then and now, pigs are easy (and economical) animals to raise; they don't need a ton of space to roam, they can eat nearly anything, and they reproduce quickly, so if you have pigs you're never without. They even help reduce food waste, eating surplus crops. And they're there just for eating, whereas cows also produce milk and dairy, and sheep yield dairy and wool fiber. While we cover the larger, more common cuts of the pig in this book, every last bit can be eaten—another reason for its versatility.

But the pigs of today aren't the porkers of yesterday. Calls to limit eating animal fats in the 1950s and 1960s led to concern over the percentage of fat on an average pig, and swine were fed diets to create a leaner (now almost 70 percent less fatty) pig that's less likely to contribute to heart concerns—and more likely to dry out and taste bland. Not to worry, however. Although pork is often referred to as the "other white meat," it doesn't have to be cooked to the same temperature as chicken; if it is, the meat will be dry and tough. We think the lean cuts—like tenderloin—are best cooked to 145 degrees. At this point, the meat will still have a tinge of pink in the center and be plenty tasty. (The USDA doesn't use this catchphrase anyway: Pork isn't white until it's cooked, so it's classified as a red meat.)

What about trichinosis? Better farming practices have all but eliminated the trichina parasite from American-raised pork. According to the Centers for Disease Control and Prevention, the number of trichinosis cases averages 12 per year—and most of those cases have been linked to wild game, not commercially raised pork. Also, the trichina parasite is killed when the temperature of the meat rises to 137 degrees, so cooking pork to 145 degrees should do the job.

Pink pork isn't completely without risk. All meat (including beef) may be subject to cross-contamination with several pathogens, such as salmonella. This can happen during processing, at the supermarket, or in your home. To reduce this risk, some food safety experts recommend cooking all meat to 160 degrees—that is, until it is well done. But if you think it's worth taking the small risk to enjoy a rosy steak, you might as well to do the same with pork.

A PIG BY ANY OTHER NAME

You can call pigs hogs and swine—they won't mind, as they're all names for the same thing. More specifically, a sow is a female pig that's given birth. Baby pigs are piglets, nursery pigs, grow-finish pigs, or shoats. A young pig of three to six weeks old is separated from its mother and called a weaner—and here the breeding process begins. Female weaners grow into gilts. A male pig for breeding

is a boar. You may have seen suckling pig on menus—it's very tender as it's a piglet slaughtered before weaning. A feeder pig is the next size up in weight class, followed by a grower pig, and a finisher pig. A finisher pig, as you might guess, weighing more than 200 pounds, is more than ready for slaughter.

SHOULD YOU PAY ATTENTION TO PIG BREEDS?

We discussed different breeds of cattle (see page 30), but do pig breeds, especially those called "heritage," matter much for eating? They're often touted for being fattier (a good thing in today's lean-pork world), juicier, and far more flavorful. Some popular pedigreed breeds are Berkshire (known as Kurobutain in Japan) and Duroc—and they come along with a premium price tag. We tasted mail-order 100 percent Berkshire pork chops; chops from Berkshire pork pigs mixed with other breeds; and other "heritage" breeds, which all had a deeper, more crimson color than supermarket chops, which were generally ghostly pale. The heritage blends tasted close to, maybe a little better than, supermarket versions, while Berkshire pork was juicy, smoky, and intensely porky—even bacon-like.

We learned that color does matter in pork: It reflects the meat's pH, which is a huge driver of quality in pork. In mammals, normal pH is around 7. But even small differences in pH can have a significant impact on pork's flavor and texture. Berkshire pigs are bred to have a slightly higher pH than normal, which in turn makes their meat darker, firmer, more flavorful, and better able to retain water. In fact, a high pH can be even more important than fat in determining flavor. Conversely, pork with low pH is paler, softer, and relatively bland.

In addition to genetics, pH is influenced by husbandry, along with slaughtering and processing methods. Berkshire pigs are raised in low-stress environments that keep them calm. And the calmer the animal, the more evenly blood flows through its system, distributing flavorful juices throughout. Berkshire pigs are also slaughtered with methods that minimize stress, which causes a buildup of lactic acid in the muscles and lowers pH. Chilling the meat very rapidly after slaughter is yet another factor that affects pH, which begins to decline immediately once blood flow stops. Increasingly, commercial producers are adopting similar measures in slaughtering and processing in an effort to keep the pH of their pork as high as possible. The bottom line? Berkshire pork won't become a regular purchase for most of us, but we think our favorite sample is worth the occasional splurge.

And what truly is the reason for the premium price tag on Berkshire pigs? Heritage breeds lose that aforementioned ease of breeding. They take two or three times longer to mature and they need to consume two to three times as much food to gain the proper weight.

PORK SHOPPING

Pork at the store is always from domesticated pigs. Wild boar is the term for meat from wild pigs. Old pork is pretty simple to spot: It will be gray to even green in color and smell rancid.

Because modern supermarket pork is so lean and therefore some-what bland and prone to dryness if overcooked, many producers now inject their fresh pork products with a sodium solution. So-called enhanced pork is now the only option at many super-markets, especially for lean cuts like the tenderloin. To be sure, read the label; if the pork has been enhanced it will have an ingre-dient label, while natural pork will not have ingredients. (Note that "natural" here means something different than it does for beef—it's about processing, not how the pork was raised. You may see the term "naturally raised" on a product, but this isn't regulated so it can be ignored when you're shopping. Look to individual brands if you have ethical concerns.)

Enhanced pork is injected with a solution of water, salt, sodium phosphates, sodium lactate, potassium lactate, sodium diacetate, and varying flavor agents, generally adding 7 to 15 percent extra weight. While enhanced pork does cook up juicier (it's been pumped full of water!), we find the texture almost spongy, and the flavor is often unpleasantly salty. We prefer the genuine pork flavor of natural pork, in some cuts even more emphatically than others (see recipe headnotes), and we brine lean cuts to keep them juicy. If you must buy enhanced pork, follow our instructions in recipe headnotes for decreasing or omitting salt. Note that enhanced pork loses six times more moisture when frozen and thawed than does natural pork—yet another reason to avoid it.

PORK GRADING

The inspection process by the USDA or the state is the same for pork as it is for beef. You will find a seal that says "passed and inspected by USDA" on healthy-to-eat pork. There's not much else to pay attention to here as there are only two grades, acceptable and unacceptable, and the latter isn't sold. What makes pork unacceptable? A low proportion of lean meat to fat and bone, and soft and watery meat.

While there are no grading labels, there are qualities (color, firmness) to look for that the National Pork Board (pork.org) organizes in the below categories. These can help serve as visual guidelines when shopping.

PSE (pale, soft, exudative): If the meat is pale and soft it won't hold on to as much moisture as darker pork; when cooked it has a greater tendency to become tough and dry. These qualities aren't uncommon to pork in the supermarket, however. Brining or salting can help pork that falls into this category.

RFN (reddish pink, firm, nonexudative): This is the best pork: It doesn't exude a lot of moisture and is tender and juicy when cooked.

DFD (dark reddish purple, firm, nonexudative): This meat is quite dry to the touch and very firm. It spoils quickly and can have a mushy texture. Avoid.

And marbling: This one is pretty obvious. The more marbled, the better the flavor. Pick marbled pork first.

ORGANIC PORK

If pork is organic, the way it was raised lives up to a certain ethi-cal standard. The pigs have more room to move, can go inside and outside, are not raised in stalls, and rest on organic dry bedding materials. Since the pigs can go outside, producers take measures to prevent parasites. The pigs' diet is all organic, without medica-tions, growth hormones, or any other synthetic enhancements. Only pork raised in this manner receives the USDA seal for organic products.

BRINING PORK

While salting can be used with a wide variety of meat, brining is often preferable for lean pork. Brining works pretty much the same way as salting. (For information on salting and brining, see page 10.) Salt in the brine seasons the meat and promotes a change in its protein structure, reducing its overall toughness and creating gaps that fill up with water and keep the meat juicy and flavorful. Brining works faster than salting and can also result in juicier lean cuts since it adds, rather than merely retains, moisture— which is why we often prefer brining to salting in lean cuts of pork such as pork tenderloin. Note that brining inhibits browning, and it entails fitting a brining bowl or container in the fridge. (See page 11 for general rules on water and salt amounts and brining times for different types of cuts.)

BLADE SHOULDER

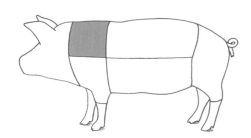

AN ANIMAL'S SHOULDER IS an animal's shoulder. That is, whether we're talking about a big cow, or a rotund pig, or a comparatively skinny lamb, the shoulder primal serves the same movement purposes and will be hardy, tough, full of connective tissue, relatively fatty—and absolutely succulent when cooked slowly. And to keep the meat at prime collagen-melting temperature for as long as possible without losing too much moisture, we cook pork shoulder at a low temperature, too. Unlike fairer parts of the pig, the shoulder has a darker color owing to the abundance of the red, oxygen-storing pigment known as myoglobin that is found there.

A pig's shoulder is generally split into two primals, the blade shoulder (sometimes referred to as the upper shoulder) discussed here and the arm shoulder (see page 238)—otherwise you'd be cooking a gigantic, complex piece of bone-in meat. The whole blade shoulder weighs about 14 pounds, plenty enough, and is the thicker portion of the shoulder with more fat coursing through it. (Be careful when shopping and ask questions if you can: Both shoulder parts can be labeled simply "pork shoulder," which can cause confusion. While we have recipe-specific preferences, they can generally be swapped if necessary in recipes.) Pork shoulder's flavor is rich and meaty as you would expect from this area of the pig, but it also has a lovely sweetness. It's one of our favorite parts of the pig to cook and eat.

Pork Butt Roast

Cost: ▪▪◻◻ Flavor: ▪▪◻◻

Best cooking methods: roast, braise, stew, slow roast, slow cook, sous vide, grill roast, barbecue
Texture: tough; rich, tender, succulent once slowly cooked
Alternative names: Boston shoulder, pork butt, pork shoulder roast, Boston butt

"Pork butt" doesn't seem like an anatomically correct labeling, but the butt is indeed from the shoulder of the pig and not from the rear. (Rumor has it that in Revolutionary New England, this cut was stored in specialty barrels called "butts." And the technique for cutting this roast was originated in Boston.) This large blade roast is available bone-in (and can weigh up to 8 pounds if so) or boneless. A bone-in roast can be impressive to present; a boneless roast lends itself to being pulled or shredded. Pork butt is often sold with a fat cap intact. Sometimes we leave it on for its moistening fat; sometimes we call for it to be trimmed to keep a dish from being greasy. Often we crosshatch it to encourage rendering and crisping, or so it can hold a salt or spice rub. As with the chuck-eye roast from the shoulder of the cow (see page 35), sometimes we'll pull apart pork butt at the seams to create two roasts or to trim the fat therein; sometimes we'll cut it up for stews.

MEAT PREP *Crosshatching Pork Butt Roast*

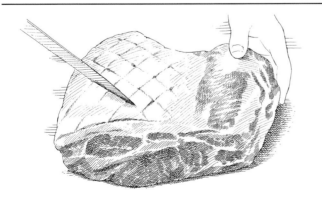

Using sharp knife, cut slits 1 inch apart in crosshatch pattern in fat cap of roast, being careful not to cut into meat.

MEAT PREP *Cutting Pork Butt into Stew Meat*

1. Trim hard, waxy fat from surface of meat, leaving just thin layer.

2. Slice meat crosswise into slabs of desired thickness.

3. Cut slabs lengthwise into strips of desired thickness.

4. Cut each strip crosswise into cubes, trimming as needed.

TRIM THIS, LEAVE THAT

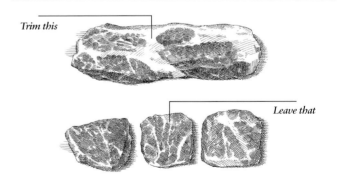

Trim this

Leave that

If your recipe calls for trimming a pork butt roast, most often for cutting it up for a stew or braise, it's hard to know exactly what to trim. The cut is well marbled throughout, and you don't want to trim away too much of the fat and connective tissue that gives the meat a rich, moist texture. The key is to remove any hard, waxy fat from the surface of the whole roast and to leave a thin layer; don't worry about removing any interior fat at this point. A boning knife can make this task easier (see page 17). Once you've got your smaller chunks and cubes, remove the hard knobs of waxy fat as they become accessible. Don't worry about removing every last bit.

MEAT PREP *Shredding Pork*

Using 2 forks, shred pork into bite-size pieces.

Pork Butt Steaks

Cost: ■■▯▯ **Flavor:** ■■■▯
Best cooking methods: braise, slow cook, sous vide, barbecue
Texture: tough; rich, tender, succulent once slowly cooked
Alternative names: pork steak, Boston butt steak, blade steak

The pork steak, slabs of pork cut from a pork butt, originated at a supermarket in St. Louis in the 1950s. If you're not from the Midwest, you may have never heard of the cut, much less seen it in the supermarket. But in St. Louis it's so popular that you can buy packs of steaks in the supermarket refrigerator case. These steaks are as delicious as pork butt and thus delicious no matter *where* you cook them—a fine addition to your repertoire. You'll just need to cut them yourself. These cannot be seared like many meat cuts with steak in the name—they must be cooked low and slow like pork butt to break down the abundant connective tissue.

MEAT PREP *Cutting Pork Butt into Steaks*

1. Slice pork crosswise in half and remove any large pieces of fat.

2. Rotate and stand each half of the pork butt on its cut end. Cut each half into three or four 1-inch-thick steaks.

Blade-Cut Pork Chops

Cost: ■■▯▯ **Flavor:** ■■■▯
Best cooking methods: braise, slow cook, grill
Texture: fatty, tough, juicy
Alternative names: shoulder chop, pork chop end cut

There are three pork chop types to parse in this book, and we start by introducing blade-cut pork chops, as they're cut from the upper shoulder. This makes them the toughest of the chops, less likely to be seared but instead braised or slow-cooked like their shoulder roast parent. They're also more marbled and fattier than chops cut from the loin, so they're more deeply flavored. They can be a little harder to find at the market than other pork chops.

There's a band of fatty connective tissue and shoulder meat along the outer edge of blade chops. This matter can contribute body and flavor to a braise—but it also causes the chops to buckle. We trim away the band, and in one recipe, Red Wine–Braised Pork Chops (page 234), we chop the band up and save the pieces for searing and adding to the braise. (They even taste great on the side after the recipe is cooked.)

MEAT PREP *Trimming Blade-Cut Pork Chops*

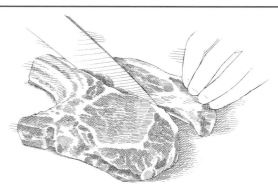

Trim off swath of fatty meat and any cartilage running along edge of chop.

Slow-Roasted Pork Shoulder

SLOW-ROASTED PORK SHOULDER WITH PEACH SAUCE

Serves 8 to 12 | bone-in pork butt roast

WHY THIS RECIPE WORKS Slow roasting can transform a tough, complex piece of pork butt into something succulent, tender, and truly special. To achieve "special," we rubbed a bone-in pork butt roast with salt and sugar and refrigerated it overnight, allowing the salt to penetrate deep into the meat. Five to 6 hours of roasting pushed the meat well beyond its "done" mark, but the cut's substantial collagen and fat kept it moist while it achieved ultimate tenderness (see "Overcooking for a Cause" on page 15 for more information). Meanwhile, the thick fat cap rendered to form a bacon-like crust. Elevating the pork shoulder on a V-rack and pouring water into the roasting pan kept the pork's drippings from burning as the meat roasted. Finally, a fruity sauce with sweet and tart elements cut the pork's richness. Add more water to the roasting pan as necessary to prevent the fond from burning.

PORK ROAST

1 (6- to 8-pound) bone-in pork butt roast
⅓ cup kosher salt
⅓ cup packed light brown sugar

PEACH SAUCE

10 ounces frozen peaches, cut into 1-inch pieces, or 2 fresh peaches, peeled, pitted, and cut into ½-inch wedges
2 cups dry white wine
½ cup granulated sugar
5 tablespoons unseasoned rice vinegar, divided
2 sprigs fresh thyme
1 tablespoon whole-grain mustard

1. For the pork roast: Using sharp knife, cut slits 1 inch apart in crosshatch pattern in fat cap of roast, being careful not to cut into meat. Combine salt and sugar in bowl. Rub salt mixture over entire roast and into slits. Wrap roast tightly in double layer of plastic wrap and refrigerate for at least 12 hours or up to 24 hours.

2. Adjust oven rack to lowest position and heat oven to 325 degrees. Line large roasting pan with aluminum foil. Unwrap roast and brush any excess salt mixture from surface. Season roast with pepper. Set V-rack in roasting pan, spray with vegetable oil spray, and place roast on rack. Add 1 quart water to roasting pan.

3. Cook roast, basting twice during cooking, until roast is extremely tender and pork near (but not touching) bone registers 190 degrees, 5 to 6 hours. (If pan begins to smoke and sizzle, add additional water.) Transfer roast to carving board and let rest for 1 hour. Transfer liquid in roasting pan to fat separator and let liquid settle for 5 minutes. Pour off ¼ cup jus and set aside; discard fat and reserve remaining jus for another use.

4. For the peach sauce: Bring peaches, wine, sugar, ¼ cup vinegar, ¼ cup defatted jus, and thyme sprigs to simmer in small saucepan; cook, stirring occasionally, until reduced to 2 cups, about 30 minutes. Stir in remaining 1 tablespoon vinegar and mustard. Discard thyme sprigs, cover, and keep warm.

5. Using sharp paring knife, cut around inverted T-shaped bone until it can be pulled free from pork (use clean dish towel to grasp bone). Slice pork and serve, passing sauce separately.

VARIATION

Slow-Roasted Pork Shoulder with Cherry Sauce
Substitute 10 ounces fresh or frozen pitted cherries for peaches, red wine for white wine, and red wine vinegar for rice vinegar and add ¼ cup ruby port along with defatted jus. Increase granulated sugar to ¾ cup, omit thyme sprigs and mustard, and reduce mixture to 1½ cups.

CIDER-BRAISED PORK ROAST

Serves 8 | bone-in pork butt roast

WHY THIS RECIPE WORKS Pork and apples are as classic as meat and potatoes, so for this recipe, we paired a flavorful bone-in pork butt roast with apple cider. Rubbing the meat with a brown sugar–salt mixture and refrigerating it overnight seasoned the meat, complemented its natural sweetness, and helped keep it juicy. Apple cider worked perfectly as a braising medium. After braising the pork, we supplemented the liquid with more apple flavor in the form of thick apple butter and apple cider vinegar along with a slurry of cornstarch for a beautiful sauce with body and sheen. Apple wedges seared in flavorful pork fat united the elements of this hearty roast and were a sweet side. If you can't find Braeburn apples, substitute Jonagold.

TUTORIAL
Slow-Roasted Pork Shoulder

To achieve some of the ultimate in pork—succulent pull-apart meat and a crisp, burnished fat cap—follow these simple steps.

1. Using sharp knife, cut slits 1 inch apart in crosshatch pattern in fat cap of roast, being careful not to cut into meat.

2. Rub salt mixture over entire roast and into slits. Wrap roast tightly in double layer of plastic wrap and refrigerate for at least 12 hours or up to 24 hours.

3. Brush excess salt from roast. Season with pepper. Place roast on V-rack and add 1 quart water to roasting pan.

4. Cook roast, basting twice during cooking, until roast is extremely tender and pork near (but not touching) bone registers 190 degrees, 5 to 6 hours.

5. Using sharp paring knife, cut around inverted T-shaped bone until it can be pulled free from pork (use clean dish towel to grasp bone).

6. Slice pork and serve, passing sauce separately.

1 (5- to 6-pound) bone-in pork butt roast
¼ cup packed brown sugar, for dry rub
¼ cup kosher salt
3 tablespoons vegetable oil
1 onion, halved and sliced thin
6 garlic cloves, smashed and peeled
2 cups apple cider, divided
6 sprigs fresh thyme
2 bay leaves
1 cinnamon stick
2 Braeburn apples, cored and cut into 8 wedges each
¼ cup apple butter
1 tablespoon cornstarch
1 tablespoon cider vinegar

1. Using sharp knife, trim fat cap on roast to ¼ inch. Cut slits 1 inch apart in crosshatch pattern in fat cap, being careful not to cut into meat. Place roast on large sheet of plastic wrap. Combine sugar and salt in bowl and rub mixture over entire roast and into slits. Wrap roast tightly in double layer of plastic, place on plate, and refrigerate for 18 to 24 hours.

2. Adjust oven rack to middle position and heat oven to 275 degrees. Unwrap roast and pat dry with paper towels, brushing away any excess salt mixture from surface. Season roast with pepper.

3. Heat oil in Dutch oven over medium-high heat until just smoking. Sear roast until well browned on all sides, about 3 minutes per side. Turn roast fat side up. Scatter onion and garlic around roast and cook until fragrant and beginning to brown, about 2 minutes. Add 1¾ cups cider, thyme sprigs, bay leaves, and cinnamon stick and bring to simmer. Cover, transfer to oven, and braise until fork slips easily in and out of meat and meat registers 190 degrees, 2¼ to 2¾ hours.

4. Transfer roast to carving board, tent with aluminum foil, and let rest for 30 minutes. Strain braising liquid through fine-mesh strainer into fat separator; discard solids and let liquid settle for at least 5 minutes.

5. About 10 minutes before roast is done resting, wipe out pot with paper towels. Spoon 1½ tablespoons of clear, separated fat from top of fat separator into now-empty pot and heat over medium-high heat until shimmering. Season apples with salt and pepper. Space apples evenly in pot, cut side down, and cook until well browned on both cut sides, about 3 minutes per side. Transfer to platter and tent with foil.

6. Wipe out pot with paper towels. Return 2 cups defatted braising liquid to now-empty pot and bring to boil over high heat. Whisk in apple butter until incorporated. Whisk cornstarch and remaining ¼ cup cider together in bowl and add to

Cider-Braised Pork Roast

pot. Return to boil and cook until thickened, about 1 minute. Off heat, add vinegar and season with salt and pepper to taste. Cover sauce and keep warm.

7. Using sharp paring knife, cut around inverted T-shaped bone until it can be pulled free from pork (use clean dish towel to grasp bone). Slice pork and transfer to platter with apples. Pour 1 cup sauce over pork and apples. Serve, passing remaining sauce separately.

CHINESE BARBECUE ROAST PORK SHOULDER

Serves 8 to 12 | bone-in pork butt roast

WHY THIS RECIPE WORKS This Chinese barbecue pork is reminiscent of char siu (see page 233) but in roast form and features succulent pork slathered in a sticky, sweet-salty glaze. We soaked bone-in pork butt in a bold marinade of soy sauce, hoisin, Chinese rice wine, ginger, sesame oil, five-spice powder, and white pepper before roasting. To prevent overbrowning in the oven, we covered the pork with foil for most of the cooking time and basted it twice with the flavorful pan drippings; an hour or so uncovered allowed the pork to take on plenty of flavor-boosting color. Before pulling the roast from the oven, we brushed it with a sticky, sweet glaze, and while the pork rested, we used the meaty pan drippings to create a potent sauce. You can substitute dry sherry for Chinese rice wine. A longer marinating time is preferable. Let the meat rest for a full hour before serving or it will not be sufficiently tender.

1 (6- to 8-pound) bone-in pork butt roast
1¾ cups sugar, divided
1 cup soy sauce
¾ cup hoisin sauce
½ cup Chinese rice wine or dry sherry
¼ cup grated fresh ginger
2 tablespoons toasted sesame oil
4 garlic cloves, minced
2 teaspoons five-spice powder
½ teaspoon ground white pepper
2 scallions, sliced thin on bias
2 teaspoons rice vinegar, plus extra as needed

1. Using sharp knife, cut slits 1 inch apart in crosshatch pattern in fat cap of roast, being careful not to cut into meat. Whisk 1 cup sugar, soy sauce, hoisin, rice wine, ginger, oil, garlic, five-spice powder, and pepper together in bowl. Measure out 1½ cups marinade and set aside. Transfer pork butt to 1-gallon zipper-lock bag and pour in remaining marinade. Press out as much air as possible from bag and seal; refrigerate roast for at least 12 hours or up to 24 hours, flipping pork butt halfway through marinating.

2. Whisk reserved marinade and remaining ¾ cup sugar together in medium saucepan. Bring to simmer over medium heat and cook, stirring occasionally, until sugar has dissolved and glaze has thickened and measures about 2 cups, about 2 minutes.

3. Adjust oven rack to lowest position and heat oven to 325 degrees. Set V-rack in large roasting pan and spray with vegetable oil spray. Remove pork butt from marinade, letting excess drip off, and place fat side up on prepared V-rack. Add 4 cups water to pan.

4. Cover pan with aluminum foil and roast for 4 hours, basting pork butt halfway through roasting. Uncover, baste pork butt, and continue to roast until extremely tender and pork near (but not touching) bone registers 190 degrees, 1 to 2 hours. (If pan begins to smoke and sizzle, add additional water.)

5. Brush pork butt with ⅓ cup glaze and roast for 20 minutes, brushing pork with glaze twice more during roasting. Transfer pork butt to carving board and let rest for 1 hour.

6. Transfer liquid in roasting pan to fat separator and let settle for 5 minutes. Combine remaining glaze, ¼ cup defatted liquid, scallions, and vinegar in serving bowl; discard remaining liquid. Season sauce with extra vinegar to taste. Using sharp paring knife, cut around inverted T-shaped bone until it can be pulled free from pork (use clean dish towel to grasp bone). Slice pieces of pork ¼ inch thick. Serve, passing sauce separately.

SLOW-COOKER SOUTHWESTERN PORK ROAST

Serves 8 to 10 | boneless pork butt roast
Cooking time: 9 to 10 hours on low or 6 to 7 hours on high

WHY THIS RECIPE WORKS Pork butt roast is a great candidate for braising in the slow cooker—its fat and connective tissue break down over the long cooking time, resulting in tender, silky meat. For our pot roast we found that halving a large roast to make two smaller roasts (2 to 2½ pounds each) yielded fork-tender meat more consistently and in less time than cooking a larger whole roast. To get enough flavor into our dish, we browned the roasts first, then browned onions deeply. To distinguish our pork pot roast from our beef ones, we put a Southwestern spin on it, seasoning the roast liberally with chili powder, oregano, salt, and pepper. We also added some of the spices to a mixture of canned tomato sauce and spicy chipotle chile to make a boldly flavored braising liquid.

1 tablespoon chili powder
1 teaspoon dried oregano
1 teaspoon table salt
1 teaspoon pepper
1 (4- to 5-pound) boneless pork butt roast, trimmed and halved
1 tablespoon vegetable oil
2 onions, chopped
2 tablespoons all-purpose flour
1 (15-ounce) can tomato sauce
2 teaspoons minced canned chipotle chile in adobo sauce
3 tablespoons minced fresh cilantro

1. Combine chili powder, oregano, salt, and pepper in bowl. Pat pork dry with paper towels and rub with half of spice mixture. Tie 3 pieces of kitchen twine around each piece of pork to create 2 evenly shaped roasts. Heat oil in 12-inch skillet over medium-high heat until just smoking. Brown roasts on all sides, 7 to 10 minutes; transfer to plate.

2. Add onions to fat left in skillet and cook over medium heat until softened and lightly browned, about 8 minutes. Stir in flour and remaining spice mixture and cook until fragrant, about 1 minute. Stir in tomato sauce and chipotle, scraping up any browned bits and smoothing out any lumps; transfer to slow cooker.

3. Nestle roasts into slow cooker, adding any accumulated juices. Cover and cook until pork is tender and fork slips easily in and out of meat, 9 to 10 hours on low or 6 to 7 hours on high.

4. Transfer roasts to carving board, tent with aluminum foil, and let rest for 20 minutes.

5. Strain sauce into fat separator, reserving solids, and let sit for 5 minutes. Combine defatted sauce, reserved solids, and cilantro in bowl. Season with salt and pepper to taste. Remove twine from roasts, slice meat against grain ½ inch thick, and arrange on serving dish. Spoon 1 cup sauce over meat and serve, passing remaining sauce separately.

CARNITAS

Serves 8 to 10 | boneless pork butt roast

WHY THIS RECIPE WORKS For our carnitas at home, we were after soft, ultrarich pork with lightly crisped edges. We wanted to let the flavor of the meaty pork butt shine, and that meant cooking the pork in lard with no extra liquid, seasonings, or spices. Cooking the meat in a Dutch oven in a 300-degree oven helped it cook evenly. Another bonus was that the corners of pork that poked above the surface of the fat browned well and developed beautiful, lightly crisped edges. Chopping the meat into bite-size pieces made it ideal for packing into warmed corn tortillas. We developed this recipe using Morrell Snow Cap Lard, but you can substitute 4 cups of peanut or vegetable oil. The pork doesn't need to be cut into perfect 2-inch pieces; a little variation in size is fine. Serve with tomatillo salsa.

  4 pounds boneless pork butt roast, cut into 2-inch pieces
1½ tablespoons kosher salt
  2 pounds lard, cut into 8 pieces
24 (6-inch) corn tortillas, warmed
    Finely chopped onion
    Coarsely chopped fresh cilantro
    Lime wedges

1. Adjust oven rack to lower-middle position and heat oven to 300 degrees. Sprinkle pork with salt. Melt lard in large Dutch oven over medium-low heat. Add pork, increase heat to medium-high, and cook until bubbling vigorously all over, about 5 minutes. Transfer to oven and cook, uncovered, until pork is tender, about 2½ hours.

2. Remove pot from oven and let stand for 30 minutes. Using spider skimmer or tongs, transfer pork to carving board; chop into bite-size pieces. Transfer pork to bowl and season with salt to taste. Divide pork among warm tortillas and garnish with onion and cilantro. Serve with lime wedges.

PORCHETTA

Serves 8 to 10 | boneless pork butt roast

WHY THIS RECIPE WORKS Porchetta—fall-apart tender, rich pieces of slow-cooked pork, infused with the flavors of garlic, fennel, rosemary, and thyme and served with pieces of crisp skin on a crusty roll—is one of Italy's greatest street foods. To take it inside, we opted for accessible pork butt over the traditional whole pig. For extra-crispy "skin," we crosshatched the fat cap, rubbed it with a mixture of salt and baking soda, and refrigerated the roast overnight to help dry it out. For quicker cooking, we cut the roast into two pieces and tied each into a compact cylinder. We then cooked the roasts in a covered roasting pan, trapping steam to cook the meat evenly and keep it moist. Finally, we uncovered the pan and browned and crisped the outer layer of the roasts. Look for a roast with a substantial fat cap. If fennel seeds are unavailable, substitute ¼ cup of ground fennel. A longer refrigeration time is preferred.

  3 tablespoons fennel seeds
  ½ cup fresh rosemary leaves (2 bunches)
  ¼ cup fresh thyme leaves (2 bunches)
12 garlic cloves, peeled
  2 tablespoons plus 1 teaspoon kosher salt, divided
  4 teaspoons pepper, divided
  ½ cup extra-virgin olive oil
  1 (5- to 6-pound) boneless pork butt roast, trimmed
  ¼ teaspoon baking soda

1. Grind fennel seeds in spice grinder or mortar and pestle until finely ground. Transfer ground fennel to food processor and add rosemary, thyme, garlic, 2 teaspoons salt, and 1 tablespoon pepper. Pulse mixture until finely chopped, 10 to 15 pulses. Add oil and process until smooth paste forms, 20 to 30 seconds.

2. Using sharp knife, cut slits 1 inch apart in crosshatch pattern in fat cap of roast, being careful not to cut into meat. Cut roast in half with grain into 2 equal pieces. Turn each roast on its side so fat cap is facing away from you, bottom of roast is facing toward you, and newly cut side is facing up. Starting 1 inch from short end of each roast, use boning or paring knife to make slit that starts 1 inch from top of roast and ends 1 inch from bottom, pushing knife completely through roast. Repeat making slits, spaced 1 to 1½ inches apart, along length of each roast, stopping 1 inch from opposite end (you should have 6 to 8 slits, depending on size of roast).

3. Turn roast so fat cap is facing down. Rub sides and bottom of roasts with 2 teaspoons salt, taking care to work salt into slits from both sides. Rub herb paste onto sides and bottom of each roast, taking care to work paste into slits from both sides. Flip roast so that fat cap is facing up. Using 3 pieces of kitchen twine per roast, tie each roast into compact cylinder.

TUTORIAL
Porchetta

This Italian specialty may seem intimidating to make at home, but it's far from it when you follow our steps.

1. Using sharp knife, cut slits 1 inch apart in fat cap of roast in crosshatch pattern, being careful not to cut into meat. Cut roast in half with grain into 2 equal pieces.

2. Turn each roast on its side so fat cap is facing away from you and newly cut side is facing up. Starting 1 inch from short end of each roast, make slit that starts 1 inch from top of roast and ends 1 inch from bottom, pushing knife completely through roast.

3. Repeat making slits, spaced 1 to 1½ inches apart, along length of each roast, stopping 1 inch from opposite end.

4. Turn roast so fat cap is facing down. Rub sides and bottom of each roast with salt and work into slits. Rub herb paste onto sides and bottom of each roast and work into slits. Tie each roast into compact cylinder.

5. Rub fat cap of each roast with salt–baking soda mixture. Cook, covered, at 325 degrees until pork registers 180 degrees, 2 to 2½ hours.

6. Remove twine from roasts. Continue to cook at 500 degrees until exteriors of roasts are well browned and interiors register 190 degrees, 20 to 30 minutes. Let rest for 20 minutes and slice ½ inch thick.

4. Combine baking soda, remaining 1 tablespoon salt, and remaining 1 teaspoon pepper in small bowl. Rub fat cap of each roast with salt–baking soda mixture, taking care to work mixture into crosshatches. Transfer roasts to wire rack set in rimmed baking sheet and refrigerate, uncovered, for at least 6 hours or up to 24 hours.

5. Adjust oven rack to middle position and heat oven to 325 degrees. Transfer roasts, fat side up, to large roasting pan, leaving at least 2 inches between roasts. Cover tightly with aluminum foil. Cook until pork registers 180 degrees, 2 to 2½ hours.

6. Remove pan from oven and increase oven temperature to 500 degrees. Carefully discard foil and transfer roasts to large plate. Discard liquid in pan. Line pan with foil. Remove twine from roasts; return roasts to pan, directly on foil; and return pan to oven. Cook until exteriors of roasts are well browned and interiors register 190 degrees, 20 to 30 minutes. Transfer roasts to carving board and let rest for 20 minutes. Slice roasts ½ inch thick, transfer to platter, and serve.

South Carolina Pulled Pork

SOUTH CAROLINA PULLED PORK

Serves 8 | boneless pork butt roast

WHY THIS RECIPE WORKS In South Carolina, pit masters dress pulled pork in a savory mustard-based sauce nicknamed "Carolina gold." We rubbed a boneless pork butt with a spice rub that included dry mustard to highlight the mustard in the sauce; the rub also helped the meat develop a flavorful crust. Brushing the pork with the sauce before it went, covered, into a low oven produced a second hit of mustardy bite; we found that a combination of grill smoking and oven roasting reduced the cooking time from all day to 4 or 5 hours. Tossing the shredded pork with the remaining sauce gave the meat a final layer of flavor. If you'd like to use wood chunks instead of wood chips when using a charcoal grill, substitute four medium wood chunks, soaked in water for 1 hour, for the wood chip packets.

PORK
- 3 tablespoons dry mustard
- 2 tablespoons table salt
- 1½ tablespoons packed light brown sugar
- 2 teaspoons pepper
- 2 teaspoons paprika
- ¼ teaspoon cayenne pepper
- 1 (4- to 5-pound) boneless pork butt roast, trimmed
- 4 cups wood chips

BARBECUE SAUCE
- ½ cup yellow mustard
- ½ cup packed light brown sugar
- ¼ cup distilled white vinegar
- 2 tablespoons Worcestershire sauce
- 1 tablespoon hot sauce
- 1 teaspoon table salt
- 1 teaspoon pepper

1. **For the pork:** Combine mustard, salt, sugar, pepper, paprika, and cayenne in bowl. Pat pork dry with paper towels and rub with spice mixture. Wrap meat in plastic wrap and let sit at room temperature for at least 1 hour or refrigerate for up to 24 hours. (If refrigerated, let sit at room temperature for 1 hour before grilling.)

2. Just before grilling, soak wood chips in water for 15 minutes, then drain. Using large piece of heavy-duty aluminum foil, wrap 2 cups soaked chips in 8 by 4½-inch foil packet. (Make sure chips do not poke holes in sides or bottom of packet.) Repeat with remaining 2 cups chips. Cut 2 evenly spaced 2-inch slits in top of each packet.

3a. **For a charcoal grill:** Open bottom vent halfway. Light large chimney starter half filled with charcoal briquettes (3 quarts). When top coals are partially covered with ash, pour into steeply banked pile against 1 side of grill. Place wood chip packets on coals. Set cooking grate in place, cover, and open lid vent half-way. Heat grill until hot and wood chips are smoking, about 5 minutes.

3b. For a gas grill: Remove cooking grate and place wood chip packets directly on primary burner. Set cooking grate in place, turn all burners to high, cover, and heat grill until hot and wood chips are smoking, about 15 minutes. Turn primary burner to medium-high and turn other burner(s) off. (Adjust primary burner [or, if using 3-burner grill, primary burner and second burner] as needed to maintain grill temperature around 325 degrees.)

4. Clean and oil cooking grate. Place roast on cooler side of grill. Cover (positioning lid vent over roast if using charcoal) and cook until pork has dark, rosy crust, about 2 hours. During final 20 minutes of grilling, adjust oven rack to lower-middle position and heat oven to 325 degrees.

5. For the barbecue sauce: Whisk all ingredients in bowl until smooth. Measure out ½ cup sauce for cooking; set aside remaining sauce for tossing with pork.

6. Transfer pork to large roasting pan and brush evenly with the ½ cup sauce for cooking. Cover pan tightly with foil and transfer to oven. Roast until fork slips easily in and out of meat, 2 to 3 hours.

7. Remove pork from oven and let rest, still covered with foil, for 1 hour. When cool enough to handle, unwrap pork and pull meat into thin shreds, discarding excess fat and gristle. Toss pork with reserved sauce and serve.

INDOOR PULLED PORK WITH SWEET AND TANGY BARBECUE SAUCE

Serves 6 to 8 | boneless pork butt roast

WHY THIS RECIPE WORKS We wanted moist, shreddable meat with deep smoke flavor and the flavorful dark crust known as bark—all done indoors. To mimic the moist heat of a grill, we covered the pork for the first part of the oven time, trapping steam. We uncovered it for the remainder of the time to help the meat develop a substantial crust. Liquid smoke infused our brine with the flavor of the outdoors. If the pork is enhanced, do not brine in step 1. Sweet paprika can be substituted for the smoked paprika. Covering the pork with parchment paper and then aluminum foil prevents the mustard from eating holes in the foil. You can substitute 2 cups of your favorite barbecue sauce thinned with ½ cup of the defatted pork cooking liquid for the sauce in step 5.

PORK
- 1 cup table salt for brining
- ½ cup plus 2 tablespoons sugar, divided
- 3 tablespoons plus 2 teaspoons liquid smoke, divided
- 5 pounds boneless pork butt roast, trimmed and cut in half horizontally
- ¼ cup yellow mustard
- 2 tablespoons smoked paprika
- 2 tablespoons pepper
- 2 teaspoons table salt
- 1 teaspoon cayenne pepper

SAUCE
- 1½ cups ketchup
- ¼ cup molasses
- 2 tablespoons Worcestershire sauce
- 1 tablespoon hot sauce
- ½ teaspoon table salt
- ½ teaspoon pepper

1. For the pork: Dissolve 1 cup salt, ½ cup sugar, and 3 tablespoons liquid smoke in 4 quarts cold water in large container. Submerge pork in brine, cover, and refrigerate for 1½ to 2 hours.

2. While pork brines, combine mustard and remaining 2 teaspoons liquid smoke in bowl; set aside. Combine paprika, pepper, salt, cayenne, and remaining 2 tablespoons sugar in second bowl; set aside.

3. Adjust oven rack to lower-middle position and heat oven to 325 degrees. Set wire rack in aluminum foil–lined rimmed baking sheet. Remove pork from brine and thoroughly pat dry with paper towels. Rub mustard mixture over entire surface of each piece of pork. Sprinkle entire surface of each piece with paprika mixture. Place pork on prepared wire rack. Place piece of parchment paper over pork, then cover with sheet of foil, sealing edges to prevent moisture from escaping. Roast pork for 3 hours.

4. Remove pork from oven; discard foil and parchment. Carefully pour off liquid in bottom of sheet into fat separator and reserve for sauce. Return pork to oven and roast, uncovered, until well browned and tender and meat registers 200 degrees, about 1½ hours. Transfer pork to dish, tent with foil, and let rest for 20 minutes.

5. For the sauce: While pork rests, pour ½ cup defatted cooking liquid from fat separator into medium bowl; whisk in all sauce ingredients.

6. Using 2 forks, shred pork into bite-size pieces. Toss with 1 cup sauce and season with salt and pepper to taste. Serve, passing remaining sauce separately.

Pork Gyro

VARIATION

Indoor Pulled Pork with Lexington Vinegar Barbecue Sauce

Substitute 1 cup cider vinegar, ½ cup ketchup, ½ cup water, 1 tablespoon sugar, ¾ teaspoon salt, ¾ teaspoon red pepper flakes, and ½ teaspoon pepper for sauce ingredients. Whisk all ingredients into ½ cup defatted cooking liquid as directed in step 5.

PORK GYRO

Serves 8 | boneless pork butt roast

WHY THIS RECIPE WORKS Without using the traditional setup of a live fire and/or a rotating spit, we managed to mimic the typical cooking method of this Greek American favorite in just three steps. To jump-start the cooking and preserve moisture, we first covered the pork, which we marinated in a garlic, oil, and spice mixture, in aluminum foil and steamed it in a 350-degree oven. Uncovering the pork and continuing to roast it helped dry out its exterior. Finally, a stint under the broiler gave the meat a crisp, well-charred crust. We cooked it to 160 degrees so we could slice it thinly for making sandwiches, as is traditional. We made the most of the broiler's heat by toasting pita breads while the meat rested. A cooling homemade tzatziki sauce finished everything off right.

GYRO

    1 (4-pound) boneless pork butt roast, trimmed
    ½ cup plus 1 tablespoon extra-virgin olive oil, divided
    6 garlic cloves, minced
  1½ tablespoons dried oregano
  1½ tablespoons kosher salt, for marinade
    1 tablespoon ground coriander
    1 tablespoon paprika
    2 teaspoons pepper
    8 (8-inch) pita breads
    1 romaine lettuce heart (6 ounces), sliced thin
    1 small red onion, halved and sliced thin
       Lemon wedges

TZATZIKI

    1 English cucumber, halved lengthwise and seeded, divided
  1½ cups plain Greek yogurt
    2 tablespoons extra-virgin olive oil
    1 tablespoon lemon juice
    1 tablespoon chopped fresh dill
  1½ teaspoons kosher salt
    1 large garlic clove, minced
    ½ teaspoon pepper

1. For the gyro: Slice pork lengthwise into 4 equal steaks, about 1 inch thick (if steaks are thicker than 1 inch, press them with your hand to 1-inch thickness). Place pork in 1-gallon zipper-lock bag. Whisk ½ cup oil, garlic, oregano, salt, coriander, paprika, and pepper together in bowl. Add marinade to bag with pork. Seal bag and turn to distribute marinade evenly. Refrigerate for at least 1 hour or up to 24 hours.

2. Adjust oven rack 6 inches from broiler element and heat oven to 350 degrees. Line rimmed baking sheet with aluminum foil and set wire rack in sheet. Remove pork from marinade and place on prepared wire rack; discard marinade.

3. Cover sheet tightly with foil and transfer to oven. Roast until pork registers 100 degrees, about 40 minutes. Remove sheet from oven and carefully remove foil so steam escapes away from you. Return sheet to oven and continue to roast until pork registers 160 degrees, 20 to 25 minutes longer.

4. For the tzatziki: While pork roasts, shred 1 cucumber half on large holes of box grater. Combine shredded cucumber, yogurt, oil, lemon juice, dill, salt, garlic, and pepper in bowl. Refrigerate until ready to serve. Slice remaining cucumber thin and set aside.

5. Leave sheet in oven and turn on broiler. Broil until pork is well browned on top side only, about 10 minutes. Transfer pork to carving board and let rest for 5 minutes.

6. Brush 1 side of pitas with remaining 1 tablespoon oil. Place 4 pitas oiled side up on now-empty wire rack. Broil until pitas are soft and lightly toasted, about 1 minute. Repeat with remaining 4 pitas. Slice pork crosswise very thin. Toss pork with accumulated juices on carving board. Divide pork evenly among pitas and top with lettuce, onion, sliced cucumber, and tzatziki. Serve with lemon wedges.

HOMEMADE SAUSAGES AND PEPPERS

Serves 4 to 6 | boneless pork butt roast

WHY THIS RECIPE WORKS Store-bought Italian sausages vary widely, so for more reliable results, we made our own in the food processor. Grinding our own meat gave us control over the fat content; we started with carefully trimmed pork butt and then incorporated fatty salt pork. We found that a 70:30 ratio of meat to fat made for the juiciest, most flavorful sausages. After adding traditional Italian seasonings, we shaped the mixture into rough sausage links without fussy casings. We browned the sausages on all sides and simmered them with peppers and onions in a simple tomato sauce to build flavor. Tangy balsamic vinegar counterbalanced the sweet peppers. Make sure to rinse the salt pork well; otherwise, the sausages will be too salty. You should have about 2 pounds of meat once the pork butt has been trimmed. Serve these sausages as is or in toasted buns.

12 ounces salt pork, rind removed, cut into ½-inch pieces

3 pounds boneless pork butt roast, pulled apart at seams, trimmed, and cut into ½-inch pieces

2 green or red bell peppers, cored and quartered lengthwise

2 onions, quartered through root end

¾ teaspoon baking soda

3 garlic cloves, peeled and smashed

2 teaspoons dried oregano, divided

1½ teaspoons fennel seeds, cracked

½ teaspoon pepper

¼ teaspoon red pepper flakes

1 tablespoon vegetable oil

¼ cup tomato paste

½ cup chicken broth

1 tablespoon balsamic vinegar

1. Rinse salt pork and pat dry with paper towels. Arrange salt pork and pork butt separately in single layer in rimmed baking sheet. Freeze until very firm and starting to harden around edges but still pliable, about 45 minutes.

2. Working in batches, use food processor fitted with slicing disk to process bell peppers and onions until thinly sliced; set aside.

3. Fit now-empty processor with chopping blade. Sprinkle baking soda evenly over pork butt. Working in 6 batches, pulse pork butt in processor until ground into ⅛-inch pieces, about 10 pulses, stopping to redistribute meat as needed; transfer to large bowl.

4. Pulse salt pork, garlic, 1½ teaspoons oregano, fennel seeds, pepper, and pepper flakes in again-empty processor to smooth paste, about 30 seconds, scraping down sides of bowl as needed. Transfer salt pork mixture to bowl with pork butt and knead with your hands until well combined.

5. Divide sausage mixture into 12 lightly packed balls, then gently shape into 5 by 1-inch cylinders. Refrigerate sausages until ready to cook. (Sausages can be covered and refrigerated for up to 1 day.)

6. Heat oil in 12-inch nonstick skillet over medium heat until shimmering. Brown half of sausages on all sides, about 10 minutes; transfer to plate. Repeat with remaining sausages.

7. Pour off all but 1 tablespoon fat from skillet, add tomato paste and remaining ½ teaspoon oregano, and cook until fragrant, about 30 seconds. Stir in bell peppers, onions, and broth.

8. Nestle sausages into vegetable mixture along with any accumulated juices and bring to simmer. Reduce heat to low, cover, and simmer until sausages and vegetables are tender, about 15 minutes. Stir in vinegar and season with salt and pepper to taste. Serve.

RAGÙ BIANCO

Serves 4 to 6 | boneless pork butt roast

WHY THIS RECIPE WORKS Tomatoes didn't show up in Italian ragus until the 1800s. To take things back, our white ragu (ragù bianco) skips tomatoes in favor of bright lemon and rich cream. We ensured plenty of savoriness in this lighter sauce by creating fond twice. We first browned finely chopped pancetta, onion, and fennel in a Dutch oven and then added water and a touch of cream to create a braising liquid. A pork shoulder, which we halved crosswise to make cooking faster and shredding easier, simmered in this liquid in the oven, where a second fond formed on the sides of the pot. After scraping this second fond into the sauce, we added plenty of lemon juice before incorporating the pasta. You can substitute tagliatelle for the pappardelle, if desired.

4 ounces pancetta, chopped

1 large onion, chopped fine

1 large fennel bulb, 2 tablespoons fronds chopped, stalks discarded, bulb halved, cored, and chopped fine, divided

4 garlic cloves, minced

1½ teaspoons table salt, plus salt for cooking pasta

2 teaspoons minced fresh thyme

1 teaspoon pepper

⅓ cup heavy cream

1 (1½-pound) boneless pork butt roast, well trimmed and cut in half across grain

1½ teaspoons grated lemon zest plus ¼ cup juice (2 lemons)

12 ounces pappardelle

2 ounces Pecorino Romano cheese, grated (1 cup), plus extra for serving

1. Adjust oven rack to middle position and heat oven to 350 degrees. Cook pancetta and ⅔ cup water in Dutch oven over medium-high heat, stirring occasionally, until water has evaporated and dark fond forms on bottom of pot, 8 to 10 minutes. Add onion and fennel bulb and cook, stirring occasionally, until vegetables soften and start to brown, 5 to 7 minutes. Stir in garlic, salt, thyme, and pepper and cook until fragrant, about 30 seconds.

2. Stir in cream and 2 cups water, scraping up any browned bits. Add pork and bring to boil over high heat. Cover, transfer to oven, and cook until pork is tender, about 1½ hours. Transfer pork to large plate and let cool for 15 minutes. Cover pot so fond will steam and soften. Using spatula, scrape browned bits from sides of pot and stir into sauce. Stir in lemon zest and juice.

3. While pork cools, bring 4 quarts water to boil in large pot. Using 2 forks, shred pork into bite-size pieces, discarding any large pieces of fat or connective tissue. Return pork and any juices to Dutch oven. Cover and keep warm.

Ragù Bianco

cooking, we used half of our crumbs to absorb the excess liquid in the casserole. Then we uncovered the pot, added the remaining crumbs, and let the dish cook until they were crisp. If you can't find fresh French garlic sausage, Irish bangers or bratwurst may be substituted.

   2 tablespoons table salt for brining
   1 pound (2½ cups) dried cannellini beans, picked over and rinsed
   2 celery ribs
   4 sprigs fresh thyme
   1 bay leaf
1½ pounds fresh French garlic sausage
   4 ounces salt pork, rinsed
  ¼ cup vegetable oil, divided
1½ pounds boneless pork butt roast, cut into 1-inch chunks
   1 large onion, chopped fine
   2 carrots, peeled and cut into ¼-inch pieces
   4 garlic cloves, minced
   1 tablespoon tomato paste
  ½ cup dry white wine
   1 (14.5-ounce) can diced tomatoes
   4 cups chicken broth
   4 large slices hearty white sandwich bread, torn into rough pieces
  ½ cup chopped fresh parsley

4. Add pasta and 1 tablespoon salt to boiling water and cook, stirring occasionally, until al dente. Reserve 2 cups cooking water, then drain pasta and add it to Dutch oven. Add Pecorino and ¾ cup reserved cooking water and stir until sauce is slightly thickened and cheese is fully melted, 2 to 3 minutes. If desired, stir in remaining reserved cooking water, ¼ cup at a time, to adjust sauce consistency. Season with salt and pepper to taste and sprinkle with fennel fronds. Serve immediately, passing extra Pecorino separately.

FRENCH PORK AND WHITE BEAN CASSEROLE

Serves 8 to 10 | boneless pork butt roast

WHY THIS RECIPE WORKS Though it may look humble, traditional cassoulet requires ingredients that can be difficult to find in the U.S. and a whole lot of love and effort. The traditional version is a masterpiece, but we wanted to add a simple braise that combined pork and white beans to our repertoire, too. We used the even, constant heat of the oven for most of the cooking so that the cook would be largely off-duty. To replace the common luxury addition of duck confit, we used salt pork, which provided all the necessary richness. Pork shoulder fit the bill as the requisite stewing pork. We opted to keep the fresh French garlic sausage. A crispy bread-crumb crust covers the braise. To achieve crispness even with covered

1. Dissolve salt in 3 quarts cold water in large bowl or container. Add beans and soak at room temperature for 8 to 24 hours. Drain and rinse well.

2. Adjust oven rack to lower-middle position and heat oven to 300 degrees. Using kitchen twine, tie together celery, thyme sprigs, and bay leaf. Place sausage and salt pork in medium saucepan and add cold water to cover by 1 inch; bring to boil over high heat. Reduce heat to simmer and cook for 5 minutes. Transfer sausage to cutting board; let cool slightly, then cut into 1-inch pieces. Remove salt pork from water; set aside.

3. Heat 2 tablespoons oil in Dutch oven over medium-high heat until just smoking. Add sausage and brown on all sides, 8 to 12 minutes; transfer to bowl. Add pork shoulder and brown on all sides, 8 to 12 minutes total. Add onion and carrots; cook, stirring constantly, until onion is translucent, about 2 minutes. Add garlic and tomato paste and cook, stirring constantly, until fragrant, about 30 seconds. Return sausage to pot; add wine, scraping up any browned bits. Cook until slightly reduced, about 30 seconds. Stir in tomatoes, celery bundle, and reserved salt pork.

4. Stir in broth and beans, pressing beans into even layer. If any beans are completely exposed, add up to 1 cup water to submerge (beans may still break surface of liquid). Increase heat to high, bring to simmer, and cover; transfer pot to oven.

Cook until beans are tender, about 1½ hours. Discard celery bundle and salt pork. (Alternatively, dice salt pork and return it to casserole.) Using wide spoon, skim fat from surface and discard. Season with salt and pepper to taste. Increase oven temperature to 350 degrees and bake, uncovered, for 20 minutes.

5. Meanwhile, pulse bread and remaining 2 tablespoons oil in food processor until crumbs are no larger than ⅛ inch, 8 to 10 pulses. Transfer to bowl, add parsley, and toss to combine. Season with salt and pepper to taste.

6. Sprinkle ½ cup bread-crumb mixture evenly over casserole; bake, covered, for 15 minutes. Remove lid and bake 15 minutes longer. Sprinkle remaining bread-crumb mixture over casserole and bake until topping is golden brown, about 30 minutes. Let rest for 15 minutes before serving.

FEIJOADA

Serves 6 to 8 | boneless pork butt roast

WHY THIS RECIPE WORKS This Brazilian black bean and pork stew is traditionally loaded with a bevy of pork cuts, as well as pig parts such as feet, ears, tail, and snout. Considered one of Brazil's national dishes, it's as much an event as it is a meal. For a version with fewer cuts of meat that still felt celebratory, we used three pork cuts that packed a punch and required minimal prep work: boneless pork butt roast, bacon, and smoky linguiça sausage. We discovered that a little baking soda gave the stew a more striking color because it helped the black beans keep their dark hue; without it, the beans turned grayish. A homemade hot sauce was a traditional accompaniment that brought pleasing heat to the finished braise and cut through its richness.

STEW

- 1 (3½- to 4-pound) boneless pork butt roast, pulled apart at seams, trimmed, and cut into 1½-inch pieces
- 3 tablespoons vegetable oil, divided
- 4 slices bacon, chopped fine
- 1 onion, chopped fine
- ½ teaspoon table salt, divided
- 4 garlic cloves, minced
- 1 tablespoon chili powder
- 1 teaspoon ground cumin
- 1 teaspoon ground coriander
- 7 cups water
- 1 pound (2½ cups) dried black beans, picked over and rinsed
- 2 bay leaves
- ⅛ teaspoon baking soda
- 1 pound linguiça sausage, cut into ½-inch pieces

HOT SAUCE

- 2 tomatoes, cored, seeded, and chopped fine
- 1 onion, chopped fine
- 1 small green bell pepper, stemmed, seeded, and chopped fine
- 1 jalapeño chile, stemmed, seeded, and minced
- ⅓ cup white wine vinegar
- 3 tablespoons extra-virgin olive oil
- 1 tablespoon minced fresh cilantro
- ½ teaspoon table salt

1. **For the stew:** Adjust oven rack to lower-middle position and heat oven to 325 degrees. Pat pork dry with paper towels and season with salt and pepper. Heat 1 tablespoon oil in Dutch oven over medium-high heat until just smoking. Add half of pork and brown well on all sides, 7 to 10 minutes; transfer to large bowl. Repeat with 1 tablespoon oil and remaining pork. Add bacon to fat left in pot and cook over medium heat until crispy, 5 to 7 minutes.

2. Stir in remaining 1 tablespoon oil, onion, and ¼ teaspoon salt and cook until onion is softened, about 5 minutes. Stir in garlic, chili powder, cumin, and coriander and cook until fragrant, about 30 seconds. Stir in water, beans, bay leaves, baking soda, remaining ¼ teaspoon salt, and pork and any accumulated juices and bring to simmer. Cover, transfer pot to oven, and cook for 1½ hours. Remove pot from oven and stir in linguiça. Cover, return pot to oven, and cook until meat and beans are fully tender, about 30 minutes.

3. **For the hot sauce:** While the stew cooks, combine all ingredients in bowl and let sit at room temperature until flavors meld, about 30 minutes. (Sauce can be refrigerated for up to 2 days.)

4. Remove pot from oven and discard bay leaves. (Stew can be refrigerated for up to 2 days; add water as needed to loosen consistency when reheating.) Season with salt and pepper to taste. Serve with hot sauce.

CHILE VERDE CON CERDO

Serves 6 to 8 | boneless pork butt roast

WHY THIS RECIPE WORKS Chile verde is a vibrant Mexican stew of pork simmered in a tangy tomatillo and green chile sauce. Braising is a cooking technique that's more or less the same everywhere, so we followed our standard approach: We gently braised the pork in the oven and allowed the meat's fat and collagen to thoroughly break down, making it supple. To build a savory fond, we browned the pork trimmings rather than dry out the surface of the meat itself. Broiling the tomatillos, poblanos, jalapeño, and garlic concentrated their flavors and added welcome smokiness. Seasoning the chili with warm spices and sugar softened its acidity and heat.

Chile Verde con Cerdo

Omitting broth and/or water minimized the amount of liquid in the pot, so that the salsa—the only source of liquid—reduced to a tight, flavorful sauce. If your jalapeño is shorter than 3 inches long, you may wish to use two. If fresh tomatillos are unavailable, substitute three (11-ounce) cans of tomatillos, drained, rinsed, and patted dry; broil as directed. Serve with white rice and/or warm corn tortillas.

- 1 (3½- to 4-pound) boneless pork butt roast, trimmed and cut into 1½-inch pieces, trimmings reserved
- 1 tablespoon plus 1 teaspoon kosher salt, divided
- 1 cup water
- 1½ pounds tomatillos, husks and stems removed, rinsed well and dried
- 5 poblano chiles, stemmed, halved, and seeded
- 1 large onion, peeled, cut into 8 wedges through root end
- 5 garlic cloves, unpeeled
- 1 jalapeño chile, stemmed and halved
- 1 tablespoon vegetable oil
- 1 teaspoon dried oregano
- 1 teaspoon ground cumin
- ⅛ teaspoon ground cinnamon
  Pinch ground cloves
- 2 bay leaves
- 2 teaspoons sugar
- 1 teaspoon pepper
- ½ cup minced fresh cilantro, plus extra for serving
  Lime wedges

1. Toss pork pieces with 1 tablespoon salt in large bowl. Cover and refrigerate for 1 hour. Meanwhile, chop pork trimmings coarse. Transfer to Dutch oven. Add water and bring to simmer over high heat. Cook, adjusting heat to maintain vigorous simmer and stirring occasionally, until all liquid evaporates and trimmings begin to sizzle, about 12 minutes. Continue to cook, stirring frequently, until dark fond forms on bottom of pot and trimmings have browned and crisped, about 6 minutes longer. Using slotted spoon, discard trimmings. Pour off all but 2 tablespoons fat; set aside pot.

2. Adjust 1 oven rack to lower-middle position and second rack 6 inches from broiler element and heat broiler. Line rimmed baking sheet with aluminum foil. Place tomatillos, poblanos, onion, garlic, and jalapeño on prepared sheet and drizzle with oil. Arrange chiles skin side up. Broil until chile skins are blackened and vegetables begin to soften, 10 to 13 minutes, rotating sheet halfway through broiling. Transfer poblanos, jalapeño, and garlic to cutting board.

3. Turn off broiler and heat oven to 325 degrees. Transfer tomatillos, onion, and any accumulated juices to food processor. When poblanos, jalapeño, and garlic are cool enough to handle,

remove and discard skins (it's OK if some small bits of chile skin remain). Remove seeds from jalapeño and reserve. Add poblanos, jalapeño, and garlic to processor. Pulse until mixture is coarsely pureed, about 10 pulses, scraping down sides of bowl as needed. If spicier chili is desired, add reserved jalapeño seeds and pulse 3 times.

4. Heat reserved fat in Dutch oven over medium heat until just shimmering. Add oregano, cumin, cinnamon, and cloves and cook, stirring constantly, until fragrant, about 30 seconds. Stir in tomatillo mixture, bay leaves, sugar, pepper, and remaining 1 teaspoon salt, scraping up any browned bits. Stir in pork and bring to simmer. Cover, transfer to oven, and cook until pork is tender, about 1½ hours, stirring halfway through cooking.

5. Remove pot from oven and let sit, covered, for 10 minutes. Discard bay leaves. Using heatproof rubber spatula, scrape browned bits from sides of pot. Stir in any fat that has risen to top of chili. Stir in cilantro; season with salt and pepper to taste. Serve, passing lime wedges and extra cilantro separately.

PRESSURE-COOKER SHREDDED PORK TACOS

Serves 6 to 8 | boneless pork butt roast

WHY THIS RECIPE WORKS Tender shredded pork butt makes for a flavorful and indulgent taco filling. When we used an electric pressure cooker, the pieces of pork became so tender during cooking that we didn't even need to shred them; they simply broke down when we stirred. Orange juice and zest, chipotle chile in adobo, and a halved onion (which we removed after cooking) gave the pork a spiced and floral aroma and flavor. To crisp the meat after cooking, we simply cooked it uncovered until the liquid evaporated so the meat could brown. Some lime juice, added at the end, enhanced the bright citrus notes. Cilantro and thinly sliced radishes added freshness, color, and crunch to our tacos.

- 1 (3- to 4-pound) boneless pork butt roast, pulled apart at seams, trimmed, and cut into 2-inch pieces
- 6 (3-inch) strips orange zest plus ½ cup juice
- 2 onions (1 halved through root end, 1 chopped fine)
- 1 tablespoon minced canned chipotle chile in adobo sauce
- 1 tablespoon minced fresh oregano or 1 teaspoon dried
- 1 tablespoon sugar
- 1 teaspoon ground cumin
- 1 teaspoon table salt
- ½ teaspoon pepper
- 1 bay leaf

Sous Vide Char Siu

2 tablespoons lime juice, plus lime wedges for serving
18 (6-inch) corn tortillas, warmed
Fresh cilantro leaves
Thinly sliced radishes

1. Combine pork, orange zest and juice, halved onion, chipotle, oregano, sugar, cumin, salt, pepper, and bay leaf in electric pressure cooker.

2. Lock lid in place and close pressure release valve. Select high pressure cook function and cook for 25 minutes. Turn off pressure cooker and let pressure release naturally for 15 minutes. Quick-release any remaining pressure, then carefully remove lid, allowing steam to escape away from you.

3. Discard orange zest, onion halves, and bay leaf. Let braising liquid settle, then skim excess fat from surface using large spoon. Cook pork, uncovered, using highest sauté or browning function until liquid is mostly reduced, 20 to 30 minutes. Continue to cook, stirring occasionally to break up pork, until liquid has completely evaporated and pork begins to crisp around edges, about 10 minutes. Stir lime juice into pork and season with salt and pepper to taste. Serve pork with warm tortillas, cilantro, radishes, chopped onion, and lime wedges.

SOUS VIDE CHAR SIU

Serves 8 to 10 | boneless pork butt roast
Sous vide time: 12 to 16 hours

WHY THIS RECIPE WORKS The smell of fatty, sweet, slow-roasted char siu is familiar to anyone who frequents Chinatown. "Char siu" literally means "fork roast," since it is usually skewered with long forks and roasted over a fire. We wanted pork that struck a balance between chewy, juicy, and just tender. An extended cooking time facilitated by sous vide rendered just enough collagen to tenderize the meat without having it fall apart. A quick glaze and broil made the pork fragrant and deliciously shellacked. To help give the pork its traditional vibrant color, we used red food dye and pink curing salt, though neither are required. Pink curing salt #1, which can be purchased online or in stores specializing in meat curing, is a mixture of table salt and nitrites; it is also called Prague Powder #1, Insta Cure #1, or DQ Curing Salt #1. Serve in steamed buns or over rice.

1 cup soy sauce
1 cup sugar
¾ cup hoisin sauce
½ cup Shaoxing Chinese rice wine or dry sherry
¼ cup grated fresh ginger
2 tablespoons toasted sesame oil
4 garlic cloves, minced
1 tablespoon red food coloring (optional)
2 teaspoons five-spice powder
½ teaspoon ground white pepper
⅛ teaspoon pink curing salt (optional)
1 4-pound boneless pork butt roast, trimmed
¾ cup honey

1. Whisk soy sauce; sugar; hoisin; rice wine; ginger; sesame oil; garlic; food coloring, if using; five-spice powder; and pepper together in large bowl. Measure out 1 cup marinade and set aside in refrigerator. Whisk pink curing salt, if using, into remaining marinade.

2. Slice pork crosswise into ¾-inch-thick steaks. Add steaks to marinade with pink salt and toss to coat. Cover and refrigerate for at least 10 hours or up to 16 hours.

3. Using sous vide circulator, bring water to 149°F in 7-quart container.

4. Remove steaks from marinade, letting excess drip off. Divide pork between two 1-gallon zipper-lock freezer bags. Seal bags, pressing out as much air as possible. Gently lower bags into prepared water bath until steaks are fully submerged, and then clip top corner of each bag to side of water bath container,

allowing remaining air bubbles to rise to top of bag. Reopen 1 corner of zipper, release remaining air bubbles, and reseal bag. Cover and cook for at least 12 hours or up to 16 hours.

5. Whisk honey and reserved marinade together in medium saucepan. Cook over medium heat, stirring frequently, until reduced to about 1 cup, 4 to 8 minutes.

6. Adjust oven rack 6 inches from broiler element and heat broiler. Set wire rack in aluminum foil–lined rimmed baking sheet and spray with vegetable spray. Transfer steaks to prepared rack and pat dry with paper towels. Brush top of steaks with half of glaze and broil until mahogany, 2 to 6 minutes per side. Brush both sides of steaks with remaining glaze and broil until top is dark mahogany and lightly charred, 2 to 6 minutes. Transfer steaks, charred side up, to cutting board and let rest for 10 minutes. Slice steaks crosswise ½ inch thick and serve.

To make ahead: Pork can be rapidly chilled in ice bath (see page 8) and then refrigerated in zipper-lock bags after step 4 for up to 3 days. To reheat, return sealed bags to water bath set to 149°F for 30 minutes and then proceed with step 5.

Red Wine–Braised Pork Chops

RED WINE–BRAISED PORK CHOPS

Serves 4 | blade-cut pork chops

WHY THIS RECIPE WORKS Pork chops are less cumbersome to braise than a roast and easy to transform into a flavorful dinner. We trimmed fit-for-braising blade-cut pork chops of excess fat and connective tissue to prevent them from buckling during braising and cooking unevenly. Although the move was at first utilitarian, there was an added benefit. We used those trimmings to build a rich braising liquid with depth and sweetness and a bit of tang from a combination of red wine and ruby port. Fresh ginger and allspice infused the braising liquid with warm notes, while woodsy thyme complemented the wine. When the chops were done braising, we quickly reduced the braising liquid to a tasty sauce, enriched with a swirl of butter. The pork scraps can be removed when straining the sauce in step 4 and served alongside the chops.

3 tablespoons table salt for brining
4 (10- to 12-ounce) bone-in blade-cut pork chops, 1 inch thick
2 teaspoons vegetable oil
2 onions, halved and sliced thin
5 sprigs fresh thyme, plus ¼ teaspoon minced
2 garlic cloves, peeled
2 bay leaves
1 (½-inch) piece ginger, peeled and crushed
⅛ teaspoon ground allspice
½ cup red wine

¼ cup ruby port
2 tablespoons plus ½ teaspoon red wine vinegar, divided
1 cup chicken broth
2 tablespoons unsalted butter
1 tablespoon minced fresh parsley

1. Dissolve salt in 1½ quarts cold water in large container. Submerge chops in brine, cover, and refrigerate for 1 hour.

2. Adjust oven rack to lower-middle position and heat oven to 275 degrees. Remove chops from brine and pat dry with paper towels. Trim off cartilage, meat cap, and fat opposite rib bones. Cut trimmings into 1-inch pieces. Heat oil in Dutch oven over medium-high heat until shimmering. Add trimmings and brown on all sides, 6 to 9 minutes.

3. Reduce heat to medium and add onions, thyme sprigs, garlic, bay leaves, ginger, and allspice. Cook, stirring occasionally, until onions are golden brown, 5 to 10 minutes. Stir in wine, port, and 2 tablespoons vinegar and cook until reduced to thin syrup, 5 to 7 minutes. Add broth, spread pork trimmings mixture into even layer, and bring to simmer. Arrange chops on top of pork trimmings mixture and cover; transfer pot to oven.

4. Cook until meat is tender, 1¼ to 1½ hours. Remove from oven and let chops rest in pot, covered, for 30 minutes. Transfer chops to serving platter and tent with aluminum foil. Strain

braising liquid through fine-mesh strainer set over large bowl; discard solids. Transfer braising liquid to fat separator. Let liquid settle for 5 minutes.

5. Wipe now-empty pot clean with paper towels. Return defatted braising liquid to pot and cook over medium-high heat until reduced to 1 cup, 3 to 7 minutes. Off heat, whisk in butter, minced thyme, and remaining ½ teaspoon vinegar. Season with salt and pepper to taste. Pour sauce over chops, sprinkle with parsley, and serve.

FILIPINO PORK ADOBO

Serves 4 | blade-cut pork chops

WHY THIS RECIPE WORKS Adobo may be the national dish of the Philippines, but thanks to the country's melting-pot ancestry, the recipes are remarkably varied. What most agree on, however, is that the dish is easy to prepare, the ingredients are few, and the finished product—tender meat napped with a rich, bracing sauce—boasts bold, well-developed flavors. The vinegary sauce that is the hallmark of this dish is traditionally used as both a marinade and a braising liquid, but we found that marinating with the acidic sauce made the meat mushy; plus, our sauce was already so flavorful that any flavor benefit of the marinade was lost anyway. Instead, we built savory flavor by browning bone-in blade-cut pork chops, whose high fat content protected them from drying out during braising. As the pork simmered, the sauce reduced and thickened, creating a silky, creamy, coating consistency. Serve with rice.

SAUCE
1 (14-ounce) can coconut milk
6 tablespoons cider vinegar
¼ cup low-sodium soy sauce
8 garlic cloves, peeled and smashed
2 bay leaves
1 teaspoon pepper

PORK
4 (6- to 8-ounce) bone-in blade-cut pork chops, ¾ inch thick, trimmed
1 tablespoon vegetable oil
1 scallion, sliced thin

1. **For the sauce:** Bring all ingredients to simmer in medium saucepan over medium heat. Cook, stirring occasionally, until thickened and reduced to 2 cups, about 15 minutes.

2. Strain sauce through fine-mesh strainer into bowl and season with pepper to taste.

3. **For the pork:** Adjust oven rack to middle position and heat oven to 300 degrees. Cut 2 slits, about 2 inches apart, through outer layer of fat and silverskin on each chop. Pat chops dry with paper towels and season with pepper. Heat oil in Dutch oven over medium-high heat until just smoking. Brown half of chops, about 4 minutes per side; transfer to plate. Repeat with remaining chops; transfer to plate.

4. Stir sauce into now-empty pot, scraping up any browned bits. Return chops and any accumulated juices to pot and bring to simmer over medium heat. Cover, transfer pot to oven, and cook until chops are tender and fork slips easily in and out of meat, 1 to 1½ hours.

5. Remove pot from oven. Transfer chops to serving dish and let rest for 5 to 10 minutes. Using large spoon, skim excess fat from surface of sauce. Adjust consistency with hot water as needed. Season with salt and pepper to taste. Spoon 1 cup sauce over chops and sprinkle with scallion. Serve, passing remaining sauce separately.

SLOW-COOKER BRAISED PORK CHOPS WITH CAMPFIRE BEANS

Serves 4 | blade-cut pork chops
Cooking time: 7 to 8 hours on low or 4 to 5 hours on high

WHY THIS RECIPE WORKS Beans are a classic accompaniment to pork dishes, in different iterations in different regions, and we wanted to complement our meaty pork chops with a side of hearty barbecue beans. To create a deeply flavored sauce, we used a small amount of ketchup and molasses for the necessary sweetness and viscosity and then amped up the flavor with onion, chili powder, and liquid smoke. Canned pinto beans turned creamy and tender in the slow cooker as they absorbed the smoky flavor of the sauce and helped to braise the chops. We chose blade-cut pork chops, which contain a good amount of fat and connective tissue that help them stay tender and juicy during hours of braising. To really wake up the flavor of the beans before serving, we stirred in cider vinegar and Dijon mustard for a hit of piquant freshness. You will need an oval slow cooker for this recipe.

Grilled Lemongrass Pork Chops

1 onion, chopped fine
2 garlic cloves, minced
1 teaspoon chili powder
1 tablespoon vegetable oil
2 (15-ounce) cans pinto or navy beans, rinsed
¼ cup ketchup
1 tablespoon molasses
½ teaspoon liquid smoke
4 (8- to 10-ounce) bone-in blade-cut pork chops, ¾ inch thick, trimmed
1 tablespoon cider vinegar
1 tablespoon Dijon mustard
2 scallions, sliced thin

1. Microwave onion, garlic, chili powder, and oil in bowl, stirring occasionally, until onion is softened, about 5 minutes; transfer to slow cooker. Stir in beans, ketchup, molasses, and liquid smoke.

2. Cut 2 slits about 2 inches apart through fat on edges of each pork chop. Season chops with salt and pepper and nestle into slow cooker. Cover and cook until pork is tender, 7 to 8 hours on low or 4 to 5 hours on high.

3. Transfer chops to serving dish, tent with aluminum foil, and let rest for 5 minutes. Using large spoon, skim fat from surface of sauce. Transfer 1 cup beans to bowl and mash with potato masher until mostly smooth. Stir mashed beans, vinegar, mustard, and scallions into remaining beans, and season with salt and pepper to taste. Serve chops with beans.

GRILLED LEMONGRASS PORK CHOPS

Serves 4 | blade-cut pork chops

WHY THIS RECIPE WORKS Juicy pork chops, charred until crisp and imbued with aromatic lemongrass, are a favorite across Vietnam and are pleasingly easy to re-create at home on a hot grill. The key is the marinade, comprised of lemongrass with garlic and shallot and the signature fish sauce–sugar combination, which adds a sweet-savory profile. Because quick marinades don't penetrate far into meat, we opted for thin pork chops (around ½ inch thick) in order to maximize the surface area of the pork. Blade chops, with their intramuscular fat, stayed juicy on the grill. The salt from the soy sauce and fish sauce acted as a quick brine for the pork, further preventing drying out. The molasses-like sweetness from brown sugar helped the meat pick up deep browning in the relatively short time the meat was on the grill. We served the chops with nuoc cham, an intensely flavored mixture of lime juice, fish sauce, sugar, water, garlic, and chiles.

3 lemongrass stalks, trimmed to bottom 6 inches and chopped
1 shallot, chopped coarse
¼ cup packed brown sugar
3 garlic cloves, chopped
2 tablespoons fish sauce
1 tablespoon vegetable oil
2 teaspoons soy sauce
8 (6-ounce) bone-in blade-cut pork chops, ½ inch thick, trimmed
1 recipe Nuoc Cham (recipe follows)

1. Process lemongrass, shallot, sugar, and garlic in food processor until finely ground, about 30 seconds, scraping down sides of bowl as needed. Add fish sauce, oil, and soy sauce and process until incorporated, about 10 seconds; transfer to bowl.

2. Using kitchen shears, snip interior portion of fat surrounding loin muscle of each chop in 2 places, about 2 inches apart. Rub chops all over with lemongrass mixture and transfer to 13 by 9-inch baking dish. Cover and refrigerate for at least 1 hour or up to 24 hours, turning pork once or twice.

3a. For a charcoal grill: Open bottom vent completely. Light large chimney starter mounded with charcoal briquettes (7 quarts). When top coals are partially covered with ash, pour evenly over grill. Set cooking grate in place, cover, and open lid vent completely. Heat grill until hot, about 5 minutes.

3b. For a gas grill: Turn all burners to high, cover, and heat grill until hot, about 15 minutes. Leave all burners on high.

4. Clean and oil cooking grate. Place chops on grill and cook (covered if using gas), without moving them, until well charred on first side, 3 to 5 minutes. Flip chops and continue to cook on second side until well charred and meat registers 140 degrees, 2 to 4 minutes. Transfer chops to serving platter, tent with aluminum foil, and let rest for 5 minutes. Serve, passing nuoc cham separately.

Nuoc Cham
Makes 1 cup; serves 4

3 tablespoons sugar, divided
1 small Thai chile, stemmed and minced
1 garlic clove, minced
⅔ cup hot water
5 tablespoons fish sauce
¼ cup lime juice (2 limes)

Using mortar and pestle (or on cutting board using flat side of chef's knife), mash 1 tablespoon sugar, Thai chile, and garlic to fine paste. Transfer to medium bowl and add hot water and remaining 2 tablespoons sugar. Stir until sugar is dissolved. Stir in fish sauce and lime juice.

ARM SHOULDER

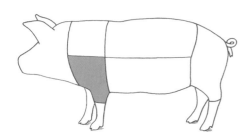

THE LOWER ARM END OF the pork's shoulder is triangular in shape with a tapered end where it moves down toward the foreleg. It has less intramuscular fat and marbling than the blade shoulder and is also tougher. Unlike the pork butt, which usually comes with just a fat cap, roasts from this area are commonly sold with the skin on, which can become a delightfully crisp treat on a picnic shoulder roast. A roast from the arm shoulder can be used in a recipe for pork butt (see page 215) but that's not always recommended, as it is a tougher cut with a more complex structure of muscle, fat, connective tissue, and some unpleasant sinewy parts. It's also very commonly cured and smoked to create a lovely picnic ham (not to be confused with true hams from the rear of the cow; see page 305).

Picnic Shoulder Roast

Cost: ▪▫▫▫ Flavor: ▪▪▫▫
Best cooking methods: roast, braise, slow cook, grill roast
Texture: tough but mostly tender once slow-cooked
Alternative names: fresh picnic, shoulder arm picnic, pork shoulder

While we consider the pork butt (see page 215) the more versatile pork shoulder roast, picnic shoulder does have great merits, especially when we want that crispy, crackling exterior. It's also more affordable, so it's an economical choice for slow-cooking applications. Boneless picnic roasts are often sold in netting to keep the pieces together, and once that netting is removed, the meat unfolds into a somewhat uneven layer, so it's a bit trickier to cook than pork butt. That's why when we call for picnic roast, we always call for its bone-in form, weighing about 8 pounds; we prefer the butt for boneless applications.

SHOULDER CHEAT SHEET

Still find pork shoulder confusing as a whole? Here's a quick list summarizing the differences and similarities between a pork butt roast and a picnic shoulder roast so you know what to pick up when shopping.

PORK BUTT	PICNIC SHOULDER
Also known as "pork shoulder" or "Boston butt"	Also known as "pork shoulder" or "picnic roast"
Well marbled with fat	Typically has less intramuscular fat and marbling
Often has fat cap	Frequently sold with skin on
Rectangular, uniform shape	Tapered, triangular shape
Sold bone-in or boneless	Sold bone-in or boneless

When to Use Pork Butt

Since pork butt has more fat marbling throughout the meat and a more uniform shape, it's the best cut for stewing and braising as well as for making fall-apart-tender pulled pork for a barbecue or for tacos. If a recipe calls for a choice between pork shoulder and pork butt, we highly recommend choosing pork butt.

When to Use Picnic Shoulder

Pork shoulder is our cut of choice when making a pork roast that traditionally has crackling-crisp skin (such as our Cuban-Style Grill-Roasted Pork on page 243), since the cut is sold with the skin on. We only cook this roast whole—we don't cut it for stew, and we don't "pull it," as for pulled pork or tacos.

Smoked Picnic Ham

Cost: ▪▫▫▫ Flavor: ▪▪▫▫
Best cooking methods: bake
Texture: rich and meaty
Alternative names: smoked pork shoulder

When smoked and cured, the picnic shoulder is a delicious ham. Well, it's a ham in name only. Like true cured hams from the pig's back end, it comes fully cooked, but it has a lot more fat than those hams so it needs extra cooking (beyond heating through) for it to be palatable. It's worth it: Once it's cooked further, the economical picnic ham becomes intensely flavorful with an incredibly desirable crackling exterior. When cooking for a crowd, we buy a larger smoked picnic ham with the bone in, but you can also purchase a shankless roast (sometimes, confusingly, called smoked Boston butt).

PORK PERNIL

Serves 8 to 10 | picnic shoulder roast

WHY THIS RECIPE WORKS Pernil is a Puerto Rican dish of heavily seasoned, long-cooked pork with supremely crispy skin. We used a bone-in pork picnic shoulder and rubbed it with a flavorful herb and spice paste called a sofrito. We started cooking the pork skin side down in a roasting pan—first covered, to create steam, and then uncovered. We then moved the roast to a V-rack with the skin side up to start drying out the skin, and finally we cranked up the heat and finished the roast at 500 degrees for just long enough to render the skin a deep mahogany brown. This skin-focused approach reaped big rewards. A quick sauce of pan drippings, cilantro, and lime finished the dish. Crimp the foil tightly over the edges of the roasting pan in step 2 to minimize evaporation.

1½ cups chopped fresh cilantro leaves and stems, divided
1 onion, chopped coarse
¼ cup kosher salt
¼ cup olive oil
10 garlic cloves, peeled
2 tablespoons pepper
1 tablespoon dried oregano
1 tablespoon ground cumin
1 (7-pound) bone-in skin-on pork picnic shoulder roast
1 tablespoon grated lime zest plus ⅓ cup juice (3 limes)

1. Pulse 1 cup cilantro, onion, salt, oil, garlic, pepper, oregano, and cumin in food processor until finely ground, about 15 pulses, scraping down sides of bowl as needed. Pat pork dry with paper towels and rub cilantro mixture all over pork. Wrap pork in plastic wrap and refrigerate for at least 12 hours or up to 24 hours.

2. Adjust oven rack to lower-middle position and heat oven to 450 degrees. Pour 8 cups water into large roasting pan. Unwrap pork and place skin side down in pan. Cover pan tightly with aluminum foil and roast for 1½ hours. Remove foil, reduce oven temperature to 375 degrees, and roast for 2½ hours.

3. Remove pan from oven. Spray V-rack with vegetable oil spray. Gently slide metal spatula under pork to release skin from pan. Using 2 large wads of paper towels, grasp ends of pork and transfer to V-rack, skin side up. Wipe skin dry with paper towels. Set V-rack with pork in roasting pan. If pan looks dry, add 1 cup water. Roast until pork registers 195 degrees, about 1 hour. (Add water as needed to keep bottom of pan from drying out.)

4. Line rimmed baking sheet with foil. Remove pan from oven. Transfer V-rack with pork to prepared sheet, place sheet in oven, and increase oven temperature to 500 degrees. Roast until pork skin is well browned and crispy (when tapped lightly with tongs,

skin will sound hollow), 15 to 30 minutes, rotating sheet halfway through roasting. Transfer pork to carving board and let rest for 30 minutes.

5. Meanwhile, pour juices from pan into fat separator. Let liquid settle for 5 minutes, then pour 1 cup defatted juices into large bowl (if necessary, add water to equal 1 cup). Whisk lime zest and juice and remaining ½ cup cilantro into juices.

6. Using sharp knife, remove skin from pork in 1 large piece. Chop skin into bite-size pieces and set aside. Trim and discard excess fat from pork. Remove pork from bone and chop coarse. Transfer pork to bowl with cilantro-lime sauce and toss to coat. Serve pork, with crispy skin on side.

GLAZED PICNIC HAM (SMOKED SHOULDER)

Serves 12 to 16 | smoked picnic ham

WHY THIS RECIPE WORKS Although our picnic ham was already technically fully cooked, its extra fat meant that it needed extra cooking (not just heating through, like ham from the pig's leg) to become palatable. To create a moist environment for the fat to properly render, we placed the pork on a rack in a large roasting pan and covered it with foil. We found that slowly roasting the meat at a low temperature produced the best finished ham. A sweet, spicy glaze of brown sugar, Dijon mustard, clove, cayenne pepper, and balsamic vinegar balanced the salty richness of the meat.

1 (8- to 10-pound) bone-in smoked picnic ham
3 tablespoons dry mustard, divided
1 teaspoon pepper
1 cup packed dark brown sugar
½ cup Dijon mustard
½ cup balsamic vinegar
¼ teaspoon cayenne pepper
⅛ teaspoon ground cloves
1 tablespoon cider vinegar or water

1. Adjust oven rack to lowest position and heat oven to 325 degrees. Line large roasting pan with aluminum foil. Using sharp knife, remove skin from ham and trim fat to ¼-inch thickness. Cut slits 1 inch apart in crosshatch pattern in fat, being careful not to cut into meat. Combine 1 tablespoon dry mustard and pepper in small bowl. Rub ham all over with spice rub. Set ham on V-rack set inside prepared roasting pan. Cover pan tightly with foil. Bake until ham registers 140 degrees, 2 to 3 hours.

2. Meanwhile, bring sugar, Dijon mustard, balsamic vinegar, cayenne, cloves, and remaining 2 tablespoons dry mustard to boil in medium saucepan. Reduce heat to low and simmer until

Pork Pernil

Glazed Picnic Ham

reduced to 1 cup, 15 to 20 minutes. (Glaze can be refrigerated for up to 3 days. Microwave glaze until bubbling around edges before using.)

3. Remove ham from oven and let sit for 5 minutes. Increase oven temperature to 450 degrees. Discard foil and brush ham evenly with ½ cup glaze. Return ham to oven and bake until dark brown and caramelized, 25 to 30 minutes. Stir cider vinegar into remaining glaze. Transfer ham to carving board, tent with foil, and let rest for 30 minutes. Carve and serve with glaze.

CUBAN-STYLE GRILL-ROASTED PORK

Serves 8 to 10 | picnic shoulder roast

WHY THIS RECIPE WORKS Roast pork in Cuba is perfection: crackling-crisp skin and tender meat infused with flavor. To speed up cooking for our version, we used a combination cooking method: cooking the pork on the grill until our initial supply of coals died down, and then finishing it in the oven. To give the pork added flavor, we again combined methods, first brining the pork in a powerful solution that included two heads of garlic and orange juice, and then rubbing a flavor paste into slits cut all over the pork. Let the meat rest for a full hour before serving or it will not be as tender. Traditional accompaniments include black beans, rice, and fried plantains. Serve the pork with Mojo Sauce (recipe follows), if desired.

PORK
- 1 (7- to 8-pound) bone-in, skin-on pork picnic shoulder roast
- 3 cups sugar for brining
- 2 cups table salt for brining
- 2 garlic heads, unpeeled, cloves separated and crushed
- 4 cups orange juice (8 oranges) for brining

PASTE
- 12 garlic cloves, chopped coarse
- 2 tablespoons ground cumin
- 2 tablespoons dried oregano
- 1 tablespoon table salt
- 1½ teaspoons pepper
- 6 tablespoons orange juice
- 2 tablespoons distilled white vinegar
- 2 tablespoons vegetable oil

1. For the pork: Cut 1-inch-deep slits (1 inch long) all over roast, spaced about 2 inches apart. Dissolve sugar and salt in 6 quarts cold water in large container. Stir in garlic and orange juice. Submerge pork in brine, cover, and refrigerate for 18 to 24 hours. Remove pork from brine and pat dry with paper towels.

2. For the paste: Pulse garlic, cumin, oregano, salt, and pepper in food processor to coarse paste, about 10 pulses. With processor running, add orange juice, vinegar, and oil and process until smooth, about 20 seconds. Rub all over roast and into slits. Wrap roast in plastic wrap and let sit at room temperature for 1 hour.

3a. For a charcoal grill: Open bottom vent halfway. Light large chimney starter three-quarters filled with charcoal briquettes (4½ quarts). When top coals are partially covered with ash, pour into steeply banked pile against side of grill. Set cooking grate in place, cover, and open lid vent halfway. Heat grill until hot, about 5 minutes.

3b. For a gas grill: Turn all burners to high, cover, and heat grill until hot, about 15 minutes. Turn primary burner to medium-high and turn off other burner(s). (Adjust primary burner [or, if using 3-burner grill, primary burner and second burner] as needed to maintain grill temperature of 325 degrees.)

4. Clean and oil cooking grate. Make two ½-inch folds on long side of 18-inch length of aluminum foil to form reinforced edge. Place foil in center of cooking grate, with reinforced edge over hotter side of grill. Place roast, skin side up, on cooler side of grill so that it covers about one-third of foil. Lift and bend edges to shield sides of pork, tucking in edges. Cover (position lid vent over meat if using charcoal) and cook for 2 hours. During final 20 minutes of grilling, adjust oven rack to lower-middle position and heat oven to 325 degrees. Transfer pork to wire rack set in rimmed baking sheet. Roast pork in oven until skin is browned and crisp and meat registers 190 degrees, 3 to 4 hours.

5. Transfer roast to carving board and let rest for 1 hour. Remove skin in 1 large piece. Scrape off and discard fat from top of roast and from underside of skin. Cut meat away from bone in 3 or 4 large pieces, then slice ¼ inch thick. Cut skin into strips. Serve.

Mojo Sauce
Makes 1 cup; serves 8 to 10

- ½ cup olive oil
- 4 garlic cloves, minced to paste
- 2 teaspoons kosher salt
- ½ teaspoon ground cumin
- ¼ cup distilled white vinegar
- ¼ cup orange juice
- ¼ teaspoon dried oregano
- ⅛ teaspoon pepper

Heat oil in medium saucepan over medium heat until shimmering. Add garlic, salt, and cumin and cook, stirring, until fragrant, about 30 seconds. Remove pan from heat and whisk in vinegar, orange juice, oregano, and pepper. Transfer sauce to bowl and let cool completely. Whisk sauce to recombine before serving.

LOIN

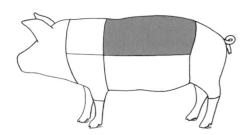

THE PORK LOIN IS THE money section of the pig. Spanning from the shoulder (see page 214) to the leg (see page 304), it includes a lot of cuts—and a lot that are universally desirable. The loin is the leanest, most tender, most fine-grained part of the animal because the back and spine area isn't worked much. It's a long primal; pigs are bred to have up to 17 ribs on each side. (By comparison, other animals in this book have up to 13.) You can buy an entire pork loin (trimmed), a tenderloin, rib roasts, or the pork loin's individual cuts and cutlets. The amount of fat and collagen varies depending on the exact cut. The only one we don't recommend is the sirloin chop, a tough, dry muscle mosaic containing loin, tenderloin, and part of the hip.

In recent decades, pigs have been bred to be leaner, so the loin, while supremely tender, can cook up drier and less flavorful than it did from pigs in the past if not treated with care, more like chicken than beef. This means we often brine pork loin, which we rarely do for beef, and sometimes we salt it. (For more information on brining lean pork, see page 10.)

In approaching the enormous pork loin, we've decided to break down its cuts as if reading a book, from left to right (or, in the case of an animal, front to back), following the loin from its tougher more flavorful end abutting the shoulder through its supremely tender center.

Blade-End Pork Rib Roast

Cost: ■■□□ Flavor: ■■■□
Best cooking methods: roast, grill roast
Texture: moist, can be chewy with fat pockets
Alternative names: pork seven-rib roast, pork five-rib roast, pork loin rib end, rib-end roast

The name makes the cut easy to identify on the long loin: It's from the front of the pork loin nearest the blade shoulder. Because of this placement it can be chewy, as its structure is more complex than other loin roasts.

But this really is stellar swine. We more often use its boneless counterpart (below), but it can be employed as a substitute for a center-cut rib roast in a pinch (see page 246), and it's glorious if slowly barbecued, tasting great kissed with smoke. It should be tied at even intervals since it doesn't sit evenly like other rib roasts.

Boneless Blade-End Pork Loin

Cost: ■■□□ Flavor: ■■■□
Best cooking methods: roast, grill roast
Texture: tender once adequately cooked
Alternative names: blade roast, blade-end roast

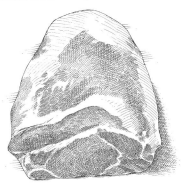

This boneless version of the blade-end pork rib roast has great flavor. Center-cut pork loin (see page 248) is the norm in pork loin recipes, and we default to it and use it quite often because that user-friendly cut is much easier to find at the supermarket. But unless we're stuffing it, we actually would choose to roast the blade-end roast in most cases (and it can be used in all of our recipes that call for boneless pork loin). At a good price point when you *can* find it, this cut has great richness and is nicely tender when cooked properly.

Country-Style Ribs

Cost: ■■□□ Flavor: ■■■□
Best cooking methods: braise, stew, stir fry, grill
Texture: meaty, tender
Alternative names: country ribs

These ribs aren't the ones used for those finger-licking, fall-off-the-bone barbecue ribs that the pig is known for (although you can certainly grill and sauce them; see page 256). They're equally great for other reasons, though. These meaty, tender bone-in or boneless ribs are cut from the upper side of the rib cage from the fatty blade end of the loin, so they contain a mix of darker meat from the shoulder and lighter meat from the loin. Butchers usually cut them into individual ribs and package several ribs together. The combination of good rib flavor and fat and easy shape means these ribs are incredibly versatile—almost like well-marbled pork chops—and perhaps underutilized. But not by us. They can be braised and shredded for pasta sauce (see page 256), pounded flat and grilled (see page 256) for a fork-and-knife cut of meat, or sliced for stir-fries (see page 263). Don't be alarmed if a single package of country-style ribs contains a motley assortment of pieces. It's common to find small and large bones, dark and light meat, and varied marbling.

Center-Cut Pork Rib Roast

Cost: ▪▪◻◻ **Flavor:** ▪▪◻◻
Best Cooking Methods: roast, grill roast
Texture: lean, tender
Alternative names: rack of pork, pork loin rib half, center-cut pork roast

This is the prime rib of pork, the lamb rack of pork—minus the expense. Although slightly less flavorful, it's more uniform, easier to cook evenly, and easier to carve than the blade-end pork rib roast. This mild, fairly lean roast consists of a single muscle with a protective fat cap. It may be cut with anywhere from five to eight ribs. Because the bones (and nearby fat) are still attached, we find this roast a better option than the center-cut loin roast (which is cut from the same muscle but lacks the bones and fat) for roasting for a special occasion or holiday, or for grill roasting. Crosshatched, that fat cap becomes deliciously crisp, makes a beautiful presentation, and also bastes the meat. We often cook this roast much like prime rib, removing the ribs, salting it, reattaching the ribs, and roasting it low and slow for even cooking—then we broil it to crisp the fat cap. It's fairly easy to carve because of its cylindrical shape, uniform for a rib roast. Rib roasts can be cut into large slabs between the ribs to create thick bone-in chops or the roast can be cut off the bone and carved.

MORE BONES ABOUT IT

In addition to the rib bones, a pork rib roast can come with the chine bone attached. Sometimes it's called a backbone. Below see how to identify it. You should ask your butcher to remove as much of this bone as possible to facilitate carving. (Sometimes butchers merely crack it between the ribs).

With Chine Bone

Without Chine Bone

MEAT PREP *Preparing Center-Cut Rib Roast*

1. Using sharp knife, remove roast from bones, running knife down length of bones and closely following contours.

2. Trim surface fat to ¼ inch and score with crosshatch slits; rub roast with salt mixture and refrigerate.

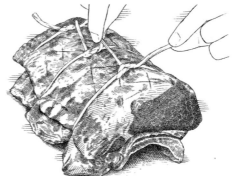

3. Place roast back on ribs; using kitchen twine, tie roast to bones between ribs.

MEAT PREP *Cutting Pork Rib Roast into Chops*

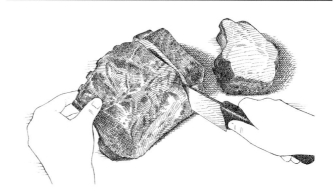

Stand roast on carving board with bones pointing up and cut between bones into separate chops.

MEAT PREP *Cutting Pork Rib Roast into Thin, Boneless Slices*

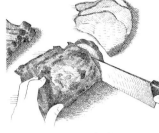

1. Holding tip of bones with 1 hand, use sharp knife to cut along the rib to sever meat from bones.

2. Set meat cut side down on carving board and slice against grain into ½-inch-thick slices.

Pork Rib Chops

Cost: ■■□□□   Flavor: ■■□□□

Best cooking methods: pan sear, grill, braise
Texture: juicy, tender but with good chew
Alternative names: none

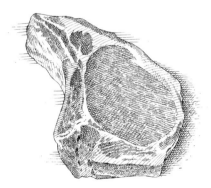

As the name suggests, these pork chops are cut from the rib section of the loin, so they have a relatively high fat content and are unlikely to dry out during cooking. They're the most flavorful of the loin chops and the most impressive to receive, seared until golden, in the center of a plate. These chops are easily identified by the bone that runs along one side and the one large eye of loin muscle. Note that rib chops are also sold boneless; in fact, most boneless chops you'll find are cut from the rib chop. The bone-in version is our tippity-top chop.

THE THICK AND THIN OF PORK CHOPS

Chops can be sold thick-cut or thin-cut, the thicker ones taking more time to cook (obviously) and seeming a bit more special, and the thinner ones being more casual and weeknight-ready. You shouldn't approach the chops the same. Thin chops can be simply seared quickly on both sides; thick chops require more special treatment to be perfect. We presalt them, bring up their internal temperature in a low oven (you can also achieve this by cooking them sous vide), and then sear them in a smoking pan, much like thick-cut steaks (see page 77), for a deep crust and a juicy interior.

CURLY CHOPS

When searing pork chops, you may have noticed that they can buckle in the pan, especially thinner ones. In addition to being unattractive, it results in uneven browning since all of the chop can't be in contact with the pan. When exposed to the high heat of the pan, the ring of fat and connective tissue that surrounds the exterior tightens, causing the curling. Here's how we prevent this.

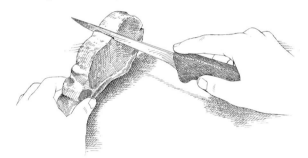

Cut slits about 2 inches apart into fat and underlying silverskin, opposite bone of chop.

Crown Roast

Cost: ■■▫▫▫   Flavor: ■■▫▫▫
Best cooking methods: roast
Texture: lean, tender
Alternative names: crown rib roast

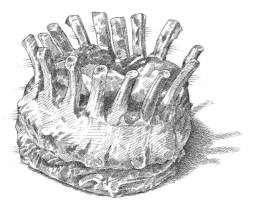

Perhaps the prettiest treatment for pork and thus a good center-piece, this cut is fashioned by tying two bone-in center-cut rib or center-cut loin roasts together. We find that a crown roast with 16 to 20 ribs is the best choice, as smaller roasts are more difficult to cook evenly. And look out: Because of this roast's shape and size, it's prone to overcooking. You can't cook it like any old larger roast. As you'll see in our recipe for Crown Roast of Pork (page 266), we do not cook it directly on the bottom of a roasting pan because the perimeter overcooks by the time the interior ring is done.

MEAT PREP *Tying a Crown Roast*

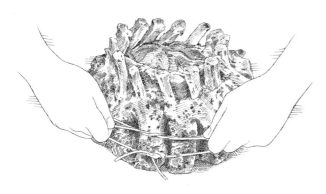

Make 2 loops around widest part of roast with kitchen twine and tie securely.

Center-Cut Pork Loin

Cost: ■■▫▫▫   Flavor: ■■▫▫▫
Best cooking methods: roast, grill roast
Texture: juicy, tender
Alternative names: center-cut pork roast

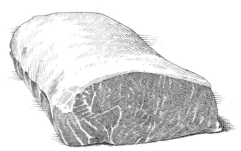

Essentially the back of the pig, this evenly shaped roast might be the most popular pork roast and the one we call for the most. It has less fat than a rib or a blade roast, and while its pristine—almost white when cooked—meat isn't robust, it is juicy and tender. (That said, while we call for center-cut pork loin in pork loin recipes, if you have a choice at the store, buy a boneless blade-end pork loin [see page 245]—the cuts can be used interchangeably, but the latter is very hard to find, so our recipes assume you won't.) Because this cut is so lean, we nearly always brine it to help it stay moist during roasting (see page 10). If you can, buy a center-cut roast with a decent fat cap; this will serve as a protectant. Because of its even cylindrical shape, this roast is particularly great for butterflying, stuffing, and tying back together, and it fits nicely in most vessels.

We strongly prefer the flavor of natural pork, but lean, mild pork loin is very often enhanced (injected with a salt solution; see page 213). If that's the case, you'll need to reduce the amount of salt in the recipe. We give instruction in headnotes when necessary.

BONELESS PORK CHOPS

We call for boneless pork chops quite often in our recipes—they're easy to cook evenly and they're weeknight-friendly. They're often cut from rib chops (see page 247), sometimes from center-cut chops. But when we want to ensure that they are thick and evenly weighted, we skip buying ready-made chops and cut them ourselves from a center-cut pork loin. These are the most consistent boneless chops.

TWO WAYS TO STUFF A LOIN

Stuffing a pork loin points up its flavor. Round and long, the roast can be filled via a pocket (which will present as a line of filling down the middle) or double butterflied and rolled (which will present as a spiral of filling). When butterflying a skinnier roast, a single bisecting cut suffices. But to open up a wide pork roast, we make two parallel cuts to expose more surface area to seasoning.

MEAT PREP *Pocket Method*

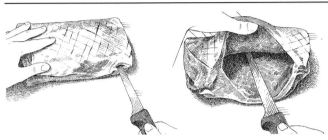

1. Starting ½ inch from end of roast, insert knife into middle of roast, with blade parallel to work surface.

2. Cut along side of pork, stopping ½ inch short of other end. Pull open roast and use gentle strokes to cut deeper pocket.

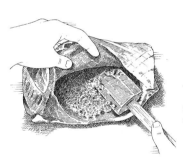

3. Spread filling evenly into pocket, making sure it reaches corners.

4. Fold roast over to original shape and tie at even intervals along its length with 3 pieces of kitchen twine.

MEAT PREP *Double Butterfly*

1. Holding chef's knife parallel to cutting board, insert knife one-third of way up from bottom of roast and cut horizontally, stopping ½ inch before edge. Open up flap.

2. Make another horizontal cut into thicker portion of roast about ½ inch from bottom, stopping about ½ inch before edge. Open up this flap, smoothing out rectangle of meat.

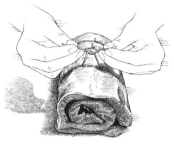

3. Spread open pork loin with filling.

4. Starting from short side, fold roast back together like business letter (keeping fat on outside) and tie at 1-inch intervals.

Center-Cut Pork Chops

Cost: ▪▪▫▫ Flavor: ▪▪▫▫
Best cooking methods: pan sear, grill
Texture: lean, tender, can dry out
Alternative names: top loin chops, loin chops

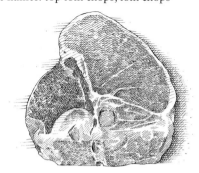

These chops can be identified by the bone that divides the loin meat from the tenderloin muscle, which makes them look like smaller versions of T-bone steaks. The lean tenderloin section cooks more quickly than the loin section, making these chops a challenge. They have good flavor, but since they contain less fat than the rib chops, they are not quite as moist. They're better suited to the grill because the bone prevents them from lying flat when they're cooked in a skillet. We do not use them in our recipes but they are common to find.

Pork Tenderloin

Cost: ▪▪▫▫ Flavor: ▪▫▫▫
Best cooking methods: broil, roast, pan sear, sous vide, stir fry
Texture: lean, delicate
Alternative names: none

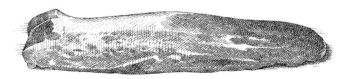

Pork tenderloin is cut from the back of the pork loin. Much like a beef tenderloin, pork tenderloin is supertender, superlean—and not superflavorful. A sauce or a flavored butter is often recommended to dress up the plain roast (see pages 20–25 for some ideas). But if you prize tenderness it's the cut for you, and also one of the simplest to cook. Tenderloin is tops in convenience: It cooks much faster and easier than other roasts because it's so small, usually weighing just about 1 pound, and evenly shaped. It's a great candidate for broiling. Overcook it, though, and its texture is ruined, as it has no lubricating marbling.

Tenderloins are often sold two to a package. Like center-cut pork loin, many tenderloins sold in the supermarket are enhanced; look at labels and buy one that has no ingredients other than pork if you can. You need to remove the silverskin from a tenderloin before cooking it. This inedible membrane will cause the small roast to buckle and cook unevenly. A boning knife makes this easy.

MEAT PREP *Trimming Silverskin*

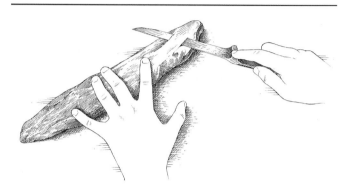

Slip sharp thin knife under silverskin and trim off tenderloin.

WEEKDAY WARRIOR

Because of its size, quick-cooking pork tenderloin is one of the few roasts you can present on a weekday with ease. But it's also super weeknight-friendly because of what it can transform into. Cut a tenderloin into meaty steaks with more surface for browning (see page 284), into pork cutlets for crispy schnitzel (see page 283), or into medallions to be cooked with a surrounding sauce (see page 283). They all cook quickly and easily. Here we show how to fashion each of them.

MEAT PREP *Steaks*

1. Pound tenderloin to even thickness according to recipe.

2. Slice tenderloin in half crosswise.

MEAT PREP *Cutlets*

1. Cut tenderloin in half at about 20-degree angle. Using same angle, cut each half in half again, cutting tapered tail pieces slightly thicker than middle pieces.

2. Place pork between 2 sheets of parchment paper or plastic wrap and pound to even thickness between ⅛ and ¼ inch.

MEAT PREP *Medallions*

1. Cut tenderloin crosswise into 1½-inch medallions.

2. Score tapered end pieces and fold in half at incision; tie to make sure top and bottom surfaces are flat.

Baby Back Ribs

Cost: ■■⬜⬜ Flavor: ■■⬜⬜
Best cooking methods: roast, grill, barbecue
Texture: lean, can dry out
Alternative names: loin back ribs, riblets

Baby back ribs are cut from the section of the rib cage closest to the backbone. Loin center-cut roasts and chops come from the same part of the pig, which explains why baby back ribs can be expensive, and popular. This location also explains why baby back ribs are much leaner than spareribs (found near the belly; see page 293)—and why they need special attention to keep from drying out on the grill. They either need to be cooked low and slow, like barbecue, or according to a trick we use for our Grilled Glazed Baby Back Ribs (page 289) where we simmer them in water before putting them on the grill to cut down the time they require. We like to buy meaty ribs—racks as close to 2 pounds as possible—to provide substantial, satisfying portions. Sometimes a recipe will call for removing the ribs' thin protective membrane; see page 293 for steps to do so.

BARBECUE GLAZED PORK ROAST

Serves 6 | blade-end pork rib roast

WHY THIS RECIPE WORKS The marriage of smoke and swine may be divine, but rarely does it make for an elegant centerpiece. We wanted big barbecue flavor in a sliceable, dinner party–worthy roast. A blade-end bone-in pork rib roast was the perfect cut. It has great marbling (and thus great flavor), a nice fat cap (which let the roast stay on the grill longer), bones that help the meat stay moist, and the sliceable presentation we were looking for. Basting the roast with the sauce (in a disposable pan on the grill) for the last half of cooking gave the pork a flavorful shellacked crust. Look for a roast with a ¼-inch fat cap; if you end up with a thicker fat cap, trim it to ¼ inch. For a spicier roast, use the larger amount of hot sauce. If you'd like to use wood chunks instead of wood chips when using a charcoal grill, substitute 2 medium wood chunks, soaked in water for 1 hour, for the wood chip packets.

Barbecue Glazed Pork Roast

1 (4- to 5-pound) blade-end or center-cut bone-in
   pork rib roast, chine bone removed
⅓ cup packed brown sugar, divided
1 tablespoon kosher salt
1½ teaspoons pepper
1 teaspoon paprika
½ teaspoon garlic powder
2 cups wood chips
1½ cups ketchup
1½ cups apple juice
3 tablespoons cider vinegar
1 tablespoon Worcestershire sauce
1 tablespoon yellow mustard seeds
1–2 teaspoons hot sauce
1 (13 by 9-inch) disposable aluminum pan

1. Pat roast dry with paper towels. Using sharp knife, cut ½-inch-deep slits, spaced ½ inch apart, in crosshatch pattern through fat cap. Combine 1 teaspoon sugar, salt, pepper, paprika, and garlic powder in small bowl and rub all over roast, making sure to rub spice mixture into crosshatch. Wrap roast with plastic wrap and refrigerate for 6 to 24 hours. Just before grilling, soak wood chips in water for 15 minutes, then drain. Using large piece of heavy-duty aluminum foil, wrap soaked chips in 8 by 4 ½-inch foil packet. (Make sure chips do not poke holes in sides or bottom of packet.) Cut 2 evenly spaced 2-inch slits in top of packet.

2a. For a charcoal grill: Open bottom vent completely and arrange 3 quarts unlit charcoal briquettes over half of grill. Light large chimney starter filled with charcoal briquettes (6 quarts). When top coals are partially covered with ash, pour evenly over unlit coals. Place wood chip packet on coals. Set cooking grate in place, cover, and open lid vent completely. Heat grill until hot and wood chips are smoking, about 5 minutes.

2b. For a gas grill: Remove cooking grate and place wood chip packet directly on primary burner. Set grate in place, turn all burners to high, cover, and heat grill until hot and wood chips are smoking, about 15 minutes. Leave primary burner on high and turn off other burner(s).

3. Clean and oil cooking grate. Place roast meat side up on cooler side of grill, with rib bones facing fire. Cook, covered, until meat registers 90 to 100 degrees, about 1 hour.

4. Meanwhile, whisk ketchup, juice, vinegar, Worcestershire, mustard seeds, hot sauce, and remaining sugar in disposable pan until sugar dissolves. Place disposable pan on grill and transfer roast to disposable pan with glaze. Spoon glaze over roast. Continue to cook on cooler side of grill, covered, basting roast with glaze every 15 minutes, until meat registers 140 degrees, 45 minutes to 1¼ hours.

5. Remove disposable pan from grill; tent roast with foil and let rest in glaze for 30 minutes. Transfer roast to carving board and pour glaze into serving vessel, skimming off fat as needed. (You should have about 2 cups glaze.) Carve roast in between ribs into thick chops. Serve, passing glaze separately.

GRILL-ROASTED PORK LOIN

Serves 6 | boneless blade-end pork loin

WHY THIS RECIPE WORKS Succulent pork roast with a peppered crust and smoke-flavored meat is an impressive dinner. But in the dry heat, the lean loin loses much of its moisture before it's done on the grill. Brining keeps the meat juicy (and even more flavorful). We used a two-step grilling process, searing the roast directly over hot coals for a nice crust and finishing it gently over indirect heat. If using enhanced pork, do not brine in step 1 and add 1 tablespoon salt to the pepper. If you'd like to use wood chunks instead of wood chips when using a charcoal grill, substitute two medium wood chunks, soaked in water for 1 hour, for the wood chip packet.

¼ cup salt for brining
1 (2½- to 3-pound) boneless blade-end pork loin roast, trimmed and tied at 1½-inch intervals
2 tablespoons extra-virgin olive oil
1 tablespoon pepper
2 cups wood chips

1. Dissolve salt in 2 quarts cold water in large container. Submerge roast in brine, cover, and refrigerate for 1 to 1½ hours. Remove roast from brine and pat dry with paper towels. Rub roast with oil, then sprinkle with pepper. Let sit at room temperature for 1 hour.

2. Just before grilling, soak wood chips in water for 15 minutes, then drain. Using large piece of heavy-duty aluminum foil, wrap soaked chips in 8 by 4½-inch foil packet. (Make sure chips do not poke holes in sides or bottom of packet.) Cut 2 evenly spaced 2-inch slits in top of packet.

3a. For a charcoal grill: Open bottom vent halfway. Light large chimney starter three-quarters filled with charcoal briquettes (4½ quarts). When top coals are partially covered with ash, pour evenly over half of grill. Place wood chip packet on coals. Set cooking grate in place, cover, and open lid vent halfway. Heat grill until hot and wood chips are smoking, about 5 minutes.

3b. For a gas grill: Remove cooking grate and place wood chip packet directly on primary burner. Set grate in place, turn all burners to high, cover, and heat grill until hot and wood chips are smoking, about 15 minutes. Leave primary burner on high and turn off other burner(s). (Adjust primary burner [or, if using 3-burner grill, primary burner and second burner] as needed to maintain grill temperature of 300 to 325 degrees.)

4. Clean and oil cooking grate. Place roast fat side up on hotter side of grill and cook (covered if using gas) until well browned, 10 to 12 minutes, turning as needed. Slide roast to cooler side of grill, parallel with and as close as possible to heat. Cover (position lid vent over roast if using charcoal) and cook for 20 minutes.

Rotate roast 180 degrees, cover, and cook until pork registers 140 degrees, 10 to 30 minutes. Transfer roast to carving board, tent with foil, and let rest for 20 minutes. Remove twine and slice ½ inch thick. Serve.

SMOKED PORK LOIN WITH DRIED-FRUIT CHUTNEY

Serves 6 | boneless blade-end pork loin

WHY THIS RECIPE WORKS For a recipe that satisfied that meaty, smoky pork craving without a full day of grilling, we looked to quicker-cooking pork loin. Letting the roast sit overnight rubbed with a mixture of salt and brown sugar seasoned it, kept it juicy, and ensured a caramelized exterior. Low-and-slow indirect cooking was key for an evenly cooked, juicy roast, so we poured lit coals over a layer of unlit coals to create a fire that wouldn't require refueling. We strongly prefer natural pork in this recipe. If using enhanced pork, omit the salt in step 1. This recipe requires refrigerating the salted meat for at least 6 hours or up to 24 hours before cooking. A blade-end roast is our preferred cut here, but a center-cut boneless loin roast can also be used. Except for mesquite, any variety of wood chip will work; we prefer hickory. If you'd like to use wood chunks instead of wood chips when using a charcoal grill, substitute two medium wood chunks, soaked in water for 1 hour, for the wood chip packet.

PORK
½ cup packed light brown sugar
¼ cup kosher salt
1 (3½- to 4-pound) boneless blade-end pork loin roast, trimmed
2 cups wood chips
1 (13 by 9-inch) disposable aluminum roasting pan (if using charcoal) or 1 (9-inch) disposable aluminum pie plate (if using gas)

CHUTNEY
¾ cup dry white wine
½ cup dried apricots, diced
½ cup dried cherries
¼ cup white wine vinegar
3 tablespoons water
3 tablespoons packed light brown sugar
1 shallot, minced
2 tablespoons grated fresh ginger
1 tablespoon unsalted butter
1 tablespoon Dijon mustard
1½ teaspoons dry mustard

Smoked Pork Loin with Dried-Fruit Chutney

1. **For the pork:** Combine sugar and salt in small bowl. Tie roast with twine at 1-inch intervals. Rub sugar-salt mixture evenly over entire surface of roast. Wrap roast tightly in plastic wrap, transfer to rimmed baking sheet, and refrigerate for at least 6 hours or up to 24 hours.

2. Just before grilling, soak wood chips in water for 15 minutes, then drain. Using large piece of heavy-duty aluminum foil, wrap soaked chips in 8 by 4½-inch foil packet. (Make sure chips do not poke holes in sides or bottom of packet.) Cut 2 evenly spaced 2-inch slits in top of packet.

3a. **For a charcoal grill:** Open bottom vent halfway. Arrange 25 unlit charcoal briquettes over half of grill and place disposable pan filled with 3 cups water on other side of grill. Light large chimney starter two-thirds filled with charcoal briquettes (4 quarts). When top coals are partially covered with ash, pour evenly over unlit briquettes. Place wood chip packet on coals. Set cooking grate in place, cover, and open lid vent halfway. Heat grill until hot and wood chips are smoking, about 5 minutes.

3b. **For a gas grill:** Remove cooking grate and place wood chip packet directly on primary burner. Place disposable pie plate filled with 1 inch water directly on other burner(s). Set grate in place, turn all burners to high, cover, and heat grill until hot and wood chips are smoking, about 15 minutes. Turn primary burner to medium and turn off other burner(s). (Adjust primary burner as needed to maintain grill temperature around 300 degrees.)

4. Clean and oil cooking grate. Unwrap roast and pat dry with paper towels. Place roast on grill directly over disposable pan about 7 inches from heat source. Cover (position lid vent over roast if using charcoal) and cook until meat registers 140 degrees, 1½ to 2 hours, rotating roast 180 degrees after 45 minutes.

5. **For the chutney:** Combine wine, apricots, cherries, vinegar, water, sugar, shallot, and ginger in medium saucepan. Bring to simmer over medium heat. Cover and cook until fruit is softened, 10 minutes. Uncover and reduce heat to medium-low. Add butter, Dijon, and dry mustard and continue to cook until slightly thickened, 4 to 6 minutes longer. Remove saucepan from heat and season chutney with kosher salt. Transfer to bowl and let stand at room temperature.

6. Transfer roast to cutting board, tent with foil, and let stand for 30 minutes. Discard twine. Slice roast ¼ inch thick and serve with chutney.

POSOLE

Serves 6 to 8 | boneless country-style ribs

WHY THIS RECIPE WORKS Recipes for New Mexican posole range from oversimplified afterthoughts to over-the-top opuses; we wanted to streamline the process while maintaining posole's complex flavor. We browned boneless pork ribs before adding them to the pot to increase their porky flavor; browning drained hominy in the ribs' rendered fat turned it sweet, toasty, and chewy and infused it with the same meaty richness. Sautéed onions and garlic pureed with the chiles created a gentle, caramelized sweetness. Serve the posole with sliced radishes and green cabbage, chopped avocado, hot sauce, and lime wedges.

¾ ounce dried ancho chiles (about 3 chiles)
8 cups chicken broth, divided
2 pounds boneless country-style pork ribs, trimmed
3 tablespoons vegetable oil, divided
3 (15-ounce) cans white hominy, rinsed
2 onions, chopped
5 garlic cloves, minced
1 tablespoon minced fresh oregano
½ teaspoon table salt
½ teaspoon pepper
1 tablespoon lime juice

1. Adjust oven rack to middle position and heat oven to 350 degrees. Place chiles on baking sheet and bake until puffed and fragrant, about 6 minutes. When chiles are cool enough to handle, remove stems and seeds. Combine chiles and 1 cup broth in medium bowl. Cover and microwave until bubbling, about 2 minutes. Let stand until softened, 10 to 15 minutes.

2. Pat pork dry with paper towels and season with salt and pepper. Heat 2 tablespoons oil in Dutch oven over medium-high heat until just smoking. Cook pork until well browned all over, about 10 minutes. Transfer pork to plate. Add hominy to now-empty pot and cook, stirring frequently, until fragrant and hominy begins to darken, 2 to 3 minutes. Transfer hominy to medium bowl.

3. Heat remaining 1 tablespoon oil in now-empty pot over medium heat until shimmering. Add onions and cook until softened, about 5 minutes. Stir in garlic and cook until fragrant, about 30 seconds. Puree onion mixture with softened chile mixture in blender. Combine remaining 7 cups broth, pureed onion-chile mixture, pork, oregano, salt, and pepper in now-empty pot and bring to boil. Reduce heat to low and simmer, covered, until meat is tender, 1 to 1½ hours. Transfer pork to clean plate. Add hominy to pot and simmer, covered, until tender, about 30 minutes. Skim fat from broth. Shred pork into bite-size pieces, discarding fat. Return pork to pot and cook until heated through, about 1 minute. Off heat, add lime juice and season with salt and pepper to taste. Serve.

SLOW-COOKER SUNDAY GRAVY

Makes about 16 cups; serves 10 to 12 | bone-in country-style ribs
Cooking time: 9 to 10 hours on low or 6 to 7 hours on high

WHY THIS RECIPE WORKS Italian gravy—the ultimate Sunday comfort supper—is a hearty tomato sauce cooked with everything meat, from meatballs to pork chops. We wanted a more modest gravy with all of the flavor of elaborate versions, so we limited ourselves to three essential meaty components. Sausage was a must for sweet, spicy complexity, and our need for something beefy was fulfilled by flank steak. What brings this sauce together, however, is a cut that braises to fall-apart tenderness. Because a large roast would be inconvenient, we turned to bone-in country-style ribs. The ribs cooked slowly until the meat fell off the bones, and the bones deepened the flavor of the sauce. We used the flavorful drippings left behind from browning the sausage to sauté our aromatics, which infused the whole dish with flavor. And a combination of drained diced tomatoes, tomato puree, and tomato paste ensured a rich, thick sauce. This makes enough gravy to sauce 3 pounds of pasta.

  1 tablespoon extra-virgin olive oil
  2 pounds hot or sweet Italian sausage, divided
  2 onions, chopped fine
  1 (6-ounce) can tomato paste
12 garlic cloves, minced
  2 tablespoons minced fresh oregano or 2 teaspoons dried
½ cup dry red wine
  1 (28-ounce) can diced tomatoes, drained
  1 (28-ounce) can tomato puree
  2 pounds bone-in country-style pork ribs, trimmed
1½ pounds flank steak, trimmed
¼ cup chopped fresh basil

1. Heat oil in Dutch oven over medium-high heat until just smoking. Brown half of sausage on all sides, about 5 minutes; transfer to slow cooker. Repeat with remaining sausage; transfer to slow cooker.

2. Add onions to fat left in pot and cook over medium heat until softened and lightly browned, 5 to 7 minutes. Stir in tomato paste, garlic, and oregano and cook until fragrant, about 1 minute. Stir in wine, scraping up any browned bits; transfer to slow cooker. Stir in tomatoes and tomato puree.

3. Season ribs and steak with salt and pepper and nestle into slow cooker. Cover and cook until pork and beef are tender and fork slips easily in and out of meat, 9 to 10 hours on low or 6 to 7 hours on high.

4. Transfer sausages, ribs, and steak to cutting board and let cool slightly. Using 2 forks, shred ribs and steak into rough 1-inch pieces; discard fat and bones. Slice sausages in half crosswise. Using large spoon, skim fat from surface of sauce. Stir in meat and sausages and season with salt and pepper to taste. Before serving, stir in 2 tablespoons basil for every 8 cups sauce.

SWEET AND TANGY GRILLED COUNTRY-STYLE PORK RIBS

Serves 4 to 6 | bone-in country-style ribs

WHY THIS RECIPE WORKS The trick to grilling country-style ribs with the bone is to remember they're not like other ribs—you need to get both kinds of meat, light and dark, to cook evenly. We started with a simple dry rub of chili powder, cayenne, salt, and brown sugar, which would encourage browning while adding a complex sweetness. Though cooking the ribs to 175 degrees delivered perfect dark meat, the light meat was woefully dry. On the flip side, pulling the ribs off the grill when they hit 135 to 140 degrees produced juicy light meat but chewy, underdone dark meat. A compromise was in order: 150 degrees. The fat in the ribs moistened the light meat enough that the slight overcooking wasn't noticeable, while the dark meat still had a little tug to it but was nevertheless tender. We basted the ribs with barbecue sauce that caramelized on them. Carefully trim the pork to reduce the number of flare-ups when the pork is grilled.

PORK

4 teaspoons packed brown sugar
1 tablespoon kosher salt
1 tablespoon chili powder
⅛ teaspoon cayenne pepper
4 pounds bone-in country-style pork ribs, trimmed

SAUCE

1 cup ketchup
5 tablespoons molasses
3 tablespoons cider vinegar
2 tablespoons Worcestershire sauce
2 tablespoons Dijon mustard
¼ teaspoon pepper
2 tablespoons vegetable oil
⅓ cup grated onion
1 garlic clove, minced
1 teaspoon chili powder
¼ teaspoon cayenne pepper

**Sweet and Tangy Grilled
Country-Style Pork Ribs**

with ¼ cup sauce for basting. Cover and cook for 6 minutes. Flip ribs and brush with remaining ¼ cup sauce for basting. Cover and continue to cook until pork registers 150 degrees, 5 to 10 minutes longer. Transfer ribs to platter, tent with foil and let rest for 10 minutes. Serve, passing reserved sauce separately.

SLOW-COOKER SPICY PORK CHILI WITH BLACK-EYED PEAS

Serves 6 | boneless country-style ribs
Cooking Time: 6 to 8 hours on low or 4 to 6 hours on high
WHY THIS RECIPE WORKS More classical versions of chili (see page 53) are a comfort-food favorite, but the formula can be applied for vibrant, healthful, flavorful twists on the norm. For this slow-cooker chili, we paired sweet potatoes with a Southern staple: earthy black-eyed peas. To preserve the bright color and flavor of the chunks of sweet potato, we wrapped them in an insulating foil packet. Pork seemed like a natural here so we added country-style ribs, which became meltingly tender. A hefty dose of bold aromatics, including chili powder and chipotle chile, ensured that this chili made a statement. Serve with your favorite chili garnishes.

2 onions, chopped fine
6 garlic cloves, minced
2 tablespoons chili powder
2 tablespoons tomato paste
2 teaspoons canola oil
1½ teaspoons minced canned chipotle chile in adobo sauce
3 (15-ounce) cans black-eyed peas, rinsed
3 cups chicken broth, divided
½ teaspoon table salt
1½ pounds boneless country-style pork ribs, trimmed of all visible fat and cut into 1½-inch pieces
1½ pounds sweet potatoes, peeled and cut into ½-inch pieces
2 tablespoons minced fresh cilantro

1. For the pork: Combine sugar, salt, chili powder, and cayenne in bowl. Pat ribs dry. Rub mixture all over ribs. Wrap ribs in plastic and refrigerate for at least 1 hour or up to 24 hours.

2. For the sauce: Whisk ketchup, molasses, vinegar, Worcestershire, mustard, and pepper together in bowl. Heat oil in medium saucepan over medium heat until shimmering. Add onion and garlic; cook until onion is softened, 2 to 4 minutes. Add chili powder and cayenne and cook until fragrant, about 30 seconds. Whisk in ketchup mixture and bring to boil. Reduce heat to medium-low and simmer for 5 minutes. Transfer ½ cup of sauce to small bowl for basting and set aside remaining sauce for serving. (Sauce can be refrigerated for up to 1 week.)

3a. For a charcoal grill: Open bottom vent halfway. Light large chimney starter filled with charcoal briquettes (6 quarts). When top coals are partially covered with ash, pour evenly over half of grill. Set cooking grate in place, cover, and open lid vent halfway. Heat grill until hot, about 5 minutes.

3b. For a gas grill: Turn all burners to high, cover, and heat grill until hot, about 15 minutes. Leave primary burner on high and turn off other burner(s). (Adjust primary burner as needed to maintain grill temperature around 350 degrees.)

4. Clean and oil cooking grate. Unwrap ribs. Place ribs on hotter side of grill and cook until well browned on both sides, 4 to 7 minutes. Move ribs to cooler side of grill and brush top side

1. Microwave onions, garlic, chili powder, tomato paste, oil, and chipotle in bowl, stirring occasionally, until onions are softened, about 5 minutes; transfer to slow cooker.

2. Process one-third of peas and 1 cup broth in blender until smooth, about 30 seconds; transfer to slow cooker. Stir in remaining peas, remaining 2 cups broth, and salt, then stir in pork. Wrap potatoes in foil packet; lay packet on top of stew. Cover and cook until pork is tender, 6 to 8 hours on low or 4 to 6 hours on high. Transfer foil packet to plate. Carefully open packet (watch for steam) and stir potatoes with any accumulated juice into chili. Stir in cilantro and season with salt and pepper to taste. Serve.

BRAISED RIBS WITH BLACK-EYED PEAS AND COLLARD GREENS

Serves 6 to 8 | boneless country-style ribs

WHY THIS RECIPE WORKS There's a simple Southern side dish in which black-eyed peas, collard greens, and a smoked ham hock are stewed together for hours until the beans are creamy, the greens are velvety soft, and the broth is suffused with the smoky sweetness of the ham. Our goal was to expand this dish into a full-blown meal with the addition of a heftier cut of meat. Country-style ribs are resilient to braising, making them a perfect, more substantial replacement for the ham hock. With this addition, the dish was flavorful, more robust, and porky, but we missed the smokiness provided by ham hocks, so we added some bacon. Problem solved. Pickled red onion was a brilliant finish, cutting through the richness and enlivening the dish.

2 pounds boneless country-style pork ribs, trimmed
1 teaspoon vegetable oil
4 ounces bacon, sliced crosswise into ¼-inch strips
1 red onion, chopped
1 large celery rib, chopped fine
6 garlic cloves, minced
1 pound (2½ cups) dried black-eyed peas, picked through and rinsed
3½ cups chicken broth
1 cup water
2 bay leaves
1 pound collard greens, stemmed and sliced thin
1 recipe Spicy Pickled Onion (recipe follows)

1. Adjust oven rack to lower-middle position and heat oven to 300 degrees. Dry ribs thoroughly with paper towels and season with salt and pepper. Heat oil in Dutch oven over medium-high heat until just smoking. Place ribs in single layer and cook, without moving them, until well browned, about 5 minutes. Flip ribs and continue to cook until brown on second side, about 4 minutes longer; transfer ribs to plate.

2. Pour off fat in pot and return to medium heat. Add bacon and cook, stirring frequently, until most of fat has rendered, about 3 minutes. Add onion and celery; cook, stirring occasionally, until softened and beginning to brown, about 6 minutes. Add garlic and cook until fragrant, about 30 seconds. Add black-eyed peas, broth, water, bay leaves, and browned ribs, bring to simmer, and cover; transfer pot to oven. Cook until black-eyed peas are tender and sharp knife slips easily in and out of meat, about 1 hour.

3. Transfer ribs to carving board and tent with aluminum foil. Stir collard greens into now-empty pot and cook until wilted and tender, 4 to 8 minutes. Discard bay leaves. Season with salt and pepper to taste. Serve with ribs and pickled onion.

Spicy Pickled Onion
Makes about 2 cups

¾ cup red wine vinegar
2 tablespoons sugar
½ teaspoon table salt
¼ teaspoon red pepper flakes
2 bay leaves
1 red onion, halved and sliced thin

Bring vinegar, sugar, salt, pepper flakes, and bay leaves to boil over medium-high heat in small saucepan. Add onion, return to boil, and cook for 1 minute. Transfer to shallow bowl and refrigerate until cooled.

FRIED BROWN RICE WITH PORK AND SHRIMP

Serves 6 | boneless country-style ribs

WHY THIS RECIPE WORKS Using short-grain brown rice puts a modern spin on fried rice and provides a hearty base to stand up to the barbecue pork, shrimp, and scrambled eggs in this dish. To balance the nuttier flavor of brown rice, we used more ginger, garlic, and soy sauce than we do for white-rice recipes. Staggering the cooking was the key to ensuring that every component was perfectly cooked—no rubbery shrimp or eggs. The superlative porkiness of boneless country-style ribs made them the best choice for this dish. We coated small pieces of pork with a sweet-spicy mixture of hoisin, honey, five-spice powder, and cayenne. We cooked the pork without moving it so it would develop maximum browning and caramelization—and therefore maximum flavor.

2 cups short-grain brown rice
¾ teaspoon table salt, divided, plus salt for cooking rice
10 ounces boneless country-style pork ribs, trimmed
1 tablespoon hoisin sauce
2 teaspoons honey
⅛ teaspoon five-spice powder
Small pinch cayenne pepper
4 teaspoons vegetable oil, divided
8 ounces large shrimp (26 to 30 per pound), peeled, deveined, tails removed, and cut into ½-inch pieces
3 eggs, lightly beaten
1 tablespoon toasted sesame oil
6 scallions, white and green parts separated and sliced thin on bias
2 garlic cloves, minced
1½ teaspoons grated fresh ginger
2 tablespoons soy sauce
1 cup frozen peas

Braised Ribs with Black-Eyed Peas and Collard Greens

5. Heat sesame oil in now-empty skillet over medium-high heat until shimmering. Add scallion whites and cook, stirring frequently, until well browned, about 1 minute. Stir in garlic and ginger and cook until fragrant and beginning to brown, 30 to 60 seconds. Add soy sauce and half of rice and stir until all ingredients are fully incorporated, making sure to break up clumps of ginger and garlic. Reduce heat to medium-low and add remaining rice, pork mixture, and peas. Stir until all ingredients are evenly incorporated and heated through, 2 to 4 minutes. Remove from heat and stir in scallion greens. Serve.

PINCHOS MORUNOS

Serves 4 | boneless country-style ribs

WHY THIS RECIPE WORKS Pinchos morunos is a dish normally served as part of a tapas spread, but it works equally well as an entrée. To develop our version of these Spanish pork kebabs, we used country-style ribs for both their convenience and their ability to remain juicy and tender when grilled in 1-inch chunks. To increase juiciness, we brined the pork for 30 minutes before cutting it into cubes and coating it with a robust spice paste that included garlic, lemon, ginger, coriander, smoked paprika, and fresh oregano. And because country-style ribs contain a mix of lighter loin meat and darker shoulder meat, we kept the light meat and dark meat on separate skewers and cooked each to its ideal temperature (140 and 155 degrees, respectively) to ensure that the light meat didn't overcook and the dark meat wasn't chewy. You will need four or five 12-inch metal skewers for this recipe. If your pork is enhanced, do not brine it in step 1.

- 3 tablespoons table salt for brining
- 2 pounds boneless country-style pork ribs, trimmed
- ¼ cup vegetable oil
- 2 tablespoons lemon juice, plus lemon wedges for serving
- 6 garlic cloves, minced
- 1 tablespoon grated fresh ginger
- 2 teaspoons minced fresh oregano, divided
- 2 teaspoons smoked paprika
- 1 teaspoon ground coriander
- 1 teaspoon table salt
- ½ teaspoon ground cumin
- ½ teaspoon pepper
- ¼ teaspoon cayenne pepper

1. Bring 3 quarts water to boil in large pot. Add rice and 2 teaspoons salt. Cook, stirring occasionally, until rice is tender, about 35 minutes. Drain well and return to pot. Cover and set aside.

2. Meanwhile, cut pork into 1-inch pieces and slice each piece against grain ¼ inch thick. Combine pork with hoisin, honey, five-spice powder, cayenne, and ½ teaspoon salt and toss to coat; set aside.

3. Heat 1 teaspoon vegetable oil in 12-inch nonstick skillet over medium-high heat until shimmering. Add shrimp in single layer and cook, without moving, until golden brown, about 90 seconds. Stir and continue to cook until opaque throughout, about 90 seconds longer. Push shrimp to 1 side of skillet. Add 1 teaspoon vegetable oil to cleared side of skillet. Add eggs to clearing and sprinkle with remaining ¼ teaspoon salt. Using rubber spatula, stir eggs gently until set but still wet, about 30 seconds. Stir eggs into shrimp and continue to cook, breaking up large pieces of egg, until eggs are fully cooked, about 30 seconds longer. Transfer shrimp-egg mixture to clean bowl.

4. Heat remaining 2 teaspoons vegetable oil in now-empty skillet over medium-high heat until shimmering. Add pork in even layer. Cook pork, without moving, until well browned, 2 to 3 minutes. Flip pork and cook, without moving, until cooked through and caramelized on second side, 2 to 3 minutes. Transfer to bowl with shrimp-egg mixture.

1. Dissolve 3 tablespoons salt in 1½ quarts cold water in large container. Submerge ribs in brine and let stand at room temperature for 30 minutes. Meanwhile, whisk oil, lemon juice, garlic, ginger, 1 teaspoon oregano, paprika, coriander, salt, cumin, pepper, and cayenne in small bowl until combined.

2. Remove pork from brine and pat dry with paper towels. Cut ribs into 1-inch chunks; place dark meat and light meat in separate bowls. Divide spice paste proportionately between bowls and toss to coat. Thread light and dark meat onto separate skewers (do not crowd pieces). Place dark meat kebabs on left side of rimmed baking sheet and light meat kebabs on right side.

3a. For a charcoal grill: Open bottom vent completely. Light large chimney starter filled with charcoal briquettes (6 quarts). When top coals are partially covered with ash, pour evenly over half of grill. Set cooking grate in place, cover, and open lid vent completely. Heat grill until hot, about 5 minutes.

3b. For a gas grill: Turn all burners to high, cover, and heat grill until hot, about 15 minutes. Leave primary burner on high and turn off other burner(s).

4. Clean and oil cooking grate. Place dark meat on hotter side of grill and cook for 6 minutes. Flip dark meat and add light meat to hotter side of grill. Cook for 4 minutes, then flip all kebabs. Continue to cook, flipping kebabs every 4 minutes, until dark meat is well charred and registers 155 degrees and light meat is lightly charred and registers 140 degrees, 4 to 8 minutes longer. Transfer to serving platter, tent with aluminum foil, and let rest for 5 minutes. Remove pork from skewers, toss to combine, sprinkle with remaining 1 teaspoon oregano, and serve, passing lemon wedges separately.

VIETNAMESE SUMMER ROLLS

Serves 4 | boneless country-style ribs

WHY THIS RECIPE WORKS Boneless country-style pork ribs add heft and flavor to the traditional noodles, fresh herbs, and mild shrimp in Vietnamese summer rolls. We used the same water for cooking the pork and the shrimp, which infused additional pork flavor into the milder shrimp, and indirect heat kept the shrimp from becoming tough. If Thai basil is unavailable, increase the mint and cilantro to 1½ cups each. A wooden surface will draw moisture away from the wrappers, so assemble the rolls directly on your counter or on a plastic cutting board. If part of the wrapper starts to dry out while you are forming the rolls, moisten it with your dampened fingers. One serving (three rolls) makes a light meal, but these rolls can also be halved crosswise using a sharp, wet knife and served as an appetizer. These rolls are best served immediately. If you like, serve Nuoc Cham (page 237) along with the Peanut-Hoisin Sauce.

Vietnamese Summer Rolls

PEANUT-HOISIN SAUCE
- 1 Thai chile, sliced thin
- 1 garlic clove, minced
- 1 teaspoon kosher salt
- ⅔ cup water
- ⅓ cup creamy peanut butter
- 3 tablespoons hoisin sauce
- 2 tablespoons tomato paste
- 1 tablespoon distilled white vinegar

SUMMER ROLLS
- 6 ounces rice vermicelli
- 10 ounces boneless country-style pork ribs, trimmed
- 2 teaspoons kosher salt for cooking pork
- 18 medium-large shrimp (31 to 40 per pound), peeled, deveined, and tails removed
- 1 cup fresh mint leaves
- 1 cup fresh cilantro leaves and thin stems
- 1 cup Thai basil leaves
- 12 (8½-inch) round rice paper wrappers
- 12 leaves red or green leaf lettuce, thick ribs removed
- 2 scallions, sliced thin on bias

1. **For the peanut-hoisin sauce:** Using mortar and pestle (or on cutting board using flat side of chef's knife), mash Thai chile, garlic, and salt to fine paste. Transfer to medium bowl. Add water, peanut butter, hoisin, tomato paste, and vinegar and whisk until smooth.

2. **For the summer rolls:** Bring 2 quarts water to boil in medium saucepan. Stir in noodles. Cook until noodles are tender but not mushy, 3 to 4 minutes. Drain noodles and rinse with cold water until cool. Drain noodles again, then spread on large plate to dry.

3. Bring 2 quarts water to boil in now-empty saucepan. Add pork and salt. Reduce heat, cover, and simmer until thickest part of pork registers 150 degrees, 8 to 12 minutes. Transfer pork to cutting board, reserving water.

4. Return water to boil. Add shrimp and cover. Let stand off heat until shrimp are opaque throughout, about 3 minutes. Drain shrimp and rinse with cold water until cool. Transfer to cutting board. Pat shrimp dry and halve lengthwise. Transfer to second plate.

5. When pork is cool enough to handle, cut each rib crosswise into 2-inch lengths. Slice each 2-inch piece lengthwise ⅛ inch thick (you should have at least 24 slices) and transfer to plate with shrimp. Tear mint, cilantro, and Thai basil into 1-inch pieces and combine in bowl.

6. Fill large bowl with cold water. Submerge 1 wrapper in water until wet on both sides, no longer than 2 seconds. Shake gently over bowl to remove excess water, then lay wrapper flat on work surface (wrapper will be fairly stiff but will continue to soften as you assemble roll). Repeat with second wrapper and place next to first wrapper. Fold 1 lettuce leaf and place on lower third of first wrapper, leaving about ½-inch margin on each side. Spread ⅓ cup noodles on top of lettuce, then sprinkle with 1 teaspoon scallions. Top scallions with 2 slices pork. Spread ¼ cup herb mixture over pork.

7. Bring lower edge of wrapper up and over herbs. Roll snugly but gently until long sides of greens and noodles are enclosed. Fold in sides to enclose ends. Arrange 3 shrimp halves, cut side up, on remaining section of wrapper. Continue to roll until filling is completely enclosed in neat cylinder. Transfer roll to serving platter, shrimp side up, and cover with plastic wrap. Repeat with second moistened wrapper. Repeat with remaining wrappers and filling, keeping completed rolls covered with plastic. Uncover and serve with sauce. (Leftovers can be wrapped tightly and refrigerated for up to 24 hours, but wrappers will become chewier and may break in places.)

SHU MAI

Serves 8 to 10 | boneless country-style ribs

WHY THIS RECIPE WORKS Flavor-packed, bite-size steamed Chinese dumplings are an irresistible appetizer—and our recipe serves a crowd. The moist, flavorful filling in our steamed dumplings boasts pork and shrimp, shiitake mushroom caps, minced cilantro, fresh ginger, and water chestnuts. The combination of country-style pork ribs and shiitake mushrooms makes for an intensely savory, meaty filling. For maximum control and consistent results, we ground our own pork at home; grinding half of the meat to a fine consistency and keeping the other half coarse ensured that the filling would be tender. The smaller pieces helped hold the dumplings together. Powdered gelatin and cornstarch kept the filling moist. Do not trim the excess fat from the ribs; the fat adds flavor and moisture. Use any size shrimp except popcorn shrimp; there's no need to halve shrimp smaller than 26 to 30 per pound. Serve with chili oil.

- 2 tablespoons soy sauce
- ½ teaspoon unflavored gelatin
- 1 pound boneless country-style pork ribs, trimmed and cut into 1-inch pieces, divided
- 8 ounces shrimp, peeled, tails removed, halved lengthwise
- ¼ cup chopped water chestnuts
- 4 dried shiitake mushroom caps (about ¾ ounce), soaked in hot water 30 minutes, squeezed dry, and chopped fine
- 2 tablespoons cornstarch
- 2 tablespoons minced fresh cilantro
- 1 tablespoon toasted sesame oil
- 1 tablespoon Shaoxing wine or dry sherry
- 1 tablespoon rice vinegar
- 2 teaspoons sugar
- 2 teaspoons grated fresh ginger
- ½ teaspoon table salt
- ½ teaspoon pepper
- 1 (1-pound) package 5½-inch square egg roll wrappers
- ¼ cup finely grated carrot (optional)

1. Combine soy sauce and gelatin in small bowl. Set aside to allow gelatin to bloom, about 5 minutes.

2. Meanwhile, place half of pork in food processor and pulse until coarsely ground into ⅛-inch pieces, about 10 pulses; transfer to large bowl. Add shrimp and remaining pork to food processor and pulse until coarsely chopped into ¼-inch pieces, about 5 pulses. Add to more finely ground pork. Stir in soy sauce mixture, water chestnuts, mushrooms, cornstarch, cilantro, sesame oil, wine, vinegar, sugar, ginger, salt, and pepper.

3. Divide egg roll wrappers into 3 stacks. Using 3-inch biscuit cutter, cut two 3-inch rounds from each stack. Cover with moist paper towels to prevent drying.

TUTORIAL
Shu Mai

Grinding your own pork, wrapping your own dumplings, and steaming them to perfection might sound like a job for the pros. We break it down so it's a job for anyone.

1. Place half of pork in food processor and pulse until coarsely ground into ⅛-inch pieces, about 10 pulses; transfer to large bowl.

2. Add shrimp and remaining pork to food processor and pulse until coarsely chopped into ¼-inch pieces, about 5 pulses. Add to more finely ground pork.

3. Stir in soy sauce mixture, water chestnuts, mushrooms, cornstarch, cilantro, sesame oil, wine, vinegar, sugar, ginger, salt, and pepper.

4. Place heaping tablespoon of filling in center of each round.

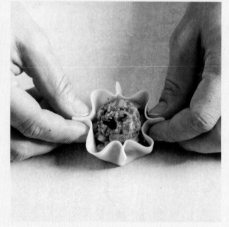

5. Form dumplings by pinching opposing sides of wrapper with your fingers until you have 8 equidistant pinches.

6. Gather up sides of dumpling and squeeze gently to create "waist." Hold dumpling in your hand and gently but firmly pack down filling with your finger.

4. Working with 6 rounds at a time, brush edges of each round lightly with water. Place heaping tablespoon of filling in center of each round. Form dumplings by pinching opposing sides of wrapper with your fingers until you have 8 equidistant pinches. Gather up sides of dumpling and squeeze gently to create "waist." Hold dumpling in your hand and gently but firmly pack down filling with your finger. Transfer to parchment paper–lined baking sheet, cover with damp kitchen towel, and repeat with remaining wrappers and filling. Top center of each dumpling with pinch of grated carrot, if using.

5. Cut piece of parchment paper slightly smaller than diameter of steamer basket and place in basket. Poke about 20 small holes in parchment and lightly coat with vegetable oil spray. Place batches of dumplings on parchment, making sure they are not touching. Set steamer over simmering water and cook, covered, until no longer pink, 8 to 10 minutes. Serve immediately.

PORK LO MEIN

Serves 4 | boneless country-style ribs

WHY THIS RECIPE WORKS Pork lo mein needs pork with big flavor but also natural tenderness—two things that don't always come together. They do in country-style ribs, however. We trimmed their surface fat to prevent an overly greasy dish and cut them into thin strips to create more surface area for the flavorful, classic marinade. A trick, just a few drops of liquid smoke, provided a flavor reminiscent of traditional Chinese barbecue pork. A quick sear in a cast-iron skillet gave us tender and juicy meat with a crisp, browned exterior. Use a cast-iron skillet for this recipe if you have one; it will help create the best sear on the pork. When shopping for Chinese rice wine, look for one that is amber in color; if it's not available, sherry may be used as a substitute. It is important that the noodles are cooked at the last minute to avoid clumping.

- 3 tablespoons soy sauce
- 2 tablespoons oyster sauce
- 2 tablespoons hoisin sauce
- 1 tablespoon toasted sesame oil
- ¼ teaspoon five-spice powder
- 1 pound boneless country-style pork ribs, trimmed and sliced crosswise into ⅛-inch pieces
- ¼ teaspoon liquid smoke (optional)
- ½ cup chicken broth
- 1 teaspoon cornstarch
- 2 garlic cloves, minced
- 2 teaspoons grated fresh ginger
- 1½ tablespoons vegetable oil, divided
- ¼ cup Shaoxing wine or dry sherry, divided

- 8 ounces shiitake mushrooms, stemmed and halved if small or quartered if large
- 16 scallions, white parts sliced thin, green parts cut into 1-inch pieces
- 1 small head napa cabbage (1½ pounds), halved, cored, and sliced crosswise into ½-inch strips (4 cups)
- 1 (9-ounce) package fresh Chinese lo mein noodles or 8 ounces dried linguine
- 1 tablespoon Asian chili-garlic sauce

1. Whisk soy sauce, oyster sauce, hoisin sauce, sesame oil, and five-spice powder together in medium bowl. Transfer 3 tablespoons soy sauce mixture to large zipper-lock bag; add pork and liquid smoke, if using. Press out as much air as possible and seal bag, making sure that all pieces are coated with marinade. Refrigerate for at least 15 minutes or up to 1 hour. Whisk broth and cornstarch into remaining soy sauce mixture; set aside. Mix garlic, ginger, and ½ teaspoon vegetable oil in second small bowl; set aside.

2. Heat 1 teaspoon vegetable oil in 12-inch cast-iron or nonstick skillet over high heat until just smoking. Add half of pork in single layer, breaking up clumps with wooden spoon. Cook, without stirring pork, for 1 minute. Continue to cook, stirring occasionally, until browned, 2 to 3 minutes. Add 2 tablespoons wine to skillet; cook, stirring constantly, until liquid is reduced and pork is well coated, 30 to 60 seconds. Transfer pork to medium bowl and repeat with 1 teaspoon vegetable oil, remaining pork, and remaining 2 tablespoons wine. Wipe skillet clean with paper towels.

3. Return now-empty skillet to high heat, add 1 teaspoon vegetable oil, and heat until just smoking. Add mushrooms and cook, stirring occasionally, until light golden brown, 4 to 6 minutes. Add scallions and continue to cook, stirring occasionally, until scallions are wilted, 2 to 3 minutes longer; transfer vegetables to bowl with pork.

4. Add remaining 1 teaspoon vegetable oil and cabbage to now-empty skillet; cook, stirring occasionally, until cabbage is spotty brown, 3 to 5 minutes. Push cabbage to sides of skillet. Add garlic mixture to center and cook, mashing mixture into skillet, until fragrant, about 30 seconds. Stir mixture into cabbage. Return pork mixture to skillet and add broth mixture; simmer until thickened and ingredients are well incorporated, 1 to 2 minutes. Remove skillet from heat.

5. While cabbage is cooking, bring 4 quarts water to boil in large pot over high heat. Add noodles to boiling water and cook, stirring occasionally, until noodles are tender, 3 to 4 minutes for fresh or 10 minutes for dried. Drain noodles and return them to pot; add pork-vegetable mixture and chili-garlic sauce to noodles, tossing constantly until sauce coats noodles. Serve immediately.

SLOW-COOKER PORK PAD THAI

Serves 4 to 6 | boneless country-style ribs
Cooking time: 6 to 7 hours on low or 4 to 5 hours on high

WHY THIS RECIPE WORKS Most pad thai recipes include shrimp and egg, but we decided to sidestep tradition for our slow-cooker rendition in favor of boneless country-style pork ribs, which could take full advantage of the slow-cook time to become tender. Braising the pork in a combination of chicken broth, fish sauce, sugar, and tamarind juice created a distinct pad thai flavor profile. Tamarind juice concentrate can be found at Asian markets as well as in the international food aisle of many supermarkets. Look for tamarind juice concentrate manufactured in Thailand, which is thinner and tastes brighter than the paste concentrate produced in other countries. If you can't find it, substitute 1½ tablespoons lime juice and 1½ tablespoons water, and omit the lime wedges. Look for country-style pork ribs with lots of fat and dark meat; lean ribs will taste very dry after the extended cooking time.

 3 tablespoons toasted sesame oil
 4 scallions, white parts minced, green parts cut into 1-inch pieces
 4 garlic cloves, minced
 1 serrano chile, stemmed and sliced into thin rings
1¾ cups chicken broth
 ¼ cup sugar
 3 tablespoons tamarind juice concentrate
 3 tablespoons fish sauce, divided
1½ pounds boneless country-style pork ribs, trimmed
 8 ounces (¼-inch-wide) rice noodles
 4 ounces (2 cups) bean sprouts
 2 tablespoons rice vinegar
 ¼ cup fresh cilantro leaves
 ¼ cup dry-roasted peanuts, chopped coarse
   Lime wedges

1. Microwave oil, scallion whites, garlic, and serrano in bowl, stirring occasionally, until fragrant, about 1 minute; transfer to slow cooker. Stir in broth, sugar, tamarind juice, and 2 table-spoons fish sauce.

2. Season pork with salt and pepper and nestle into slow cooker. Cover and cook until pork is tender and fork slips easily in and out of meat, 6 to 7 hours on low or 4 to 5 hours on high.

3. Transfer pork to cutting board, let cool slightly, then pull apart into large chunks using 2 forks. Nestle noodles into cooking liquid left in slow cooker, cover, and cook on high until tender, 20 to 30 minutes.

4. Add pork to noodles and gently toss to combine. Let sit until heated through, about 5 minutes. Add bean sprouts, vinegar, scallion greens, and remaining 1 tablespoon fish sauce and toss to combine. Sprinkle with cilantro and peanuts. Serve with lime wedges.

SLOW-ROASTED BONE-IN PORK RIB ROAST

Serves 6 to 8 | center-cut pork rib roast

WHY THIS RECIPE WORKS To guarantee a juicy, flavorful, and beautifully browned roast (without searing), we applied a brown sugar and salt rub and let the meat rest overnight. Removing the bones allowed the rub to penetrate the meat, and tying them back in place before roasting safeguarded the pork's juices. Roasting low and slow prevented overcooking and allowed the crosshatched fat cap to melt and baste the pork. A final blast under the broiler crisped and caramelized the brown sugar for a perfect mahogany crust, and a rich accompanying sauce made for a perfect finish. This recipe requires refrigerating the salted meat for at least 6 hours and up to 24 hours before cooking (a longer salting time is preferable). For easier carving, ask the butcher to remove the chine bone. We strongly prefer natural pork in this recipe. If using enhanced pork, do not salt in step 1.

 1 (4- to 5-pound) center-cut bone-in pork rib roast, chine bone removed
 2 tablespoons packed dark brown sugar
 1 tablespoon kosher salt
1½ teaspoons pepper

1. Using sharp knife, remove roast from bones, running knife down length of bones and following contours as closely as possible. Reserve bones. Combine sugar and salt in small bowl. Pat roast dry with paper towels. If necessary, trim thick spots of surface fat layer to about ¼-inch thickness. Using sharp knife, cut slits spaced 1 inch apart in crosshatch pattern in surface fat layer, being careful not to cut into meat. Rub roast evenly with sugar mixture. Refrigerate, uncovered, for at least 6 hours or up to 24 hours.

2. Adjust oven rack to lower-middle position and heat oven to 250 degrees. Pat roast dry with paper towels and season with pepper. Place roast back on ribs so bones fit where they were cut; tie roast to bones with lengths of kitchen twine between ribs. Transfer roast, fat side up, to wire rack set in rimmed baking sheet. Roast until pork registers 140 to 145 degrees, 3 to 4 hours.

TUTORIAL
Slow-Roasted Bone-In Pork Rib Roast

Consider this pork rib roast instead of prime rib roast for the next holiday for a change of pace. Here's how to make it.

1. Using sharp knife, remove roast from bones, running knife down length of bones and following contours as closely as possible. Reserve bones.

2. Using sharp knife, cut slits, spaced 1 inch apart in crosshatch pattern in surface fat layer, being careful not to cut into meat. Rub roast evenly with sugar mixture. Refrigerate.

3. Pat roast dry with paper towels and season with pepper. Place roast back on ribs so bones fit where they were cut; tie roast to bones with lengths of kitchen twine between ribs.

4. Transfer roast, fat side up, to wire rack set in rimmed baking sheet. Roast until pork registers 140 to 145 degrees, 3 to 4 hours.

5. Let roast rest for 30 minutes. Adjust oven rack 8 inches from broiler element and heat broiler. Broil roast until top of roast is well browned and crispy, 2 to 6 minutes.

6. Remove twine and remove meat from ribs. Slice pork ¾ inch thick.

3. Remove roast from oven (leave roast on sheet) and let rest for 30 minutes.

4. Adjust oven rack 8 inches from broiler element and heat broiler. Return roast to oven and broil until top of roast is well browned and crispy, 2 to 6 minutes.

5. Transfer roast to carving board. Remove twine and remove meat from ribs. Slice pork ¾ inch thick. Serve.

GRILL-ROASTED BONE-IN PORK RIB ROAST

Serves 6 to 8 | center-cut pork rib roast

WHY THIS RECIPE WORKS To prepare our center-cut pork rib—often referred to as the pork equivalent of prime rib or rack of lamb—for the grill, we scored the fat cap to help the rendered drippings baste the meat during cooking. For a deeply browned, crisp crust, we salted the roast and refrigerated it for at least 6 hours before grilling. All that was left to do was to position the pork correctly, bones pointed away from the coals, on the cooler side of a banked fire and let it roast gently to perfection for a little more than an hour. A thick mahogany crust developed without the need for searing. A longer salting time is preferable. We strongly prefer natural pork in this recipe. If using enhanced pork, omit salt in step 1. If you'd like to use wood chunks instead of wood chips when using a charcoal grill, substitute 1 medium wood chunk, soaked in water for 1 hour, for the wood chip packets.

  1 (4- to 5-pound) center-cut bone-in pork rib roast, chine bone removed
  4 teaspoons kosher salt
  1 cup wood chips
1½ teaspoons pepper

1. Pat roast dry with paper towels. If necessary, trim thick spots of surface fat layer to about ¼-inch thickness. Using sharp knife, cut slits spaced 1 inch apart in crosshatch pattern in surface fat layer, being careful not to cut into meat. Rub roast evenly with salt. Refrigerate for at least 6 hours or up to 24 hours.

2. Just before grilling, soak wood chips in water for 15 minutes, then drain. Using large piece of heavy-duty aluminum foil, wrap soaked chips in 8 by 4½-inch foil packet. (Make sure chips do not poke holes in sides or bottom of packet.) Cut 2 evenly spaced 2-inch slits in top of packet.

3a. For a charcoal grill: Open bottom vent halfway. Light large chimney starter filled with charcoal briquettes (6 quarts). When top coals are partially covered with ash, pour into steeply

banked pile against side of grill. Place wood chip packet on coals. Set cooking grate in place, cover, and open lid vent halfway. Heat grill until hot and wood chips are smoking, about 5 minutes.

3b. For a gas grill: Remove cooking grate and place wood chip packet directly on primary burner. Set cooking grate in place, turn all burners to high, cover, and heat grill until hot and wood chips are smoking, about 15 minutes. Turn primary burner to medium-high and turn off other burner(s). (Adjust primary burner [or, if using 3-burner grill, primary burner and second burner] as needed to maintain grill temperature around 325 degrees.)

4. Clean and oil cooking grate. Pat roast dry with paper towels and season with pepper. Place roast on grill with meat near, but not over, heat source and bones facing away from coals and flames. Cover (position lid vent over meat if using charcoal) and cook until meat registers 140 degrees, 1¼ to 1½ hours.

5. Transfer roast to carving board and let rest for 30 minutes. Carve roast into thick slices by cutting between ribs, and serve.

CROWN ROAST OF PORK

Serves 10 to 12 | crown roast

WHY THIS RECIPE WORKS A crown roast yields enough meat to feed a holiday crowd and offers a dramatic presentation, but its shape presents serious cooking challenges. Simply roasting it overcooked the meat on the outside and undercooked it around the inner circle. The solution? We turned the roast upside down to allow more air to circulate and to expose the thickest part of the roast to the heat. Ask your butcher to make this roast for you (see page 248). Wrapping kitchen twine around the widest part of the roast provides more support when the roast is flipped. Use small red potatoes measuring 1 to 2 inches in diameter for this recipe.

  3 tablespoons kosher salt
  3 tablespoons minced fresh thyme
  2 tablespoons minced fresh rosemary
  5 garlic cloves, minced
  1 tablespoon pepper
  1 (8- to 10-pound) pork crown roast, trimmed
  2 pounds small red potatoes, unpeeled
10 ounces shallots, peeled and halved
  2 Golden Delicious apples, peeled, cored, and halved
  8 tablespoons unsalted butter, melted, divided
½ cup apple cider
  1 cup chicken broth

Indoor Barbecue Pork Chops

INDOOR BARBECUE PORK CHOPS

Serves 4 to 6 | pork rib chops

WHY THIS RECIPE WORKS To make easy "barbecue" pork chops without firing up the grill, we started with ½-inch-thick bone-in rib chops. The bone added flavor and prevented the chops from overcooking, while the thin cut meant a higher ratio of flavorful spiced and sauced exterior to mild meat (plus a faster cooking time). A potent dry rub gave the chops a spicy, caramelized crust, and some added cornstarch ensured even browning. We finished the chops in a simple sauce of ketchup, cider vinegar, extra dry rub, and liquid smoke, making for a tangy-sweet pork chop with just-off-the-grill flavor.

    3   tablespoons packed brown sugar, divided
    1   tablespoon paprika
    1   tablespoon kosher salt
    1   teaspoon pepper
    ½   teaspoon cayenne pepper
    1   tablespoon cornstarch
    8   (5- to 7-ounce) bone-in pork rib chops, ½ inch thick,
        trimmed
    1   tablespoon vegetable oil
    4   tablespoons unsalted butter
    ½   cup ketchup
    1   tablespoon cider vinegar
    1   teaspoon liquid smoke

1. Combine salt, thyme, rosemary, garlic, and pepper in bowl; set aside 2 teaspoons salt-herb mixture. Pat roast dry with paper towels and rub remaining salt-herb mixture all over roast. Wrap kitchen twine twice around widest part of roast and tie tightly. Refrigerate roast, covered, for at least 6 hours or up to 24 hours.

2. Adjust oven rack to lower-middle position and heat oven to 475 degrees. Set V-rack in large roasting pan. Toss potatoes, shallots, apples, 4 tablespoons melted butter, and reserved salt-herb mixture in large bowl; transfer to pan. Arrange roast bone side down in V-rack and brush with remaining 4 tablespoons melted butter. Roast until meat is well browned and registers 110 degrees, about 1 hour. Remove roast from oven and reduce oven temperature to 300 degrees. Using 2 large wads of paper towels, flip roast bone side up. Pour apple cider into bottom of pan and return pan to oven. Roast until meat registers 140 degrees, 30 to 50 minutes. Transfer roast to carving board, tent with aluminum foil, and let rest for 15 to 20 minutes.

3. Transfer apples to blender and potatoes and shallots to bowl. Pour pan juices into fat separator. Let liquid settle for 5 minutes, then pour defatted juices into blender. Add broth to blender with apples and process until smooth, about 1 minute. Transfer sauce to medium saucepan and bring to simmer over medium heat. Season with salt and pepper to taste. Remove twine from roast, slice between bones, and serve with vegetables and sauce.

1. Combine 1 tablespoon sugar, paprika, salt, pepper, and cayenne in bowl. Transfer 2 tablespoons spice mixture to second bowl and stir in cornstarch; reserve remaining spice mixture for sauce. Using kitchen shears, snip through fat surrounding loin muscle of each chop in 2 places, about 2 inches apart. Pat chops dry with paper towels and sprinkle all over with cornstarch mixture.

2. Heat oil in 12-inch nonstick skillet over medium-high heat until just smoking. Add 4 chops to skillet and cook until browned and meat registers 140 degrees, about 2 minutes per side. Transfer chops to rimmed baking sheet and tent with aluminum foil. Repeat with remaining 4 chops.

3. Add butter to now-empty skillet and melt over medium heat. Add reserved spice mixture and cook until fragrant, about 30 seconds. Carefully whisk in ketchup, vinegar, liquid smoke, and remaining 2 tablespoons sugar; bring to simmer; and remove from heat. Return chops to skillet one at a time, turn to coat with sauce, and transfer to platter. Stir any accumulated juices from sheet into remaining sauce. Serve chops, passing remaining sauce separately.

Pan-Seared Thick-Cut Pork Chops

PAN-SEARED THICK-CUT PORK CHOPS

Serves 4 | pork rib chops

WHY THIS RECIPE WORKS If cooked properly, a simple pork rib chop on the bone, large and impressive at 12 ounces, is appealing, with a brown sear on succulent meat that's tender with just enough bite. For a seared pork chop that lived up to our ideal, we turned the conventional method upside down, first cooking chops (that we salted and rested before cooking) in a low oven and then searing them in a superhot pan. Slowly cooking the meat first rather than starting it in the smoking pan allowed enzymes to break down protein, tenderizing the thick chops. The salted surface gently dried out in the oven and then became beautifully caramelized in the pan—making pan-seared pork chops that had a perfect juicy interior and nicely caramelized exterior. They're great on their own or served with one of the pan sauces in the variations. If using enhanced pork, do not salt in step 1.

> 4 (12-ounce) bone-in pork rib chops, 1½ inches thick, trimmed
> 2 teaspoons kosher salt
> 1–2 tablespoons vegetable oil

1. Cut 2 slits, about 2 inches apart, through outer layer of fat and silverskin on each pork chop. Sprinkle entire surface of each chop with ½ teaspoon kosher salt and place on wire rack set in rimmed baking sheet. Let sit at room temperature for 45 minutes.

2. Adjust oven rack to middle position and heat oven to 275 degrees. Pat chops dry with paper towels and season with pepper. Transfer sheet to oven and cook until pork registers 120 to 125 degrees, 30 to 45 minutes.

3. Heat 1 tablespoon oil in 12-inch skillet over high heat until just smoking. Place 2 chops in skillet and sear until well browned and crusty, 2 to 3 minutes, lifting once halfway through cooking to redistribute fat underneath. Flip chops and cook until well browned on second side, 2 to 3 minutes. Transfer chops to plate and repeat with remaining 2 chops, adding 1 tablespoon oil if skillet is dry.

4. Reduce heat to medium. Use tongs to stand 2 pork chops on their sides. Holding chops together with tongs, return to skillet and sear sides of chops (with exception of bone side) until browned and pork registers 145 degrees, about 2 minutes; transfer to clean plate. Repeat with remaining 2 chops; transfer to plate, tent with aluminum foil, and rest for 10 minutes. Serve.

VARIATIONS

Pan-Seared Thick-Cut Pork Chops with Cilantro and Coconut Pan Sauce

While chops are resting, pour off all but 1 teaspoon fat from skillet and return skillet to medium heat. Add 1 minced large shallot, 1 tablespoon grated fresh ginger, and 2 minced garlic cloves and cook, stirring constantly, until softened, about 1 minute. Add ¼ cup chicken broth, ¾ cup coconut milk, and 1 teaspoon sugar, scraping up any browned bits. Off heat, stir in ¼ cup chopped fresh cilantro and 2 teaspoons lime, then whisk in 1 tablespoon chilled butter. Season with salt and pepper to taste, and serve with chops.

Pan-Seared Thick-Cut Pork Chops with Garlic and Thyme Pan Sauce

While chops are resting, pour off all but 1 teaspoon fat from skillet and return skillet to medium heat. Add 1 minced large shallot and 2 minced garlic cloves and cook, stirring constantly, until softened, about 1 minute. Add ¾ cup chicken broth and ½ cup dry white wine, scraping up any browned bits. Simmer until reduced to ½ cup, 6 to 7 minutes. Off heat, stir in 1 teaspoon minced thyme and ¼ teaspoon white wine vinegar, then whisk in 3 tablespoons chilled butter, 1 tablespoon at a time. Season with salt and pepper to taste, and serve with chops.

SOUS VIDE THICK-CUT PORK CHOPS

Serves 4 | pork rib chops

WHY THIS RECIPE WORKS Because pork chops don't have a lot of fat to provide insulation, traditional preparations can cause the pork to go from perfect to overcooked in a flash. For pork that was perfectly tender and juicy from edge to edge, we used an immersion circulator for even, unattended cooking. We placed the pork and a bit of vegetable oil in the bag before cooking in the hot water bath. Our thick-cut chops cooked at 140°F for 2 to 3 hours before a quick sear in a screaming hot pan. For great browning, we made sure to pat the pork dry thoroughly before searing it in a hot skillet.

> 4 (12 ounce) bone-in pork rib or center-cut chops, about 1½ inches thick, trimmed
> 6 tablespoons vegetable oil, divided

1. Using sous vide circulator, bring water to 140°F in 7-quart container.

2. Season chops with salt and pepper. Divide chops and ¼ cup oil between two 1-gallon zipper-lock freezer bags and toss to coat. Arrange chops in single layer and seal bags, pressing out as much air as possible. Gently lower bags into prepared water bath

until chops are fully submerged, and then clip top corner of each bag to side of water bath container, allowing remaining air bubbles to rise to top of bag. Reopen 1 corner of zipper, release remaining air bubbles, and reseal bag. Cover and cook for at least 2 hours or up to 3 hours.

3. Transfer chops to paper towel–lined plate and let rest for 5 to 10 minutes. Pat chops dry with paper towels. Heat 1 tablespoon oil in 12 inch skillet over medium-high heat until just smoking. Place 2 chops in skillet and cook until well browned on first side, 1 to 2 minutes, lifting once halfway through cooking to redistribute fat underneath each chop. Flip chops and continue to cook until well browned on second side, 1 to 2 minutes. Transfer chops to plate and tent with aluminum foil. Repeat with remaining 1 tablespoon oil and chops. Serve.

To make ahead: Chops can be rapidly chilled in ice bath (see page 8) and then refrigerated in zipper-lock bag after step 2 for up to 3 days. To reheat, return sealed bag to water bath set to 140°F for 30 minutes and then proceed with step 3.

Texas Thick-Cut Smoked Pork Chops

TEXAS THICK-CUT SMOKED PORK CHOPS

Serves 8 | pork rib chops

WHY THIS RECIPE WORKS Massive pork chops can deliver Texas-size pit-smoked flavor with the help of the grill and the right method. We bought extra-thick bone-in chops to help keep their lean meat from drying out on the grill, then brined them in a saltwater solution with some sugar added to promote browning and to keep them juicy. A spice mixture of salt, pepper, onion powder, and granulated garlic sprinkled on before grilling added flavor, and roasting the chops over mesquite chips infused the meat's crust with fragrant smoke. A half-grill fire allowed us to gently cook the chops through on the cooler side, retaining most of their juices along the way. For a last big shot of flavor, we called on a homemade bacony barbecue sauce bright with vinegar to reinforce the chops' smoky grilled taste. Each chop can easily serve two people. Grate the onion for the sauce on the large holes of a box grater. Our preferred hot sauce is Frank's RedHot Original Cayenne Pepper Sauce. We prefer mesquite wood chips in this recipe.

PORK
- 3 tablespoons table salt for brining
- 3 tablespoons sugar for brining
- 4 (18- to 20-ounce) bone-in pork rib chops, 2 inches thick, trimmed
- 2 tablespoons pepper
- 1½ tablespoons table salt
- 2 teaspoons onion powder
- 2 teaspoons granulated garlic

BARBECUE SAUCE
- 2 slices bacon
- ¼ cup grated onion
- ⅛ teaspoon table salt
- ¾ cup cider vinegar
- 1¼ cups chicken broth
- 1 cup ketchup
- 2 tablespoons hot sauce
- ½ teaspoon liquid smoke
- ¼ teaspoon pepper
- 2 cups wood chips

1. **For the pork:** Dissolve 3 tablespoons salt and sugar in 1½ quarts cold water in large container. Submerge chops in brine, cover, and refrigerate for 1 hour. Combine pepper, salt, onion powder, and granulated garlic in bowl; set aside.

2. **For the barbecue sauce:** Meanwhile, cook bacon in medium saucepan over medium heat until fat begins to render and bacon begins to brown, 4 to 6 minutes. Add onion and salt and cook until softened, 2 to 4 minutes. Stir in vinegar, scraping up any browned bits, and cook until slightly thickened, about 2 minutes.

3. Stir in broth, ketchup, hot sauce, liquid smoke, and pepper. Bring to simmer and cook until slightly thickened, about 15 minutes, stirring occasionally. Discard bacon and season with salt and pepper to taste. Remove from heat, cover, and keep warm.

4. Just before grilling, soak wood chips in water for 15 minutes, then drain. Using large piece of heavy-duty aluminum foil, wrap soaked chips in 8 by 4½-inch foil packet. (Make sure chips do not poke holes in sides or bottom of packet.) Cut 2 evenly spaced 2-inch slits in top of packet. Remove chops from brine and pat dry with paper towels. Season chops all over with reserved spice mixture.

5a. For a charcoal grill: Open bottom vent completely. Light large chimney starter three-quarters filled with charcoal briquettes (4½ quarts). When top coals are partially covered with ash, pour evenly over half of grill. Place wood chip packet on coals. Set cooking grate in place, cover, and, open lid vent completely. Heat grill until hot and wood chips are smoking, about 5 minutes.

5b. For a gas grill: Remove cooking grate and place wood chip packet directly on primary burner. Set cooking grate in place, turn all burners to high, cover, and heat grill until hot and wood chips are smoking, about 15 minutes. Turn primary burner to medium-high and turn off other burner(s). (Adjust primary burner [or, if using 3-burner grill, primary burner and second burner] as needed to maintain grill temperature around 325 degrees.)

6. Clean and oil cooking grate. Arrange chops on cooler side of grill with bone ends toward fire. Cover (position lid vent over chops if using charcoal) and cook until chops register 140 degrees, 45 to 50 minutes, flipping halfway through cooking.

7. Transfer chops to serving dish and let rest for 10 minutes. Brush chops generously with warm sauce and serve, passing remaining sauce separately.

GRILLED THIN-CUT PORK CHOPS

Serves 4 to 6 | pork rib chops

WHY THIS RECIPE WORKS Thin-cut chops that go directly from package to grill are often pale and unappetizing, and by the time you get a nice char from the grill, the insides have dried out. You need to use a little technique (and plenty of butter) to get them nicely charred and juicy. Salting the chops before freezing them (yes, freezing them) for 30 minutes acted like a brine and ensured well-seasoned, juicy chops. The freezing also caused rapid evaporation on the surface of the meat, which contributed to the development of a good crust when the chops were grilled. Freezing them also allowed them to stay on the grill longer, giving them more time to develop that crust we were looking for. Softened butter mixed with brown sugar encouraged caramelization and added richness to the otherwise rather lean meat. Finishing with even more butter, along with chives, mustard, and lemon zest, helped add zip and some brightness.

6 (3-ounce) bone-in pork rib or center-cut chops, about ½ inch thick, trimmed
¾ teaspoon table salt
4 tablespoons unsalted butter, softened, divided
1 teaspoon packed brown sugar
½ teaspoon pepper
1 teaspoon minced fresh chives
½ teaspoon Dijon mustard
½ teaspoon grated lemon zest

1. Set wire rack in rimmed baking sheet. Pat chops dry with paper towels. Cut 2 slits, about 2 inches apart, through outer layer of fat and silverskin on each chop. Rub chops with salt. Arrange on prepared rack and freeze until firm, at least 30 minutes or up to 1 hour. Combine 2 tablespoons butter, sugar, and pepper in small bowl; set aside. Mix chives, mustard, lemon zest, and remaining 2 tablespoons butter in second small bowl and refrigerate until firm, about 15 minutes. (Butter-chive mixture can be refrigerated, covered, for up to 24 hours.)

2a. For a charcoal grill: Open bottom vent completely. Light large chimney starter filled with charcoal briquettes (6 quarts). When top coals are partially covered with ash, pour evenly over grill. Set cooking grate in place, cover, and open lid vent completely. Heat grill until hot, about 5 minutes.

2b. For a gas grill: Turn all burners to high, cover, and heat grill until hot, about 15 minutes. Leave all burners on high.

3. Pat chops dry with paper towels. Spread butter-sugar mixture evenly over both sides of each chop. Place chops on grill and cook, covered, until well browned and pork registers 145 degrees, 6 to 8 minutes, flipping chops halfway through cooking. Transfer chops to platter and top with chilled butter-chive mixture. Tent with aluminum foil and let rest for 5 minutes. Serve.

VARIATIONS
Ginger Grilled Thin-Cut Pork Chops
Substitute ½ teaspoon minced fresh thyme for chives, 1 teaspoon grated fresh ginger for mustard, and grated orange zest for lemon zest.

Olive Tapenade Grilled Thin-Cut Pork Chops
Substitute ½ teaspoon minced fresh oregano for chives and 1½ teaspoons black olive tapenade for mustard.

Spicy Grilled Thin-Cut Pork Chops
Substitute minced fresh cilantro for chives, 1½ teaspoons Asian chili-garlic sauce for mustard, and grated lime zest for lemon zest.

ROAST PORK LOIN WITH SWEET POTATOES AND CILANTRO SAUCE

Serves 6 | center-cut pork loin

WHY THIS RECIPE WORKS This modern take on a roast pork dinner features meat and potatoes, freshened up. We partnered tender spice-rubbed pork loin with caramelized sweet potatoes and a lively green herb sauce. Roasting the meat in a moderate 375-degree oven and turning it halfway through roasting ensured juicy, perfectly cooked pork. A mixture of ground coriander, cumin, and salt gave the pork's exterior color and flavor and complemented the fresh cilantro sauce. To complete the meal, we tossed sweet potato chunks with some olive oil and a pinch of cayenne pepper and roasted them along with the pork. Look for a roast with a thin fat cap (about ¼ inch thick) and don't trim. If using enhanced pork, do not brine but do season with salt in step 1. This sauce uses two entire bunches of cilantro, including the stems.

PORK AND POTATOES
¼ cup table salt for brining
¼ cup sugar for brining
1 (2½- to 3-pound) boneless center-cut pork loin roast, trimmed, tied at 1½-inch intervals, brined if desired
1 teaspoon ground coriander
1 teaspoon ground cumin
3 pounds sweet potatoes, peeled, quartered, and cut into 2-inch pieces
3 tablespoons extra-virgin olive oil
⅛ teaspoon cayenne pepper

CILANTRO SAUCE
2½ cups fresh cilantro leaves and stems, trimmed (2 bunches)
½ cup extra-virgin olive oil
4 teaspoons lime juice
2 garlic cloves, minced
½ teaspoon sugar

1. For the pork and potatoes: Dissolve salt and sugar in 2 quarts cold water in large container. Submerge pork in brine, cover, and refrigerate for 1½ to 2 hours.

2. Adjust oven rack to lower-middle position and heat oven to 375 degrees. Pat roast dry with paper towels. Season with salt and sprinkle with coriander and cumin.

3. Toss sweet potatoes in bowl with oil and cayenne, season with salt and pepper, and spread evenly into large roasting pan. Lay roast, fat side up, on top of potatoes. Roast until pork registers 140 degrees, 50 minutes to 1 hour 10 minutes, turning roast over halfway through roasting.

4. For the cilantro sauce: Meanwhile, pulse all ingredients in food processor until cilantro is finely chopped, 10 to 15 pulses, scraping down sides of bowl as needed. Season with salt and pepper to taste.

5. Remove pan from oven. Transfer roast to carving board and let rest for 20 minutes. While roast rests, increase oven temperature to 450 degrees and continue to roast potatoes until nicely browned, about 10 minutes. Remove twine from roast and slice ½ inch thick. Serve with potatoes and cilantro sauce.

HERB-CRUSTED PORK LOIN

Serves 6 | center-cut pork loin

WHY THIS RECIPE WORKS A fresh herb crust enlivens a boneless pork roast and provides bold herb presence in every bite. To add flavor from the inside out, we started by cutting a deep, wide pocket in the roast and filling it with a flavorful herb paste (see page 249). We also scored the fat cap before searing it briefly in a very hot skillet. The seared, crosshatched layer gave the paste something to grip on to and helped unify the crust and meat. A relatively low oven allowed the roast to cook evenly and the crust to get crisp and golden brown. Look for a roast with a thin fat cap (about ¼ inch thick) and don't trim. If using enhanced pork, do not brine and omit the salt in step 4.

1 (2½- to 3-pound) boneless center-cut pork loin roast, trimmed
¼ cup table salt for brining
¼ cup sugar for brining
1 slice hearty white sandwich bread, torn into quarters
1 ounce Parmesan or Pecorino Romano cheese, grated (½ cup), divided
1 shallot, minced
¼ cup plus 2 teaspoons extra-virgin olive oil, divided
¼ teaspoon table salt, divided
¼ teaspoon pepper, divided
⅓ cup fresh parsley or basil leaves
2 tablespoons minced fresh thyme
1 teaspoon minced fresh rosemary or ½ teaspoon dried
1 garlic clove, minced

1. Using sharp knife, cut slits 1 inch apart in crosshatch pattern in fat cap of roast, being careful not to cut into meat. Create pocket in roast by inserting knife ½ inch from end of roast and cutting along side of pork, stopping ½ inch short of other end. Pull open roast and use gentle strokes to cut deeper pocket.

2. Dissolve ¼ cup salt and sugar in 2 quarts cold water in large container. Submerge pork in brine, cover, and refrigerate for 1½ to 2 hours. Remove roast from brine and pat dry with paper towels.

Enchaud Perigordine

3. Adjust oven rack to lower-middle position and heat oven to 325 degrees. Set wire rack in rimmed baking sheet lined with aluminum foil. Pulse bread in food processor until coarsely ground, about 16 pulses (you should have 1 cup crumbs). Transfer crumbs to bowl and add 2 tablespoons Parmesan, shallot, 1 tablespoon oil, ⅛ teaspoon salt, and ⅛ teaspoon pepper. Using fork, toss mixture until crumbs are evenly coated with oil.

4. Pulse parsley, thyme, rosemary, garlic, remaining 6 tablespoons Parmesan, 3 tablespoons oil, remaining ⅛ teaspoon salt, and remaining ⅛ teaspoon pepper in now-empty processor until smooth, about 12 pulses. Transfer herb paste to bowl.

5. Spread ¼ cup herb paste inside roast and tie roast at 1½-inch intervals with kitchen twine. Season roast with salt and pepper.

6. Heat remaining 2 teaspoons oil in 12-inch skillet over medium-high heat until just smoking. Brown roast well on all sides, about 10 minutes. Transfer roast, fat side up, to prepared sheet.

7. Remove twine from roast. Spread remaining herb paste over roast and top with bread-crumb mixture. Transfer sheet with roast to oven and cook until pork registers 140 degrees, 50 minutes to 1¼ hours. Remove roast from oven and let rest on sheet for 20 minutes. Transfer roast to carving board, taking care not to squeeze juices out of pocket in roast. Slice roast ½ inch thick. Serve.

Herb-Crusted Pork Loin with Mustard and Caraway
Substitute 1 tablespoon minced garlic for shallot in bread-crumb mixture, substitute 4 teaspoons whole-grain mustard and 1 tablespoon toasted caraway seeds for rosemary, and reduce oil in step 4 to 2 tablespoons.

ENCHAUD PERIGORDINE

Serves 4 to 6 | center-cut pork loin

WHY THIS RECIPE WORKS Enchaud Perigordine is a regional French dish that's impressive but quite simple: slow-cooked pork loin in a pot. But given that American pork is so lean, this cooking method can lead to bland, stringy pork when made stateside. We gave our loin special treatment. Butterflying the pork allowed us to salt a higher surface area for a roast that was well seasoned throughout. To ensure good flavor and texture, we lowered the oven temperature (to 225 degrees) and removed the roast from the oven when it was medium-rare. Searing just three sides of the roast, rather than all four, prevented the bottom of the roast from overcooking from direct contact with the pot. And while we eliminated the hard-to-find trotter (or pig's foot), we added butter for richness and sprinkled in gelatin to lend body to the sauce. If using enhanced pork, reduce the salt to 2 teaspoons (1 teaspoon per side) in step 2.

2 tablespoons unsalted butter, divided
6 garlic cloves, sliced thin, divided
1 (2½-pound) boneless center-cut pork loin roast, trimmed
1 tablespoon kosher salt
1 teaspoon sugar
2 teaspoons herbes de Provence
2 tablespoons vegetable oil, divided
1 Granny Smith apple, peeled, cored, halved, and cut into ¼-inch pieces
1 onion, chopped fine
⅓ cup dry white wine
2 sprigs fresh thyme
1 bay leaf
1 tablespoon unflavored gelatin
¼–¾ cup chicken broth
1 tablespoon chopped fresh parsley

1. Adjust oven rack to lower-middle position and heat oven to 225 degrees. Melt 1 tablespoon butter in 8-inch skillet over medium-low heat. Add half of garlic and cook, stirring frequently, until golden, 5 to 7 minutes. Transfer mixture to bow and refrigerate.

PORK – *Loin* **273**

TUTORIAL
Enchaud Perigordine

Don't save pot roast for beef. Follow these steps for one of the most elegant pot-roasted meat dishes.

1. Position roast fat side up. Insert knife one-third of way up from bottom of roast along 1 long side and cut horizontally, stopping ½ inch before edge. Open up flap.

2. Keeping knife parallel to cutting board, cut through thicker portion of roast about ½ inch from bottom of roast, keeping knife level with first cut and stopping about ½ inch before edge. Open up this flap.

3. Sprinkle sugar over inside of loin, then spread with cooled garlic mixture.

4. Starting from short side, fold roast back together like business letter and tie crosswise with kitchen twine at 1-inch intervals. Sprinkle tied roast with herbes de Provence and season with pepper.

5. Brown roast on fat side and sides (do not brown bottom of roast), 5 to 8 minutes. Transfer to large plate.

6. After starting sauce return roast to pot; place large sheet of aluminum foil over pot and cover tightly with lid. Transfer pot to oven and cook until meat registers 140 degrees, 50 minutes to 1½ hours.

2. Position roast fat side up. Insert knife one-third of way up from bottom of roast along 1 long side and cut horizontally, stopping ½ inch before edge. Open up flap. Keeping knife parallel to cutting board, cut through thicker portion of roast about ½ inch from bottom of roast, keeping knife level with first cut and stopping about ½ inch before edge. Open up this flap. If uneven, cover with plastic wrap and use meat pounder to even out. Sprinkle salt evenly over both sides of loin (½ tablespoon per side) and rub into roast until slightly tacky. Sprinkle sugar over inside of loin, then spread with cooled garlic mixture. Starting from short side, fold roast back together like business letter (keeping fat on outside) and tie crosswise with kitchen twine at 1-inch intervals. Sprinkle tied roast evenly with herbes de Provence and season with pepper.

3. Heat 1 tablespoon oil in Dutch oven over medium heat until just smoking. Add roast, fat side down, and brown on fat side and sides (do not brown bottom of roast), 5 to 8 minutes. Transfer to large plate. Add remaining 1 tablespoon oil, apple, and onion; cook, stirring frequently, until onion is softened and browned, 5 to 7 minutes. Stir in remaining garlic and cook until fragrant, about 30 seconds. Stir in wine, thyme, and bay leaf; cook for 30 seconds. Return roast, fat side up, to pot; place large sheet of aluminum foil over pot and cover tightly with lid. Transfer pot to oven and cook until meat registers 140 degrees, 50 minutes to 1½ hours (short, thick roasts will take longer than long, thin ones).

4. Transfer roast to carving board, tent with foil, and let rest for 20 minutes. While roast rests, sprinkle gelatin over ¼ cup broth in bowl and let sit until gelatin softens, about 5 minutes. Discard thyme sprigs and bay leaf. Pour jus into 2-cup liquid measuring cup and add broth as needed to equal 1¼ cups. Return jus to pot and bring to simmer over medium heat. Whisk softened gelatin mixture, parsley, and remaining 1 tablespoon butter into jus and season with salt and pepper to taste; remove from heat and cover to keep warm. Slice roast into ½-inch-thick slices, adding any accumulated juices to sauce. Serve, passing sauce separately.

SLOW-COOKER PORK LOIN WITH WARM SPICED CHICKPEA SALAD

Serves 6 to 8 | center-cut pork loin
Cooking time: 2 to 3 hours on low
WHY THIS RECIPE WORKS Inspired by the lively flavors of Moroccan cuisine, we set out to create a satisfying meal featuring moist pork loin and a spice-infused chickpea salad, and we wanted to use the slow cooker. A combination of coriander, cumin, and cloves created an authentic and flavorful base for our side dish; dried apricots, roasted red peppers, and shallots added at the end offset the savory, spiced chickpeas with a touch of sweetness. We cooked the onion and bloomed the spices in the same skillet we used to brown the pork, which gave them extra flavor. In the slow cooker, the pork loin infused the chickpea mixture with flavor; once the pork was done, we let it rest for 20 minutes to help the lean meat retain its juices when sliced. A wider, shorter pork loin (about 8 inches long) fits best in the slow cooker. An ⅛-inch-thick layer of fat on top of the roast is ideal. Check the pork's temperature after 2 hours of cooking and continue to monitor it until it registers 140 degrees.

1 (3- to 4-pound) boneless center-cut pork loin roast, trimmed and tied at 1-inch intervals
2 tablespoons extra-virgin olive oil, divided
1 onion, chopped fine
2 garlic cloves, minced
1 teaspoon ground coriander
½ teaspoon ground cumin
¼ teaspoon ground cloves
½ cup chicken broth
3 (15-ounce) cans chickpeas, rinsed
½ cup dried apricots, chopped
½ cup jarred roasted red peppers, rinsed, patted dry, and chopped
1 shallot, sliced thin
¼ cup chopped fresh mint
1 tablespoon white wine vinegar

1. Pat pork dry with paper towels and season with salt and pepper. Heat 1 tablespoon oil in 12-inch skillet over medium-high heat until just smoking. Brown roast on all sides, 7 to 10 minutes; transfer to plate.

2. Heat remaining 1 tablespoon oil in now-empty skillet over medium heat until shimmering. Add onion and cook until softened and lightly browned, 5 to 7 minutes. Add garlic, coriander, cumin, and cloves and cook until fragrant, about 30 seconds. Stir in broth, scraping up any browned bits; transfer to slow cooker.

3. Stir chickpeas into slow cooker. Nestle roast, fat side up, into slow cooker, adding any accumulated juices. Cover and cook until pork registers 140 degrees, 2 to 3 hours on low.

4. Transfer roast to carving board, tent with aluminum foil, and let rest for 20 minutes.

5. Stir apricots, red peppers, and shallot into chickpea mixture and let sit until heated through, about 5 minutes. Stir in mint and vinegar and season with salt and pepper to taste. Remove twine from roast and slice meat ½ inch thick. Serve with salad.

PRESSURE-COOKER PORK LOIN WITH BLACK MOLE SAUCE

Serves 6 | center-cut pork loin

WHY THIS RECIPE WORKS Pork loin roasts are perfect blank canvases for intensely flavored sauces, so we decided to pair our roast with a rich, complex mole sauce. We decided to create a mole negro, or black mole sauce, which contains dried chiles, spices, cocoa, tomatillos, tomatoes, and dried fruit, along with nuts and seeds for body. Mole sauces are usually cooked separately from the meat, but with the electric pressure cooker we could cook the pork and the sauce at the same rate in only one vessel. To make sure the roast cooked evenly, we cut it in half, and we cut the tomatoes and tomatillos into relatively large pieces and placed the pork on top so that it wasn't submerged in liquid. If using enhanced pork, do not brine the roast. If using the slow cook function, begin checking the pork's temperature after 1 hour and continue to monitor it until it is done. Serve with rice.

Pressure-Cooker Pork Loin with Black Mole Sauce

¼ cup table salt for brining

¼ cup sugar

1 (2½- to 3-pound) boneless center-cut pork loin roast, trimmed and halved crosswise

3 pasilla chiles, stemmed, seeded, and torn into ½-inch pieces (¾ cup)

1 tablespoon vegetable oil

1 onion, chopped

1 teaspoon table salt

2 garlic cloves, minced

2 teaspoons minced fresh oregano or ½ teaspoon dried

⅛ teaspoon ground cloves

⅛ teaspoon ground cinnamon

1 cup chicken broth, plus extra as needed

1 tomato, cored and quartered

8 ounces tomatillos, husks and stems removed, rinsed well, dried, and halved

3 tablespoons dry-roasted peanuts

2 tablespoons sesame seeds, toasted, divided

2 tablespoons raisins

1 tablespoon unsweetened cocoa powder

½ teaspoon pepper

1. Dissolve ¼ cup salt and sugar in 2 quarts cold water in large container. Submerge roast in brine, cover, and refrigerate for 1½ to 2 hours. Remove roast from brine and pat dry with paper towels.

2. Using highest sauté or browning function, toast pasillas in electric pressure cooker, stirring frequently, until fragrant, 2 to 6 minutes; transfer to bowl.

3. Tie 3 pieces of kitchen twine around each piece of pork to create 2 evenly shaped roasts. Heat oil in now-empty pressure cooker until shimmering. Add onion and salt and cook until onion is softened, 3 to 5 minutes. Stir in garlic, oregano, cloves, and cinnamon and cook until fragrant, about 30 seconds. Stir in broth, scraping up any browned bits. Stir in tomato, tomatillos, peanuts, 1 tablespoon sesame seeds, raisins, cocoa, pepper, and pasillas. Place roasts fat side up on top of tomato-tomatillo mixture so they sit above liquid.

4. Lock lid in place and close pressure release valve. Select high pressure cook function and cook for 14 minutes. Turn off pressure cooker and let pressure release naturally for 15 minutes. Quick-release any remaining pressure, then carefully remove lid, allowing steam to escape away from you.

5. Transfer pork to carving board, tent with aluminum foil, and let rest for 5 to 10 minutes.

6. Transfer cooking liquid to blender and process until smooth, 1 to 2 minutes. Adjust consistency with extra hot broth as needed. Season with salt and pepper to taste. Remove twine from roasts, slice ¼ inch thick, and transfer to serving dish. Spoon 1 cup sauce over pork and sprinkle with remaining 1 tablespoon sesame seeds. Serve, passing remaining sauce separately.

MUSTARDY APPLE BUTTER–GLAZED PORK CHOPS

Serves 4 | boneless pork chops

WHY THIS RECIPE WORKS Slow roasting is an ideal way to make tender, superjuicy glazed pork chops. The hands-off approach leaves time for you to make a side dish to complete the meal. We started by stirring together apple butter and Dijon mustard—thick and intensely flavored ingredients that wouldn't run off the chops when heated. Next, we adjusted the balance of flavors with sweet maple syrup, salty-savory soy sauce, and tangy cider vinegar. We applied a thin coating to boneless pork chops and roasted them in a low oven until the meat was juicy and tender and the glaze formed a tacky layer. Finally, we applied a second, substantial coating of glaze and broiled the chops until the glaze was bubbly and started to char. If your broiler has multiple temperature settings, use the highest. We like the consistency that Musselman's Apple Butter gives the glaze; if you're using another brand, you may need to thin the glaze with up to 1 tablespoon of water.

    3 tablespoons apple butter
    2 tablespoons maple syrup
    1 tablespoon Dijon mustard
    1 teaspoon soy sauce
    ½ teaspoon cider vinegar
    1 teaspoon kosher salt
    4 (6- to 8-ounce) boneless pork chops, ¾ to 1 inch thick, trimmed
    2 teaspoons minced fresh parsley

1. Adjust oven rack to middle position and heat oven to 275 degrees. Line rimmed baking sheet with aluminum foil and set wire rack in sheet. Spray rack with vegetable oil spray. Stir apple butter, maple syrup, mustard, soy sauce, and vinegar together in small bowl.

2. Sprinkle salt evenly over both sides of chops. Place chops on prepared wire rack and brush 1 teaspoon glaze on top and sides of each chop. Roast until meat registers 135 to 137 degrees, 40 to 45 minutes.

3. Remove sheet from oven and heat broiler. Brush 1 tablespoon glaze on top and sides of each chop. Return sheet to oven and broil until glaze is bubbly and slightly charred in spots, 3 to 6 minutes. Let rest for 5 minutes. Sprinkle with parsley and serve.

VARIATION

Spicy Gochujang-Glazed Pork Chops

Omit apple butter, mustard, and vinegar. Decrease maple syrup to 1 tablespoon and increase soy sauce to 1 tablespoon; place in small bowl. Add 4 teaspoons gochujang paste, 4 teaspoons white miso, 1 tablespoon orange juice, and 1 minced garlic clove and stir to combine. Proceed with recipe as directed.

CRISPY PAN-FRIED PORK CHOPS

Serves 4 | boneless pork chops

WHY THIS RECIPE WORKS A breaded coating can be just the thing to give lean, boneless pork chops a boost. First we dredged center-cut loin chops in cornstarch to help them form a crisp sheath once fried. Next we dipped the chops in a mixture of buttermilk, Dijon mustard, and garlic; the buttermilk brought a lighter texture and tangy flavor to the breading, and the mustard and garlic perked up the breading's flavor. To achieve the supercrunchy coating we wanted, we added cornflakes, which provided a craggy texture. To ensure that our breading stayed strongly adhered, we lightly scored the pork chops before breading them and let the breaded chops rest briefly before adding them to the pan. Don't let the chops drain on the paper towels for longer than 30 seconds, or the heat will steam the crust and make it soggy. You can substitute ¾ cup of store-bought cornflake crumbs for the whole cornflakes. If using store-bought crumbs, omit the processing step and mix the crumbs with the cornstarch, salt, and pepper.

    ⅔ cup cornstarch, divided
    1 cup buttermilk
    2 tablespoons Dijon mustard
    1 garlic clove, minced
    3 cups (3 ounces) cornflakes
    ½ teaspoon table salt
    ½ teaspoon pepper
    8 (3- to 4-ounce) boneless pork chops, ½ to ¾ inch thick, trimmed
    ⅔ cup vegetable oil for frying, divided
    Lemon wedges

1. Spread ⅓ cup cornstarch in shallow dish. Whisk buttermilk, mustard, and garlic in second shallow dish until combined. Process cornflakes, salt, pepper, and remaining ⅓ cup cornstarch in food processor until cornflakes are finely ground, about 10 seconds. Transfer cornflake mixture to third shallow dish.

2. Adjust oven rack to middle position and heat oven to 200 degrees. Set wire rack in rimmed baking sheet. Using sharp knife, cut ¹⁄₁₆-inch-deep slits, spaced ½ inch apart, on both sides of chops in crosshatch pattern. Season chops with salt and pepper. Working with 1 chop at a time, dredge chops in cornstarch; shake off excess. Using tongs, coat with buttermilk mixture; let excess drip off. Coat with cornflake mixture; gently pat off excess. Transfer chops to prepared wire rack and let chops stand for 10 minutes.

3. Heat ⅓ cup oil in 12-inch nonstick skillet over medium-high heat until shimmering. Place 4 chops in skillet and cook until golden brown and crispy on first side, 2 to 5 minutes. Carefully flip chops and continue to cook until second side is golden

brown and crispy and chops register 145 degrees, 2 to 5 minutes longer. Transfer chops to paper towel–lined plate and let drain for 30 seconds on each side. Transfer chops to clean wire rack set in rimmed baking sheet, then transfer sheet to oven to keep warm. Discard oil in skillet and wipe skillet clean with paper towels. Repeat with remaining ⅓ cup oil and remaining 4 chops. Serve with lemon wedges.

VARIATIONS

Crispy Pan-Fried Pork Chops with Spicy Rub

Combine 1½ teaspoons ground cumin, 1½ teaspoons chili powder, ¾ teaspoon ground coriander, ⅛ teaspoon ground cinnamon, and ⅛ teaspoon red pepper flakes in bowl. Coat chops with spice rub after seasoning with salt (omit pepper) in step 2.

Crispy Pan-Fried Pork Chops with Three-Pepper Rub

Combine 1½ teaspoons pepper, 1½ teaspoons white pepper, ¾ teaspoon ground coriander, ¾ teaspoon ground cumin, ¼ teaspoon red pepper flakes, and ¼ teaspoon ground cinnamon in bowl. Coat chops with spice rub after seasoning with salt (omit pepper) in step 2.

DEVILED PORK CHOPS

Serves 4 | boneless pork chops

WHY THIS RECIPE WORKS Most recipes call for pan-searing or broiling pork chops, but here we opted to slow-roast them in a low oven. This way, they retained as much moisture as possible—a must for lean cuts to taste juicy—and cooked evenly from edge to edge, no flipping required. The lower heat also encouraged enzymes within the pork to break down some of the muscle protein, leading to more tender meat. To punch up their mild flavor, we "deviled" the chops by painting them with a bold, complex-tasting paste of spicy Dijon mustard mixed with dry mustard, minced garlic, and cayenne and black peppers. For textural contrast and visual appeal, we coated the tops of the chops with crispy panko bread crumbs. If using enhanced pork, do not add salt to the mustard paste in step 2. Serve the pork chops with mashed potatoes, rice, or buttered egg noodles.

  2 tablespoons unsalted butter
  ½ cup panko bread crumbs
1⅛ teaspoons kosher salt, divided
  ¼ cup Dijon mustard
  2 teaspoons packed brown sugar
1½ teaspoons dry mustard
  1 teaspoon pepper
  ½ teaspoon garlic, minced to paste
  ¼ teaspoon cayenne pepper
  4 (6- to 8-ounce) boneless pork chops, ¾ to 1 inch thick, trimmed

1. Adjust oven rack to middle position and heat oven to 275 degrees.

2. Melt butter in 10-inch skillet over medium heat. Add panko and cook, stirring frequently, until golden brown, 3 to 5 minutes. Transfer to bowl and sprinkle with ⅛ teaspoon salt. Stir Dijon, sugar, dry mustard, pepper, garlic, cayenne, and remaining 1 teaspoon salt in second bowl until smooth.

3. Set wire rack in rimmed baking sheet and spray with vegetable oil spray. Pat chops dry with paper towels. Transfer chops to prepared wire rack, spacing them 1 inch apart. Brush 1 tablespoon mustard mixture over top and sides of each chop (leave bottoms uncoated). Spoon 2 tablespoons toasted panko evenly over top of each chop and press lightly to adhere.

4. Roast until meat registers 140 degrees, 40 to 50 minutes. Remove from oven and let rest on rack for 10 minutes before serving.

PAN-SEARED THICK-CUT BONELESS PORK CHOPS WITH PEACHES AND SPINACH

Serves 4 | boneless pork chops

WHY THIS RECIPE WORKS Quick-cooking boneless pork chops lend themselves well to a weeknight meal, so we set out to create a recipe with a side dish built in for ultimate efficiency. To ensure chops of equal size, we bought a boneless center-cut pork loin roast and cut the chops ourselves. We seasoned them with salt, pepper, and citrusy coriander and seared them in a skillet, flipping them frequently to help them cook through evenly. While the pork rested, we cooked our side in the same pan. This way, the fond left by the pork contributed deep flavor to the peaches, onion, and wilted spinach. Look for a pork loin that is 7 to 8 inches long and 3 to 3½ inches in diameter. Do not use enhanced pork. This recipe works best in a cast-iron skillet, but a 12-inch stainless-steel skillet will work.

  2 teaspoons ground coriander
  ¾ teaspoon table salt, divided
  ¼ teaspoon pepper
  1 (2½- to 3-pound) boneless center-cut pork loin roast, trimmed
  3 tablespoons vegetable oil, divided
  2 ripe peaches, halved, pitted, and cut into 1-inch wedges
  1 red onion, chopped
 12 ounces (12 cups) baby spinach
  1 tablespoon minced fresh tarragon

Pan-Seared Thick-Cut Boneless Pork Chops with Peaches and Spinach

1. Combine coriander, ½ teaspoon salt, and pepper in small bowl. Cut roast crosswise into 4 chops of equal thickness. Pat chops dry with paper towels, then season with coriander mixture.

2. Heat 12-inch cast-iron skillet over medium heat for 5 minutes. Add 1 tablespoon oil and heat until just smoking. Add chops and cook, without moving, until lightly browned on both sides, about 2 minutes per side. Flip chops and continue to cook, flipping every 2 minutes, until well browned and meat registers 140 degrees, 12 to 14 minutes. Transfer chops to cutting board, tent with aluminum foil, and let rest.

3. While pork rests, add 1 tablespoon oil to now-empty skillet and heat over medium-low heat until shimmering. Add peaches, cut side down, and cook until caramelized on first side, about 2 minutes. Flip and continue to cook until caramelized on second side and tender, about 2 minutes. Transfer to serving bowl.

4. Add remaining 1 tablespoon oil to now-empty skillet and heat over medium heat until shimmering. Add onion and remaining ¼ teaspoon salt and cook, stirring occasionally, until softened and lightly browned, 2 to 4 minutes.

5. Add spinach to skillet 1 handful at a time and cook until wilted and tender, about 2 minutes. Off heat, season with salt and pepper to taste. Sprinkle peaches with tarragon and serve alongside pork and spinach.

PEPPER-CRUSTED PORK TENDERLOIN WITH ASPARAGUS AND BALSAMIC PAN SAUCE

Serves 4 | pork tenderloin

WHY THIS RECIPE WORKS This elegant take on pork tenderloin uses a stovetop-to-oven roasting method to achieve flavorful browning and ensure that the meat cooks through evenly. We started by seasoning the tenderloins with salt, pepper, and a hefty dose of fresh rosemary to build potent flavor and then seared them in a hot skillet before transferring them to the oven to finish cooking. We then took advantage of the flavorful fond left behind in the pan to build a quick side dish of sautéed asparagus. Once the asparagus was tender, we topped it with a sprinkle of creamy goat cheese to complement its fresh vegetal flavor. We finished this easy dinner by making a quick balsamic vinegar–butter sauce in the same skillet. If using enhanced pork, omit the salt in step 1.

1 tablespoon plus ¼ teaspoon pepper, divided
1 tablespoon minced fresh rosemary
1¼ teaspoons table salt, divided
2 (12- to 16-ounce) pork tenderloins, trimmed
2 tablespoons vegetable oil, divided
2 pounds asparagus, trimmed and cut on bias into 2-inch lengths
¼ cup chicken broth
2 ounces goat cheese, crumbled (½ cup)
¼ cup balsamic vinegar
2 tablespoons unsalted butter

1. Adjust oven rack to middle position and heat oven to 450 degrees. Set wire rack in rimmed baking sheet. Combine 1 tablespoon pepper, rosemary, and 1 teaspoon salt in bowl. Pat tenderloins dry with paper towels; sprinkle with rosemary mixture.

2. Heat 1 tablespoon oil in 12-inch skillet over medium-high heat until just smoking. Brown tenderloins well on all sides, about 10 minutes. Transfer tenderloins to prepared rack and roast until pork registers 145 degrees, about 15 minutes. Transfer tenderloins to carving board and let rest for 10 minutes.

3. Meanwhile, heat remaining 1 tablespoon oil in now-empty skillet over medium-high heat until shimmering. Add asparagus, broth, remaining ¼ teaspoon pepper, and remaining ¼ teaspoon salt and cook, covered, until tender, about 5 minutes; transfer asparagus to serving dish and top with goat cheese. Reduce heat to medium-low, add vinegar to now-empty skillet, and simmer until thickened, scraping up any browned bits, about 1 minute. Off heat, whisk in butter. Slice pork ½ inch thick, arrange on serving dish with asparagus, and drizzle with sauce. Serve.

BROILED PORK TENDERLOIN

Serves 4 to 6 | pork tenderloin

WHY THIS RECIPE WORKS Quicker-cooking pork tenderloin is a great candidate for broiling but many recipes yield pallid, overcooked pork or spottily browned roasts with undercooked interiors. A smart trick, cooking in a disposable aluminum pan, reflected the radiant heat of the broiler toward the pork, enhancing browning. Since some ovens heat faster than others and are likely to cycle off if preheated at an intense heat for too long, we preheated the oven to 325 degrees before putting in the roasts and turning on the broiler. The broiler created a significant carryover cooking effect, so we pulled the roasts when they hit 125 to 130 degrees instead of 140 degrees so they'd be perfect after their 10-minute rest. If using enhanced pork, reduce the salt to 1½ teaspoons. A 3-inch-deep aluminum pan is essential. Do not make this recipe with a drawer broiler.

- 2 (1-pound) pork tenderloins, trimmed
- 2 teaspoons kosher salt
- 1¼ teaspoons vegetable oil
- ½ teaspoon pepper
- ¼ teaspoon baking soda
- 1 (13 by 9-inch) disposable aluminum roasting pan

1. Adjust oven rack 4 to 5 inches from broiler element and heat oven to 325 degrees. Fold thin tip of each tenderloin under about 2 inches to create uniformly shaped roasts. Tie tenderloins crosswise with kitchen twine at 2-inch intervals, making sure folded tip is secured underneath. Trim excess twine close to meat to prevent it from scorching under broiler.

2. Mix salt, oil, and pepper in small bowl until salt is evenly coated with oil. Add baking soda and stir until well combined. Rub mixture evenly over pork. Place tenderloins in disposable pan, evenly spaced from sides of pan and each other.

3. Turn oven to broil. Immediately place tenderloins in oven and broil for 5 minutes. Flip tenderloins and continue to broil until golden brown and meat registers 125 to 130 degrees, 8 to 14 minutes. Remove disposable pan from oven, tent with aluminum foil, and let rest for 10 minutes. Discard twine, slice tenderloins ½ inch thick, and serve.

SESAME-CRUSTED PORK TENDERLOIN WITH CELERY SALAD

Serves 4 | pork tenderloin

WHY THIS RECIPE WORKS To add excitement to a weeknight pork tenderloin dinner, we chose to coat the mild tenderloins in nutty, crunchy sesame seeds. Searing the tenderloins on all sides toasted the sesame seeds, enhancing their flavor and turning them an attractive golden brown. Once the seeds were toasted, we transferred the pork to the oven to gently finish cooking. To round out the meal, we made a quick salad of crisp celery and chewy, mildly sweet dried currants, a refreshing and unique contrast to the rich, nutty sesame seed–crusted pork. Allowing the celery and currants to marinate in a tart lemon-thyme vinaigrette helped hydrate the currants and slightly soften the celery's bite.

- 6 tablespoons extra-virgin olive oil, divided
- 3 tablespoons lemon juice
- 1 teaspoon minced fresh thyme
- 1 small garlic clove, minced
- 1 teaspoon table salt
- ½ teaspoon pepper
- 6 celery ribs, sliced thin on bias
- 3 tablespoons dried currants
- 2 (1-pound) pork tenderloins, trimmed
- ½ cup sesame seeds
- 4 ounces goat cheese, crumbled (1 cup)

1. Adjust oven rack to middle position and heat oven to 375 degrees. Set wire rack in rimmed baking sheet. Whisk ¼ cup oil, lemon juice, thyme, garlic, salt, and pepper together in large bowl. Add celery and currants and toss to combine; set aside.

2. Pat pork dry with paper towels and season with salt and pepper. Spread sesame seeds on large plate and roll pork in seeds until fully coated. Heat remaining 2 tablespoons oil in 12-inch nonstick skillet over medium-high heat until shimmering. Add pork and cook until seeds are lightly browned on all sides, about 5 minutes. Transfer pork to prepared wire rack. Roast until meat registers 135 degrees, 12 to 15 minutes. Transfer pork to carving board and let rest for 5 minutes. Transfer salad to platter and sprinkle with goat cheese. Slice pork ½ inch thick and serve with salad.

**Sesame-Crusted Pork Tenderloin
with Celery Salad**

TUTORIAL
Pork Schnitzel

A creative frying method achieves schnitzel with a trademark wrinkly-crisp, puffed coating that's easy to accomplish.

1. Cut tenderloin on angle into 4 equal pieces.

2. Working with 1 piece at a time, place pork cut side down between 2 sheets of parchment paper or plastic wrap and pound with meat pounder to even ⅛- to ¼-inch thickness.

3. Dredge cutlets thoroughly in flour, shaking off excess; dip in egg mixture, letting excess drip off to ensure very thin coating; and coat evenly with bread crumbs. Let coating dry for 5 minutes.

4. Lay 2 cutlets in pot of hot oil and cook, shaking pot gently and continuously, until cutlets are wrinkled and light golden brown on both sides, 1 to 2 minutes per side.

5. Transfer cutlets to paper towel–lined plate and flip cutlets several times to blot excess oil.

6. Serve cutlets sprinkled with parsley; capers; and hard-cooked egg, if using, passing lemon wedges separately.

PORK SCHNITZEL

Serves 4 | pork tenderloin

WHY THIS RECIPE WORKS It's difficult to achieve pork schnitzel's signature crisp, wrinkled, puffy coating. For our take, we pounded pork tenderloin into long, thin cutlets that would fit two at a time in the pan. We followed the usual flour, egg, and bread-crumb sequence for breading the cutlets, with a couple of important twists: Microwaving the bread allowed us to make extra-dry crumbs for enhanced crispness, and a tablespoon of vegetable oil whisked into the egg helped the coating puff and separate from the meat. But the real breakthrough was in the frying method. Instead of sautéing the cutlets, we cooked them in a Dutch oven in an inch of oil, shaking the pot to get some of the oil over the top of the meat. The extra heat quickly puffed the coating. The 2 cups of oil called for in this recipe may seem like a lot, but this amount is necessary to achieve the traditional wrinkled texture on the finished cutlets. When properly cooked, the cutlets absorb very little oil. Use a Dutch oven that holds 6 quarts or more.

7 slices hearty white sandwich bread, crusts removed, cut into ¾-inch cubes
½ cup all-purpose flour
2 large eggs, plus 1 hard-cooked large egg, yolk and white separated and passed through fine-mesh strainer (optional)
1 tablespoon vegetable oil
1 (1¼-pound) pork tenderloin, trimmed
2 cups vegetable oil for frying
2 tablespoons chopped fresh parsley
2 tablespoons capers, rinsed
Lemon wedges

1. Place bread on large plate. Microwave for 4 minutes, stirring well halfway through microwaving. Microwave at 50 percent power until bread is dry and few pieces start to lightly brown, 3 to 5 minutes, stirring every minute. Process bread in food processor to very fine crumbs, about 45 seconds. Transfer bread crumbs (you should have about 1¼ cups) to shallow dish. Spread flour in second shallow dish. Beat 2 eggs with 1 tablespoon oil in third shallow dish.

2. Set wire rack in rimmed baking sheet and line plate with triple layer of paper towels. Cut tenderloin on angle into 4 equal pieces. Working with 1 piece at a time, place pork cut side down between 2 sheets of parchment paper or plastic wrap and pound with meat pounder to even ⅛- to ¼-inch thickness. Pat cutlets dry with paper towels and season with salt and pepper. Working with 1 cutlet at a time, dredge cutlets thoroughly in flour, shaking off excess; dip in egg mixture, letting excess drip off to ensure very thin coating; and coat evenly with bread crumbs, pressing on crumbs to adhere. Transfer breaded cutlets to prepared rack in single layer; let coating dry for 5 minutes.

3. Heat 2 cups oil in large Dutch oven over medium-high heat to 375 degrees. Lay 2 cutlets in pot, without overlapping them, and cook, shaking pot gently and continuously, until cutlets are wrinkled and light golden brown on both sides, 1 to 2 minutes per side. Transfer cutlets to paper towel–lined plate and flip cutlets several times to blot excess oil. Return oil to 375 degrees and repeat with remaining cutlets. Serve cutlets sprinkled with parsley; capers; and hard-cooked egg, if using, passing lemon wedges separately.

PORK MEDALLIONS WITH RED PEPPER SAUCE

Serves 4 | pork tenderloin

WHY THIS RECIPE WORKS Mild, tender pork tenderloin is the perfect cut for turning into visually appealing medallions and serving with a bright, balanced sauce for a quick dinner. Jarred roasted red peppers were a convenient and flavorful option for the sauce, saving us the trouble and time of roasting peppers ourselves. We processed slivered toasted almonds (for richness and body), water (to achieve the right consistency), olive oil, sherry vinegar (for a hit of acidity to offset the peppers' sweetness), garlic, honey, and smoked paprika along with the peppers until the mixture was smooth and then set the sauce aside. All that was left to do was season the tenderloin medallions, cook them in a skillet over medium-high heat until they registered 140 degrees, and then allow them to rest for 5 minutes before serving them with the sauce. A sprinkling of slivered almonds contributed delicate crunch.

1 cup jarred roasted red peppers, rinsed and patted dry
¼ cup plus 2 tablespoons slivered almonds, toasted, divided
¼ cup water
¼ cup extra-virgin olive oil, divided
1 tablespoon sherry vinegar
2 garlic cloves, chopped
1 teaspoon honey
½ teaspoon smoked paprika
½ teaspoon table salt
2 (12-ounce) pork tenderloins, trimmed and cut crosswise into 1½-inch medallions

1. Process red peppers, ¼ cup almonds, water, 3 tablespoons oil, vinegar, garlic, honey, paprika, and salt in blender until smooth, about 45 seconds. Transfer to bowl; set aside.

2. Pat pork dry with paper towels and season with salt and pepper. Heat remaining 1 tablespoon oil in 12-inch nonstick skillet over medium-high heat until just smoking. Add pork, cut side down, and cook until well browned and meat registers 140 degrees, about 4 minutes per side. Transfer to plate, tent with foil, and let rest for 5 minutes. Serve pork with red pepper sauce, sprinkled with remaining 2 tablespoons almonds.

GRILLED PORK TENDERLOIN WITH GRILLED PINEAPPLE-RED ONION SALSA

Serves 4 to 6 | pork tenderloin

WHY THIS RECIPE WORKS To produce relatively skinny pork tenderloins with a rich crust and a tender, juicy interior, we used a half-grill fire and seared them on the hotter side of the grill. This allowed the exterior to develop flavorful browning before the interior was cooked through. Then we moved the meat to the cooler side of the grill to finish the cooking gently. Seasoning the meat with a mixture of salt, cumin, and chipotle chile powder added smoky, savory flavor, and a touch of sugar encouraged browning. To add bright flavor and make the most of the fire, we grilled pineapple and red onion and, while the cooked pork rested, combined them with cilantro, a serrano chile, lime juice, and a bit of reserved spice mixture to make a quick salsa. We prefer unenhanced pork in this recipe, but enhanced pork (pork injected with a salt solution) can be used. Pineapples don't ripen further once picked, so be sure to purchase a fragrant fruit that gives slightly when pressed.

PORK
- 1½ teaspoons kosher salt
- 1½ teaspoons sugar
- ½ teaspoon ground cumin
- ½ teaspoon chipotle chile powder
- 2 (12- to 16-ounce) pork tenderloins, trimmed

SALSA
- ½ pineapple, peeled, cored, and cut lengthwise into 6 wedges
- 1 red onion, cut into 8 wedges through root end
- 4 teaspoons extra-virgin olive oil, divided
- ½ cup minced fresh cilantro
- 1 serrano chile, stemmed, seeded, and minced
- 2 tablespoons lime juice, plus extra for seasoning

1. For the pork: Combine salt, sugar, cumin, and chile powder in small bowl. Measure out ½ teaspoon spice mixture and set aside. Rub remaining spice mixture evenly over surface of both tenderloins. Transfer to large plate or rimmed baking sheet and refrigerate while preparing grill.

2a. For a charcoal grill: Open bottom vent completely. Light large chimney starter filled with charcoal briquettes (6 quarts). When top coals are partially covered with ash, pour evenly over half of grill. Set cooking grate in place, cover, and open lid vent completely. Heat grill until hot, about 5 minutes.

2b. For a gas grill: Turn all burners to high, cover, and heat grill until hot, about 15 minutes. Leave primary burner on high and turn off other burner(s).

3. Clean and oil cooking grate. Place tenderloins on hotter side of grill. Cover and cook, turning tenderloins every 2 minutes, until well browned on all sides, about 8 minutes.

4. For the salsa: Brush pineapple and onion with 1 teaspoon oil. Move tenderloins to cooler side of grill (6 to 8 inches from heat source) and place pineapple and onion on hotter side of grill. Cover and cook until pineapple and onion are charred on both sides and softened, 8 to 10 minutes, flipping pineapple and onion halfway through cooking, and until pork registers 140 degrees, 12 to 17 minutes, turning tenderloins every 5 minutes. As pineapple and onion and tenderloins reach desired level of doneness, transfer pineapple and onion to plate and transfer tenderloins to carving board. Tent tenderloins with aluminum foil and let rest for 10 minutes.

5. While tenderloins rest, chop pineapple coarse. Pulse cilantro, serrano, lime juice, pineapple, onion, reserved spice mixture, and remaining 1 tablespoon oil in food processor until mixture is roughly chopped, 4 to 6 pulses. Transfer to bowl and season with salt and extra lime juice to taste. Slice tenderloins crosswise ½ inch thick. Serve with salsa.

PERFECT PAN-SEARED PORK TENDERLOIN STEAKS

Serves 4 | pork tenderloin

WHY THIS RECIPE WORKS Pork tenderloin steaks have ample surface area for browning, so we wanted to make sure to sear them right. After salting the pork tenderloins we dried them well so that moisture didn't inhibit browning; instead of patting the steaks dry we let them sit between paper towels for 10 minutes. We opted to use the reverse searing technique, first cooking the steaks gently in the oven at a relatively low temperature so that the meat cooked evenly from edge to edge and was moist and tender. We then finished them by searing them in a very hot skillet until they were well browned on both sides. Choose tenderloins that are equal in size to ensure that the pork cooks at the same rate. If using enhanced pork, reduce the salt in step 2 to ¼ teaspoon per steak. Open the oven as infrequently as possible in step 2. If the meat is not yet up to temperature, wait at least 5 minutes before taking its temperature again.

- 2 (1-pound) pork tenderloins, trimmed
- 1 teaspoon table salt, divided
- ¼ teaspoon pepper, divided
- 2 tablespoons vegetable oil

Grilled Pork Kebabs with Hoisin and Five-Spice

GRILLED PORK KEBABS WITH HOISIN AND FIVE-SPICE

Serves 4 | pork tenderloin

WHY THIS RECIPE WORKS The intense heat of grilling can create flavorful charring on the outside of mild pork tenderloin. To boost this effect, we increased the surface area of the pork by cutting it into bite-size pieces, coated it with a potent hoisin and five-spice powder glaze, and then threaded it onto skewers for easier grilling. Salting the meat before cooking it helped it hold on to moisture, making it less likely to overcook on the grill, and spraying the meat with oil not only minimized sticking but also helped the five-spice powder bloom, preventing a raw spice flavor. Cooking the kebabs quickly over a hot fire was the last step in preventing moisture loss and dry meat. We thickened our sweet hoisin glaze with cornstarch to help it cling to the pork and reserved a small amount to brush on halfway through grilling to ensure that each piece of moist, juicy pork boasted some crusty char and a sticky, finger-licking coating. You will need four 12-inch metal skewers for this recipe.

2 (12-ounce) pork tenderloins, trimmed and cut into 1-inch pieces
1 teaspoon kosher salt
1½ teaspoons five-spice powder
¾ teaspoon garlic powder
½ teaspoon cornstarch
4½ tablespoons hoisin sauce
  Vegetable oil spray
2 scallions, sliced thin

1. Toss pork and salt together in large bowl. Set aside for 20 minutes. Meanwhile, whisk five-spice powder, garlic powder, and cornstarch together in bowl. Add hoisin to five-spice mixture and stir to combine. Measure out 1½ tablespoons hoisin mixture and set aside.

2. Add remaining hoisin mixture to pork and toss to coat. Thread pork onto four 12-inch metal skewers, leaving ¼ inch between pieces. Spray both sides of meat generously with oil spray.

3a. For a charcoal grill: Open bottom vent completely. Light large chimney starter filled with charcoal briquettes (6 quarts). When top coals are partially covered with ash, pour evenly over half of grill. Set cooking grate in place, cover, and open lid vent completely. Heat grill until hot, about 5 minutes.

3b. For a gas grill: Turn all burners to high, cover, and heat grill until hot, about 15 minutes. Leave primary burner on high and turn off other burner(s).

1. Adjust oven rack to middle position and heat oven to 275 degrees. Set wire rack in rimmed baking sheet and lightly spray rack with vegetable oil spray.

2. Pound each tenderloin to 1-inch thickness. Halve each tenderloin crosswise. Sprinkle each steak with ½ teaspoon salt and ⅛ teaspoon pepper. Place steaks on prepared wire rack and cook until meat registers between 137 and 140 degrees, 25 to 35 minutes.

3. Move steaks to 1 side of rack. Line cleared side with double layer of paper towels. Transfer steaks to paper towels, cover with another double layer of paper towels, and let stand for 10 minutes.

4. Pat steaks until surfaces are very dry. Heat oil in 12-inch skillet over medium-high heat until just smoking. Increase heat to high, place steaks in skillet, and sear until well browned on both sides, 1 to 2 minutes per side. Transfer to carving board and let stand for 5 minutes. Slice steaks against grain ¾ inch thick and transfer to serving platter. Season with salt to taste, and serve.

4. Clean and oil cooking grate. Place skewers on hotter side of grill and grill until well charred, 3 to 4 minutes. Flip skewers, brush with reserved hoisin mixture, and continue to grill until second side is well charred and meat registers 145 degrees, 3 to 4 minutes longer. Transfer to serving platter, tent with foil, and let rest for 5 minutes. Sprinkle with scallions and serve.

VARIATION
Grilled Pork Kebabs with Sweet Sriracha Glaze
Substitute 3 tablespoons packed brown sugar and 1½ tablespoons sriracha for five-spice powder, garlic powder, and hoisin sauce. Increase cornstarch to 1 teaspoon. Substitute ¼ cup minced fresh cilantro for scallions.

SOUS VIDE PORK TENDERLOIN STEAKS WITH SCALLION-GINGER RELISH

Serves 4 | pork tenderloin

WHY THIS RECIPE WORKS For pork tenderloin that was perfectly tender and juicy from edge to edge, with no fear of overcooking, we knew our immersion circulator would do the trick. We began by lightly pounding the pork to create two flat sides that would be easy to sear. Halving the tenderloins crosswise created moderately sized steaks for us to work with. Submerged in a 140-degree water bath, the pork was guaranteed to remain moist and tender and to cook evenly throughout. Once the pork was cooked through, we removed it from the water bath, patted it thoroughly dry, and seared it quickly in a very hot skillet to give it appealing browning. A zippy scallion-ginger relish contributed welcome freshness and flavor. If using enhanced pork, reduce the salt in step 2 to ¼ teaspoon per steak.

2 (1-pound) pork tenderloins, trimmed
1 teaspoon table salt, divided
¼ teaspoon pepper, divided
½ cup vegetable oil, divided
6 scallions, white and green parts separated and sliced thin
2 teaspoons grated fresh ginger
½ teaspoon ground white pepper
½ teaspoon grated lime zest plus 2 teaspoons juice
2 teaspoons soy sauce

1. Using sous vide circulator, bring water to 140°F in 7-quart container.

2. Pound tenderloins to 1-inch thickness. Halve each tenderloin crosswise to create 4 steaks total. Sprinkle each steak with ½ teaspoon salt and ⅛ teaspoon pepper. Place steaks and

2 tablespoons oil in 1-gallon zipper-lock freezer bag. Seal bag, pressing out as much air as possible. Gently lower bag into prepared water bath until pork is fully submerged, then clip top corner of bag to side of pot, allowing remaining air bubbles to rise to top of bag. Open 1 corner of zipper, release air bubbles, and reseal bag. Cover pot with plastic wrap and cook steaks for at least 1 hour or up to 2 hours.

3. While steaks cook, combine scallion whites, ginger, pepper, and lime zest in heatproof bowl. Heat ¼ cup oil in small saucepan over medium heat until shimmering. Pour oil over scallion mixture. (Mixture will bubble.) Stir until well combined. Let cool completely, about 15 minutes. Stir in scallion greens, lime juice, and soy sauce. Set aside to allow flavors to meld.

3. Line wire rack with double layer of paper towels and place in rimmed baking sheet. Transfer steaks to paper towels, cover with another double layer of paper towels, and let stand for 10 minutes.

4. Pat steaks until surfaces are very dry. Heat remaining 2 tablespoons oil in 12-inch skillet over medium-high heat until just smoking. Increase heat to high, place steaks in skillet, and sear until well browned on both sides, 1 to 2 minutes per side. Transfer to carving board and let stand for 5 minutes. Slice against grain ¾ inch thick and transfer to serving platter. Season with salt to taste, and serve with relish.

MU SHU PORK

Serves 4 | pork tenderloin

WHY THIS RECIPE WORKS Mandarin-style pancakes are the traditional wrapper for mu shu pork filling and the hallmark of the dish. We started there. We used hot water in the dough for two important reasons: It makes the dough less sticky because the starches absorb hot water more quickly than cold water, and it makes the dough easier to roll out because the gluten proteins don't coil as tightly, and thus don't snap back as much when rolled out. As for the pork and vegetable filling, the prep can be done while the dough rests. We brined sliced pork tenderloin in soy sauce, which kept it tender and moist, while sherry, sugar, ginger, and white pepper punched up the meat's flavor. Rehydrated dried shiitake mushrooms provided a pleasantly chewy texture, and their soaking liquid added depth to our stir-fry sauce. Cabbage and sliced bamboo shoots bulked up the vegetable portion of the meal. We strongly recommend weighing the flour for the pancakes. For an accurate measurement of boiling water, bring a full kettle of water to a boil and then measure out the desired amount.

Mu Shu Pork

PANCAKES

1½ cups (7½ ounces) all-purpose flour
¾ cup boiling water
2 teaspoons toasted sesame oil
½ teaspoon vegetable oil

STIR-FRY

1 cup water
1 ounce dried shiitake mushrooms, rinsed
¼ cup soy sauce, divided
2 tablespoons dry sherry, divided
1 teaspoon sugar
1 teaspoon grated fresh ginger
¼ teaspoon ground white pepper
1 (12-ounce) pork tenderloin, trimmed, halved horizontally, and sliced thin against grain
2 teaspoons cornstarch
2 teaspoons plus 2 tablespoons vegetable oil, divided
2 eggs, beaten
6 scallions, white and green parts separated and sliced thin on bias, divided
1 (8-ounce) can bamboo shoots, rinsed and sliced into matchsticks
3 cups thinly sliced green cabbage
Hoisin sauce

1. **For the pancakes:** Using wooden spoon, mix flour and boiling water in bowl to form rough dough. When cool, transfer dough to lightly floured counter and knead until it forms ball that is tacky but no longer sticky, about 4 minutes (dough will not be perfectly smooth). Cover loosely with plastic wrap and let rest for 30 minutes.

2. Roll dough into 12-inch-long log on lightly floured counter and cut into 12 equal pieces. Turn each piece cut side up and pat into rough 3-inch disk. Brush 1 side of 6 disks with sesame oil; top each oiled side with 1 unoiled disk and press lightly to form 6 pairs. Roll disks into 7-inch rounds, lightly flouring counter as needed.

3. Heat vegetable oil in 12-inch nonstick skillet over medium heat until shimmering. Using paper towels, carefully wipe out oil. Place 1 dough round in skillet and cook, without moving it, until air pockets begin to form between layers and underside is dry, 40 to 60 seconds. Flip pancake and cook until few light brown spots appear on second side, 40 to 60 seconds. Transfer to plate and, when cool enough to handle, peel apart into 2 pancakes. Stack pancakes moist side up and cover loosely with plastic. Repeat with remaining dough rounds. Cover pancakes tightly and keep warm. Wipe skillet clean with paper towels. (Pancakes can be wrapped tightly in plastic, then aluminum foil, and refrigerated for up to 3 days or frozen for up to 2 months. Thaw wrapped pancakes at room temperature. Unwrap and place on plate. Invert second plate over pancakes and microwave until warm and soft, 1 to 1½ minutes.)

4. **For the stir-fry:** Microwave water and mushrooms in covered bowl until steaming, about 1 minute. Let sit until softened, about 5 minutes. Drain mushrooms in fine-mesh strainer set over bowl, reserve ⅓ cup liquid, discard mushroom stems, and slice caps thin.

5. Combine 2 tablespoons soy sauce, 1 tablespoon sherry, sugar, ginger, and white pepper in large bowl. Add pork and toss to combine. Whisk together cornstarch, reserved mushroom liquid, remaining 2 tablespoons soy sauce, and remaining 1 tablespoon sherry; set aside.

6. Heat 2 teaspoons oil in now-empty skillet over medium-high heat until shimmering. Add eggs and scramble quickly until set but not dry, about 15 seconds. Transfer eggs to bowl and break into ¼- to ½-inch pieces with fork. Heat 1 tablespoon oil in now-empty skillet over medium-high heat until shimmering. Add scallion whites and cook, stirring frequently, until well browned, 1 to 1½ minutes. Add pork mixture. Spread into even layer and cook, without stirring, until well browned on 1 side, 1 to 2 minutes. Stir and continue to cook, stirring frequently, until all pork is opaque, 1 to 2 minutes longer. Transfer to bowl with eggs.

7. Heat remaining 1 tablespoon oil in now-empty skillet over medium-high heat until shimmering. Whisk mushroom liquid mixture to recombine. Add bamboo shoots and mushrooms to skillet and cook, stirring frequently, until heated through, about 1 minute. Add cabbage, all but 2 tablespoons scallion greens, and mushroom liquid mixture and cook, stirring constantly, until liquid has evaporated and cabbage is wilted but retains some crunch, 2 to 3 minutes. Add pork and eggs and stir to combine. Transfer to platter; top with remaining 2 tablespoons scallion greens. Spread about ½ teaspoon hoisin in center of each warm pancake. Spoon stir-fry over hoisin and serve.

BARBECUE BABY BACK RIBS

Serves 4 | baby back ribs

WHY THIS RECIPE WORKS Ribs are a favorite of barbecue enthusiasts everywhere, but grilling them at home can go awry without the proper method. We wanted a recipe for baby back ribs that would produce juicy, tender, and fully seasoned meat with an intense, mouth-watering smokiness; in short, ribs that would be well worth the time, money, and effort. These ribs are fairly lean, so for pork that was so flavorful they wouldn't even need barbecue sauce, we first brined them in a salt, sugar, and water solution and then rubbed them with a spice and sugar mixture before throwing them on the grill. Grilling the ribs low and slow ensured that the meat would be moist. For a more potent spice flavor, coat the ribs with the spice rub as directed and refrigerate them overnight, wrapped tightly in plastic wrap.

Barbecue Baby Back Ribs

If you'd like to use wood chunks instead of wood chips when using a charcoal grill, substitute two medium wood chunks, soaked in water for 1 hour, for the wood chip packet.

½ cup table salt for brining
½ cup granulated sugar for brining
2 (2-pound) racks baby back ribs, trimmed, membrane removed
3½ teaspoons paprika
1¾ teaspoons ground cumin
1½ teaspoons chili powder
1½ teaspoons packed dark brown sugar
1 teaspoon white pepper
¾ teaspoon dried oregano
¾ teaspoon table salt
¾ teaspoon pepper
½ teaspoon cayenne pepper
2 cups wood chips, soaked in water for 15 minutes and drained

1. Dissolve ½ cup salt and granulated sugar in 4 quarts cold water in large container. Submerge ribs in brine, cover, and refrigerate for 1 hour. Remove ribs from brine, rinse under running water, and pat dry with paper towels.

2. Combine paprika, cumin, chili powder, brown sugar, white pepper, oregano, salt, pepper, and cayenne in small bowl. Rub each rack with 1 tablespoon spice rub and refrigerate for

30 minutes. Using large piece of heavy-duty aluminum foil, wrap soaked chips in 8 by 4½-inch foil packet. (Make sure chips do not poke holes in sides or bottom of packet.) Cut 2 evenly spaced 2-inch slits in top of packet.

3a. For a charcoal grill: Open bottom vent halfway. Light large chimney starter three-quarters filled with charcoal briquettes (4½ quarts). When top coals are partially covered with ash, pour evenly over half of grill. Place wood chip packet on coals. Set cooking grate in place, cover, and open lid vent halfway. Heat grill until hot and wood chips are smoking, about 5 minutes.

3b. For a gas grill: Remove cooking grate and place wood chip packet directly on primary burner. Set grate in place, turn all burners to high, cover, and heat grill until hot and wood chips are smoking, about 15 minutes. Leave primary burner on high and turn off other burner(s).

4. Clean and oil cooking grate.

5a. For a charcoal grill: Place ribs on cooler side of grill and cook, covered, for 2 hours, until grill temperature drops to about 250 degrees, flipping, switching, and rotating ribs every 30 minutes so that rack that was nearest fire is on outside. Add 10 fresh briquettes to pile of coals. Cover and continue to cook (grill temperature should register 275 to 300 degrees), flipping, switching, and rotating ribs every 30 minutes, until meat easily pulls away from bone, 1½ to 2 hours longer.

5b. For a gas grill: Place ribs on cooler side of grill and cook for about 4 hours, covered, flipping, switching, and rotating ribs every 30 minutes, until meat easily pulls away from bone.

6. Transfer ribs to cutting board, cut between bones to separate ribs, and serve.

GRILLED GLAZED BABY BACK RIBS

Serves 4 to 6 | baby back ribs

WHY THIS RECIPE WORKS As much as we love the smoky, supertender results of hours of barbecuing, we simply don't have that kind of time most nights, so we set out to develop a method for weeknight ribs. We started smaller, faster-cooking baby back ribs in the oven. But wrapping the ribs in foil and baking them before grilling wasn't the time-saver we'd hoped for, so we moved to the stove. A new-to-us method, gently simmering the ribs, allowed us to get the temperature up to 195 degrees gently. Then we simply charred them quickly on the grill. This produced reasonably tender, nicely chewy, and beautifully lacquered ribs. And they took only an hour, including a 10-minute rest. For the glazes, we paired no-cook ingredients that would color quickly over the fire. Meaty chew and nicely glazed char all on a weeknight. Since this recipe is relatively quick-cooking, we remove the ribs' membrane.

    2 tablespoons table salt for brining
    2 (2-pound) racks baby back ribs, trimmed, membrane removed, and each rack cut in half
    1 recipe glaze (recipes follow)

1. Dissolve salt in 2½ quarts water in Dutch oven; fully submerge ribs in pot. Bring to simmer over high heat. Reduce heat to low, cover, and cook at bare simmer until thickest part of ribs registers 195 degrees, 15 to 25 minutes. While ribs are simmering, set up grill. (If ribs come to temperature before grill is ready, leave in pot, covered, until ready to use.)

2a. For a charcoal grill: Open bottom vent halfway. Light large chimney starter filled with charcoal briquettes (6 quarts). When top coals are partially covered with ash, pour evenly over grill. Set cooking grate in place, cover, and open lid vent halfway. Heat grill until hot, about 5 minutes.

2b. For a gas grill: Turn all burners to high, cover, and heat grill until hot, about 15 minutes. Turn all burners to medium-high.

3. Clean and oil cooking grate. Remove ribs from pot and pat dry with paper towels. Brush both sides of ribs with ⅓ cup glaze. Grill ribs, uncovered, flipping and rotating as needed, until glaze is caramelized and charred in spots, 15 to 20 minutes, brushing with another ⅓ cup glaze halfway through cooking. Transfer ribs to cutting board, brush both sides with remaining glaze, tent with aluminum foil, and let rest for 10 minutes. Cut ribs between bones to separate, and serve.

Lime Glaze
Makes about 1 cup; serves 4 to 6

    ⅔ cup lime juice (6 limes)
    ⅓ cup ketchup
    ¼ cup packed brown sugar
    1 teaspoon salt

Whisk all ingredients together in bowl.

Spicy Marmalade Glaze
Makes about 1 cup; serves 4 to 6

    ⅔ cup orange marmalade
    ⅓ cup cider vinegar
    2 tablespoons hot sauce
    ¾ teaspoon salt

Whisk all ingredients together in bowl.

SWEET-AND-SOUR RIBS
Serves 4 to 6 | baby back ribs
WHY THIS RECIPE WORKS For ribs that we could make any season, we wanted something different from Southern barbecue. Enter these sticky, glossy indoor sweet-and-sour baby backs. For a dead-simple cooking method that would result in juicy ribs with a burnished color, we found that roasting them for about 2 hours at 325 degrees was just right. Saucing the ribs three times—at the outset, before the last 10 minutes of roasting, and before serving—made them shine. For a less spicy sauce, remove the jalapeño seeds before slicing.

SAUCE
    1 cup orange juice
    ½ cup sugar
    ⅓ cup cider vinegar
    2 tablespoons ketchup
    2 tablespoons soy sauce
    1½ tablespoons cornstarch
    1 tablespoon fish sauce
    2 tablespoons vegetable oil
    2 jalapeño chiles, stemmed and sliced into thin rings
    2 garlic cloves, minced
    1 teaspoon minced fresh ginger

RIBS
    2 (2-pound) racks baby back ribs, trimmed
    1 tablespoon kosher salt
    1 teaspoon pepper
    4 scallions, sliced thin on bias

1. For the sauce: Whisk orange juice, sugar, vinegar, ketchup, soy sauce, cornstarch, and fish sauce together in bowl. Heat oil in medium saucepan over medium-high heat until shimmering. Add jalapeños, garlic, and ginger and cook until fragrant, about 30 seconds. Stir in orange juice mixture and bring to boil. Cook, stirring occasionally, until thickened, about 3 minutes. Transfer ½ cup sauce to bowl, leaving jalapeños behind, and set aside.

2. For the ribs: Adjust oven rack to middle position and heat oven to 325 degrees. Line rimmed baking sheet with aluminum foil and set wire rack in sheet. Sprinkle ribs all over with salt and pepper. Place ribs on prepared wire rack and brush all over with reserved ½ cup sauce. Arrange ribs meat side up. Roast until tender (fork inserted into meat will meet no resistance) and middle of rib rack registers at least 205 degrees, 2 to 2½ hours.

3. Brush tops of ribs with ¼ cup remaining sauce. Return ribs to oven and roast until sauce sets, about 10 minutes. Let ribs cool for 5 minutes. Reheat remaining sauce over medium heat until hot, about 4 minutes. Cut ribs between bones. Toss ribs, half of scallions, and remaining sauce together in large bowl. Transfer to platter and sprinkle with remaining scallions. Serve.

TUTORIAL
Grilled Glazed Baby Back Ribs

Grill-touched ribs on the table on a weeknight, in an hour? Go from stove to grill to achieve this following these steps.

1. Remove membrane from ribs. Cut rack of ribs in half.

2. Dissolve salt in 2½ quarts water in Dutch oven; fully submerge ribs in pot. Bring to simmer over high heat.

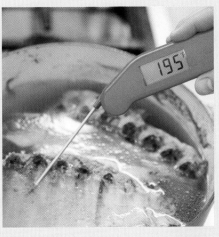

3. Reduce heat to low, cover, and cook at bare simmer until thickest part of ribs registers 195 degrees, 15 to 25 minutes.

4. Remove ribs from pot and pat dry with paper towels. Brush both sides of ribs with ⅓ cup glaze.

5. Grill ribs, uncovered, flipping and rotating as needed, until glaze is caramelized and charred in spots, 15 to 20 minutes, brushing with another ⅓ cup glaze halfway through cooking.

6. Transfer ribs to cutting board, brush both sides with remaining glaze, tent with aluminum foil, and let rest for 10 minutes. Cut ribs between bones to separate, and serve.

SIDE

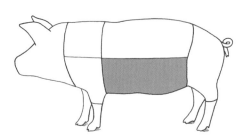

IF YOU LIKE RICH, UNCTUOUS meat, things get good here—this long primal cut of meat is the fattiest part of the pig. The pork side is also called the pork belly, so it's home, to, yes, delicious pork belly and the products that come from it: salt pork, bacon, and pancetta. It's also where spareribs are found, so you can understand why they're our preferred rib for barbecuing—that fat melts during slow grilling to baste the succulent meat. This part of the pig is unique in that no roasts come from it, but we love the delicacies that are created from it just as much.

St. Louis–Style Spareribs

Cost: ▪▪▍▍ Flavor: ▪▪▍▍
Best cooking methods: roast, barbecue
Texture: tender-chewy
Alternative names: St. Louis spareribs, spareribs

Whole spareribs from the underside of the pig are untrimmed, containing the brisket bone and surrounding meat, so each rack can weigh upward of 5 pounds. Some racks of spareribs are so big they barely fit on the grill. That's why we use this more manageable cut, called the St. Louis–style sparerib, because the brisket bone and surrounding meat are trimmed off to produce a narrower, rectangular rack that usually weighs in at a relatively svelte 3 pounds. Spareribs are larger and less lean than baby back ribs so they dry out far less quickly and cook more consistently.

REMOVING THE MEMBRANE FROM RIBS

Depending on the recipe, we may remove the membrane on a rack of ribs. In some applications, the papery membrane on the underside is chewy and unpleasant to eat, and its protective qualities aren't necessary. (In other applications, it can crisp up appealingly.) The membrane is very thin, so removing it should not expose the rib bones. Here's how to easily remove it.

1. Using tip of paring knife, loosen edge of membrane on rack.

2. Using paper towel for grip, pull membrane off slowly. (It should come off in single piece.)

8 STEPS TO SENSATIONAL RIBS

Sure, we have delicious recipes for ribs from around the world: Tuscan-style, Chinese-style, and jerk-spiced. But when we think spareribs we also tend to think of the barbecue world. We don't have a barbecue rig—you probably don't either—so we've come up with some universal steps to making great ribs on an everyday charcoal grill. While recipes vary depending on the ribs and the style, these steps are standard for the test kitchen.

1. Rub
Rub both sides of the ribs with a spice mixture, pressing so it adheres.

2. Prepare the Grill
Pour hot coals onto half of the grill, according to your recipe. This creates a low, slow oven out of your grill, perfect for cooking ribs.

3. Add Smoke
Place wood chips over the coals, cover the grill, and let them heat for 5 minutes for smoky flavor—without a smoker.

4. Start Cool
Place the ribs on the cooler side of the grill to cook low and slow without the exterior burning before the interior is tender.

5. Brush
If you're mopping dry ribs or saucing wet ribs, this is the time to do it. The ribs will drink up the flavor in the remaining cooking time and caramelize slightly.

6. Bake
You don't have a huge smoker so it's best to finish the ribs in the oven so they can fully tenderize without having to rebuild a burnt-out charcoal setup.

7. Fork
Insert a fork into the ribs to check that they are tender but not falling off the bone (195 to 200 degrees). If the fork pulls right out, the ribs are done. If not, the meat needs to cook longer.

8. Relax
Let the ribs rest for 30 minutes when they come out of the oven. The juices will redistribute for moist ribs.

Center-Cut Pork Belly

Cost: ▪▪◻◻   **Flavor:** ▪▪◻◻
Best Cooking Methods: roast, braise, sous vide cure
Texture: rich, meaty
Alternative names: none

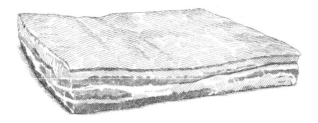

Bacon might be the belly treat you eat most often but uncured pork belly itself is a sumptuous cut of meat. This boneless cut that lines the underside of the pig (not the stomach itself) features alternating layers of flavorful, well-marbled meat and buttery fat, which, when properly cooked, turns silky and supple. Even more appealing is the contrast between that luscious texture and the skin, which can cook up crispy and airy (you'll want to buy it with the skin on). Sometimes, however, it's lovingly braised as for ramen. In applications like this, it's all about the texture of the meat and the melting qualities of the fat—no browning or crisp is needed so you'll remove the skin so it's not flabby or chewy. Long a staple in Asian and Latin cuisines, pork belly has become increasingly popular in upscale restaurants of all kinds and has started showing up in regular supermarkets.

Because of this layering of meat and fat, pork belly is often cured. Curing, or the act of preserving food, has been in practice since ancient times. It involves the addition of salt, which helps to deprive bacteria and mold of water as well as tenderize the meat; sugar, which alleviates the heavy salt flavor; and curing salt (for more information, see "The Cure"). Salt pork, most typically used as an infusing flavoring agent in our recipes, is the simplest of the cured belly meats—it's simply salt and pork. Pancetta is cured with more than just salt; the curing seasoning includes spices as well. Bacon is cured and then smoked. (Learn how to make your own on page 299.) If you want to think in reverse, fresh pork belly is simply unsliced, uncured, unsmoked bacon. (Note that Canadian bacon is made from pork loin, not the belly.)

THE CURE

A common curing agent is pink salt, a mixture of table salt and sodium nitrite and, depending on the type, also sodium nitrate. It's been used since the early 1900s to cure meat—it adds flavor and slows rancidity and bacteria growth. It's also what gives the meat its rosy color. We choose to use this product in our home-made bacon recipe (see page 299). You can omit it, but it's a smart safety measure. Plus, bacon made without it just doesn't taste as good. If you're avoiding nitrites or nitrates, you're better off avoiding cured pork.

Pink salt is the most common label, but curing salt goes by many names, including DQ Curing Salt and Insta Cure #1. You can find it in specialty food stores or online. (Do not substitute Morton's Tender Quick or Insta Cure #2.)

Rosticciana

ROSTICCIANA

Serves 4 to 6 | St. Louis–style spareribs

WHY THIS RECIPE WORKS With no sauce and minimal seasoning, these Tuscan grilled pork ribs forgo the hallmarks of American barbecue in favor of one distinct feature: juicy, unembellished pork. We started by removing the tough, papery membranes from two racks of St. Louis–style spareribs. Cutting the ribs into two-rib sections created more surface area for flavorful browning, and salting them for an hour prior to grilling ensured that they cooked up juicy and well seasoned. Grilling the ribs over a medium-hot (rather than blazing) fire also helped prevent the meat from drying out, as did removing them from the fire when their temperature reached between 175 and 185 degrees—and they still came off the fire in about 20 minutes. Drizzling the pork with a vinaigrette made from Tuscan ingredients—minced rosemary and garlic and lemon juice—balanced its richness without obscuring its meaty flavor. When portioning the meat into two-rib sections, start at the thicker end of the rack. If you are left with a three-rib piece at the tapered end, grill it as such. Take the temperature of the meat between the bones.

RIBS

- 2 (2½- to 3-pound) racks St. Louis–style spareribs, trimmed, membrane removed, and each rack cut into 2-rib sections
- 2 teaspoons kosher salt
- 1 tablespoon vegetable oil
- 1 teaspoon pepper

VINAIGRETTE

- ¼ cup extra-virgin olive oil
- 2 garlic cloves, minced
- 1 teaspoon minced fresh rosemary
- 2 tablespoons lemon juice

1. For the ribs: Pat ribs dry with paper towels. Rub evenly on both sides with salt and place on wire rack set in rimmed baking sheet. Let stand at room temperature for 1 hour.

2. For the vinaigrette: Combine oil, garlic, and rosemary in small bowl and microwave until fragrant and just starting to bubble, about 30 seconds. Stir in lemon juice and set aside.

3a. For a charcoal grill: Open bottom vent completely. Light large chimney starter filled with charcoal briquettes (6 quarts). When top coals are partially covered with ash, pour evenly over grill. Set cooking grate in place, cover, and open lid vent completely. Heat grill until hot, about 5 minutes.

3b. For a gas grill: Turn all burners to high, cover, and heat grill until hot, about 15 minutes. Turn all burners to medium-high.

4. Clean and oil cooking grate. Brush meat side of ribs with oil and sprinkle with pepper. Place ribs meat side down on grill. Cover and cook until meat side begins to develop spotty browning and light but defined grill marks, 4 to 6 minutes. Flip ribs and cook, covered, until second side is lightly browned, 4 to 6 minutes, moving ribs as needed to ensure even browning. Flip again and cook, covered, until meat side is deeply browned with slight charring and thick ends of ribs register 175 to 185 degrees, 4 to 6 minutes.

5. Transfer ribs to cutting board and let rest for 10 minutes. Cut ribs between bones and serve, passing vinaigrette separately.

JERK PORK RIBS

Serves 4 to 6 | St. Louis–style spareribs

WHY THIS RECIPE WORKS Although many American cooks employ jerk seasoning as a spicy coating for grilled chicken, it was originally used in Jamaican cooking to season pork. As a nod to this, we developed a recipe for boldly seasoned jerk pork ribs. We chose St. Louis–style spareribs for their uniform shape, a quality that helps them cook evenly. Letting the ribs marinate in our jerk paste for at least 1 hour infused them with fiery yet fruity flavor. Roasting them in a low 275-degree oven for 4 hours turned them meltingly tender. And brushing them with another coat of jerk paste cut with tangy vinegar gave them a bright, fresh crust. We recommend wearing rubber gloves when handling the habaneros—they're hot! If you are spice-averse, remove the seeds and ribs from the habaneros or substitute jalapeños, which are less spicy.

- 8 scallions, chopped coarse
- ¼ cup vegetable oil
- ¼ cup molasses, divided
- 3 tablespoons chopped fresh ginger
- 2 tablespoons ground allspice
- 1–2 habanero chiles, stemmed
- 3 garlic cloves, peeled
- 1 tablespoon dried thyme
- 1 tablespoon table salt
- 2 (2½- to 3-pound) racks St. Louis–style spareribs, trimmed
- 3 tablespoons cider vinegar
  Lime wedges

1. Process scallions, oil, 3 tablespoons molasses, ginger, allspice, habaneros, garlic, thyme, and salt in blender until smooth, 1 to 2 minutes, scraping down sides of blender jar as needed. Transfer ¼ cup jerk paste to bowl, cover, and refrigerate until needed. Place ribs on rimmed baking sheet and brush all over with remaining paste. Cover sheet tightly with plastic wrap and refrigerate for at least 1 hour or up to 24 hours.

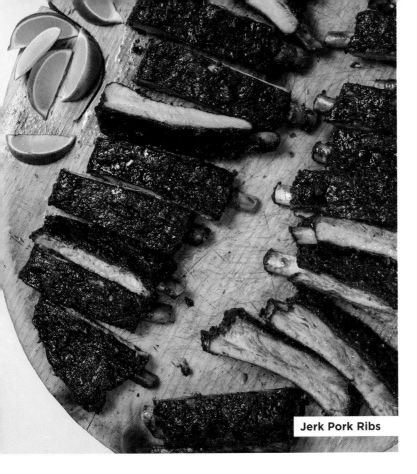

Jerk Pork Ribs

hot oven to color and crisp their exteriors. It's not necessary to remove the membrane on the bone side of the ribs. These ribs are chewier than American-style ribs; if you prefer them more tender, cook them for an additional 15 minutes in step 1. Serve the ribs alone as an appetizer or with vegetables and rice as a main course. You can serve the first batch immediately or tent them with foil to keep them warm.

- 1 (6-inch) piece fresh ginger, peeled and sliced thin
- 8 garlic cloves, peeled
- 1 cup honey
- ¾ cup hoisin sauce
- ¾ cup soy sauce
- ½ cup Chinese rice wine or dry sherry
- 2 teaspoons five-spice powder
- 1 teaspoon red food coloring (optional)
- 1 teaspoon ground white pepper
- 2 (2½- to 3-pound) racks St. Louis–style spareribs, trimmed and cut into individual ribs
- 2 tablespoons toasted sesame oil

1. Pulse ginger and garlic in food processor until finely chopped, 10 to 12 pulses, scraping down sides of bowl as needed. Transfer ginger-garlic mixture to Dutch oven. Add honey; hoisin; soy sauce; ½ cup water; rice wine; five-spice powder; food coloring, if using; and pepper and whisk until combined. Add ribs and stir to coat (ribs will not be fully submerged). Bring to simmer over high heat, then reduce heat to low, cover, and cook for 1¼ hours, stirring occasionally.

2. Adjust oven rack to middle position and heat oven to 425 degrees. Using tongs, transfer ribs to large bowl. Strain braising liquid through fine-mesh strainer set over large container, pressing on solids to extract as much liquid as possible; discard solids. Let cooking liquid settle for 10 minutes. Using wide, shallow spoon, skim fat from surface and discard.

3. Return braising liquid to pot and add sesame oil. Bring to boil over high heat and cook until syrupy and reduced to 2½ cups, 16 to 20 minutes.

4. Set wire rack in aluminum foil–lined rimmed baking sheet and pour ½ cup water into sheet. Transfer half of ribs to pot with braising liquid and toss to coat. Arrange ribs bone side up on prepared rack, letting excess glaze drip off. Roast until edges of ribs start to caramelize, 5 to 7 minutes. Flip ribs and continue to roast until second side starts to caramelize, 5 to 7 minutes longer. Transfer ribs to serving platter; repeat process with remaining ribs. Serve.

To make ahead: At end of step 3, refrigerate ribs and glaze separately, covered, for up to 2 days. When ready to serve, bring glaze and half of ribs to simmer in Dutch oven over medium heat, then proceed with step 4.

2. Adjust oven rack to middle position and heat oven to 275 degrees. Line second rimmed baking sheet with aluminum foil and set wire rack in sheet. Unwrap ribs and place, meat side up, on prepared wire rack. Roast until tender and fork inserted into meat meets no resistance, 4 to 4½ hours.

3. Stir vinegar and remaining 1 tablespoon molasses into reserved jerk paste. Brush meat side of racks with vinegar mixture. Return ribs to oven and roast until sauce sets, about 10 minutes. Transfer ribs to carving board, tent with foil, and let rest for 20 minutes. Slice racks between ribs. Serve with lime wedges.

CHINESE BARBECUE SPARERIBS

Serves 6 to 8 as an appetizer or 4 to 6 as a main course | St. Louis–style spareribs

WHY THIS RECIPE WORKS Chinese barbecue ribs are usually marinated for several hours and then slow-roasted and basted repeatedly to build up a thick crust. We skipped both of those time-consuming steps and instead braised the ribs, cut into individual pieces to speed cooking and create more surface area, in a highly seasoned liquid, which helped the flavor penetrate thoroughly and quickly. Then we strained, defatted, and reduced the braising liquid to make a full-bodied glaze in which we tossed the ribs before roasting them on a rack in a

MEMPHIS BARBECUE SPARERIBS

Serves 4 to 6 | St. Louis–style spareribs

WHY THIS RECIPE WORKS For a relatively fast barbecue spareribs recipe, we opted for a grill-to-oven approach. We rubbed the spareribs with a sugar-and-spice mixture and then used a modified two-level fire and a chimney starter to extend the life of the flame without opening the grill. Putting a pan of water underneath the cooking grate on the cooler side of the grill helped keep the temperature stable and our spareribs moister. We transferred the barbecue ribs to a wire rack set over a rimmed baking sheet and cooked them in a moderate oven until they reached 195 degrees—we were rewarded with tender and thick-crusted Memphis-style barbecue spareribs. Keep the membrane on these ribs; it prevents some of the fat from rendering out and is authentic to this style of ribs.

Memphis Barbecue Spareribs

- 1 recipe Spice Rub (recipe follows)
- 2 (2½- to 3-pound) racks St. Louis–style spareribs, trimmed
- ½ cup apple juice
- 3 tablespoons cider vinegar
- 1 (13 by 9-inch) disposable aluminum roasting pan (if using charcoal) or 2 (9-inch) disposable aluminum pie plates (if using gas)
- ¾ cup wood chips, soaked in water for 15 minutes and drained

1. Rub 2 tablespoons spice rub on each side of each rack of ribs. Let ribs sit at room temperature while preparing grill.

2. Combine apple juice and vinegar in small bowl and set aside.

3a. For a charcoal grill: Open bottom vent halfway and evenly space 15 unlit charcoal briquettes on 1 side of grill. Place disposable pan filled with 2 cups water on other side of grill. Light large chimney starter one-third filled with charcoal briquettes (2 quarts). When top coals are partially covered with ash, pour evenly over unlit coals. Sprinkle soaked wood chips over lit coals. Set cooking grate in place, cover, and open lid vent halfway. Heat grill until hot and wood chips are smoking, about 5 minutes.

3b. For a gas grill: Remove cooking grate. Place soaked wood chips in pie plate with ¼ cup water and set over primary burner. Place second pie plate filled with 2 cups water on other burner(s). Set grate in place, turn all burners to high, cover, and heat grill until hot and wood chips are smoking, about 15 minutes. Turn primary burner to medium-high and turn off other burner(s). (Adjust primary burner as needed to maintain grill temperature of 250 to 275 degrees.)

4. Clean and oil cooking grate. Place ribs meat side down on cooler side of grill, over water-filled pan. Cover (position lid vent over meat if using charcoal) and cook until ribs are deep red and smoky, about 1½ hours, brushing with apple juice mixture and flipping and rotating racks halfway through cooking. About 20 minutes before removing ribs from grill, adjust oven rack to lower-middle position and heat oven to 300 degrees.

5. Transfer ribs to wire rack set in rimmed baking sheet. Brush top of each rack of ribs with 2 tablespoons apple juice mixture. Pour 1½ cups water into sheet; roast for 1 hour. Brush ribs with remaining apple juice mixture and continue to cook until meat is tender and registers 195 degrees, 1 to 2 hours longer. Transfer ribs to cutting board, tent with aluminum foil, and let rest for 15 minutes. Slice ribs between bones and serve.

Spice Rub

Makes about ½ cup; serves 4 to 6
For a less spicy rub, you can reduce the cayenne to ½ teaspoon.

- 2 tablespoons paprika
- 2 tablespoons packed light brown sugar
- 1 tablespoon table salt
- 2 teaspoons chili powder
- 1½ teaspoons pepper
- 1½ teaspoons garlic powder
- 1½ teaspoons onion powder
- 1½ teaspoons cayenne pepper
- ½ teaspoon dried thyme

Combine all ingredients in bowl.

SLOW-COOKER SWEET-AND-SOUR BARBECUE SPARERIBS

Serves 6 to 8 | St. Louis–style spareribs
Cooking time: 7 to 8 hours on low or 4 to 5 hours on high

WHY THIS RECIPE WORKS These ribs are the ultimate in sticky, succulent goodness—and they come from your slow cooker. For fall-off-the-bone-tender barbecue pork spareribs with grilled flavor, we started by covering the ribs with a potent ginger, garlic, and spice rub that would complement the sweet-and-sour profile we were after. To fit two racks of spareribs into the slow cooker, we cut them in half and stood the racks upright around the slow cooker's perimeter, overlapping them slightly. We found that leaving the membrane coating the underside of the ribs attached helped hold the racks together as they cooked. Once the ribs were fully tender, we transferred them to a wire rack set in a baking sheet and brushed them with our simple sweet-and-sour barbecue sauce, made sweet with pineapple preserves, ketchup, and dark brown sugar, and sour with white vinegar. Then we broiled the ribs to develop a lightly charred exterior. You will need an oval slow cooker for this recipe.

- 2 tablespoons grated fresh ginger, divided
- 6 garlic cloves, minced, divided
- 1 tablespoon ground allspice
- 2 teaspoons table salt
- ½ teaspoon pepper
- 2 (2½- to 3-pound) racks St. Louis–style spareribs, trimmed, halved
- ½ cup pineapple preserves
- ¼ cup ketchup
- ¼ cup packed dark brown sugar
- 1 tablespoon distilled white vinegar
- 1 tablespoon soy sauce
- ¼ teaspoon red pepper flakes

1. Combine 1 tablespoon ginger, two-thirds of garlic, allspice, salt, and pepper in bowl. Pat ribs dry with paper towels; rub with spice mixture.

2. Arrange ribs upright in slow cooker, with thick ends pointing down and meaty sides against wall (ribs will overlap). Cover and cook until ribs are just tender, 7 to 8 hours on low or 4 to 5 hours on high.

3. Adjust oven rack 4 inches from broiler element and heat broiler. Set wire rack in aluminum foil–lined rimmed baking sheet; coat with vegetable oil spray. Transfer ribs meaty side up to prepared rack; let sit until surface is dry, about 10 minutes.

4. Whisk pineapple preserves, ketchup, sugar, vinegar, soy sauce, pepper flakes, remaining 1 tablespoon ginger, and remaining garlic in bowl until sugar is dissolved. Brush ribs with half of sauce; broil until sauce is bubbling and beginning to char, about 5 minutes. Brush ribs with remaining sauce, tent with foil, and let rest for 10 minutes. Cut ribs in between bones to separate. Serve.

DIY BACON

Makes about 3½ pounds; serves 28 | pork belly

WHY THIS RECIPE WORKS There's no denying it: We love bacon. Maybe it's the smoky maple scent that wafts from the skillet. Or the crispy bits of fat intertwined with the chewy streaks of meat. Or the irresistible flavor it imparts to everything it comes into contact with. Bacon is just plain good. And what could be better than the store-bought stuff? Making your own. We aimed to start with a relatively inexpensive slab of pork belly and create our own personal blend of salt, sugar, and seasonings to flavor it with, for homemade bacon that would easily surpass anything we'd find at the grocery store. Do not use iodized salt—we developed this recipe using Diamond Crystal kosher salt. Measurement varies among brands of kosher salt. If you use Morton kosher salt, which has larger crystals, measure out ⅓ cup for this recipe.

- 1 cup maple sugar, for curing bacon
- ½ cup Diamond Crystal kosher salt, for curing bacon
- 1 tablespoon peppercorns, cracked
- 2 teaspoons minced fresh thyme
- ¾ teaspoon pink salt, for curing bacon
- 1 bay leaf, crumbled
- 1 (4-pound) center-cut pork belly, skin removed
- 4 medium hickory wood chunks

1. Combine sugar, kosher salt, peppercorns, thyme, pink salt, and bay leaf in small bowl. Place pork belly in 13 by 9-inch glass baking dish and rub all sides and edges of pork belly with dry cure mixture. Cover dish tightly with plastic wrap and refrigerate until pork feels firm yet still pliable, 7 to 10 days, flipping meat every other day.

2. Before smoking, soak wood chunks in water for 1 hour, then drain. Thoroughly rinse pork with cold water and pat dry with paper towels.

3. Open bottom vent of smoker completely. Arrange 1½ quarts unlit charcoal briquettes in center of smoker in even layer. Light large chimney starter three-quarters filled with charcoal briquettes (4½ quarts). When top coals are partially covered with ash, pour evenly over unlit coals. Place wood chunks on coals. Assemble smoker and fill water pan with water according to manufacturer's instructions. Cover smoker and open lid vent completely. Heat smoker until hot and wood chunks are smoking, about 5 minutes.

4. Clean and oil smoking grate. Place pork belly meat side down in center of smoker. Cover (positioning lid vent over pork) and smoke until pork registers 150 degrees, 1½ to 2 hours.

5. Remove bacon from smoker and let cool to room temperature before slicing. Bacon can be wrapped tightly with plastic and refrigerated for up to 1 month or frozen for up to 2 months.

CRISPY SLOW-ROASTED PORK BELLY

Serves 8 to 10 | pork belly

WHY THIS RECIPE WORKS Pork belly is a boneless cut featuring alternating layers of well-marbled meat and buttery fat, which, when properly cooked, turns silky and sumptuous with a crown of crisp skin. To tackle this special cut, we started by scoring the skin and rubbing it with a mixture of salt and brown sugar. We then air-dried the belly overnight in the refrigerator to dehydrate the skin. Roasting the pork belly low and slow further dried the skin and broke down the tough collagen, making the meat juicy and supple. We finished by frying the belly skin side down, which caused it to dramatically puff up and crisp. A quick, bracing mustard sauce balanced the richness of the belly. A longer refrigeration time for the seasoned pork belly is preferable. Be sure to ask for a flat, rectangular center-cut section of skin-on pork belly that is 1½ inches thick with roughly equal amounts of meat and fat. Serve with white rice and steamed greens or boiled potatoes and salad.

PORK

- 1 (3-pound) skin-on center-cut fresh pork belly, about 1½ inches thick
- 2½ tablespoons kosher salt, divided
- 2 tablespoons packed dark brown sugar
  Vegetable oil

MUSTARD SAUCE

- ⅔ cup Dijon mustard
- ⅓ cup cider vinegar
- ¼ cup packed dark brown sugar
- 1 tablespoon hot sauce
- 1 teaspoon Worcestershire sauce

1. **For the pork:** Using sharp knife, slice pork belly lengthwise into 3 strips about 2 inches wide, then cut slits, spaced 1 inch apart in crosshatch pattern, in surface fat layer, being careful not to cut into meat. Combine 2 tablespoons salt and sugar in bowl. Rub salt mixture into bottom and sides of pork belly (do not rub into skin). Season skin of each strip evenly with ½ teaspoon salt. Place pork belly, skin side up, in 13 by 9-inch baking dish and refrigerate, uncovered, for at least 12 hours or up to 24 hours.

2. Adjust oven rack to middle position and heat oven to 250 degrees. Set wire rack in rimmed baking sheet and spray with vegetable oil spray. Transfer pork belly, skin side up, to wire rack and roast until pork registers 195 degrees and paring knife inserted in pork meets little resistance, 3 to 3½ hours, rotating sheet halfway through roasting.

3. **For the mustard sauce:** Whisk all ingredients together in bowl; set aside.

4. Transfer pork belly, skin side up, to large plate. (Pork belly can be held at room temperature for up to 1 hour.) Pour fat from sheet into 1-cup liquid measuring cup. Add vegetable oil as needed to equal 1 cup and transfer to 12-inch skillet. Arrange pork belly skin side down in skillet (strips can be sliced in half crosswise if skillet won't fit strips whole) and place over medium heat until bubbles form around pork belly. Continue to fry, tilting skillet occasionally to even out hot spots, until skin puffs, crisps, and turns golden, 6 to 10 minutes. Transfer pork belly skin side up to carving board and let rest for 5 minutes. Flip pork belly skin side down and slice ½ inch thick (being sure to slice through original score marks). Reinvert slices and serve with sauce.

VARIATION
Crispy Slow-Roasted Pork Belly with Tangy Hoisin Sauce
Omit mustard sauce. Whisk ½ cup hoisin, 4 teaspoons rice vinegar, 1 teaspoon grated fresh ginger, and 2 thinly sliced scallions together in bowl and serve with pork.

Crispy Slow-Roasted Pork Belly

SOUS VIDE SICHUAN TWICE-COOKED PORK BELLY

Serves 4 | pork belly
Sous vide time: 8 to 9 hours

WHY THIS RECIPE WORKS Twice-cooked pork belly is traditionally made by simmering a pork belly in water, slicing it thin, and crisping it in a hot wok with vegetables and a fiery sauce. We substituted a sous vide method for the initial simmer so that we wouldn't leave any flavor in the pot. Be sure to ask for a flat, rectangular center-cut section of skinless pork belly that's 1½ inches thick with roughly equal amounts of meat and fat. If you can only find skin-on pork belly, prepare it as directed and then cut off skin before slicing in step 3. Asian broad bean chili paste (or sauce) is also known as doubanjiang or toban djan. Bird chiles are dried red Thai chiles. You can substitute green bell peppers for the cubanelle peppers, if desired. The pork belly has a tendency to splatter during searing in step 4; use a splatter guard to minimize oil splattering. Be sure to double-bag the pork to protect against seam failure.

Ultimate Pork Ramen

1 (1½-pound) skinless center-cut fresh pork belly, about 1½ inches thick
¼ cup Asian broad bean chili paste, divided
1 teaspoon vegetable oil
2 cubanelle peppers, stemmed, seeded, and cut into 1-inch pieces
2 garlic cloves, minced
1 tablespoon grated fresh ginger
10 bird chiles, finely ground (1 tablespoon)
¼ cup Shaoxing Chinese rice wine or dry sherry
¼ cup water
2 tablespoons hoisin sauce
2 teaspoons fermented black beans, chopped coarse
8 scallions, white parts sliced thin, green parts cut into 1-inch pieces

1. Using sous vide circulator, bring water to 170°F in 7-quart container.

2. Rub pork with 1 tablespoon chili paste and place in 1-gallon zipper-lock freezer bag. Seal bag, pressing out as much air as possible. Place bag in second 1-gallon zipper-lock freezer bag and seal bag. Gently lower bag into prepared water bath until pork is fully submerged, and then clip top corner of bag to side of water bath container, allowing remaining air bubbles to rise to top of bag. Reopen 1 corner of zipper, release remaining air bubbles, and reseal bag. Cover and cook for at least 8 hours or up to 9 hours.

3. Fill large bowl halfway with ice and water. Submerge zipper-lock bag in ice bath and let sit until pork is chilled, about 15 minutes. Transfer pork to cutting board and pat dry with paper towels. Transfer congealed cooking liquid to small bowl. Slice pork lengthwise into 2-inch-wide strips, and then slice strips crosswise into ¼-inch-thick pieces.

4. Heat oil in 12-inch nonstick skillet over medium-high heat until shimmering. Add half of pork in even layer and cook until browned, 2 to 3 minutes per side; transfer to bowl. Repeat with remaining pork. Pour off all but 2 tablespoons fat from skillet.

5. Add peppers to fat left in skillet and cook over medium-high, without stirring, until lightly charred, about 3 minutes. Stir in garlic, ginger, and ground bird chiles and cook until fragrant, about 30 seconds. Stir in rice wine and water, scraping up any browned bits, and cook until liquid is reduced by half, about 15 seconds.

6. Stir in remaining 3 tablespoons chili paste, reserved cooking liquid, hoisin, and fermented black beans. Add pork and scallion greens and toss to coat. Transfer to serving dish and sprinkle with scallion whites.

To make ahead: After chilling, pork belly can be refrigerated in zipper-lock bag for up to 3 days. To reheat, return sealed bag to water bath set to 170°F for 30 minutes and then proceed with step 3.

ULTIMATE PORK RAMEN

Serves 6 to 8 | pork belly

WHY THIS RECIPE WORKS We found that to achieve a broth flavorful enough for this revered Japanese soup, we'd have to go low and slow in the oven for 6 to 12 hours and take no shortcuts with the meat products. We used pigs' trotters for bones; they provided pork flavor while their collagen added body to the broth. Chicken parts balanced the trotters' intensity, and shiitake mushrooms, ginger, garlic, and miso lent complex notes. To accompany our broth, we made a style of pork belly known as chashu, a common ramen topping. We marinated pork belly and then slow-roasted it as the broth cooked in the oven. We filled each bowl of noodles with thinly sliced chashu and broth and topped it with scallions and enoki mushrooms. Ask your butcher to split the trotters for you; they will yield more flavor. If you can't find kombu, leave it out. If fresh ramen noodles or enoki mushrooms are unavailable, 18 ounces of dried ramen noodles and thinly sliced white mushrooms may be substituted. Use a Dutch oven that holds 6 quarts or more for this recipe. The finished broth in step 4 should taste overseasoned; the addition of noodles before serving will temper the flavor of the broth. We like to serve this ramen with chili oil and shichimi togarashi. Sometimes we top it with halved soft-cooked eggs.

BROTH AND PORK BELLY

- 1 pound center-cut fresh pork belly, about 1½ inches thick, skin removed
- ¼ cup soy sauce
- 2 teaspoons packed brown sugar
- 1 teaspoon grated fresh ginger, plus 1 (1½-inch) piece ginger, peeled and sliced into ½-inch-thick rounds
- 1 tablespoon vegetable oil
- 1 onion, quartered
- 4 ounces shiitake mushrooms, stems removed and reserved, caps chopped
- 6 garlic cloves, peeled and smashed
- 2 pounds whole chicken legs, backs, and/or wings, hacked with meat cleaver into 2-inch pieces
- 2 pounds pigs' trotters, split lengthwise
- 12 cups water, plus extra as needed
- ½ cup white miso
- 1 teaspoon table salt
- ½ teaspoon pepper
- 1 (4-inch) square piece kombu

SOUP

- 1¾ pounds fresh ramen noodles
- 3 scallions, sliced thin on bias
- 4 ounces enoki mushrooms, trimmed

1. For the broth and pork belly: Using sharp knife, make ¼-inch-deep slits, spaced ¼ inch apart in crosshatch pattern, in fat layer of pork belly. Combine soy sauce, sugar, and grated ginger in bowl, then add to 1-gallon zipper-lock bag along with pork. Press out as much air as possible, seal bag, and refrigerate for at least 1 hour or up to 24 hours, flipping bag halfway through marinating.

2. While pork marinates, adjust oven racks to upper-middle and lower-middle positions and heat oven to 200 degrees. Heat oil in large Dutch oven over medium-high heat until shimmering. Add onion, shiitake mushroom stems and caps, garlic, and ginger rounds and cook until fragrant, about 1 minute. Add chicken and pigs' trotters. Cover, reduce heat to medium-low, and cook until chicken and pork release their juices, about 15 minutes, scraping bottom of pot occasionally to release fond. Whisk water, miso, salt, and pepper in bowl until combined, then add to pot and bring to boil. Cover, transfer pot to lower rack in oven, and cook until broth is flavorful, at least 6 hours or up to 12 hours.

3. Three hours before broth is finished, increase oven temperature to 250 degrees. Set wire rack in aluminum foil–lined rimmed baking sheet and spray rack with vegetable oil spray. Transfer pork belly fat side up to prepared rack, place on upper rack in oven, and cook until pork is tender and registers 195 degrees, about 3 hours.

4. Transfer pork belly to cutting board and let rest while finishing soup. Transfer broth to stovetop, stir in kombu, and let sit for 10 minutes. Set fine-mesh strainer over large bowl or container and line with triple layer of cheesecloth. Discard chicken and pigs' trotters. Strain broth through prepared strainer and let settle for 5 minutes; discard solids. Using wide, shallow spoon, skim excess fat from surface of broth. Return broth to now-empty pot and season with salt to taste. (You should have 12 cups broth; add extra water as needed to equal 12 cups. Broth and pork belly can be refrigerated for up to 4 days or frozen for up to 1 month; thaw frozen broth and pork completely before proceeding.)

5. For the soup: Meanwhile, bring 4 quarts water to boil in large pot. Add noodles and cook until tender but still have some chew. Drain noodles and distribute evenly among individual bowls.

6. Bring broth to rolling boil over high heat. Slice pork thin and shingle evenly over noodles. Ladle hot broth into each bowl and top with scallions and enoki mushrooms. Serve immediately.

LEG

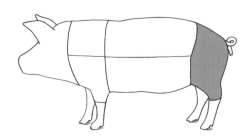

WHEN WE REFER TO THE LEG as a pig primal, we mean the rear and legs, often referred to as the "ham." And from the ham are various, well, hams—rump-end (sirloin) hams, shank-end hams, fresh hams, smoked hams, cured hams, bone-in hams, boneless hams, whole hams, half hams, ham steaks, and ham hocks. The "ham" we met in the pig's shoulder (see page 239) is not a true ham, but that roast has a meaty texture and flavor and so is considered an alternative.

Most of us think of true ham as a pink haunch that's smoked, fully cooked, and ready to eat. Fresh ham is none of those things: It's simply the pig's upper hind leg, a big pork roast. And it might be your perfect pig if you like full-flavored pork dishes like ribs and pulled pork. Whole fresh hams can weigh up to 25 pounds, so they're usually broken down into the sirloin end closer to the torso, and the tapered shank end. The interior is not as fatty as you might think, and fresh hams can benefit from brining or salting since they're not enhanced.

Then of course there are the fully cooked, cured hams with their pretty pink flesh and satisfying salty flavor. You want to pay attention to the labeling: Cooked ham is commonly wet-cured with a brining solution (often water, salt, phosphates or nitrates, and sugar). This makes the meat taste more seasoned and less likely to dry out when reheated at home. But it also allows the producer to make more money by increasing the weight of the ham with water. Officially, a cooked ham product is labeled by the percentage of protein by weight. The added water affects the weight: The more water you add, the lower the percentage of protein in the meat. The USDA bases its grading scale (on the following page) on this protein percentage.

(continued)

Ham: At least 20.5 percent protein by weight; 0 to 2 percent added water; meatiest, with the most flavor, but a little dry when cooked; often has to be special ordered.

Ham with Natural Juices: 18.5 percent to 20.5 percent protein by weight; 7 to 8 percent water; smoky and strongly pork-flavored; saltier and moister than "ham," a favorite.

Ham, Water Added: 17 percent to 18.5 percent protein by weight; no more than 10 percent added water; dulled but still acceptable ham flavor; very moist but verging on rubbery.

Ham and Water Product: Less than 17 percent protein by weight; more than 10 percent added water; spongy, bouncy, salty, processed-tasting.

The leg is marvelously meaty and thus also gives us delicious charcuterie like prosciutto, which goes through a few processes: curing, smoking, and air-drying. Move down the leg, where the shank joins the foot, and you get ham hocks, which are significantly less meaty but intensely flavorful. We'll sort through the hams and hocks in the following sections.

COUNTRY OR CITY HAM

Europe has its fabled dry-cured hams—prosciutto in Italy, jamón ibérico in Spain—but did you know that we've got one, too? Country ham is a strong, salty, dry-cured product produced primarily in Virginia, North Carolina, Tennessee, Kentucky, and Missouri. Other hams on our list—city hams—are all made by injecting or soaking a fresh ham in brine and are sold cooked, to be simply heated and served. But with the increased interest in artisanal and local foods and anything pig, plus the ease of internet mail ordering, these small-town hams are becoming more popular.

While city hams can be ready for market in 24 hours, country hams cure for anywhere from three months to a year. Traditionally, this was a way to preserve the meat in pre-refrigeration days: Hogs were slaughtered in the fall; the hams were rubbed with salt, sugar, and spices and then left to cure during the winter, with the salt drawing out moisture. Come spring, they were cleaned and hung, and some were smoked. Finally, in the warm summer months, the hams were aged. The heat accelerated enzymatic activity, which imparted the robust, pungent flavors that one producer has described as the ham's "country twang." This centuries-old seasonal style of making country ham is known as an "ambient" cure. Today, virtually all commercial cured-ham makers use special aging rooms to mimic the seasons, with temperature, airflow, and humidity under carefully monitored control. Note that mold on country ham isn't a sign of spoilage; it's a natural effect of the curing and aging process.

Country hams are as big as they come, with the hock and the pelvic bone in, weighing in at about 13 to 15 pounds. You can cook them as is and serve them with biscuits. Or you can use them as a flavoring agent, adding small amounts to scrambled eggs, cheese grits, macaroni and cheese, or even risotto.

MEAT PREP *Carving Country Ham*

1. Place ham on carving board, fat cap side up. Cut small wedge at shank end.

2. Carve very thin slices along leg bone, moving toward hip joint.

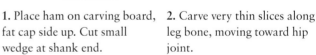
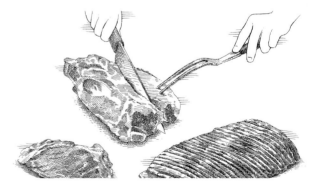

3. Once you reach hip joint, remove remaining meat from each side of leg bone in 1 large piece. Slice each chunk very thin.

Sirloin-Half Fresh Ham

Cost: ▪▫▫▫   Flavor: ▪▪▫▫
Best cooking methods: roast
Texture: complex bone structure cross-cutting ham
Alternative names: none

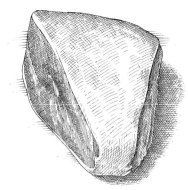

The leg is divided into two cuts—the tapered shank end and the more rounded sirloin end up top. The bone structure of the sirloin end makes carving tricky, so we favor a shank-end fresh ham, but you can use a sirloin-half if it's the only fresh ham you can find. Its flavor is quite good. As the name implies, fresh ham isn't cured—it's a ham because of the meaty area it comes from—and therefore it needs to be cooked, not just heated. We roast fresh hams or cook them on the grill.

MEAT PREP
Checking the Temperature of Sirloin-Half Fresh Ham

With ham placed skin-side up, insert thermometer into center of roast, close to but not touching the bone.

MEAT PREP *Carving Sirloin-Half Fresh Ham*

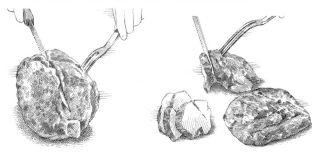

1. Carve ham into 3 pieces around bones.

2. Lay large boneless pieces flat and slice into ½-inch pieces.

Shank-End Fresh Ham

Cost: ▪▫▫▫   Flavor: ▪▪▫▫
Best cooking methods: roast, grill roast
Texture: meaty
Alternative names: none

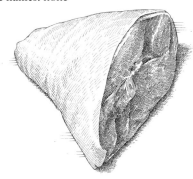

The more tapered ham from the shank end is our preferred fresh ham, as access to the meat is easier than with a sirloin-half. This cut is usually covered in a thick layer of fat and skin, which should be scored before roasting.

BRINING BIG, SALTING SUBSTANTIAL

We pretreat fresh ham for moist results. Yes, the exterior of the meat is quite fatty, but the interior isn't particularly well marbled. This isn't a small loin roast—if we call for brining, you'll need a large (about 16-quart) bucket or stockpot, which you'll be filling with a gallon of water plus the salt and seasonings. If we call for a dry brine, you need quite a bit—around ⅓ cup of kosher salt. And we crosshatch the ham so the salt really reaches the meat. Make sure you have a big enough space in your fridge ready for the ham; you'll wrap the salted ham in plastic wrap and then refrigerate it for at least 12 or up to 24 hours so the salt really penetrates the meat.

MEAT PREP *Preparing Ham Skin*

 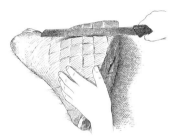

1. Place ham flat side down on cutting board. Using sharp knife, remove skin, rcent leaving ½- to ¼-inch layer of fat intact.

2. Cut 1-inch diagonal cross-hatch pattern in fat, being careful not to cut into meat.

MEAT PREP
Checking the Temperature of Shank-End Fresh Ham

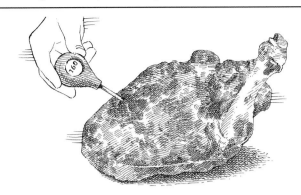

With ham placed cut side down, insert thermometer through fat into meat.

MEAT PREP *Carving Shank-End Fresh Ham*

1. Carve ham lengthwise alongside bone.

2. Lay large boneless pieces flat and slice into ½-inch pieces.

Spiral-Sliced Bone-In Ham

Cost: ◾◾⬜⬜   Flavor: ◾◾◾⬜

Best cooking methods: roast, sous vide
Texture: tender and meaty
Alternative names: spiral-cut ham

On to cured ham: Cured hams are available boneless, semiboneless, bone-in, whole, and half. Phew. We call for bone-in half hams, and spiral-sliced ham is our favorite wet-cured ham because the meat isn't pumped up with water (the label should read "ham with natural juices"; see page 305) and because it's so easy to carve—it's essentially partly presliced, a machine slicing the ham in a spiral around the bone so its shape is unaffected. Despite the name, spiral-sliced hams are not fully sliced and you must finish the job of freeing the cooked slices from the bone, but a parallel cut along the bone yields lovely slices.

Unless a recipe specifies otherwise, make sure to buy a spiral-sliced ham with the bone in; it will taste better, with more flavor than a boneless one. Spiral-sliced ham is very rarely found boneless and we assume bone-in in our recipes. Although packages are not labeled as such, look for a ham from the shank rather than from the sirloin end. You can pick out the shank ham by its tapered, more pointed end opposite the flat cut side of the ham. The sirloin ham has more rounded or blunt ends. (The shape differences mirror those in the fresh hams.)

MEAT PREP *Carving Spiral-Sliced Ham*

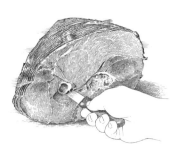

1. With ham on its side, cut all the way around bone with paring knife to free attached slices.

2. Switch to carving or chef's knife and slice horizontally above bone to remove entire top section.

3. Slice along bone to remove the remaining meat.

4. Carefully cut between slices of each half to fully separate them.

Uncut Half Ham

Cost: ▪▪▫▫▫ **Flavor:** ▪▪▫▫▫
Best Cooking Methods: slow cook, grill
Texture: meaty, a bit bouncy
Alternative names: none

This cured ham, available bone-in or boneless, is also half of the leg primal but lacks the spiral slicing. (Smaller, oval processed hams also exist.) And we do have exceptions to our spiral-sliced rule: An uncut half ham is best for the slow cooker and grill (see page 316) because it doesn't have sliced spaces that could cause drying out during long cooking. And while boneless versions aren't our favorite (boneless hams are compressed to a solid mass after the bone is removed, which can result in a "processed" texture), if we need a boneless ham to cut down before cooking, as in our recipe for Hoppin' John (page 318), this is the cut to go with. It also has a layer of fat that, if cooked with dry heat, can crisp. Buy this ham if we call simply for a "half ham" in our recipe. As usual, we prefer the shank end. Be on alert for how much water is added (see page 305).

Ham Steak

Cost: ▪▪▫▫▫ **Flavor:** ▪▪▫▫▫
Best Cooking Methods: sear, slow cook
Texture: tender, meaty
Alternative names: none

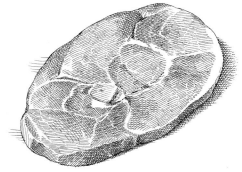

Want ham without hassle? Try a steak. A slab of salty ham is lean; we cook steaks quickly over medium-high heat in butter or incorporate them into dishes to add sweet-smoky flavor. We prefer bone-in steak, cut crosswise from a ham. These are superior to individual (processed) steaks, although you may choose these ham steaks if a recipe calls for a small amount, to be cut up.

Ham Hocks

Cost: ▪▪▫▫▫ **Flavor:** ▪▪▫▫▫
Best Cooking Methods: braise
Texture: filled with bone, fat, and connective tissue
Alternative names: none

These joint areas contain a great deal of bone, fat, and connective tissue. They're used to lend complex flavor and a rich, satiny texture to soups. And they do contain a good amount of meat; they just need to be braised or slow-cooked for long periods of time to break down the connective tissue so you can access it. Once tender, the meat can be picked off the bone, shredded, and added to soups, stews, chilis, or, as is traditional in the American South, greens (see page 320) or beans (see page 323). Ham hocks are usually sold smoked or cured, although fresh ones are available, too.

MEAT PREP *Getting the Meat from Ham Hocks*

Remove meat from ham hocks. Shred, discarding skin and bones.

TUTORIAL
Roast Fresh Ham

A fresh ham isn't just heated like a cured ham. This special roast requires special treatment, illustrated here.

1. Using sharp knife, remove skin from ham and trim fat to ½- to ¼-inch thickness. Cut slits 1 inch apart in crosshatch pattern in fat, being careful not to cut into meat.

2. Place ham on its side. Cut one 4-inch horizontal pocket about 2 inches deep in center of flat side of ham, being careful not to poke through opposite side.

3. Combine sugar, salt, rosemary, and thyme in bowl. Rub half of sugar mixture in ham pocket.

4. Tie 1 piece of kitchen twine tightly around base of ham. Rub exterior of ham with remaining sugar mixture. Wrap ham in plastic wrap and refrigerate for 12 to 24 hours.

5. Unwrap ham and place in oven bag flat side down. Tie top of oven bag closed. Place ham, flat side down, on V-rack and cut ½-inch slit in top of bag.

6. Cut off top of oven bag and push down with tongs, allowing accumulated juices to spill into roasting pan; discard oven bag.

ROAST FRESH HAM

Serves 12 to 14 | shank-end fresh ham

WHY THIS RECIPE WORKS Unlike the hams that most people are familiar with, fresh ham is neither cured nor smoked. This big cut is basically just an oddly shaped bone-in, skin-on pork roast, and slow roasting turned it tender and flavorful. In order to make it easier to season the meat, we removed its thick skin, cut slits into the fat underneath (including one bigger pocket in the meat end of the ham), and rubbed it all over with salt, sugar, and herbs. Roasting the ham in an oven bag helped it retain plenty of moisture. A simple tangy glaze brushed on toward the end of roasting made for a flavorful finish. Be sure to cut a slit in the oven bag so it doesn't burst. This recipe requires a turkey-size oven bag. A longer refrigeration time is preferable.

- 1 (8- to 10-pound) bone-in, skin-on shank-end fresh ham
- ⅓ cup packed brown sugar
- ⅓ cup kosher salt
- 3 tablespoons minced fresh rosemary
- 1 tablespoon minced fresh thyme
- 1 large oven bag
- 2 tablespoons maple syrup
- 2 tablespoons molasses
- 1 tablespoon soy sauce
- 1 tablespoon Dijon mustard
- 1 teaspoon pepper

1. Using sharp knife, remove skin from ham and trim fat to ½- to ¼-inch thickness. Cut slits 1 inch apart in crosshatch pattern in fat, being careful not to cut into meat. Place ham on its side. Cut one 4-inch horizontal pocket about 2 inches deep in center of flat side of ham, being careful not to poke through opposite side.

2. Combine sugar, salt, rosemary, and thyme in bowl. Rub half of sugar mixture in ham pocket. Tie 1 piece of kitchen twine tightly around base of ham. Rub exterior of ham with remaining sugar mixture. Wrap ham tightly in plastic wrap and refrigerate for at least 12 hours or up to 24 hours.

3. Adjust oven rack to lowest position and heat oven to 325 degrees. Set V-rack in large roasting pan and spray with vegetable oil spray. Unwrap ham and place in oven bag flat side down. Tie top of oven bag closed with kitchen twine. Place ham, flat side down, on V-rack and cut ½-inch slit in top of oven bag. Roast until extremely tender and pork near (but not touching) bone registers 160 degrees, 3½ to 5 hours. Remove ham from oven and let rest in oven bag on V-rack for 1 hour. Heat oven to 450 degrees.

4. Whisk maple syrup, molasses, soy sauce, mustard, and pepper together in bowl. Cut off top of oven bag and push down with tongs, allowing accumulated juices to spill into roasting pan; discard oven bag. Leave ham sitting flat side down on V-rack.

5. Brush ham with half of glaze and roast for 10 minutes. Brush ham with remaining glaze, rotate pan, and roast until deep amber color, about 10 minutes. Move ham to carving board, flat side down, and let rest for 30 minutes. Pour pan juices into fat separator and let liquid settle for 5 minutes. Carve ham ¼ inch thick, arrange on serving dish, and moisten lightly with defatted pan juices. Serve, passing remaining pan juices separately.

SOUTH CAROLINA SMOKED FRESH HAM

Serves 8 to 10 | shank-end fresh ham

WHY THIS RECIPE WORKS The usual go-to cut of pork for backyard barbecue is the pork shoulder, but in certain corners of South Carolina, many pitmasters swear by fresh ham. We started by salting a ham and letting it sit overnight, which seasoned it and kept the meat moist. A double-pronged cooking approach did the trick. We smoked the meat on a grill for 2 hours before transferring it to a 300-degree oven to cook until it reached an internal temperature of 200 degrees. We then cranked the oven temperature up to 400 degrees and roasted the skin on a baking sheet until it was brown and crispy. This gave us plenty of crispy skin to mix in with the shredded ham. A vinegary mustard sauce was just the contrast the sandwich needed. If you'd like to use wood chunks instead of wood chips when using a charcoal grill, substitute 2 medium wood chunks, soaked in water for 1 hour, for the wood chip packet.

HAM
- 1 (6- to 8-pound) bone-in, skin-on shank-end fresh ham
- 2 tablespoons kosher salt
- 2 cups wood chips

MUSTARD SAUCE
- 1½ cups yellow mustard
- ½ cup cider vinegar
- 6 tablespoons packed brown sugar
- 2 tablespoons ketchup
- 2 teaspoons hot sauce
- 2 teaspoons Worcestershire sauce
- 1 teaspoon pepper

  Hamburger buns

1. For the ham: Pat ham dry with paper towels. Place ham on large sheet of plastic wrap and rub all over with salt. Wrap tightly in plastic and refrigerate for 18 to 24 hours.

2. Just before grilling, soak wood chips in water for 15 minutes, then drain. Using large piece of heavy-duty aluminum foil, wrap soaked chips in 8 by 4½-inch foil packet. (Make sure chips do not poke holes in sides or bottom of packet.) Cut 2 evenly spaced 2-inch slits in top of packet.

3a. For a charcoal grill: Open bottom vent completely. Light large chimney starter three-quarters filled with charcoal briquettes (4½ quarts). When top coals are partially covered with ash, pour evenly over half of grill. Place wood chip packet on coals. Set cooking grate in place, cover, and open lid vent completely. Heat grill until hot and wood chips are smoking, about 5 minutes.

3b. For a gas grill: Remove cooking grate and place wood chip packet directly on primary burner. Set cooking grate in place, turn all burners to high, cover, and heat grill until hot and wood chips are smoking, about 15 minutes. Turn primary burner to medium-high and turn off other burner(s). (Adjust primary burner as needed to maintain grill temperature of 300 degrees.)

4. Clean and oil cooking grate. Unwrap ham and place flat side down on cooler side of grill. Cover grill (position lid vent directly over ham if using charcoal) and cook for 2 hours. Thirty minutes before ham comes off grill, adjust oven rack to middle position and heat oven to 300 degrees.

5. For the mustard sauce: Meanwhile, whisk all ingredients together in bowl. (Sauce can be refrigerated for up to 1 week.)

6. Transfer ham to 13 by 9-inch baking pan, flat side down. Cover pan tightly with foil. Transfer to oven and roast until fork inserted into ham meets little resistance and meat registers 200 degrees, about 2½ hours.

7. Remove pan from oven and increase oven temperature to 400 degrees. Line rimmed baking sheet with foil. Using tongs, remove ham skin in 1 large piece. Place skin fatty side down on prepared sheet. Transfer to oven and roast until skin is crispy and sounds hollow when tapped with fork, about 25 minutes, rotating sheet halfway through roasting. Tent ham with foil and let rest while skin roasts.

8. Transfer ham to carving board. Strain accumulated juices from pan through fine-mesh strainer set over bowl; discard solids. Trim and discard excess fat from ham. Remove bone and chop meat into bite-size pieces; transfer to large bowl.

9. When cool enough to handle, chop skin fine. Microwave reserved ham juices for 1 minute to rewarm. Add juices and chopped skin to ham and toss to combine. Season with salt to taste. Serve on buns, topped with mustard sauce.

ROAST COUNTRY HAM

Serves 12 to 15 | bone-in country ham

WHY THIS RECIPE WORKS Tradition dictates that country ham—the South's salty, aged cousin to today's spiral-cut hams—requires a lengthy soak before it's cooked. We quickly discovered that soaking the ham had no added benefits, so we skipped it altogether. We scrubbed the mold off the ham, trimmed off the skin, and scored the surface. We placed the ham fat side up in a roasting pan and, to ensure a moist ham, added water and covered the pan with aluminum foil. After baking the ham, we applied a brown sugar glaze, returned the ham to the oven to set the glaze, and let it rest on a carving board before slicing it and serving it with the traditional Jezebel sauce. Use hams aged six months or less for this recipe. Mold on country ham is not a sign of spoilage; it is a natural effect of the curing and aging process. Serve the ham on biscuits. Leftover ham is delicious in scrambled eggs, cheese grits, and macaroni and cheese.

HAM
1 (13- to 15-pound) 3- to 6-month-old bone-in country ham
½ cup packed light brown sugar
1 tablespoon dry mustard
2 teaspoons pepper

JEZEBEL SAUCE
⅓ cup pineapple preserves
⅓ cup apple jelly
⅓ cup yellow mustard
⅓ cup prepared horseradish
1½ teaspoons pepper
¼ teaspoon cayenne pepper

1. For the ham: Adjust oven rack to middle position and heat oven to 325 degrees. Using clean, stiff-bristled brush, scrub ham under cold running water to remove any surface mold. Transfer ham to cutting board and trim off dry meat, skin, and all but ¼ inch of fat. Using sharp knife, cut slits ½ inch apart in crosshatch pattern in fat cap of ham, being careful not to cut into meat.

2. Transfer ham to large roasting pan fat side up, add 4 cups water, and cover pan tightly with aluminum foil. Roast until thickest part of meat registers 140 degrees, 4 to 5 hours. Remove ham from oven, discard foil, and increase oven temperature to 450 degrees.

3. Combine sugar, mustard, and pepper in bowl and rub over top of ham. Return ham to oven and cook, uncovered, until glazed and lacquered, 12 to 17 minutes. Transfer ham to carving board and let rest for 30 minutes.

South Carolina Smoked Fresh Ham

4. For the Jezebel sauce: Combine all ingredients in blender and process until smooth, 20 to 30 seconds. Carve ham into thin slices and serve with sauce.

RISOTTO WITH CABBAGE AND COUNTRY HAM

Serves 4 as a main course or 6 as a first course | bone-in country ham

WHY THIS RECIPE WORKS Ham is typically a special-occasion centerpiece. We wanted to take advantage of its potent salty, umami flavor to enhance the flavors of a simple risotto. We started with just a few ounces of minced country ham (another cured pork product such as pancetta or prosciutto would work well also) and sautéed it with a chopped onion to bring out its flavor. Inspired by northern Italian cuisine, we added some shredded green cabbage and let it cook down to concentrate its flavors. Next we incorporated our Arborio rice. While the traditional risotto-making method calls for adding hot liquid to the rice about half a cup at a time, this requires constant stirring to keep the rice from scorching. To save work, we found that we preferred a deluge-then-stir method that started out with a lot of broth. When the risotto absorbed the first batch of liquid, we added the remaining broth in small increments.

 3 tablespoons extra-virgin olive oil
2–4 ounces leftover Roast Country Ham (page 312), minced
 1 onion, chopped
 ½ small cabbage, shredded
 3 cups water
 2 cups chicken broth
 2 cups Arborio rice or medium-grain rice
 1 teaspoon table salt
 ½ cup dry white wine
 1 ounce Parmesan or Asiago cheese, grated (½ cup), plus extra for serving

1. Heat oil in Dutch oven over medium heat. Add ham and onion and cook, stirring occasionally, until onion softens, 3 to 5 minutes. Add cabbage, cover pot, and cook, stirring occasionally until cabbage is very soft, limp, and beginning to brown, about 15 minutes.

2. Combine water and broth in 8-cup liquid measuring cup. Add rice and salt to pot, then add 3 cups broth mixture and bring to boil, stirring occasionally. Reduce heat to simmer and cook, stirring occasionally, until bottom of pot is dry when rice is pulled back with spoon, 8 to 10 minutes.

Sous Vide Spiral-Sliced Bone-In Ham

3. Add wine and cook, stirring frequently, until wine is absorbed. Add broth mixture in ½-cup increments, stirring constantly until each addition is absorbed; cook until rice is creamy but still somewhat firm in center, 10 to 12 minutes longer. (If all of broth mixture is used before rice is cooked, add water in ½ cup increments.)

4. Stir in Parmesan until incorporated. Serve, passing extra Parmesan separately.

SPIRAL-SLICED HAM GLAZED WITH CIDER-VINEGAR CARAMEL

Serves 12 to 14 | spiral-sliced bone-in ham

WHY THIS RECIPE WORKS Many recipes for spiral ham produce meat that's parched and leathery on the exterior with a glaze that flavors only the outermost edge. For moist meat throughout, we placed our ham in an oven bag, which traps juices and creates a moist environment that cooks it in less time than the dry air of the oven would, and reheated it in a 250-degree oven. We then brushed it with a sweet-tart caramel glaze. Since the sugar in the mixture was already caramelized, the glaze needed only a few minutes in a hot oven to acquire a deep mahogany sheen. Finally, we thinned some of the remaining caramel with ham juices to create a sauce to accompany the smoky, salty ham. We recommend a shank-end ham because the bone configuration makes it easier to carve; look for a half ham with a tapered, pointed end. This recipe requires a turkey-size oven bag.

1 (7- to 10-pound) spiral-sliced bone-in half ham, preferably shank end
1 large oven bag
1¼ cups sugar
½ cup water
3 tablespoons light corn syrup
1¼ cups cider vinegar
½ teaspoon pepper
¼ teaspoon five-spice powder

1. Adjust oven rack to lower-middle position and heat oven to 250 degrees. Line rimmed baking sheet with aluminum foil and set wire rack in sheet. Unwrap ham and, if necessary, discard plastic disk covering bone. Place ham cut side down in oven bag. Insert temperature probe (if using) through top of ham into center. Tie bag shut and place ham cut side down on prepared wire rack. Bake until center registers 110 degrees, 3½ to 4½ hours.

2. Bring sugar, water, and corn syrup to boil in large saucepan over medium-high heat. Cook, without stirring, until mixture is straw-colored, 6 to 8 minutes. While sugar mixture cooks, microwave vinegar in bowl until steaming, about 90 seconds; set aside. Once sugar mixture is straw-colored, reduce heat to low and continue to cook, swirling saucepan occasionally, until mixture is dark amber-colored and just smoking and registers 360 to 370 degrees, 2 to 5 minutes longer. Off heat, add warm vinegar a little at a time, whisking after each addition (some caramel may harden but will melt as sauce continues to cook). When bubbling subsides, add pepper and five-spice powder. Cook over medium-high heat, stirring occasionally, until reduced to 1⅓ cups, 5 to 7 minutes.

3. Remove sheet from oven and increase oven temperature to 450 degrees. Once oven reaches temperature, remove ham from bag and transfer to carving board. Reserve ¼ cup juices from bag; discard bag and remaining juices. Remove wire rack, leaving foil in place, and return ham to sheet, cut side down. Brush ham evenly with ⅓ cup caramel. Transfer sheet to oven and cook until glaze is bubbling and starting to brown in places, 5 to 7 minutes. Add reserved juices to remaining 1 cup caramel and whisk to combine.

4. Slice ham and serve, passing caramel sauce separately.

SOUS VIDE SPIRAL-SLICED BONE-IN HAM

Serves 12 to 14 | spiral-sliced bone-in ham
Sous vide time: 3 to 8 hours

WHY THIS RECIPE WORKS A glazed holiday ham is one of those old-school traditions that will never go out of style. Since it's already cooked, there are not too many places to go awry. All you have to do is reheat the ham, glaze it, and you're good to go. We wanted to make it even better and more foolproof. Reheating the ham sous vide guaranteed that the meat was evenly heated from edge to edge, eliminating cold spots and the need to maul our beautiful ham with an instant-read thermometer. Since cooking sous vide all but eliminates evaporation, the meat stayed moist and flavorful. To finish this holiday centerpiece, we lacquered our ham with a couple of coats of cherry-port glaze in a hot oven, which gave the exterior a rich mahogany sheen. For easy carving, we prefer a shank-end spiral-sliced ham, but a sirloin-end ham will also work. Make sure that vacuum-sealed ham has no visible tears or breaks in the packaging to ensure that the ham reheats properly. Note that this recipe requires a 12-quart container.

1 (7-pound) spiral-sliced bone-in half ham, preferably shank end
½ cup ruby port
½ cup cherry preserves
1 cup packed dark brown sugar
1 teaspoon pepper

1. Using sous vide circulator, heat water to 140°F in 12-quart container.

2. Place ham in 2-gallon zipper-lock freezer bag and seal bag, pressing out as much air as possible. Gently lower bag into prepared water bath until ham is fully submerged, and then clip top corner of bag to side of water bath container, allowing remaining air bubbles to rise to top of bag. Reopen 1 corner of zipper, release remaining air bubbles, and reseal bag. Cover and cook for at least 3 hours or up to 8 hours.

3. Cook port in small saucepan over medium heat until reduced to 2 tablespoons, about 5 minutes. Stir in cherry preserves, sugar, and pepper and cook, stirring occasionally, until sugar dissolves and mixture is thick, syrupy, and reduced to 1 cup, 5 to 10 minutes; set aside.

4. Adjust oven rack to lower-middle position and heat oven to 475 degrees. Set wire rack in aluminum foil–lined rimmed baking sheet and spray with vegetable oil spray. Transfer ham, cut side down, to prepared rack and brush with half of glaze. Cook ham until glaze becomes sticky, 5 to 10 minutes. Brush ham with remaining glaze and cook until glaze becomes sticky and light mahogany, 5 to 10 minutes. Carve and serve.

SLOW-COOKER GLAZED HAM

Serves 10 to 12 | bone-in uncut half ham
Cooking time: 5 to 6 hours on low

WHY THIS RECIPE WORKS We've all seen beautifully bronzed hams emerge from the oven, so why not from the slow cooker? We lacquered hams with every thick, sticky, sugary coating we could think of, but every glaze slid right off during slow cooking. The glaze definitely needed to be applied after the ham was brought to temperature in the slow cooker. Our goal was to make a stovetop glaze that would have a thick, coating consistency without having to make a trip to the oven. Ultimately we found that equal parts dark brown sugar and apple jelly thickened with a tablespoon of cornstarch gave us the ideal consistency, along with some Dijon mustard and pepper for balancing zest. Do not substitute spiral-cut ham, as it dries out during slow cooking. You will need an oval slow cooker for this recipe.

 1 (6- to 8-pound) bone-in half ham, preferably shank end
 ½ cup packed dark brown sugar
 ½ cup apple jelly
 2 tablespoons Dijon mustard
 1 tablespoon cornstarch
 1 teaspoon pepper

1. Using sharp knife, remove skin from ham and trim fat to ¼-inch thickness. Cut slits 1 inch apart in crosshatch pattern in fat, being careful not to cut into meat. Place ham cut side down in slow cooker. Add 1 cup water, cover, and cook until fat is rendered and ham registers 100 degrees, 5 to 6 hours on low.

2. Bring sugar, jelly, mustard, cornstarch, and pepper to boil in small saucepan over medium-high heat. Cook, whisking often, until glaze begins to darken and is slightly thickened, 2 to 3 minutes. Let glaze cool for 5 minutes.

3. Transfer ham to carving board, brush evenly with glaze, and let rest for 20 minutes. Carve ham and serve.

GRILL-ROASTED HAM

Serves 12 to 14 | bone-in uncut half ham

WHY THIS RECIPE WORKS Once you taste a grill-roasted ham, you'll never look at your holiday ham the same. Roasting ham on the grill reinforces its smoky flavor and builds a crispy charred exterior. To keep the ham moist, we opted for a bone-in uncut ham for its protective layer of fat. We treated the meat with a traditional dry barbecue rub; it stayed put

and the sugar in it caramelized nicely into a tasty, crunchy coating. We kept the ham safe from flare-ups by elevating it on a V-rack and placing it on the cooler side of a half-grill fire; when the meat reached 100 degrees we switched the ham to the hotter side. For a makeshift rotisserie, we skewered the ham to give ourselves two handles with which to safely rotate the hefty ham for a well-rounded crust. Do not use a spiral-sliced ham; it will dry out on the grill. You will need two 12-inch metal skewers for this recipe. This recipe requires letting the rubbed ham sit for 1½ hours before cooking.

 1 (7- to 10-pound) bone-in half ham, preferably shank end
 ¼ cup packed dark brown sugar
 2 tablespoons paprika
 1 teaspoon pepper
 ¼ teaspoon cayenne pepper

1. Using sharp knife, remove skin from ham and trim fat to ¼-inch thickness. Cut slits 1 inch apart in crosshatch pattern in fat, being careful not to cut into meat. Combine sugar, paprika, pepper, and cayenne in small bowl. Rub spice mixture all over ham. Transfer to V-rack and let sit at room temperature for 1½ hours. Thread ham with two 12-inch metal skewers on both sides of bone.

2a. For a charcoal grill: Open bottom vent halfway. Light large chimney starter filled with charcoal briquettes (6 quarts). When top coals are partially covered with ash, pour over half of grill. Set cooking grate in place, cover, and open lid vent halfway. Heat grill until hot, about 5 minutes.

2b. For a gas grill: Turn all burners to high, cover, and heat grill until hot, about 15 minutes. Leave primary burner on high and turn off other burner(s).

3. Clean and oil cooking grate. Place V-rack with ham on cooler side of grill. Cover and cook until meat registers 100 degrees, about 1½ hours.

4a. For a charcoal grill: Using pot holders, transfer V-rack with ham to rimmed baking sheet or roasting pan. Light 25 coals. When coals are covered with fine gray ash, remove grill grate and scatter over top of spent coals. Replace grill grate and position V-rack directly over coals.

4b. For a gas grill: Turn all burners to low.

5. Cook (covered if using gas) until ham is lightly charred on all sides, about 30 minutes, turning ham every 5 minutes. Transfer to carving board and let rest for 30 minutes. Carve and serve.

Grill-Roasted Ham

HOPPIN' JOHN

Serves 8 | boneless uncut half ham

WHY THIS RECIPE WORKS In the Lowcountry of South Carolina and Georgia, eating hoppin' John—a humble slow-cooked dish of rice, black-eyed peas, and ham hocks—at the start of a new year is said to bring good luck. Hoping to turn out a quicker version of this hearty dish, we started by swapping ham hocks for more readily available bacon and boneless ham. After browning the bacon, we used the rendered fat to brown slices of boneless ham. We cooked onion, celery, garlic, and thyme before adding the black-eyed peas, broth, and ham. Rinsing the rice and covering the hoppin' John with aluminum foil ensured tender, toothsome rice. We stirred in the reserved bacon and ham and served up our one-pot meal. Small boneless hams are available in the meat case at most supermarkets. If you can't find one, you can substitute an equal weight of ham steak. Covering the surface of the dish with aluminum foil after adding the rice helps ensure that the rice cooks evenly. Serve with hot sauce, if desired.

- 6 slices bacon, chopped
- 1 (1- to 1½-pound) boneless half ham, cut into ¾-inch-thick planks
- 1 onion, chopped fine
- 2 celery ribs, minced
- 4 garlic cloves, minced
- ½ teaspoon dried thyme
- 4 cups chicken broth
- 2 pounds frozen black-eyed peas
- 2 bay leaves
- 1½ cups long-grain white rice
- 3 scallions, sliced thin

1. Cook bacon in Dutch oven over medium heat until crispy, 5 to 7 minutes. Using slotted spoon, transfer bacon to paper towel–lined plate. Pour off all but 1 tablespoon fat from pot and brown ham, about 3 minutes per side. Transfer ham to plate with bacon.

2. Add onion and celery to pot and cook until softened, about 5 minutes. Stir in garlic and thyme and cook until fragrant, about 30 seconds. Add broth, peas, bay leaves, and ham and bring to boil. Reduce heat to low and simmer, covered, until peas are just tender, about 20 minutes. Transfer ham to cutting board and cut into ½-inch pieces.

3. Place rice in fine-mesh strainer and rinse under cold running water until water runs clear, about 1 minute. Drain rice well and stir into pot. Place square of aluminum foil directly on surface of simmering liquid. Simmer, covered, until liquid is absorbed and rice is tender, about 20 minutes, stirring and repositioning foil twice during cooking. Remove from heat and let stand, covered, for 10 minutes. Discard bay leaves. Fluff rice with fork. Stir in scallions, bacon, and ham. Serve.

St. Paul Sandwiches

HAM STEAK WITH RED-EYE GRAVY

Serves 4 | ham steak

WHY THIS RECIPE WORKS When we took this Southern classic for a spin here in the test kitchen, we found that most gravy made from coffee, as is traditional, was inedible—when coffee boils, it becomes extremely bitter. To get the flavor without the bitterness, we used instant espresso powder. Maple syrup balanced the coffee, and sautéed onion added depth to the gravy, while finishing it with butter gave a silky texture. For the ham, we went with bone-in steaks, but found them so lean that they needed a boost; bacon did the trick, adding smoky, porky flavor and rendering enough flavorful fat to brown the ham steaks in. Pat the ham steak dry before cooking so it will brown well. Before pouring the gravy over the ham in step 2, discard any accumulated juices on the platter, as they will make the gravy too salty.

- 1 (1¼-pound) bone-in ham steak
- 2 slices bacon
- 2 tablespoons finely chopped onion
- 1 teaspoon all-purpose flour
- 1½ cups chicken broth
- 1 tablespoon maple syrup
- 3 tablespoons unsalted butter, cut into 3 pieces and chilled
- 2 teaspoons instant espresso powder

1. Pat ham dry with paper towels and season with pepper. Cook bacon in 12-inch skillet over medium heat until crispy, 7 to 9 minutes. Remove bacon from skillet and reserve for another use. Add ham to fat left in skillet and cook until well browned on first side, about 5 minutes. Flip ham and cook on second side until lightly browned, about 2 minutes. Transfer ham to platter and tent with aluminum foil.

2. Add onion to now-empty skillet and cook until just beginning to brown, about 1 minute. Stir in flour and cook for 15 seconds. Whisk in broth and maple syrup, scraping up any browned bits. Bring to simmer and cook until mixture is reduced to ¾ cup and slightly thickened, 5 to 7 minutes. Off heat, whisk in butter and espresso powder. Season with pepper to taste. Discard any accumulated ham juices on platter. Carve ham into 4 equal portions. Pour gravy over ham and serve.

ST. PAUL SANDWICHES

Serves 4 | ham steak

WHY THIS RECIPE WORKS Despite its name, the St. Paul sandwich originated in St. Louis. The filling for this sandwich is an egg foo yong patty—a deep-fried omelet filled with bean sprouts, onions, and meat. We chose easy-to-chop precooked ham steak for the meat for ease. Often the egg foo yong is deep-fried in an oil-filled wok for a fluffy, frizzled sandwich-size patty; we cooked ours in just ½ cup of oil in a nonstick skillet. Transferring the ham patties to a paper towel–lined plate after shallow-frying them kept them from being greasy. Iceberg lettuce, tomatoes, pickles, and mayonnaise made for a sandwich that had a mash-up of salty and tangy flavors and soft yet crispy textures. Be sure to pat the ham steak dry with paper towels before adding it to the bowl with eggs in step 1; this will keep it from splattering as it cooks in step 2.

    4 large eggs
    ½ teaspoon table salt
    ½ teaspoon white pepper
    ½ teaspoon granulated garlic
    2 ounces (1 cup) mung bean sprouts, chopped coarse
    1 cup chopped onion
    5 ounces ham steak, patted dry and cut into ½-inch pieces
    ½ cup vegetable oil for frying
    ¼ cup mayonnaise
    8 slices hearty white sandwich bread
    2 cups shredded iceberg lettuce
    8 thin tomato slices
   16 dill pickle chips

1. Beat eggs, salt, white pepper, and granulated garlic together in medium bowl. Stir in bean sprouts, onion, and ham until thoroughly combined.

2. Heat oil in 12-inch nonstick skillet over medium heat until just smoking. Using ½-cup dry measuring cup, portion 4 evenly spaced scoops of egg mixture in skillet. (Eggs may run together; this is OK.) Cover and cook, without stirring, until bottoms of egg foo yong patties are browned and tops are set, about 5 minutes.

3. Using spatula, cut and separate egg foo yong patties in skillet. Flip each patty and continue to cook, covered, until browned on second side, about 3 minutes longer. Transfer egg foo yong patties to paper towel–lined plate and let drain for 1 minute.

4. Spread mayonnaise on 1 side of each piece of bread. Top each of 4 slices of bread with ½ cup lettuce, 1 egg foo yong patty, 2 tomato slices, 4 pickles, and 1 slice of bread. Serve.

PRESSURE-COOKER MACARONI AND CHEESE WITH HAM AND PEAS

Serves 8 | ham steak

WHY THIS RECIPE WORKS When you want macaroni and cheese, you're usually stuck with two options: the stuff from the box or the lusciously cheesy casserole that requires multiple steps. With the pressure cooker, we discovered we could have the best of both: a simple, streamlined cooking process as well as a flavorful, ultracheesy sauce. We didn't even need to wait for a pot of water to come to a boil. While stovetop pasta recipes call for cooking pasta in a large amount of water that then gets drained away, we relied instead on the absorption method, combining 3 cups of water with a pound of pasta before turning the cooker on. (Since the pressure cooker is a closed environment, we didn't need to worry about evaporation.) Because dairy curdles when cooked under pressure, we waited to add the cheese until the end. Evaporated milk thickened the sauce, and a combination of cheddar and Monterey Jack melted beautifully for a creamy, cheesy mac and cheese. Chopped ham steak and peas made for flavorful additions to fancify this favorite.

    1 pound elbow macaroni or small shells
    3 cups water
 1½ teaspoons table salt
    2 teaspoons dry mustard
    ⅛ teaspoon cayenne pepper
    2 (12-ounce) cans evaporated milk
    8 ounces ham steak, cut into ½-inch pieces
    1 cup frozen peas
    4 ounces sharp cheddar cheese, shredded (1 cup)
    4 ounces Monterey Jack cheese, shredded (1 cup)

1. Combine macaroni, water, salt, mustard, and cayenne in recent electric pressure cooker.

2. Lock lid in place and close pressure release valve. Select high pressure cook function and cook for 5 minutes. Turn off pressure cooker and quick-release pressure. Carefully remove lid, allowing steam to escape away from you.

3. Stir evaporated milk, ham, and peas into macaroni mixture and cook using highest sauté or browning function until sauce has thickened and macaroni is fully tender, 2 to 10 minutes. Turn off pressure cooker. Stir in cheddar and Monterey Jack cheeses, 1 handful at a time, until cheese has melted and sauce is smooth. Season with salt and pepper to taste. Serve.

SLOW-COOKER SPLIT PEA SOUP

Serves 6 to 8 | ham steak
Cooking time: 8 to 10 hours on low or 5 to 7 hours on high

WHY THIS RECIPE WORKS To give our split pea soup a rich, smoky flavor, we used a 1-pound ham steak in addition to a smoked ham hock. To ensure that our base of aromatics and vegetables would be properly cooked, we microwaved onions, celery, butter, garlic, and thyme for a few minutes before adding the mixture to the slow cooker along with the ham, water, and peas. After the soup was done, we removed the ham steak and ham hock. We then shredded the ham steak (and discarded the ham hock) and returned the meat to the soup. Merely whisking the soup right before serving ensured that all the peas had broken down and that the soup was smooth. Ham hocks often can be found near the ham and bacon in the supermarket.

 2 onions, chopped fine
 1 celery rib, chopped fine
 2 tablespoons unsalted butter
 3 garlic cloves, minced
 1 tablespoon minced fresh thyme or ¾ teaspoon dried
 ¾ teaspoon table salt
 ¼ teaspoon red pepper flakes
 7 cups water
 1 pound (2 cups) split peas, picked over and rinsed
 1 pound ham steak, quartered
 1 (12-ounce) smoked ham hock, rinsed
 2 bay leaves

1. Microwave onions, celery, butter, garlic, thyme, salt, and pepper flakes in bowl, stirring occasionally, until onions are softened, about 5 minutes; transfer to slow cooker. Stir in water, peas, ham steak, ham hock, and bay leaves. Cover and cook until peas are tender, 8 to 10 hours on low or 5 to 7 hours on high.

2. Transfer ham steak to cutting board, let cool slightly, then shred into bite-size pieces using 2 forks. Discard ham hock and bay leaves.

3. Whisk soup vigorously until peas are broken down and soup thickens, about 30 seconds. Stir in ham and let sit until heated through, about 5 minutes. Season with salt and pepper to taste. Serve.

SOUTHERN-STYLE COLLARD GREENS

Serves 6 to 8 | ham hocks

WHY THIS RECIPE WORKS This Southern recipe is made by braising collard greens with a salty smoked pork product. Over a long cooking time, the pork and greens intermingle and turn the cooking water into a supersavory pot liquor (or "pot likker"). We found that two smoked ham hocks provided the best deeply smoky pork flavor. Plus, after a long braising time, it was easy to pull the savory little chunks of meat off the hocks to add back to the greens. If you can't find ham hocks, you can substitute 6 slices of bacon and 3 ounces of ham steak cut into ½-inch pieces. Be sure to remove the rind from the ham before cutting it into pieces. Add the bacon and ham in place of the ham hocks in step 2, but discard the bacon before serving. Do not drain off the cooking liquid before serving. This flavorful, savory pot liquor should be sipped while eating the collards. Any leftover pot liquor can be used as a soup base. We like to serve the greens with cornbread.

 2 pounds collard greens
 2 tablespoons unsalted butter
 1 onion, chopped
 6 cups water
 2 (12-ounce) smoked ham hocks
 3 garlic cloves, smashed and peeled
 2¼ teaspoons table salt
 2 teaspoons sugar
 ⅛ teaspoon red pepper flakes
   Hot sauce

1. Adjust oven rack to lower-middle position and heat oven to 300 degrees. Trim collard stems to base of leaves; discard trimmings. Cut leaves into roughly 2-inch pieces. Place collard greens in large bowl and cover with water. Swish with your hand to remove grit. Repeat with fresh water, as needed, until grit no longer appears in bottom of bowl. Remove collard greens from water and set aside (you needn't dry them).

Southern-Style Collard Greens

2. Melt butter in large Dutch oven over medium heat. Add onion and cook until lightly browned, 6 to 8 minutes. Add water, ham hocks, garlic, salt, sugar, and pepper flakes and bring to boil over high heat. Add collard greens (pot may be full) and stir until collard greens wilt slightly, about 1 minute. Cover, transfer to oven, and cook until collard greens are very tender, about 1½ hours.

3. Transfer ham hocks to cutting board and let cool for 10 minutes. Remove meat from ham hocks, chop, and return to pot; discard skin and bones. Season collard greens with salt to taste. Serve with hot sauce.

SENATE NAVY BEAN SOUP

Serves 6 to 8 | ham hocks

WHY THIS RECIPE WORKS The origins of this mainstay of the U.S. Senate cafeteria may be up for debate, but its list of ingredients is simple and clear: navy beans, ham hocks, onions, celery, and (sometimes) potatoes. Since many of the versions we tried yielded bland, stodgy soups, we built layers of flavor by first brining the beans and then doubling up on the smoked ham hock to infuse the dish with even more porky flavor. We added the aromatics to the soup near the end of cooking so that they would retain their savory punch and texture next to the tenderness of the fully cooked beans. And while mashed potatoes are traditionally used to help thicken the soup, we found that cooking diced potatoes in the soup worked just as well, especially after a few strokes with a potato masher. The finished texture of the soup should be creamy but not too thick. Eight to 10 strokes with a potato masher should be adequate. We use whole cloves because ground cloves turn the soup an unsightly gray color.

> 3 tablespoons table salt for soaking beans
> 1 pound (2½ cups) navy beans, picked over and rinsed
> 1 tablespoon vegetable oil
> 1 onion, chopped fine
> 2 celery ribs, chopped fine
> 1 teaspoon table salt
> 2 garlic cloves, minced
> 3 whole cloves
> 2 (12-ounce) smoked ham hocks
> 8 ounces russet potatoes, peeled and cut into ¼-inch pieces
> ½ teaspoon pepper
> 1 tablespoon cider vinegar

1. Dissolve 3 tablespoons salt in 4 quarts cold water in large container. Add beans and soak at room temperature for at least 8 hours or up to 24 hours. Drain and rinse well.

2. Heat oil in Dutch oven over medium heat until shimmering. Add onion, celery, and salt and cook until softened, 8 to 10 minutes. Stir in garlic and cook until fragrant, about 30 seconds. Transfer onion mixture to bowl.

3. Insert cloves into skin of 1 ham hock. Add 8 cups water, beans, and ham hocks to now-empty pot and bring to boil over high heat. Reduce heat to medium-low and simmer, covered with lid slightly ajar, until beans are tender, 45 minutes to 1 hour, stirring occasionally.

4. Stir potatoes and onion mixture into soup and simmer, uncovered, until potatoes are tender, 10 to 15 minutes; remove pot from heat. Transfer ham hocks to cutting board and let cool slightly. Discard cloves, then shred meat, discarding bones and skin.

5. Using potato masher, gently mash beans and potatoes until soup is creamy and lightly thickened, 8 to 10 strokes. Add pepper and shredded meat and return to simmer over medium heat. Stir in vinegar. Season with salt and pepper to taste, and serve.

TEXAS-STYLE PINTO BEANS

Serves 8 | ham hocks

WHY THIS RECIPE WORKS Texas-style pinto beans are tender whole beans long-simmered with pork and served up in the velvety, savory broth they cook in. For supercreamy beans, we soaked dried pinto beans overnight in salted water. To cook them, we covered them with fresh water and added a bit more salt and a smoked ham hock, which provided rich pork flavor. We then simmered them uncovered for 1½ hours to reduce and concentrate the cooking liquid and give it smoky complexity and meaty, buttery sweetness. If you can't find a ham hock, substitute 4 ounces of salt pork, omit the salt in step 2, and season to taste once finished. Monitor the water level as the beans cook. Don't let it fall below the level of the beans before they're done. If it does, add more water. Good garnishes include finely chopped onion, dill pickles, jalapeños, and/or tomatoes. Use the meat from the ham hock within a few days to flavor another dish.

> 1½ tablespoons table salt, for soaking beans
> 1 pound (2½ cups) dried pinto beans, picked over and rinsed
> 1 (10-ounce) smoked ham hock
> 1 teaspoon table salt

Texas-Style Pinto Beans

fat gave body to the cooking liquid and smokiness and shine to the beans. To finish the dish, we mashed some of the beans with bean cooking liquid and a sofrito of onion and bell pepper. We then stirred this in with the rest of the beans, plenty of lime juice, and the shredded ham hock. These beans are hearty and satisfying and sure to get you through the tough winter months. Be sure to double-bag the beans to protect against seam failure.

  1 pound (2½ cups) dried black beans, picked over and rinsed
  1 (12-ounce) smoked ham hock, rinsed
1¼ teaspoon table salt
  2 bay leaves
¼ teaspoon baking soda
  2 tablespoons extra-virgin olive oil
  1 onion, chopped fine
  1 green bell pepper, stemmed, seeded, and chopped fine
  6 garlic cloves, minced
  2 tablespoons minced fresh oregano or 2 teaspoons dried
1½ teaspoons ground cumin
½ cup minced fresh cilantro
  1 tablespoon lime juice, plus extra for seasoning

1. Using sous vide circulator, bring water to 194°F in 7-quart container.

2. Combine 5 cups water, beans, ham hock, 1 teaspoon salt, bay leaves, and baking soda in 1-gallon zipper-lock freezer bag. Seal bag, pressing out as much air as possible. Place bag in second 1-gallon zipper-lock freezer bag and seal. Gently lower bag into prepared water bath until beans are fully submerged, and then clip top corner of bag to side of water bath container, allowing remaining air bubbles to rise to top of bag. Reopen 1 corner of zipper, release remaining air bubbles, and reseal bag. Cover and cook for at least 20 hours or up to 24 hours.

3. Drain beans, reserving 1½ cups cooking liquid; discard bay leaves. Transfer ham hock to cutting board, let cool slightly, then shred into bite-size pieces using 2 forks; discard fat, skin, and bones.

4. Heat oil in Dutch oven over medium heat until shimmering. Add onion, bell pepper, and remaining ¼ teaspoon salt and cook, stirring occasionally, until softened, about 5 minutes. Stir in garlic, oregano, and cumin and cook until fragrant, about 1 minute. Reduce heat to low, add reserved cooking liquid and one-third of beans, and mash with potato masher until mostly smooth. Stir in remaining beans, shredded ham hock, cilantro, and lime juice. Season with salt, pepper, and extra lime juice to taste. Serve.

To make ahead: Beans can be refrigerated for up to 3 days. To serve, bring to a simmer in medium saucepan or heat in microwave for 2 minutes, stirring halfway.

1. Dissolve 1½ tablespoons salt in 2 quarts cold water in large container. Add beans and soak at room temperature for at least 8 hours or up to 24 hours. Drain and rinse well. (Soaked beans can be stored in zipper-lock bag and frozen for up to 1 month.)

2. Combine 12 cups water, ham hock, beans, and salt in Dutch oven. Bring to boil over high heat. Reduce heat to medium-low and simmer, uncovered, stirring occasionally, until beans are tender, about 1½ hours, skimming any foam from surface with spoon. Remove from heat and let stand for 15 minutes. Reserve ham hock for another use. Season with salt to taste. Serve.

SOUS VIDE CUBAN BLACK BEANS

Serves 6 | ham hocks
Sous vide time: 20 to 24 hours

WHY THIS RECIPE WORKS Sous vide cooking provides a foolproof method for creamy, evenly cooked beans with virtually no messy bean blowouts. For our take on Cuban black beans, we cooked the beans with a smoked ham hock for an extended period of time in a solution of baking soda, salt, and water. This moderately alkaline environment sped up the deterioration of each bean's pectin-rich exterior, leading to softer, creamier beans; plus, the ham hock broke down beautifully over the 20-plus hours of cooking. The rendered

PART 3

lamb

LAMB CUTS

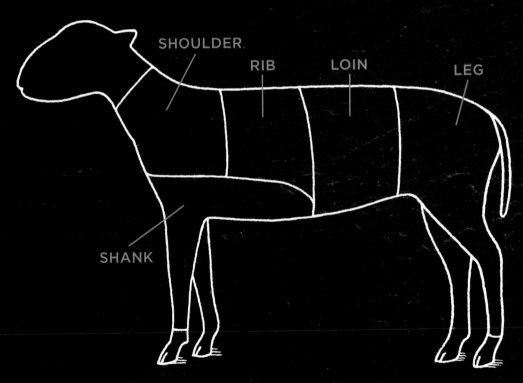

SHOULDER.

RIB

LOIN

LEG

SHANK

LAMB IS A STAPLE IN NEW ZEALAND, Australia, and the Middle East. But the flavor of lamb, which *we* wholeheartedly love, has a reputation for being a bit divisive in the United States, although interest in lamb is rising given that it's relatively inexpensive; it takes well to a variety of cooking methods, such as roasting, stewing, and grilling; and its rich flavor is unmatched.

We like to think of that flavor as unique, a pleasant but not jarring departure from beef—something with a bit more character that can stand up to complex spice rubs and punchy sauces (see pages 20–25 for some examples) that we love to have the opportunity to treat meat with. Others might find it a bit too grassy in flavor, some calling it gamy. The truth is, though, lamb can be loved by all once you learn the different cuts and also where their flavor comes from.

You see, it's not the muscle itself—the majority of what you eat when you're sitting down to a plate of meat—but the fat that's more important in determining this flavor. Research has shown that unique branched-chain fatty acids (BCFAs) are responsible for much of the gamy flavor we associate with lamb. So a fattier cut of lamb will taste more like, well, lamb. With this knowledge, you have a greater ability to cook lamb to your tastes. As we break down the cuts in this chapter, you'll learn which ones are fattier, and therefore more lamb-y. Lower-fat cuts will taste sweeter. And if you pick lamb fed with at least a little grain in its diet (see page 328), you're already guaranteed milder flavor. Lamb flavor can also be controlled in the kitchen by adjusting fat content through trimming. Removing some, or all, of the fat cap on a rack of lamb, for example, will create an even milder end product, while leaving it intact will boost lamb flavor. There's nothing stopping even the pickiest meat eaters from cooking with lamb.

While eating lamb is now just becoming more popular here, the history of breeding sheep is a long one; they were the first domesticated animals in ancient times in the Middle East. And every meat-eating culture and religion consumes lamb, unlike beef and pork, which are barred from some diets. Europeans arriving in America discovered vast lands; however, sheep need fairly little pasture compared with cows, so beef became "American" while lamb became "other." We hope to blur those lines.

SORTING SHEEP

Sheep aren't bred just for meat, of course. They can be meat sheep, wool sheep, or dual-purpose sheep. Most breeds in the United States are named for where in the United Kingdom they originated, and each tastes a bit different, with flavors ranging from delicate and sweet to robust. A female sheep is a ewe and a male sheep is a ram. And a sheep 14 months old or younger is a lamb. Anything older is labeled mutton, which is rarely eaten in the United States.

In the States, most lamb is slaughtered between four and eight months, though milk-fed or "hothouse" lamb is slaughtered at six to eight weeks. The younger the lamb, the more tender the meat. Why? The tenderness of cooked lamb is directly related to the number of chemical cross-links holding the collagen proteins together. The number of cross-links increases with the age of the animal, and as the number increases, the process of breaking down collagen to soluble gelatin becomes more difficult, requiring longer cooking times.

GRAIN AND GRASS

Grass-fed and grain-fed lamb taste different. This is because when lambs eat grain—even if their diet is just finished with grain, as is most common in the United States—it impacts the composition of the animal's fat, where most of its unique flavor resides. A grain-based diet reduces the concentration of the medium-length branched-chain fatty acids, the ones we've said give lamb its distinctive flavor. This means that grain-fed lamb has a less intense "lamb" flavor and can taste slightly sweeter.

LAMB SHOPPING

While almost all the beef and pork sold in American markets is raised domestically, you can purchase imported (usually from New Zealand or Australia) as well as domestic lamb, and you may want to think about your choice based on your flavor preferences. Domestic lamb is distinguished by its larger size and milder flavor, which comes from a diet of grass that's finished with grain; we prefer it in the test kitchen. Lamb imported from Australia or New Zealand features a far gamier taste, as they are raised on just pasture-fed mixed grasses.

As we've mentioned, younger lamb has a milder flavor that many prefer. One indication of slaughter age at the supermarket is size. A whole leg of lamb weighing 9 pounds is likely to have come from an older animal than a whole leg weighing just 6 pounds. This is a very imperfect system, because there are bones and cutting techniques to consider in determining weight. A better indication is the lamb's appearance: The lighter the color, the younger the meat will be. Dark red to purple lamb is on the older side. Younger lamb also has bones that are moist, red, and porous at the ends, not white and calcified-looking.

And don't worry about whether lamb is labeled "spring" or not. This is an outdated way of looking at lamb's age. It was once thought that lambs born in the spring would be slaughtered in the fall and therefore of good age. This is no longer relevant as lambs are born year round and brought to market before they're a year old.

Lamb Provenance

DOMESTIC LAMB

Diet of grass and grain, larger size, sweeter-tasting meat.

IMPORTED LAMB

Diet of grass only, smaller size, gamier-tasting meat.

Making the Grade

Like beef, lamb is assigned quality grades by the USDA: prime, choice, good, and utility. These grades are based on maturity, leanness, and something called carcass conformation, essentially the ability of a lamb's body to yield more retail cuts. The great majority of lamb sold at the supermarket is choice and very good—if you want the heavier marbling of prime lamb, you may need to search smaller butchers or special order. Very often lamb isn't even labeled because 90 percent is choice or prime. We don't put too much stock into investigating to find a certain grade as we do with beef.

Organic Lamb

Like with other meats, the USDA regulates this labeling on lamb. The rules: no antibiotics, no hormones, no GMO feed, no pesticides on the land. As it is for other meats, "natural" is an obscure, hard-to-regulate term that does little to help determine what lamb you're eating.

Lamb and Mint Make Magic

In 2011, researchers published an article in *Scientific Reports* called "Flavor Network and the Principles of Food Pairings," introducing a complicated, graphic flavor network that "captures the flavor compounds shared by culinary ingredients." The theory goes that foods that share similar flavor compounds complement each other, tasting better together (even seemingly incongruous ingredients—think blue cheese and chocolate). This theory can expand to include not only ingredients that share the same flavor compounds, but also those that share compounds that have similar chemical structures. Many science-minded chefs, including Heston Blumenthal at the Fat Duck in London, are on board. There are even companies—like the well-named FoodPairing.com—that exist to help bartenders and chefs discover "unseen pairings based on science."

What does this tell us about lamb? Lamb is traditionally served with fresh mint in recipes originating in places like England and the Middle East. Does science explain why these two ingredients pair so well? Let's start with the unique flavor of lamb. Roasted and grilled lamb has a flavor unlike any other cooked meat, distinguished by the release of volatile aroma compounds in the fat during cooking. The majority of these compounds are branched-chain fatty acids.

And mint? Mint is rich with branched-chain ketones, which are chemically related to lamb's BCFAs and have similar, though not identical, aromas. This means, according to the theory of food pairing, that lamb and mint are a scientific match. (The dominant flavor compounds in mint are not found in other herbs, like tarragon or basil. But it's important to note that this doesn't mean other herbs taste bad with lamb.) In addition, researchers have found another interesting compound in lamb that originates from the animal's diet. This compound, called 2,3-octanedione, is formed when the lamb consumes fresh clover and ryegrass. It is stored in the lamb's fat and, according to this theory, chemically bridges the gap between the BCFAs and the branched-chain ketones, with a similar sweet, fruity aroma that complements the aroma of mint.

SHOULDER

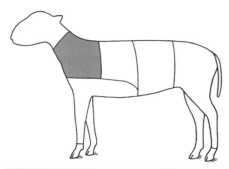

WATCH OUT, BEEF STEW; LAMB is a most delightful meat to stew or braise, giving dishes from Ireland, like our stew on page 336, to Morocco, like Lamb Tagine with Apricots and Olives (page 333) more complex, distinct flavor than beef can, even with classic flavor boosters. As with other animals, lamb stew meat typically comes from the shoulder, the area that extends from the neck of the lamb through the fourth rib. Low in cost, meat from this area is rich and flavorful, although it contains a fair amount of connective tissue and can be tough if not cooked slowly and lovingly, most likely braised or stewed as with the chuck of the cow (see pages 34–37). Welcome the robust flavors of the world into your home with dishes made with lamb shoulder. The shoulder can also be cut into chops of the same texture, with blade chops coming from the upper portion of the shoulder and round bone chops coming from the lower portion.

Lamb Shoulder Roast

Cost: ■■⬜⬜ Flavor: ■■⬜⬜
Best cooking methods: braise, stew, slow cook
Texture: tough, strewn with connective tissue, tender once slow-cooked
Alternative names: square-cut shoulder roast

As far as roasts go, lamb shoulder is less common than lamb leg (see page 349) but a worthwhile cut to seek out. In the test kitchen, we mostly braise or stew lamb shoulder roasts. You could do more, but they're a large, complex construction of muscles and connective tissue so they're tough to navigate without cooking up, well, tough. (Because of this, we use only boneless lamb shoulder.) And the opportunities to introduce flavor through these mediums are vast as you'll see with the pleasantly intense flavors of Lamb Pot Roast with Coriander, Fennel, and Figs (page 332) or Lamb Vindaloo (page 332). An exception to the slow-cooking rule: Arrosticini (page 334), Italian lamb skewers that are unique in that the meat cubes are cut much smaller than kebabs you may be used to and are meant to be cooked a little longer (past medium-rare) and to have some satisfying chew.

Note that lamb shoulder can come with the bone in, often the whole shoulder and upper arm, weighing as much as 8 pounds. Since we braise or cut up lamb shoulder for stew, we don't purchase shoulder with the bone—it's an added hassle—and choose a boneless roast, which is the same cut with, yes, the bones removed. Boneless lamb shoulder is plenty rich in connective tissue to create the right amount of gelatin for a silky sauce. This boneless roast can weigh up to 6 pounds.

Blade Chops

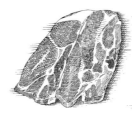

Cost: ■■⬜⬜ Flavor: ■■■⬜
Best cooking methods: braise, slow cook, grill
Texture: chewy but not tough
Alternative names: shoulder chops

You can think of lamb blade chops a lot like pork blade chops (see page 216) if you're more familiar with those. They certainly aren't shaped the same (lamb blade chops are roughly rectangular) nor do they taste the same, but their applications and texture are similar.

Lamb blade chops contain a piece of the chine bone (the backbone of the animal) and a thin piece of the blade bone (the shoulder blade of the animal). Like the shoulder from where they come, these chops are meant for braising, although, like pork blade chops, they can be grilled successfully. You can cook them to eat them whole with fork and knife as in Braised Lamb Shoulder Chops with Tomatoes and Red Wine (page 334) or to shred or break them into pieces for soups and stews that don't require the large yield that a shoulder roast would provide. Similar to a shoulder roast, they can stand up to robust flavors, and we take the opportunity to be bold, with briny capers, sharp vinegars, complex spice blends, salty soy, spicy pepper pastes, and more.

Round Bone Chops

Cost: ■■⬜⬜ Flavor: ■■■⬜
Best cooking methods: braise, slow cook, grill
Texture: leaner than blade chops, chewy but not tough
Alternative names: shoulder chops, arm chops

If you ask for a lamb shoulder chop, you'll most likely get a blade chop. But while blade chops come from the meatier upper blade portion of the shoulder, there are also oval-shaped round bone chops that come from the lower, leaner arm shoulder, nearer the leg. Each chop contains a cross-section of the arm bone so that the chop looks a bit like a small ham steak. In addition to the arm bone, there's also a tiny line of riblets on the side of each chop. These chops have bold lamb flavor and aren't tough, despite some chewiness. They can be used interchangeably with blade chops.

LAMB POT ROAST WITH CORIANDER, FENNEL, AND FIGS

Serves 8 to 10 | lamb shoulder roast

WHY THIS RECIPE WORKS We often cut up lamb shoulder as it's a complex group of muscles, but slow-braising a shoulder breaks down the collagen and fats that add flavor and body to the cooking liquid and produces fall-apart tender meat. We followed a classic oven-braising method to even cooking, but what really elevated this dish was to simmer the lamb in ruby port along with rosemary and aromatics. After the long braise, the liquid turned rich and deeply flavored. While the lamb rested, we defatted the liquid, reduced it, and then stirred in figs, creating a sauce that had a great balance of salty, sweet, and tart notes. For even more flavor, and to help the lamb stay juicy throughout cooking, we seasoned the roast inside and out with a mixture of ground coriander, ground fennel seeds, and salt. A sprinkling of parsley added pleasant freshness.

1 tablespoon ground coriander
2 teaspoons ground fennel
1½ teaspoons table salt
1½ teaspoons pepper
1 (4- to 5-pound) boneless lamb shoulder roast, trimmed
2 tablespoons extra-virgin olive oil
1 onion, chopped fine
5 garlic cloves, minced
2 cups ruby port
2 sprigs fresh rosemary
12 ounces fresh figs, stemmed and quartered
¼ cup chopped fresh parsley

1. Combine coriander, fennel, salt, and pepper in bowl. Place roast with rough interior side (which was against bone) facing up on cutting board and sprinkle with 4 teaspoons spice mixture. Starting from short side, roll roast tightly and tie with kitchen twine at 1-inch intervals. Sprinkle exterior with remaining spice mixture. Transfer to plate, cover, and refrigerate for at least 1 hour or up to 24 hours.

2. Adjust oven rack to lower-middle position and heat oven to 300 degrees. Pat roast dry with paper towels. Heat oil in Dutch oven over medium-high heat until just smoking. Brown roast on all sides, 8 to 10 minutes; transfer to plate.

3. Pour off all but 1 tablespoon fat from pot. Add onion and cook over medium heat until softened, about 5 minutes. Stir in garlic and cook until fragrant, about 30 seconds. Stir in port, scraping up any browned bits, and bring to simmer. Return roast to pot, adding any accumulated juices. Add rosemary sprigs, cover, and transfer pot to oven. Cook until lamb is tender and fork slips easily in and out of meat, 2¼ to 2¾ hours, flipping roast halfway through cooking.

Lamb Pot Roast with Coriander, Fennel, and Figs

4. Remove pot from oven. Transfer roast to carving board, tent with aluminum foil, and let rest while finishing sauce. Discard rosemary sprigs and strain braising liquid through fine-mesh strainer into fat separator; reserve solids. Allow braising liquid to settle for 5 minutes. Add defatted braising liquid and reserved solids to now-empty pot and bring to simmer over medium-high heat. Cook until slightly thickened and reduced to 1½ cups, about 10 minutes. Stir in figs and cook until heated through, about 2 minutes. Season with salt and pepper to taste.

5. Remove twine from roast. Slice meat ½ inch thick and transfer to platter. Spoon sauce over lamb and sprinkle with parsley. Serve.

LAMB VINDALOO

Serves 6 to 8 | lamb shoulder roast

WHY THIS RECIPE WORKS Vindaloo is a complex dish that originated in Goa, a region on India's western coast. Because Goa was once a Portuguese colony, much of the local cuisine incorporates Indian and Portuguese ingredients and techniques. In fact, the word vindaloo comes from the Portuguese words for wine vinegar ("vinho") and garlic ("alhos"). It's no surprise, then, that the sauce napping tender chunks of lamb (in this version) is much about the interplay of sweet, sour, and pungent flavors—the pungency provided by the garlic, along with spices and chiles. Most vindaloo recipes simply call for water as the cooking liquid because, in theory, its neutral flavor allows the flavors of the meat and spices to shine. However, we found that we preferred chicken broth, which added richness and body to the stewing liquid and still let the lamb flavor come through. Two tablespoons of red wine vinegar and 1 teaspoon of sugar provided the right sweet-sour balance. In order to give it time to soften and mix with the other flavors, we added the vinegar at the beginning of cooking. The diced tomatoes provided further acidity.

1 (3½ - to 4-pound) boneless lamb shoulder roast, trimmed and cut into 1½-inch pieces
3 tablespoons vegetable oil, divided
3 onions, chopped
¼ teaspoon table salt
8 garlic cloves, minced
1 tablespoon paprika
¾ teaspoon ground cumin
½ teaspoon ground cardamom
¼ teaspoon cayenne pepper
¼ teaspoon ground cloves
3 tablespoons all-purpose flour
1½ cups chicken broth
1 (14.5-ounce) can diced tomatoes
2 tablespoons red wine vinegar
1 tablespoon mustard seeds
2 bay leaves
1 teaspoon sugar
¼ cup minced fresh cilantro

1. Adjust oven rack to lower-middle position and heat oven to 325 degrees. Pat lamb dry with paper towels and season with salt and pepper. Heat 1 tablespoon oil in Dutch oven over medium-high heat until just smoking. Brown half of lamb on all sides, 7 to 10 minutes; transfer to bowl. Repeat with 1 tablespoon oil and remaining lamb; transfer to bowl.

2. Add remaining 1 tablespoon oil to pot and return to medium heat until shimmering. Add onions and salt and cook, stirring occasionally, until softened, 5 to 7 minutes. Stir in garlic, paprika, cumin, cardamom, cayenne, and cloves and cook until fragrant, about 30 seconds. Stir in flour and cook for 1 minute.

3. Gradually whisk in broth, scraping up browned bits and smoothing out any lumps. Stir in tomatoes and their juice, vinegar, mustard seeds, bay leaves, sugar, and browned lamb and any accumulated juices, bring to simmer, and cover; transfer pot to oven. Cook until meat is tender, about 2 hours. Remove bay leaves. Stir in cilantro, season with salt and pepper to taste, and serve.

LAMB TAGINE WITH APRICOTS AND OLIVES

Serves 6 | lamb shoulder roast

WHY THIS RECIPE WORKS Tagines—generously spiced, assertively flavored stews slow-cooked in earthenware vessels of the same name—are a North African specialty. They can include all manner of meats, vegetables, and fruit but we set our sights on a popular version: fork-tender lamb, sweet dried apricots, and briny olives. We started with a boneless lamb shoulder roast and flavored it with a handful of assertive spices: cumin, ginger, cinnamon, cayenne, coriander, and paprika. Whole apricots remained leathery in the stew; chopping them into small bits and adding them toward the end softened them and maintained their flavor. Tagines typically get lemon notes from preserved lemon, which can be hard to find. Two broad ribbons of lemon zest did the trick, and the high heat drew out the zest's oils and mellowed them. Adding grated zest and lemon juice just before serving reinforced the bright flavor. Greek olives are not traditional, but they're easier to find than Moroccan olives. If the olives are particularly salty, rinse them.

1 (3½- to 4-pound) boneless lamb shoulder roast, trimmed and cut into 1½-inch pieces
3 tablespoons extra-virgin olive oil, divided
3 onions, halved and sliced through root end into ¼-inch-thick pieces
4 (2-inch) strips lemon zest, plus ½ teaspoon grated zest plus ¼ cup juice (2 lemons)
¼ teaspoon table salt
10 garlic cloves (8 minced, 2 minced to paste)
2½ teaspoons paprika
1 teaspoon ground cumin
½ teaspoon ground ginger
½ teaspoon ground coriander
½ teaspoon ground cinnamon
¼ teaspoon cayenne pepper
¼ cup all-purpose flour
4 cups chicken broth
2 tablespoons honey
1 pound carrots, peeled and sliced 1 inch thick
2 cups pitted Greek green olives, halved
1 cup dried apricots, chopped
¼ cup minced fresh cilantro

1. Adjust oven rack to lower-middle position and heat oven to 325 degrees. Pat lamb dry with paper towels and season with salt and pepper. Heat 1 tablespoon oil in Dutch oven over medium-high heat until just smoking. Brown half of lamb on all sides, 7 to 10 minutes; transfer to bowl. Repeat with 1 tablespoon oil and remaining lamb; transfer to bowl.

2. Add remaining 1 tablespoon oil to pot and heat over medium heat until shimmering. Add onions, lemon zest strips, and salt and cook until onions are softened, 5 to 7 minutes. Stir in minced garlic, paprika, cumin, ginger, coriander, cinnamon, and cayenne and cook until fragrant, about 30 seconds. Stir in flour and cook for 1 minute.

3. Slowly whisk in broth, scraping up any browned bits and smoothing out any lumps. Stir in honey and browned lamb with any accumulated juices, bring to simmer, and cover; transfer pot to oven. Cook for 1 hour. Stir in carrots and continue to cook in oven until lamb is tender, 1 to 1½ hours longer.

4. Remove tagine from oven and discard lemon zest strips. Stir in olives and apricots, cover, and let stand off heat for 5 minutes. Stir in cilantro, lemon zest and juice, and garlic paste. Season with salt and pepper to taste, and serve.

ARROSTICINI

Serves 6 to 8 | lamb shoulder roast

WHY THIS RECIPE WORKS The roots of these grilled lamb skewers are steeped in the long shepherding tradition of the Abruzzo region of Italy; lore has it that the mountain shepherds would roast pieces of mutton over the fire as a quick and easy meal while they traveled. Today, arrosticini is a popular street food—the meat is cut into tiny cubes by machine, cooked over a specialized grill, and eaten directly off the skewer. Arrosticini can be made with lamb or mutton, but either way its exterior should be well browned, with the meat basted in its own flavorful fat and cooked until tender. We used our half-grill fire setup, which produced a concentrated, blazing-hot fire. We cut the lamb into ½-inch chunks and packed it tightly on skewers to prevent it from overcooking. After a quick stint on the grill, it was so flavorful that all it needed was a dash of salt and pepper. You can substitute 2½ pounds lamb shoulder chops (blade or round bone) for the lamb shoulder. You will need twelve 12-inch metal skewers for this recipe.

 2 pounds boneless lamb shoulder roast, trimmed and cut into ½-inch pieces
1½ teaspoons kosher salt
 1 teaspoon pepper
 3 tablespoons extra-virgin olive oil

1. Pat lamb dry with paper towels and sprinkle with salt and pepper. Tightly thread lamb onto twelve 12-inch metal skewers, leaving top 3 inches of each skewer exposed. Brush skewers with oil.

2a. **For a charcoal grill:** Open bottom vent completely. Light large chimney starter filled with charcoal briquettes (6 quarts). When top coals are partially covered with ash, pour evenly over half of grill. Set cooking grate in place, cover, and open lid vent completely. Heat grill until hot, about 5 minutes.

2b. **For a gas grill:** Turn all burners to high, cover, and heat grill until hot, about 15 minutes. Leave all burners on high.

3. Clean and oil cooking grate. Place skewers on hotter side of grill, and cook (covered if using gas), turning frequently, until well browned on all sides, 5 to 7 minutes. Serve.

BRAISED LAMB SHOULDER CHOPS WITH TOMATOES AND RED WINE

Serves 4 | lamb shoulder chops

WHY THIS RECIPE WORKS This dish will remind you not to overlook lamb shoulder chops in favor of rib chops (see page 341). Although shoulder chops have chew, they're not particularly tough. This meant they didn't require a long time in the pot before becoming tender; a relatively quick stovetop braise of just 15 to 20 minutes was all it took to yield fork-tender meat (another good reason to cook them). The robust flavor of shoulder chops called for a braising liquid that could double as an equally bold sauce. After sautéing some onion and garlic, we deglazed the pan with red wine. Tomatoes balanced out the acidity of the wine. Once the lamb was done cooking, we removed it from the sauce to rest before stirring in parsley and allowing the sauce to reduce for a few more minutes. We came up with two variations that also embrace brash flavors to bring out the best in this weekday-friendly braise.

 4 (8- to 12-ounce) lamb shoulder chops (blade or round bone), about ¾ inch thick, trimmed
 2 tablespoons extra-virgin olive oil, divided
 1 small onion, chopped fine
 2 small garlic cloves, minced
⅓ cup dry red wine
 1 cup canned whole peeled tomatoes, chopped
 2 tablespoons minced fresh parsley

1. Pat chops dry with paper towels and season with salt and pepper. Heat 1 tablespoon oil in 12-inch skillet over medium-high heat until just smoking. Brown chops, in batches if necessary, 4 to 5 minutes per side; transfer to plate. Pour off fat from skillet.

Braised Lamb Shoulder Chops
with Tomatoes and Red Wine

2. Heat remaining 1 tablespoon oil in now-empty skillet over medium heat until shimmering. Add onion and cook until softened, about 5 minutes. Stir in garlic and cook until fragrant, about 30 seconds. Stir in wine, scraping up any browned bits. Bring to simmer and cook until reduced by half, 2 to 3 minutes. Stir in tomatoes.

3. Nestle chops into skillet along with any accumulated juices and return to simmer. Reduce heat to low, cover, and simmer gently until chops are tender and fork slips easily in and out of meat, 15 to 20 minutes. Transfer chops to platter and tent with aluminum foil.

4. Stir parsley into sauce and simmer until sauce thickens, 2 to 3 minutes. Season with salt and pepper to taste. Spoon sauce over chops and serve.

VARIATIONS
Braised Lamb Shoulder Chops with Capers, Balsamic Vinegar, and Red Pepper
Add 1 diced red bell pepper with onion and stir in 2 tablespoons rinsed capers and 2 tablespoons balsamic vinegar with parsley.

Braised Lamb Shoulder Chops with Figs and Warm Spices
Soak ⅓ cup dried figs in ⅓ cup warm water for 30 minutes. Drain, reserving liquid, and cut figs into quarters. Add 1 teaspoon ground coriander, ½ teaspoon ground cumin, ½ teaspoon cinnamon, and ⅛ teaspoon cayenne pepper to skillet with garlic. Omit red wine and replace with ⅓ cup fig soaking water. Add 2 tablespoons honey with tomatoes. Stir in figs with parsley.

IRISH STEW

Serves 6 | lamb shoulder chops

WHY THIS RECIPE WORKS At its most traditional, Irish stew is made with just lamb, onions, potatoes, and water. The raw ingredients are layered in the pot and cooked until tender. The dish is nutritious and sustaining. We wanted a rich, deeply flavored stew as delicious as it was filling. For a traditional stew, we would cut the meat off the bone into pieces, but we found it essential to add the bones to the pot as well; it gave the stew richness and a velvety texture. The stew got deeply flavored back notes from caramelized onion, so all we needed was water in addition as chicken broth muted the flavor of the lamb. Broken-down potatoes (along with some flour for assistance) thickened the stew and gave it heft. All our homey stew needed was a side of Irish soda bread. Though we prefer lamb chops cut 1½ inches thick here, 1-inch-thick chops will suffice.

4½ pounds lamb shoulder chops (blade or round bone), 1 to 1½ inches thick, trimmed, meat removed from bones and cut into 1½-inch pieces, bones reserved
3 tablespoons vegetable oil, divided
2½ pounds onions, chopped coarse
1¼ teaspoons table salt, divided
¼ cup all-purpose flour
3 cups water, divided
1 teaspoon dried thyme
2 pounds Yukon Gold potatoes, peeled and cut into 1-inch pieces
¼ cup minced fresh parsley

1. Adjust oven rack to lower-middle position and heat oven to 300 degrees. Season lamb with salt and pepper.

2. Heat 1 tablespoon oil in Dutch oven over medium-high heat until shimmering. Add half of lamb to pot so that individual pieces are close together but not touching. Cook, without moving lamb, until well browned, 2 to 3 minutes. Using tongs, flip lamb pieces and continue to cook until most sides are well browned, about 5 minutes longer; transfer to bowl. Add 1 tablespoon oil to pot, swirl to coat pot, and repeat with remaining lamb; transfer to bowl and set aside.

3. Reduce heat to medium, add remaining 1 tablespoon oil, and swirl to coat pot. Add onions and ¼ teaspoon salt and cook, stirring frequently and scraping up any browned bits, until onions have browned, about 8 minutes. Add flour and stir until onions are evenly coated, 1 to 2 minutes.

4. Stir in 1½ cups water, scraping up any remaining browned bits. Gradually add remaining 1½ cups water, stirring constantly and scraping pan edges to dissolve flour. Add thyme and remaining 1 teaspoon salt and bring to simmer. Add reserved bones, then meat and accumulated juices. Return to simmer and cover; transfer pot to oven. Cook for 1 hour.

5. Remove pot from oven and place potatoes on top of meat and bones. Cover and return pot to oven. Cook until lamb is tender, about 1 hour. Stir potatoes into liquid, wait 5 minutes, then skim off any fat that rises to top. Stir in parsley and season with salt and pepper to taste. Discard bones and serve.

VARIATION
Irish Stew with Carrots and Turnips
Substitute 3 carrots, peeled and sliced ¼ inch thick, and 8 ounces turnips, peeled and cut into 1-inch-thick pieces, for half of potatoes.

Irish Stew with Carrots and Turnips

SHARBA

Serves 6 to 8 | lamb shoulder chops

WHY THIS RECIPE WORKS We wanted to develop a soup reminiscent of sharba, a Libyan staple dish that traditionally includes lamb, mint, chickpeas, orzo, and plenty of warm spices, with a humble spice cabinet. We started by searing chunks of lamb shoulder chops to produce fond, and then braised the meat slowly in a soup base built on onion, tomatoes, dried mint, and a pared-down blend of spices. Looking for a way to reinforce the mint flavor without making the soup taste like peppermint, we landed on adding the dried mint in stages, stirring in some at the beginning of braising and some at the very end before serving. With this simple change, the dish took on a subtle but refreshing mint aroma that did not overpower the warmer flavors of our comforting, aromatic soup.

1 pound lamb shoulder chops (blade or round bone), 1 to 1½ inches thick, trimmed and halved
1 tablespoon extra-virgin olive oil
1 onion, chopped fine
4 plum tomatoes, cored and cut into ¼-inch pieces
2 tablespoons tomato paste
1½ teaspoons dried mint, crumbled, divided
1 teaspoon ground turmeric
1 teaspoon paprika

1 teaspoon table salt
½ teaspoon ground cinnamon
¼ teaspoon ground cumin
¼ teaspoon pepper
10 cups chicken broth
1 (15-ounce) can chickpeas, rinsed
1 cup orzo

1. Adjust oven rack to lower-middle position and heat oven to 325 degrees. Pat lamb dry with paper towels and season with salt and pepper. Heat oil in Dutch oven over medium-high heat until just smoking. Brown lamb, about 4 minutes per side; transfer to plate. Pour off all but 2 tablespoons fat from pot.

2. Add onion to fat left in pot and cook over medium heat until softened, about 5 minutes. Stir in tomatoes and cook until softened and juice has evaporated, about 2 minutes. Stir in tomato paste, 1 teaspoon mint, turmeric, paprika, salt, cinnamon, cumin, and pepper and cook until fragrant, about 1 minute. Stir in broth, scraping up any browned bits, and bring to boil.

3. Stir in chickpeas, then nestle lamb into pot along with any accumulated juices. Cover, place pot in oven, and cook until fork slips easily in and out of lamb, about 1 hour.

4. Transfer lamb to cutting board, let cool slightly, then shred into bite-size pieces using 2 forks, discarding excess fat and bones. Meanwhile, stir orzo into soup, bring to simmer over medium heat, and cook until tender, 10 to 12 minutes. Stir in shredded lamb and cook until heated through, about 2 minutes. Off heat, stir in remaining ½ teaspoon mint and let sit until fragrant, about 1 minute. Serve.

HARIRA

Serves 8 | lamb shoulder chops

WHY THIS RECIPE WORKS Harira is a heavily spiced, intensely flavored Moroccan soup of lentils, tomatoes, chickpeas, and often chicken or lamb that is rich and soul-satisfying. For this version we used inexpensive lamb shoulder chops, which were the right thickness to cut into pieces for this soup. After searing pieces of lamb and setting them aside, we built the stock with onion, tomato, and spices and then simmered the lamb, lentils, and chickpeas in the oven for even cooking and a hands-off method. We shredded the lamb before stirring it back in, and the fall-apart texture of this meat made us swoon. This version was balanced, warming, and near perfect, but we wanted just a little more zing. We chose to finish the soup by stirring in a healthy portion of homemade harissa paste, which imparted spice, heat, and depth. You can substitute store-bought harissa, though spiciness can vary greatly by brand. French green lentils (lentilles du Puy) also work well here.

HARISSA

5 tablespoons extra-virgin olive oil
1½ tablespoons paprika
4 garlic cloves, minced
2 teaspoons ground coriander
¾ teaspoon ground cumin
¼ teaspoon cayenne pepper
⅛ teaspoon table salt

SOUP

1 pound lamb shoulder chops (blade or round bone),
   trimmed of all visible fat and cut into 2-inch pieces
1 tablespoon extra-virgin olive oil
1 onion, chopped fine
1 teaspoon grated fresh ginger
1 teaspoon ground cumin
½ teaspoon paprika
¼ teaspoon ground cinnamon
¼ teaspoon pepper
¼ teaspoon cayenne pepper
   Pinch saffron threads, crumbled
1 tablespoon all-purpose flour
10 cups chicken broth
1 cup dried brown lentils, picked over and rinsed
4 plum tomatoes (about 1 pound), cored and cut into
   ¾-inch pieces
1 (15-ounce) can chickpeas, rinsed
⅓ cup minced fresh cilantro

1. **For the harissa:** Combine all ingredients in medium bowl; microwave on high until bubbling and fragrant, 15 to 30 seconds. Set aside to cool.

2. **For the soup:** Adjust oven rack to lower-middle position and heat oven to 325 degrees. Season lamb with salt and pepper. Heat oil in Dutch oven over medium-high heat until just smoking. Brown lamb on all sides, about 8 minutes; transfer to plate. Pour off all but 2 tablespoons fat from pot.

3. Reduce heat to medium, add onion to fat left in pot and cook until softened, 5 to 7 minutes. Stir in ginger, cumin, paprika, cinnamon, pepper, cayenne, and saffron and cook until fragrant, about 30 seconds. Stir in flour and cook for 1 minute. Gradually whisk in broth, scraping up any browned bits and smoothing out any lumps. Return lamb and any accumulated juices to pot, bring to simmer, and cook for 10 minutes. Add lentils, cover, place pot in oven, and cook until fork slips easily in and out of lamb and lentils are tender, about 50 minutes.

4. Remove lamb from pot; let cool slightly; then, using 2 forks, shred lamb into bite-size pieces, discarding pieces of fat. Meanwhile, stir in tomatoes and chickpeas and continue to simmer until flavors meld, about 10 minutes longer. Stir in shredded

Grilled Lamb Shoulder Chops

lamb and let it heat through, about 2 minutes. Stir in cilantro and ¼ cup harissa and season with salt and pepper to taste. Serve, passing extra harissa separately.

GRILLED LAMB SHOULDER CHOPS

Serves 4 | lamb shoulder chops

WHY THIS RECIPE WORKS When done right, grilled lamb shoulder chops are juicy and tender, with just a touch of gamy richness and satisfying chew. To grill this relatively fatty cut while avoiding flare-ups caused by rendered fat dripping onto the coals, we built a two-level fire: We started the chops on the hotter side to give them a well-browned crust and then slid them to the cooler side to finish cooking through. Look for lamb shoulder chops that are at least ¾ inch thick, since they are less prone to overcook. If you can find only chops that are ½ inch thick, reduce the cooking time on the cooler side of the grill by about 30 seconds on each side.

4 (8- to 12-ounce) lamb shoulder chops (blade or round
   bone), ¾ to 1 inch thick, trimmed
2 tablespoons extra-virgin olive oil

1a. For a charcoal grill: Open bottom vent completely. Light large chimney starter filled with charcoal briquettes (6 quarts). When top coals are partially covered with ash, pour two-thirds evenly over half of grill, then pour remaining coals over other half of grill. Set cooking grate in place, cover, and open lid vent completely. Heat grill until hot, about 5 minutes.

1b. For a gas grill: Turn all burners to high, cover, and heat grill until hot, about 15 minutes. Leave primary burner on high and turn other burner(s) to medium.

2. Clean and oil cooking grate. Rub chops with oil and season with salt and pepper. Place chops on hotter side of grill and cook (covered if using gas) until well browned, about 2 minutes per side. Slide chops to cooler side of grill and continue to cook until meat registers 120 to 125 degrees (for medium-rare), 2 to 4 minutes longer per side. Transfer chops to large platter, tent with aluminum foil, and let rest for 5 minutes before serving.

SPICED RED PEPPER–RUBBED GRILLED LAMB SHOULDER CHOPS

Serves 4 | lamb shoulder chops

WHY THIS RECIPE WORKS Lamb is lovely paired with strong flavors from around the world—and the added flavor from grilling elevates any of these pairings even more. We proved this point by rubbing shoulder chops with a red pepper rub that got its flavor from two peppers: sweetness from red bell pepper and spicy freshness from serrano chile. We cooked the two and pureed them with bright lemon and mint and warm spices for a complex, substantial rub that we marinated the chops with before grilling them. Our equally bold variations include a simple but complementary garlic-rosemary rub and a zippy soy-shallot one.

- 3 tablespoons extra-virgin olive oil, divided
- ½ red bell pepper, chopped coarse
- ½ serrano or jalapeño chile, stemmed, seeded, and chopped coarse
- 2 teaspoons lemon juice
- 1½ teaspoons chopped fresh mint
- 1 garlic clove, minced
- ½ teaspoon ground cumin
- ½ teaspoon dried summer savory
- ¼ teaspoon ground cinnamon
- 4 (8- to 12-ounce) lamb shoulder chops (blade or round bone), ¾ to 1 inch thick, trimmed

1. Heat 1 tablespoon oil in 8-inch skillet over medium-high heat until shimmering. Add bell pepper and serrano and cook, stirring frequently, until just beginning to soften, about 2 minutes. Reduce heat to medium-low and continue to cook until softened, about 5 minutes longer.

2. Transfer bell pepper mixture to food processor. Add lemon juice, mint, garlic, cumin, savory, cinnamon, and remaining 2 tablespoons oil and process until almost smooth (some chunky pieces of bell pepper will remain), about 20 seconds.

3. Rub chops with pepper paste. Transfer chops to 13 by 9-inch baking dish, cover with plastic wrap, and refrigerate for at least 20 minutes or up to 24 hours.

4a. For a charcoal grill: Open bottom vent completely. Light large chimney starter filled with charcoal briquettes (6 quarts). When top coals are partially covered with ash, pour two-thirds evenly over half of grill, then pour remaining coals over other half of grill. Set cooking grate in place, cover, and open lid vent completely. Heat grill until hot, about 5 minutes.

4b. For a gas grill: Turn all burners to high, cover, and heat grill until hot, about 15 minutes. Leave primary burner on high and turn other burner(s) to medium.

5. Clean and oil cooking grate. Season chops with salt and pepper. Place chops on hotter side of grill and cook (covered if using gas) until well browned, about 2 minutes per side. Slide chops to cooler side of grill and continue to cook until meat registers 120 to 125 degrees (for medium-rare) or 130 to 135 degrees (for medium), 2 to 4 minutes longer per side. Transfer chops to large platter, tent with aluminum foil, and let rest for 5 minutes before serving.

VARIATIONS

Grilled Lamb Shoulder Chops with Garlic-Rosemary Marinade

Combine 2 tablespoons extra-virgin olive oil, 1 tablespoon minced fresh rosemary, 2 minced large garlic cloves, and pinch cayenne pepper in small bowl and substitute for pepper paste.

Grilled Lamb Shoulder Chops with Soy-Shallot Marinade

Combine ¼ cup minced shallot or scallion, 3 tablespoons lemon juice, 2 tablespoons vegetable oil, 2 tablespoons minced fresh thyme, 2 tablespoons minced fresh parsley, and 2 tablespoons soy sauce in bowl; season with pepper to taste and transfer to zipper-lock bag. Place chops in bag with marinade and toss to coat; press out as much air as possible and seal bag. Refrigerate chops for at least 20 minutes or up to 1 hour. Omit pepper paste in step 3 and salt and pepper in step 5.

RIB AND LOIN

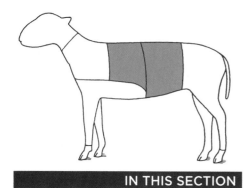

IF YOU'RE A CASUAL LAMB EATER, or someone who eats it for the holidays, you're probably most familiar with the pricier, prettier rib-area cuts of lamb—a crusted rack with trimmed upstanding bones, or maybe a sophisticated plate of chops from the same cut. And there's a lot to love about the rib—it's the prime land of the lamb landscape. The rib area is directly behind the shoulder and extends from the fifth to the 12th rib. Meat from this area has a fine, tender grain due to its lack of exercise, and a mild flavor from its low fat content. The loin extends from the last rib down to the hip area. It's usually cut into loin chops (and this is the only cut from the loin we cook), which are a good, flavorful substitute for rib chops.

Rack of Lamb

Cost: ■■□□ Flavor: ■■□□
Best cooking methods: roast, grill
Texture: extremely tender
Alternative names: rack roast, rib roast

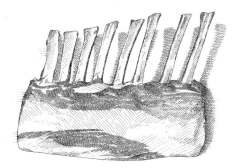

The rack is all eight ribs from the rib section. It's as "prime" as beef prime rib but some of its beauty, beyond flavor, is that is cooks a whole lot faster, and its smaller size (1¾ to 2 pounds; we usually cook two) also makes it more manageable for a smaller number of guests. It's a lovely centerpiece that can be served adorned (along with an herby sauce, with a crumb crust, or with grill smoke) or simply salt-and-peppered. For the mildest flavor, trim the fat from a rack. Like a pork rib roast (see page 246), rack of lamb has an associated chine bone. It's usually removed when you purchase the rack; in the event it isn't, have the butcher do this for you so it's easy to cut between the ribs.

MEAT PREP *Trimming Fat from a Rack of Lamb*

1. If rack has fat cap, peel back thick outer layer of fat from racks and use boning knife to cut any tissue connecting fat cap to rack.

2. Trim fat to ⅛ to ¼ inch.

FRENCH FLAIR

Traditionally rack of lamb is spiffed up via frenching, a process that involves cutting away the sinew, fat, and small bits of meat that cover the bones. We instruct you on how to do it below, but you can have your butcher do this for you. Often the rack comes frenched—and thus oven ready—automatically.

1. Make straight cut along top side of bones, 1 inch up from small eye of meat.

2. Remove any fat above this line and scrape any remaining meat or fat from exposed bones.

Rib Chops

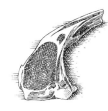

Cost: ■■■□ Flavor: ■■□□
Best cooking methods: pan sear, grill
Texture: extremely tender
Alternative names: rack chops, frenched chops

These chops have the most refined flavor and tender texture. The meat is mild and sweet. For best results, don't cook these lean chops past medium-rare since they don't have a lot of intramuscular fat. This cut is easily recognized by the bone that runs along one side. As with a rack of lamb, ask your butcher to "french" the chops by scraping away the fat from the end of the bone. Since they're small, there's a lot of potential for overcooking, so you'll want to seek evenly sized chops for even doneness temperatures.

Loin Chops

Cost: ■■■□ Flavor: ■■■□
Best cooking methods: pan sear, grill
Texture: tender and fine-grained on the smaller side of the T-bone; a bit chewier on the larger side
Alternative names: none

Like rib chops, loin chops are tender and have a mild, sweet flavor. The chops look like miniature T-bone steaks, with the bone separating a larger piece of top loin and a smaller piece of very tender tenderloin. They're so small that there is less discrepancy to worry about between the sides when cooking as with a T-bone steak.

ROASTED RACK OF LAMB WITH ROASTED RED PEPPER RELISH

Serves 4 to 6 | rack of lamb

WHY THIS RECIPE WORKS Rack of lamb is impressive, but its size also makes it a manageable roast for busy times. (It roasts for just a little over an hour.) To ensure that our rack of lamb had a rosy, juicy interior and a nicely browned exterior, we used the reverse searing method: We slowly roasted the lamb in a 250-degree oven until the meat registered 120 to 125 degrees and then gave it a quick sear in a very hot skillet. We seasoned the rack with a warm cumin-spiked salt before roasting, and we sprinkled the chops with a bit more before serving. While the lamb was in the oven, we made a simple relish of convenient jarred red peppers, fresh parsley, olive oil, lemon, and garlic, allowing the flavors to meld for at least an hour before serving it alongside the lamb. We prefer domestic lamb; if using smaller imported racks, season each rack with ½ teaspoon of the salt mixture in step 1 and reduce the cooking time to 50 minutes.

LAMB

- 2 (1¾- to 2-pound) racks of lamb, fat trimmed to ⅛ to ¼ inch and rib bones frenched
- 2 tablespoons kosher salt
- 1 teaspoon ground cumin
- 1 tablespoon vegetable oil

RELISH

- ½ cup jarred roasted red peppers, rinsed, patted dry, and chopped fine
- ½ cup minced fresh parsley
- ¼ cup extra-virgin olive oil
- ¼ teaspoon lemon juice
- ⅛ teaspoon garlic, minced to paste

1. For the lamb: Adjust oven rack to middle position and heat oven to 250 degrees. Using sharp knife, cut slits, spaced ½ inch apart in crosshatch pattern in surface fat layer, being careful not to cut into meat. Combine salt and cumin in bowl. Rub ¾ teaspoon salt mixture over entire surface of each rack and into slits. Reserve remaining salt mixture. Place racks, bone side down, on wire rack set in rimmed baking sheet. Roast until meat registers 120 to 125 degrees (for medium-rare), about 1 hour 5 minutes.

2. For the relish: While lamb roasts, combine all relish ingredients in bowl. Season with salt and pepper to taste. Let stand at room temperature for at least 1 hour before serving

3. Heat vegetable oil in 12-inch skillet over high heat until just smoking. Place 1 rack, bone side up, in skillet and cook until well browned, 1 to 2 minutes. Transfer to carving board. Pour off all but 1 teaspoon fat from skillet and repeat browning with second rack. Tent racks with aluminum foil and let rest for

20 minutes. Cut between ribs to separate chops and sprinkle cut side of chops with ½ teaspoon salt mixture. Serve, passing relish and remaining salt mixture separately.

VARIATION

Roasted Rack of Lamb with Sweet Mint-Almond Relish

Substitute ground anise for cumin in salt mixture. Omit red pepper relish. While lamb roasts, combine ½ cup minced fresh mint; ¼ cup sliced almonds, toasted and chopped fine; ¼ cup extra-virgin olive oil; 2 tablespoons red currant jelly; 4 teaspoons red wine vinegar; and 2 teaspoons Dijon mustard in bowl. Season with salt and pepper to taste. Let stand at room temperature for at least 1 hour before serving.

CRUMB-CRUSTED RACK OF LAMB

Serves 4 to 6 | rack of lamb

WHY THIS RECIPE WORKS A flavorful crust makes a rack of lamb worthy of any special occasion. For our crust, we put Dijon mustard to work in two ways: helping the crumbs adhere while adding tangy flavor. Panko bread crumbs gave our crust a big crunch, and a surprising addition—anchovies—added umami oomph. To ensure that the crust was golden brown, we toasted our bread-crumb mixture before pressing it onto the lamb. Trimming the lamb and searing the racks to render fat before coating them with the crumb mixture and roasting helped minimize the gamy flavor. We prefer domestic lamb; if using smaller imported racks, season each rack with ¾ teaspoon salt mixture in step 2 and reduce the cooking time by 5 minutes.

- 1 cup panko bread crumbs
- 2 tablespoons plus 1 teaspoon extra-virgin olive oil, divided
- 2 tablespoons minced fresh thyme
- 6 garlic cloves, minced
- 4 anchovy fillets, rinsed, patted dry, and minced (optional)
- 4 teaspoons kosher salt, divided
- 1 teaspoon pepper
- 2 tablespoons minced fresh parsley
- 1 tablespoon grated lemon zest
- 2 (1¾- to 2-pound) racks of lamb, fat trimmed to ⅛ inch and rib bones frenched
- ¼ cup Dijon mustard

1. Adjust oven rack to middle position and heat oven to 300 degrees. Combine panko; 2 tablespoons oil; thyme; garlic; anchovies, if using; 2 teaspoons salt; and pepper in 12-inch nonstick skillet. Cook over medium heat, stirring frequently and breaking up any clumps, until golden brown, about 5 minutes. Transfer to shallow dish. Stir in parsley and lemon zest.

TUTORIAL
Crumb-Crusted Rack of Lamb

Follow these steps to make this centerpiece look and taste as special as the occasion at which you serve it.

1. Trim fat on racks to ⅛ inch. Pat lamb dry and sprinkle each rack with 1 teaspoon salt and season with pepper.

2. Heat oil in skillet over medium-high heat until just smoking. Place 1 rack in skillet and cook until well browned, 2 to 4 minutes per side, using tongs as necessary to stand up rack to brown loin portion. Transfer to wire rack. Pour off all but 1 teaspoon fat from skillet and repeat with remaining rack. Let cool for 5 minutes.

3. Brush lamb all over with mustard.

4. Working with 1 rack at a time, transfer lamb to panko mixture, turning to coat all sides and pressing gently to adhere.

5. Roast until lamb register 120 to 125 degrees (for medium-rare). Let rest for 15 minutes.

6. Cut between bones to separate chops.

2. Wipe skillet clean with paper towels. Set wire rack in rimmed baking sheet. Pat lamb dry with paper towels, sprinkle each rack with 1 teaspoon salt, and season with pepper. Heat remaining 1 teaspoon oil in now-empty skillet over medium-high heat until just smoking. Place 1 rack in skillet and cook until well browned, 2 to 4 minutes per side, using tongs as necessary to stand up rack to brown loin portion. Transfer to prepared wire rack. Pour off all but 1 teaspoon fat from skillet and repeat cooking with remaining rack of lamb. Let lamb cool for 5 minutes.

3. Brush lamb all over with mustard. Working with 1 rack at a time, transfer lamb to panko mixture, turning to coat all sides and pressing gently to adhere. Return lamb to wire rack, fat side up. Roast until lamb registers 120 to 125 degrees (for medium-rare), about 40 minutes. Transfer to carving board and let rest for 15 minutes. Cut between bones to separate chops. Serve.

GRILLED RACK OF LAMB

Serves 4 to 6 | rack of lamb
WHY THIS RECIPE WORKS With its juicy, pink meat, rich crust, and impressive presentation, rack of lamb is a bona fide showstopper. But grill this piece of meat improperly and you've made a costly mistake. We came up with a technique that would deliver perfect results every time. To avoid flare-ups, we needed fairly lean racks, so we started by trimming away excess fat. We placed a disposable aluminum pan in the middle of the grill between two piles of coals; placing the lamb over the pan ensured that the pan would catch the rendering fat, preventing flare-ups. For flavorful meat and a crust that wasn't scorched, we applied a wet rub during the last few minutes of grilling. We prefer domestic lamb; if using smaller imported racks, check for doneness sooner.

- 4 teaspoons vegetable oil, divided
- 4 teaspoons minced fresh rosemary
- 2 teaspoons minced fresh thyme
- 2 garlic cloves, minced
- 2 (1½- to 1¾-pound) racks of lamb (8 ribs each), trimmed and frenched
- 1 (13 by 9-inch) disposable aluminum roasting pan (if using charcoal)

1. Combine 1 tablespoon oil, rosemary, thyme, and garlic in bowl; set aside. Pat lamb dry with paper towels, rub with remaining 1 teaspoon oil, and season with salt and pepper.

2a. **For a charcoal grill:** Open bottom vent completely and place disposable pan in center of grill. Light large chimney starter filled with charcoal briquettes (6 quarts). When top coals are partially covered with ash, pour into 2 even piles on either side of disposable pan. Set cooking grate in place, cover, and open lid vent completely. Heat grill until hot, about 5 minutes.

2b. **For a gas grill:** Turn all burners to high, cover, and heat grill until hot, about 15 minutes. Leave primary burner on high and turn off other burner(s).

3. Clean and oil cooking grate. Place racks, bone side up, on cooler part of grill with meaty side very close to, but not quite over, hotter part of grill. Cover and cook until meat is lightly browned, faint grill marks appear, and fat has begun to render, 8 to 10 minutes.

4. Flip racks bone side down and slide to hotter part of grill. Cook until well browned on bone side, 3 to 4 minutes. Brush racks with herb mixture, flip bone side up, and cook until well browned on meaty side, 3 to 4 minutes.

5. Stand up racks, leaning them against each other for support, and cook until bottoms are well browned and meat registers 120 to 125 degrees (for medium-rare), 3 to 8 minutes.

6. Transfer racks to carving board, tent with aluminum foil, and let rest for 15 to 20 minutes. Cut between ribs to separate chops and serve.

VARIATION
Grilled Rack of Lamb with Sweet Mustard Glaze
Omit rosemary. Add 3 tablespoons Dijon mustard, 2 tablespoons honey, and ½ teaspoon grated lemon zest to herb mixture in step 1. Set aside 2 tablespoons glaze and brush racks with remaining glaze as directed in step 4. Brush racks with reserved glaze after removing from grill in step 6.

CAST IRON LAMB CHOPS WITH MINT AND ROSEMARY RELISH

Serves 4 | rib or loin chops
WHY THIS RECIPE WORKS Lamb and cast-iron cookware have great chemistry. The intense heat of a preheated cast-iron skillet can produce a rich crust on lamb while melting away its abundant fat. We wanted to develop a technique that would ensure that this delicate cut had no risk of overcooking. Searing the chops quickly on both sides over medium-high heat and then gently finishing them over lower heat created crispy crusts and juicy interiors. We seasoned the chops with just salt and pepper, and to add flavor and complement the lamb, we created a quick olive oil–based mint and rosemary relish. The bold combination of mint and rosemary, along with garlic, spicy red pepper flakes, and tart red wine vinegar, was the perfect pairing for the lamb.

Cast Iron Lamb Chops with
Mint and Rosemary Relish

RELISH

½ cup minced fresh mint

5 tablespoons extra-virgin olive oil

2 teaspoons minced fresh rosemary

2 teaspoons red wine vinegar

1 garlic clove, minced

⅛ teaspoon red pepper flakes

LAMB

8 (5- to 6-ounce) lamb rib or loin chops, 1¼ to 1½ inches thick, trimmed

2 tablespoons vegetable oil

1. Adjust oven rack to middle position, place 12-inch cast-iron skillet on rack, and heat oven to 500 degrees.

2. For the relish: While oven heats, combine all ingredients in serving bowl. Season with salt and pepper to taste; set aside for serving.

3. For the lamb: Pat chops dry with paper towels and season with salt and pepper. When oven reaches 500 degrees, remove skillet from oven using pot holders and place over medium-high heat; turn off oven. Being careful of hot skillet handle, add oil and heat until just smoking. Cook chops, without moving them, until lightly browned on first side, about 2 minutes. Flip chops and cook until lightly browned on second side, about 2 minutes.

4. Flip chops, reduce heat to medium-low, and cook until well browned and meat registers 120 to 125 degrees (for medium-rare), 3 to 5 minutes, flipping chops halfway through cooking. Transfer chops to serving platter, tent with aluminum foil, and let rest for 5 to 10 minutes. Serve with relish.

VARIATION

Lamb Chops with Onion and Balsamic Relish

Omit mint relish. While chops rest, pour off all but 1 tablespoon fat from skillet. Add 1 finely chopped small red onion and ¼ teaspoon table salt and cook over medium heat until softened and lightly browned, about 5 minutes. Stir in 2 minced garlic cloves and cook until fragrant, about 30 seconds. Off heat, stir in 2 tablespoons balsamic vinegar. Transfer onion mixture to small serving bowl and let cool slightly. Stir in 3 tablespoons extra-virgin olive oil and 2 tablespoons minced fresh parsley. Season with salt and pepper to taste. Serve with chops.

Sumac Lamb Loin Chops with Carrots, Mint, and Paprika

SUMAC LAMB LOIN CHOPS WITH CARROTS, MINT, AND PAPRIKA

Serves 4 | loin chops

WHY THIS RECIPE WORKS Lamb loves bright flavors (see page 329), so we used a combination of fresh mint, sweet paprika, and the bright, citrusy Middle Eastern spice sumac to amp up the flavor of mild lamb loin chops. We sprinkled the sumac directly onto the lamb chops along with some salt and pepper and then seared the meat in a hot skillet until the chops were browned and their interiors were medium-rare (making sure to use chops that were at least ¾ to 1 inch thick ensured that they didn't overcook before their exteriors were brown). For a simple side, we boiled some carrots until they were just tender before combining them with paprika, lemon juice, and mint; the sweetness of the cooked carrots complemented the lamb. A cooling, nutty tahini sauce enhanced with garlic and lemon tied the whole meal together.

SAUCE

- 3 tablespoons tahini
- 3 tablespoons plain Greek yogurt
- 2 tablespoons water
- 1 tablespoon lemon juice
- 1 small garlic clove, minced
- ¼ teaspoon table salt

LAMB AND CARROTS

- 8 (4-ounce) lamb loin or rib chops, ¾ to 1 inch thick, trimmed
- 1 tablespoon ground sumac, plus extra for seasoning
- 2 tablespoons extra-virgin olive oil, divided, plus extra for drizzling
- 1 pound carrots, peeled and cut into 1½- to 2-inch lengths, thick pieces quartered lengthwise and medium pieces halved lengthwise
- 2 teaspoons table salt
- 1 tablespoon lemon juice, divided
- ½ teaspoon paprika
- 2 tablespoons chopped fresh mint, divided

1. For the sauce: Whisk tahini, yogurt, water, lemon juice, garlic, and salt in bowl until combined.

2. For the lamb and carrots: Pat lamb dry with paper towels. Sprinkle sumac evenly over lamb and season with salt and pepper. Heat 1 tablespoon oil in 12-inch skillet over medium-high heat until just smoking. Cook chops until well browned and meat registers 120 to 125 degrees (for medium-rare), 4 to 6 minutes per side. Transfer chops to platter, tent with aluminum foil, and let rest.

3. While lamb is cooking, bring 2 cups water to boil in medium saucepan over high heat. Add carrots and salt, cover, and cook until tender throughout, about 6 minutes (start timer as soon as carrots go into water). Drain carrots and return to now-empty pan.

4. Add 1 teaspoon lemon juice, paprika, and remaining 1 tablespoon oil to carrots and stir until combined. Stir in 1 tablespoon chopped mint. Season with salt, pepper, and remaining 2 teaspoons lemon juice to taste.

5. Sprinkle remaining 1 tablespoon mint over lamb, drizzle with extra oil to taste, and season with extra sumac to taste. Serve chops with carrots and sauce.

GRILLED LAMB LOIN OR RIB CHOPS

Serves 4 | loin or rib chops

WHY THIS RECIPE WORKS Lamb loin and rib chops can be up to 1½ inches thick so the challenge in developing our grilled lamb chops recipe was to find a way to cook the delicate meat through gently without overbrowning its exterior. We found that using a two-level fire was best—the chops could be seared on the hotter side of the grill until they developed a rich crust and then moved to the cooler side to cook through. This method also reduced the potential for flare-ups, which often occur when lamb's abundant fat renders and drips onto the hot coals. A minimalist rub of olive oil, salt, and pepper was all the embellishment these beautifully charred and perfectly medium-rare chops needed, but for a change of pace we rubbed them with a fresh herb paste.

- 8 lamb loin or rib chops, 1¼ to 1½ inches thick, trimmed
- 2 tablespoons extra-virgin olive oil

1. Rub chops with oil and season with salt and pepper.

2a. For a charcoal grill: Open bottom vent completely. Light large chimney starter filled with charcoal briquettes (6 quarts). When top coals are partially covered with ash, pour two-thirds evenly over half of grill, then pour remaining coals over other half of grill. Set cooking grate in place, cover, and open lid vent completely. Heat grill until hot, about 5 minutes.

2b. For a gas grill: Turn all burners to high, cover, and heat grill until hot, about 15 minutes. Leave primary burner on high and turn other burner(s) to medium.

3. Clean and oil cooking grate. Place chops on hotter side of grill. Cook (covered if using gas), turning as needed, until nicely charred on both sides, 2 to 4 minutes. Slide chops to cooler part of grill and cook, turning as needed, until meat registers 120 to 125 degrees (for medium-rare), 6 to 9 minutes.

4. Transfer chops to platter, tent with aluminum foil, and let rest for 5 to 10 minutes. Serve.

VARIATION

Grilled Lamb Loin or Rib Chops with Herb and Garlic Paste

Combine ¼ cup extra-virgin olive oil, 3 minced garlic cloves, 1 tablespoon chopped fresh parsley, 2 teaspoons chopped fresh sage, 2 teaspoons chopped fresh thyme, 2 teaspoons chopped fresh rosemary, and 2 teaspoons chopped fresh oregano in small bowl. Rub chops with herb paste and refrigerate for at least 20 minutes or up to 24 hours. Omit oil, season chops with salt and pepper, and grill as directed.

LEG AND SHANKS

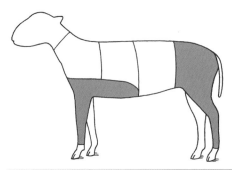

WHEN IT COMES TO LAMB, the leg might be the most complex primal to break down. The leg area runs from the hip down to the hoof. It may be sold whole or broken into smaller roasts. The whole leg generally weighs 6 to 10 pounds (although smaller legs are available from younger lambs).

An entire leg of lamb consists of three main parts: The wide part up near the hip is the butt end (which includes the sirloin, or hip meat); below that is the shank end, with the shank (or ankle) at the very bottom. Like with the ham (leg) from the back of a pig (see page 304) we prefer the shank-end leg of lamb, which is easier to work with, yields more delicious meat, and looks impressive. Make sure the butcher has removed the hip bone and aitchbone or carving will be very difficult.

(continued)

Leg roasts are also sold boneless, butterflied often for even cooking or stuffing and rolling.

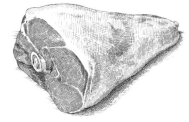

Sirloin-Half Leg of Lamb   *Shank-End Leg of Lamb*

Because lamb is young, leg of lamb is quite tender, in contrast to the equivalent cut of beef, and so makes a superlative roast—it doesn't require low, moist cooking. However, you can certainly braise leg of lamb; we like to cut boneless leg of lamb into chunks and serve it in a wonderful curry (see page 357).

Our preferred bone-in shank-end leg of lamb will often have the shank attached. But shanks are also wonderful eating on their own, although they're cooked completely differently when detached from the leg. They indeed do need moist, slow cooking to become luscious. The two hindshanks run down from the lamb's leg primal, while the two foreshanks technically come from a different primal, the Foreshank/Breast. We don't devote a section to or discuss the whole breast, however, as it's difficult to cook and nearly impossible to find.

Bone-In Leg of Lamb

Cost: ■■▢▢   **Flavor:** ■■▢▢
Best cooking methods: roast, grill
Texture: generally tender but features a range of textures
Alternative names: whole leg, semiboneless leg of lamb, sirloin-on leg

While we've broken down the lamb leg divisions, at the end of the day, a whole bone-in leg is cumbersome to deal with. But this big cut is absolutely delicious roasted or grilled—a cut you can throw intriguing flavor at. If you purchase a whole leg, you'll be delighted with a festive, grand-looking roast with the shank bone sticking out proudly—it looks like a giant version of a Renaissance fair turkey leg. Another nifty thing about a bone-in leg of lamb? Its tapered shape offers a range of doneness throughout the roast to please all tastes, and you can achieve a great crust. Grilling it, in particular, is a nod to earlier times when animals were butchered more simply and large cuts were cooked over a live fire. This is the lamb cut for when you want to go all out.

You might see a bone-in leg of lamb as described here actually called "semiboneless." This sounds confusing but it's what you want; it just means that the hipbone and aitchbone are removed, which is important. This is the most common preparation, but if you happen to find a leg with the whole bone, ask the butcher to remove these parts for proper cooking.

Boneless Leg of Lamb

Cost: ■■◻◻ Flavor: ■■◻◻
Best cooking methods: braise, roast, sous vide, grill
Texture: tender
Alternative names: none

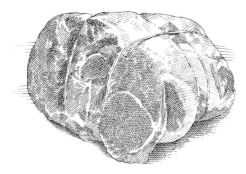

While a bone-in leg of lamb is hugely impressive (and just plain huge), a boneless leg of lamb is much more manageable, so you can eat it much more often. A whole boneless leg, preferably from the shank end again, will weigh 5 to 8 pounds and will feed a crowd. To make sure you're getting exactly what you want, it pays to be overly explicit with the butcher and ask for "a whole boneless leg of lamb, but without the sirloin attached."

If, as is more often the case, you're just making dinner, you'll want a "half" leg of lamb, which is usually the right size for four to six people. These typically weigh in at around 3½ to 4 pounds, but you can find smaller or larger pieces. Again, we most often prefer the shank end.

BUTTERFLIED LEG OF LAMB

Usually the boneless roast comes butterflied into a single piece of varying thickness, but we call specifically for that when needed for good measure. (The other method for removing the bone is called corkscrewing.) So while you don't have to butterfly it at home (phew!), you generally should pound it out to even thickness (easy!). Cook it as is for a delicious roast that's a breeze to carve (see page 355) or stuff it with flavor and roll and tie it for braising, roasting, or grilling. Sometimes this butterflied piece is already rolled and tied. Unroll it and start over to stuff it with your aromatic filling of choice.

MEAT PREP *Carving a Butterflied Leg of Lamb*

1. Position meat so that long side is facing you. Slice lamb with grain into 3 equal pieces.

2. Turn each piece to cut against grain into ¼-inch-thick slices.

Lamb Shanks

Cost: ■■◻◻ Flavor: ■■◻◻
Best cooking methods: braise
Texture: tender once fully braised
Alternative names: none

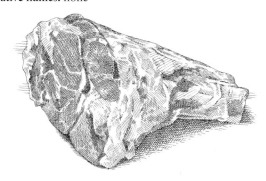

A lamb shank is a personally satisfying thing to eat. You're served an individual one, it's got plenty of meat (more than shanks of other animals), and there's an aesthetically pleasing bone sticking out, off of which, if cooked properly, the meat easily cuts. As these are ankles of lamb, you can imagine that they are strewn with connective tissue that makes them very tough—until lovingly braised. And they provide a lot of body to the braising liquid between the contributions from that bone and that tissue.

**Pomegranate-Glazed Roast
Bone-In Leg of Lamb**

POMEGRANATE-GLAZED ROAST BONE-IN LEG OF LAMB

Serves 8 to 10 | bone-in leg of lamb

WHY THIS RECIPE WORKS Talk about an impressive centerpiece—a roasted leg of lamb boasts a browned, crusty, gleaming exterior and juicy, ultrarich meat. Because of its large, awkward shape, stovetop searing isn't an option for this cut, but we found that we got great results using a combination of a low-and-slow roasting technique plus an "oven sear," where we started the lamb in a 250-degree oven before cranking up the heat to 450 degrees for the last 20 minutes. Adding water to the roasting pan during the high-heat finish helped prevent the pan drippings from burning and smoking out the kitchen. To flavor the lamb, we used a simple Middle Eastern–inspired pomegranate glaze, which we brushed on the meat twice during cooking and a final time before serving for a perfectly lacquered roast.

LAMB
1 (6- to 8-pound) bone-in leg of lamb, trimmed
1 tablespoon vegetable oil

POMEGRANATE GLAZE
2 cups pomegranate juice
⅓ cup sugar
3 sprigs fresh thyme

1. For the lamb: Pat roast dry with paper towels, rub with oil, and season with kosher salt and pepper. Cover roast with plastic wrap and let sit at room temperature for at least 1 hour or up to 2 hours.

2. For the pomegranate glaze: Meanwhile, simmer pomegranate juice, sugar, and thyme sprigs together in small saucepan over medium heat until thickened and mixture measures about ½ cup, about 20 minutes. Discard thyme sprigs. Measure out and reserve half of glaze for serving.

3. Adjust oven rack to lowest position and heat oven to 250 degrees. Set wire rack inside aluminum foil–lined rimmed baking sheet. Transfer roast to prepared rack, fat side up, and brush with about half of remaining glaze. Roast until meat registers 100 degrees, about 1¾ hours.

4. Brush roast with remaining glaze and pour ¼ cup water into sheet. Increase oven temperature to 450 degrees and roast until lamb registers 125 degrees (for medium-rare), about 20 minutes.

5. Transfer roast to carving board and brush with half of glaze reserved for serving. Let rest for 30 minutes. Brush with remaining glaze reserved for serving and carve roast. Serve.

GRILLED BONE-IN LEG OF LAMB WITH CHARRED-SCALLION SAUCE

Serves 10 to 12 | bone-in leg of lamb

WHY THIS RECIPE WORKS This grand cut is impressive enough for any celebration, but its tapered shape also means that even cooking is a challenge, especially over a live flame. To help us avoid flare-ups while still giving the roast a charred exterior and medium-rare interior, we set up a half-grill fire and started the leg of lamb on the cooler side of the grill before searing it over the hotter side. We smeared a powerful paste of fresh thyme, dried oregano, garlic, lemon zest, and plenty of salt and pepper onto the leg of lamb and refrigerated it overnight to season the meat. We finished our dish with a rich sauce of charred scallions mixed with extra-virgin olive oil, red wine vinegar, parsley, and garlic. For an accurate temperature reading in step 5, insert your thermometer into the thickest part of the leg until you hit bone, then pull it ½ inch away.

LAMB
12 garlic cloves, minced
2 tablespoons vegetable oil
2 tablespoons kosher salt
1½ tablespoons pepper
1 tablespoon fresh thyme leaves
1 tablespoon dried oregano
2 teaspoons finely grated lemon zest
1 teaspoon ground coriander
1 (8-pound) bone-in leg of lamb, trimmed

SCALLION SAUCE
¾ cup extra-virgin olive oil
¼ cup chopped fresh parsley
1 tablespoon red wine vinegar
2 garlic cloves, minced
1 teaspoon pepper
¾ teaspoon kosher salt
¼ teaspoon red pepper flakes
12 scallions, trimmed

1. For the lamb: Combine garlic, oil, salt, pepper, thyme, oregano, lemon zest, and coriander in bowl. Place lamb on rimmed baking sheet and rub all over with garlic paste. Cover with plastic wrap and refrigerate for at least 12 hours or up to 24 hours.

2. For the scallion sauce: Combine oil, parsley, vinegar, garlic, pepper, salt, and pepper flakes in bowl; set aside.

3a. For a charcoal grill: Open bottom vent completely. Light large chimney starter filled with charcoal briquettes (6 quarts). When top coals are partially covered with ash, pour evenly over half of grill. Set cooking grate in place, cover, and open lid vent completely. Heat grill until hot, about 5 minutes.

TUTORIAL
Grilled Bone-In Leg of Lamb with Charred-Scallion Sauce

A bone-in leg of lamb is a mammoth piece of meat, but it doesn't have to be a mammoth challenge. Follow these steps to grilling it to perfection.

1. Place lamb on rimmed baking sheet and rub all over with garlic-herb paste. Cover with plastic wrap and refrigerate for at least 12 hours or up to 24 hours.

2. Open bottom vent of charcoal grill completely. Light large chimney starter filled with charcoal briquettes (6 quarts). When top coals are partially covered with ash, pour evenly over half of grill.

3. Clean and oil cooking grate. Place scallions on hotter side of grill. Cook until lightly charred on both sides, about 3 minutes per side; transfer to plate.

4. Place lamb fat side up on cooler side of grill, parallel to fire. Cover grill (position lid vent directly over lamb) and cook until thickest part of meat (½ inch from bone) registers 120 degrees, 1¼ hours to 1¾ hours.

5. Transfer lamb, fat side down, to hotter side of grill. Cook (covered if using gas) until fat side is well browned, 7 to 9 minutes. Let rest for 30 minutes, then slice thin.

6. Meanwhile, cut scallions into ½-inch pieces, then stir into reserved sauce mixture. Season sauce with salt and pepper to taste, and serve with lamb.

3b. For a gas grill: Turn all burners to high, cover, and heat grill until hot, about 15 minutes. Leave primary burner on high and turn off other burner(s). (Adjust primary burner [or, if using 3-burner grill, primary burner and second burner] as needed to maintain grill temperature between 350 and 400 degrees.)

4. Clean and oil cooking grate. Place scallions on hotter side of grill. Cook (covered if using gas) until lightly charred on both sides, about 3 minutes per side. Transfer scallions to plate.

5. Uncover lamb and place fat side up on cooler side of grill, parallel to fire. (If using gas, it may be necessary to angle thicker end of lamb toward hotter side of grill to fit.) Cover grill (position lid vent directly over lamb if using charcoal) and cook until thickest part of meat (½ inch from bone) registers 120 degrees, 1¼ hours to 1¾ hours.

6. Transfer lamb, fat side down, to hotter side of grill. Cook (covered if using gas) until fat side is well browned, 7 to 9 minutes. Transfer lamb to carving board, fat side up, and tent with aluminum foil. Let rest for 30 minutes.

7. Cut scallions into ½-inch pieces, then stir into reserved sauce mixture. Season sauce with salt and pepper to taste. Slice lamb thin and serve with sauce.

Harissa-Rubbed Roast Boneless Leg of Lamb with Warm Cauliflower Salad

HARISSA-RUBBED ROAST BONELESS LEG OF LAMB WITH WARM CAULIFLOWER SALAD

Serves 6 to 8 | boneless leg of lamb

WHY THIS RECIPE WORKS As seen in our lamb recipes a few times, the robust, fragrant flavor profile of North African cuisine is another perfect pairing with rich, meaty lamb. We took advantage of the broad surface area of a boneless leg of lamb by rubbing it with quick homemade harissa paste before rolling it up and tying it to make a compact roast. We seared the exterior of the meat on all sides to build up some browning before applying more harissa and moving the lamb to the oven where it finished roasting to a juicy medium-rare. To prepare a quick vegetable side, we tossed cauliflower florets with the flavorful pan drippings and roasted them until they were tender and browned before combining them with shredded carrots, sweet raisins, cilantro, and toasted almonds. If you can't find Aleppo pepper, you can substitute ¾ teaspoon paprika and ¾ teaspoon finely chopped red pepper flakes.

½ cup extra-virgin olive oil, divided
6 garlic cloves, minced
2 tablespoons paprika
1 tablespoon ground coriander
1 tablespoon ground dried Aleppo pepper
1 teaspoon ground cumin
¾ teaspoon caraway seeds
1½ teaspoons table salt, divided
1 (3½- to 4-pound) boneless half leg of lamb, trimmed and pounded to ¾-inch thickness
1 head cauliflower (2 pounds), cored and cut into 1-inch florets
½ teaspoon pepper
½ red onion, sliced ¼ inch thick
1 cup shredded carrots
½ cup raisins
¼ cup fresh cilantro leaves
2 tablespoons sliced almonds, toasted
1 tablespoon lemon juice, plus extra for seasoning

1. Combine 6 tablespoons oil, garlic, paprika, coriander, Aleppo pepper, cumin, caraway seeds, and 1 teaspoon salt in bowl and microwave until bubbling and very fragrant, about 1 minute, stirring halfway through microwaving. Let cool to room temperature.

2. Adjust oven rack to lower-middle position and heat oven to 375 degrees. Set V-rack in large roasting pan and spray with vegetable oil spray. Lay roast on cutting board with rough interior side (which was against bone) facing up and rub with 2 tablespoons spice paste. Roll roast and tie with kitchen twine at 1½-inch intervals, then rub exterior with 1 tablespoon oil.

3. Heat remaining 1 tablespoon oil in 12-inch skillet over medium-high heat until just smoking. Brown lamb on all sides, about 8 minutes. Brush lamb all over with remaining spice paste and place fat side down in prepared V-rack. Roast until thickest part registers 125 degrees (for medium-rare), 50 minutes to 1 hour 10 minutes, flipping lamb halfway through roasting. Transfer lamb to carving board, tent with aluminum foil, and let rest while making salad.

4. Increase oven temperature to 475 degrees. Pour all but 3 tablespoons fat from pan; discard any charred drippings. Add cauliflower, pepper, and remaining ½ teaspoon salt to pan and toss to coat. Cover with aluminum foil and roast until cauliflower is softened, about 5 minutes.

5. Remove foil and spread onion evenly over cauliflower. Roast until vegetables are tender and cauliflower is golden brown, 10 to 15 minutes, stirring halfway through roasting. Transfer vegetable mixture to serving bowl, add carrots, raisins, cilantro, almonds, and lemon juice and toss to combine. Season with salt, pepper, and extra lemon juice to taste. Slice leg of lamb ½ inch thick and serve with salad.

LEG OF LAMB EN COCOTTE

Serves 6 to 8 | boneless leg of lamb

WHY THIS RECIPE WORKS Cooking en cocotte isn't just for beef (see page 112); in fact, we use the technique for just about any protein, including leg of lamb. Since lamb's gamy flavor comes mostly from the fat, we trimmed as much as possible before cooking to give the finished roast a milder flavor that we appreciated for this simply presented application, especially since the meat cooks in the pot in its own juices. We added sprigs of rosemary and a handful of sliced garlic cloves to the pot with the lamb before it went into the oven and their aroma perfumed the meat. In just an hour, we had a simple, beautifully flavored dish to add to our en cocotte repertoire and a lamb roast that sliced like a dream into tender pieces, made even more succulent with a pour of lamb jus from the pot before serving.

1 (4- to 5-pound) boneless half leg of lamb, trimmed and tied
2 tablespoons extra-virgin olive oil
8 garlic cloves, peeled and sliced thin
2 sprigs fresh rosemary

1. Adjust oven rack to lowest position and heat oven to 250 degrees. Pat lamb dry with paper towels and season with salt and pepper.

2. Heat oil in Dutch oven over medium-high heat until just smoking. Brown lamb well on all sides, 7 to 10 minutes, reducing heat if pot begins to scorch. Transfer lamb to large plate.

3. Pour off fat from pot. Add garlic and rosemary and nestle lamb, with any accumulated juices, into pot. Place large piece of aluminum foil over pot and cover tightly with lid; transfer pot to oven. Cook until lamb registers 120 to 125 degrees (for medium-rare), 45 minutes to 1 hour.

4. Transfer lamb to carving board, tent with foil, and let rest for 20 minutes. Remove rosemary from pot, then cover to keep jus warm. Remove twine, slice lamb ¼ inch thick, and transfer to serving platter. Spoon jus over lamb and serve.

ROAST BUTTERFLIED LEG OF LAMB WITH CORIANDER, CUMIN, AND MUSTARD SEEDS

Serves 10 to 12 | boneless butterflied leg of lamb

WHY THIS RECIPE WORKS Boneless butterflied leg of lamb is usually cooked in one of two ways. Because it comes rolled up and tied, you can treat it like a regular roast and just season and cook it as is. Or you can unroll it, fill it with seasoning, and roll and tie it again before cooking. But you can also unroll a boneless leg of lamb, pound it to even out the thickness, and cook the meat flat; you get the same flavor, and the uniform thickness encourages faster, even cooking. For this roasting method, we started the meat in a very low oven and then finished with a blast under the broiler for juicy, tender roasted lamb with a burnished, crisp crust. Scoring the fat cap, rubbing the roast with salt and letting it sit for an hour gave us well-seasoned, tender meat. A spice-infused oil spread beneath the slab of meat both seasoned the lamb and provided the basis for a quick sauce; we toasted the spices right on the sheet pan meant for the lamb to bloom their flavor. The 2 tablespoons of salt in step 1 is for a 6-pound leg. If using a larger leg (7 to 8 pounds), add an additional teaspoon of salt for every pound.

LAMB

- 1 (6- to 8-pound) boneless butterflied leg of lamb
- 2 tablespoons kosher salt
- ⅓ cup vegetable oil
- 3 shallots, sliced thin
- 4 garlic cloves, peeled and smashed
- 1 (1-inch) piece ginger, sliced into ½-inch-thick rounds and smashed
- 1 tablespoon coriander seeds
- 1 tablespoon cumin seeds
- 1 tablespoon mustard seeds
- 3 bay leaves
- 2 (2-inch) strips lemon zest

SAUCE

- ⅓ cup chopped fresh mint
- ⅓ cup chopped fresh cilantro
- 1 shallot, minced
- 2 tablespoons lemon juice

1. **For the lamb:** Place roast on cutting board with fat cap facing down. Using sharp knife, trim any pockets of fat and connective tissue from underside of roast. Flip roast over, trim fat cap to between ⅛ and ¼ inch thick, and pound to even 1-inch thickness. Using sharp knife, cut slits ½ inch apart in crosshatch pattern in fat cap of roast, being careful not to cut into meat. Rub salt over entire roast and into slits. Let sit, uncovered, at room temperature for 1 hour.

2. Meanwhile, adjust oven racks to upper-middle and lower-middle positions and heat oven to 250 degrees. Stir oil, shallots, garlic, ginger, coriander seeds, cumin seeds, mustard seeds, bay leaves, and lemon zest together in rimmed baking sheet and bake on lower rack until spices are softened and fragrant and shallots and garlic turn golden, about 1 hour. Remove sheet from oven and discard bay leaves.

3. Thoroughly pat roast dry with paper towels and transfer, fat side up, to sheet (directly on top of spices). Roast on lower rack until lamb registers 120 degrees, 30 to 40 minutes. Remove sheet from oven and heat broiler. Broil roast on upper rack until surface is well browned and charred in spots and lamb registers 125 degrees (for medium-rare), 3 to 8 minutes.

4. Remove sheet from oven and transfer roast to carving board (some spices will cling to roast); let rest for 20 minutes.

5. **For the sauce:** Meanwhile, carefully pour pan juices through fine-mesh strainer into medium bowl, pressing on solids to extract as much liquid as possible; discard solids. Stir in mint, cilantro, shallot, and lemon juice. Add any accumulated lamb juices to sauce and season with salt and pepper to taste.

6. With long side facing you, slice roast with grain into 3 equal pieces. Turn each piece and slice against grain ¼ inch thick. Serve with sauce. (Briefly warm sauce in microwave if it has cooled and thickened.)

VARIATION

Roast Butterflied Leg of Lamb with Coriander, Rosemary, and Red Pepper

Omit cumin and mustard seeds. Toss 6 sprigs fresh rosemary and ½ teaspoon red pepper flakes with oil mixture in step 2. Substitute parsley for cilantro in sauce.

CAST IRON ROASTED BONELESS LEG OF LAMB WITH HERBED BREAD-CRUMB CRUST

Serves 6 to 8 | boneless leg of lamb

WHY THIS RECIPE WORKS We wanted a foolproof method for boneless leg of lamb with a crisp crust and perfectly cooked interior. Whole boneless legs of lamb are impractical for the average dinner table, but a half leg is just the right amount for six to eight people. We relied on our cast-iron skillet to jump-start the crust on the stovetop. Moving the roast to a gentle 375-degree oven guaranteed a juicy, tender interior. A savory crumb crust with fresh herbs, garlic, and Parmesan was the ideal complement to the tender lamb. Applying the crust partway through cooking (after removing the twine) ensured that it would stay in place. A quick blast under the broiler helped the crumbs turn crisp and brown. We usually prefer the shank end of the leg of lamb; here we prefer the sirloin end for its more uniform shape, though either will work well.

- ¼ cup minced fresh parsley
- 3 tablespoons minced fresh rosemary
- 3 tablespoons extra-virgin olive oil, divided
- 2 tablespoons minced fresh thyme
- 3 garlic cloves, peeled
- ¾ cup panko bread crumbs
- 1 ounce Parmesan cheese, grated (½ cup)
- 1 (3½- to 4-pound) boneless half leg of lamb, untied, trimmed
- 1 tablespoon Dijon mustard

1. Adjust oven rack to middle position and heat oven to 375 degrees. Process parsley, rosemary, 1 teaspoon oil, thyme, and garlic in food processor until finely ground, scraping down sides of bowl as needed, about 1 minute. Measure out 1½ tablespoons herb mixture and set aside. Combine remaining herb mixture, panko, Parmesan, and 1 tablespoon oil in bowl; set aside.

Cast Iron Roasted Boneless Leg of Lamb with Herbed Bread-Crumb Crust

LAMB CURRY WITH WHOLE SPICES

Serves 4 to 6 | boneless leg of lamb

WHY THIS RECIPE WORKS A homemade Indian-style curry is bound to taste more complex and vibrant when made with whole spices. For this recipe, our first move was to toast whole spices in oil. Garlic, onion, and ginger deepened the flavor, while jalapeño offered subtle spice. Instead of browning the meat, we simply stirred it into the pot along with crushed tomatoes and cooked the mixture until the liquid evaporated and the oil separated. This classic Indian technique allowed the spices to bloom in the oil, which was then absorbed by the meat. We then added water and simmered the mixture until the meat was tender. A little cilantro provided a fresh finish. You can substitute a scant ½ teaspoon of cayenne pepper for the jalapeño, adding it to the skillet with the other ground dried spices. Feel free to increase the amounts of the aromatics (garlic, ginger, jalapeños, and onions) or the dried spices. For a creamier curry, use yogurt rather than the crushed tomatoes.

SPICE BLEND

1½ cinnamon sticks
4 whole cloves
4 green cardamom pods
8 black peppercorns
1 bay leaf

CURRY

¼ cup vegetable oil
1 onion, sliced thin
1½ pounds boneless leg of lamb, trimmed and cut into ¾-inch cubes
⅔ cup canned crushed tomatoes
4 large garlic cloves, minced
1 tablespoon grated fresh ginger
2 teaspoons ground cumin
2 teaspoons ground coriander
1 teaspoon ground turmeric
½ teaspoon table salt
2 cups water
1 jalapeño chile, stemmed, halved, and seeded
4 medium red potatoes, peeled and cut into ¾-inch cubes
¼ cup chopped fresh cilantro

2. Position roast with rough interior side (which was against bone) facing up on cutting board. Cover roast with plastic wrap and pound to even ¾-inch thickness with meat pounder. Rub surface of roast with 2 teaspoons oil and season with salt and pepper. Spread reserved herb mixture evenly over surface of meat, leaving 1-inch border on all sides. Starting from short side, roll roast tightly, then tie with kitchen twine at 1-inch intervals. Season with salt and pepper.

3. Heat 12-inch cast-iron skillet over medium heat for 5 minutes. Add remaining 1 tablespoon oil and heat until just smoking. Brown roast on all sides, 8 to 12 minutes. Transfer skillet to oven and roast until meat registers 110 to 115 degrees, 25 to 35 minutes.

4. Using pot holders, remove skillet from oven; heat broiler. Transfer roast to carving board and remove twine. Brush top and sides of roast with mustard, then firmly press bread-crumb mixture onto coated sides with your hands to form solid, even coating that adheres to meat.

5. Being careful of hot skillet handle, return roast to skillet and broil until crust is golden brown and meat registers 120 to 125 degrees (for medium-rare), about 5 minutes. Transfer roast to carving board and let rest for 20 minutes. Slice roast ½ inch thick. Serve.

1. For the spice blend: Combine all ingredients in small bowl.

2. For the curry: Heat oil in Dutch oven over medium-high heat until shimmering. Add spice blend and cook, stirring with wooden spoon until cinnamon sticks unfurl and cloves pop, about 5 seconds. Add onion and cook until softened, 3 to 4 minutes.

Sous Vide Spice-Rubbed Leg
of Lamb with Chermoula

3. Stir in lamb, tomatoes, garlic, ginger, cumin, coriander, turmeric, and salt and cook, stirring frequently, until liquid evaporates, oil separates and turns orange, and spices begin to fry, 5 to 7 minutes. Continue to cook, stirring constantly, until spices are very fragrant, about 30 seconds longer.

4. Add water and jalapeño. Bring to simmer, then reduce heat to low, cover, and simmer until meat is tender, 30 to 40 minutes.

5. Add potatoes and cook until tender, about 15 minutes. Stir in cilantro, simmer for 3 minutes, season with salt to taste, and serve.

VARIATION
Lamb Curry with Figs and Fenugreek
Omit whole spice blend and potatoes. Add ½ teaspoon fenugreek along with cumin, coriander, and turmeric in step 3 and ¼ cup dried figs, chopped coarse, along with water in step 4.

SOUS VIDE SPICE-RUBBED LEG OF LAMB WITH CHERMOULA

Serves 6 to 8 | boneless butterflied half leg of lamb
Sous vide time: 20 to 24 hours
WHY THIS RECIPE WORKS Cooking a leg of lamb can be a little intimidating. But swapping in a boneless leg of lamb for bone-in and cooking sous vide provided us with a number of benefits: thorough seasoning, a great ratio of crust to meat, and perfectly even cooking. To balance out the potential gamy flavor in lamb, we rubbed ours with an intense paste of complex warm spices (savory, spicy, and a little sweet) and let it marinate to intensify the flavors. Circulating the lamb for 24 hours at a low temperature yielded a rosy, medium-rare interior from edge to edge that was about as tender as filet mignon. We coated the lamb with even more paste as soon as it came out of the bath before blasting it under the broiler to char and crisp up the exterior. With a bright, tangy North African chermoula sauce on top to play with the spice flavors rubbed on the lamb, this is one lamb roast that's sure to impress.

- 5 tablespoons extra-virgin olive oil
- 4 teaspoons paprika
- 1 tablespoon ground cumin
- 1 teaspoon garlic powder
- 1 teaspoon table salt
- ¾ teaspoon pepper
- ¾ teaspoon ground turmeric
- ¼ teaspoon cayenne pepper
- ¼ teaspoon ground cinnamon
- ¼ teaspoon ground ginger
- ¼ cup oil-packed sun-dried tomatoes, patted dry
- ¼ cup pitted brine-cured green olives
- 1 3-pound boneless half leg of lamb
- 1 recipe Chermoula (page 21)

1. Whisk oil, paprika, cumin, garlic powder, salt, pepper, turmeric, cayenne, cinnamon, and ginger in small bowl. Microwave until bubbling and fragrant, about 3 minutes, stirring halfway through microwaving. Transfer spice mixture to food processor. Add tomatoes and olives and process until smooth paste forms, about 1 minute, scraping down sides of bowl as needed. Measure out half of paste and transfer to refrigerator.

2. Place lamb on cutting board with fat cap facing down. Using sharp knife, trim any pockets of fat and connective tissue from underside of lamb. Flip lamb over, trim fat cap to between ⅛ and ¼ inch thick, and pound roast to even 1-inch thickness. Cut slits in surface layer of fat, spaced 1 inch apart in crosshatch pattern, being careful not to cut into meat. Season both sides of lamb with salt and rub with remaining spice paste. Place lamb in 2-gallon zipper-lock freezer bag and arrange in even layer. Seal bag, pressing out as much air as possible. Refrigerate lamb for at least 4 hours or up to 24 hours.

3. Using sous vide circulator, bring water to 131°F in 7-quart container.

4. Gently lower bag into prepared water bath until lamb is fully submerged, and then clip top corner of bag to side of water bath container, allowing remaining air bubbles to rise to top of bag. Reopen 1 corner of zipper, release remaining air bubbles, and reseal bag. Cover and cook for at least 20 hours or up to 24 hours.

5. Adjust oven rack 6 inches from broiler element and heat broiler. Set wire rack in aluminum foil–lined rimmed baking sheet and spray with vegetable oil spray. Transfer lamb, fat side up, to prepared rack and let rest for 10 to 15 minutes.

6. Pat lamb dry with paper towels, then spread reserved paste over top. Broil until lightly charred, 6 to 8 minutes. Transfer lamb to carving board and slice thin against grain. Serve with chermoula.

To make ahead: Lamb can be rapidly chilled in ice bath (see page 8) and then refrigerated in zipper-lock bag after step 4 for up to 3 days. To reheat, return sealed bag to water bath set to 131°F for 1 hour and then proceed with step 5.

LAMB SHANKS BRAISED WITH LEMON AND MINT

Serves 6 | lamb shanks

WHY THIS RECIPE WORKS Braising lamb shank turns this richly flavored but tough cut of meat meltingly tender. But the high fat content of lamb all too often leads to a greasy sauce. We avoided this pitfall by trimming the shanks well and then browning them before adding liquid to get a head start on rendering their fat. We also made sure to defat the braising liquid after the shanks had cooked. We used more liquid than is called for in many braises to guarantee that plenty would remain in the pot despite about an hour of uncovered cooking. For appropriately robust flavor, we stirred bright lemon and mint into the braising liquid before serving. If you're using smaller shanks than the ones called for in this recipe, you'll need to reduce the braising time. Côtes du Rhône works particularly well here.

6 (12- to 16-ounce) lamb shanks, trimmed
2 tablespoons vegetable oil, divided
3 carrots, peeled and cut into 2-inch pieces
2 onions, sliced thick
2 celery ribs, cut into 2-inch pieces
2 tablespoons tomato paste
2 tablespoons minced fresh mint, divided
4 garlic cloves, minced
Pinch table salt
2 cups dry white wine
3 cups chicken broth
1 tablespoon grated lemon zest, plus 1 lemon, quartered

1. Adjust oven rack to middle position and heat oven to 350 degrees. Pat lamb shanks dry with paper towels and season with salt. Heat 1 tablespoon oil in Dutch oven over medium-high heat until just smoking. Brown 3 shanks on all sides, 7 to 10 minutes. Transfer shanks to large plate and repeat with remaining 1 tablespoon oil and remaining 3 shanks.

2. Pour off all but 2 tablespoons fat from pot. Add carrots, onions, celery, tomato paste, 1 tablespoon mint, garlic, and salt and cook until vegetables just begin to soften, 3 to 4 minutes. Stir in wine, then broth, scraping up browned bits; add lemon quarters and bring to simmer. Nestle shanks, along with any accumulated juices, into pot.

3. Return to simmer and cover; transfer pot to oven. Cook for 1½ hours. Uncover and continue to cook until tops of shanks are browned, about 30 minutes. Flip shanks and continue to cook until remaining sides are browned and fork slips easily in and out of shanks, 15 to 30 minutes longer.

4. Remove pot from oven and let rest for 15 minutes. Using tongs, transfer shanks and vegetables to large plate and tent with aluminum foil. Skim fat from braising liquid and season with salt and pepper to taste. Stir in lemon zest and remaining 1 tablespoon mint. Return shanks to braising liquid to warm through before serving.

VARIATIONS

Lamb Shanks Braised with Ras el Hanout
Serve with couscous and one or more of the following: sautéed onion, lemon zest, parsley, mint, toasted almonds, and additional ras el hanout.

Add 2 minced ancho chile peppers (or 2 or 3 minced jalapeños) to onions, carrots, and celery in step 2. Substitute 2 tablespoons ras el hanout for mint in step 2. Omit lemon in step 2 and lemon zest and mint in step 4.

Lamb Shanks Braised with Red Wine and Herbes de Provence
Substitute dry red wine for white wine. Omit lemon in step 2 and lemon zest in step 4. Substitute 1 tablespoon herbes de Provence for mint in step 2. Omit mint in step 4.

BRAISED LAMB SHANKS WITH BELL PEPPERS AND HARISSA

Serves 4 | lamb shanks

WHY THIS RECIPE WORKS Harissa and lamb show up together often—and for good reason. The strong flavor of lamb can really take a pepper punch. This recipe is unique in that the harissa actually infuses the braising liquid for a seductively (but not overwhelmingly) spicy sauce. Chicken broth served as a mild medium in which to meld the rich flavors of the lamb, the sweet peppers, and the aromatic harissa. To keep our sauce clean and light, we trimmed our shanks of all visible fat before cooking them, and we strained and defatted the cooking liquid after braising. We blended braised bell peppers into the cooking liquid to complete our sauce, thickening and sweetening it, and we sprinkled the dish with fresh mint for a bright finish.

4 (10- to 12-ounce) lamb shanks, trimmed
1 tablespoon extra-virgin olive oil
1 onion, chopped fine
4 bell peppers (red, orange, and/or yellow), stemmed, seeded, and cut into 1-inch pieces
½ teaspoon table salt
¼ cup harissa, divided
2 tablespoons tomato paste

Moroccan Lamb and White Beans

5. Transfer sauce to now-empty pot and stir in vinegar and remaining 1 tablespoon harissa. Return shanks and any accumulated juices to pot, bring to gentle simmer over medium heat, and cook, spooning sauce over shanks occasionally, until heated through, about 5 minutes. Season with salt and pepper to taste. Transfer shanks to serving platter, spoon 1 cup sauce over top, and sprinkle with mint. Serve, passing remaining sauce separately.

MOROCCAN LAMB AND WHITE BEANS

Serves 6 to 8 | lamb shanks

WHY THIS RECIPE WORKS We like loubia, a dish of white beans and lamb stewed in a warm-spiced, tomatoey base, because it's a comforting, cozy weekend meal. Khlii, a Moroccan preserved meat, is often used, but khlii is difficult to find in the United States; we decided to use more easily accessible lamb shank instead. A healthy dose of Moroccan-inspired spices gave the dish a deeply flavorful backbone, and some white wine provided welcome acidity. A combination of mostly chicken broth and a little water gave the cooking medium savory depth without making it too salty. We chose dried beans over canned so that the beans would cook at the same rate as the lamb shank, leaving us with creamy, richly flavored beans and melt-in-your-mouth-tender pieces of lamb. You can substitute 1 pound of lamb shoulder chops (blade or round bone), 1 to 1½ inches thick, trimmed and halved, for the lamb shank; reduce the browning time in step 2 to 8 minutes.

- 3 tablespoons table salt for brining
- 1 pound (2½ cups) dried great Northern beans, picked over and rinsed
- 1 (12- to 16-ounce) lamb shank, trimmed
- 1 tablespoon extra-virgin olive oil, plus extra for serving
- 1 onion, chopped
- 1 red bell pepper, stemmed, seeded, and chopped fine
- 2 tablespoons tomato paste
- 3 garlic cloves, minced
- 2 teaspoons paprika
- 2 teaspoons ground cumin
- 1½ teaspoons ground ginger
- ¼ teaspoon cayenne pepper
- ⅛ teaspoon pepper
- ½ cup dry white wine
- 4 cups chicken broth
- 2 tablespoons minced fresh parsley

1. Dissolve salt in 4 quarts cold water in large container. Add beans and soak at room temperature for at least 8 hours or up to 24 hours. Drain and rinse well.

- 4 garlic cloves, minced
- 2½ cups chicken broth
- 2 bay leaves
- 1 tablespoon red wine vinegar
- 2 tablespoons minced fresh mint

1. Adjust oven rack to lower-middle position and heat oven to 350 degrees. Pat shanks dry with paper towels and season with salt and pepper. Heat oil in Dutch oven over medium-high heat until just smoking. Brown shanks on all sides, 8 to 10 minutes; transfer to bowl.

2. Add onion, peppers, and salt to fat left in pot and cook over medium heat until softened, about 5 minutes. Stir in 3 tablespoons harissa, tomato paste, and garlic and cook until fragrant, about 30 seconds. Stir in broth and bay leaves, scraping up any browned bits, and bring to simmer.

3. Nestle shanks into pot and return to simmer. Cover, transfer pot to oven, and cook until lamb is tender and fork slips easily in and out of meat and peppers begin to break down, 2 to 2½ hours, turning shanks halfway through cooking. Transfer shanks to bowl, tent with aluminum foil, and let rest while finishing sauce.

4. Strain braising liquid through fine-mesh strainer into fat separator; discard bay leaves and transfer solids to blender. Let braising liquid settle for 5 minutes, then pour defatted liquid into blender with solids and process until smooth, about 1 minute.

2. Adjust oven rack to lower-middle position and heat oven to 350 degrees. Pat lamb dry with paper towels and season with salt and pepper. Heat oil in Dutch oven over medium-high heat until just smoking. Brown lamb on all sides, 10 to 15 minutes; transfer to plate. Pour off all but 2 tablespoons fat from pot.

3. Add onion and bell pepper and cook over medium heat until softened and lightly browned, 5 to 7 minutes. Stir in tomato paste, garlic, paprika, cumin, ginger, cayenne, and pepper and cook until fragrant, about 30 seconds. Stir in wine, scraping up any browned bits. Stir in broth, 1 cup water, and beans and bring to boil.

4. Nestle lamb into beans along with any accumulated juices and cover; transfer pot to oven. Cook until fork slips easily in and out of lamb and beans are tender, 1½ to 1¾ hours, stirring every 30 minutes.

5. Transfer lamb to cutting board, let cool slightly, then shred into bite-size pieces using 2 forks; discard excess fat and bone. Stir shredded lamb and parsley into beans and season with salt and pepper to taste. Adjust consistency with extra hot water as needed. Serve, drizzling individual portions with extra oil.

PRESSURE-COOKER SPICED LAMB SHANKS WITH FIGS

Serves 6 | lamb shanks

WHY THIS RECIPE WORKS Lamb shanks are an ideal cut for pressure cooking: The moist heat breaks down the shanks' collagen-rich connective tissue to produce fall-apart-tender meat. Since lamb shanks have such robust flavor, we wanted our braising liquid to double as an equally bold serving sauce. Browning the shanks before adding aromatics and liquid produced fond, which contributed complex flavor to the dish. We bloomed some warm spices (coriander, cumin, and cinnamon) in the lamb's rendered fat to enhance their flavor and added dried figs to balance out the dish's savory notes. While the shanks rested, we reduced the braising liquid into a satiny sauce and stirred in a bit of honey to complement the figs' sweetness, tying the dish together. To avoid a greasy dish, be sure to trim the shanks of all visible fat and to defat the sauce thoroughly.

6 (10- to 12-ounce) lamb shanks, trimmed
2 tablespoons extra-virgin olive oil
1 onion, chopped fine
¼ teaspoon table salt
2 tablespoons tomato paste
2 garlic cloves, minced
1 teaspoon ground coriander
½ teaspoon ground cumin
½ teaspoon ground cinnamon
⅛ teaspoon cayenne pepper
½ cup dry red wine
1 (14.5-ounce) can diced tomatoes
¾ cup dried figs, stemmed and halved
½ cup chicken broth
2 tablespoons honey
2 tablespoons minced fresh mint

1. Pat shanks dry with paper towels and season with salt and pepper. Using highest sauté or browning function, heat oil in electric pressure cooker for 5 minutes (or until just smoking). Brown half of shanks on all sides, 8 to 10 minutes; transfer to plate. Repeat with remaining shanks; transfer to plate.

2. Add onion and salt to fat left in pressure cooker and cook until onion is softened and lightly browned, 5 to 7 minutes. Stir in tomato paste, garlic, coriander, cumin, cinnamon, and cayenne and cook until fragrant, about 1 minute. Stir in wine, scraping up any browned bits, then stir in tomatoes and their juice, figs, and broth. Nestle shanks into pressure cooker, adding any accumulated juices.

3. Lock lid in place and close pressure release valve. Select high pressure cook function and cook for 1 hour. Turn off pressure and let pressure release naturally for 15 minutes. Quick-release any remaining pressure, then carefully remove lid, allowing steam to escape away from you.

4. Transfer shanks to serving dish, tent with aluminum foil, and let rest while finishing sauce.

5. Using highest sauté or browning function, cook sauce until slightly thickened, 8 to 10 minutes. Turn off pressure cooker. Let sauce settle, then skim excess fat from surface using large spoon. Stir in honey and season with salt and pepper to taste. Spoon 1 cup sauce over shanks and sprinkle with mint. Serve, passing remaining sauce separately.

Pressure-Cooker Spiced Lamb Shanks with Figs

PART 4

ground meat

GROUND MEAT, WHETHER GROUND BEEF, veal, pork, or lamb, is a staple in American homes, the star of such iconic dishes as juicy burgers (seared, grilled, or stacked); shiny, glazed homestyle meatloaf (whether just beef or a mix of beef, veal, and pork); and spicy hard-shell taco filling. Ground meats also introduce international dishes to the table, filling dumplings or pita or topping creamy hummus for a hearty dish. And oh, you will find there are many, many ways to meatball.

Unsurprisingly, ground meats taste of the meats they were ground from. What is most important is the fat content of the ground meat, which is determined largely by the specific cut of meat it's ground from. Some recipes take well to lean ground meats whereas others require the moisture of something with a higher percentage of fat. In the pages that follow, you'll discover the best cuts—cuts you've learned about in the preceding pages of this collection—for grinding meat with this consideration in mind.

Grinding meat yourself, as you'll learn, is often the best way to determine the outcome of your dish. Recipes that call for home-grinding are peppered throughout the other parts of this book that highlight the larger cut the meat is ground from. All recipes in this part of the book call for ground meat; you'll have all the tools you need to make an informed purchase of ground meat or you can choose to grind it yourself, in a food processor.

GOOD REASON TO GRIND IT YOURSELF

The best ground meat is meat you grind yourself. (And you don't need a meat grinder; see below and page 127 for an example of how we do it in a food processor that can be applied universally.) The second-best ground meat is meat your butcher grinds for you. And the third-best ground meat is meat you buy packaged at the supermarket. Buying ground meat at the supermarket is kind of a gamble; unless your butcher grinds to order, there's no way to know what you're actually getting. The cut, fat content, and texture of store-ground meat can vary widely. It's often overprocessed to a pulp, so it cooks up heavy and dense no matter how much care you take. But when grinding your own meat, you're in the driver's seat. The coarser texture you can achieve is great for burgers because it makes them looser and more tender. You know exactly what cut you're using and how marbled it is. And you need only a food processor.

A serious reason to consider home-grinding for beef in particular: Regardless of where the meat is processed, ground pork, poultry, and beef are safe to eat as long as they are cooked to 160 degrees—the temperature at which potential pathogens are deactivated. But since ground meat is frequently served at temperatures lower than 160 degrees, foodborne illness can be an issue. Meat processing plants have stringent guidelines intended to prevent cross-contamination, but anyone who reads the news knows that outbreaks of salmonella and the harmful 0157:H7 strain of *E. coli* routinely occur. However, only ground beef—not whole cuts—is considered risky. This is because contaminants do not penetrate the surface of a steak or a roast, and any that may be present on the surface will be killed during cooking, making the meat safe even if the interior is served rare. The risk occurs during grinding, when the exterior of the meat is distributed into the interior, taking any potential pathogens along with it.

As long as you follow safe food-handling guidelines—including frequent and thorough hand washing, thorough cleaning of surfaces, and storing meat at or below 40 degrees—we believe that grinding beef at home is safer than buying ground beef at the store since the chance of a single cut of beef (that you then grind at home) being contaminated is relatively slim. Conversely, a single portion of preground store beef can be an amalgam of various grades of meat from different parts of many different cattle. In fact, a typical hamburger may contain meat from hundreds of different animals. And obviously, the more cattle that go into your burger the greater the odds of contamination.

Getting the Right Grind

Underprocessed meat will lead to gristly bits. If you're making burgers, this could mean patties that don't hold together. Overprocessed meat becomes rubbery and dense as it cooks. Perfectly ground meat contains pieces that are fine enough to ensure tenderness but coarse enough that a burger patty will stay loose. Here are the steps to perfection.

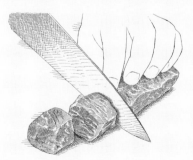

1. Cut meat into ½-inch pieces.

2. Arrange ½-inch pieces of meat in single layer on rimmed baking sheet. Freeze until firm and starting to harden around edges but still pliable, 15 to 25 minutes.

3. Working in batches, pulse meat in food processor, stopping to redistribute meat as needed for an even grind according to recipe. Spread ground meat over sheet, discarding any long strands of gristle and large chunks of fat.

SUPERMARKET SAFETY

If you are dead set on buying your ground meat at the supermarket, we highly recommend you seek a grocer that offers fresh ground meat, which usually means there is an in-house grinder who starts with larger primal cuts. Many supermarkets purchase bulk packages of ground beef from beef-processing plants (sometimes referred to as "tubed" meat), which they sometimes regrind and supplement with meat scraps before packing into smaller parcels.

To see how commercially ground meat stacks up to freshly ground, we made tacos and hamburgers using both types. In tacos, heady spices like chili powder overwhelmed any subtle flavor differences in the meat, but the simply seasoned hamburgers elicited an altogether different response. Here, tasters picked out the just-ground meat, favoring its "fresh," "beefy" flavor. Once again, freshly ground minimizes the risk of foodborne illness with fewer animal parts in the mix. And, bonus, if you find a butcher who will grind to order, you can even choose the grind size.

Ground Beef

The most commonly found ground meat in the United States, ground beef is available in the most versions at the store, varying in fat percentage, cut, and branding (such as Angus ground beef). Many recipes call simply for "ground beef." The USDA defines "ground beef" as ground fresh and/or frozen beef from primal cuts and trimmings containing no more than 30 percent fat. But that doesn't really help us understand the difference between ground round, ground chuck, and ground sirloin at the store. And what about fat content, which can go as low as 7 percent?

To find out if the cut matters, we prepared hamburgers, Bolognese sauce, and meatloaf using each type of ground beef from the supermarket; differences between the cuts were obvious and noted across the board. Ground round, which can contain as little as 11 percent fat, and generically labeled ground beef consistently ranked poorly in our tests, with ground round described as "tough" and "chewy," "livery" even. "Ground beef" can be any cut or combination of cuts, so consistency is a problem. And it may have as much as 30 percent fat, so greasiness can be an issue. Tasters dismissed it in all applications as "mushy," with an "old boiled beef taste." Tasters preferred ground chuck, which typically contains 15 to 20 percent fat, and sirloin, which typically contains around 15 percent. Sirloin was favored for dishes in which other ingredients added fat, whereas chuck was preferred in burgers.

As a general rule, we like 85 percent lean ground beef for dishes with the perfect richness; you can typically have great success with that. We will state otherwise in the ingredient list of our recipes when something different is preferred for the best outcome in that case. While purchasing or grinding yourself is your call, if a recipe calls for 85 percent lean ground beef, you can most definitely choose to grind chuck-eye roast (see page 35). Want to go all out? For the ultimate, *ultimate* big-league ground beef blend, you can use two parts skirt steak, one part boneless short ribs, and one part flap meat. This blend is so ultimate, we recommend splurging only for burgers. Follow the same grinding steps on page 367.

Make sure not to buy ground beef that looks brown. A brown color in store-bought ground beef is a sign that the meat is not freshly ground; it won't be as tender and flavorful as fresher, redder ground meat. We did not notice a difference in the taste, texture, or flavor of dishes made with grass-fed versus grain-fed beef. If you see ground beef labeled "hamburger," it means that the beef can contain added seasonings, ingredients, or fat.

Ground Veal

Ground veal won't win a personality test. We never use it alone—its flavor is meek. But veal, as we've learned (see pages 196–198), wins the tenderness test. That means it gets along well with others, and we use it with ground beef and pork when we want an ultra-tender ground meat dish without a lot of chew, like meatloaf. (Note that you don't want to buy ground meat labeled "meatloaf mix"—it could come from any part of the animal.)

Ground Pork

Ground pork has a somewhat sweet but mild enough flavor and can take on intense flavorings. There's not much choice in pork fat percentages, so we just call for ground pork. Ground pork may retain some of its pink color after it cooks, making it difficult to judge doneness. If it's used for something like a burger, take its temperature to make sure it's fully cooked. We don't grind pork as often as we do beef because it's a pricier operation, but when we do, we like to use pork butt roast or country-style ribs (see pages 215 and 245).

Ground Lamb

If you're able to ask for your lamb ground or are grinding yourself, cuts from the shoulder or leg are preferable for their fat content. That said, if the lamb is prepackaged it is probably from fattier areas and will be fine. Unlike with ground beef, grass and grain make a difference for ground lamb. Grass-fed is more intense and less sweet than grain-fed. This flavor-packed meat is widely available so be sure to try it as a deliciously earthy but also convenient option and alternative to ground beef.

Spaghetti and Meatballs

SPAGHETTI AND MEATBALLS

Serves 8 to 10 | ground beef

WHY THIS RECIPE WORKS It doesn't get much better than sitting down to a heaping pile of spaghetti topped with juicy, flavor-packed meatballs, all married together by a bright tomato sauce. Our version of this classic hits every mark while being relatively fuss-free. While most meatball recipes call for equal amounts of pork and beef, we opted to use more beef than pork—and we chose 80 percent ground beef. This mixture was juicy from the fatty beef but still drier and leaner than a 50-50 beef-pork mix so it was better able to maintain its shape through cooking. For the pork, we used a small amount of Italian sausage, which boosted the meaty flavor without adding a lot more fat. We brought the meatballs together with a panade: a binding paste of milk and bread that keeps ground meat moist when it's cooked above medium-rare. Instead of browning the meatballs on the stovetop, we utilized the oven to prevent splattering and make them more hands-off. Finishing the meatballs in the tomato sauce flavored both components and tied the dish together before serving. We prefer to use ground chuck in this recipe, if you can find it.

SAUCE

¼ cup extra-virgin olive oil
3 onions, chopped fine
8 garlic cloves, minced
1 tablespoon dried oregano
½ teaspoon red pepper flakes
1 (6-ounce) can tomato paste
1 cup dry red wine
4 (28-ounce) cans crushed tomatoes
1 cup water
1 ounce Parmesan cheese, grated (½ cup)
¼ cup chopped fresh basil

MEATBALLS AND PASTA

4 slices hearty white sandwich bread, torn into pieces
¾ cup milk
8 ounces sweet Italian sausage, casings removed
2 ounces Parmesan cheese, grated (1 cup)
½ cup minced fresh parsley
2 large eggs
2 garlic cloves, minced
1½ teaspoons table salt, plus salt for cooking pasta
2½ pounds 80 percent lean ground beef
2 pounds spaghetti

1. For the sauce: Heat oil in Dutch oven over medium-high heat until shimmering. Add onions and cook until golden, 10 to 15 minutes. Stir in garlic, oregano, and pepper flakes and cook until fragrant, about 30 seconds. Transfer half of onion mixture to bowl; set aside for meatballs.

2. Stir tomato paste into onion mixture left in pot and cook over medium-high heat until fragrant, about 1 minute. Stir in wine and cook until slightly thickened, about 2 minutes. Stir in tomatoes and water and simmer over low heat until sauce is no longer watery, 45 minutes to 1 hour. Stir in Parmesan and basil and season with salt and pepper to taste.

3. For the meatballs and pasta: While sauce simmers, line 2 rimmed baking sheets with aluminum foil and spray with vegetable oil spray. Adjust oven racks to upper-middle and lower-middle positions and heat oven to 475 degrees. Mash bread and milk in large bowl until smooth. Mix in reserved onion mixture, sausage, Parmesan, parsley, eggs, garlic, and salt. Add beef and knead with your hands until well combined.

4. Shape meat mixture into 30 meatballs (about ¼ cup each) and place on prepared sheets, spaced evenly apart. Roast meatballs until well browned, about 20 minutes. Transfer meatballs to pot with sauce and simmer for 15 minutes.

5. Meanwhile, bring 8 quarts water to boil in 12-quart pot. Add pasta and 2 tablespoons salt and cook, stirring often, until al dente. Reserve ½ cup cooking water, then drain pasta and return it to pot. Add several spoonfuls of sauce (without meatballs) and toss to combine. Add reserved cooking water as needed to adjust consistency. Serve pasta with remaining sauce and meatballs.

HEARTY BEEF LASAGNA

Serves 10 to 12 | ground beef

WHY THIS RECIPE WORKS Many recipes for meat lasagna can take all day to make. We wanted the same meaty, creamy, cheesy result in a more manageable amount of time. Ninety percent lean ground beef offered bold and familiar flavor without adding grease. To amp up the meatiness in our lasagna, we used 1½ pounds of the beef and just one can of tomatoes—a much higher meat-to-tomato ratio than usual, putting beef in the recipe title. To prevent the meat from turning dry and pebbly, we employed a panade. It ensured a soft texture and also made the meat sauce easier to layer. Wedeveloped this recipe using dried curly-edged lasagna noodles; do not use no-boil noodles. There are about 20 individual noodles in a 1-pound box of lasagna noodles, enough for this recipe.

Hearty Beef Lasagna

LASAGNA

    Vegetable oil spray
17 curly-edged lasagna noodles
    Table salt for cooking noodles
12 ounces mozzarella cheese, shredded (3 cups), divided
¼ cup grated Pecorino Romano cheese

MEAT SAUCE

 2 slices hearty white sandwich bread, torn into small pieces
¼ cup milk
1½ pounds 90 percent lean ground beef
¾ teaspoon table salt
½ teaspoon pepper
1 tablespoon extra-virgin olive oil
1 onion, chopped fine
6 garlic cloves, minced
1 teaspoon dried oregano
¼ teaspoon red pepper flakes
1 (28-ounce) can crushed tomatoes

CREAM SAUCE

8 ounces (1 cup) cottage cheese
4 ounces Pecorino Romano cheese, grated (2 cups)
1 cup heavy cream
2 garlic cloves, minced
1 teaspoon cornstarch
¼ teaspoon table salt
¼ teaspoon pepper

1. For the lasagna: Adjust oven rack to middle position and heat oven to 375 degrees. Spray rimmed baking sheet and 13 by 9-inch baking dish with vegetable oil spray. Bring 4 quarts water to boil in large Dutch oven. Add noodles and 1 tablespoon salt and cook, stirring often, until al dente. Drain noodles and transfer them to prepared sheet. Using tongs, gently turn noodles to coat lightly with oil spray. Cut 2 noodles in half crosswise.

2. For the meat sauce: Mash bread and milk in medium bowl until smooth. Add beef, salt, and pepper and knead with your hands until well combined; set aside. Heat oil in now-empty Dutch oven over medium heat until shimmering. Add onion and cook until softened, about 5 minutes. Stir in garlic, oregano, and pepper flakes and cook until fragrant, about 1 minute.

3. Add beef mixture, breaking meat into small pieces with wooden spoon, and cook until no longer pink, about 4 minutes. Stir in tomatoes and bring to simmer, scraping up any browned bits. Reduce heat to medium-low and simmer until flavors have melded, about 5 minutes.

4. For the cream sauce: Whisk all ingredients in bowl until combined.

5. Lay 3 noodles lengthwise in prepared dish with ends touching 1 short side of dish, leaving gap at far end. Lay 1 half noodle crosswise to fill gap (if needed).

6. Spread 1½ cups meat sauce over noodles, followed by ½ cup cream sauce and finally ½ cup mozzarella. Repeat layering of noodles, meat sauce, cream sauce, and mozzarella 3 more times, switching position of half noodle to opposite end of dish each time.

7. Lay remaining 3 noodles over top (there is no half noodle for top layer). Spread remaining cream sauce over noodles, followed by remaining 1 cup mozzarella. Sprinkle Pecorino over top.

8. Spray sheet of aluminum foil with oil spray and cover lasagna. Set lasagna on rimmed baking sheet. Bake for 30 minutes. Discard foil and continue to bake until top layer of lasagna is spotty brown, 25 to 30 minutes longer. Let lasagna cool for 30 minutes. Slice and serve.

To make ahead: At end of step 7, cover dish with greased aluminum foil and refrigerate for up to 24 hours. When ready to eat, bake lasagna as directed in step 8, increasing covered baking time to 55 minutes.

Pastitsio

PASTITSIO

Serves 6 | ground beef

WHY THIS RECIPE WORKS For our rendition of this impressively stratified Greek spiced meat and creamy macaroni casserole, we started by treating the raw ground beef with baking soda, which made it better able to hold on to moisture (see page 16), and we skipped browning to avoid toughening the meat. Don't use ground beef that's less than 93 percent lean or the dish will be greasy. We like the richness of whole milk for this dish, but you can substitute 2 percent low-fat milk, if desired. Do not use skim milk. Kasseri is a semifirm sheep's-milk cheese from Greece. If it's unavailable, substitute a mixture of 1½ ounces (¾ cup) grated Pecorino Romano and 3 ounces (¾ cup) shredded Provolone, adding ½ cup to the ziti in step 4, ½ cup to the béchamel, and the remaining ½ cup to the top of the béchamel. We strongly recommend using a spider skimmer to transfer the pasta to the baking dish, but a slotted spoon will work. To accommodate all the components, use a baking dish that is at least 2¼ inches tall.

MEAT SAUCE

- 1 tablespoon plus ½ cup water, divided
- ¾ teaspoon table salt
- ¼ teaspoon baking soda
- 8 ounces 93 percent lean ground beef
- 1 tablespoon vegetable oil
- ½ cup finely chopped onion
- 3 garlic cloves, minced
- 1¼ teaspoons ground cinnamon
- 1 teaspoon dried oregano
- 1 teaspoon dried mint
- 1 teaspoon paprika
- ⅛ teaspoon red pepper flakes
- ⅛ teaspoon pepper
- ¼ cup red wine
- ⅓ cup tomato paste

BÉCHAMEL AND PASTA

- 2 tablespoons unsalted butter
- 2 tablespoons all-purpose flour
- 1 garlic clove, minced
- ½ teaspoon table salt
- ¼ teaspoon grated nutmeg
- ⅛ teaspoon pepper
- 4 cups whole milk
- 8 ounces (2½ cups) ziti
- 4 ounces kasseri cheese, shredded (1 cup)
- 1 large egg, lightly beaten

1. For the meat sauce: Combine 1 tablespoon water, salt, and baking soda in medium bowl. Add beef and toss until thoroughly combined. Set aside.

2. Heat oil in medium saucepan over medium heat until shimmering. Add onion and cook, stirring frequently, until softened, about 3 minutes. Stir in garlic, cinnamon, oregano, mint, paprika, pepper flakes, and pepper and cook until fragrant, 1 to 2 minutes. Add wine and cook, stirring occasionally, until mixture is thickened, 2 to 3 minutes. Add tomato paste, beef mixture, and remaining ½ cup water and cook, breaking up meat into pieces no larger than ¼ inch with wooden spoon, until beef has just lost its pink color, 3 to 5 minutes. Bring to simmer; cover, reduce heat to low, and simmer for 30 minutes, stirring occasionally. Off heat, season with salt to taste. (Meat sauce can be refrigerated in airtight container for up to 3 days. Heat through before proceeding with step 3.)

3. For the béchamel and pasta: Adjust oven rack to middle position and heat oven to 375 degrees. Spray 8-inch square baking dish with vegetable oil spray and place on rimmed baking sheet. Melt butter in large saucepan over medium heat. Add flour, garlic, salt, nutmeg, and pepper and cook, stirring constantly, until golden and fragrant, about 1 minute. Slowly whisk in milk and bring to boil. Add pasta and return to simmer, stirring frequently to prevent sticking. When mixture reaches simmer, cover and let stand off heat, stirring occasionally, for 15 minutes (pasta will not be fully cooked).

4. Using spider skimmer, transfer pasta to prepared dish, leaving excess béchamel in saucepan. Sprinkle ⅓ cup kasseri over pasta and stir to combine. Using spatula, gently press pasta into even layer. Add ⅓ cup kasseri to béchamel and whisk to combine. Whisk egg into béchamel. Spread meat sauce over pasta and, using spatula, spread into even layer. Top with béchamel. Sprinkle remaining ⅓ cup kasseri over béchamel. Bake until top of pastitsio is puffed and spotty brown, 40 to 50 minutes. Let cool for 20 minutes. Serve.

TACOS DORADOS

Serves 4 | ground beef

WHY THIS RECIPE WORKS To make tacos dorados, a Mexican preparation of crispy tacos in which corn tortillas are stuffed with a beef filling before being folded in half and fried, we first tossed ground beef with a bit of baking soda to help it stay juicy before adding it to a savory base of sautéed onion, spices, and tomato paste. Next, we stirred in some shredded cheese to make the filling more cohesive. To build the tacos, we brushed corn tortillas with oil, warmed them in the oven to make them pliable, and stuffed them with the filling. Finally, we pan-fried the tacos in two batches until they were supercrispy. Arrange the tacos so that they face the same direction in the skillet to make them easy to fit and flip. To ensure crispy tacos, cook the tortillas until they are deeply browned. To garnish, open each taco like a book and load it with your preferred toppings; close it to eat.

1 tablespoon water
¼ teaspoon baking soda
12 ounces 90 percent lean ground beef
7 tablespoons vegetable oil, divided
1 onion, chopped fine
1½ tablespoons chili powder
1½ tablespoons paprika
1½ teaspoons ground cumin
1½ teaspoons garlic powder
1 teaspoon table salt
2 tablespoons tomato paste
2 ounces cheddar cheese, shredded (½ cup), plus extra
   for serving
12 (6-inch) corn tortillas
   Shredded iceberg lettuce
   Chopped tomato
   Sour cream
   Pickled jalapeño slices
   Hot sauce

1. Adjust oven rack to middle position and heat oven to
400 degrees. Combine water and baking soda in large bowl.
Add beef and mix until thoroughly combined. Set aside.

2. Heat 1 tablespoon oil in 12-inch nonstick skillet over medium
heat until shimmering. Add onion and cook, stirring occasionally, until softened, 4 to 6 minutes. Add chili powder, paprika,
cumin, garlic powder, and salt and cook, stirring frequently, until
fragrant, about 1 minute. Stir in tomato paste and cook until
paste is rust-colored, 1 to 2 minutes. Add beef mixture and cook,
using wooden spoon to break meat into pieces no larger than
¼ inch, until beef is no longer pink, 5 to 7 minutes. Transfer
beef mixture to bowl; stir in cheddar until cheese has melted and
mixture is homogeneous. Wipe skillet clean with paper towels.

3. Thoroughly brush both sides of tortillas with 2 tablespoons
oil. Arrange tortillas, overlapping, on rimmed baking sheet in
2 rows (6 tortillas each). Bake until tortillas are warm and
pliable, about 5 minutes. Remove tortillas from oven and
reduce oven temperature to 200 degrees.

4. Place 2 tablespoons filling on 1 side of 1 tortilla. Fold and
press to close tortilla (edges will be open, but tortilla will remain
folded). Repeat with remaining tortillas and remaining filling.
(At this point, filled tortillas can be covered and refrigerated for
up to 12 hours.)

5. Set wire rack in second rimmed baking sheet and line rack
with double layer of paper towels. Heat remaining ¼ cup oil in
now-empty skillet over medium-high heat until shimmering.
Arrange 6 tacos in skillet with open sides facing away from you.
Cook, adjusting heat so oil actively sizzles and bubbles appear
around edges of tacos, until tacos are crispy and deeply browned

on 1 side, 2 to 3 minutes. Using tongs and thin spatula, carefully
flip tacos. Cook until deeply browned on second side, 2 to
3 minutes, adjusting heat as necessary.

6. Remove skillet from heat and transfer tacos to prepared wire
rack. Blot tops of tacos with double layer of paper towels.
Place sheet with fried tacos in oven to keep warm. Return skillet
to medium-high heat and cook remaining tacos. Serve tacos
immediately, passing extra cheddar, lettuce, tomato, sour cream,
jalapeños, and hot sauce separately.

GORDITAS

Serves 6 | ground beef

WHY THIS RECIPE WORKS To make tender gordita shells
("gordita" means "little fat one" in Spanish), we started with
corn flour (masa harina), which forms a dough with less
structure (read: toughness) than dough made with wheat
flour. Rather than use the typical cooking method of griddling
without fat, we fried the corn cakes to give them exteriors
with clear corn flavor and a captivating crispness. A version
of picadillo—a mixture of ground beef, cubed potato, and
plenty of seasoning—worked perfectly as a filling. We further
stuffed the gorditas with shredded iceberg lettuce and diced
tomatoes for freshness and then topped it all off with hot sauce
and tangy shredded Colby Jack cheese. We developed this
recipe using Maseca Instant Corn Masa Flour. Monterey Jack or
cheddar cheese can be substituted for the Colby Jack. Use a
Dutch oven that holds 6 quarts or more for this recipe. Add hot
sauce, shredded iceberg lettuce, diced tomatoes, and shredded
cheese to your filled gorditas, if desired.

FILLING
1 pound 85 percent lean ground beef
1 russet potato, peeled and cut into ¼-inch pieces
1 teaspoon table salt
1 teaspoon pepper
1 onion, chopped fine
1 tomato, cored and chopped fine
3 garlic cloves, minced
1½ teaspoons ground cumin
2 teaspoons all-purpose flour
¾ cup water

DOUGH
5 cups (20 ounces) masa harina
2 teaspoons table salt
3⅔ cups water, room temperature
3 ounces Colby Jack cheese, shredded (¾ cup)
1½ quarts vegetable oil for frying

Gorditas

1. **For the filling:** Combine beef, potato, salt, and pepper in 12-inch nonstick skillet. Cook over medium-high heat until beef and potato begin to brown, 6 to 8 minutes, breaking up meat with wooden spoon. Add onion and tomato and cook until softened, 4 to 6 minutes. Add garlic and cumin and cook until fragrant, about 30 seconds.

2. Stir in flour and cook for 1 minute. Stir in water and bring to boil. Cook until slightly thickened, about 1 minute. Off heat, season with salt and pepper to taste. Cover and set aside.

3. **For the dough:** Line baking sheet with parchment paper. Whisk masa harina and salt together in large bowl. Add room-temperature water and Colby Jack and knead with your hands until mixture is fully combined. (Mixture should have texture of Play-Doh and easily hold fingerprint.)

4. Divide dough into 12 level ½-cup portions and place on large plate; divide any remaining dough evenly among portions. Working with 1 portion at a time (keep remaining dough covered with damp dish towel), roll dough into smooth ball between your wet hands, then return it to plate. Cut sides of 1-quart zipper-lock bag, leaving bottom seam intact.

5. Enclose 1 dough ball in split bag. Using clear plate or dish (so you can see size of dough round), press dough into 4-inch round, about ½ inch thick. Smooth any cracks around edges of round; transfer to prepared sheet. Repeat with remaining dough balls, placing second sheet of parchment on top once sheet is filled so you can stack dough rounds as needed. Cover with damp dish towel. (Dough rounds can be covered tightly with plastic wrap, without dish towel, and refrigerated for up to 2 hours.)

6. Set wire rack in rimmed baking sheet and line with triple layer of paper towels. Add oil to large Dutch oven until it measures about ¾ inch deep and heat over medium-high heat to 375 degrees.

7. Fry 4 dough rounds until golden brown on both sides, 5 minutes per side. Adjust burner, if necessary, to maintain oil temperature between 350 and 375 degrees. Transfer fried rounds to prepared rack to drain. Return oil to 375 degrees and repeat with remaining dough rounds in 2 batches. Let fried rounds cool for 10 minutes. While rounds are cooling, reheat filling.

8. Insert paring knife into side of fried dough rounds and split 180 degrees to create pocket. Stuff each pocket with ⅓ cup filling and serve.

Double-Decker Drive-Thru Burgers

DOUBLE-DECKER DRIVE-THRU BURGERS

Serves 4 | ground beef

WHY THIS RECIPE WORKS Introduced by a certain fast-food chain, the double-decker—two all-beef patties, special sauce, lettuce, cheese, pickles, and onions on a sesame seed bun—has solidified its place in American culture. We knew a large, 12-inch skillet would be essential to cook the eight patties for our double stacks, but we still needed to cook the burgers in two batches to avoid overcrowding the pan, which would cause our patties to steam rather than fry. To keep the thin patties from shrinking too much, we weighted them with a foil-lined pot as they cooked. Once the first set of patties had cooked, we topped each with a slice of cheese and placed them in a warm oven; in the time it took the cheese to melt, the second batch of quick-cooking patties was ready. For this burger's hallmark flavor, we topped them with our Classic Burger Sauce (page 23), along with some shredded lettuce, pickles, and finely chopped onion to re-create this delicious drive-thru classic at home.

    1   pound 85 percent lean ground beef
    ½   teaspoon table salt
    ¼   teaspoon pepper
    1   teaspoon vegetable oil
    4   slices American cheese (4 ounces)

½ cup Classic Burger Sauce (page 23), divided, plus extra for serving
4 hamburger buns, plus 4 bun bottoms, divided
2 cups shredded iceberg lettuce, divided
¼ cup finely chopped onion, rinsed
¼ cup dill pickle chips

1. Adjust oven rack to middle position and heat oven to 250 degrees. Wrap bottom of Dutch oven with aluminum foil. Cut sides off 1-quart zipper-lock bag, leaving bottom seam intact.

2. Divide ground beef into eight 2-ounce portions, then roll each portion into ball. Working with 1 ball at a time, enclose in split bag. Using clear pie plate (so you can see size of patty), press ball into even 3½-inch patty. Remove patty from bag and transfer to platter. Sprinkle patties with salt and pepper.

3. Heat oil in 12-inch skillet over high heat until just smoking. Place 4 patties in skillet and weight with prepared pot. Cook until well browned on first side, 60 to 90 seconds. Flip patties, return pot, and continue to cook until browned on second side, about 60 seconds. Transfer burgers to rimmed baking sheet, top with cheese, and keep warm in oven. Pour off all but 1 teaspoon fat from skillet and repeat with remaining 4 patties; transfer to sheet.

4. Spread ¼ cup burger sauce over 4 bun bottoms, then top with 1 cup lettuce and cheeseburgers. Spread remaining ¼ cup sauce over remaining 4 bun bottoms, then top with remaining 1 cup lettuce, remaining burgers, onions, and pickle chips. Place second set of burger stacks on top of first and top with bun tops. Serve, passing extra sauce separately.

BEST GROUND BEEF CHILI

Serves 8 to 10 | ground beef

WHY THIS RECIPE WORKS Perfectly tender—not pebbly—ground beef, a judicious amount of beans, and a stew with nice body are requisites for a chili with the title "Best." But it's the chiles that give this chili its blue-ribbon flavor: Toasted dried anchos provided deep, fruity flavor, while smoky chipotle in adobo heated things up. To keep the meat tender and help it hold on to moisture, we first treated it with salt and baking soda. Cornmeal was perfect for thickening and adding a subtle corn flavor, but since we like serving the chili with tortilla chips, we found it easier to use those. Before serving, we made sure to stir in the fat that collected on the top, since it contains much of the bloomed flavor from the fat-soluble spices. We prefer the robust flavor of Mexican oregano, but you can substitute any dried oregano. For a spicier chili, use the larger amount of chipotle. Don't skim the fat from the chili; it's an important source of flavor. You can serve the chili with any additional favorite toppings and tortilla chips.

2 tablespoons plus 2 cups water, divided
1 teaspoon table salt
¾ teaspoon baking soda
2 pounds 85 percent lean ground beef
3 ounces (6 to 8) dried ancho chiles, stemmed, seeded, and torn into ½-inch pieces (1½ cups)
1 ounce tortilla chips, crushed (¼ cup)
2 tablespoons cumin seeds
4 teaspoons coriander seeds
1 tablespoon paprika
1 tablespoon garlic powder
2 teaspoons dried Mexican oregano
1½ teaspoons black peppercorns
½ teaspoon dried thyme
1 (14.5-ounce) can whole peeled tomatoes
1 tablespoon vegetable oil
1 yellow onion, chopped fine
3 garlic cloves, minced
1–2 teaspoons minced canned chipotle chile in adobo sauce
1 (15-ounce) can pinto beans
2 teaspoons sugar
2 tablespoons cider vinegar
Lime wedges
Coarsely chopped fresh cilantro
Chopped red onion

1. Adjust oven rack to lower-middle position and heat oven to 275 degrees. Combine 2 tablespoons water, salt, and baking soda in medium bowl. Add beef and toss until thoroughly combined. Set aside for 20 minutes.

2. Meanwhile, toast anchos in Dutch oven over medium-high heat, stirring frequently, until fragrant, 2 to 6 minutes; reduce heat if they begin to smoke. Transfer to food processor and let cool for 5 minutes. Add tortilla chips, cumin seeds, coriander seeds, paprika, garlic powder, oregano, peppercorns, and thyme to food processor with anchos and process until finely ground, about 3 minutes; transfer to bowl. Process tomatoes and their juice in now-empty processor until smooth, about 30 seconds.

3. Heat oil in now-empty pot over medium-high heat until shimmering. Add yellow onion and cook until softened, about 5 minutes. Stir in garlic and cook until fragrant, about 30 seconds. Add beef and cook, breaking up meat into ¼-inch pieces with wooden spoon, until browned and fond begins to form on pot bottom, 12 to 14 minutes. Add ancho mixture and chipotle and cook, stirring frequently, until fragrant, 1 to 2 minutes. Stir in beans and their liquid, sugar, processed tomatoes, and remaining 2 cups water, scraping up any browned bits, and bring to simmer. Cover, transfer pot to oven, and cook, stirring occasionally, until beef is tender and chili is slightly thickened, 1½ to 2 hours. Remove pot from oven and let sit, uncovered, for 10 minutes. Add vinegar and stir chili well to recombine. Season with salt to taste. Serve, passing lime wedges, cilantro, and red onion separately.

Mapo Tofu

MAPO TOFU

Serves 4 to 6 | ground beef

WHY THIS RECIPE WORKS We started our version of this signature Sichuan dish by poaching cubed tofu in chicken broth to help the cubes stay intact. For the sauce, we used plenty of ginger and garlic along with four Sichuan pantry powerhouses: Asian broad bean chili paste, fermented black beans, Sichuan chili powder, and Sichuan peppercorns. A small amount of ground beef acted as a seasoning to complement the other components. Ground pork can be used in place of the beef, if desired. Asian broad bean chili paste (or sauce) is also known as doubanjiang or toban djan. Our favorite, Pixian, is available online; Lee Kum Kee Chili Bean Sauce is a good supermarket option. If you can't find Sichuan chili powder, substitute an equal amount of Korean red pepper flakes (gochugaru). In a pinch, use 2½ teaspoons of ancho chile powder and ½ teaspoon of cayenne pepper. If you can't find fermented black beans, you can use an equal amount of fermented black bean paste or sauce or 2 additional teaspoons of Asian broad bean chili paste.

    1 tablespoon Sichuan peppercorns
    12 scallions
    28 ounces soft tofu, cut into ½-inch cubes
    2 cups chicken broth
    ⅓ cup Asian broad bean chili paste
    9 garlic cloves, peeled
    1 (3-inch) piece ginger, peeled and cut into ¼-inch rounds
    1 tablespoon fermented black beans
    6 tablespoons vegetable oil, divided
    1 tablespoon Sichuan chili powder
    8 ounces 85 percent lean ground beef
    2 tablespoons hoisin sauce
    2 teaspoons toasted sesame oil
    2 tablespoons water
    1 tablespoon cornstarch

1. Place peppercorns in small bowl and microwave until fragrant, 15 to 30 seconds. Let cool completely. Once cool, grind in spice grinder or mortar and pestle (you should have 1½ teaspoons).

2. Using side of chef's knife, lightly crush white parts of scallions, then cut scallions into 1-inch pieces. Place tofu, broth, and scallions in large bowl and microwave, covered, until steaming, 5 to 7 minutes. Let stand while preparing remaining ingredients.

3. Process chili paste, garlic, ginger, and black beans in food processor until coarse paste forms, 1 to 2 minutes, scraping down sides of bowl as needed. Add ¼ cup vegetable oil, chili powder, and 1 teaspoon peppercorns and continue to process until smooth paste forms, 1 to 2 minutes longer; transfer spice paste to bowl.

4. Heat 1 tablespoon vegetable oil and beef in large saucepan over medium heat; cook, breaking up meat with wooden spoon, until meat just begins to brown, 5 to 7 minutes; transfer beef to bowl.

5. Add remaining 1 tablespoon vegetable oil and spice paste to now-empty saucepan and cook, stirring frequently, until paste darkens and oil begins to separate from paste, 2 to 3 minutes. Gently pour tofu with broth into saucepan, followed by hoisin, sesame oil, and beef. Cook, stirring gently and frequently, until dish comes to simmer, 2 to 3 minutes. Whisk water and cornstarch together in small bowl. Add cornstarch mixture to saucepan and continue to cook, stirring frequently, until thickened, 2 to 3 minutes longer. Transfer to serving dish, sprinkle with remaining peppercorns, and serve.

HUMMUS WITH BAHARAT-SPICED BEEF

Serves 12 to 14 | ground beef

WHY THIS RECIPE WORKS This hummus is velvety-smooth, creamy, and satisfyingly rich. For a balanced garlic flavor, we steeped minced garlic in fresh lemon juice and salt, which deactivated alliinase, the enzyme that gives the allium its harsh bite. We used plenty of lemon juice to give the hummus a bright flavor. Topping hummus with spiced beef is common throughout the Middle East and turns this dip into a hearty meal. Eighty-five percent lean ground beef provided the topping with the requisite richness, and with a few pantry spices, we made our own baharat—a warm, savory Middle Eastern spice blend. Our favorite tahini, Ziyad Tahini Sesame Paste, is made with gently roasted sesame seeds, which gives it a light color and a mild flavor. If Ziyad is unavailable, look for a similarly light tahini such as Roland Tahini Pure Sesame Paste or Kevala Organic Sesame Tahini. The hummus will thicken slightly over time; add warm water, 1 tablespoon at a time, as needed to restore its creamy consistency. Serve with crudités and pita bread or crackers.

HUMMUS
    2 (15-ounce) cans chickpeas, rinsed
    ½ teaspoon baking soda
    4 garlic cloves, peeled
    ⅓ cup lemon juice (2 lemons), plus extra for seasoning
    1 teaspoon table salt
    ¼ teaspoon ground cumin
    ½ cup tahini, stirred well
    2 tablespoons extra-virgin olive oil, plus extra for drizzling

TOPPING

- 2 teaspoons water
- ½ teaspoon table salt
- ¼ teaspoon baking soda
- 8 ounces 85 percent lean ground beef
- 1 tablespoon extra-virgin olive oil
- ¼ cup finely chopped onion
- 2 garlic cloves, minced
- 1 teaspoon hot smoked paprika
- 1 teaspoon ground cumin
- ¼ teaspoon pepper
- ¼ teaspoon ground coriander
- ⅛ teaspoon ground cloves
- ⅛ teaspoon ground cinnamon
- ⅓ cup pine nuts, toasted, divided
- 2 teaspoons lemon juice
- 1 teaspoon chopped fresh parsley

1. For the hummus: Combine chickpeas, baking soda, and 6 cups water in medium saucepan and bring to boil over high heat. Reduce heat and simmer, stirring occasionally, until chickpea skins begin to float to surface and chickpeas are creamy and very soft, 15 to 25 minutes.

2. While chickpeas cook, mince garlic using garlic press or rasp-style grater. Measure out 1 tablespoon garlic and set aside; discard remaining garlic. Whisk lemon juice, salt, and reserved garlic together in small bowl and let sit for 10 minutes. Strain garlic-lemon mixture through fine-mesh strainer set over bowl, pressing on solids to extract as much liquid as possible; discard solids.

3. Drain chickpeas in colander and return to saucepan. Fill saucepan with cold water and gently swish chickpeas with your fingers to release skins. Pour off most of water into colander to collect skins, leaving chickpeas behind in saucepan. Repeat filling, swishing, and draining 3 or 4 times until most skins have been removed (this should yield about ¾ cup skins); discard skins. Transfer chickpeas to colander to drain.

4. Process chickpeas, garlic-lemon mixture, ¼ cup water, and cumin in food processor until smooth, about 1 minute, scraping down sides of bowl as needed. Add tahini and oil and process until hummus is smooth, creamy, and light, about 1 minute, scraping down sides of bowl as needed. (Hummus should have pourable consistency similar to yogurt. If too thick, loosen with water, adding 1 teaspoon at a time.) Season with salt and extra lemon juice to taste. (Hummus can be refrigerated for up to 5 days. Let sit, covered, at room temperature for 30 minutes before serving.) Transfer to wide, shallow serving bowl. Using back of spoon, make 1-inch-deep well in center of hummus, leaving 1-inch border.

5. For the topping: Combine water, salt, and baking soda in large bowl. Add beef and toss to combine. Let sit for 5 minutes.

6. Heat oil in 12-inch nonstick skillet over medium heat until shimmering. Add onion and garlic and cook, stirring occasionally, until onion is softened, 3 to 4 minutes. Add paprika, cumin, pepper, coriander, cloves, and cinnamon and cook, stirring constantly, until fragrant, about 30 seconds. Add beef and cook, breaking up meat with wooden spoon, until beef is no longer pink, about 5 minutes. Add ¼ cup pine nuts and lemon juice and toss to combine. Spoon topping into well in hummus. Sprinkle with parsley and remaining pine nuts. Serve.

EGYPTIAN EGGAH WITH GROUND BEEF AND SPINACH

Serves 4 to 6 | ground beef

WHY THIS RECIPE WORKS Eggah, a thick Egyptian omelet, often features boldly spiced fillings in a hearty egg base. We started by choosing traditional Egyptian fillings: ground beef, spinach, and leeks. Using 90 percent lean ground beef ensured that our eggah didn't turn out greasy. A mixture of cumin, cinnamon, and cilantro enhanced the North African flavor profile. We precooked our filling and let it cool slightly before adding it to the beaten eggs. We cooked the egg mixture in a hot skillet and then flipped it halfway through cooking using two plates. Eggah can be served hot, warm, or at room temperature. You will need a 10-inch nonstick skillet with a tight-fitting lid for this recipe.

- 8 ounces (8 cups) baby spinach
- 4 teaspoons extra-virgin olive oil, divided
- 1 pound leeks, whites and light green parts only, halved lengthwise, sliced thin, and washed thoroughly
- 8 ounces 90 percent lean ground beef
- 1 garlic clove, minced
- 1 teaspoon ground cumin
- 1 teaspoon table salt, divided
- ½ teaspoon pepper, divided
- ¼ teaspoon ground cinnamon
- 8 large eggs
- ¼ cup minced fresh cilantro

1. Place spinach and ¼ cup water in large bowl, cover, and microwave until spinach is wilted and decreased in volume by about half, about 5 minutes. Remove bowl from microwave and keep covered for 1 minute. Transfer spinach to colander and gently press to release liquid. Transfer spinach to cutting board and chop coarse. Return to colander and press again.

2. Heat 1 teaspoon oil in 10-inch nonstick skillet over medium heat until shimmering. Add leeks and cook until softened, about 5 minutes. Add ground beef and cook, breaking up meat with

Egyptian Eggah with Ground Beef and Spinach

wooden spoon, until beginning to brown, 5 to 7 minutes. Stir in garlic, cumin, ½ teaspoon salt, ¼ teaspoon pepper, and cinnamon and cook until fragrant, about 30 seconds. Stir in spinach until heated through, about 1 minute; transfer to bowl and let cool slightly.

3. Beat eggs, 2 tablespoons water, remaining ½ teaspoon salt, and remaining ¼ teaspoon pepper with fork in large bowl until thoroughly combined and mixture is pure yellow; do not overbeat. Gently fold in spinach mixture and cilantro, making sure to scrape all of spinach mixture out of skillet.

4. Heat remaining 1 tablespoon oil in now-empty skillet over medium-high heat until just smoking. Add egg mixture and cook, shaking skillet and folding mixture constantly for 15 seconds. Smooth top of egg mixture, reduce heat to medium, cover, and cook, gently shaking skillet every 30 seconds, until bottom is golden brown and top is lightly set, about 3 minutes.

5. Off heat, run heat-resistant rubber spatula around edge of skillet and shake skillet gently to loosen eggah; it should slide around freely in skillet. Slide eggah onto large plate, then invert onto second large plate and slide back into skillet browned side up. Tuck edges of eggah into skillet with rubber spatula. Continue to cook over medium heat, gently shaking skillet every 30 seconds, until second side is golden brown, about 2 minutes. Slide eggah onto cutting board and let cool slightly. Slice and serve hot, warm, or at room temperature.

STUFFED CABBAGE ROLLS

Serves 4 | ground beef and ground pork

WHY THIS RECIPE WORKS When done right, cabbage rolls are comfort food at its finest: softened cabbage leaves filled with ground meat and simmered in a smooth tomato sauce flavored with warm spices, sugar, and vinegar. Many recipes, however, yield blown-out rolls filled with chewy, flavorless meat and bland rice swimming in a sugary sauce. For our cabbage rolls, canned tomato sauce had a smooth texture tasters liked and was thin enough to properly coat the rolls without becoming pasty. Sautéed onions and garlic provided a savory foundation, and ground ginger, cinnamon, and nutmeg added the requisite warm spice flavor to the sauce. Tasters preferred brown sugar to white for its more complex flavor and red wine vinegar to white for its bite. We supplemented the beef filling with bratwurst, a mild German sausage, to boost the meaty flavor. A panade helped keep the filling soft and moist. If the baked cabbage rolls appear dry after the foil is removed, spoon some sauce over them.

1 head green cabbage (2 pounds), cored
1 tablespoon vegetable oil
1 onion, chopped fine
3 garlic cloves, minced
1 teaspoon ground ginger
½ teaspoon ground cinnamon
¼ teaspoon ground nutmeg
1 (28-ounce) can tomato sauce
¼ cup packed light brown sugar
3 tablespoons red wine vinegar
1 teaspoon table salt, divided
½ teaspoon pepper, divided
2 slices hearty white sandwich bread, torn into 1-inch pieces
½ cup milk
12 ounces 85 percent lean ground beef
12 ounces bratwurst, casings removed

1. Adjust oven rack to middle position and heat oven to 375 degrees. Place cabbage in large bowl, cover tightly with plastic wrap, and microwave until outer leaves are pliable and translucent, 3 to 6 minutes. Using tongs, carefully remove wilted outer leaves; set aside. Repeat until you have 15 to 17 large, intact leaves.

2. Heat oil in Dutch oven over medium-high heat until shimmering. Add onion and cook until golden, about 5 minutes. Add garlic, ginger, cinnamon, and nutmeg and cook until fragrant, about 30 seconds. Transfer half of onion mixture to small bowl and set aside. Off heat, add tomato sauce, sugar, vinegar, ½ teaspoon salt, and ¼ teaspoon pepper to pot with remaining onion mixture and stir until sugar dissolves. (Cooled sauce can be refrigerated for up to 24 hours.)

TUTORIAL
Stuffed Cabbage Rolls

As with burritos or spring rolls, it's helpful to have visual cues to follow for anything rolled. Here's how to make neat meat-filled cabbage bundles.

1. Working with 1 cabbage leaf at a time, cut along both sides of rib at base of leaf to form narrow triangle; remove rib.

2. Continue cutting up center of leaf about 1 inch above triangle.

3. Slightly overlap cut ends of cabbage.

4. Place 2 heaping tablespoons of meat mixture on each leaf about ½ inch from bottom of where cut ends overlap. Fold bottom of leaf over filling and fold in sides.

5. Roll leaf tightly around filling.

6. Repeat with remaining leaves and remaining filling. Arrange rolls seam side down in 13 by 9-inch baking dish.

3. Pulse bread and milk in food processor until smooth paste forms, 8 to 10 pulses. Add beef, bratwurst, reserved onion mixture, remaining ½ teaspoon salt, and remaining ¼ teaspoon pepper and pulse until well combined, about 10 pulses.

4. Working with 1 cabbage leaf at a time, cut along both sides of rib at base of leaf to form narrow triangle; remove rib. Continue cutting up center of leaf about 1 inch above triangle, then slightly overlap cut ends of cabbage. Place 2 heaping tablespoons of meat mixture on each leaf about ½ inch from bottom of where cut ends overlap. Fold bottom of leaf over filling and fold in sides. Roll leaf tightly around filling. Repeat with remaining leaves and remaining filling. Arrange rolls seam side down in 13 by 9-inch baking dish. (Unbaked rolls can be refrigerated for up to 24 hours.)

5. Pour sauce over rolls, cover dish tightly with aluminum foil, and bake until sauce is bubbling and rolls are heated through, about 45 minutes. Remove foil and bake until sauce is slightly thickened and cabbage is tender, about 15 minutes. Serve.

STUFFED BELL PEPPERS WITH SPICED BEEF, CURRANTS, AND FETA

Serves 4 | ground beef

WHY THIS RECIPE WORKS Stuffed bell peppers are a simple entrée enjoyed throughout the Mediterranean. We found that briefly blanching the peppers curbed their raw crunch but ensured that they were sturdy enough to hold our hearty filling. To keep our recipe streamlined, we used the same water to blanch the peppers and cook the rice (simple long-grain white rice was preferred). A generous dose of spices ensured that our ground beef stuffing wasn't bland, and some sautéed garlic and onion rounded out the aromatic profile. Chopped toasted almonds brought some welcome crunch, and a little feta helped bind everything together and further boosted flavor. We found that we could make our stuffing while the peppers and rice cooked, keeping the process efficient.

4 red, yellow, or orange bell peppers, ½ inch trimmed off tops, cores and seeds discarded
¼ teaspoon table salt, plus salt for cooking peppers and rice
½ cup long-grain white rice
1 tablespoon extra-virgin olive oil, plus extra for serving
1 onion, chopped fine
3 garlic cloves, minced
2 teaspoons grated fresh ginger
2 teaspoons ground cumin
¾ teaspoon ground cardamom
½ teaspoon red pepper flakes
¼ teaspoon ground cinnamon

10 ounces 90 percent lean ground beef
1 (14.5-ounce) can diced tomatoes, drained with 2 tablespoons juice reserved
¼ cup currants
2 teaspoons chopped fresh oregano or ½ teaspoon dried
2 ounces feta cheese, crumbled (½ cup), divided
¼ cup slivered almonds, toasted and chopped

1. Bring 4 quarts water to boil in large pot. Add bell peppers and 1 tablespoon salt and cook until just beginning to soften, 3 to 5 minutes. Using tongs, remove peppers from pot, drain excess water, and place peppers cut side up on paper towels. Return water to boil, add rice, and cook until tender, about 13 minutes. Drain rice and transfer to large bowl; set aside.

2. Adjust oven rack to middle position and heat oven to 350 degrees. Heat oil in 12-inch skillet over medium-high heat until shimmering. Add onion and salt and cook until softened and lightly browned, 5 to 7 minutes. Stir in garlic, ginger, cumin, cardamom, pepper flakes, and cinnamon and cook until fragrant, about 30 seconds. Add ground beef and cook, breaking up meat with wooden spoon, until no longer pink, about 4 minutes. Off heat, stir in tomatoes and reserved juice, currants, and oregano, scraping up any browned bits. Transfer mixture to bowl with rice. Add ¼ cup feta and almonds and gently toss to combine. Season with salt and pepper to taste.

3. Place peppers cut side up in 8-inch square baking dish. Pack each pepper with rice mixture, mounding filling on top. Bake until filling is heated through, about 30 minutes. Sprinkle remaining ¼ cup feta over peppers and drizzle with extra oil. Serve.

MEXICAN MEATBALL SOUP

Serves 6 to 8 | ground pork

WHY THIS RECIPE WORKS Meatballs as soup filling are common in different parts of the world and just as comforting as meatballs with spaghetti. Mexican versions feature tender, flavorful meatballs cooked in a vibrant, complex broth that's spiked with chiles and herbs and grounded by earthy toasted corn. For a flavorful broth base we landed on a mix of chicken stock, canned diced tomatoes, chili powder, and chipotle in adobo. Adding tortillas that had been pulsed in the food processor layered in toasted corn flavor while giving the broth body. A panade of ground corn tortillas and broth added to the meatball mix of sweet and savory ground pork, garlic, and cilantro gave us the tender, juicy texture we were after. We simply dropped these meatballs into our simmering broth to cook them through. A #60 scoop will make quick work of portioning the meatballs, and moistening your hands with water will make them easier to shape.

MEATBALLS
    7 (6-inch) corn tortillas, quartered
    1 cup fresh cilantro leaves and stems
    1 large egg
    2 tablespoons chicken broth
    4 garlic cloves, chopped coarse
    1 teaspoon salt
    ¼ teaspoon pepper
    1 pound ground pork

SOUP
    1 (14.5-ounce) can diced tomatoes
    1 onion, quartered
 1½ tablespoons chili powder
    4 garlic cloves, chopped coarse
    2 teaspoons minced canned chipotle chile in adobo sauce
    1 teaspoon dried oregano
    1 teaspoon table salt
    ¼ teaspoon pepper
    1 tablespoon vegetable oil
    6 cups chicken broth
    2 zucchini, cut into ½-inch pieces
    2 carrots, peeled and cut into ½-inch pieces
      Lime wedges
    ¼ cup chopped fresh cilantro

1. **For the meatballs:** Pulse tortillas in food processor until finely chopped, with no pieces larger than ½ inch, 15 to 20 pulses. Set aside ¾ cup processed tortillas for soup. Add cilantro, egg, broth, garlic, salt, and pepper to processor with remaining tortillas and process until smooth, about 1 minute, scraping down sides of bowl as needed.

2. Transfer tortilla mixture to large bowl. Add pork and mix with your hands until thoroughly combined. Using your dampened hands, pinch off and roll 1-tablespoon-size pieces of mixture into balls and transfer to plate (you should have about 32 meatballs. Cover with plastic wrap and refrigerate until ready to use. (Meatballs can be refrigerated for up to 24 hours.)

3. **For the soup:** In clean, dry processor, process tomatoes and their juice, onion, chili powder, garlic, chipotle, oregano, salt, and pepper until smooth, about 30 seconds, scraping down sides of bowl as needed.

4. Heat oil in Dutch oven over medium-high heat until shimmering. Add tomato mixture and cook, stirring occasionally, until well browned and starting to stick to bottom of pot, 10 to 12 minutes.

5. Stir in broth, zucchini, carrots, and reserved processed tortillas. Add meatballs to pot and bring to boil. Reduce heat to medium and simmer until meatballs are cooked through and vegetables are tender, about 15 minutes. Season with salt and pepper to taste. Serve with lime wedges, sprinkling individual portions with cilantro.

ITALIAN PORK BURGERS WITH BROCCOLI RABE

Serves 4 | ground pork

WHY THIS RECIPE WORKS The combination of charred pork, fennel, rosemary, and garlic is a heady one. The succulent meat's flavor is both lightened by this fragrant spice blend and enhanced by it. We were sure this Italian-inspired combination would translate into burger form; it was just a matter of figuring out the logistics. The patty was the easy part: We took a basic pork burger (which remained juicy thanks to a panade of bread and milk) and stirred in ground fennel and fresh rosemary. Some soy sauce accentuated meatiness. Lettuce was too pallid a partner for this burger, so we tried a cooked green. We loved how the bitterness of sautéed broccoli rabe complemented the seared, herb-infused meat. A little honey balanced any residual bitterness from the rabe and a pinch of red pepper flakes provided a bit of heat. Finally, a bright lemon-garlic mayonnaise pulled the dish together.

SAUCE
    ¼ cup mayonnaise
    ½ teaspoon grated lemon zest
    1 small garlic clove, minced

BURGERS
    1 slice hearty white sandwich bread, torn into 1-inch pieces
    1 shallot, minced
    2 tablespoons milk
    4 teaspoons soy sauce
    1 teaspoon ground fennel
    1 teaspoon minced fresh rosemary
    ½ teaspoon pepper
 1½ pounds ground pork
    4 teaspoons extra-virgin olive oil, divided
    2 garlic cloves, sliced thin
    8 ounces broccoli rabe, trimmed and cut into ½-inch pieces
    1 teaspoon table salt, divided
      Pinch red pepper flakes
    2 teaspoons honey
    4 hamburger buns, toasted if desired

1. **For the sauce:** Combine mayonnaise, lemon zest, and garlic in bowl; refrigerate for at least 15 minutes. (Sauce can be refrigerated for up to 3 days.)

2. **For the burgers:** Using fork, mash bread, shallot, milk, soy sauce, fennel, rosemary, and pepper to paste in large bowl. Break ground pork into small pieces and add to bowl with bread mixture. Gently knead with your hands until well combined. Divide pork mixture into 4 equal portions, then gently shape each portion into ¾-inch-thick patty. Using your fingertips, press center of each patty down until about ½ inch thick, creating slight indentation; set aside.

Italian Pork Burgers with Broccoli Rabe

3. Heat 1 tablespoon oil and garlic in 12-inch nonstick skillet over medium heat until garlic is golden brown and fragrant, 2 to 4 minutes. Add broccoli rabe, ½ teaspoon salt, and pepper flakes and cook, stirring occasionally, until tender, 3 to 5 minutes. Off heat, stir in honey. Transfer to bowl and cover to keep warm. Wipe skillet clean with paper towels.

4. Sprinkle patties with remaining ½ teaspoon salt. Heat remaining 1 teaspoon oil in 12-inch nonstick skillet over medium heat until just smoking. Transfer patties to skillet indentation side up and cook until well browned on first side, 4 to 6 minutes. Flip patties, reduce heat to medium-low, and continue to cook until browned on second side and meat registers 150 degrees, 5 to 7 minutes. Transfer burgers to platter and let rest for 5 minutes. Spread mayonnaise on bun tops. Serve burgers on buns, topped with broccoli rabe, passing extra mayonnaise separately.

GROUND PORK TACOS WITH ALMONDS AND RAISINS

Serves 4 | ground pork

WHY THIS RECIPE WORKS For a ground meat taco filling with complexity, we turned to picadillo Oaxaqueño, a savory-sweet Mexican preparation of ground pork with onions, raisins, and warm spices. We started by softening the onion and then added the garlic and spices so that their flavors would bloom. After sautéing the pork briefly, we added chicken broth and tomato sauce along with the raisins, for depth. But we found that we needed to rein in the filling's sweetness. We tried cutting down on the tomato sauce, but tasters missed the rich flavor; in the end, adding cider vinegar and some smoky chipotle did the trick. Depending on the fat level of the ground pork, you may need to drain off some excess grease. Serve with shredded cheese, shredded lettuce, chopped tomatoes, chopped onion, diced avocado, chopped cilantro, and sour cream or Mexican crema.

- 1 tablespoon vegetable oil
- 1 small onion, chopped fine
- 2 garlic cloves, minced
- ½ teaspoon minced canned chipotle chile in adobo sauce
- ½ teaspoon ground cinnamon
- ⅛ teaspoon ground cloves
- 1 pound ground pork
- 1 cup chicken broth
- ½ cup canned tomato sauce
- 2 tablespoons chopped raisins
- 1 tablespoon cider vinegar
- ½ teaspoon table salt
- ½ teaspoon pepper
- ¼ cup slivered almonds, toasted
- 8 taco shells, warmed

1. Heat oil in 12-inch nonstick skillet over medium heat until shimmering. Add onion and cook until softened, 5 to 7 minutes. Stir in garlic, chipotle, cinnamon, and cloves and cook until fragrant, about 30 seconds. Stir in pork and cook, breaking up meat with wooden spoon, until no longer pink, about 5 minutes.

2. Stir in broth, tomato sauce, raisins, vinegar, salt, and pepper and simmer until thickened, about 10 minutes. Stir in almonds and season with salt and pepper to taste. Divide filling evenly among taco shells and serve.

CHILES RELLENOS WITH PORK

Serves 4 | ground pork

WHY THIS RECIPE WORKS Chiles rellenos are poblano chiles that are stuffed with a savory filling, battered, and deep-fried. Traditional recipes take hours to prepare; we wanted a streamlined version that didn't sacrifice any flavor. The fillings for chiles rellenos vary widely, but we were drawn to a boldly flavored ground pork filling seasoned with tomatoes, almonds, raisins, and warm spices. Although most recipes call for peeling the peppers before stuffing them, we found this step unnecessary; we simply broiled the peppers to soften them. Instead of the traditional (and fussy) egg white batter, we opted for an easy-to-make batter of flour, cornstarch, and seltzer. A quick dredge in cornstarch dried out the surface of the chiles and helped the batter to adhere. If using poblano chiles smaller than 4 ounces, increase the total number of chiles to 12 to accommodate the filling. Use a Dutch oven that holds 6 quarts or more. Serve with hot sauce.

FILLING

- 1 tablespoon vegetable oil
- 2 garlic cloves, minced
- 1 teaspoon minced fresh oregano or ¼ teaspoon dried
- ½ teaspoon minced canned chipotle chile in adobo sauce
- ½ teaspoon ground cinnamon
- ⅛ teaspoon ground cloves
- 1 pound ground pork
- 1 (8-ounce) can tomato sauce
- ¼ cup raisins
- 1 tablespoon cider vinegar
- ¼ teaspoon table salt
- 2 ounces Monterey Jack cheese, shredded (½ cup)
- ¼ cup slivered almonds, toasted and chopped

Ground Pork Tacos with Almonds and Raisins

4. Set wire rack in rimmed baking sheet. Stuff poblanos with meat mixture, leaving ½ inch room at top. Seal open end by weaving toothpick through top of chile. Place ⅔ cup cornstarch in shallow bowl; coat stuffed poblanos thoroughly with cornstarch and place on prepared wire rack.

5. Add oil to large Dutch oven and bring to 375 degrees over medium-high heat. Whisk flour, baking powder, salt, and remaining ⅔ cup cornstarch together in large bowl. Slowly whisk in seltzer until just combined (some lumps will remain). Coat 1 poblano with batter and add to hot oil; repeat with 3 more poblanos. Fry chiles, turning as needed, until golden and crisp, about 6 minutes, adjusting burner as needed to maintain oil temperature of 325 degrees.

6. Transfer fried chiles to prepared rack and remove toothpicks. Repeat with remaining chiles. (Chiles can be held in 200-degree oven for 30 minutes.)

PASTA ALLA NORCINA

Serves 6 | ground pork

WHY THIS RECIPE WORKS Pasta alla norcina is an Umbrian pasta dish that showcases ultratender, flavorful local sausage in a light cream sauce. For an authentic-tasting version, we chose to make our own sausage (no meat grinder needed). We soaked ground pork in a strong baking soda mixture; salt dissolved some of the pork's protein fibers, and the baking soda raised the pH of the meat and improved its water-holding capacity so that it stayed juicy, like Umbrian pork. We flavored the mix with rosemary, nutmeg, and garlic. To ensure the juiciest sausage, we seared the meat in the form of a patty before chopping it into small pieces and gently finishing it in the sauce of cream, wine, and mushrooms. White mushrooms can be substituted for the cremini and short pasta such as mezzi rigatoni or shells for the orecchiette.

1¼ teaspoons kosher salt, divided, plus salt for cooking pasta
¼ teaspoon baking soda
8 ounces ground pork
3 garlic cloves, minced, divided
1¼ teaspoons minced fresh rosemary, divided
1¼ teaspoons pepper, divided
⅛ teaspoon ground nutmeg
8 ounces cremini mushrooms, trimmed
2 tablespoons plus 1 teaspoon vegetable oil, divided
¾ cup heavy cream
1 pound orecchiette
½ cup dry white wine
1½ ounces Pecorino Romano cheese, grated (¾ cup)
3 tablespoons minced fresh parsley
1 tablespoon lemon juice

POBLANOS
8 poblano chiles (4 ounces each)
1⅓ cups cornstarch, divided
5 cups vegetable oil
⅔ cup all-purpose flour
1 teaspoon baking powder
1 teaspoon table salt
1 cup seltzer

1. **For the filling:** Cook oil, garlic, oregano, chipotle, cinnamon, and cloves in 12-inch nonstick skillet over medium heat until fragrant, about 1 minute. Stir in ground pork and cook, breaking up meat with wooden spoon, until no longer pink, about 5 minutes. Stir in tomato sauce, raisins, vinegar, and salt and simmer until most of liquid has evaporated, 3 to 5 minutes.

2. Transfer meat mixture to bowl and mash into fine pieces with potato masher. Let meat cool slightly, then stir in Monterey Jack and almonds. Season with salt and pepper to taste.

3. **For the poblanos:** Position oven rack 4 inches from broiler element and heat broiler. Line rimmed baking sheet with aluminum foil. Lay poblanos on sheet and broil until skin is charred and puffed but flesh is still firm, about 8 minutes, flipping after 5 minutes. Transfer poblanos to bowl, cover, and steam for 10 minutes. Gently remove any loosened pieces of poblano skin, cut off stem end, and remove seeds (you do not need to remove all of skin or seeds).

Chinese Pork Dumplings

1. Spray large plate with vegetable oil spray. Dissolve 1⅛ teaspoons salt and baking soda in 4 teaspoons water in medium bowl. Add pork and fold gently to combine; let stand for 10 minutes.

2. Add 1 teaspoon garlic, ¾ teaspoon rosemary, ¾ teaspoon pepper, and nutmeg to pork and smear with rubber spatula until well combined and tacky, 10 to 15 seconds. Transfer pork mixture to greased plate and form into rough 6-inch patty. Pulse mushrooms in food processor until finely chopped, 10 to 12 pulses.

3. Heat 2 teaspoons oil in 12-inch skillet over medium-high heat until just smoking. Add patty and cook, without moving it, until bottom is browned, 2 to 3 minutes. Flip patty and continue to cook until second side is well browned, 2 to 3 minutes longer (very center of patty will be raw). Remove pan from heat, transfer sausage to cutting board, and chop into ⅛- to ¼-inch pieces. Transfer sausage to bowl and add cream; set aside.

4. Bring 4 quarts water to boil in large Dutch oven. Add pasta and 2 tablespoons salt and cook, stirring often, until al dente. Reserve 1½ cups cooking water, then drain pasta and return it to pot.

5. While pasta cooks, return now-empty skillet to medium heat. Add 1 tablespoon oil, mushrooms, and remaining ⅛ teaspoon salt; cook, stirring frequently, until mushrooms are browned, 5 to 7 minutes. Stir in remaining 2 teaspoons oil, remaining garlic, remaining ½ teaspoon rosemary, and remaining ½ teaspoon pepper; cook until fragrant, about 30 seconds. Stir in wine, scraping up any browned bits, and cook until completely evaporated, 1 to 2 minutes. Stir in sausage-cream mixture and ¾ cup reserved cooking water and simmer until meat is no longer pink, 1 to 3 minutes. Off heat, stir in Pecorino until smooth.

6. Add sauce, parsley, and lemon juice to pasta and toss well to coat. Adjust consistency with remaining reserved cooking water as needed and season with salt and pepper to taste. Serve.

CHINESE PORK DUMPLINGS

Makes 40 dumplings | ground pork

WHY THIS RECIPE WORKS If you have the right recipe, Chinese dumplings can be as fun to make as they are to eat. For our pork filling, we added vegetable oil and sesame oil to ground pork, mimicking the richness of the traditionally used fatty pork shoulder. Mixing the filling in the food processor developed myosin, a protein that helps the filling hold together when cooked. Our recipe makes 40 dumplings, so you can cook some right away and freeze some for later. For dough that has the right moisture level, weigh the flour. For an accurate measurement of boiling water, bring a full kettle of water to a boil and then measure out the desired amount. To ensure that the dumplings seal completely, use minimal flour

when working with the dough so it remains slightly tacky. Keep all the dough covered with a damp towel except when rolling and shaping. A shorter, smaller-diameter rolling pin works well here, but a conventional pin will also work.

DOUGH
- 2½ cups (12½ ounces) all-purpose flour
- 1 cup boiling water

FILLING
- 5 cups 1-inch napa cabbage pieces
- ½ teaspoon table salt, plus salt for salting cabbage
- 12 ounces ground pork
- 1½ tablespoons soy sauce, plus extra for dipping
- 1½ tablespoons toasted sesame oil
- 1 tablespoon vegetable oil, plus 2 tablespoons for pan frying (optional)
- 1 tablespoon Shaoxing or dry sherry
- 1 tablespoon hoisin sauce
- 1 tablespoon grated fresh ginger
- ¼ teaspoon ground white pepper
- 4 scallions, chopped fine
  Black or rice vinegar
  Chili oil

1. **For the dough:** Place flour in food processor. With processor running, add boiling water. Continue to process until dough forms ball and clears sides of bowl, 30 to 45 seconds longer. Transfer dough to counter and knead with your hands until smooth, 2 to 3 minutes. Wrap dough in plastic wrap and let rest for 30 minutes.

2. **For the filling:** While dough rests, scrape any excess dough from now-empty processor bowl and blade. Pulse cabbage in processor until finely chopped, 8 to 10 pulses. Transfer cabbage to medium bowl and stir in ½ teaspoon salt; let sit for 10 minutes. Using your hands, squeeze excess moisture from cabbage. Transfer cabbage to small bowl and set aside.

3. Pulse pork, soy sauce, sesame oil, 1 tablespoon vegetable oil, rice wine, hoisin, ginger, pepper, and salt in now-empty food processor until blended and slightly sticky, about 10 pulses. Scatter cabbage over pork mixture. Add scallions and pulse until vegetables are evenly distributed, about 8 pulses. Transfer pork mixture to small bowl and, using rubber spatula, smooth surface. Cover with plastic and refrigerate.

4. Line 2 rimmed baking sheets with parchment paper. Dust lightly with flour; set aside. Unwrap dough and roll into 12-inch cylinder and cut cylinder into 4 equal pieces. Set 3 pieces aside and cover with plastic. Roll remaining piece into 8-inch cylinder. Cut cylinder in half and cut each half into 5 equal pieces. Place dough pieces on 1 cut side on lightly floured counter and lightly dust with flour. Using palm of your hand, press each dough piece into 2-inch disk. Cover disks with damp towel.

5. Roll 1 disk into 3½-inch round (wrappers needn't be perfectly round) and re-cover disk with damp towel. Repeat with remaining disks. (Do not overlap disks.) Using rubber spatula, mark filling with cross to divide into 4 equal portions. Transfer 1 portion to small bowl and refrigerate remaining filling. Working with 1 wrapper at a time (keep remaining wrappers covered), place scant 1 tablespoon filling in center of wrapper. Brush away any flour clinging to surface of wrapper. Lift side of wrapper closest to you and side farthest away and pinch together to form 1½-inch-wide seam in center of dumpling. (When viewed from above, dumpling will have rectangular shape with rounded open ends.) Lift left corner farthest away from you and bring to center of seam. Pinch to seal. Pinch together remaining dough on left side to seal. Repeat pinching on right side. Gently press dumpling into crescent shape and transfer to prepared sheet. Repeat with remaining wrappers and filling in bowl. Repeat dumpling-making process with remaining 3 pieces dough and remaining 3 portions filling.

6a. To pan fry: Brush 12-inch nonstick skillet with 1 tablespoon vegetable oil. Evenly space 16 dumplings, flat sides down, around edge of skillet and place four in center. Cook over medium heat until bottoms begin to turn spotty brown, 3 to 4 minutes. Off heat, carefully add ½ cup water (water will sputter). Return skillet to heat and bring water to boil. Cover and reduce heat to medium-low. Cook for 6 minutes. Uncover, increase heat to medium-high, and cook until water has evaporated and bottoms of dumplings are crispy and browned, 1 to 3 minutes. Transfer dumplings to platter, crispy sides up. (To cook second batch of dumplings, let skillet cool for 10 minutes. Rinse skillet under cool water and wipe dry with paper towels. Repeat cooking process with 1 tablespoon vegetable oil and remaining dumplings.)

6b. To boil: Bring 4 quarts water to boil in large Dutch oven over high heat. Add 20 dumplings, a few at a time, stirring gently to prevent them from sticking. Return to simmer, adjusting heat as necessary to maintain simmer. Cook dumplings for 7 minutes. Drain well.

7. Serve dumplings hot, passing vinegar, chili oil, and extra soy sauce separately for dipping.

To make ahead: Freeze uncooked dumplings on rimmed baking sheet until solid. Transfer to zipper-lock bag and freeze for up to 1 month. To pan-fry, increase water to ⅔ cup and covered cooking time to 8 minutes. To boil, increase cooking time to 8 minutes.

BUN CHA

Serves 4 to 6 | ground pork

WHY THIS RECIPE WORKS Vietnamese bun cha—a vibrant mix of grilled pork, crisp salad, and delicate rice vermicelli, all united by a bold and zesty sauce known as nuoc cham—is an ideal meal for a hot summer night. For juicy pork patties, we mixed baking soda into supermarket ground pork to help it retain moisture on the grill. Look for dried rice vermicelli in the Asian section of your supermarket. We prefer the more delicate springiness of vermicelli made from 100 percent rice flour to those that include a secondary starch such as cornstarch. If you can find only the latter, just cook them longer—up to 12 minutes. For a less spicy sauce, use only half the Thai chile. For the cilantro, use the leaves and the thin, delicate stems, not the thicker stems close to the root. To serve, place platters of noodles, salad, sauce, and pork patties on the table and allow diners to combine components to their taste. The sauce is potent, so use it sparingly.

NOODLES AND SALAD
8 ounces rice vermicelli
1 head Boston lettuce (8 ounces), torn into bite-size pieces
1 English cucumber, peeled, quartered lengthwise, seeded, and sliced thin on bias
1 cup fresh cilantro leaves and stems
1 cup fresh mint leaves, torn if large

SAUCE
1 small Thai chile, stemmed and minced
3 tablespoons sugar, divided
1 garlic clove, minced
⅔ cup hot water
5 tablespoons fish sauce
¼ cup lime juice (2 limes)

PORK PATTIES
1 large shallot, minced
1 tablespoon fish sauce
1½ teaspoons sugar
½ teaspoon baking soda
½ teaspoon pepper
1 pound ground pork

1. For the noodles and salad: Bring 4 quarts water to boil in large pot. Stir in noodles and cook until tender but not mushy, 4 to 12 minutes. Drain noodles and rinse under cold running water until cool. Drain noodles very well, spread on large plate, and let stand at room temperature to dry. Arrange lettuce, cucumber, cilantro, and mint separately on large platter and refrigerate until needed.

Congee with Stir-Fried Pork

CONGEE WITH STIR-FRIED PORK

Serves 4 to 6 | ground pork

WHY THIS RECIPE WORKS Great congee features soft, barely intact grains gently bound by their silky, viscous cooking liquid; the result should be a fluid porridge that's thick and creamy enough to suspend toppings. We simmered the rice vigorously in broth to encourage the grains to break down in about 45 minutes, partially covering the pot to help the contents cook quickly while minimizing evaporation. We made a savory, stir-fried pork topping by briefly soaking the pork in a salty baking soda solution that helped it stay juicy. We seasoned the meat with soy sauce, Shaoxing wine, white pepper, and a touch of sugar and added a little cornstarch to thicken the sauce. Sometimes we top the congee with halved soft-cooked eggs.

CONGEE
- ¾ cup long-grain white rice
- 1 cup chicken broth
- ¾ teaspoon table salt

STIR-FRIED PORK
- 8 ounces ground pork
- 1 tablespoon water
- ¼ teaspoon table salt
- ⅛ teaspoon baking soda
- 1 garlic clove, minced
- 1 teaspoon minced fresh ginger
- 1 teaspoon soy sauce, plus extra for serving
- 1 teaspoon Shaoxing wine or dry sherry
- 1 teaspoon cornstarch
- ½ teaspoon sugar
- ¼ teaspoon white pepper
- 1 teaspoon vegetable oil

  Scallions, sliced thin on bias
  Fresh cilantro leaves
  Dry-roasted peanuts, chopped coarse
  Chili oil
  Chinese black vinegar

1. For the congee: Place rice in fine-mesh strainer and rinse under cold running water until water runs clear. Drain well and transfer to Dutch oven. Add broth, salt, and 9 cups water and bring to boil over high heat. Reduce heat to maintain vigorous simmer. Cover pot, tucking wooden spoon horizontally between pot and lid to hold lid ajar. Cook, stirring occasionally, until mixture is thickened, glossy, and reduced by half, 45 to 50 minutes.

2. For the stir-fried pork: While rice cooks, toss pork, water, salt, and baking soda in bowl until thoroughly combined. Add garlic, ginger, soy sauce, Shaoxing wine, cornstarch, sugar, and white pepper and toss until thoroughly combined.

2. For the sauce: Using mortar and pestle (or on cutting board using flat side of chef's knife), mash Thai chile, 1 tablespoon sugar, and garlic to fine paste. Transfer to medium bowl and add hot water and remaining 2 tablespoons sugar. Stir until sugar is dissolved. Stir in fish sauce and lime juice. Set aside.

3. For the pork patties: Combine shallot, fish sauce, sugar, baking soda, and pepper in medium bowl. Add pork and mix until well combined. Shape pork mixture into 12 patties, each about 2½ inches wide and ½ inch thick.

4a. For a charcoal grill: Open bottom vent completely. Light large chimney starter filled with charcoal briquettes (6 quarts). When top coals are partially covered with ash, pour evenly over half of grill. Set cooking grate in place, cover, and open lid vent completely. Heat grill until hot, about 5 minutes.

4b. For a gas grill: Turn all burners to high, cover, and heat grill until hot, about 15 minutes. Leave all burners on high.

5. Clean and oil cooking grate. Cook patties (directly over coals if using charcoal; covered if using gas) until well charred, 3 to 4 minutes per side. Transfer patties to bowl with sauce and gently toss to coat. Let stand for 5 minutes.

6. Transfer patties to serving plate, reserving sauce. Serve noodles, salad, sauce, and pork patties separately.

3. Heat oil in 12-inch nonstick skillet over medium-high heat until just smoking. Add pork mixture and cook, breaking meat into ¼-inch pieces with wooden spoon, until pork is no longer pink and just beginning to brown. Serve congee in bowls, spooning pork over congee and passing scallions, cilantro, peanuts, oil, vinegar, and extra soy sauce separately.

MEATBALL STEW WITH PAPRIKA AND SAFFRON

Serves 6 to 8 | ground pork and ground beef

WHY THIS RECIPE WORKS We started with the meatballs for our stew, opting for a tender, flavorful combination of ground pork and beef. Manchego cheese, shallot, parsley, and olive oil provided even more interest to the meat mix. We rolled ½-inch meatballs and then placed them in the refrigerator to firm up. For a full-flavored broth, we started with a sofrito of onion, bell pepper, and garlic, then added enough saffron threads for a potent but not overwhelming impact. Paprika contributed sweetness to the broth while also reinforcing its sunset-orange hue, and red pepper flakes delivered just enough heat. We deglazed the pot with white wine for brightness, poured in chicken broth, and then dropped in the meatballs. Finally, we added body to the soup with a traditional picada.

PICADA
- ¼ cup slivered almonds
- 2 slices hearty white sandwich bread, torn into quarters
- 2 tablespoons extra-virgin olive oil
- ⅛ teaspoon salt
  Pinch pepper

MEATBALLS
- 2 slices hearty white sandwich bread, torn into quarters
- ⅓ cup whole milk
- 8 ounces ground pork
- 1 ounce Manchego cheese, grated (½ cup)
- 3 tablespoons minced fresh parsley
- 1 shallot, minced
- 2 tablespoons extra-virgin olive oil
- ½ teaspoon table salt
- ½ teaspoon pepper
- 8 ounces 80 percent lean ground beef

SOUP
- 1 tablespoon extra-virgin olive oil
- 1 onion, chopped fine
- 1 red bell pepper, stemmed, seeded, and cut into ¾-inch pieces
- 2 garlic cloves, minced
- 1 teaspoon paprika
- ¼ teaspoon saffron threads, crumbled
- ⅛ teaspoon red pepper flakes

Glazed Meatloaf

- 1 cup dry white wine
- 8 cups chicken broth
- 2 tablespoons minced fresh parsley

1. For the picada: Adjust oven rack to middle position and heat oven to 375 degrees. Pulse almonds in food processor to fine crumbs, about 20 pulses. Add bread, oil, salt, and pepper and pulse bread to coarse crumbs, about 10 pulses. Spread mixture evenly in rimmed baking sheet and bake, stirring often, until golden brown, about 10 minutes. Set aside to cool.

2. For the meatballs: Using fork, mash bread and milk together into paste in large bowl. Stir in ground pork, Manchego, parsley, shallot, oil, salt, and pepper until combined. Add ground beef and knead until combined. Using your dampened hands, pinch off and roll 2-teaspoon-size pieces of mixture into balls and arrange in rimmed baking sheet (you should have 30 to 35 meatballs). Cover with plastic wrap and refrigerate until firm, at least 30 minutes.

3. For the soup: Heat oil in large Dutch oven over medium-high heat until shimmering. Add onion and bell pepper and cook until softened and lightly browned, 8 to 10 minutes. Stir in garlic, paprika, saffron, and pepper flakes and cook until fragrant, about 30 seconds. Stir in wine, scraping up any browned bits, and cook until almost completely evaporated, about 1 minute. Stir in broth and bring to simmer. Gently add meatballs and simmer until cooked through, 10 to 12 minutes. Off heat, stir in picada and parsley and season with salt and pepper to taste. Serve.

HOMEMADE BREAKFAST SAUSAGE

Serves 8 | ground pork

WHY THIS RECIPE WORKS Commercially made breakfast sausage always disappoints when it comes to flavor, tasting either too sweet or salty or too bland or highly seasoned, so we decided to make our own. We started with ground pork with some fat in it (lean meat was neither fatty nor flavorful enough) and amped up its mild flavor with classic breakfast sausage ingredients: garlic, sage, thyme, and cayenne pepper. A spoonful of maple syrup sweetened the patties nicely and was appropriate for breakfast fare. To combine the meat mixture, we kneaded it gently with our hands but were careful not to overmix it, which would toughen the meat. To form even patties, we found that a greased measuring cup worked like a charm. Avoid lean or extra-lean ground pork; it makes the sausage dry, crumbly, and less flavorful.

    2 pounds ground pork
    1 tablespoon maple syrup
    2 teaspoons dried sage
 1½ teaspoons pepper
    1 teaspoon salt
    1 garlic clove, minced
  ½ teaspoon dried thyme
  ⅛ teaspoon cayenne pepper
    2 tablespoons unsalted butter, divided

1. Combine pork, maple syrup, sage, pepper, salt, garlic, thyme, and cayenne in large bowl. Gently mix with your hands until well combined. Using greased ¼-cup measure, divide mixture into 16 patties and place on rimmed baking sheet. Cover patties with plastic wrap, then gently flatten each one to ½-inch thickness.

2. Melt 1 tablespoon butter in 12-inch nonstick skillet over medium heat. Cook half of patties until well browned and cooked through, 6 to 10 minutes. Transfer to paper towel–lined plate and tent with aluminum foil. Wipe out skillet. Repeat with remaining butter and patties. Serve.

GLAZED MEATLOAF

Serves 6 to 8 | ground beef and ground pork

WHY THIS RECIPE WORKS An old-fashioned meatloaf with tender meat topped with a shining, sweet-tangy glaze that offsets the loaf's richness can be a satisfying dinner centerpiece anytime. Since this dish is all about the meat we stuck with the flavorful and classic combination of equal parts ground beef and sweet ground pork. As for seasoning, we kept with tradition: salt, pepper, Dijon mustard, Worcestershire sauce, thyme, parsley, sautéed onion, and garlic. To add moisture and structure, we used a panade of milk and saltines. Combining the panade in a food processor and then pulsing it with the meat gave the loaf the most cohesive, tender structure. To evaporate the surface moisture that was inhibiting the formation of a crust, we broiled the loaf prior to baking and glazing.

GLAZE

    1 cup ketchup
  ¼ cup packed brown sugar
 2½ tablespoons cider vinegar
  ½ teaspoon hot sauce

MEATLOAF

    2 teaspoons vegetable oil
    1 onion, chopped fine
    2 garlic cloves, minced
  17 square or 19 round saltines
  ⅓ cup whole milk
    1 pound 90 percent lean ground beef
    1 pound ground pork
    2 large eggs plus 1 large yolk
  ⅓ cup finely chopped fresh parsley
    2 teaspoons Dijon mustard
    2 teaspoons Worcestershire sauce
  ½ teaspoon dried thyme
    1 teaspoon table salt
  ¾ teaspoon pepper

1. **For the glaze:** Whisk all ingredients in saucepan until sugar dissolves. Reserve ¼ cup glaze mixture, then simmer remaining glaze over medium heat until slightly thickened, about 5 minutes. Cover and keep warm.

2. **For the meatloaf:** Line rimmed baking sheet with aluminum foil and coat lightly with vegetable oil spray. Heat oil in nonstick skillet over medium heat until shimmering. Cook onion until golden, about 8 minutes. Add garlic and cook until fragrant, about 30 seconds. Transfer to large bowl.

3. Process saltines and milk in food processor until smooth, about 30 seconds. Add beef and pork and pulse until well combined, about 10 pulses. Transfer meat mixture to bowl with cooled onion mixture. Add eggs and yolk, parsley, mustard, Worcestershire, thyme, salt, and pepper to bowl and mix with your hands until combined.

4. Adjust 1 oven rack to middle position and second rack 4 inches from broiler element; heat broiler. Transfer meat mixture to prepared baking sheet and shape into 9 by 5-inch loaf. Broil on upper rack until well browned, about 5 minutes. Brush 2 tablespoons unreduced glaze over top and sides of loaf and then return to oven and broil until glaze begins to brown, about 2 minutes.

5. Transfer meatloaf to lower rack and brush with remaining unreduced glaze. Reduce oven temperature to 350 degrees and bake until meatloaf registers 160 degrees, 40 to 45 minutes. Transfer to cutting board, tent with foil, and let rest for 20 minutes. Slice and serve, passing remaining reduced glaze at table.

RAGÙ ALLA BOLOGNESE

Makes about 6 cups | ground beef, ground pork, and ground veal

WHY THIS RECIPE WORKS There are many different ways to interpret what "real" Bolognese sauce is. But it should always be hearty and rich but not cloying, with a velvety, clinging texture. For our version we used six types of meats: ground beef, pork, and veal; pancetta; mortadella (bologna-like Italian deli meat); and chicken livers. These meats and the combination of red wine and tomato paste gave us a rich, complex sauce with balanced acidity. The final addition of gelatin lent the sauce an ultrasilky texture. Leftover sauce can be refrigerated for up to three days or frozen for up to one month. Eight teaspoons of gelatin is equivalent to one (1-ounce) box of gelatin.

  1 cup chicken broth
  1 cup beef broth
  8 teaspoons unflavored gelatin
  1 onion, chopped coarse
  1 large carrot, peeled and chopped coarse
  1 celery rib, chopped coarse
  4 ounces pancetta, chopped
  4 ounces mortadella, chopped
  6 ounces chicken livers, trimmed
  3 tablespoons extra-virgin olive oil
12 ounces 85 percent lean ground beef
12 ounces ground veal
12 ounces ground pork
  3 tablespoons minced fresh sage
  1 (6-ounce) can tomato paste
  2 cups dry red wine

1. Combine chicken broth and beef broth in bowl; sprinkle gelatin over top and let sit until softened, about 5 minutes.

2. Pulse onion, carrot, and celery in food processor until finely chopped, about 10 pulses, scraping down sides of bowl as needed; transfer to separate bowl. Pulse pancetta and mortadella in now-empty processor until finely chopped, about 25 pulses; transfer to third bowl. Process chicken livers in again-empty processor until pureed, about 5 seconds; refrigerate until ready to use.

3. Heat oil in Dutch oven over medium-high heat until shimmering. Add ground beef, veal, and pork and cook, breaking up meat with wooden spoon, until all liquid has evaporated and meat begins to sizzle, 10 to 15 minutes. Stir in pancetta mixture and sage and cook until pancetta is translucent, 5 to 7 minutes, adjusting heat as needed to keep fond from burning. Stir in chopped vegetables and cook until softened, 5 to 7 minutes. Stir in tomato paste and cook until rust-colored and fragrant, about 3 minutes.

4. Stir in wine, scraping up any browned bits, and simmer until thickened, about 5 minutes. Stir in broth mixture, return to bare simmer, and cook until sauce has thickened (wooden spoon should leave trail when dragged through sauce), about 1½ hours.

5. Stir in chicken livers and bring to brief simmer. Season with salt and pepper to taste. (Sauce can be refrigerated for up to 3 days or frozen for up to 1 month.)

KEFTEDES

Serves 8 to 10 | ground lamb

WHY THIS RECIPE WORKS This Greek dish can be found on many restaurant menus and gives lamb its rightful turn in meatballs. We wanted to make our own version with tender, juicy ground lamb; lemony brightness; and bold yet balanced seasoning from garlic, spices, and herbs. We chose crushed saltine crackers and milk as a panade to keep the meatballs tender and juicy. Lemon zest and a hefty dose of minced garlic added punch and pungency, and citrusy coriander and earthy cumin provided complexity. Aromatic mint and scallions, as well as dried oregano with its slight licorice undertones, provided the best herb mix. We roasted the meatballs and then served them cocktail-style with a smooth and creamy tahini and yogurt dip. The zippy flavor and cooling nature of the sauce was the perfect finish for these rich, spiced, sophisticated meatballs, as was a refreshing garnish of complementary fresh mint.

MEATBALLS
20 square saltines
 ½ cup milk
 ½ cup chopped fresh mint, plus mint leaves for sprinkling
  6 scallions, minced
  2 tablespoons dried oregano
  5 garlic cloves, minced
  1 tablespoon grated lemon zest
  2 teaspoons ground cumin
  2 teaspoons ground coriander
1½ teaspoons pepper
1¼ teaspoons table salt
  2 pounds ground lamb

Keftedes

SAUCE

- 1 cup plain whole-milk yogurt
- ½ cup tahini
- ¼ cup lemon juice (2 lemons)
- 1 teaspoon table salt
- ½ teaspoon pepper

1. **For the meatballs:** Adjust oven rack to upper-middle position and heat oven to 450 degrees. Set wire rack in aluminum foil–lined rimmed baking sheet.

2. Place saltines in large zipper-lock bag, seal bag, and crush fine with rolling pin (you should end up with 1 scant cup crushed saltines). Combine saltines and milk in large bowl, mashing with rubber spatula until paste forms, about 1 minute.

3. Add chopped mint, scallions, oregano, garlic, lemon zest, cumin, coriander, pepper, and salt to saltine mixture and mash until thoroughly combined. Add lamb and mix with your hands until thoroughly combined.

4. Divide mixture into 40 portions (1 heaping tablespoon each). Roll portions between your wet hands to form 1½-inch meatballs and evenly space on prepared wire rack. Roast until meatballs are lightly browned, about 20 minutes.

5. **For the sauce:** While meatballs roast, whisk all ingredients together in bowl; set aside.

6. Using tongs, transfer meatballs to serving platter. Serve with sauce and sprinkle with mint leaves.

HOISIN-GLAZED LAMB BURGERS

Serves 4 | ground lamb

WHY THIS RECIPE WORKS Mediterranean and Middle Eastern approaches to lamb are popular, so we were interested in going in a different direction for these burgers. To play up the lamb's intense umami notes, we turned to hoisin sauce, which packs a spicy, salty, sweet, and savory punch from chiles, garlic, fermented soy, and sugar. For complex flavor throughout, we used it twice: folded into the ground lamb and brushed onto the cooked burgers as they rested for a beautiful lacquered effect. The lamb's naturally meaty flavor was both tempered and complemented by these additions, and the burgers were juicier to boot. To round out the flavors and add texture, we topped the burgers with scallions, carrot, and cucumber, all of which we first marinated in rice vinegar. This brought freshness along with some bright color and satisfying crunch. Avoid pickling the cucumber and carrots for longer than 1 hour or they will begin to turn limp and gray.

Hoisin-Glazed Lamb Burgers

PICKLES

- 3 tablespoons rice vinegar
- ¼ teaspoon table salt
- ¼ English cucumber, halved lengthwise and sliced thin
- 1 small carrot, peeled and cut into 2-inch-long matchsticks
- 2 scallions, sliced thin on bias

BURGERS

- 1½ pounds ground lamb
- ¼ cup hoisin sauce, divided, plus extra for serving
- 1 teaspoon five-spice powder
- ½ teaspoon table salt
- 1 teaspoon vegetable oil
- 4 hamburger buns, toasted if desired

1. **For the pickles:** Whisk vinegar and salt in medium bowl until salt has dissolved. Stir in cucumber and carrot and refrigerate for at least 15 minutes or up to 1 hour. Drain vegetables, return to now-empty bowl, and stir in scallions; set aside for serving.

2. **For the burgers:** Break ground lamb into small pieces in large bowl. Add 2 tablespoons hoisin and five-spice powder and gently knead with your hands until well combined. Divide lamb mixture into 4 equal portions, then gently shape each portion into ¾-inch-thick patty. Using your fingertips, press center of each patty down until about ½ inch thick, creating slight indentation.

3. Sprinkle patties with salt. Heat oil in 12-inch nonstick skillet over medium heat until just smoking. Transfer patties to skillet indentation side up and cook until well browned on first side, 2 to 4 minutes. Flip patties, reduce heat to medium-low, and continue to cook until browned on second side and meat registers 120 to 125 degrees (for medium-rare) or 130 to 135 (for medium), 3 to 5 minutes. Transfer burgers to platter, brush with remaining 2 tablespoons hoisin, and let rest for 5 minutes. Serve burgers on buns, topped with pickled vegetables, passing extra hoisin separately.

LAMB RAGU WITH PAPPARDELLE

Serves 4 | ground lamb

WHY THIS RECIPE WORKS Traditional ragu is simmered for hours, but using rich, meaty ground lamb as the base for our ragu helped us achieve a flavorful sauce that tasted like it had been simmered all day—but in 30 minutes. Ground lamb is tender and juicy, and its strong flavor provided the backbone for the sauce. Its fat helped add additional richness to the dish. Aromatics, carrots, and fennel complemented the lamb and rounded out the flavor and texture of the ragu. We found that adding fresh basil before serving was essential: Its brightness balanced out the decadent sauce. The wide strands of pappardelle allowed for plenty of sauce to cling to each noodle. You can substitute tagliatelle for the pappardelle, if desired. Serve with grated Parmesan cheese.

   1 pound ground lamb
   1 onion, chopped fine
   2 carrots, peeled and chopped fine
   4 garlic cloves, sliced thin
1½ teaspoons ground fennel
   1 teaspoon dried oregano
   ½ teaspoon table salt, plus salt for cooking pasta
   ½ teaspoon pepper
   1 (28-ounce) can crushed tomatoes
   1 pound pappardelle
   ½ cup torn fresh basil

1. Combine lamb, onion, carrots, garlic, fennel, oregano, salt, and pepper in 12-inch nonstick skillet. Cook over medium-high heat, breaking up meat with wooden spoon, until meat is cooked through and carrots are tender, about 8 minutes. Stir in tomatoes and reduce heat to medium. Cook, covered, until sauce has thickened slightly, about 15 minutes.

2. Meanwhile, bring 4 quarts water to boil in large pot. Add pasta and 1 tablespoon salt and cook, stirring often, until al dente. Reserve 1 cup cooking water, then drain pasta and return it to pot.

3. Add sauce and ¼ cup reserved cooking water to pasta and toss to combine. Adjust consistency with remaining reserved cooking water as needed. Stir in basil and season with salt and pepper to taste. Serve.

MOUSSAKA

Serves 6 to 8 | ground lamb

WHY THIS RECIPE WORKS For a manageable recipe for Greek moussaka, we quickly determined that roasting presented a better option than frying, producing a less oily, slick casserole. We cut the eggplant into cubes rather than slices before roasting so that they would fit on two baking sheets and could be cooked all at once. To reduce greasiness and gamy lamb flavor (ground lamb is almost always fatty), we opted to drain off most of the fat after browning it when making our meat sauce. We then turned to the béchamel for our moussaka recipe, toying with butter, flour, and milk ratios until we made an extremely thick béchamel that sat on top of the casserole instead of running into the other layers. Myzithra cheese is added to the béchamel in traditional versions, but we found a good substitute in Parmesan. When buying eggplants, look for those that are glossy, feel firm, and are heavy for their size. Do not substitute low-fat or nonfat milk in the sauce.

   4 pounds eggplant, peeled and cut into ¾-inch cubes
   3 tablespoons olive oil
   2 teaspoons table salt, divided
   ¼ teaspoon pepper
   2 pounds ground lamb
   1 onion, chopped fine
   4 garlic cloves, minced
   ¾ teaspoon ground cinnamon
   2 tablespoons tomato paste
   1 (28-ounce) can tomato puree
   ½ cup dry red wine
   1 tablespoon minced fresh oregano or 1 teaspoon dried
   1 teaspoon sugar
   3 tablespoons unsalted butter
   ¼ cup all-purpose flour
   2 cups whole milk
   2 ounces Parmesan cheese, grated (1 cup)
     Pinch ground nutmeg

1. Adjust oven racks to upper-middle and lower-middle positions and heat oven to 450 degrees. Line 2 rimmed baking sheets with aluminum foil and spray with vegetable oil spray. Toss eggplant with oil, 1 teaspoon salt, and pepper. Spread eggplant evenly over prepared sheets and bake until light golden brown, 40 to 50 minutes, switching and rotating sheets halfway through roasting time. Set aside to cool.

2. Meanwhile, cook lamb in large Dutch oven over medium-high heat, breaking meat into small pieces with wooden spoon, until meat is no longer pink and fat has rendered, about 5 minutes. Drain lamb in fine-mesh strainer, reserving drippings.

3. Return 2 tablespoons of reserved lamb drippings to now-empty pot and set it over medium heat until shimmering. Add onion and remaining 1 teaspoon salt and cook until softened and lightly browned, 5 to 7 minutes. Stir in garlic and cinnamon and cook until fragrant, about 30 seconds. Stir in tomato paste and cook for 30 seconds. Stir in drained lamb, tomato puree, wine, oregano, and sugar. Bring to simmer, reduce heat to low, cover partially, and cook, stirring occasionally, until juices have evaporated and filling has thickened, 25 to 30 minutes. Season with salt and pepper to taste. Reduce oven to 400 degrees.

4. While lamb filling simmers, melt butter in medium saucepan over medium-high heat. Add flour and cook, stirring constantly, for 1 minute. Gradually whisk in milk. Bring to simmer and cook, whisking often, until béchamel thickens and no longer tastes of flour, about 5 minutes. Off heat, whisk in Parmesan and nutmeg and season with salt and pepper to taste; cover and set aside.

5. Spread roasted eggplant evenly into 13 by 9-inch baking dish. Spread lamb filling over eggplant, then pour béchamel evenly over top.

6. Bake until top of casserole is light golden brown, 25 to 35 minutes. Serve.

ARAYES

Serves 4 to 6 | ground lamb

WHY THIS RECIPE WORKS Seasoned with herbs and warm spices, pressed between pita rounds, and grilled, these Middle Eastern lamb sandwiches offer a flavorful alternative to the everyday burger on a bun. Along with traditional cumin, coriander, and onion, we added lemon zest to our meat mixture as well as cayenne for heat and paprika for its complementary pepper flavor. The grill made the pita really crisp, providing contrast to the texture of the filling. As the sandwiches cooked, the lamb released fat and juices into the bread to help it crisp up. To balance the sandwiches' richness, we serve them with a bright and cooling yogurt-tahini sauce. You can substitute 85 percent lean ground beef for the ground lamb, if desired. This recipe works best with ¼-inch-thick pitas that are fresh and pliable. To determine which side of the pita is thicker, look closely at the pattern of browning across its surface; the more fragile side is usually covered with char marks in a dotted-line pattern. Serve with a dressed green salad if desired.

SAUCE
- 1 cup plain Greek yogurt
- ½ cup minced fresh mint
- 2 tablespoons lemon juice
- 2 tablespoons tahini
- 2 tablespoons extra-virgin olive oil
- ½ teaspoon table salt

SANDWICHES
- 1 onion, cut into 1-inch pieces
- 1 cup fresh cilantro leaves
- ¼ cup extra-virgin olive oil
- 1 tablespoon grated lemon zest plus 3 tablespoons juice
- 1 tablespoon ground coriander
- 1 tablespoon ground cumin
- 1 tablespoon paprika
- 2 teaspoons table salt
- 1½ teaspoons pepper
- ½ teaspoon cayenne pepper
- ¼ teaspoon ground cinnamon
- 2 pounds ground lamb
- 4 (8-inch) pita breads

1. For the sauce: Whisk all ingredients together in bowl. Set aside.

2. For the sandwiches: Pulse onion and cilantro in food processor until finely chopped, 10 to 12 pulses, scraping down sides of bowl as needed. Transfer mixture to large bowl. Stir in oil, lemon zest and juice, coriander, cumin, paprika, salt, pepper, cayenne, and cinnamon. Add lamb and gently knead with your hands until thoroughly combined.

3. Using kitchen shears, cut around circumference of each pita and separate into 2 halves. Place 4 thicker halves on counter, interior side up. Divide lamb mixture into 4 equal portions and place 1 portion in center of each pita half. Using spatula, gently spread lamb mixture into even layer, leaving ½-inch border around edge. Top each lamb portion with 1 thinner pita half. Press each sandwich firmly until lamb mixture spreads to ¼ inch from edge of pita. Transfer sandwiches to large plate, cover with plastic wrap, and set aside. (Sandwiches can be left at room temperature for up to 1 hour before grilling.)

4a. For a charcoal grill: Open bottom vent completely. Light large chimney starter two-thirds filled with charcoal briquettes (4 quarts). When top coals are partially covered with ash, pour evenly over grill. Set cooking grate in place, cover, and open lid vent completely. Heat grill until hot, about 5 minutes.

4b. For a gas grill: Turn all burners to high, cover, and heat grill until hot, about 15 minutes. Turn all burners to medium-high.

Spicy Lamb with Lentils and Yogurt

1 pound ground lamb
¾ teaspoon table salt, divided, plus salt for cooking lentils
¼ teaspoon baking soda
1 cup lentilles du Puy, picked over and rinsed
3 garlic cloves, minced
1 tablespoon tomato paste
2 teaspoons garam masala
1 teaspoon red pepper flakes
1 teaspoon grated fresh ginger
1 tablespoon vegetable oil
1 onion, chopped
2 naan breads
2 tomatoes, cored and cut into ½-inch pieces
¾ cup chopped fresh cilantro, divided
¾ cup plain Greek yogurt

1. Toss lamb with 2 tablespoons water, ½ teaspoon salt, and baking soda in bowl until thoroughly combined; set aside for 20 minutes.

2. While lamb sits, bring lentils, 4 cups water, and 1 teaspoon salt to boil in medium saucepan over high heat. Reduce heat to low and simmer until lentils are just tender, 18 to 22 minutes. Drain well.

3. Adjust oven rack to middle position and heat oven to 400 degrees. Combine garlic, tomato paste, garam masala, pepper flakes, and ginger in small bowl. Heat oil in 12-inch skillet over medium heat until shimmering. Add onion and remaining ¼ teaspoon salt and cook until softened and lightly browned, 5 to 7 minutes. Stir in garlic mixture and cook, stirring constantly until bottom of skillet is dark brown, 1 to 2 minutes.

4. Add 1 cup water and bring to boil, scraping up any browned bits. Reduce heat to medium-low, add lamb in 2-inch chunks to skillet, and bring to gentle simmer. Cover and cook until lamb is cooked through, 10 to 12 minutes, stirring and breaking up lamb chunks with 2 forks halfway through cooking. Uncover skillet, increase heat to medium, stir in drained lentils, and cook until liquid is mostly absorbed, 3 to 5 minutes.

5. While lamb cooks, place naan on rimmed baking sheet and bake until warmed through, about 5 minutes.

6. Off heat, stir tomatoes, ½ cup cilantro, and 2 tablespoons yogurt into lentils and season with salt and pepper to taste. Sprinkle with remaining ¼ cup cilantro. Serve with naan and remaining yogurt.

5. Clean and oil cooking grate. Place sandwiches on grill, cover, and cook until bottoms are evenly browned and edges are starting to crisp, 7 to 10 minutes, moving sandwiches as needed to ensure even cooking. Flip sandwiches, cover grill, and continue to cook until second sides are evenly browned and edges are crispy, 7 to 10 minutes longer. Transfer sandwiches to cutting board and cut each in half crosswise. Transfer sandwiches to platter and serve, passing sauce separately.

SPICY LAMB WITH LENTILS AND YOGURT

Serves 4 | ground lamb

WHY THIS RECIPE WORKS This skillet recipe combines earthy lentils with warm-spiced ground lamb for a hearty but not fussy meal. Cilantro and tomatoes added freshness, while Greek yogurt stirred in at the end brought the dish together. We created a full-flavored fond by sautéing our aromatics and then deglazing the pan to dissolve all that complex flavor into the dish. Garam masala and red pepper flakes added the punch of warm-spiced flavor we were looking for in the lamb. Adding a tiny amount of baking soda helped tenderize the ground lamb by raising its pH. Note that you will need ¾ cup of cilantro, so shop accordingly. We prefer how small green lentilles du Puy, or French green lentils, hold their shape in this recipe; we do not recommend substituting other types of lentils here.

LAMB KOFTE

Serves 4 to 6 | ground lamb

WHY THIS RECIPE WORKS In the Middle East, kebabs called kofte feature ground meat mixed with lots of spices and fresh herbs that is formed around metal skewers and quickly grilled. We like them dressed with a za'atar yogurt sauce; the kebabs' spices and deep savor are complemented by welcome herbal freshness and tang from the za'atar while the creaminess from the also-tart yogurt cuts through the richness. For the kofte, the biggest challenge was getting the patties' sausage-like texture right. We found that adding a small amount of powdered gelatin to the ground lamb helped the meat firm up and hold fast to the skewer. Ground pine nuts added to the meat prevented toughness and contributed their own pleasant texture and a boost in richness. A concentrated charcoal fire setup mimicked the intense heat of a kofte grill. Serve with rice pilaf, or make sandwiches with warm pita bread, sliced red onion, tomatoes, and fresh mint; just make sure to drizzle with the spiced sauce. You will need eight 12-inch metal skewers for this recipe.

- ½ cup pine nuts
- 4 garlic cloves, peeled
- 1½ teaspoons smoked hot paprika
- 1 teaspoon table salt
- 1 teaspoon ground cumin
- ½ teaspoon pepper
- ¼ teaspoon ground coriander
- ¼ teaspoon ground cloves
- ⅛ teaspoon ground nutmeg
- ⅛ teaspoon ground cinnamon
- 1½ pounds ground lamb
- ½ cup grated onion, drained
- ⅓ cup minced fresh parsley
- ⅓ cup minced fresh mint
- 1½ teaspoons unflavored gelatin
- 1 (13 by 9-inch) disposable aluminum roasting pan (if using charcoal)
- 1 cup Za'atar Yogurt Sauce (page 22)

1. Process pine nuts, garlic, paprika, salt, cumin, pepper, coriander, cloves, nutmeg, and cinnamon in food processor until coarse paste forms, 30 to 45 seconds. Transfer mixture to large bowl. Add lamb, onion, parsley, mint, and gelatin and knead with your hands until thoroughly combined and mixture feels slightly sticky, about 2 minutes. Divide mixture into 8 equal portions. Shape each portion into 5-inch-long cylinder about 1 inch in diameter. Using eight 12-inch metal skewers, thread 1 cylinder onto each skewer, pressing gently to adhere. Transfer kebabs to lightly greased baking sheet, cover with plastic wrap, and refrigerate for at least 1 hour or up to 24 hours.

2a. For a charcoal grill: Using skewer, poke 12 holes in bottom of disposable pan. Open bottom vent completely and place pan in center of grill. Light large chimney starter two-thirds filled with charcoal briquettes (4 quarts). When top coals are partially covered with ash, pour into disposable pan. Set cooking grate in place, cover, and open lid vent completely. Heat grill until hot, about 5 minutes.

2b. For a gas grill: Turn all burners to high, cover, and heat grill until hot, about 15 minutes. Leave all burners on high.

3. Clean and oil cooking grate. Place kebabs on grill (directly over coals if using charcoal) at 45-degree angle to bars. Cook (covered if using gas) until browned and meat easily releases from grill, 4 to 7 minutes. Flip kebabs and continue to cook until meat is browned on second side and registers 160 degrees, about 6 minutes. Transfer kebabs to serving platter and serve, passing yogurt sauce separately.

STUFFED ZUCCHINI

Serves 4 | ground lamb

WHY THIS RECIPE WORKS For perfectly baked zucchini, we scooped out the seeds to reduce moisture, roasted the unstuffed zucchini cut side down to achieve a flavorful sear, and returned the zucchini to the hot oven—packed with our robust filling—for a final burst of heat before serving. For a rich, gently-spiced stuffing, we paired ground lamb with a trio of elements popular in Moroccan cuisine: sweet dried apricots; buttery pine nuts; and aromatic ras el hanout, a North African spice blend that includes coriander, cardamom, cinnamon, and more. After browning the lamb, we poured off all but a small amount of the fat to keep our filling from tasting too greasy; to offset the filling's meaty texture and add a mild, wheaty chew, we incorporated a small amount of bulgur. It's important to use smaller, in-season zucchini, which have thinner skins and fewer seeds. You can find ras el hanout in the spice aisle of most well-stocked supermarkets.

- 4 zucchini (8 ounces each), trimmed, halved lengthwise, and seeded
- 2 tablespoons plus 1 teaspoon extra-virgin olive oil, divided
- 8 ounces ground lamb
- ½ teaspoon table salt
- ¼ teaspoon pepper
- 1 onion, chopped fine
- 4 garlic cloves, minced
- 2 teaspoons ras el hanout
- ⅔ cup chicken broth
- ½ cup medium-grind bulgur, rinsed
- ¼ cup dried apricots, chopped fine
- 2 tablespoons pine nuts, toasted
- 2 tablespoons minced fresh parsley

Lamb Kofte

Potato, Swiss Chard, and Lamb
Hash with Poached Eggs

1. Adjust oven racks to upper-middle and lowest positions, place rimmed baking sheet on lower rack, and heat oven to 400 degrees. Brush cut sides of zucchini with 2 tablespoons oil and season with salt and pepper. Lay zucchini cut side down in hot sheet and roast until slightly softened and skins are wrinkled, 8 to 10 minutes. Remove zucchini from oven and flip cut side up on sheet; set aside.

2. Meanwhile, heat remaining 1 teaspoon oil in large saucepan over medium-high heat until just smoking. Add lamb, salt, and pepper and cook, breaking up meat with wooden spoon, until browned, 3 to 5 minutes. Using slotted spoon, transfer lamb to paper towel–lined plate.

3. Pour off all but 1 tablespoon fat from saucepan. Add onion to fat left in saucepan and cook over medium heat until softened, about 5 minutes. Stir in garlic and ras el hanout and cook until fragrant, about 30 seconds. Stir in broth, bulgur, and apricots and bring to simmer. Reduce heat to low, cover, and simmer gently until bulgur is tender, 16 to 18 minutes.

4. Off heat, lay clean dish towel underneath lid and let pilaf sit for 10 minutes. Add pine nuts and parsley to pilaf and gently fluff with fork to combine. Season with salt and pepper to taste.

5. Pack each zucchini half with bulgur mixture, about ½ cup per zucchini half, mounding excess. Place baking sheet on upper rack and bake zucchini until heated through, about 6 minutes. Serve.

POTATO, SWISS CHARD, AND LAMB HASH WITH POACHED EGGS

Serves 4 | ground lamb

WHY THIS RECIPE WORKS We set out to create a simple breakfast hash with bold flavors and ground lamb, which you don't often see at breakfast. We decided on russet potatoes as our base for their fluffy interiors and crisp exteriors. The deeply savory ground lamb provided richness; warm spices such as cumin, coriander, and paprika offered balanced flavor. Tasters liked the addition of slightly bitter, vegetal Swiss chard; we started cooking the stems before adding the leaves so that the stems would fully soften by the time the leaves were wilted. Because we were combining ingredients that cook at different rates, we cooked each element separately before mixing them together. Once we added the mixture to the skillet, we packed it down to ensure good contact with the hot pan, which encouraged deep browning. Flipping the hash in portions was easier than flipping the whole thing at once. Finally, we cooked the eggs right in the hash, in indentations that we made with

a spoon. You will need a 12-inch nonstick skillet with a tight-fitting lid for this recipe. If the potatoes aren't getting brown in step 4, turn up the heat.

1½ pounds russet potatoes, peeled and cut into ½-inch pieces
2 tablespoons extra-virgin olive oil, divided
¾ teaspoon table salt, divided
¼ teaspoon pepper
1½ pounds Swiss chard, stems sliced ¼ inch thick, leaves sliced into ½-inch-wide strips
8 ounces ground lamb
1 onion, chopped fine
3 garlic cloves, minced
2 teaspoons paprika
1 teaspoon ground cumin
1 teaspoon ground coriander
¼ teaspoon cayenne pepper
4 large eggs
1 tablespoon minced fresh chives

1. Toss potatoes with 1 tablespoon oil, ½ teaspoon salt, and pepper in bowl. Cover and microwave until potatoes are translucent around edges, 7 to 9 minutes, stirring halfway through microwaving; drain well.

2. Heat remaining 1 tablespoon oil in 12-inch nonstick skillet over medium-high heat until shimmering. Add chard stems and remaining ¼ teaspoon salt and cook until softened and lightly browned, 5 to 7 minutes. Stir in chard leaves, 1 handful at a time, and cook until mostly wilted, about 4 minutes; transfer to bowl with potatoes.

3. Cook lamb in now-empty skillet over medium-high heat, breaking up meat with wooden spoon, until beginning to brown, about 5 minutes. Stir in onion and cook until softened and lightly browned, 5 to 7 minutes. Stir in garlic, paprika, cumin, coriander, and cayenne and cook until fragrant, about 30 seconds.

4. Stir in chard-potato mixture. Using back of spatula, gently pack chard-potato mixture into skillet and cook, without stirring, for 2 minutes. Flip hash, 1 portion at a time, and lightly repack into skillet. Repeat flipping process every few minutes until potatoes are well browned, 6 to 8 minutes.

5. Off heat, make 4 shallow indentations (about 2 inches wide) in hash using back of spoon, pushing hash up into center and around edges of skillet (bottom of skillet should be exposed in each indentation). Crack 1 egg into each indentation and season with salt and pepper. Cover and cook over medium-low heat until whites are just set and yolks are still runny, 4 to 5 minutes. Sprinkle with chives and serve immediately.

nutritional information
FOR OUR RECIPES

We calculate the nutritional values of our recipes per serving; if there is a range in the serving size, we used the highest number of servings to calculate the nutritional values. We entered all the ingredients, using weights for important ingredients such as most vegetables. We also used our preferred brands in these analyses. We did not include additional salt or pepper for food that's "seasoned to taste."

	Cal	Total Fat (g)	Sat Fat (g)	Chol (mg)	Sodium (mg)	Total Carb (g)	Dietary Fiber (g)	Total Sugars (g)	Protein (g)
BEEF - CHUCK									
Classic Pot Roast	330	14	4	130	580	4	0	2	44
Pot Roast with Root Vegetables	460	14	4	130	650	33	6	9	47
Bresato al Barolo	550	19	7	185	590	6	0	2	63
Pot-au-Feu	400	14	4	130	810	18	4	5	49
Chuck Roast in Foil	540	16	6	195	1360	27	4	6	70
Roasted Beef Chuck with Horseradish-Parsley Sauce	590	46	14	140	920	2	1	1	41
Best Beef Stew	570	21	6	160	530	24	2	5	56
Boeuf Bourguignon	610	24	10	175	1080	19	2	7	58
Rigatoni alla Genovese	440	9	3.5	55	530	58	3	9	25
Carne Guisada	530	16	5	90	1210	53	2	5	39
Slow-Cooker Pot Roast with Tomatoes and Red Wine	500	24	8	160	860	13	3	7	55
Pressure-Cooker Beef Stew with Tomatoes, Olives, and Orange Zest	360	11	3	100	1360	24	3	5	38
Sous Vide Pepper–Crusted Beef Roast	290	12	3.5	125	1110	2	1	0	42
Barbecue Chuck Roast	320	11	4.5	145	670	0	0	0	50
Shredded Barbecue Beef	410	12	4.5	150	1050	24	0	20	50
Grilled Chuck Steaks	540	24	7	220	1110	2	0	1	75
Ultimate Beef Chili	530	19	6	135	940	36	11	6	50
Braised Steaks with Root Vegetables	400	14	5	115	310	27	6	7	38
Braised Steaks with Mushrooms and Tomatoes	370	14	5	115	440	19	4	6	39
Pressure-Cooker Beef and Barley Soup	190	6	1.5	40	920	17	3	3	17
Thai Beef with Chiles and Shallots	540	31	8	155	830	15	2	7	52
Chipotle Beef Tamales	560	32	12	100	910	44	5	4	27
Smoked Herb-Rubbed Flat-Iron Steaks	240	14	5	85	660	1	0	0	25
BEEF - RIB									
Best Roast Prime Rib	710	58	23	160	350	0	0	0	44
Boneless Rib Roast with Yorkshire Pudding and Jus	740	50	20	200	480	23	0	4	44
One-Pan Roasted Prime Rib and Vegetables	810	60	24	160	640	17	4	7	46

	Cal	Total Fat (g)	Sat Fat (g)	Chol (mg)	Sodium (mg)	Total Carb (g)	Dietary Fiber (g)	Total Sugars (g)	Protein (g)
BEEF - RIB *(cont.)*									
Grill-Smoked Prime Rib	710	59	23	160	260	0	0	0	44
Sous Vide Prime Rib	760	62	24	170	300	0	0	0	46
Butter-Basted Rib Steak	700	61	26	155	690	1	0	0	36
Grilled Cowboy-Cut Steaks	410	26	10	130	170	0	0	0	39
Bulgogi	530	33	10	65	1910	36	3	27	27
Spice-Rubbed Rib Eyes	390	26	9	120	170	1	0	0	37
Grilled Bourbon Steaks	540	41	15	110	330	2	0	1	36
Hibachi-Style Steaks and Vegetables	670	50	20	130	1570	14	3	8	40
Simple Hibachi-Style Fried Rice	370	11	3.5	145	640	56	0	3	10
Yum-Yum Sauce	210	23	5	15	520	1	0	1	1
White Mustard Sauce	140	13	7	35	590	3	0	2	2
Sweet Ginger Sauce	50	0	0	0	870	12	0	11	1
BEEF - SHORT LOIN									
Holiday Strip Roast	480	29	9	160	850	3	1	0	52
Thick-Cut Strip Steaks	340	15	4.5	120	420	0	0	0	52
Red Wine–Mushroom Pan Sauce	150	9	4	15	110	6	0	3	1
Sun-Dried Tomato Relish	15	0.5	0	0	130	3	0	2	0
Tequila-Poblano Pan Sauce	150	8	5	25	75	2	1	1	0
Quick Pan-Seared Strip Steaks	310	12	4.5	120	130	0	0	0	52
Cast Iron Steaks with Herb Butter	480	30	12	150	420	1	0	0	52
Cast Iron Steaks with Blue Cheese–Chive Butter	490	30	12	150	610	0	0	0	54
Garlic Steaks	550	37	13	150	550	2	0	0	52
One-Pan Steak with Sweet Potatoes and Scallions	570	19	5	120	2040	45	8	18	56
Steak Frites	720	30	12	150	430	52	0	1	59
Grilled Frozen Steaks with Arugula and Parmesan	580	37	9	130	1120	3	1	1	60
Grilled Argentine Steaks with Chimichurri Sauce	450	26	6	120	860	3	1	0	53
Ultimate Charcoal-Grilled Steaks	310	12	4.5	120	690	0	0	0	52
Sous Vide Seared Steaks	310	12	4.5	120	420	0	0	0	52
Red Wine–Peppercorn Pan Sauce	150	12	6	25	115	6	0	3	1
Pressure-Cooker Beef Pho	360	5	1.5	40	710	54	0	1	25
Thick-Cut Porterhouse Steaks	330	19	6	135	240	0	0	0	38
Grilled Thick-Cut Porterhouse Steaks	390	26	9	145	700	0	0	0	38
Bistecca alla Fiorentina	390	26	9	145	660	0	0	0	38
Grilled Steaks with Garlic Essence	390	26	9	145	660	0	0	0	38
BEEF - TENDERLOIN									
Peppercorn-Crusted Beef Tenderloin	790	37	12	296	590	9	3	1	102
Green Peppercorn–Crusted Beef Tenderloin	770	37	12	295	790	2	1	1	101
Pink Peppercorn–Crusted Beef Tenderloin	770	37	12	295	590	4	1	1	101
White Peppercorn–Crusted Beef Tenderloin	780	37	12	295	580	5	1	1	101
Roast Beef Tenderloin	530	35	16	190	550	1	0	0	50
Horseradish-Crusted Beef Tenderloin	470	31	9	120	930	11	1	3	35
Roast Beef Tenderloin with Mushroom and Caramelized Onion Stuffing	560	33	13	170	420	6	1	3	51
Beef Wellington	660	40	11	205	750	25	0	2	47
Duxelles	35	3	1.5	10	150	2	0	1	1

	Cal	Total Fat (g)	Sat Fat (g)	Chol (mg)	Sodium (mg)	Total Carb (g)	Dietary Fiber (g)	Total Sugars (g)	Protein (g)
BEEF - TENDERLOIN (*cont.*)									
Grill-Roasted Beef Tenderloin	420	21	7	160	680	1	0	0	53
Filets Mignons with Sage-Buttered Mushrooms and Black Pepper Polenta	870	55	26	250	370	29	0	2	63
Pepper-Crusted Filets Mignons	740	54	16	190	390	7	3	0	54
Blue Cheese–Chive Butter	110	11	7	30	190	0	0	0	2
Port-Cherry Reduction	260	3	2	10	15	31	0	20	1
Bacon-Wrapped Filets Mignons	500	28	9	170	700	1	0	0	57
Grilled Filets Mignons	460	22	8	185	115	0	0	0	61
BEEF - SIRLOIN									
Coffee-Chipotle Top Sirloin Roast	320	12	3.5	145	860	2	1	0	50
Rosemary-Garlic Top Sirloin Roast	310	12	3	145	860	1	0	0	49
Beef en Cocotte with Caramelized Onions	300	14	3.5	110	220	5	1	2	37
Beef en Cocotte with Creamy Mushroom Barley	560	19	4	145	460	38	7	2	57
Baltimore Pit Beef	480	19	4	120	960	34	1	3	45
Pan-Seared Inexpensive Steaks	280	10	4	120	380	0	0	0	44
Pan-Seared Inexpensive Steaks with Mustard-Cream Pan Sauce	410	22	9	145	730	2	0	1	45
Pan-Seared Inexpensive Steaks with Tomato-Caper Pan Sauce	340	14	4	120	630	4	1	2	45
Steak Marsala	350	20	8	80	340	10	1	4	24
Steak and Potato Salad	370	16	3	60	380	30	2	10	26
Grilled Steak with New Mexican Chile Rub	240	8	3	90	350	5	1	2	34
Barbecue Tri-Tip	320	19	0	105	590	1	0	0	33
Santa Maria Salsa	30	0	0	0	590	6	2	4	1
Sirloin Steak with Couscous Salad	590	32	7	95	1240	24	3	4	49
Mongolian Beef	470	8	1.5	55	1000	65	1	24	30
Steak Tips with Mushroom-Onion Gravy	220	8	1.5	55	560	6	1	3	28
Sirloin Steak Tips with Charro Beans	600	15	3	115	1840	46	13	2	66
Beef Shashlik	220	7	2	80	280	3	0	2	34
Grilled Beef Teriyaki	500	6	2.5	115	1670	37	0	35	53
Juicy Pub-Style Burgers	830	50	14	160	1130	25	2	8	57
Juicy Pub-Style Burgers with Crispy Shallots and Blue Cheese	980	62	21	185	1520	30	3	10	65
Juicy Pub-Style Burgers with Peppered Bacon and Aged Cheddar	1120	76	26	220	1590	28	3	8	70
Juicy Pub-Style Burgers with Pan-Roasted Mushrooms and Gruyère	1030	66	20	190	1480	30	3	10	68
BEEF - ROUND									
Grilled London Broil	410	23	8	100	2490	8	0	5	40
Bottom Round Roast Beef with Zip-Style Sauce	650	34	14	245	480	4	0	2	76
Slow-Roast Beef	340	11	3	150	290	0	0	0	58
Smoked Roast Beef	300	8	2.5	135	470	2	0	1	51
Beef on Weck Sandwiches	370	11	2	70	880	33	1	3	33
Slow-Cooker Roast Beef with Warm Garden Potato Salad	420	15	3.5	105	330	22	2	3	45
BEEF - BRISKET									
Brisket Carbonnade	870	53	20	280	370	12	1	5	78
Braised Brisket with Pomegranate, Cumin, and Cilantro	870	52	21	275	560	20	2	12	77
Brisket with Pasilla Chile Sauce	860	52	20	280	960	15	3	5	79
Slow-Cooker Barbecue Brisket	620	36	14	200	370	14	1	11	55

	Cal	Total Fat (g)	Sat Fat (g)	Chol (mg)	Sodium (mg)	Total Carb (g)	Dietary Fiber (g)	Total Sugars (g)	Protein (g)
BEEF - BRISKET *(cont.)*									
Ropa Vieja	470	32	9	120	460	9	2	4	34
Russian Beef and Cabbage Soup	310	19	6	80	840	8	3	4	26
Home-Corned Beef and Vegetables	680	38	15	215	280	20	4	6	62
Barbecue Burnt Ends	750	42	17	240	620	25	0	22	66
Texas Barbecue Brisket	900	60	23	285	420	0	0	0	83
BEEF - PLATE									
Pan-Seared Skirt Steak with Zucchini and Scallion Sauce	740	63	14	125	490	7	2	3	37
Bun Bo Xao	560	24	6	85	840	58	2	6	30
Steak Taco Salad	610	39	13	110	1540	30	8	6	38
Philly Cheesesteaks	1130	58	22	215	1890	77	0	7	72
Cornish Pasties	870	50	28	205	1660	71	2	4	31
Grilled Mojo-Marinated Skirt Steak	370	26	8	115	880	4	0	2	32
Grilled Steak Fajitas	600	32	10	115	870	39	2	7	38
Grilled Steak Sandwiches	970	69	16	115	1190	24	1	3	36
Texas Smoked Beef Ribs	1040	82	33	245	2710	4	1	0	67
BEEF - FLANK									
Pan-Seared Flank Steak with Mustard-Chive Butter	320	20	8	105	200	1	0	1	32
Pan-Seared Flank Steak with Garlic-Anchovy Butter	320	20	8	105	180	1	0	1	32
Pan-Seared Flank Steak with Sriracha-Lime Butter	320	20	8	105	210	1	0	1	32
Steak Tacos	690	37	7	135	105	36	1	1	51
Braciole	480	23	7	100	740	31	1	19	38
Arrachera en Adobo	860	35	12	180	1780	67	3	18	70
Beef Stir-Fry with Bell Peppers and Black Pepper Sauce	350	22	4.5	70	1130	12	2	6	24
Yakisoba with Beef, Shiitakes, and Cabbage	280	9	2	60	1070	30	2	26	18
Sesame-Orange Spice Blend	29	2	0	0	2	3	1	0	1
Flank Steak with Red Curry Potatoes	600	34	16	95	780	37	0	1	35
Nam Tok	220	9	3.5	70	290	10	2	3	25
Negimaki	230	8	3	75	980	8	1	6	27
Grilled Beef Satay	430	25	10	90	720	18	0	11	34
Peanut Sauce	230	20	9	0	360	9	1	4	6
BEEF - SHORT RIBS									
Red Wine–Braised Short Ribs with Bacon, Parsnips, and Pearl Onions	630	31	12	130	1310	23	4	7	42
Pomegranate-Braised Beef Short Ribs with Prunes and Sesame	340	19	6	75	390	15	3	7	25
Braised Boneless Beef Short Ribs	580	32	12	155	650	4	0	1	51
Braised Boneless Beef Short Ribs with Guinness and Prunes	550	32	12	155	650	9	1	3	52
Panang Beef Curry	500	38	20	90	450	7	1	2	33
Beef Short Rib Ragu	340	18	7	90	750	7	1	3	32
Sous Vide Short Rib "Pot Roast"	830	48	18	235	80	0	1	3	77
Pressure-Cooker Tamarind Braised Beef Short Ribs	610	32	12	165	650	14	0	11	55
Pub-Style Steak and Ale Pie	720	40	20	210	850	31	1	2	52
Carne Deshebrada	580	24	9	110	1020	47	5	9	41
Cabbage-Carrot Slaw	30	0	0	0	170	7	2	4	1
Kalbi	290	17	7	90	410	3	0	2	30

	Cal	Total Fat (g)	Sat Fat (g)	Chol (mg)	Sodium (mg)	Total Carb (g)	Dietary Fiber (g)	Total Sugars (g)	Protein (g)
BEEF - SHORT RIBS *(cont.)*									
Grill-Roasted Beef Short Ribs with Mustard Glaze	350	16	7	90	1700	13	1	11	30
Grill-Roasted Beef Short Ribs with Blackberry Glaze	380	16	7	90	1670	20	3	14	31
Grill-Roasted Beef Short Ribs with Hoisin-Tamarind Glaze	370	16	7	90	1460	24	1	8	30
Grilled Boneless Short Ribs with Argentine Pepper Sauce	420	29	10	110	780	3	1	1	36
BEEF - SHANKS AND OXTAILS									
Etli Kuru Fasulye	510	27	10	170	870	16	4	5	52
Alcatra	520	21	8	155	600	5	1	1	63
Rich Beef Stock	20	0	0	0	276	0	0	0	4
Beef Barley Soup with Mushrooms and Thyme	190	6	1	30	560	15	3	3	17
Hearty Beef Shank and Vegetable Soup	570	18	5	170	1060	20	1	2	77
VEAL									
Italian Veal Stew	320	13	2.5	115	580	13	2	5	32
Blanquette de Veau	430	22	12	155	390	18	4	8	34
Pan-Seared Veal Chops	180	8	2	115	350	0	0	0	27
Pan-Seared Veal Chops with Spinach and Gremolata	270	11	2.5	115	500	8	5	0	32
Grilled Veal Rib Chops	160	5	1.5	115	320	0	0	0	27
Grilled Veal Chops with Herb Paste	300	19	3.5	115	320	1	0	0	27
Porcini-Rubbed Grilled Rib Veal Chops	370	26	4.5	115	710	2	1	0	28
Veal Scaloppini with Lemon-Parsley Sauce	505	31	9	155	172	19	1	3	38
Veal Scaloppini with Porcini-Marsala Sauce	550	31	9	135	175	23	2	6	38
Cotoletta alla Valdostana	440	31	18	185	470	9	0	1	30
Osso Buco	440	18	3	120	560	13	2	5	40
Sous Vide Osso Buco	400	17	2	105	910	16	2	7	35
Pressure-Cooker Veal Shanks with Sweet and Spicy Pepperonata	340	13	2.5	120	930	15	2	11	40
PORK - BLADE SHOULDER									
Slow-Roasted Pork Shoulder with Peach Sauce	630	32	11	160	2450	27	1	25	45
Slow-Roasted Pork Shoulder with Cherry Sauce	670	32	11	160	2400	36	1	33	45
Cider-Braised Pork Roast	630	37	12	160	600	27	1	22	46
Chinese Barbecue Roast Pork Shoulder	630	32	10	145	1710	40	0	35	44
Slow-Cooker Southwestern Pork Roast	360	23	8	105	500	5	1	2	31
Carnitas	320	11	3	65	140	32	0	4	23
Porchetta	330	21	5	95	600	3	1	0	30
South Carolina Pulled Pork	310	11	3.5	100	2320	19	1	17	32
Indoor Pulled Pork with Sweet and Tangy Barbecue Sauce	390	10	3.5	100	970	43	1	38	31
Indoor Pulled Pork with Lexington Vinegar Sauce	250	9	3.5	100	560	7	0	6	31
Pork Gyro	620	34	9	85	1190	40	2	3	37
Homemade Sausages and Peppers	660	56	20	125	1890	9	2	5	29
Ragù Bianco	480	18	8	110	1140	48	2	4	29
French Pork and White Bean Casserole	650	38	12	85	1350	43	17	5	29
Feijoada	630	28	9	130	1200	42	2	8	49
Chile Verde con Cerdo	240	10	3	80	670	11	3	7	26
Pressure-Cooker Shredded Pork Tacos	350	10	2.5	80	390	37	1	8	28
Sous Vide Char Siu	390	10	2.5	65	1850	51	0	45	24
Red Wine–Braised Pork Chops	550	23	9	170	620	11	1	5	58
Filipino Pork Adobo	570	34	19	155	920	6	0	0	59

	Cal	Total Fat (g)	Sat Fat (g)	Chol (mg)	Sodium (mg)	Total Carb (g)	Dietary Fiber (g)	Total Sugars (g)	Protein (g)
PORK - BLADE SHOULDER *(cont.)*									
Slow-Cooker Braised Pork Chops with Campfire Beans	520	16	4.5	115	760	39	8	9	52
Grilled Lemongrass Pork Chops	660	23	7	200	1620	32	0	24	76
Nuoc Cham	70	0	0	0	860	15	0	10	3
PORK - ARM SHOULDER									
Pork Pernil	350	19	6	130	1490	4	1	1	39
Glazed Picnic Ham (Smoked Shoulder)	420	16	5	125	3240	19	0	18	46
Cuban-Style Grill-Roasted Pork	380	17	5	130	1110	16	1	9	40
Mojo Sauce	70	7	1	0	140	1	0	0	0
PORK - LOIN									
Barbecue Glazed Pork Roast	540	23	4.5	115	1370	41	0	35	41
Grill-Roasted Pork Loin	310	19	6	105	560	2	0	0	34
Smoked Pork Loin with Dried-Fruit Chutney	600	22	8	155	2960	45	0	37	48
Posole	430	18	4	110	1550	28	5	6	36
Slow-Cooker Sunday Gravy	330	15	5	95	780	16	3	7	36
Sweet and Tangy Grilled Country-Style Pork Ribs	600	22	6	225	1430	32	1	27	63
Slow-Cooker Spicy Pork Chili with Black-Eyed Peas	410	9	2.5	85	1150	47	10	9	34
Braised Ribs with Black-Eyed Peas and Collard Greens	460	13	4	95	580	44	2	10	38
Fried Brown Rice with Pork and Shrimp	410	13	2.5	165	1330	55	5	4	23
Pinchos Morunos	460	27	6	170	880	3	1	0	48
Vietnamese Summer Rolls	550	17	3.5	90	870	69	3	8	32
Shu Mai	230	4.5	1	60	640	29	0	2	17
Pork Lo Mein	450	17	3	105	1460	36	5	23	34
Slow-Cooker Pork Pad Thai	450	17	4	85	610	45	1	11	29
Slow-Roasted Bone-In Pork Rib Roast	360	21	4.5	110	530	4	0	3	38
Grill-Roasted Bone-In Pork Rib Roast	350	21	4.5	110	660	0	0	0	38
Crown Roast of Pork	670	40	18	180	1840	22	3	7	58
Indoor Barbecue Pork Chops	310	15	7	85	850	16	0	12	25
Pan-Seared Thick-Cut Pork Chops	310	13	3.5	115	680	0	0	0	44
Pan-Seared Thick-Cut Pork Chops with Cilantro and Coconut Pan Sauce	430	25	13	120	720	5	0	2	46
Pan-Seared Thick-Cut Pork Chops with Garlic and Thyme Pan Sauce	420	22	9	135	790	3	0	1	45
Sous Vide Thick-Cut Pork Chops	460	31	5	115	120	0	0	0	44
Texas Thick-Cut Smoked Pork Chops	360	10	3.5	145	2290	14	1	9	49
Grilled Thin-Cut Pork Chops	140	10	5	50	330	1	0	1	11
Ginger Grilled Thin-Cut Pork Chops	140	10	5	50	320	1	0	1	11
Olive Tapenade Grilled Thin-Cut Pork Chops	140	10	5	50	340	1	0	1	11
Spicy Grilled Thin-Cut Pork Chops	140	10	5	50	360	1	0	1	11
Roast Pork Loin with Sweet Potatoes and Cilantro Sauce	600	31	5	95	210	42	8	13	38
Herb-Crusted Pork Loin	340	18	4	100	280	5	0	1	37
Herb-Crusted Pork Roast with Mustard and Caraway	290	13	3	95	280	5	1	1	35
Enchaud Perigordine	330	15	4.5	105	660	10	2	5	36
Slow-Cooker Pork Loin with Warm Spiced Chickpea Salad	340	11	2.5	85	440	23	6	6	36
Pressure-Cooker Pork Loin with Black Mole Sauce	350	13	2.5	95	660	20	3	14	37

	Cal	Total Fat (g)	Sat Fat (g)	Chol (mg)	Sodium (mg)	Total Carb (g)	Dietary Fiber (g)	Total Sugars (g)	Protein (g)
PORK - LOIN *(cont.)*									
Mustardy Apple Butter–Glazed Pork Chops	240	5	1.5	95	520	13	0	11	32
Spicy Gochujang-Glazed Pork Chops	220	5	1.5	95	850	9	0	6	33
Crispy Pan-Fried Pork Chops	410	19	3	95	680	21	1	5	34
Crispy Pan-Fried Pork Chops with Spicy Rub	410	19	3	95	680	21	1	5	34
Crispy Pan-Fried Pork Chops with Three-Pepper Rub	410	19	3	95	680	21	1	5	34
Deviled Pork Chops	300	11	5	110	760	11	0	3	33
Pan-Seared Thick-Cut Boneless Pork Chops with Peaches and Spinach	460	20	3.5	145	610	14	4	8	54
Pepper-Crusted Pork Tenderloin with Asparagus and Balsamic Pan Sauce	400	19	7	125	910	15	5	9	42
Broiled Pork Tenderloin	170	4	1	95	500	0	0	0	30
Sesame-Crusted Pork Tenderloin with Celery Salad	630	40	10	155	880	12	4	6	54
Pork Schnitzel	420	11	2	180	410	40	0	4	37
Pork Medallions with Red Pepper Sauce	370	22	3.5	105	550	6	1	4	36
Grilled Pork Tenderloin with Grilled Pineapple–Red Onion Salsa	200	6	1	70	340	13	2	9	23
Perfect Pan-Seared Pork Tenderloin Steaks	300	12	2	140	700	0	0	0	45
Grilled Pork Kebabs with Hoisin and Five-Spice	280	5	1.5	140	690	10	0	5	46
Grilled Pork Kebabs with Sweet Sriracha Glaze	280	4.5	1.5	140	510	12	0	11	45
Sous Vide Pork Tenderloin Steaks with Scallion-Ginger Relish	490	33	3.5	140	850	2	1	1	46
Mu Shu Pork	510	17	2.5	145	1150	56	3	7	30
Barbecue Baby Back Ribs	410	23	8	150	1060	4	2	2	48
Grilled Glazed Baby Back Ribs with Lime Glaze	320	15	5	100	930	16	0	13	32
Grilled Glazed Baby Back Ribs with Spicy Marmalade Glaze	350	15	5	100	900	23	0	21	32
Sweet-and-Sour Ribs	420	20	6	100	1180	27	1	22	33
PORK - SIDE									
Rosticciana	480	27	7	200	550	1	0	0	56
Jerk Pork Ribs	510	25	7	200	1350	14	1	11	56
Chinese Barbecue Spareribs	700	21	6	200	2540	62	0	51	61
Memphis Barbecue Spareribs	420	16	5	200	1370	10	1	7	56
Slow-Cooker Sweet-and-Sour Barbecue Spare Ribs	970	55	18	215	2040	61	1	43	61
DIY Bacon	430	43	16	60	530	2	0	2	8
Crispy Slow-Roasted Pork Belly	750	72	26	100	1310	8	0	8	13
Crispy Slow-Roasted Pork Belly with Tangy Hoisin Sauce	740	73	26	100	1090	9	0	6	13
Sous Vide Sichuan Twice-Cooked Pork Belly	390	37	13	50	370	3	0	1	7
Ultimate Pork Ramen	600	42	16	40	1770	43	1	3	14
PORK - LEG									
Roast Fresh Ham	380	15	5	140	1470	9	0	9	46
South Carolina Smoked Fresh Ham	420	17	6	160	990	10	0	9	52
Roast Country Ham	870	62	21	240	200	18	0	16	57
Risotto with Cabbage and Country Ham	340	18	6	55	320	25	2	5	17
Spiral-Sliced Ham Glazed with Cider-Vinegar Caramel	550	36	12	135	95	22	0	22	33
Sous Vide Spiral-Sliced Bone-In Ham	560	36	12	135	95	24	0	23	33
Slow-Cooker Glazed Ham	690	47	16	185	180	18	0	17	44
Grill-Roasted Ham	680	51	18	195	130	4	0	4	47
Hoppin' John	590	25	9	75	480	59	6	2	32

	Cal	Total Fat (g)	Sat Fat (g)	Chol (mg)	Sodium (mg)	Total Carb (g)	Dietary Fiber (g)	Total Sugars (g)	Protein (g)
PORK - LEG (cont.)									
Ham Steak with Red-Eye Gravy	330	20	9	95	2110	5	0	4	30
St. Paul Sandwiches	530	26	4.5	205	1360	49	1	8	20
Pressure-Cooker Macaroni and Cheese with Ham and Peas	460	17	9	60	1060	52	1	9	26
Slow-Cooker Split-Pea Soup	410	12	4.5	70	1140	39	15	6	36
Southern-Style Collard Greens	260	15	6	80	1030	6	3	2	23
Senate Navy Bean Soup	440	15	4.5	70	730	41	9	3	35
Texas-Style Pinto Beans	280	5	1.5	30	510	36	13	3	21
Sous Vide Cuban Black Beans	450	13	3.5	50	680	50	1	8	29
LAMB - SHOULDER									
Lamb Pot Roast with Coriander, Fennel, and Figs	430	18	7	120	520	15	2	10	38
Lamb Vindaloo	390	21	7	120	430	10	2	3	39
Lamb Tagine with Apricots and Olives	680	34	10	165	1400	42	5	24	53
Arrosticini	200	13	4	60	290	0	0	0	18
Braised Lamb Shoulder Chops with Tomatoes and Red Wine	730	56	25	170	320	6	1	3	45
Braised Lamb Shoulder Chops with Capers, Balsamic Vinegar, and Red Pepper	760	56	25	170	420	11	2	7	45
Braised Lamb Shoulder Chops with Figs and Warm Spices	780	56	25	170	320	23	3	17	46
Irish Stew	1020	66	29	200	730	46	3	7	59
Irish Stew with Carrots and Turnips	980	66	29	200	770	38	4	1	58
Sharba	320	14	6	35	1180	31	2	4	17
Harira	390	23	7	35	900	25	7	4	19
Grilled Lamb Shoulder Chops	610	50	22	145	160	0	0	0	39
Spiced Red Pepper–Rubbed Grilled Lamb Shoulder Chops	650	53	22	145	160	2	1	1	39
Grilled Lamb Shoulder Chops with Garlic-Rosemary Marinade	620	50	22	145	160	1	0	0	39
Grilled Lamb Shoulder Chops with Soy-Shallot Marinade	570	43	21	145	630	3	1	1	40
LAMB - RIB AND LOIN									
Roasted Rack of Lamb with Roasted Red Pepper Relish	880	67	28	255	1350	1	0	1	69
Roasted Rack of Lamb with Sweet Mint-Almond Relish	920	69	29	255	1330	6	1	4	70
Crumb-Crusted Rack of Lamb	890	61	28	260	530	12	1	0	71
Grilled Rack of Lamb	420	22	9	165	170	0	0	0	55
Grilled Rack of Lamb with Sweet Mustard Glaze	450	22	9	165	350	6	0	5	55
Cast Iron Lamb Chops with Mint and Rosemary Relish	410	29	7	105	110	1	0	0	38
Lamb Chops with Onion and Balsamic Relish	370	22	6	105	260	6	1	4	38
Sumac Lamb Loin Chops with Carrots, Mint, and Paprika	380	22	6	85	1480	16	4	6	34
Grilled Loin or Rib Lamb Chops	250	14	4	80	90	0	0	0	30
Grilled Lamb Loin or Rib Lamb Chops with Herb and Garlic Paste	380	28	6	80	90	1	0	0	30
LAMB - LEG AND SHANKS									
Pomegranate-Glazed Roast Bone-In Leg of Lamb	500	33	6	125	160	10	0	10	40
Grilled Bone-In Leg of Lamb with Charred-Scallion Sauce	450	27	7	140	810	3	1	0	45
Harissa-Rubbed Roast Boneless Leg of Lamb with Warm Cauliflower Salad	440	24	6	110	620	18	4	10	38
Leg of Lamb en Cocotte	550	30	13	255	180	1	0	0	69
Roast Butterflied Leg of Lamb with Coriander, Cumin, and Mustard Seeds	400	20	5	150	860	3	1	0	49
Roast Butterflied Leg of Lamb with Coriander, Rosemary, and Red Pepper	400	20	5	150	860	3	1	1	48

	Cal	Total Fat (g)	Sat Fat (g)	Chol (mg)	Sodium (mg)	Total Carb (g)	Dietary Fiber (g)	Total Sugars (g)	Protein (g)
LAMB - LEG AND SHANKS *(cont.)*									
Cast Iron Roasted Boneless Leg of Lamb with Herbed Bread-Crumb Crust	300	15	4	105	200	6	0	0	36
Lamb Curry with Whole Spices	340	15	3	60	370	28	4	4	24
Lamb Curry with Figs and Fenugreek	360	15	3	60	380	32	5	7	24
Sous Vide Spice-Rubbed Leg of Lamb with Chermoula	290	17	4.5	95	480	3	1	0	30
Lamb Shanks Braised with Lemon and Mint	480	27	10	120	540	13	2	5	33
Lamb Shanks Braised with Ras el Hanout	490	27	10	120	580	13	2	5	33
Lamb Shanks Braised with Red Wine and Herbes de Provence	480	27	10	120	530	12	2	5	33
Braised Lamb Shanks with Bell Peppers and Harissa	370	22	8	100	930	12	3	7	28
Moroccan Lamb and White Beans	290	6	1.5	15	390	40	12	4	18
Pressure-Cooker Spiced Lamb Shanks with Figs	430	23	9	100	460	25	2	18	28
GROUND MEAT - BEEF									
Spaghetti and Meatballs	880	27	9	120	1500	109	7	24	49
Hearty Beef Lasagna	430	23	13	95	770	29	2	7	28
Pastitsio	470	22	10	100	940	43	1	12	25
Tacos Dorados	640	41	8	65	970	49	3	7	26
Gorditas	700	33	8	65	1330	77	8	1	28
Double-Decker Drive-Thru Burgers	640	32	11	90	1290	39	4	12	36
Best Ground Beef Chili	310	17	5	60	570	18	4	3	21
Mapo Tofu	400	28	3.5	25	950	11	2	3	19
Hummus with Baharat-Spiced Beef	170	12	2	10	440	9	2	0	7
Egyptian Eggah with Ground Beef and Spinach	220	13	4	270	540	7	2	2	17
Stuffed Cabbage Rolls	730	44	14	125	2420	50	7	29	34
Stuffed Bell Peppers with Spiced Beef, Currants, and Feta	420	18	6	60	660	42	6	15	22
GROUND MEAT - PORK									
Mexican Meatball Soup	290	16	5	65	1250	22	3	6	14
Italian Pork Burgers with Broccoli Rabe	800	54	16	130	1350	33	4	9	39
Ground Pork Tacos with Almonds and Raisins	540	38	10	80	790	26	5	6	24
Chiles Rellenos with Pork	700	43	13	95	930	50	6	15	28
Pasta alla Norcina	570	26	12	70	400	62	2	3	20
Chinese Pork Dumplings	320	13	4	30	400	35	1	1	13
Bun Cha	400	17	6	55	850	45	1	9	18
Congee with Stir-Fried Ground Pork	190	9	3	25	580	19	0	1	8
Meatball Stew with Paprika and Saffron	380	25	7	45	890	17	1	5	15
Homemade Breakfast Sausage	330	27	11	90	350	2	0	2	19
Glazed Meatloaf	360	17	6	145	810	25	0	16	24
GROUND MEAT - VEAL									
Ragù alla Bolognese	720	47	16	230	1130	11	1	6	47
GROUND MEAT - LAMB									
Keftedes	310	20	7	65	650	12	2	2	20
Hoisin-Glazed Lamb Burgers	660	37	14	165	2110	32	1	8	47
Lamb Ragu with Pappardelle	830	27	11	145	730	103	2	11	40
Moussaka	600	39	18	110	1160	31	9	16	32
Arayes	660	45	20	120	490	29	2	2	36
Spicy Lamb with Lentils and Yogurt	660	35	16	90	840	49	6	8	37

	Cal	Total Fat (g)	Sat Fat (g)	Chol (mg)	Sodium (mg)	Total Carb (g)	Dietary Fiber (g)	Total Sugars (g)	Protein (g)
GROUND MEAT - VEAL *(cont.)*									
Lamb Kofte	380	31	12	85	480	4	1	1	22
Stuffed Zucchini	420	24	6	40	460	38	7	19	16
Potato, Swiss Chard, and Lamb Hash with Poached Eggs	460	24	8	225	920	40	6	4	23
EAT WITH MEAT - SPICE RUBS AND SAUCES (PER 1-TABLESPOON SERVING)									
Barbecue Rub	30	0	0	0	90	7	1	5	1
Classic Steak Rub	15	0.5	0	0	0	3	2	0	1
Herbes de Provence	10	0	0	0	0	2	1	0	0
Five-Spice Powder	10	0	0	0	0	2	1	0	0
Jerk Rub	35	0	0	0	0	8	1	5	1
Southwestern Rub	25	1	0	0	90	4	2	0	1
Salsa Verde	100	9	1.5	0	100	3	0	0	1
Lemon-Basil Salsa Verde	90	9	1.5	0	100	3	0	0	1
Salsa Verde with Arugula	90	9	1.5	0	100	3	0	0	1
Chermoula	60	7	1	0	50	1	0	0	0
Chimichurri	45	4.5	0.5	0	100	1	0	0	0
Mint Persillade	70	7	1	0	90	1	0	0	1
Gremolata	5	0	0	0	0	1	0	0	0
Hollandaise Sauce	90	9	6	50	30	0	0	0	0
Yogurt-Herb Sauce	10	0.5	0	0	5	1	0	1	1
Za'atar Yogurt Sauce	10	0.5	0	0	5	1	0	1	1
Horseradish–Sour Cream Sauce	15	1	0.5	5	140	1	0	1	0
Gorgonzola Vinaigrette	45	4.5	1	5	100	0	0	0	1
Romesco	20	1	0	0	80	1	0	1	0
Spicy Avocado–Sour Cream	35	3	1.5	5	10	1	0	0	0
Classic Burger Sauce	50	5	0.5	0	90	2	0	2	0
Onion-Balsamic Relish	90	8	1	0	105	4	0	3	0
Tangy Corn Relish	15	0	0	0	75	3	0	2	0
Cilantro-Mint Chutney	10	0.5	0	0	40	1	0	1	1
Green Tomato Chutney	25	0	0	0	75	6	0	6	0
Red Bell Pepper Chutney	25	0	0	0	75	5	0	0	0
Spiced Apple Chutney	25	0	0	0	0	6	0	5	0
Classic Basil Pesto	110	12	1.5	0	20	1	0	0	1
Toasted Walnut and Parsley Pesto	100	11	1.5	0	20	1	0	0	1
Sun-Dried Tomato Pesto	60	6	1	0	35	1	0	0	1
Chipotle-Cilantro Compound Butter	110	11	7	30	0	2	0	1	0
Chive-Lemon Miso Compound Butter	100	11	7	30	0	0	0	0	0
Parsley-Caper Compound Butter	100	11	7	30	35	0	0	0	0
Parsley-Lemon Compound Butter	100	11	7	30	0	0	0	0	0
Tarragon-Lime Compound Butter	100	11	7	30	0	0	0	0	0
Tapenade Compound Butter	120	13	7	120	2	1	0	0	0

conversions AND EQUIVALENTS

The recipes in this book were developed using standard U.S. measures following U.S. government guidelines. The charts below offer equivalents for U.S. and metric measures. All conversions are approximate and have been rounded up or down to the nearest whole number.

EXAMPLE

1 teaspoon = 4.9292 milliliters, rounded up to 5 milliliters
1 ounce = 28.3495 grams, rounded down to 28 grams

VOLUME CONVERSIONS

U.S.	METRIC
1 teaspoon	5 milliliters
2 teaspoons	10 milliliters
1 tablespoon	15 milliliters
2 tablespoons	30 milliliters
¼ cup	59 milliliters
⅓ cup	79 milliliters
½ cup	118 milliliters
¾ cup	177 milliliters
1 cup	237 milliliters
1¼ cups	296 milliliters
1½ cups	355 milliliters
2 cups (1 pint)	473 milliliters
2½ cups	591 milliliters
3 cups	710 milliliters
4 cups (1 quart)	0.946 liter
1.06 quarts	1 liter
4 quarts (1 gallon)	3.8 liters

WEIGHT CONVERSIONS

OUNCES	GRAMS
½	14
¾	21
1	28
1½	43
2	57
2½	71
3	85
3½	99
4	113
4½	128
5	142
6	170
7	198
8	227
9	255
10	283
12	340
16 (1 pound)	454

CONVERSIONS FOR COMMON BAKING INGREDIENTS

Because measuring by weight is far more accurate than measuring by volume, and thus more likely to produce reliable results, in our recipes we provide ounce measures in addition to cup measures for many ingredients. Refer to the chart below to convert these measures into grams.

INGREDIENT	OUNCES	GRAMS
Flour		
1 cup all-purpose flour*	5	142
1 cup cake flour	4	113
1 cup whole-wheat flour	5½	156
Sugar		
1 cup granulated (white) sugar	7	198
1 cup packed brown sugar (light or dark) sugar	7	198
1 cup confectioners' sugar	4	113
Butter†		
4 tablespoons (½ stick or ¼ cup)	2	57
8 tablespoons (1 stick or ½ cup)	4	113
16 tablespoons (2 sticks or 1 cup)	8	227

* U.S. all-purpose flour, the most frequently used flour in this book, does not contain leaveners, as some European flours do. These leavened flours are called self-rising or self-raising. If you are using self-rising flour, take this into consideration before adding leaveners to a recipe.

† In the United States, butter is sold both salted and unsalted. We recommend unsalted butter. If you are using salted butter, take this into consideration before adding salt to a recipe.

OVEN TEMPERATURE

FAHRENHEIT	CELSIUS	GAS MARK
225	105	¼
250	120	½
275	135	1
300	150	2
325	165	3
350	180	4
375	190	5
400	200	6
425	220	7
450	230	8
475	245	9

CONVERTING TEMPERATURES FROM AN INSTANT-READ THERMOMETER

We include doneness temperatures in many of the recipes in this book. We recommend an instant-read thermometer for the job. (See page 11 for a chart of common Meat Doneness Temperatures.) Use the simple formula below to convert Fahrenheit degrees to Celsius:

Subtract 32 degrees from the Fahrenheit reading, then divide the result by 1.8 to find the Celsius reading.

To convert 160°F to Celsius:
160°F − 32 = 128°
128° ÷ 1.8 = 71.11°C, rounded down to 71°C

TAKING THE TEMPERATURE OF MEAT AND POULTRY

Since the temperature of beef and pork will continue to rise as the meat rests—an effect called carryover cooking—they should be removed from the oven, grill, or pan when they are 5 to 10 degrees below the desired serving temperature. Carryover cooking doesn't apply to poultry (it lacks the dense muscle structure of beef and pork and doesn't retain heat as well), so it should be cooked to the desired serving temperature. The following temperatures should be used to determine when to stop the cooking process.

INGREDIENT	TEMPERATURE
Beef/lamb	
Rare	115 to 120 degrees (120 to 125 degrees after resting)
Medium-rare	120 to 125 degrees (125 to 130 degrees after resting)
Medium	130 to 135 degrees (135 to 140 degrees after resting)
Medium-well	140 to 145 degrees (145 to 150 degrees after resting)
Well-done	150 to 155 degrees (155 to 160 degrees after resting)
Pork	
Chops and tenderloin	145 degrees (150 degrees after resting)
Loin roasts	140 degrees (145 degrees after resting)
Chicken	
White meat	160 degrees
Dark meat	175 degrees

Index

Note: Page references in *italics* indicate photographs.